Grades 4-8

NotebookReference

Webster's Thesaurus Second Edition

AMERICAN
EDUCATION
PUBLISHING™

Columbus, Ohio

School Specialty Publishing

Copyright © 2006 School Specialty Publishing.

Published by American Education Publishing, an imprint of School Specialty
Publishing, a member of the School Specialty Family.

Send all inquiries to:
School Specialty Publishing
8720 Orion Place
Columbus, OH 43240-2111

ISBN 0-7696-4344-2

3 4 5 6 PAT 12 11 10 09

Proofreading Marks

lowercase: **/** ̷Sister

capitalize: **≡** <u>ohio</u>

delete: **ℓ** ~~word~~

transpose: **∿** sheep⁀wool

insert: **∧** a ∧sunset
(beautiful)

add... a comma: ⌄

a period: ⊙

a colon: ⌃

a semicolon: ⌃

a quotation mark: ⌄⌄

an apostrophe: ⌄

The thesaurus is a useful tool for expanding vocabulary, which adds variety to speech and writing.

A thesaurus is a compilation of words and phrases that are similar in meaning. The name for these like words is *synonyms*; words that are opposite in meaning are called *antonyms*.

This *Thesaurus* from School Specialty Publishing is organized alphabetically, using a base of common words and their variants. Synonyms (*SYN.*) are listed first, followed by antonyms (*ANT.*) when applicable. We believe you will find this to be a handy and reliable reference book.

A

a (SYN.) any, one.

abandon (SYN.) relinquish, resign, surrender, leave, give up, cease, forsake, desert, quit, vacate, abjure, discard, evacuate, withdraw. (ANT.) keep, stay, maintain, embrace, adopt, join, engage, retain.

abandoned (SYN.) depraved, wicked, deserted, desolate, forsaken, rejected, cast off, degraded, loose, unrestrained, marooned, immoral, evil. (ANT.) befriended, cherished, chaste, moral, respectable, virtuous, righteous.

abase (SYN.) humble, reduce, bring down, degrade, demote, mock, scorn, belittle, shame. (ANT.) exalt, cherish, elevate, uplift, dignify.

abash (SYN.) disconcert, bewilder, confuse, put off. (ANT.) comfort, relax, hearten.

abashed (SYN.) confused, ashamed, embarrassed, mortified, humiliated.

abate (SYN.) lessen, curtail, reduce, decrease, restrain, decline, stop, moderate, subside, slow, diminish, slacken. (ANT.) grow, prolong, increase, extend, intensify, quicken, enhance, accelerate.

abbey (SYN.) nunnery, convent, cloister.

abbot (SYN.) friar, monk.

abbreviate (SYN.) shorten, lessen, abridge, condense, curtail, reduce, cut, trim, restrict, clip, contract. (ANT.) lengthen, increase, expand, extend, prolong, enlarge.

abbreviation (SYN.) abridgment, reduction, shortening, condensation. (ANT.) expansion, extension, amplification, lengthening dilation.

abdicate (SYN.) relinquish, renounce, vacate, waive, desert, forsake, abolish, quit, abandon, surrender, resign. (ANT.) maintain, stay, retain, uphold.

abdomen (SYN.) paunch, belly, stomach.

abduct (SYN.) carry off, take, kidnap.

aberrant (SYN.) capricious, devious, irregular, unnatural, abnormal. (ANT.) regular, usual, fixed, ordinary.

aberration (SYN.) oddity, abnormality, irregularity, deviation, monster, abortion, eccentricity. (ANT.) conformity, normality.

abet (SYN.) support, connive, encourage, conspire, help, incite, aid, assist. (ANT.) deter, check, hinder, frustrate, oppose, discourage, resist.

abettor (SYN.) accomplice, ally, confederate, associate, accessory. (ANT.) opponent, enemy.

abeyance (SYN.) cessation, pause, inactivity, rest, suspension, recess, dormancy, remission. (ANT.) ceaseless, continuation.

abhor (SYN.) hate, loathe, execrate, avoid, scorn, detest, despise.

abhorrent (SYN.) loathsome, horrible, detestable, nauseating, hateful, despicable, disgusting, foul, offensive, terrible, revolting.

abide (SYN.) obey, accept, tolerate, endure, dwell, stay, reside.

ability (SYN.) aptness, capability, skill, faculty, talent. (ANT.) incapacity, incompetency, weakness, ineptitude, inability.

abject (SYN.) sordid, infamous, miserable, wretched, mean, base, contempt.

abjure (SYN.) relinquish, renounce, vacate, waive, desert, quit, leave, forsake, foreswear, abdicate, resign, surrender. (ANT.) maintain, uphold, stay.

able (SYN.) qualified, competent, fit, capable, skilled, efficient, clever, talented, adequate, skillful. (ANT.) inadequate, trained, incapable, weak, incompetent, unable.

abnegation (SYN.) rejection, renunciation, self-denial, abandonment, refusal, relinquishment, abjuration.

abnormal (SYN.) uncommon, unnatural, odd, irregular, monstrous. (ANT.) natural, usual, normal, average.

aboard (SYN.) on board.

abode (SYN.) dwelling, habitat, home, residence, address, quarters, lodging place, domicile.

abolish (SYN.) end, eradicate, annul, cancel, revoke, destroy, invalidate, overthrow, obliterate, abrogate, erase, exterminate, wipe out, eliminate. (ANT.) promote, restore, continue, establish, sustain.

abominable (SYN.) foul, dreadful, hateful, revolting, vile, odious, loathsome, detestable, bad, horrible, terrible, awful, disgusting. (ANT.) delightful, pleasant, agreeable, commendable, admirable, noble.

abominate (SYN.) despise, detest, hate, dislike, abhor, loathe. (ANT.) like, cherish, approve, admire.

abomination (SYN.) freak, detestation, hatred, disgust, revulsion, horror.

abort (SYN.) flop, fizzle, miscarry, abandon, cancel.

abortion (SYN.) miscarriage, fiasco, disaster, failure, defeat.

abortive (SYN.) unproductive, vain, unsuccessful, useless, failed, futile. (ANT.) rewarding, effective, profitable, successful.

abound (SYN.) swarm, plentiful, filled, overflow, teem. (ANT.) scarce, lack.

about (SYN.) relating to, involving, concerning, near, around, upon, almost, approximately, of, nearby, ready to, nearly.

about-face (SYN.) reversal, backing out, shift, switch.

above (SYN.) higher than, overhead, on, upon, over, superior to. (ANT.) under, beneath, below.

aboveboard (SYN.) forthright, open, frank, honest, overt, plain, straightforward, guileless, trustworthy. (ANT.) sneaky, wily.

abracadabra (SYN.) voodoo, magic, charm, spell.

abrasion (SYN.) rubbing, roughness, scratching, scraping, friction, chap, chafe, chapping, scrape.

abrasive (SYN.) rough, hurtful, sharp, galling, annoying, grating, cutting, irritating, caustic. (ANT.) pleasant, soothing, comforting, agreeable, smooth.

abreast (SYN.) beside, side by side, alongside.

abridge (SYN.) condense, cut, abbreviate, make shorter, contract, shorten, reduce, summarize, curtail. (ANT.) increase, lengthen, expand, extend.

abridgment (SYN.) digest, condensation, summary, abbreviation, shortening. (ANT.) lengthening, expansion, enlargement.

abroad (SYN.) away, overseas, broadly, widely. (ANT.) at home, privately, secretly.

abrogate (SYN.) rescind, withdraw, revoke, annul, cancel, abolish, repeal.

abrupt (SYN.) sudden, unexpected, blunt, curt, precipitous, sharp, hasty, unannounced, harsh, precipitate, brusque, rude, rough, short, steep. (ANT.) foreseen, smooth, warm, courteous, gradual, smooth, expected, anticipated.

abscess (SYN.) pustule, sore, wound, inflammation.

absence (SYN.) nonexistence, deficiency, lack, need, shortcoming. (ANT.) attendance, completeness, existence, presence.

absent (SYN.) gone, away, truant, departed, inattentive, lacking, not present, out, off. (ANT.) attending, attentive, present.

absent-minded (SYN.) inattentive, daydreaming, preoccupied, absorbed, bemused, dreaming, forgetful. (ANT.) observant, attentive, alert.

absolute (SYN.) unconditional, entire, actual, complete, thorough, total, perfect, essential, supreme, ultimate, unrestricted, positive, unqualified, whole. (ANT.) partial, conditional, dependent, accountable, restricted, qualified, limited, fragmentary.

absolutely (SYN.) positively, really, doubtlessly. (ANT.) doubtfully, uncertainly.

absolution (SYN.) pardon, forgiveness, acquittal, mercy, amnesty, remission.

absolutism (SYN.) autarchy, dictatorship, authoritarianism.

absolve (SYN.) exonerate, discharge, acquit, pardon, forgive, clear, excuse. (ANT.) blame, convict, charge, accuse.

absorb (SYN.) consume, swallow up, engulf, assimilate, imbibe, engage, engross, take in, integrate, incorporate, occupy. (ANT.) discharge, dispense, emit, exude, leak, eliminate, bore, tire, weary, drain.

absorbent (SYN.) permeable, spongy, pervious, porous. (ANT.) waterproof, impervious.

absorbing (SYN.) interesting, engaging, exciting, engrossing, entertaining, thrilling, intriguing, pleasing, fascinating. (ANT.) dull, boring, tedious, tiresome.

abstain (SYN.) forbear, forego, decline, resist, withhold, refrain. (ANT.) pursue.

abstemious (SYN.) abstinent, sparing, cautious, temperate, ascetic, self-disciplined, continent, sober. (ANT.) uncontrolled, indulgent, abandoned, excessive.

abstinence (SYN.) fasting, self-denial, continence, forbearance, sobriety, refrain. (ANT.) gluttony, greed, excess, self-indulgence.

abstract (SYN.) theoretical,

ideal, part, appropriate, steal, separate, purloin, nonconcrete, summarize. (ANT.) return, concrete, unite, add, replace, specific, clear, particular, restore.

abstracted (SYN.) preoccupied, absent-minded, parted, removed, stolen, abridged, taken away. (ANT.) replaced, returned, alert, united, added.

abstraction (SYN.) idea, image, generalization, thought, opinion, impression, notion. (ANT.) matter, object, substance.

abstruse (SYN.) arcane, obscure, complicated, abstract, esoteric, metaphysical. (ANT.) uncomplicated, direct, obvious, simple.

absurd (SYN.) ridiculous, silly, unreasonable, foolish, irrational, nonsensical, impossible, inconsistent, preposterous, self-contradictory, unbelievable. (ANT.) rational, sensible, sound, meaningful, consistent, reasonable.

absurdity (SYN.) foolishness, nonsense, farce, drivel, joke, senselessness, folly.

abundance (SYN.) ampleness, profusion, copiousness, plenty. (ANT.) insufficiency, want, absence, dearth, scarcity.

abundant (SYN.) ample, overflowing, plentiful, rich, teeming, profuse, abounding. (ANT.) insufficient, scant, not enough, scarce, deficient, rare, uncommon, absent.

abuse (SYN.) maltreatment, misuse, reproach, defamation, dishonor, mistreat, damage, ill-use, reviling, aspersion, desecration, invective, insult, outrage, profanation, perversion, disparagement, misemploy, misapply, hurt, harm, injure, scold, berate. (ANT.) plaudit, respect, appreciate, commendation, protect, praise, cherish.

abusive (SYN.) harmful, insulting, libelous, hurtful, slanderous, nasty, defamatory, injurious, scathing, derogatory. (ANT.) helpful, laudatory.

abut (SYN.) touch, border, meet, join, connect with.

abutment (SYN.) pier, buttress, bulwark, brace, support.

abysmal (SYN.) bottomless, unfathomable, yawning, overwhelming.

abyss (SYN.) depth, chasm, void, infinitude, limbo, unknowable.

academic (SYN.) learned, scholarly, theoretical, erudite, bookish, formal, pedantic.

(ANT.) ignorant, practical, simple, uneducated.

academy (SYN.) college, school.

accede (SYN.) grant, agree, comply, consent, yield, endorse, accept, admit. (ANT.) dissent, disagree, differ, oppose.

accelerate (SYN.) quicken, dispatch, facilitate, hurry, rush, speed up, forward, hasten, push, expedite. (ANT.) hinder, retard, slow, delay.

accent (SYN.) tone, emphasis, inflection, stress, consent.

accept (SYN.) take, approve, receive, allow, consent to, believe, adopt, admit. (ANT.) ignore, reject, refuse.

acceptable (SYN.) passable, satisfactory, fair, adequate, standard, par, tolerable. (ANT.) poor, substandard.

access (SYN.) entrance, approach, course, gateway, door, avenue, gain, enter.

accessible (SYN.) nearby, attainable, achievable, affable, accommodating. (ANT.) remote, unobtainable, unachievable, standoffish, forbidding, unfriendly.

accessory (SYN.) extra, addition, assistant, supplement, contributory, accomplice.

accident (SYN.) casualty, disaster, misfortune, mishap, chance, calamity, contingency, fortuity, misadventure, mischance, injury, catastrophe. (ANT.) purpose, intention, calculation.

accidental (SYN.) unintended, chance, casual, fortuitous, contingent, unplanned, unexpected, unforeseen. (ANT.) calculated, planned, willed, intended, intentional, deliberate.

acclaim (SYN.) eminence, fame, glory, honor, reputation, credit, applaud, distinction, approve, notoriety. (ANT.) infamy, obscurity, disapprove, reject, disrepute.

acclimated (SYN.) adapted, habituated, acclimatized, accommodated, seasoned, inured, used to, weathered, reconciled.

accolade (SYN.) praise, honor, acclaim, recognition, applause, kudos, bouquet, crown, testimonial, acclamation, salute.

accommodate (SYN.) help, assist, aid, provide for, serve, oblige, hold, house. (ANT.) inconvenience.

accommodating (SYN.) obliging, helpful, willing,

kind, cooperative, gracious, cordial, sympathetic, unselfish. (ANT.) unfriendly, selfish, hostile.

accommodation (SYN.) change, alteration, adaptation, convenience, adjustment, acclimatization, aid, help, boon, kindness, service, courtesy. (ANT.) inflexibility, rigidity, disservice, stubbornness, disadvantage.

accommodations (SYN.) housing, lodgings, room, place, quarters, board.

accompany (SYN.) chaperon, consort with, escort, go with, associate with, attend, join. (ANT.) abandon, quit, leave, desert, avoid, forsake.

accomplice (SYN.) accessory, ally, associate, partner in crime, assistant, sidekick, confederate. (ANT.) opponent, rival, enemy, adversary.

accomplish (SYN.) attain, consummate, achieve, do, execute, carry out, fulfill, complete, effect, perform, finish. (ANT.) fail, frustrate, spoil, neglect, defeat.

accomplished (SYN.) proficient, skilled, finished, well-trained, gifted, masterly, polished, able. (ANT.) unskilled, amateurish, crude.

accomplishment (SYN.) deed, feat, statute, operation, performance, action, achievement, transaction. (ANT.) cessation, inhibition, intention, deliberation.

accord (SYN.) concur, agree, award, harmony, conformity, agreement, give, tale, sum, statement, record, grant.

accordingly (SYN.) consequently, therefore, whereupon, hence, so, thus.

accost (SYN.) approach, greet, speak to, address. (ANT.) avoid, shun.

account (SYN.) description, chronicle, history, narration, reckoning, rate, computation, detail, narrative, relation, recital, consider, believe, deem, record, explanation, report, tale, story, anecdote, reason, statement, tale, ledger.

accountable (SYN.) chargeable, answerable, beholden, responsible, obliged, liable.

account for (SYN.) justify, explain, substantiate, illuminate, clarify, elucidate.

accredited (SYN.) qualified, licensed, deputized, certified, commissioned, vouched for, empowered. (ANT.) illicit, unofficial, unauthorized.

accrue (SYN.) amass, collect,

heap, increase, accumulate, gather, hoard. (ANT.) disperse, dissipate, waste, diminish.

accrued (SYN.) accumulated, totaled, increased, added, enlarged, amassed.

accumulate (SYN.) gather, collect, heap, increase, accrue, assemble, compile, hoard, amass. (ANT.) spend, give away, diminish, dissipate.

accumulation (SYN.) heap, collection, pile, store, hoard, stack, aggregation.

accurate (SYN.) perfect, just, truthful, unerring, meticulous, correct. (ANT.) incorrect, mistaken, false, wrong, inaccurate.

accursed (SYN.) ill-fated, cursed, condemned, doomed, bedeviled, ruined. (ANT.) fortunate, hopeful.

accusation (SYN.) charge, incrimination, indictment, arraignment. (ANT.) pardon, exoneration, absolve.

accuse (SYN.) incriminate, indict, censure, tattle, denounce, charge, arraign, impeach, blame. (ANT.) release, vindicate, exonerate, acquit, absolve, clear.

accustom (SYN.) addict, familiarize, condition.

accustomed (SYN.) familiar with, used to, comfortable with. (ANT.) strange, unusual, rare, unfamiliar.

ace (SYN.) champion, hotshot, pip, one, secret, fighter pilot.

acerbity (SYN.) bitterness, harshness, unkindness, sourness, acidity, unfriendliness, acrimony, coldness, sharpness. (ANT.) sweetness, gentleness, kindness, tenderness.

ache (SYN.) hurt, pain, throb.

achieve (SYN.) do, execute, gain, obtain, acquire, accomplish, realize, perform, complete, accomplish, finish, fulfill, reach, attain, secure, procure. (ANT.) fail, lose, fall short.

achievement (SYN.) feat, accomplishment, attainment, exploit, realization, performance, completion, deed. (ANT.) botch, dud, mess, omission, defeat, failure.

acid (SYN.) tart, sour, bitter, mordant, biting. (ANT.) base, pleasant, friendly, bland, mild, sweet.

acknowledge (SYN.) allow, admit, concede, recognize, answer, grant, accept, receive. (ANT.) reject, refuse, disavow, refute, deny.

acme (SYN.) summit, top, zenith, peak, crown. (ANT.)

bottom.

acquaint *(SYN.)* inform, teach, enlighten, notify, tell.

acquaintance *(SYN.)* fellowship, friendship, cognizance, knowledge, intimacy, familiarity, companionship, associate, colleague, companion. *(ANT.)* inexperience, unfamiliarity, ignorance.

acquiesce *(SYN.)* submit, agree, concur, assent, comply, consent, succumb. *(ANT.)* refuse, disagree, rebel, argue.

acquire *(SYN.)* amass, attain, earn, get, procure, assimilate, obtain, secure, gain, appropriate. *(ANT.)* surrender, lose, forego, forfeit.

acquirement *(SYN.)* training, skill, learning, achievement, attainment, education, information.

acquisition *(SYN.)* procurement, gain, gift, purchase, proceeds, possession, grant.

acquisitive *(SYN.)* greedy, avid, hoarding, covetous.

acquit *(SYN.)* forgive, exonerate, absolve, cleanse, pardon, excuse, discharge, found not guilty. *(ANT.)* doom, saddle, sentence, condemn.

acrid *(SYN.)* bitter, sharp, nasty, stinging, harsh. *(ANT.)* pleasant, sweet.

acrimonious *(SYN.)* sharp, sarcastic, acerb, waspish, cutting, stinging, testy. *(ANT.)* soft, kind, sweet, pleasant, soothing.

acrobat *(SYN.)* athlete, gymnast.

act *(SYN.)* deed, doing, feat, execution, accomplishment, performance, action, operation, transaction, law, decree, statute, edict, achievement, exploit, statute, judgment, routine, pretense. *(ANT.)* inactivity, deliberation, cessation.

acting *(SYN.)* behaving, performing, pretending, officiating, substituting, surrogate, temporary, delegated.

action *(SYN.)* deed, achievement, feat, activity, exploit, movement, motion, behavior, battle, performance, exercise. *(ANT.)* idleness, inertia, repose, inactivity, rest.

activate *(SYN.)* mobilize, energize, start, propel. *(ANT.)* paralyze, immobilize, stop, deaden.

active *(SYN.)* working, operative, alert, agile, nimble, supple, sprightly, busy, brisk, lively, quick, industrious, energetic, vigorous, industrious, occupied, vivacious, dynamic,

engaged. *(ANT.)* passive, inactive, idle, dormant, lazy, lethargic.

activism *(SYN.)* engagement, confrontation, agitation, commitment, aggression, fervor, zeal. *(ANT.)* detachment, lethargy, disengagement.

activist *(SYN.)* militant, doer, enthusiast.

activity *(SYN.)* action, liveliness, motion, vigor, agility, exercise, energy, quickness, enterprise, movement, briskness. *(ANT.)* idleness, inactivity, dullness, sloth.

actor *(SYN.)* performer, trouper, entertainer, thespian.

actual *(SYN.)* true, genuine, certain, factual, authentic, concrete, real. *(ANT.)* unreal, fake, bogus, nonexistent, false.

actuality *(SYN.)* reality, truth, deed, occurrence, fact, certainty. *(ANT.)* theory, fiction, falsehood, supposition.

acute *(SYN.)* piercing, severe, sudden, keen, sharp, perceptive, discerning, shrewd, astute, smart, intelligent. *(ANT.)* bland, mild, dull, obtuse, insensitive.

adamant *(SYN.)* unyielding, firm, obstinate. *(ANT.)* yielding.

adapt *(SYN.)* adjust, conform, accommodate, change, fit, alter, vary, modify. *(ANT.)* misapply, disturb.

add *(SYN.)* attach, increase, total, append, sum, affix, augment, adjoin, put together, unite, supplement. *(ANT.)* remove, reduce, deduct, subtract, detach, withdraw.

address *(SYN.)* greet, hail, accost, speak to, location, residence, home, abode, dwelling, speech, lecture, greeting, oration, presentation. *(ANT.)* avoid, pass by.

adept *(SYN.)* expert, skillful, proficient. *(ANT.)* unskillful.

adequate *(SYN.)* capable, commensurate, fitting, satisfactory, sufficient, enough, ample, suitable, plenty, fit. *(ANT.)* lacking, scant, insufficient, inadequate.

adhere *(SYN.)* stick fast, grasp, hold, keep, retain, cling, stick to, keep, cleave. *(ANT.)* surrender, abandon, release, separate, loosen.

adherent *(SYN.)* follower, supporter. *(ANT.)* renegade, dropout, defector.

adjacent *(SYN.)* next to, near, bordering, adjoining, touching, neighboring. *(ANT.)* separate, distant, apart.

adjoin *(SYN.)* connect, be

close to, affix, attach. *(ANT.)* detach, remove.

adjoining *(SYN.)* touching, bordering, next to, close to. *(ANT.)* distant, remote, separate.

adjourn *(SYN.)* postpone, defer, delay, suspend, discontinue, put off. *(ANT.)* begin, convene, assemble.

adjust *(SYN.)* repair, fix, change, set, regulate, settle, arrange, adapt, suit, accommodate, modify, vary, alter, fit.

administer *(SYN.)* supervise, oversee, direct, manage, rule, govern, control, conduct, provide, give, execute, preside, apply, contribute, help.

administration *(SYN.)* conduct, direction, management, supervision.

admirable *(SYN.)* worthy, fine, praiseworthy, commendable, excellent.

admiration *(SYN.)* pleasure, wonder, esteem, approval. *(ANT.)* disdain, disrespect, contempt.

admire *(SYN.)* approve, venerate, appreciate, respect, revere, esteem, like. *(ANT.)* abhor, dislike, despise, loathe, detest, hate.

admissible *(SYN.)* fair, justifiable, tolerable, allowable, permissible. *(ANT.)* unsuitable, unfair, inadmissible.

admission *(SYN.)* access, admittance, entrance, pass, ticket. *(ANT.)* denial.

admit *(SYN.)* allow, assent, permit, acknowledge, welcome, concede, agree, confess, accept, grant. *(ANT.)* deny, dismiss, shun, obstruct.

admittance *(SYN.)* access, entry, entrance. *(ANT.)* refusal.

admonish *(SYN.)* caution, advise against, warn, rebuke, reprove, censure. *(ANT.)* glorify, praise.

admonition *(SYN.)* advice, warning, caution, reminder, tip.

ado *(SYN.)* trouble, other, fuss, bustle, activity, excitement, commotion, action, upset, confusion, turmoil. *(ANT.)* tranquillity.

adolescent *(SYN.)* young, youthful, immature, teenage. *(ANT.)* grown, mature, adult.

adoration *(SYN.)* veneration, reverence, glorification, worship, homage.

adore *(SYN.)* revere, venerate, idolize, respect, love, cherish, esteem, honor. *(ANT.)* loathe, hate, despise.

adorn *(SYN.)* trim, bedeck, decorate, ornament, beautify, embellish, glamorize, enhance, garnish. *(ANT.)* mar, deform, deface, strip, bare.

adrift *(SYN.)* floating, afloat, drifting, aimless, purposeless, unsettled. *(ANT.)* purposeful, stable, secure, well organized.

adroit *(SYN.)* adept, apt, dexterous, skillful, clever, ingenious, expert. *(ANT.)* awkward, clumsy, graceless, unskillful, oafish.

adult *(SYN.)* full-grown, mature, grown-up. *(ANT.)* infantile, immature, baby, child.

advance *(SYN.)* further, promote, bring forward, propound, proceed, aggrandize, elevate, improve, adduce, propose, progress, move, advancement, improvement, promotion, upgrade. *(ANT.)* retard, retreat, hinder, revert, withdraw, flee, retardation.

advantage *(SYN.)* edge, profit, superiority, benefit, leverage, favor, vantage, gain. *(ANT.)* handicap, impediment, obstruction, disadvantage, detriment, hindrance, loss.

adventure *(SYN.)* undertaking, occurrence, enterprise, happening, event, project, incident, exploit.

adventurous *(SYN.)* daring, enterprising, rash, bold, chivalrous. *(ANT.)* cautious, timid, hesitating.

adversary *(SYN.)* foe, enemy, contestant, opponent, antagonist. *(ANT.)* ally, friend.

adverse *(SYN.)* hostile, counteractive, unfavorable, opposed, disastrous, contrary, antagonistic, opposite, unlucky, unfriendly, unfortunate. *(ANT.)* favorable, propitious, fortunate, friendly, beneficial.

adversity *(SYN.)* misfortune, trouble, calamity, distress, hardship, disaster. *(ANT.)* benefit, happiness.

advertise *(SYN.)* promote, publicize, make known, announce, promulgate.

advertisement *(SYN.)* commercial, billboard, want ad, handbill, flyer, poster, brochure, blurb.

advice *(SYN.)* counsel, instruction, suggestion, warning, information, caution, exhortation, admonition, recommendation, plan, tip, guidance, opinion.

advisable *(SYN.)* wise, sensible, prudent, suitable, fit, proper, fitting. (*ANT.*) *ill-considered, imprudent, inadvisable.*

advise (*SYN.*) recommend, suggest, counsel, caution, warn, admonish.

adviser (*SYN.*) coach, guide, mentor, counselor.

advocate (*SYN.*) defend, recommend, support, defender, proponent, lawyer. (*ANT.*) *opponent, adversary, oppose.*

aesthetic (*SYN.*) literary, artistic, sensitive, tasteful, well-composed. (*ANT.*) *tasteless, crude, barbaric.*

affable (*SYN.*) pleasant, courteous, sociable, friendly, amiable, gracious, approachable, communicative. (*ANT.*) *unfriendly, unsociable.*

affair (*SYN.*) event, occasion, happening, party, occurrence, matter, festivity, business, concern, liaison, infidelity.

affect (*SYN.*) alter, modify, concern, regard, move, touch, feign, pretend, influence, sway, transform, change, impress.

affected (*SYN.*) pretended, fake, sham, false, pretentious.

affection (*SYN.*) fondness, kindness, emotion, love, feeling, tenderness, attachment, endearment, liking, friendliness, warmth. (*ANT.*) *aversion, indifference, repulsion, hatred, repugnance, dislike, antipathy.*

affectionate (*SYN.*) warm, loving, tender, fond, attached. (*ANT.*) *distant, unfeeling, cold.*

affirm (*SYN.*) assert, aver, declare, swear, maintain, endorse, certify, state, ratify, pronounce, say, confirm, establish. (*ANT.*) *deny, dispute, oppose, contradict, demur, disclaim.*

afflict (*SYN.*) trouble, disturb, bother, agitate, perturb. (*ANT.*) *soothe.*

affliction (*SYN.*) distress, grief, misfortune, trouble, illness. (*ANT.*) *relief, benefit, easement.*

affluent (*SYN.*) wealthy, prosperous, rich, abundant, ample, plentiful, bountiful, well-to-do. (*ANT.*) *poor, destitute.*

afford (*SYN.*) provide, supply, yield, furnish, manage to buy.

affront (*SYN.*) offense, slur, slight, provocation, insult. (*ANT.*) *compliment.*

afraid (*SYN.*) scared, fainthearted, frightened, timid, fearful, apprehensive, cowardly, terrified. (*ANT.*) *assured, composed, courageous,* bold, confident.

after (*SYN.*) following, subsequently, behind, next. (*ANT.*) *before.*

again (*SYN.*) anew, repeatedly, afresh.

against (*SYN.*) versus, hostile, opposed to, in disagreement, touching. (*ANT.*) *pro, with, for, promoting.*

age (*SYN.*) antiquity, date, period, generation, time, senility, grow old, senescence, mature, dotage, ripen, mature, era, epoch. (*ANT.*) *youth, childhood.*

aged (*SYN.*) ancient, elderly, old. (*ANT.*) *youthful, young.*

agency (*SYN.*) office, operation.

agent (*SYN.*) performer, doer, worker, operator, instrument, manager.

aggravate (*SYN.*) intensify, magnify, annoy, irritate, increase, nettle, irk, vex, provoke, embitter, worsen. (*ANT.*) *soften, sooth, appease, pacify, mitigate, ease, relieve.*

aggregate (*SYN.*) collection, entirety, sum, accumulate, total, compile, conglomeration. (*ANT.*) *part, unit, ingredient, element.*

aggression (*SYN.*) anger, assault, attack, invasion, offense. (*ANT.*) *defense.*

aggressive (*SYN.*) hostile, offensive, belligerent, attacking, militant, pugnacious. (*ANT.*) *timid, withdrawn, passive, peaceful.*

aghast (*SYN.*) surprised, astonished, astounded, awed, thunderstruck, flabbergasted, bewildered.

agile (*SYN.*) nimble, graceful, lively, active, alert, fast, quick, athletic, spry. (*ANT.*) *inept, awkward, clumsy.*

agility (*SYN.*) quickness, vigor, liveliness, energy, activity, motion. (*ANT.*) *dullness, inertia, idleness, inactivity.*

agitate (*SYN.*) disturb, excite, perturb, rouse, shake, arouse, disconcert, instigate, inflame, provoke, jar, incite, shake, stir up, toss. (*ANT.*) *calm, placate, quiet, ease, soothe, steady.*

agitated (*SYN.*) jumpy, jittery, nervous, restless, restive, upset, disturbed, ruffled.

agony (*SYN.*) anguish, misery, pain, suffering, torture, ache, distress, throe, woe, torment, grief. (*ANT.*) *relief, ease, comfort.*

agree (*SYN.*) comply, coincide, conform, concur, assent, accede, tally, settle, harmonize, unite, yield, consent. (*ANT.*) *differ, disagree, protest, contradict, argue, refuse.*

agreeable (*SYN.*) amiable, charming, gratifying, pleasant, suitable, pleasurable, welcome, pleasing, acceptable, friendly, cooperative.

agreement (*SYN.*) harmony, understanding, unison, contract, pact, stipulation, alliance, deal, bargain, treaty, contract, arrangement, settlement, accord, concord. (*ANT.*) *variance, dissension, discord, disagreement, difference.*

agriculture (*SYN.*) farming, gardening, tillage, husbandry, cultivation, agronomy.

ahead (*SYN.*) before, leading, forward, winning, advanced. (*ANT.*) *behind.*

aid (*SYN.*) help, remedy, assist, helper, service, support, assistant, relief. (*ANT.*) *obstruct, hinder, obstacle, impede, hindrance.*

ail (*SYN.*) bother, trouble, perturb, disturb, suffer.

ailing (*SYN.*) sick, ill. (*ANT.*) *hearty, hale, well.*

ailment (*SYN.*) illness, disease, affliction, sickness.

aim (*SYN.*) direction, point, goal, object, target, direct, try, intend, intention, end, objective.

aimless (*SYN.*) directionless, adrift, purposeless.

air (*SYN.*) atmosphere, oxygen, display, reveal, expose, publicize. (*ANT.*) *conceal, hide.*

airy (*SYN.*) breezy, light, gay, lighthearted, graceful, fanciful, exposed.

aisle (*SYN.*) corridor, passageway, lane, alley, opening.

ajar (*SYN.*) slightly open.

akin (*SYN.*) alike, related, connected, similar, affiliated, allied.

alarm (*SYN.*) frighten, signal, warning, terror, apprehension, affright, consternation, fear, siren, arouse, startle, bell. (*ANT.*) *tranquility, composure, security, quiet, calm, soothe, comfort.*

alarming (*SYN.*) shocking, appalling, daunting. (*ANT.*) *comforting, calming, soothing.*

alcoholic (*SYN.*) sot, drunkard, tippler, inebriate.

alert (*SYN.*) attentive, keen, clear-witted, ready, nimble, vigilant, watchful, observant. (*ANT.*) *logy, sluggish, dulled, listless.*

alias (*SYN.*) anonym, assumed name.

alibi (*SYN.*) story, excuse.

alien (*SYN.*) foreigner, stranger, remote, strange, different, extraneous. (*ANT.*) *germane, kindred, relevant, akin, familiar, accustomed.*

alight (*SYN.*) land, debark, disembark. (*ANT.*) *embark, board.*

alive (*SYN.*) living, existing, breathing, live, lively, vivacious, animated. (*ANT.*) *inactive, dead, moribund.*

allay (*SYN.*) soothe, check, lessen, calm, lighten, relieve, soften, moderate, quiet. (*ANT.*) *intensify, worsen, arouse.*

allege (*SYN.*) testify, affirm, cite, claim, declare, maintain, state, assert. (*ANT.*) *deny, disprove, refute, contradict, gainsay.*

allegiance (*SYN.*) faithfulness, duty.

allegory (*SYN.*) fable, fiction, myth, saga, parable, legend. (*ANT.*) *history, fact.*

alleviate (*SYN.*) diminish, soothe, solace, abate, assuage, allay, soften, mitigate, extenuate, relieve, case, slacken, relax, weaken. (*ANT.*) *increase, aggravate, augment, irritate.*

alley (*SYN.*) footway, byway, path, passageway, aisle, corridor, opening, lane.

alliance (*SYN.*) combination, partnership, union, treaty, coalition, association, confederacy, marriage, pact, agreement, relation, interrelation, understanding, relationship. (*ANT.*) *separation, divorce, schism.*

allot (*SYN.*) divide, mete, assign, give, measure, distribute, allocate, share, grant, dispense, deal, apportion. (*ANT.*) *withhold, retain, keep, confiscate, refuse.*

allow (*SYN.*) authorize, grant, acknowledge, admit, let, permit, sanction, consent, concede, mete, allocate. (*ANT.*) *resist, refuse, forbid, object, prohibit.*

allowance (*SYN.*) grant, fee, portion, ration, allotment.

allude (*SYN.*) intimate, refer, insinuate, hint, advert, suggest, imply, mention. (*ANT.*) *demonstrate, specify, state, declare.*

allure (*SYN.*) attract, fascinate, tempt, charm, infatuate, captivate. (*ANT.*) *repulse.*

ally (*SYN.*) accomplice, associate, confederate, abettor, assistant, friend, partner. (*ANT.*) *rival, enemy, opponent, foe, adversary.*

almighty (*SYN.*) omnipotent,

powerful.

almost (SYN.) somewhat, nearly. (ANT.) completely, absolutely.

alms (SYN.) dole, charity, donation, contribution.

aloft (SYN.) overhead.

alone (SYN.) desolate, unaided, only, isolated, lone, secluded, lonely, deserted, solitary, single, apart, solo, separate. (ANT.) surrounded, attended, accompanied, together.

aloof (SYN.) uninterested, uninvolved, apart, away, remote, unsociable, standoffish, separate, distant. (ANT.) warm, outgoing, friendly, cordial.

also (SYN.) in addition, likewise, too, besides, furthermore, moreover, further.

alter (SYN.) adjust, vary, deviate, modify, change. (ANT.) maintain, preserve, keep.

alteration (SYN.) difference, adjustment, change, modification. (ANT.) maintenance, preservation.

altercation (SYN.) controversy, dispute, argument, quarrel.

alternate (SYN.) rotate, switch, spell, interchange. (ANT.) fix.

alternative (SYN.) substitute, selection, option, choice, replacement, possibility.

although (SYN.) though, even if, even though, despite.

altitude (SYN.) elevation, height. (ANT.) depth.

altogether (SYN.) totally, wholly, quite, entirely, thoroughly, completely. (ANT.) partly.

altruism (SYN.) benevolence, philanthropy, kindness, tenderness, generosity, charity, liberality. (ANT.) selfishness, unkindness, cruelty.

always (SYN.) evermore, forever, perpetually, ever, unceasingly, continually, constantly, eternally, everlastingly. (ANT.) never, rarely, sometimes, occasionally.

amalgamate (SYN.) fuse, unify, unite, commingle, merge, blend, combine, consolidate. (ANT.) decompose, disintegrate, separate.

amass (SYN.) collect, accumulate, heap up, gather, increase, compile, assemble, store up. (ANT.) disperse, dissipate, spend.

amateur (SYN.) beginner, dilettante, learner, dabbler, neophyte, apprentice, novice, nonprofessional, tyro. (ANT.) expert, master, adept,

professional, authority.

amaze (SYN.) surprise, flabbergast, stun, dumb-found, astound, bewilder, aghast, thunderstruck, astonish. (ANT.) bore, disinterest, tire.

ambiguous (SYN.) vague, uncertain, obscure, dubious, equivocal, unclear, deceptive. (ANT.) plain, clear, explicit, obvious, unequivocal, unmistakable, certain.

ambition (SYN.) eagerness, goal, incentive, aspiration, yearning, longing, desire. (ANT.) indifference, satisfaction, indolence, resignation.

ambitious (SYN.) aspiring, intent upon. (ANT.) indifferent, content.

amble (SYN.) saunter, stroll.

ambush (SYN.) trap, surprise, hiding place.

amend (SYN.) change, mend, better, correct, improve. (ANT.) worsen.

amends (SYN.) compensation, restitution, payment, reparation, remedy, redress.

amiable (SYN.) friendly, good-natured, gracious, pleasing, agreeable, outgoing, pleasant. (ANT.) surly, hateful, churlish, disagreeable, ill-natured, ill-tempered, cross, captious, touchy.

amid (SYN.) among, amidst, surrounded by.

amiss (SYN.) wrongly, improperly, astray, awry. (ANT.) properly, rightly, correct.

ammunition (SYN.) shot, powder, shells, bullets.

among (SYN.) between, mingled, amidst, amid, betwixt, surrounded by. (ANT.) separate, apart.

amorous (SYN.) amatory, affectionate, romantic.

amount (SYN.) sum, total, quantity, number, price, value, measure.

ample (SYN.) plentiful, large, profuse, spacious, copious, liberal, full, bountiful, abundant, great, extensive, generous, wide, enough, sufficient, roomy. (ANT.) limited, insufficient, meager, small, lacking, cramped, confined, inadequate.

amplification (SYN.) magnification, growth, waxing, accrual, enhancement, enlargement, heightening, increase. (ANT.) decrease, diminishing, reduction, contraction.

amplify (SYN.) make louder, broaden, develop, expand, enlarge, extend. (ANT.) confine, restrict, abridge, narrow.

amuse (SYN.) divert, please, delight, entertain, charm. (ANT.) tire, bore.

amusement (SYN.) diversion, pastime, entertainment, pleasure, enjoyment, recreation. (ANT.) tedium, boredom.

amusing (SYN.) pleasant, funny, pleasing, entertaining, comical. (ANT.) tiring, tedious, boring.

analogous (SYN.) comparable, corresponding, like, similar, correspondent, alike, correlative, parallel, allied, akin. (ANT.) different, opposed, incongruous.

analysis (SYN.) examination, separation, investigation.

analyze (SYN.) examine, explain, investigate, separate.

ancestral (SYN.) hereditary, inherited.

ancestry (SYN.) family, line, descent, lineage. (ANT.) posterity.

anchor (SYN.) fix, attach, secure, fasten. (ANT.) detach, free, loosen.

ancient (SYN.) aged, old-fashioned, archaic, elderly, antique, old, primitive. (ANT.) new, recent, current, fresh.

anecdote (SYN.) account, narrative, story, tale.

anesthetic (SYN.) opiate, narcotic, sedative, painkiller, analgesic.

angel (SYN.) cherub, archangel, seraph. (ANT.) demon, devil.

angelic (SYN.) pure, lovely, heavenly, good, virtuous, innocent, godly, saintly. (ANT.) devilish.

anger (SYN.) exasperation, fury, ire, passion, rage, resentment, temper, indignation, animosity, irritation, wrath, displeasure, infuriate, arouse, nettle, annoyance, exasperate. (ANT.) forbearance, patience, peace, self-control.

angry (SYN.) provoked, wrathful, furious, enraged, incensed, exasperated, maddened, indignant, irate, mad, inflamed. (ANT.) pleased, calm, satisfied, content, tranquil.

anguish (SYN.) suffering, torment, torture, distress, pain, heartache, grief, agony, misery. (ANT.) solace, relief, joy, comfort, peace, ecstasy, pleasure.

animal (SYN.) beast, creature.

animate (SYN.) vitalize, invigorate, stimulate, enliven, alive, vital, vigorous. (ANT.)

dead, inanimate.

animated (SYN.) gay, lively, spry, vivacious, active, vigorous, chipper, snappy. (ANT.) inactive.

animosity (SYN.) grudge, hatred, rancor, spite, bitterness, enmity, opposition, dislike, hostility, antipathy. (ANT.) goodwill, love, friendliness, kindliness.

annex (SYN.) join, attach, add, addition, wing, append.

annihilate (SYN.) destroy, demolish, end, wreck, abolish, erase.

announce (SYN.) proclaim, give out, make known, notify, publish, report, herald, promulgate, advertise, broadcast, state, tell, declare, publicize. (ANT.) conceal, withhold, suppress, bury, stifle.

announcement (SYN.) notification, report, declaration, bulletin, advertisement, broadcast, message.

annoy (SYN.) bother, irk, pester, tease, trouble, vex, disturb, inconvenience, molest, irritate, harry, harass. (ANT.) console, gratify, soothe, accommodate, please, calm, comfort.

annually (SYN.) yearly.

anoint (SYN.) baptize, besprinkle, purify.

answer (SYN.) reply, rejoinder, response, retort, rebuttal, respond. (ANT.) summoning, argument, questioning, inquiry, query, ask, inquire.

antagonism (SYN.) opposition, conflict, enmity, hostility, animosity. (ANT.) geniality, cordiality, friendliness.

antagonist (SYN.) adversary, rival, enemy, foe, opponent. (ANT.) ally, friend.

antagonize (SYN.) provoke, counter, oppose, embitter. (ANT.) soothe.

anthology (SYN.) treasury, collection.

anticipate (SYN.) await, foresee, forecast, hope for, expect.

anticipated (SYN.) expected, foresight, hoped, preconceived. (ANT.) dreaded, reared, worried, doubted.

antics (SYN.) horseplay, fun, merrymaking, pranks, capers, tricks, clowning.

antipathy (SYN.) hatred. (ANT.) sympathy.

antiquated (SYN.) old, outdated, old-fashioned.

antique (SYN.) rarity, curio, old, ancient, old-fashioned, archaic, out-of-date. (ANT.) new, recent, fresh.

anxiety (SYN.) care, disquiet, fear, concern, solicitude, trouble, worry, apprehension, uneasiness, distress, foreboding. (*ANT.*) *nonchalance, assurance, confidence, contentment, peacefulness, placidity, tranquillity.*

anxious (*SYN.*) troubled, uneasy, perturbed, apprehensive, worried, concerned, desirous, bothered, agitated, eager, fearful. (*ANT.*) *tranquil, calm, peaceful.*

anyway (*SYN.*) nevertheless, anyhow.

apartment (*SYN.*) suite, flat, dormitory.

apathy (*SYN.*) unconcern, indifference, lethargy. (*ANT.*) *interest, feeling.*

aperture (*SYN.*) opening, gap, pore, cavity, chasm, abyss, hole, void. (*ANT.*) *connection, bridge, link.*

apex (*SYN.*) acme, peak, tip, summit, crown, top.

apologize (*SYN.*) ask forgiveness.

apology (*SYN.*) defense, excuse, confession, justification, alibi, explanation, plea. (*ANT.*) *denial, complaint, dissimulation, accusation.*

apostate (*SYN.*) unbeliever, nonconformist, dissenter, heretic, schismatic. (*ANT.*) *saint, conformist, believer.*

appall (*SYN.*) shock, stun, dismay, frighten, terrify, horrify. (*ANT.*) *edify, please.*

appalling (*SYN.*) fearful, frightful, ghastly, horrid, repulsive, terrible, dire, awful. (*ANT.*) *fascinating, beautiful, enchanting, enjoyable.*

apparatus (*SYN.*) rig, equipment, furnishings, gear, tackle.

apparel (*SYN.*) clothing, attire, garb, garments, dress, robes.

apparent (*SYN.*) obvious, plain, self-evident, clear, manifest, transparent, unmistakable, palpable, unambiguous, ostensible, visible, seeming, evident, understandable, illusory. (*ANT.*) *uncertain, indistinct, dubious, hidden, mysterious.*

apparition (*SYN.*) illusion, ghost, phantom, vision, fantasy, dream.

appeal (*SYN.*) plea, petition, request, entreaty, plead, beseech, beg, attract. (*ANT.*) *repulse, repel.*

appear (*SYN.*) look, arrive, emanate, emerge, arise, seem, turn up. (*ANT.*) *vanish, withdraw, exist, disappear, evaporate.*

appearance (*SYN.*) advent,

arrival, aspect, demeanor, fashion, guise, apparition, manner, mien, look, presence. (*ANT.*) *disappearance, reality, departure, vanishing.*

appease (*SYN.*) calm, compose, lull, quiet, relieve, assuage, pacify, satisfy, restraint, lessen, soothe, check, ease, alleviate, still, allay, tranquilize. (*ANT.*) *excite, amuse, incense, irritate, inflame.*

append (*SYN.*) supplement, attach, add.

appendage (*SYN.*) addition, tail, supplement.

appetite (*SYN.*) zest, craving, desire, liking, longing, stomach, inclination, hunger, thirst, relish, passion. (*ANT.*) *satiety, disgust, distaste, repugnance.*

appetizer (*SYN.*) hors d'oeuvre.

applaud (*SYN.*) cheer, clap, hail, approve, praise, acclaim. (*ANT.*) *disapprove, denounce, reject, criticize, condemn.*

appliance (*SYN.*) machine, tool, instrument, device, utensil, implement.

applicable (*SYN.*) fitting, suitable, proper, fit, usable, appropriate, suited. (*ANT.*) *inappropriate, inapplicable.*

apply (*SYN.*) affix, allot, appropriate, use, employ, petition, request, devote, avail, pertain, attach, ask, administer, petition, assign, relate, utilize. (*ANT.*) *give away, demand, detach, neglect, ignore.*

appoint (*SYN.*) name, choose, nominate, designate, elect, establish, assign, place. (*ANT.*) *discharge, fire, dismiss.*

appointment (*SYN.*) rendezvous, meeting, designation, position, engagement, assignment. (*ANT.*) *discharge, dismissal.*

appraise (*SYN.*) value, evaluate, place a value on.

appreciate (*SYN.*) enjoy, regard, value, prize, cherish, admire, go up, improve, rise, respect, esteem, appraise. (*ANT.*) *belittle, misunderstand, apprehend, degrade, scorn, depreciate, undervalue.*

apprehend (*SYN.*) seize, capture, arrest, understand, dread, fear, grasp, perceive. (*ANT.*) *release, lose.*

apprehension (*SYN.*) misgiving, fear, dread, uneasiness, worry, fearfulness, anticipation, capture, seizure. (*ANT.*) *confidence, composure, selfassuredness.*

apprehensive (*SYN.*)

worried, afraid, uneasy, bothered, anxious, concerned, perturbed, troubled, fearful. (*ANT.*) *relaxed.*

apprentice (*SYN.*) amateur, recruit, novice, learner, beginner. (*ANT.*) *experienced, professional, master.*

approach (*SYN.*) greet, inlet, come near, advance, access, passageway. (*ANT.*) *avoid, pass by, retreat.*

appropriate (*SYN.*) apt, particular, proper, fitting, suitable, applicable, loot, pillage, purloin, rob, steal, embezzle, assign, becoming, apportion, authorize. (*ANT.*) *improper, contrary, inappropriate, buy, repay, restore, return, unfit, inapt.*

approval (*SYN.*) commendation, consent, praise, approbation, sanction, assent, endorsement, support. (*ANT.*) *reproach, censure, reprimand, disapprove.*

approve (*SYN.*) like, praise, authorize, confirm, endorse, appreciate, ratify, commend, sanction. (*ANT.*) *criticize, nullify, disparage, frown on, disapprove, deny.*

approximate (*SYN.*) near, approach, roughly, close. (*ANT.*) *absolute.*

apt (*SYN.*) suitable, proper, appropriate, fit, suited, disposed, liable, inclined, prone, clever, bright, alert, intelligent, receptive. (*ANT.*) *illbecoming, unsuitable, unlikely, slow, retarded, dense.*

aptitude (*SYN.*) knack, talent, gift, ability.

aptness (*SYN.*) capability, dexterity, qualification, skill, ability, aptitude. (*ANT.*) *incompetence, unreadiness, incapacity.*

aqueduct (*SYN.*) gully, pipe, canal, waterway, channel.

arbitrary (*SYN.*) unrestricted, absolute, despotic, willful, unreasonable, unconditional, authoritative. (*ANT.*) *contingent, qualified, fair, reasonable, dependent, accountable.*

arbitrate (*SYN.*) referee, settle, mediate, umpire, negotiate.

architecture (*SYN.*) structure, building, construction.

ardent (*SYN.*) fervent, fiery, glowing, intense, keen, impassioned, fervid, hot, passionate, earnest, eager, zealous, enthusiastic. (*ANT.*) *cool, indifferent, nonchalant, apathetic.*

ardor (*SYN.*) enthusiasm, rapture, spirit, zeal, fervent,

eager, glowing, eagerness. (*ANT.*) *unconcern, apathy, disinterest, indifference.*

arduous (*SYN.*) laborious, hard, difficult, burdensome, strenuous, strained. (*ANT.*) *easy.*

area (*SYN.*) space, extent, region, zone, section, expanse, district, neighborhood, size.

argue (*SYN.*) plead, reason, wrangle, indicate, prove, show, dispute, denote, imply, object, bicker, discuss, debate, disagree. (*ANT.*) *reject, spurn, ignore, overlook, agree, concur.*

argument (*SYN.*) debate, dispute, discussion, controversy. (*ANT.*) *harmony, accord, agreement.*

arid (*SYN.*) waterless, dry, flat, dull, unimaginative, stuffy. (*ANT.*) *fertile, wet, colorful.*

arise (*SYN.*) enter, institute, originate, start, open, commence, emerge, appear. (*ANT.*) *terminate, end, finish, complete, close.*

aristocrat (*SYN.*) noble, gentleman, peer, lord, nobleman, bourgeoisie. (*ANT.*) *peasant, commoner, proletariat.*

arm (*SYN.*) weapon, defend, equip, empower, fortify.

armistice (*SYN.*) truce, pact, deal, understanding, peace, treaty, contract, alliance, agreement.

army (*SYN.*) troops, legion, military, forces, militia.

aroma (*SYN.*) smell, odor, fragrance, perfume, scent.

arouse (*SYN.*) stir, animate, move, pique, provoke, kindle, disturb, excite, foment, stimulate, awaken. (*ANT.*) *settle, soothe, calm.*

arraign (*SYN.*) charge, censure, incriminate, indict, accuse. (*ANT.*) *acquit, release, vindicate, exonerate, absolve.*

arraignment (*SYN.*) imputation, charge, accusation, incrimination. (*ANT.*) *pardon, exonerate, exculpation.*

arrange (*SYN.*) classify, assort, organize, place, plan, prepare, devise, adjust, dispose, regulate, order, group, settle, adapt, catalog, systematize, distribute, prepare. (*ANT.*) *jumble, scatter, disorder, confuse, disturb, disarrange.*

arrangement (*SYN.*) display, grouping, order, array, deal.

array (*SYN.*) dress, adorn, attire, clothe, arrange, order, distribute, display, exhibit. (*ANT.*) *disorder, disorganization, disarray.*

arrest (*SYN.*) detain, hinder, restrain, seize, withhold, stop, check, obstruct, apprehend, interrupt, catch, capture. (*ANT.*) *free, release, discharge, liberate.*

arrival (*SYN.*) advent, coming. (*ANT.*) *leaving, departure.*

arrive (*SYN.*) come, emerge, reach, visit, land, appear. (*ANT.*) *exit, leave, depart, go.*

arrogance (*SYN.*) pride, insolence. (*ANT.*) *humbleness, modest, humility.*

arrogant (*SYN.*) insolent, prideful, scornful, haughty, cavalier, proud. (*ANT.*) *modest, humble.*

art (*SYN.*) cunning, tact, artifice, skill, aptitude, adroitness, painting, drawing, design, craft, dexterity, composition, ingenuity. (*ANT.*) *clumsiness, innocence, unskillfulness, honesty.*

artery (*SYN.*) aqueduct, pipe, channel.

artful (*SYN.*) clever, sly, skillful, knowing, deceitful, tricky, crafty, cunning. (*ANT.*) *artless.*

article (*SYN.*) story, composition, treatise, essay, thing, report, object.

artifice (*SYN.*) trick, clever, scheme, device.

artificial (*SYN.*) bogus, fake, affected, feigned, phony, sham, unreal, synthetic, assumed, counterfeit, unnatural, man-made, unreal, manufactured, false, feigned, pretended. (*ANT.*) *genuine, natural, true, real, authentic.*

artisan (*SYN.*) worker, craftsman, mechanic.

artist (*SYN.*) actor, actress, painter, sculptor, singer, designer.

artless (*SYN.*) innocent, open, frank, simple, honest, candid, natural, unskilled, ignorant, truthful, sincere. (*ANT.*) *artful.*

ascend (*SYN.*) rise, scale, tower, mount, go up. (*ANT.*) *fall, sink, descend, go down.*

ascertain (*SYN.*) solve, learn, clear up, answer.

ascribe (*SYN.*) attribute, assign.

ashamed (*SYN.*) shamefaced, humiliated, abashed, mortified, embarrassed. (*ANT.*) *proud.*

ask (*SYN.*) invite, request, inquire, query, question, beg, solicit, demand, entreat, claim, interrogate, charge, expect. (*ANT.*) *order, reply, insist, answer.*

askance (*SYN.*) sideways.

askew (*SYN.*) disorderly, crooked, awry, twisted.

(*ANT.*) *straight.*

asleep (*SYN.*) inactive, sleeping, dormant. (*ANT.*) *alert, awake.*

aspect (*SYN.*) appearance, look, view, outlook, attitude, viewpoint, phase, part, feature, side.

aspersion (*SYN.*) dishonor, insult, misuse, outrage, reproach, defamation, abuse, disparagement. (*ANT.*) *plaudit, respect, approval.*

asphyxiate (*SYN.*) suffocate, stifle, smother, choke, strangle, throttle.

aspiration (*SYN.*) craving, desire, hope, longing, objective, passion, ambition.

aspire (*SYN.*) seek, aim, wish for, strive, desire, yearn for.

ass (*SYN.*) mule, donkey, burro, silly, dunce, stubborn, stupid, fool.

assail (*SYN.*) assault, attack.

assassinate (*SYN.*) purge, kill, murder.

assault (*SYN.*) invade, strike, attack, assail, charge, bombard, onslaught. (*ANT.*) *protect, defend.*

assemble (*SYN.*) collect, gather, meet, congregate, connect, manufacture. (*ANT.*) *disperse, disassemble, scatter.*

assembly (*SYN.*) legislature, congress, council, parliament.

assent (*SYN.*) consent to, concede, agree, approval, accept, comply, permission. (*ANT.*) *deny, dissent, refusal, denial, refuse.*

assert (*SYN.*) declare, maintain, state, claim, express, defend, press, support, aver, uphold, consent, accept, comply, affirm, allege, emphasize. (*ANT.*) *deny, refute, contradict, decline.*

assertion (*SYN.*) statement, affirmation, declaration. (*ANT.*) *contradiction, denial.*

assess (*SYN.*) calculate, compute, estimate, levy, reckon, tax, appraise.

asset (*SYN.*) property, wealth, capitol, resources, goods.

assign (*SYN.*) apportion, ascribe, attribute, cast, allot, chose, appropriate, name, elect, appoint, distribute, designate, specify. (*ANT.*) *release, relieve, unburden, discharge.*

assignment (*SYN.*) task, job, responsibility, duty.

assimilate (*SYN.*) digest, absorb, blot up.

assist (*SYN.*) help, promote, serve, support, sustain, abet, aid, back. (*ANT.*) *prevent, impede, hamper.*

assistance (*SYN.*) backing, help, patronage, relief, succor, support. (*ANT.*) *hostility, resistance, antagonism, counteraction.*

assistant (*SYN.*) accomplice, ally, associate, confederate, abettor. (*ANT.*) *rival, enemy, adversary.*

associate (*SYN.*) affiliate, ally, join, connect, unite, combine, link, mingle, partner, mix. (*ANT.*) *separate, disconnect, divide, disrupt, estrange.*

association (*SYN.*) organization, club, union, society, fraternity, sorority, companionship, fellowship.

assorted (*SYN.*) varied, miscellaneous, classified, different, several, grouped, various. (*ANT.*) *alike, same.*

assortment (*SYN.*) collection, variety, mixture, conglomeration.

assuage (*SYN.*) calm, quiet, lessen, relieve, ease, allay, moderate, alleviate, restrain.

assume (*SYN.*) arrogate, affect, suspect, believe, appropriate, take, pretend, usurp, simulate, understand, postulate, presume, suppose. (*ANT.*) *doff, demonstrate, prove, grant, concede.*

assumption (*SYN.*) presumption, guess, supposition, conjecture, postulate.

assure (*SYN.*) promise, convince, warrant, guarantee, pledge. (*ANT.*) *equivocate, deny.*

astonish (*SYN.*) astound, amaze, surprise, shock. (*ANT.*) *tire, bore.*

astound (*SYN.*) shock, amaze, astonish, stun, surprise, floor.

asunder (*SYN.*) divided, separate, apart. (*ANT.*) *together.*

asylum (*SYN.*) shelter, refuge, home, madhouse, institution.

athletic (*SYN.*) strong, active, able-bodied, gymnastic, muscular, well-built.

atone (*SYN.*) repay, make up.

atrocious (*SYN.*) horrible, savage, brutal, ruthless, dreadful, awful, horrifying. (*ANT.*) *good, kind.*

attach (*SYN.*) connect, adjoin, annex, join, append, stick, unite, affix. (*ANT.*) *unfasten, separate, disengage.*

attack (*SYN.*) raid, assault, besiege, abuse, censure, offense, siege, denunciation, aggression, push, criticism, invade. (*ANT.*) *surrender, defense, opposition, aid, defend, protect, repel.*

attain (*SYN.*) achieve, acquire, accomplish, gain, get, reach,

win. (*ANT.*) *discard, abandon, desert.*

attainment (*SYN.*) exploit, feat, accomplishment, realization, performance. (*ANT.*) *omission, defeat, failure, neglect.*

attempt (*SYN.*) essay, experiment, trial, try, undertaking, endeavor, effort. (*ANT.*) *laziness, neglect, inaction.*

attend (*SYN.*) accompany, escort, watch, serve, care for, follow, lackey, present, frequent, protect, guard. (*ANT.*) *desert, abandon, avoid.*

attendant (*SYN.*) waiter, servant, valet.

attention (*SYN.*) consideration, heed, circumspection, notice, watchfulness, observance, application, reflection, study, care, alertness, mindfulness. (*ANT.*) *negligence, indifference, omission, oversight, disregard.*

attentive (*SYN.*) careful, awake, alive, considerate, heedful, mindful, wary. (*ANT.*) *unaware, oblivious, apathetic.*

attest (*SYN.*) testify, swear, vouch, certify.

attire (*SYN.*) apparel, dress, clothe.

attitude (*SYN.*) standpoint, viewpoint, stand, pose, aspect, position, posture.

attract (*SYN.*) enchant, interest, pull, fascinate, draw, tempt, infatuate, entice. (*ANT.*) *deter, repel, repulse, alienate.*

attractive (*SYN.*) enchanting, winning, engaging, pleasant, pleasing, seductive. (*ANT.*) *unattractive, obnoxious, repellent, repulsive, forbidding.*

attribute (*SYN.*) give, apply, place, trait, characteristic, feature, nature, credit.

audacious (*SYN.*) daring, bold, arrogant, foolhardy, cavalier, haughty, insolent. (*ANT.*) *humble, shy.*

audacity (*SYN.*) effrontery, fearlessness, temerity, boldness. (*ANT.*) *humility, meekness, circumspection, fearfulness.*

audible (*SYN.*) distinct, plain, clear. (*ANT.*) *inaudible.*

augment (*SYN.*) enlarge, increase, raise, expand, broaden, extend.

auspicious (*SYN.*) lucky, timely, favorable, promising, fortunate. (*ANT.*) *untimely, unfortunate.*

austere (*SYN.*) stern, severe, harsh, strict. (*ANT.*) *lenient, soft.*

authentic (*SYN.*) real, true,

genuine, pure, accurate, reliable, legitimate, factual. (ANT.) false, spurious, artificial, counterfeit, erroneous.

authenticate (SYN.) validate, warrant, guarantee, verify, certify.

author (SYN.) father, inventor, maker, originator, writer, composer.

authoritative (SYN.) certain, secure, commanding, sure, tried, trustworthy, safe, influential, dependable. (ANT.) uncertain, unreliable, dubious, fallible, questionable.

authority (SYN.) dominion, justification, power, permission, authorization, importance, domination, supremacy. (ANT.) incapacity, denial, prohibition, weakness, impotence.

autocrat (SYN.) monarch, ruler, tyrant.

autograph (SYN.) endorse, sign, approve.

automatic (SYN.) self-acting, mechanical, spontaneous, uncontrolled, involuntary. (ANT.) hand-operated, intentional, deliberate, manual.

automobile (SYN.) auto, car.

auxiliary (SYN.) assisting, helping, aiding.

avail (SYN.) help, profit, use, value, benefit, serve, advantage.

available (SYN.) obtainable, convenient, ready, handy, accessible, prepared. (ANT.) unavailable, out of reach, inaccessible, unobtainable.

avarice (SYN.) lust, greed.

average (SYN.) moderate, ordinary, usual, passable, fair, intermediate, medium. (ANT.) outstanding, exceptional, extraordinary, unusual.

averse (SYN.) unwilling, opposed, forced, against, involuntary. (ANT.) willing.

avert (SYN.) avoid, prevent, prohibit. (ANT.) invite.

avid (SYN.) greedy, eager.

avoid (SYN.) elude, forestall, evade, escape, dodge, avert, forbear, eschew. (ANT.) oppose, meet, confront, encounter, seek.

award (SYN.) reward, prize, medal, gift, trophy.

aware (SYN.) mindful, perceptive, formed, apprised, realizing, conscious. (ANT.) unaware, ignorant, oblivious.

away (SYN.) absent, departed, distracted, gone, not at home. (ANT.) present, attentive, attending.

awe (SYN.) surprise, respect, dread, astonishment, alarm.

awful (SYN.) frightful, horrible, awe-inspiring, dire, terrible, unpleasant. (ANT.) humble, pleasant, wonderful, commonplace.

awkward (SYN.) inept, unpolished, clumsy, gauche, rough, ungraceful. (ANT.) adroit, graceful, polished, skillful.

awry (SYN.) askew, wrong, twisted, crooked, disorderly. (ANT.) straight, right.

axiom (SYN.) fundamental, maxim, principle, theorem, adage, apothegm, byword, aphorism.

B

babble (SYN.) twaddle, nonsense, gibberish, prattle, balderdash, rubbish, chatter, baby talk, poppycock, jabber, maunder, piffle.

baby (SYN.) newborn, infant, neonate, babe, teeny, small, wee, little, undersized, midget, papoose, protect, cosset, pamper.

babyish (SYN.) infantile, childish, whiny, unreasonable, immature, puerile, foolish, dependent. (ANT.) mature, adult, sensible, reasonable, grown-up.

back (SYN.) help, assist, endorse, support, second, ratify, approve, stand by, posterior, rear. (ANT.) anterior, front, face, undercut, veto, undermine.

backbiting (SYN.) gossip, slander, abuse, malice, cattiness, aspersion, derogation, belittling, badmouthing. (ANT.) compliments, praise, loyalty, friendliness, approval.

backbone (SYN.) vertebrae, spine, pillar, support, staff, mainstay, basis, courage, determination, toughness, character. (ANT.) timidity, weakness, cowardice, spinelessness.

backbreaking (SYN.) exhausting, fatiguing, tough, tiring, demanding, wearying, wearing, difficult. (ANT.) light, relating, undemanding, slight.

back down (SYN.) accede, concede, acquiesce, yield, withdraw, renege. (ANT.) persevere, insist.

backer (SYN.) underwriter, benefactor, investor, patron, sponsor, supporter.

backfire (SYN.) flop, boomerang, fail, founder, disappoint. (ANT.) succeed.

background (SYN.) training, practice, knowledge, experience.

backing (SYN.) help, support, funds, money, assistance, grant, advocacy, subsidy, sympathy, endorsement. (ANT.) criticism, detraction, faultfinding.

backlog (SYN.) inventory, reserve, hoard, amassment, accumulation.

backslide (SYN.) relapse, revert, return, weaken, regress, renege.

backward (SYN.) dull, sluggish, stupid, loath, regressive, rearward, underdeveloped, slow, retarded. (ANT.) progressive, precocious, civilized, advanced, forward.

bad (SYN.) unfavorable, wrong, evil, immoral, sinful, faulty, improper, unwholesome, wicked, corrupt, tainted. (ANT.) good, honorable, reputable, moral, excellent.

badger (SYN.) tease, question, annoy, pester, bother, taunt, bait, provoke, torment, harass, hector.

baffle (SYN.) confound, bewilder, perplex, puzzle, mystify, confuse, frustrate. (ANT.) inform, enlighten.

bag (SYN.) catch, snare, poke, sack.

bait (SYN.) enticement, captivate, ensnare, tease, torment, pester, worry, entrap, question, entice, lure, trap, harass, tempt, badger.

balance (SYN.) poise, stability, composure, remains, residue, equilibrium, compare, weigh, equalize. (ANT.) unsteadiness, instability.

bald (SYN.) bare, hairless, nude, open, uncovered, simple. (ANT.) covered, hairy.

balk (SYN.) unwilling, obstinate, stubborn, hesitate, check, stop. (ANT.) willing.

ball (SYN.) cotillion, dance, globe, sphere, spheroid.

ballad (SYN.) poem, song, ditty.

balloon (SYN.) puff up, enlarge, swell. (ANT.) shrivel, shrink.

ballot (SYN.) choice, vote, poll.

balmy (SYN.) soft, gentle, soothing, fragrant, mild. (ANT.) tempestuous, stormy.

ban (SYN.) prohibit, outlaw, disallow, block, bar, exclude, obstruct, prohibition, taboo, forbid. (ANT.) allow, permit.

banal (SYN.) hackneyed, corny, vapid, trite, overused, humdrum. (ANT.) striking,

original, fresh, stimulating, novel.

band (SYN.) company, association, crew, group, society, belt, strip, unite, gang.

bandit (SYN.) thief, robber, highwayman, outlaw, marauder.

bang (SYN.) hit, strike, slam.

banish (SYN.) drive away, eject, exile, oust, deport, dismiss, expel. (ANT.) receive, accept, shelter, admit, harbor, embrace, welcome.

bank (SYN.) barrier, slope, storage, treasury, row, series, string, shore.

banner (SYN.) colors, standard, pennant, flag.

banquet (SYN.) feast, celebration, festival, dinner, regalement, affair.

banter (SYN.) joke, tease, jest.

bar (SYN.) counter, impediment, saloon, exclude, obstacle, barricade, obstruct, shut out, hindrance, forbid, block, barrier, obstruction. (ANT.) allow, permit, aid, encouragement.

barbarian (SYN.) brute, savage, boor, ruffian, rude, uncivilized, primitive, uncultured, coarse, cruel, barbaric, crude. (ANT.) cultured, civilized.

barbarous (SYN.) savage, remorseless, cruel, uncivilized, rude, unrelenting, merciless, crude, ruthless, inhuman. (ANT.) kind, civilized, humane, refined, tasteful.

barber (SYN.) coiffeur, hairdresser.

bare (SYN.) naked, nude, uncovered, undressed, unclothed, unfurnished, plain, barren, empty, disclose, reveal, publicize, bald, expose, scarce, mere. (ANT.) dressed, garbed, conceal, covered, hide, clothed.

barefaced (SYN.) impudent, bold, insolent, brazen, shameless, audacious, impertinent, rude.

barely (SYN.) hardly, scarcely, just.

bargain (SYN.) agreement, arrangement, deal, contract, arrange, sale.

baroque (SYN.) ornamented, elaborate, embellished, ornate.

barren (SYN.) unproductive, bare, unfruitful, infertile, sterile, childless. (ANT.) productive, fruitful, fertile.

barricade (SYN.) fence, obstruction, shut in, fortification, barrier. (ANT.) free, open, release.

barrier (SYN.) fence, wall, bar,

railing, obstacle, hindrance, fortification, restraint, impediment, limit, barricade.

barter *(SYN.)* exchange, deal, trade.

base *(SYN.)* bottom, rest, foundation, establish, found, immoral, evil, bad, wicked, depraved, selfish, worthless, cheap, debased, poor, support, stand, low, abject, menial. *(ANT.)* exalted, righteous, lofty, esteemed, noble, honored, refined, valuable.

bashful *(SYN.)* timorous, abashed, shy, coy, timid, diffident, modest, sheepish, embarrassed, shame-faced, humble, recoiling, uneasy, awkward, ashamed. *(ANT.)* fearless, outgoing, adventurous, gregarious, aggressive, daring.

basic *(SYN.)* underlying, chief, essential, main, fundamental. *(ANT.)* subsidiary, subordinate.

basis *(SYN.)* presumption, support, base, principle, groundwork, presupposition, foundation, postulate, ground, assumption, premise, essential. *(ANT.)* implication, trimming, derivative, superstructure.

basket *(SYN.)* hamper, creel, dossier, bassinet.

bastion *(SYN.)* mainstay, support, staff, tower, stronghold.

bat *(SYN.)* strike, hit, clout, stick, club, knock, crack.

batch *(SYN.)* group, set, collection, lot, cluster, bunch, mass, combination.

bath *(SYN.)* washing, shower, tub, wash, dip, soaping.

bathe *(SYN.)* launder, drench, swim, cover, medicate, immerse, wet, dip, soak, suffuse, rinse, saturate.

bathing suit *(SYN.)* maillot, swimsuit, trunks.

bathos *(SYN.)* mawkishness, soppiness, slush, sentimentality.

bathroom *(SYN.)* powder room, toilet, bath, lavatory.

baton *(SYN.)* mace, rod, staff, billy club, crook, stick, caduceus, fasces.

battalion *(SYN.)* mass, army, swarm, mob, drove, horde, gang, legion, regiment.

batten *(SYN.)* thrive, flourish, fatten, wax, expand, bloom, boom, grow. *(ANT.)* decrease, weaken, fail.

batter *(SYN.)* pound, beat, hit, pommel, wallop, bash, smash, mixture, strike.

battery *(SYN.)* series, troop, force, rally, muster, set.

battle *(SYN.)* strife, fray, combat, struggle, contest, skirmish, conflict, fight, war, flight, warfare, action, campaign, strive against. *(ANT.)* truce, concord, agreement, settlement, harmony, accept, concur, peace.

battlement *(SYN.)* parapet, crenelation, rampart, fort, bastion, stronghold, escarpment.

bauble *(SYN.)* plaything, toy, trinket.

bawd *(SYN.)* procuress, prostitute.

bawdy *(SYN.)* vulgar, smutty, filthy, dirty, obscene, pornographic.

bawl *(SYN.)* sob, shout, wail, cry loudly, bellow, weep, cry.

bawl out *(SYN.)* scold, upbraid, censure, berate, reprove, reprimand.

bay *(SYN.)* inlet, bayou, harbor, lagoon, cove, sound, gulf.

bazaar *(SYN.)* fair, market, marketplace.

beach *(SYN.)* sands, seashore, waterfront, seaside, strand, coast, shore.

beacon *(SYN.)* light, signal, watchtower, guide, flare, warning, alarm.

bead *(SYN.)* globule, drop, pill, blob.

beak *(SYN.)* nose, bill, proboscis.

beam *(SYN.)* gleam, ray, girder, cross-member, pencil, shine, glisten, smile, glitter, gleam.

beaming *(SYN.)* joyful, bright, happy, radiant, grinning. *(ANT.)* sullen, gloomy, threatening, scowling.

bear *(SYN.)* carry, support, take, uphold, suffer, convey, allow, stand, yield, endure, tolerate, produce, sustain, brook, transport, undergo, permit, suffer, abide, tolerate. *(ANT.)* evade, shun, avoid, refuse, dodge.

bearable *(SYN.)* sufferable, supportable, manageable, tolerable. *(ANT.)* terrible, painful, unbearable, awful, intolerable.

bearing *(SYN.)* course, direction, position, posture, behavior, manner, carriage, relation, reference, connection, application, deportment, air, way, conduct.

bearings *(SYN.)* orientation, whereabouts, location, direction, position, reading, course.

bear on *(SYN.)* affect, relate to.

bear out *(SYN.)* confirm, substantiate, justify, verify, prove.

bear up *(SYN.)* carry on, endure.

bear with *(SYN.)* tolerate, forbear.

beast *(SYN.)* monster, savage, brute, creature, animal.

beastly *(SYN.)* detestable, mean, low, hateful, loathsome, nasty, unpleasant, despicable, obnoxious, brutal, brutish, offensive. *(ANT.)* considerate, sympathetic, refined, humane, fine, pleasant.

beat *(SYN.)* pulse, buffet, pound, defeat, palpitate, hit, thump, belabor, knock, overthrow, thrash, pummel, rout, smite, throb, punch, subdue, pulsate, dash, strike, overpower, vanquish, conquer, batter, overcome, blow. *(ANT.)* stroke, fail, defend, surrender, shield.

beaten *(SYN.)* disheartened, dejected, licked, discouraged, hopeless, downcast, down, depressed. *(ANT.)* eager, hopeful, cheerful.

beatific *(SYN.)* uplifted, blissful, elated, happy, wonderful, joyful, divine. *(ANT.)* awful, hellish, ill-fated, accursed.

beating *(SYN.)* whipping, drubbing, flogging, lashing, scourging, walloping.

beau *(SYN.)* lover, suitor, swain, admirer.

beautiful *(SYN.)* pretty, fair, lovely, charming, comely, handsome, elegant, attractive. *(ANT.)* repulsive, hideous, unsightly, foul, homely, plainness, unattractive, ugly.

beauty *(SYN.)* handsomeness, fairness, charm, pulchritude, attractiveness, loveliness, comeliness, grace, allegiance. *(ANT.)* ugliness, disfigurement, homeliness, plainness, deformity, eyesore.

becalm *(SYN.)* calm, quiet, smooth, still, hush, repose, settle.

because *(SYN.)* inasmuch as, as, since, for.

because of *(SYN.)* as a result of, as a consequence of.

beckon *(SYN.)* call, signal, summon, motion, gesture, wave.

becloud *(SYN.)* obfuscate, confuse, befog, confound, obscure, muddle. *(ANT.)* illuminate, clarify, solve.

become *(SYN.)* change, grow, suit, be appropriate, befit.

becoming *(SYN.)* suitable, meet, befitting, appropriate, fitting, seemly, enhancing, attractive, pleasing, flattering, tasteful, smart, adorning, ornamental. *(ANT.)* unsuitable, inappropriate, incongruent, ugly, unattractive, improper.

bed *(SYN.)* layer, cot, vein, berth, stratum, couch, accumulation, bunk, cradle.

bedazzle *(SYN.)* glare, blind, dumbfound, flabbergast, bewilder, furbish, festoon.

bedeck *(SYN.)* deck, adorn, beautify, smarten, festoon, garnish.

bedevil *(SYN.)* worry, fret, irk, torment, harass, pester, nettle, tease, vex, plague. *(ANT.)* soothe, calm, delight, please.

bedlam *(SYN.)* tumult, uproar, madhouse, commotion, confusion, racket, rumpus, pandemonium. *(ANT.)* calm, peace.

bedraggled *(SYN.)* shabby, muddy, sodden, messy, sloppy. *(ANT.)* dry, neat, clean, wellgroomed.

bedrock *(SYN.)* basis, foundation, roots, basics, essentials, fundamentals, bottom, bed, substratum, core. *(ANT.)* top, dome, apex, nonessentials.

bedroom *(SYN.)* chamber, bedchamber.

beef *(SYN.)* brawn, strength, heft, gripe, sinew, fitness, huskiness, might.

beef up *(SYN.)* reinforce, vitalize, nerve, buttress, strengthen. *(ANT.)* sap, weaken, enervate, drain.

beefy *(SYN.)* solid, strong, muscular, heavy, stocky.

befall *(SYN.)* occur, come about, happen.

before *(SYN.)* prior, earlier, in advance, formerly. *(ANT.)* behind, following, afterward, latterly, after.

befriend *(SYN.)* welcome, encourage, aid, stand by. *(ANT.)* dislike, shun, desert, avoid.

befuddle *(SYN.)* stupefy, addle, confuse, rattle, disorient.

beg *(SYN.)* solicit, ask, implore, supplicate, entreat, adjure, petition, beseech, request, importune, entreat, implore. *(ANT.)* grant, cede, give, bestow, favor.

beget *(SYN.)* sire, engender, produce, create, propagate, originate, breed, generate, procreate, father. *(ANT.)* murder, destroy, kill, abort, prevent, extinguish.

beggar *(SYN.)* scrub, tatterdemalion, pauper, wretch, ragamuffin, vagabond, starveling.

begin *(SYN.)* open, enter, arise, initiate, commence, start, inaugurate, originate, institute, create. *(ANT.)*

terminate, complete, finish, close, end, stop.

beginner *(SYN.)* nonprofessional, amateur, apprentice. *(ANT.) veteran, professional.*

beginning *(SYN.)* outset, inception, origin, source, commencement, start, opening, initiation, inauguration. *(ANT.) termination, completion, end, close, consumption, closing, ending, finish.*

begrime *(SYN.)* soil, dirty, smear, muddy, splotch, tarnish. *(ANT.) wash, clean, freshen, launder.*

begrudge *(SYN.)* resent, envy, stint, withhold, grudge.

begrudging *(SYN.)* hesitant, reluctant, resentful, unwilling, forced. *(ANT.) willing, eager, quick, spontaneous.*

beguiling *(SYN.)* enchanting, interesting, delightful, intriguing, engaging, bewitching, attractive, enthralling, captivating. *(ANT.) boring, dull, tedious.*

behalf *(SYN.)* benefit, welfare, support, aid, part, interest.

behave *(SYN.)* deport, comport, manage, act, demean, bear, interact, carry, operate, conduct.

behavior *(SYN.)* manners, carriage, disposition, action, deed, bearing, deportment, conduct, demeanor. *(ANT.) rebelliousness, misbehavior.*

behead *(SYN.)* decapitate, guillotine, decollate.

behest *(SYN.)* order, command, decree, mandate, bidding.

behind *(SYN.)* after, backward, at the back, in back of. *(ANT.) frontward, ahead, before.*

behold *(SYN.)* look, see, view, notice, observe, perceive, sight. *(ANT.) overlook, ignore.*

being *(SYN.)* life, existing, existence, living, actuality, organism, individual. *(ANT.) death, nonexistence, expiration.*

belabor *(SYN.)* repeat, reiterate, pound, explain, expatiate, din.

belated *(SYN.)* late, delayed, overdue, tardy. *(ANT.) well-timed, early.*

belch *(SYN.)* emit, erupt, gush, disgorge, bubble, eructation, burp.

beleaguered *(SYN.)* bothered, annoyed, beset, harassed, badgered, vexed, plagued, victimized.

belie *(SYN.)* distort, misrepresent, twist, disappoint.

belief *(SYN.)* trust, feeling, certitude, opinion, conviction,

persuasion, credence, confidence, reliance, faith, view, creed, assurance. *(ANT.) heresy, denial, incredulity, distrust, skepticism, doubt.*

believe *(SYN.)* hold, apprehend, fancy, support, accept, conceive, suppose, imagine, trust, credit. *(ANT.) doubt, reject, distrust, disbelieve, question.*

believer *(SYN.)* adherent, follower, devotee, convert, zealot. *(ANT.) doubter, critic, scoffer, skeptic.*

belittle *(SYN.)* underrate, depreciate, minimize, decry, disparage, diminish, demean, slight, discredit, militant, depreciate, humiliate. *(ANT.) esteem, admire, flatter, overrate, commend.*

bell *(SYN.)* pealing, ringing, signal, tolling, buzzer, chime.

belligerent *(SYN.)* aggressive, warlike, hostile, offensive, combative, militant. *(ANT.) easygoing, compromising, peaceful.*

bellow *(SYN.)* thunder, roar, scream, shout, yell, howl.

bellwether *(SYN.)* leader, pilot, guide, ringleader, boss, shepherd.

belly *(SYN.)* stomach, abdomen, paunch.

belonging *(SYN.)* loyalty, relationship, kinship, acceptance, rapport.

belongings *(SYN.)* property, effects, possessions.

beloved *(SYN.)* adored, sweet, loved, cherished, prized, esteemed, valued, darling.

below *(SYN.)* under, less, beneath, underneath, lower. *(ANT.) aloft, overhead, above, over.*

belt *(SYN.)* girdle, sash, strap, cummerbund, band, waistband, whack, hit, wallop, punch.

bemoan *(SYN.)* mourn, lament, grieve, sorrow, regret, deplore.

bend *(SYN.)* turn, curve, incline, submit, bow, lean, crook, twist, yield, stoop, crouch, agree, suppress, oppress, mold, kneel, deflect, subdue, influence. *(ANT.) resist, straighten, break, stiffen.*

beneath *(SYN.)* under, below. *(ANT.) above, over.*

benediction *(SYN.)* thanks, blessing, prayer.

beneficial *(SYN.)* salutary, good, wholesome, advantageous, useful, helpful, serviceable, profitable. *(ANT.) harmful, destructive, injurious, disadvantageous, unwholesome,*

deleterious, detrimental.

benefit *(SYN.)* support, help, gain, avail, profit, account, favor, aid, good, advantage, serve, interest, behalf, service. *(ANT.) handicap, calamity, trouble, disadvantage, distress.*

benevolence *(SYN.)* magnanimity, charity, tenderness, altruism, humanity, philanthropy, generosity, liberality, beneficence, goodwill. *(ANT.) malevolence, unkindness, cruelty, selfishness, inhumanity.*

benevolent *(SYN.)* kindhearted, tender, merciful, generous, altruistic, obliging, kind, good, well-wishing, philanthropy, liberal, unselfish, kindly, disposed, openhearted, humane, benign, friendly. *(ANT.) malevolent, greedy, wicked, harsh.*

bent *(SYN.)* curved, crooked, resolved, determined, set, inclined, firm, decided. *(ANT.) straight.*

berate *(SYN.)* scold.

beseech *(SYN.)* appeal, entreat, plead, ask, beg, implore.

beset *(SYN.)* surround, attack.

besides *(SYN.)* moreover, further, except for, also, as well, furthermore.

besiege *(SYN.)* assault, attack, siege, bombard, raid, charge.

bespeak *(SYN.)* engage, reserve, indicate, show, signify, express.

best *(SYN.)* choice, prime, select. *(ANT.) worst.*

bestial *(SYN.)* brutal, beastly, savage, cruel.

bestow *(SYN.)* confer, place, put, award, give, present. *(ANT.) withdraw, withhold.*

bet *(SYN.)* gamble, give, stake, wager, pledge, ante.

betray *(SYN.)* reveal, deliver, expose, mislead, trick, deceive, exhibit, show. *(ANT.) shelter, protect, safeguard.*

betrothal *(SYN.)* marriage, engagement, contract.

better *(SYN.)* superior, preferable, improve. *(ANT.) worsen.*

between *(SYN.)* among, betwixt.

beware *(SYN.)* take care, watch out, look sharp, be careful.

bewilder *(SYN.)* perplex, confuse, mystify, baffle, puzzle, overwhelm. *(ANT.) clarify, enlighten.*

bewitch *(SYN.)* captivate, charm, delight, enchant.

beyond *(SYN.)* past, farther, exceeding.

bias *(SYN.)* slant, inclination,

proneness, turn, bent, penchant, tendency, disposition, propensity, partiality, predisposition, leaning, proclivity, prejudice, influence, warp, slanting, predilection. *(ANT.) fairness, justice, even-handedness, equity, detachment, impartiality.*

bible *(SYN.)* guide, handbook, gospel, manual, sourcebook, guidebook.

bibulous *(SYN.)* guzzling, intemperate, winebibbing, sottish, alcoholic. *(ANT.) sober, moderate.*

bicker *(SYN.)* dispute, argue, wrangle, quarrel. *(ANT.) go along with, agree.*

bid *(SYN.)* order, command, direct, wish, greet, say, offer, instruct, invite, purpose, tender, proposal.

bidding *(SYN.)* behest, request, decree, call, charge, beck, summons, solicitation, invitation, instruction, mandate.

bide *(SYN.)* stay, tarry, delay, wait, remain.

big *(SYN.)* large, huge, bulky, immense, colossal, majestic, august, monstrous, hulking, gigantic, massive, great, enormous, tremendous, outgoing, important, kind, big-hearted, considerable, generous, grand. *(ANT.) small, little, tiny, immature, petite.*

big-hearted *(SYN.)* good-natured, liberal, generous, unselfish, open-handed, unstinting, charitable, magnanimous. *(ANT.) cold, selfish, mean, uncharitable.*

bigoted *(SYN.)* intolerant, partial, prejudiced, biased, unfair, chauvinist.

bigotry *(SYN.)* bias, blindness, intolerance, unfairness, prejudice, ignorance, passion, sectarianism. *(ANT.) acceptance, open-mindedness.*

big-shot *(SYN.)* somebody, brass hat, big gun. *(ANT.) underling, nobody, cipher.*

bijou *(SYN.)* gem, bauble, jewel, ornament.

bile *(SYN.)* spleen, rancor, anger, bitterness, peevishness, ill-humor, resentment, discontent, irascibility. *(ANT.) cheerfulness, affability, pleasantness.*

bilge *(SYN.)* hogwash, drivel, gibberish, rubbish, bosh, foolishness, twaddle.

bilious *(SYN.)* petulant, crabby, ill-natured, cross, peevish, crotchety, cranky. *(ANT.) happy, agreeable, pleasant, good-natured.*

bilk (SYN.) defraud, trick, cheat, hood-wink, deceive, fleece, rook, bamboozle.

bill (SYN.) charge, invoice, account, statement, beak.

billet (SYN.) housing, quarters, berth, shelter, barrack, installation.

billingsgate (SYN.) swearing, scurrility, cursing, abuse, vulgarity, gutter, profanity.

billow (SYN.) surge, swell, rise, rush, peaking, magnification, amplification, augmentation, increase, intensification. (ANT.) lowering, decrease.

bin (SYN.) cubbyhole, box, container, chest, cubicle, crib, receptacle, can.

bind (SYN.) connect, restrain, band, fasten, oblige, obligate, engage, wrap, connect, weld, attach, tie, require, restrict. (ANT.) unlace, loose, unfasten, untie, free.

binding (SYN.) compulsory, obligatory, mandatory, compelling, unalterable, imperative, indissoluble, unconditional, unchangeable, hard-and-fast. (ANT.) adjustable, flexible, elastic, changeable.

binge (SYN.) fling, spree, carousal, toot.

birth (SYN.) origin, beginning, infancy, inception. (ANT.) decline, death, disappearance, end.

biscuit (SYN.) bun, roll, cake, muffin, bread, rusk, scone.

bit (SYN.) fraction, portion, scrap, fragment, particle, drop, speck, harness, small amount, restraint, morsel.

bite (SYN.) gnaw, chew, nip, sting, pierce, mouthful, snack, morsel.

biting (SYN.) cutting, sharp, acid, sneering, sarcastic. (ANT.) soothing, kind, gentle, agreeable.

bitter (SYN.) distasteful, sour, acrid, pungent, piercing, vicious, severe, biting, distressful, stinging, distressing, ruthless, hostile, grievous, harsh, painful, tart. (ANT.) sweet, mellow, pleasant, delicious.

bizarre (SYN.) peculiar, strange, odd, uncommon, queer, unusual. (ANT.) usual, everyday, ordinary, inconspicuous.

black (SYN.) sooty, dark, ebony, inky, swarthy, soiled, filthy, dirty, stained, somber, depressing, sad, dismal, gloomy. (ANT.) white, clean, pristine, glowing, pure, cheerful, light-skinned, sunny, bright.

blackball (SYN.) turn down, ban, blacklist, exclude, snub, reject, debar. (ANT.) accept, include, invite, ask, bid.

blacken (SYN.) tar, ink, black, darken, besoot, smudge, begrime, discredit, defile, dull, dim, tarnish, ebonize, denounce, sully, libel, blemish, defame. (ANT.) exalt, honor, whiten, brighten, shine, bleach.

blackmail (SYN.) bribe, payment, bribery, extortion, shakedown, coercion.

blackout (SYN.) faint, coma, unconsciousness, oblivion, amnesia, stupor, swoon.

bladder (SYN.) saccule, sac, vesicle, pouch, pod, cell, blister, container, cyst.

blade (SYN.) cutter, lancet, knife, sword.

blame (SYN.) upbraid, criticize, fault, guilt, accuse, rebuke, charge, implicate, impeach, tattle, condemn, indict, responsibility, censure, denounce, reproach. (ANT.) exonerate, credit, honor, absolve.

blameless (SYN.) moral, innocent, worthy, faultless. (ANT.) blameworthy, culpable, guilty.

blanch (SYN.) whiten, bleach, decolorize, peroxide, fade, wash out, dim, dull.

bland (SYN.) soft, smooth, gentle, agreeable, vapid, insipid, mild, polite. (ANT.) harsh, outspoken, disagreeable.

blandish (SYN.) praise, compliment, overpraise, cajole, puff, adulate, salve, fawn, court, toady, butter up, please, jolly. (ANT.) insult, deride, criticize, belittle.

blandisher (SYN.) adulator, booster, sycophant, eulogist, flunky. (ANT.) knocker, fault-finder, belittler.

blandishment (SYN.) applause, cajolery, honor, adulation, plaudits, acclaim, fawning, compliments. (ANT.) criticism, deprecation.

blank (SYN.) unmarked, expressionless, uninterested, form, area, void, vacant, empty. (ANT.) marked, filled, alert, animated.

blanket (SYN.) quilt, coverlet, cover, comforter, robe, padding, carpet, wrapper, mantle, envelope, housing, coat, comprehensive, universal, across-the-board, panoramic, omnibus. (ANT.) limited, detailed, restricted, precise.

blare (SYN.) roar, blast, resound, jar, scream, clang, peal, trumpet, toot, hoot.

blasphemous (SYN.) profane, irreverent, impious, godless, ungodly, sacrilegious, irreligious. (ANT.) reverent, reverential, religious, pious.

blasphemy (SYN.) profanation, impiousness, cursing, irreverence, sacrilege, abuse, swearing, contempt. (ANT.) respect, piety, reverence, devotion.

blast (SYN.) burst, explosion, discharge, blow-out.

blasted (SYN.) blighted, withered, ravaged, decomposed, spoiled, destroyed.

blastoff (SYN.) launching, expulsion, launch, shot, projection.

blatant (SYN.) shameless, notorious, brazen, flagrant, glaring, bold, obvious. (ANT.) deft, subtle, insidious, devious.

blaze (SYN.) inferno, shine, flare, marking, fire, outburst, holocaust, notch, flame. (ANT.) die, dwindle.

bleach (SYN.) pale, whiten, blanch, whitener. (ANT.) darken, blacken.

bleak (SYN.) dreary, barren, cheerless, depressing, gloomy, windswept, bare, cold, dismal, desolate, raw, chilly. (ANT.) lush, hopeful, promising, cheerful.

bleary (SYN.) hazy, blurry, fuzzy, misty, clouded, overcast, dim. (ANT.) clear, vivid, precise, clear-cut.

bleed (SYN.) pity, lose blood, grieve, sorrow.

blemish (SYN.) injury, speck, flaw, scar, disgrace, imperfection, stain, fault, blot. (ANT.) purity, embellishment, adornment, perfection.

blend (SYN.) beat, intermingle, combine, fuse, unite, consolidate, amalgamate, conjoin, mix, coalesce, intermix, join, merge, compound, combination, stir, mixture, mingle. (ANT.) separate, decompose, analyze, disintegrate.

bless (SYN.) thank, celebrate, extol, glorify, adore, delight, praise, gladden, exalt. (ANT.) denounce, blaspheme, slander, curse.

blessed (SYN.) sacred, holy, consecrated, dedicated, hallowed, sacrosanct, beatified, joyful, delighted, joyous, sainted, canonized, blissful. (ANT.) miserable, sad, dispirited, cheerless.

blessing (SYN.) sanction, favor, grace, benediction, invocation, approbation, approval, compliment, bounty, windfall, gift, benefit, advantage, kindness, felicitation, invocation. (ANT.) disapproval, execration, curse, denunciation, malediction, rebuke, displeasure, condemnation, adversity, misfortune, mishap, calamity.

blight (SYN.) decay, disease, spoil, sickness, wither, ruin, damage, harm, decaying, epidemic, affliction, destroy.

blind (SYN.) sightless, unmindful, rash, visionless, ignorant, unsighted, unconscious, discerning, heedless, oblivious, purblind, unknowing, screen, unaware, thoughtless, shade, unthinking, cover, curtain, without thought, headlong. (ANT.) discerning, sensible, calculated, perceiving, perceptive, aware.

blink (SYN.) bat, glance, flicker, wink, twinkle.

bliss (SYN.) ecstasy, rapture, glee, elation, joy, blessedness, gladness, happiness, delight, felicity, blissfulness. (ANT.) woe, sadness, sorrow, grief, unhappiness, torment, wretchedness, misery.

blissful (SYN.) happy, elated, rapturous, ecstatic, paradisiacal, joyous, enraptured.

blister (SYN.) swelling, welt, sore, blob, bubble, inflammation, boil, canker.

blithe (SYN.) breezy, merry, airy, lighthearted, light, gay, fanciful, graceful. (ANT.) morose, grouchy, low-spirited, gloomy.

blitz (SYN.) strike, onslaught, thrust, raid, lunge, drive, incursion, assault, sally.

blizzard (SYN.) storm, snowfall, gale, tempest, blast, blow, swirl.

bloat (SYN.) distend, puff up, inflate, swell. (ANT.) deflate.

blob (SYN.) bubble, blister, pellet, globule.

block (SYN.) clog, hinder, bar, impede, close, obstruct, barricade, blockade, obstruction, hindrance, obstacle, impediment, retard, check, stop. (ANT.) forward, promote, aid, clear, advance, advantage, assist, further, open.

blockade (SYN.) barrier, fortification, obstruction, barricade.

blockhead (SYN.) dunce, dolt, fool, sap, idiot, simpleton, chump, booby, bonehead, woodenhead.

blood (SYN.) murder, gore, slaughter, bloodshed, ancestry, lineage, heritage.

bloodcurdling *(SYN.)* hair-raising, terrifying, alarming, chilling, stunning, scary.

bloodless *(SYN.)* dead, torpid, dull, drab, cold, colorless, passionless, lackluster. *(ANT.)* passionate, vital, ebullient, animated, vivacious.

bloodshed *(SYN.)* murder, killing, slaying, blood bath, massacre, carnage.

bloodthirsty *(SYN.)* murderous, cruel.

bloody *(SYN.)* cruel, pitiless, bloodthirsty, inhuman, ruthless, ferocious, murderous. *(ANT.)* kind, gentle.

bloom *(SYN.)* thrive, glow, flourish, blossom, flower. *(ANT.)* wane, decay, dwindle, shrivel, wither.

blooming *(SYN.)* flush, vigorous, thriving, vital, abloom, healthy, fresh, booming. *(ANT.)* flagging, declining, withering.

blooper *(SYN.)* muff, fluff, error, bungle, botch, blunder, fumble, howler, indiscretion.

blossom *(SYN.)* bloom, flower, flourish. *(ANT.)* shrink, wither, dwindle, fade.

blot *(SYN.)* stain, inkblot, spot, ink-stain, blemish, dishonor, disgrace, spatter, obliterate, soil, dry.

blot out *(SYN.)* wipe out, destroy, obliterate, abolish, annihilate, cancel, expunge, strike out, shade, darken, shadow, overshadow, obfuscate, cloud, eclipse.

blow *(SYN.)* hit, thump, slap, cuff, box, shock, move, drive, spread, breeze, puff, whistle, inflate, enlarge.

blowout *(SYN.)* blast, explosion, burst.

blue *(SYN.)* sapphire, azure, gloomy, sad, unhappy, depressed, dejected, melancholy. *(ANT.)* cheerful, optimistic, happy.

blueprint *(SYN.)* design, plan, scheme, chart, draft, prospectus, outline, proposal, conception, project, layout.

blues *(SYN.)* dumps, melancholy, depression, doldrums, despondency, gloominess, moroseness.

bluff *(SYN.)* steep, perpendicular, vertical, abrupt, precipitous, rough, open, frank, hearty, blunt, foot, mislead, pretend, deceive, fraud, lie, fake, deceit.

blunder *(SYN.)* error, flounder, mistake, stumble.

blunt *(SYN.)* solid, abrupt, rough, dull, pointless, plain, bluff, edgeless, unceremonious, obtuse, rude, outspoken, unsharpened, rounded, worn, crude, direct, impolite, short, curt, gruff. *(ANT.)* tactful, polite, subtle, polished, suave, sharp, keen, pointed, diplomatic.

blur *(SYN.)* sully, dim, obscure, stain, dull, confuse, cloud, smear, stain, smudge. *(ANT.)* clear, clarify.

blush *(SYN.)* redden.

board *(SYN.)* embark, committee, wood, mount, cabinet, food, get on, lumber.

boast *(SYN.)* vaunt, flaunt, brag, glory, crow, exaggerate. *(ANT.)* humble, apologize, minimize, deprecate.

body *(SYN.)* remains, bulk, mass, carcass, form, company, corpus, society, firmness, group, torso, substance, collection, cadaver, trunk, group, throng, company, crowd, band. *(ANT.)* spirit, intellect, soul.

bogus *(SYN.)* counterfeit, false, pretend, fake, phony. *(ANT.)* genuine.

boil *(SYN.)* seethe, bubble, pimple, fume, cook, swelling, rage, foam, simmer, stew.

boisterous *(SYN.)* rough, violent, rowdy, noisy, tumultuous. *(ANT.)* serene.

bold *(SYN.)* daring, forward, pushy, striking, brave, dauntless, rude, prominent, adventurous, fearless, insolent, conspicuous, defiant, arrogant, cavalier, brazen, unafraid, intrepid, courageous, valiant, heroic, gallant, disrespectful, impudent, shameless. *(ANT.)* modest, bashful, cowardly, timid, retiring, flinching, fearful, timorous, polite, courteous, deferential.

bolt *(SYN.)* break away, fastener, floe, take flight, lock.

bombard *(SYN.)* shell, open fire, bomb, rake, assail, attack.

bond *(SYN.)* fastener, rope, tie, cord, connection, attachment, link, tie, promise. *(ANT.)* sever, separate, untie, disconnect.

bondage *(SYN.)* slavery, thralldom, captivity, imprisonment, servitude, confinement, vassalage, enslavement. *(ANT.)* liberation, emancipation, free, independence, freedom.

bonds *(SYN.)* chains, cuffs, fetters, shackles, irons, bracelets.

bone up *(SYN.)* learn, master, study, relearn.

bonus *(SYN.)* more, extra, premium, gift, reward, bounty.

bony *(SYN.)* lean, lank, thin, lanky, rawboned, fleshless, skinny, gangling, weight. *(ANT.)* plump, fleshy, stout.

book *(SYN.)* manual, textbook, work, booklet, monograph, brochure, tract, volume, pamphlet, treatise, publication, hardcover, paperback, novel, workbook, text.

bookish *(SYN.)* formal, scholarly, theoretical, academic, learned, scholastic, erudite. *(ANT.)* ignorant.

boom *(SYN.)* advance, grow, flourish, progress, gain, roar, beam, rumble, reverberate, thunder, prosper, swell, thrive, pole, rush. *(ANT.)* decline, fail, recession.

booming *(SYN.)* flourishing, blooming, thriving, vigorous, prospering, exuberant. *(ANT.)* waning, dying, failing, declining.

boon *(SYN.)* gift, jolly, blessing, pleasant, godsend, windfall.

boondocks *(SYN.)* sticks, backwoods.

boor *(SYN.)* lout, clown, oaf, yokel, rustic, vulgarian, ruffian.

boorish *(SYN.)* coarse, churlish, uncivil, ill-mannered, ill-bred, uncivilized, crude, uncouth. *(ANT.)* polite, cultivated, well-mannered.

boost *(SYN.)* push, lift, help, hoist, shove. *(ANT.)* depress, lower, belittle, disparage, decrease, decline, reduction, down turn.

booster *(SYN.)* supporter, fan, rooter, plugger, follower.

boot *(SYN.)* shoe, kick.

booth *(SYN.)* enclosure, cubicle, stand, compartment, box.

bootless *(SYN.)* purposeless, ineffective, profitless, useless. *(ANT.)* favorable, successful, useful.

bootlicker *(SYN.)* flunky, fawner, toady, sycophant.

booty *(SYN.)* prize, plunder, loot.

booze *(SYN.)* spirits, drink, liquor, alcohol.

border *(SYN.)* fringe, rim, verge, boundary, edge, termination, brink, limit, brim, outskirts, frontier, margin. *(ANT.)* interior, center, mainland, core, middle.

borderline *(SYN.)* unclassifiable, indeterminate, halfway, obscure, inexact, indefinite, unclear. *(ANT.)* precise, absolute, definite.

border on *(SYN.)* approximate, approach, resemble, echo, parallel, connect.

bore *(SYN.)* tire, weary, hole, perforate, pierce, drill. *(ANT.)* arouse, captivate, excite, interest.

boredom *(SYN.)* ennui, doldrums, weariness, dullness, tedium. *(ANT.)* stimulation, motive, activity, stimulus, excitement.

boring *(SYN.)* monotonous, dull, dead, flat, tedious, wearisome, trite, prosaic, humdrum, long-winded.

born *(SYN.)* hatched, produced.

borrow *(SYN.)* copy, adopt, simulate, mirror, assume, usurp, plagiarize, take. *(ANT.)* allow, advance, invent, originate, credit, lend.

bosom *(SYN.)* chest, breast, feelings, thoughts, mind, interior, marrow, heart.

boss *(SYN.)* director, employer, oversee, direct, foreman, supervisor, manager.

bossy *(SYN.)* overbearing, arrogant, domineering, lordly, tyrannical. *(ANT.)* flexible, easygoing, cooperative.

botch *(SYN.)* blunder, bungle, fumble, goof, muff, mishandle, mismanage. *(ANT.)* perform, realize.

bother *(SYN.)* haunt, molest, trouble, annoy, upset, fleeting, transient, harass, inconvenience, momentary, disturb, passing, pester, tease, irritate, worry, vex. *(ANT.)* prolonged, extended, long, protracted, lengthy, comfort, solace.

bothersome *(SYN.)* irritating, vexatious, worrisome, annoying, distressing, troublesome, disturbing.

bottle *(SYN.)* container, flask, vessel, decanter, vial, ewer, jar.

bottleneck *(SYN.)* obstacle, obstruction, barrier, block, blockage, detour.

bottom *(SYN.)* basis, fundament, base, groundwork, foot, depths, lowest part, underside, foundation, seat, buttocks, rear, behind. *(ANT.)* top, peak, apex, summit, topside.

bough *(SYN.)* branch, arm, limb.

bounce *(SYN.)* recoil, ricochet, rebound.

bound *(SYN.)* spring, vault, hop, leap, start, surrounded, jump, limit, jerk, boundary, bounce, skip, tied, shackled, trussed, fettered, certain, sure, destined, compelled, required. *(ANT.)* unfettered, free.

boundary *(SYN.)* bound,

limit, border, margin, outline, circumference, perimeter, division, frontier, edge.

boundless *(SYN.)* limitless, endless, inexhaustible, unlimited, eternal, infinite. *(ANT.)* restricted, limited.

bounteous *(SYN.)* plentiful, generous, liberal, abundant. *(ANT.)* scarce, rare.

bountiful *(SYN.)* bounteous, fertile, plentiful, generous, abundant. *(ANT.)* sparing, infertile, scarce.

bounty *(SYN.)* generosity, gift, award, bonus, reward, prize, premium.

bourgeois *(SYN.)* common, ordinary, commonplace, middle-class, conventional. *(ANT.)* upper-class, unconventional, loose, aristocratic.

bout *(SYN.)* round, contest, conflict, test, struggle, match, spell, fight.

bow *(SYN.)* bend, yield, kneel, submit, stoop.

bowels *(SYN.)* entrails, intestines, innards, guts, stomach.

bowl *(SYN.)* container, dish, pot, pottery, crock, jug, vase.

bowl over *(SYN.)* fell, floor, overturn, astound, nonplus, stagger, jar.

bow out *(SYN.)* give up, withdraw, retire, resign, abandon.

box *(SYN.)* hit, fight, crate, case, container.

boxer *(SYN.)* prizefighter, fighter.

boy *(SYN.)* male, youngster, lad, kid, fellow, buddy, youth. *(ANT.)* girl, man.

boycott *(SYN.)* picket, strike, ban, revolt, blackball.

boyfriend *(SYN.)* date, young man, sweetheart, courtier, beau.

brace *(SYN.)* strengthen, tie, prop, support, tighten, stay, strut, bind, truss, crutch.

bracelet *(SYN.)* armband, bangle, circlet.

bracing *(SYN.)* stimulating, refreshing, restorative, fortifying, invigorating.

bracket *(SYN.)* join, couple, enclose, relate, brace, support.

brag *(SYN.)* boast, flaunt, vaunt, bluster, swagger. *(ANT.)* demean, debase, denigrate, degrade, depreciate, deprecate.

braid *(SYN.)* weave, twine, wreath, plait.

brain *(SYN.)* sense, intelligence, intellect, common sense, understanding, reason. *(ANT.)* stupid, stupidity.

brake *(SYN.)* decelerate, stop, curb. *(ANT.)* accelerate.

branch *(SYN.)* shoot, limb, bough, tributary, offshoot, part, division, expand, department, divide, spread, subdivision.

brand *(SYN.)* make, trademark, label, kind, burn, trade name, mark, stamp, blaze.

brave *(SYN.)* bold, daring, gallant, valorous, adventurous, heroic, magnanimous, chivalrous, audacious, valiant, courageous, fearless, intrepid, unafraid. *(ANT.)* weak, cringing, timid, cowardly, fearful, craven.

brawl *(SYN.)* racket, quarrel, fracas, riot, fight, melee, fray, disturbance, dispute, disagreement.

brawn *(SYN.)* strength, muscle. *(ANT.)* weakness.

brazen *(SYN.)* immodest, forward, shameless, bold, brassy, impudent, insolent, rude. *(ANT.)* retiring, self-effacing, modest, shy.

breach *(SYN.)* rupture, fracture, rift, break, crack, gap, opening, breaking, quarrel, violation.

break *(SYN.)* demolish, pound, rack, smash, burst, rupture, disobey, violate, crack, infringe, crush, squeeze, transgress, fracture, shatter, wreck, crash, atomize, disintegrate, collapse, splinter, gap, breach, opening. *(ANT.)* restore, heal, join, renovate, mend, repair.

breed *(SYN.)* engender, bear, propagate, father, beget, rear, conceive, train, generate, raise, procreate, nurture, create, mother, produce, originate. *(ANT.)* murder, abort, kill.

breeze *(SYN.)* air, wind, zephyr, breath. *(ANT.)* calm.

breezy *(SYN.)* jolly, spry, active, brisk, energetic, lively, carefree, spirited.

brevity *(SYN.)* briefness, conciseness. *(ANT.)* length.

brew *(SYN.)* plot, plan, cook, ferment, prepare, scheme.

bribe *(SYN.)* buy off.

bridle *(SYN.)* control, hold, restrain, check, harness, curb, restraint, halter. *(ANT.)* release, free, loose.

brief *(SYN.)* curt, short, fleeting, passing, compendious, terse, laconic, succinct, momentary, transient, temporary, concise, compact, condensed. *(ANT.)* long, extended, prolonged, lengthy, protracted, comprehensive, extensive, exhaustive.

brigand *(SYN.)* bandit, robber, thief.

bright *(SYN.)* luminous, gleaming, clever, witty, brilliant, lucid, vivid, clear, smart, intelligent, lustrous, clever, shining, shiny, sparkling, shimmering, radiant, cheerful, lively, gay, happy, lighthearted, keen, promising, favorable, encouraging. *(ANT.)* sullen, dull, murky, dark, gloomy, dim, lusterless, boring, colorless, stupid, backward, slow.

brilliant *(SYN.)* bright, clear, smart, intelligent, sparkling, shining, alert, vivid, splendid, radiant, glittering, talented, ingenious, gifted. *(ANT.)* mediocre, dull, lusterless, second-rate.

brim *(SYN.)* border, margin, lip, rim, edge. *(ANT.)* middle, center.

bring *(SYN.)* fetch, take, carry, raise, introduce, propose. *(ANT.)* remove, withdraw.

brink *(SYN.)* limit, verge, rim, margin, edge.

brisk *(SYN.)* fresh, breezy, cool, lively, refreshing, spirited, jolly, energetic, quick, active, animated, nimble, spry, agile, sharp, keen, stimulating, invigorating. *(ANT.)* musty, faded, stagnant, decayed, hackneyed, slow, lethargic, sluggish, still, dull, oppressive.

briskness *(SYN.)* energy, exercise, motion, rapidity, agility, action, quickness, activity, vigor, liveliness, movement. *(ANT.)* inertia, idleness, sloth, dullness, inactivity.

bristle *(SYN.)* flare up, anger, rage, seethe, get mad.

brittle *(SYN.)* crumbling, frail, breakable, delicate, splintery, crisp, fragile, weak. *(ANT.)* tough, enduring, unbreakable, thick, strong, sturdy, flexible, elastic, supple.

broach *(SYN.)* set afoot, introduce, inaugurate, start, mention, launch, advance.

broad *(SYN.)* large, wide, tolerant, expanded, vast, liberal, sweeping, roomy, expansive, extended, general, extensive, full. *(ANT.)* restricted, confined, narrow, constricted, slim, tight, limited, negligible.

broadcast *(SYN.)* distribute, announce, publish, scatter, circulate, spread, send, transmit, relay.

broaden *(SYN.)* spread, widen, amplify, enlarge, extend, increase, add to, expand, stretch, deepen, magnify. *(ANT.)* tighten, narrow, constrict, straiten.

broad-minded *(SYN.)* unprejudiced, tolerant, liberal, unbigoted. *(ANT.)* prejudiced, petty, narrow-minded.

brochure *(SYN.)* booklet, pamphlet, leaflet, mailing, circular, tract, flier.

broil *(SYN.)* cook, burn, beat, roast, bake, scorch, fire, grill, singe, sear, toast.

broken *(SYN.)* flattened, rent, shattered, wrecked, destroyed, reduced, smashed, crushed, fractured, ruptured, interrupted, burst, separated. *(ANT.)* whole, integral, united, repaired.

brokenhearted *(SYN.)* disconsolate, forlorn, heartbroken, sad, grieving.

bromide *(SYN.)* banality, platitude, stereotype, commonplace, slogan, proverb.

brooch *(SYN.)* clasp, pin, breast-pin.

brood *(SYN.)* study, consider, ponder, reflect, contemplate, meditate, young, litter, offspring, think, muse, deliberate.

brook *(SYN.)* rivulet, run, branch, stream, creek.

brother *(SYN.)* comrade, man, kinsman, sibling. *(ANT.)* sister.

brotherhood *(SYN.)* kinship, kindness, fraternity, fellowship, clan, society, brotherliness, bond, association, relationship, solidarity. *(ANT.)* strife, discard, acrimony, opposition.

brotherly *(SYN.)* affectionate, fraternal, cordial, sympathetic, benevolent, philanthropic, humane, kindred, communal, altruistic.

brow *(SYN.)* forehead, eyebrow.

browbeat *(SYN.)* bully, domineer, bulldoze, intimidate, henpeck, oppress, grind.

brown study *(SYN.)* contemplation, reflection, reverie, musing, thoughtfulness, deliberation, rumination, selfcommunion.

browse *(SYN.)* scan, graze, read, feed.

bruise *(SYN.)* hurt, injure, wound, damage, abrasion, injury, contusion, mark, harm, wound.

brunt *(SYN.)* force, impact, shock, strain, oppression, severity.

brush *(SYN.)* rub, wipe, clean, bushes, remove, shrubs, broom, whisk, paintbrush, hairbrush, underbrush, thicket.

brush-off (SYN.) dismissal, snub, sight, rebuff, turndown.

brusque (SYN.) sudden, curt, hasty, blunt, rough, steep, precipitate, rugged, craggy, gruff, surly, abrupt, short, bluff. (ANT.) smooth, anticipated, courteous, expected, gradual, personable.

brutal (SYN.) brute, cruel, inhuman, rude, barbarous, gross, sensual, ferocious, brutish, coarse, bestial, carnal, remorseless, ruthless, savage, mean, pitiless, barbaric. (ANT.) kind, courteous, humane, civilized, gentle, kindhearted, mild.

brute (SYN.) monster, barbarian, beast, animal, wild, savage.

bubble (SYN.) boil, foam, seethe, froth.

buccaneer (SYN.) sea robber, privateer, pirate.

buck (SYN.) spring, jump, vault, leap.

bucket (SYN.) pot, pail, canister, can.

buckle (SYN.) hook, fastening, fastener, bend, wrinkle, clip, clasp, distort, catch, strap, fasten, collapse, yield, warp.

bud (SYN.) develop, sprout.

buddy (SYN.) companion, comrade, friend, partner, pal.

budge (SYN.) stir, move.

budget (SYN.) schedule, ration.

buff (SYN.) shine, polish, burnish, rub, wax.

buffet (SYN.) bat, strike, clout, blow, knock, beat, crack, hit, slap, cabinet, counter, server.

buffoon (SYN.) jester, fool, clown, jokester, zany, comedian, chump, boor, dolt.

bug (SYN.) fault, hitch, defect, catch, snag, failing, rub, flaw, snarl, weakness, annoy, pester, hector, vex, nag, nettle.

bugbear (SYN.) bogy, specter, demon, devil, fiend.

build (SYN.) found, rear, establish, constructed, raise, set up, erect, assemble. (ANT.) raze, destroy, overthrow, demolish, undermine.

building (SYN.) residence, structure, house, edifice.

buildup (SYN.) gain, enlargement, increase, praise, commendation, promotion, jump, expansion, uptrend, testimonial, plug, puff, blurb, endorsement, compliment. (ANT.) reduction, decrease, decline.

bulge (SYN.) lump, protuberance, bump, swelling, protrusion, extend, protrude.

(ANT.) hollow, shrink, contract, depression.

bulk (SYN.) lump, magnitude, volume, size, mass, most, majority.

bulky (SYN.) great, big, huge, large, enormous, massive, immense, clumsy, cumbersome, unwieldy. (ANT.) tiny, little, small, petite, handy, delicate.

bull (SYN.) push, force, press, drive, thrust, bump.

bulldoze (SYN.) cow, bully, coerce, thrust, push.

bulletin (SYN.) news, flash, message, statement, newsletter, circular.

bullheaded (SYN.) dogged, stiff-necked, stubborn, mulish, rigid, pigheaded, willful, tenacious, unyielding. (ANT.) flexible, submissive, compliant.

bully (SYN.) pester, tease, intimidate, harass, domineer.

bulwark (SYN.) wall, bastion, abutment, bank, dam, rampart, shoulder, parapet, backing, maintainer, embankment, safeguard, reinforcement, sustainer.

bum (SYN.) idler, loafer, drifter, hobo, wretch, dawdler, beggar, vagrant.

bumbling (SYN.) bungling, inept, blundering, clumsy, incompetent, awkward, maladroit, lumbering, ungainly. (ANT.) facile, handy, dexterous, proficient.

bump (SYN.) shake, push, hit, shove, prod, collide, knock, bang, strike.

bumpkin (SYN.) hick, yokel, rustic, yahoo.

bumptious (SYN.) arrogant, self-assertive, conceited, forward, overbearing, pushy, boastful, obtrusive. (ANT.) sheepish, self-effacing, retiring, shrinking, unobtrusive, diffident.

bumpy (SYN.) uneven, jolting, rough, jarring, rocky, coarse, irregular. (ANT.) flat, smooth, flush, polished, level.

bunch (SYN.) batch, bundle, cluster, company, collection, flock, group.

bundle (SYN.) package, mass, collection, batch, parcel, packet, box, carton, bunch.

bungalow (SYN.) ranch house, cabana, cabin, cottage, lodge, summer house, villa.

bungle (SYN.) fumble, botch, foul up, boggle, mess up, louse up, blunder.

bunk (SYN.) berth, rubbish, nonsense, couch, bed, cot.

buoyant (SYN.) light, jolly, spirited, effervescent, blithe, sprightly, lively, resilient. (ANT.) hopeless, dejected, sullen, depressed, heavy, despondent, sinking, low, pessimistic, downcast, glum.

burden (SYN.) oppress, afflict, trouble, encumber, tax, weight, load, worry, contents, trial, lade, overload. (ANT.) lighten, alleviate, ease, mitigate, console, disburden.

bureau (SYN.) office, division, department, unit, commission, chest, dresser.

bureaucrat (SYN.) clerk, official, functionary, servant, politician.

burglar (SYN.) thief, robber.

burial (SYN.) interment, funeral.

burn (SYN.) scorch, blaze, scald, sear, char, incinerate, fire, flare, combust. (ANT.) quench, extinguish.

burrow (SYN.) tunnel, search, seek, dig, excavate, hunt, den, hole.

burst (SYN.) exploded, broken, erupt.

bury (SYN.) hide, inhume, conceal, immure, cover, inter, entomb, secrete. (ANT.) reveal, display, open, raise, disinter.

business (SYN.) employment, profession, trade, work, art, vocation, occupation, company, concern, firm. (ANT.) hobby, avocation, pastime.

bustle (SYN.) noise, flurry, action, fuss, ado, stir, excitement, commotion. (ANT.) calmness, composure, serenity, peacefulness.

busy (SYN.) careful, industrious, active, patient, assiduous, diligent, perseverant. (ANT.) unconcerned, indifferent, careless, inactive, unemployed, lazy, indolent.

busybody (SYN.) gossip, tattletale, pry, meddler, snoop.

but (SYN.) nevertheless, yet, however, though, although, still.

butcher (SYN.) kill, murder, slaughter, assassinate, slay, massacre. (ANT.) save, protect, vivify, animate, resuscitate.

butt (SYN.) bump, ram, bunt, shove, jam, drive, blow, push, thrust, propulsion.

buttocks (SYN.) hind end, rump, posterior, behind, bottom, rear, butt.

button (SYN.) clasp, close, fasten, hook, buttress, support, brace, stay, frame, prop, reinforcement, bulwark.

buy (SYN.) procure, get, purchase, acquire, obtain. (ANT.) vend, sell.

buzz (SYN.) whir, hum, drone, burr.

by (SYN.) near, through, beside, with, from, at, close to.

bygone (SYN.) bypast, former, earlier, past, onetime, forgotten. (ANT.) present, current, modern.

bypass (SYN.) deviate from, go around, detour around.

bystander (SYN.) onlooker, watcher, viewer, observer, witness, kibitzer.

byway (SYN.) passage, detour, path.

byword (SYN.) adage, proverb, axiom, shibboleth, apothegm, motto, slogan.

C

cab (SYN.) coach, taxi, car, hack, taxicab, carriage.

cabin (SYN.) cottage, shack, shanty, hut, dwelling, house.

cabinet (SYN.) ministry, council, committee, case, cupboard.

cable (SYN.) wire, cord, rope, telegraph.

cache (SYN.) bury, hide, cover, store.

cad (SYN.) knave, rascal, scoundrel, rogue.

cafe (SYN.) coffeehouse.

cafeteria (SYN.) cafe, diner, restaurant.

cagey (SYN.) cunning, wary, clever, tricky, cautious, shrewd, evasive. (ANT.) innocent, straightforward, guileless, naive.

calamity (SYN.) ruin, disaster, casualty, distress, hardship, trouble, misfortune, bad luck, catastrophe. (ANT.) blessing, fortune, welfare.

calculate (SYN.) count, compute, figure, estimate, consider, tally, determine, measure, subtract, add, divide, multiply, judge, reckon. (ANT.) guess, miscalculate, assume, conjecture.

calculating (SYN.) crafty, shrewd, scheming, cunning. (ANT.) simple, guileless, direct, ingenuous.

calculation (SYN.) figuring, reckoning, computation, estimation. (ANT.) guess, assumption.

calendar (SYN.) timetable, schedule, diary.

call (SYN.) designate, name, yell, cry, ask, shout, speak, cry out, call out, exclaim,

command, term, label, phone, ring up, collect, waken, awaken, ring, wake, arouse, rouse, outcry, need, demand, claim, assemble, telephone, occasion, invite.
calling *(SYN.)* occupation, profession, trade.
callous *(SYN.)* insensitive, impenitent, obdurate, unfeeling, indurate, hard, insensible, heartless. *(ANT.) soft, compassionate, tender.*
calm *(SYN.)* appease, lull, quiet, soothe, alloy, assuage, unruffled, mild, tranquil, smooth, serene, cool, levelheaded, unexcited, aloof, detached, stillness, calmness, serenity, composure. *(ANT.) tempestuous, disturbed, emotional, turmoil, incite, inflame, roiled, incense, upheaval, excite, upset, disturb, arouse.*
campaign *(SYN.)* movement, cause, crusade.
can *(SYN.)* tin, container.
canal *(SYN.)* gully, tube, duct, waterway.
cancel *(SYN.)* eliminate, obliterate, erase, delete, nullify, repeal, revoke, cross out, expunge, void, recall, set aside, abolish, rescind. *(ANT.) perpetuate, confirm, ratify, enforce, enact.*
candid *(SYN.)* free, blunt, frank, plain, open, sincere, honest, straightforward, direct, outspoken. *(ANT.) sly, contrived, wily, scheming.*
candidate *(SYN.)* applicant, aspirant, nominee.
canine *(SYN.)* pooch, dog, puppy.
canny *(SYN.)* artful, skillful, shrewd, clever, cautious, cunning, careful.
canopy *(SYN.)* awning, screen, shelter, cover.
cant *(SYN.)* dissimulation, patois, jargon, shoptalk, deceit, argot, pretense. *(ANT.) honesty, candor, frankness, truth.*
cantankerous *(SYN.)* crabby, grouchy, irritable, surly, grumpy, irascible.
canyon *(SYN.)* gulch, gully, arroyo, ravine, gorge.
cap *(SYN.)* top, cover, crown, beat, lid, excel.
capability *(SYN.)* aptness, ability, capacity, aptitude, dexterity, power, efficiency, qualification. *(ANT.) incapacity, disability, incompetency.*
capable *(SYN.)* clever, qualified, able, efficient, competent, skilled, fit, skillful, accomplished, fitted. *(ANT.) unfitted, incapable, incompetent,*

unskilled, inept, inadequate.
capacity *(SYN.)* capability, power, ability, talent, content, skill, volume, size. *(ANT.) inability, stupidity, incapacity, impotence.*
cape *(SYN.)* pelisse, cloak, mantle, neck, point, headland, peninsula.
caper *(SYN.)* romp, frisk, cavort, frolic, gambol.
capital *(SYN.)* leading, chief, important, property, wealth, money, city, cash, assets, principal, resources, major, primary, first, funds. *(ANT.) unimportant, trivial, secondary.*
capricious *(SYN.)* undependable, erratic, inconstant, fickle, changeable, irregular, inconsistent, unstable.
captain *(SYN.)* commander, authority, supervisor, leader, skipper, master, officer.
caption *(SYN.)* heading, title, headline.
captivate *(SYN.)* fascinate, charm, delight.
captive *(SYN.)* convict, prisoner, hostage.
captivity *(SYN.)* detention, imprisonment, custody, confinement, bondage, slavery. *(ANT.) liberty, freedom.*
capture *(SYN.)* catch, grip, apprehend, clutch, arrest, snare, seize, nab, seizure, catching, grasp, take prisoner, grab, recovery, trap. *(ANT.) set free, lose, liberate, throw, free, release.*
car *(SYN.)* auto, automobile, motorcar, vehicle.
carcass *(SYN.)* remains, frame, corpse, form, bulk, mass, corpus, association, body, cadaver. *(ANT.) mind, intellect, soul.*
cardinal *(SYN.)* chief, primary, important, prime, leading, major, essential. *(ANT.) subordinate, secondary, auxiliary.*
care *(SYN.)* concern, anxiety, worry, caution, solicitude, charge, ward, attention, regard, supervision, consider, consideration, keeping, protection, attend, watch, supervise, keep, guardianship, custody. *(ANT.) neglect, disregard, indifference, unconcern, negligence.*
career *(SYN.)* occupation, profession, job, calling, vocation, trade.
carefree *(SYN.)* lighthearted, happy, unconcerned, breezy, jolly, uneasy, nonchalant, happy-go-lucky, lively.
careful *(SYN.)* prudent,

thoughtful, attentive, cautious, painstaking, scrupulous, heedful, circumspect, vigilant, guarded, discreet, watchful, wary, concerned, meticulous, thorough. *(ANT.) nice, careful, heedless, messy, careless, sloppy.*
careless *(SYN.)* imprudent, heedless, unconcerned, inattentive, lax, indiscreet, desultory, reckless, negligent. *(ANT.) careful, nice, cautious, painstaking, prudent, accurate.*
caress *(SYN.)* hug, fondle, embrace, pet, pat, stroke, kiss, cuddle. *(ANT.) spurn, vex, buffet, annoy, tease.*
cargo *(SYN.)* freight, load, freight-load, shipment.
caricature *(SYN.)* exaggeration, parody, spoof, takeoff, lampoon, satire, burlesque.
carnage *(SYN.)* massacre, liquidation, slaughter, genocide, butchery, extermination, annihilation.
carnal *(SYN.)* base, corporeal, animal, lustful, worldly, sensual, bodily, gross, fleshy, voluptuous. *(ANT.) intellectual, spiritual, exalted, temperate.*
carnival *(SYN.)* fete, fair, jamboree, festival.
carol *(SYN.)* hymn, song, ballad.
carp *(SYN.)* pick, praise, complain.
carpet *(SYN.)* mat, rug.
carping *(SYN.)* discerning, exact, captions, accurate, fastidious, important, hazardous. *(ANT.) superficial, cursory, approving, encouraging, unimportant, insignificant.*
carriage *(SYN.)* bearing, conduct, action, deed, behavior, demeanor, disposition, department.
carry *(SYN.)* convey, transport, support, bring, sustain, bear, hold, move, transfer, take. *(ANT.) drop, abandon.*
carry off *(SYN.)* seize, abduct, capture, kidnap. *(ANT.) set free, let go, liberate.*
carry on *(SYN.)* go on, continue, proceed, misbehave. *(ANT.) stop.*
carry out *(SYN.)* succeed, complete, fulfill, win, accomplish, effect.
carve *(SYN.)* hew, shape, cut, whittle, chisel, sculpt.
case *(SYN.)* state, covering, receptacle, condition, instance, example, occurrence, happening, illustration, sample, suit, action, claim, lawsuit, crate, container, carton, box.

cash *(SYN.)* currency, money.
casket *(SYN.)* coffin, box, crate.
cast *(SYN.)* fling, toss, throw, pitch, form, company, shape, sort, mold, hurl, sling, shed, direct, impart, turn, actors, players, type, variety.
caste *(SYN.)* class, grade, order, category, status, elegance, set, rank, station, social standing, denomination, excellence, genre.
castle *(SYN.)* mansion, palace, chateau.
casual *(SYN.)* chance, unexpected, informal, accidental, incidental, offhand, unplanned, relaxed, fortuitous, unintentional, spontaneous. *(ANT.) planned, expected, calculated, formal, deliberate, dressy, premeditated, pretentious.*
casualty *(SYN.)* calamity, fortuity, mishap, loss, injured, dead, wounded, accident, contingency, victim, sufferer, misfortune. *(ANT.) design, purpose, intention, calculation.*
catalog *(SYN.)* classify, roll, group, list, inventory, directory, index, record, file.
catastrophe *(SYN.)* mishap, calamity, disaster, adversity, accident, ruin. *(ANT.) fortune, boon, triumph, blessing, advantage.*
catch *(SYN.)* hook, snare, entrap, ensnare, capture, grip, apprehend, grasp, take, grab, nab, arrest, contract, seize, apprehension, latch, bolt, pin, clasp, trap. *(ANT.) lose, free, liberate, throw, release.*
catching *(SYN.)* contagious, pestilential, communicable, infectious, virulent. *(ANT.) non-communicable, healthful.*
catchy *(SYN.)* tricky, misleading, attractive.
category *(SYN.)* class, caste, kind, order, genre, rank, classification, sort, elegance, type, set, excellence.
cater *(SYN.)* coddle, oblige, serve, humor, baby, mollycoddle, pamper, spoil, indulge, provide.
cause *(SYN.)* effect, incite, create, induce, inducement, occasion, incentive, prompt, principle, determinant, reason, origin, motive.
caustic *(SYN.)* bitter, disagreeable, distasteful, acrid, sour, spiteful, pungent, tart, painful, cruel, insulting, peevish, mean, ruthless, malicious, hateful, harsh. *(ANT.) mellow, sweet, delicious, pleasant.*

caution (SYN.) heed, vigilance, care, prudence, counsel, warning, wariness, advice, warn, injunction, admonish, watchfulness. (ANT.) carelessness, heedlessness, incaution, abandon, recklessness.

cautious (SYN.) heedful, scrupulous, attentive, prudent, thoughtful, discreet, guarded, circumspect, vigilant, watchful, wary, careful. (ANT.) improvident, headstrong, heedless, foolish, forgetful, indifferent.

cavalcade (SYN.) column, procession, parade.

cavalier (SYN.) contemptuous, insolent, haughty, arrogant.

cave (SYN.) grotto, hole, shelter, lair, den, cavern.

cave in (SYN.) fall in, collapse.

cavity (SYN.) pit, hole, crater.

cavort (SYN.) caper, leap, frolic, hop, prance.

cease (SYN.) desist, stop, abandon, discontinue, relinquish, end, terminate, leave, surrender, resign. (ANT.) occupy, continue, persist, begin, endure, stay.

cede (SYN.) surrender, relinquish, yield.

celebrate (SYN.) honor, glorify, commemorate, keep, solemnize, extol, observe, commend, praise. (ANT.) decry, overlook, profane, disregard, disgrace.

celebrated (SYN.) eminent, glorious, distinguished, noted, illustrious, famed, well-known, popular, renowned, famous. (ANT.) obscure, hidden, anonymous, infamous, unknown.

celebrity (SYN.) somebody, personage, heroine, hero, dignitary, notable.

celestial (SYN.) godlike, holy, supernatural, divine, paradisiacal, utopian, transcendent, superhuman. (ANT.) diabolical, profane, mundane, wicked.

cement (SYN.) solidify, weld, fasten, secure.

cemetery (SYN.) graveyard.

censure (SYN.) denounce, reproach, upbraid, blame, disapproval, reprehend, condemn, criticism, disapprove, criticize, reprove. (ANT.) commend, approval, forgive, approve, praise, applaud, condone.

center (SYN.) heart, core, midpoint, middle, nucleus, inside, hub, focus. (ANT.) rim, boundary, edge, border, periphery, outskirts.

central (SYN.) chief, necessary, main, halfway, dominant, mid, middle, inner, focal, leading, fundamental, principal. (ANT.) side, secondary, incidental, auxiliary.

ceremonious (SYN.) correct, exact, precise, stiff, outward, external, solemn, formal. (ANT.) material, unconventional, easy, heartfelt.

ceremony (SYN.) observance, rite, parade, formality, pomp, ritual, protocol, solemnity. (ANT.) informality, casualness.

certain (SYN.) definite, assured, fixed, inevitable, sure, undeniable, positive, confident, particular, special, indubitable, secure, unquestionable. (ANT.) probable, uncertain, doubtful, questionable.

certainly (SYN.) absolutely, surely, definitely. (ANT.) dubiously, doubtfully, questionably.

certainty (SYN.) confidence, courage, security, assuredness, firmness, assertion, statement. (ANT.) humility, bashfulness, modesty, shyness.

certificate (SYN.) affidavit, document.

certify (SYN.) validate, affirm, verify, confirm, authenticate, substantiate.

certitude (SYN.) confidence, belief, conviction, feeling, faith, persuasion, trust. (ANT.) doubt, incredulity, denial, heresy.

cessation (SYN.) ending, finish, stoppage, termination, conclusion, end.

chafe (SYN.) heat, rub, warm, annoy, disturb.

chagrin (SYN.) irritation, mortification, embarrassment, annoyance, vexation, worry, bother, shame, annoy, irk, humiliation, irritate, vex, frustrate, humiliate, embarrass, mortify, exasperate, disappoint, disappointment.

chain (SYN.) fasten, bind, shackle, restrain.

chairman (SYN.) speaker.

challenge (SYN.) question, dare, call, summon, threat, invite, threaten, demand.

chamber (SYN.) cell, salon, room.

champion (SYN.) victor, winner, choice, best, conqueror, hero, support, select.

chance (SYN.) befall, accident, betide, disaster, opportunity, calamity, occur, possibility, prospect, happen, luck, fate, take place. (ANT.) design, purpose, inevitability, calculation, certainty, intention.

change (SYN.) modification, alternation, alteration, mutation, variety, exchange, shift, alter, transfigure, veer, vary, variation, substitution, substitute, vicissitude. (ANT.) uniformity, monotony, settle, remain, endure, retain, preserve, steadfastness, endurance, immutability, stability.

changeable (SYN.) fitful, fickle, inconstant, unstable, shifting, wavering. (ANT.) stable, uniform, constant, unchanging.

channel (SYN.) strait, corridor, waterway, artery, duct, canal, way, trough, groove, passageway.

chant (SYN.) singing, incantation, hymn, intone, sing, carol, psalm, song, ballad.

chaos (SYN.) confusion, jumble, turmoil, anarchy, disorder, muddle. (ANT.) organization, order, tranquility, tidiness, system.

chaotic (SYN.) confused, disorganized, disordered, messy. (ANT.) neat, ordered, systematic, organized.

chap (SYN.) break, fellow, person, crack, split, man, rough, individual, boy.

chaperon (SYN.) associate with, escort, convoy, accompany, consort with. (ANT.) avoid, desert, leave, abandon, quit.

chapter (SYN.) part, section, division.

char (SYN.) scorch, singe, burn, sear.

character (SYN.) description, class, kind, repute, mark, individuality, disposition, traits, personality, reputation, symbol, features, quality, eccentric, nature.

characteristic (SYN.) exclusive, distinctive, special, mark, feature, property, typical, unique, attribute, distinguishing, trait, quality.

charge (SYN.) arraignment, indictment, accusation, sell for, attack, assail, assault, indict, blame, allegation, care, custody, imputation. (ANT.) pardon, flee, exculpation, excuse, absolve, retreat, exoneration.

charitable (SYN.) benevolent, generous, liberal, altruistic, kind, obliging, considerate, unselfish. (ANT.) petty, mean, harsh, wicked, greedy, narrow-minded, stingy, malevolent.

charity (SYN.) benevolence, kindness, magnanimity, altruism, generosity. (ANT.) malevolence, cruelty, selfishness.

charm (SYN.) allure, spell, enchantment, attractiveness, magic, witchery, amulet, talisman, lure, enchant, bewitch, fascinate, captivate.

charmer (SYN.) siren, temptress, enchantress, vamp, seductress, seducer, enchanter.

charming (SYN.) attractive, enchanting, fascinating, alluring, appealing, winsome, agreeable, bewitching, winning. (ANT.) revolting, repugnant, repulsive.

chart (SYN.) design, plan, cabal, plot, sketch, stratagem, map, diagram, conspiracy, graph, intrigue.

charter (SYN.) lease, hire, rent, alliance.

chase (SYN.) hunt, run after, pursue, trail, follow, persist, scheme. (ANT.) escape, flee, abandon, elude, evade.

chasm (SYN.) ravine, abyss, canyon, gorge.

chaste (SYN.) clear, immaculate, innocent, sincere, bare, clean, modest, pure, decent, virtuous, virginal, sheer, absolute, spotless. (ANT.) polluted, tainted, foul, impure, sinful, worldly, sullied, defiled.

chasten (SYN.) chastise, restrain, punish, discipline.

chastise (SYN.) punish, castigate, correct. (ANT.) release, acquit, free, exonerate.

chat (SYN.) argue, jabber, blab, plead, consult, converse, lecture, discuss, talk, conversation, tattle.

chatter (SYN.) dialogue, lecture, speech, conference, talk, discourse. (ANT.) silence, correspondence, writing.

cheap (SYN.) poor, common, inexpensive, shabby, low-priced, beggary, low-cost, shoddy, mean, inferior. (ANT.) honorable, dear, noble, expensive, costly, well-made, elegant, dignified.

cheat (SYN.) deceive, fool, bilk, outwit, victimize, dupe, gull, hoodwink, circumvent, swindler, cheater, trickster, phony, fraud, defraud, charlatan, crook, chiseler, con artist, hoax, swindle.

check (SYN.) dissect, interrogate, analyze, contemplate, inquire, question, scrutinize, arrest, stop, halt, block, curb, control, investigate, review, examine, test, counterfoil, stub, barrier, watch. (ANT.) overlook, disregard, advance, foster, continue, promote, omit, neglect.

checkup (SYN.) medical examination, physical.

cheek *(SYN.)* nerve, effrontery, impudence, gall, impertinence.

cheer *(SYN.)* console, gladden, comfort, encourage, applause, encouragement, joy, glee, gaiety, mirth, soothe, sympathize, approval, solace. *(ANT.)* depress, sadden, discourage, derision, dishearten, discouragement, antagonize.

cheerful *(SYN.)* glad, jolly, joyful, gay, happy, cherry, merry, joyous, lighthearted. *(ANT.)* mournful, sad, glum, depressed, gloomy, sullen.

cherish *(SYN.)* prize, treasure, appreciate, nurse, value, comfort, hold dear, foster, nurture, sustain. *(ANT.)* disregard, neglect, deprecate, scorn, reject, undervalue, abandon.

chest *(SYN.)* bosom, breast, coffer, box, case, trunk, casket, dresser, commode, cabinet, chiffonier.

chew *(SYN.)* gnaw, munch, bite, nibble.

chic *(SYN.)* fashionable, modish, smart, stylish, trendy.

chide *(SYN.)* admonish, rebuke, scold, reprimand, criticize, reprove. *(ANT.)* extol, praise, commend.

chief *(SYN.)* chieftain, head, commander, captain, leader, principal, master, boss, leading, ruler. *(ANT.)* servant, subordinate, secondary, follower, incidental, accidental, auxiliary, attendant.

chiefly *(SYN.)* mainly, especially, mostly.

childish *(SYN.)* immature, childlike, infantile, babyish. *(ANT.)* mature, grownup.

chill *(SYN.)* coolness, cold, cool, coldness, brisk, frosty. *(ANT.)* hot, warm, heat, heated, warmth.

chilly *(SYN.)* cold, frigid, freezing, arctic, cool, icy, passionless, wintry, unfeeling. *(ANT.)* fiery, heated, passionate, ardent.

chirp *(SYN.)* peep, cheep, twitter, tweet, chirrup.

chivalrous *(SYN.)* noble, brave, polite, valorous, gallant, gentlemanly, courteous. *(ANT.)* crude, rude, impolite, uncivil.

chivalry *(SYN.)* courtesy, nobility, gallantry, knighthood.

choice *(SYN.)* delicate, elegant, file, dainty, exquisite, pure, refined, subtle, splendid, handsome, option, selection, beautiful, minute, pretty, pick, select, uncommon, rare, precious, valuable, thin, small.

(ANT.) coarse, rough, thick, blunt, large.

choke *(SYN.)* throttle, gag, strangle.

choose *(SYN.)* elect, decide between, pick, select, cull, opt. *(ANT.)* reject, refuse.

chop *(SYN.)* hew, cut, fell, mince.

chore *(SYN.)* routine, task, job, duty, work.

chronic *(SYN.)* persistent, constant, lingering, continuing, perennial, unending, sustained, permanent. *(ANT.)* fleeting, acute, temporary.

chronicle *(SYN.)* detail, history, narrative, account, description, narration. *(ANT.)* misrepresentation, confusion, distortion.

chuckle *(SYN.)* titter, laugh, giggle.

chum *(SYN.)* friend, pal, buddy, companion.

cinema *(SYN.)* effigy, film, etching, appearance, drawing, engraving, illustration, likeness, image, panorama, picture.

circle *(SYN.)* disk, ring, set, group, class, club, surround, encircle, enclose, round.

circuit *(SYN.)* circle, course, journey, orbit, revolution, tour.

circuitous *(SYN.)* distorted, devious, indirect, roundabout, swerving, crooked, tortuous. *(ANT.)* straightforward, straight, direct, honest.

circular *(SYN.)* complete, curved, bulbous, cylindrical, round, ring-like, globular, entire, rotund. *(ANT.)* straight.

circumference *(SYN.)* border, perimeter, periphery, edge.

circumspection *(SYN.)* care, worry, solicitude, anxiety, concern, caution, attention, vigilance. *(ANT.)* neglect, negligence, indifference.

circumstance *(SYN.)* fact, event, incident, condition, happening, position, occurrence, situation.

circumstances *(SYN.)* facts, conditions, factors, situation, background, grounds, means, capital, assets, rank, class.

cite *(SYN.)* affirm, assign, allege, advance, quote, mention, declare, claim, maintain. *(ANT.)* refute, gainsay, deny, contradict.

citizen *(SYN.)* native, inhabitant, national, denizen, subject, dweller, resident.

city *(SYN.)* metropolis, municipality, town.

civil *(SYN.)* courteous, cultivated, accomplished, public, municipal, respectful, genteel, polite, considerate, gracious, urban. *(ANT.)* uncouth, uncivil, impertinent, impolite, boorish.

civilization *(SYN.)* cultivation, culture, education, breeding, enlightenment, society, refinement. *(ANT.)* ignorance, vulgarity.

civilize *(SYN.)* refine, tame, polish, cultivate, instruct, teach.

claim *(SYN.)* aver, declare, allege, assert, affirm, express, state, demand, maintain, defend, uphold. *(ANT.)* refute, deny, contradict.

clamor *(SYN.)* cry, din, babble, noise, racket, outcry, row, sound, tumult, shouting, shout, uproar. *(ANT.)* hush, serenity, silence, tranquility, stillness, quiet.

clan *(SYN.)* fellowship, kindness, solidarity, family, brotherhood, association, fraternity. *(ANT.)* discord, strife, opposition, acrimony.

clandestine *(SYN.)* covert, hidden, latent, private, concealed, secret, unknown. *(ANT.)* exposed, known, conspicuous, obvious.

clarify *(SYN.)* educate, explain, expound, decipher, illustrate, clear, resolve, define, interpret, unfold. *(ANT.)* darken, obscure, baffle, confuse.

clash *(SYN.)* clank, crash, clang, conflict, disagreement, opposition, collision, struggle, mismatch, contrast, disagree, collide, interfere. *(ANT.)* accord, agreement, harmony, blend, harmonize, match, agree.

clasp *(SYN.)* grip, hold, grasp, adhere, clutch, keep, have, maintain, possess, occupy, retain, support, confine, embrace, fastening, check, detain, curb, receive. *(ANT.)* relinquish, vacate, surrender, abandon.

class *(SYN.)* category, denomination, caste, kind, genre, grade, rank, order, elegance, classification, division, sort, family, species, set, excellence.

classic *(SYN.)* masterpiece.

classification *(SYN.)* order, category, class, arrangement, ordering, grouping, organization.

classify *(SYN.)* arrange, class, order, sort, grade, group, index.

clause *(SYN.)* condition, paragraph, limitation, article.

claw *(SYN.)* hook, talon, nail, scratch.

clean *(SYN.)* mop, tidy, neat, dustless, clear, unsoiled, immaculate, unstained, untainted, pure, dust, vacuum, scour, decontaminate, wipe, sterilize, cleanse, scrub, purify, wash, sweep. *(ANT.)* stain, soil, pollute, soiled, impure, dirty.

cleanse *(SYN.)* mop, purify, wash, sweep. *(ANT.)* stain, soil, dirty, pollute.

clear *(SYN.)* fair, sunny, cloudless, transparent, apparent, limpid, distinct, intelligible, evident, unmistakable, understandable, unclouded, light, bright, certain, manifest, lucid, plain, obvious, unobstructed. *(ANT.)* obscure, unclear, muddled, confused, dark, cloudy, blocked, obstructed, questionable, dubious, blockaded, foul, overcast.

clearly *(SYN.)* plainly, obviously, evidently, definitely, surely, certainly. *(ANT.)* questionably, dubiously.

clemency *(SYN.)* forgiveness, charity, compassion, grace, mercy, leniency, pity, mildness. *(ANT.)* punishment, vengeance, retribution.

clerical *(SYN.)* ministerial, pastoral, priestly, celestial, holy, sacred, secretarial.

clerk *(SYN.)* typist, office worker, salesperson, salesclerk.

clever *(SYN.)* apt, dexterous, quick, adroit, quick-witted, talented, bright, skillful, witty, ingenious, smart, intelligent, shrewd, gifted, expert, sharp. *(ANT.)* unskilled, slow, stupid, backward, maladroit, bungling, dull, clumsy.

cleverness *(SYN.)* intellect, intelligence, comprehension, mind, perspicacity, sagacity, fun. *(ANT.)* sobriety, stupidity, solemnity, commonplace, platitude.

client *(SYN.)* patron, customer.

cliff *(SYN.)* scar, tor, bluff, crag, precipice, escarpment.

climate *(SYN.)* aura, atmosphere, air, ambience.

climax *(SYN.)* apex, culmination, peak, summit, consummation, height, acme, zenith. *(ANT.)* depth, base, anticlimax, floor.

climb *(SYN.)* mount, scale, ascend. *(ANT.)* descend.

clip *(SYN.)* snip, crop, cut, mow, clasp.

cloak *(SYN.)* conceal, cover, disguise, clothe, cape, guard, envelop, hide, mask, protect, shield. (*ANT.*) *divulge, expose, reveal, bare, unveil.*

clod (*SYN.*) wad, hunk, gobbet, lump, chunk, clot, gob, dunce, dolt, oaf, fool.

clog (*SYN.*) crowd, congest, cram, overfill, stuff.

cloister (*SYN.*) monastery, priory, hermitage, abbey, convent.

close (*SYN.*) adjacent, adjoining, immediate, unventilated, stuffy, abutting, neighboring, dear, oppressive, mean, impending, nearby, near, devoted. (*ANT.*) *afar, faraway, removed, distant.*

close (*SYN.*) seal, shut, clog, stop, obstruct, cease, conclude, complete, end, terminate, occlude, finish. (*ANT.*) *unlock, begin, open, unbar, inaugurate, commence, start.*

closet (*SYN.*) cabinet, locker, wardrobe, cupboard.

cloth (*SYN.*) fabric, goods, material, textile.

clothe (*SYN.*) garb, dress, apparel. (*ANT.*) *strip, undress.*

clothes (*SYN.*) array, attire, apparel, clothing, garb, dress, garments, raiment, drapery, vestments. (*ANT.*) *nudity, nakedness.*

clothing (*SYN.*) attire, clothes, apparel, array, dress, drapery, garments, garb, vestments. (*ANT.*) *nudity, nakedness.*

cloud (*SYN.*) fog, mist, haze, mass, collection, obscure, dim, shadow.

cloudy (*SYN.*) dim, dark, indistinct, murky, mysterious, indefinite, vague, sunless, clouded, obscure, overcast, shadowy. (*ANT.*) *sunny, clear, distinct, limpid, lucid, clarified, cloudless, brilliant, bright.*

club (*SYN.*) society, association, set, circle, organization, bat, cudgel, stick, blackjack.

clue (*SYN.*) sign, trace, hint, suggestion.

clumsy (*SYN.*) bungling, inept, rough, unpolished, bumbling, awkward, ungraceful, gauche, ungainly, unskillful, untoward. (*ANT.*) *polished, skillful, neat, graceful, dexterous, adroit.*

cluster (*SYN.*) batch, clutch, group, bunch, gather, pack, assemble, crowd.

clutch (*SYN.*) grip, grab, seize, hold.

coalition (*SYN.*) combination, association, alliance, confederacy, entente, league, treaty. (*ANT.*) *schism, separation, divorce.*

coarse (*SYN.*) unpolished, vulgar, rough, impure, rude, crude, gruff, gross. (*ANT.*) *delicate, smooth, refined, polished, genteel, cultivated, suave, fine, cultured.*

coast (*SYN.*) seaboard, seashore, beach, shore, drift, glide, ride.

coax (*SYN.*) urge, persuade, wheedle, cajole. (*ANT.*) *force, bully, coerce.*

coddle (*SYN.*) pamper, baby, spoil, indulge.

coerce (*SYN.*) constrain, compel, enforce, force, drive, oblige, impel. (*ANT.*) *prevent, persuade, convince, induce.*

coercion (*SYN.*) emphasis, intensity, energy, dint, might, potency, power, vigor, strength, compulsion, force, constraint, violence. (*ANT.*) *impotence, frailty, feebleness, weakness, persuasion.*

cognizance (*SYN.*) apprehension, erudition, acquaintance, information, learning, knowledge, lore, science, scholarship, understanding. (*ANT.*) *illiteracy, misunderstanding, ignorance.*

cognizant (*SYN.*) conscious, aware, apprised, informed, mindful, observant, perceptive. (*ANT.*) *unaware, ignorant, oblivious, insensible.*

coherent (*SYN.*) logical, intelligible, sensible, rational, commonsensical, reasonable.

coiffeur (*SYN.*) hairdresser.

coiffure (*SYN.*) haircut, hairdo.

coincide (*SYN.*) acquiesce, agree, accede, assent, consent, comply, correspond, concur, match, tally, harmonize, conform. (*ANT.*) *differ, disagree, protest, contradict.*

coincidence (*SYN.*) accident, chance. (*ANT.*) *plot, plan, prearrangement, scheme.*

coincident (*SYN.*) identical, equal, equivalent, distinguishable, same, like. (*ANT.*) *distinct, contrary, disparate, opposed.*

coincidental (*SYN.*) unpredicted, unexpected, chance, unforeseen, accidental, fortuitous.

cold (*SYN.*) cool, freezing, chilly, frigid, icy, frozen, wintry, arctic, unfriendly, indifferent, phlegmatic, stoical, passionless, chill, unemotional, heartless, unfeeling. (*ANT.*) *hot, torrid, fiery, burning, ardent, friendly, temperate, warm, passionate.*

collapse (*SYN.*) descend, decrease, diminish, fail,

downfall, failure, decline, fall, drop, sink, subside, topple. (*ANT.*) *soar, steady, limb, mount, arise.*

colleague (*SYN.*) companion, attendant, comrade, associate, crony, mate, friend, partner. (*ANT.*) *enemy, stranger, adversary.*

collect (*SYN.*) assemble, amass, concentrate, pile, accumulate, congregate, obtain, heap, gather, solicit, secure, procure, raise, get, mass, hoard, consolidate. (*ANT.*) *divide, dole, assort, dispel, distribute, disperse.*

collected (*SYN.*) cool, calm, composed, imperturbable, placid, sedate, quiet. (*ANT.*) *excited, violent, aroused, agitated.*

collection (*SYN.*) amount, conglomeration, sum, entirety, aggregation, hoard, accumulation, pile, store, aggregate, total, whole. (*ANT.*) *part, unit, particular, element, ingredient.*

collide (*SYN.*) hit, smash, crash, strike.

collision (*SYN.*) conflict, combat, duel, battle, encounter, crash, smash, fight, contention, struggle, discord. (*ANT.*) *concord, amity, harmony, consonance.*

collusion (*SYN.*) combination, cabal, intrigue, conspiracy, plot, treachery.

color (*SYN.*) hue, paint, pigment, complexion, dye, shade, tone, tincture, stain, tint, tinge. (*ANT.*) *paleness, transparency, achromatism.*

colorful (*SYN.*) impressive, vivid, striking, full-color, multicolored, offbeat, weird, unusual. (*ANT.*) *flat, dull, uninteresting.*

colossal (*SYN.*) enormous, elephantine, gargantuan, huge, immense, gigantic, prodigious. (*ANT.*) *little, minute, small, miniature, diminutive, microscopic, tiny.*

combat (*SYN.*) conflict, duel, battle, collision, encounter, fight, contest, oppose, war, contention, struggle, discord. (*ANT.*) *consonance, harmony, concord, yield, surrender, succumb, amity.*

combination (*SYN.*) association, confederacy, alliance, entente, league, compounding, mixture, blend, composite, federation, mixing, compound, blending, union. (*ANT.*) *separation, division, schism.*

combine (*SYN.*) adjoin,

associate, accompany, conjoin, connect, link, mix, blend, couple, unite, join. (*ANT.*) *detach, disjoin, divide, separate, disconnect.*

come (*SYN.*) near, approach, reach, arrive, advance. (*ANT.*) *depart, leave, go.*

comedian (*SYN.*) comic, wit, humorist, gagman, wag.

comely (*SYN.*) charming, elegant, beauteous, beautiful, fine, lovely, pretty, handsome. (*ANT.*) *hideous, repulsive, foul, unsightly.*

come-on (*SYN.*) lure, inducement, enticement, temptation, premium.

comfort (*SYN.*) contentment, ease, enjoyment, relieve, consolation, relief, cheer, console, calm, satisfaction, soothe, encourage, succor, luxury, solace. (*ANT.*) *depress, torture, discomfort, upset, misery, disturb, agitate, affliction, discompose, uncertainty, suffering.*

comfortable (*SYN.*) pleasing, agreeable, convenient, cozy, welcome, acceptable, relaxed, restful, cozy, gratifying, easy, contented, rested, satisfying, pleasurable. (*ANT.*) *miserable, distressing, tense, strained, troubling, edgy, uncomfortable.*

comical (*SYN.*) droll, funny, humorous, amusing, ludicrous, witty, ridiculous, odd, queer. (*ANT.*) *sober, solemn, sad, serious, melancholy.*

command (*SYN.*) class, method, rank, arrangement, series, sequence, point, aim, conduct, manage, guide, bid, system, succession, bidding, direct, order, demand, direction, rule, dictate, decree. (*ANT.*) *consent, obey, misdirect, distract, deceive, misguide, license, confusion.*

commandeer (*SYN.*) take possession, seize, confiscate, appropriate.

commanding (*SYN.*) imposing, masterful, assertive, authoritative, positive.

commence (*SYN.*) open, start. (*ANT.*) *stop, end, terminate, finish.*

commend (*SYN.*) laud, praise, applaud, recommend. (*ANT.*) *censure, criticize.*

commendable (*SYN.*) deserving, praiseworthy. (*ANT.*) *bad, deplorable, lamentable.*

commendation (*SYN.*) approval, applause, praise, recommendation, honor, medal. (*ANT.*) *criticism, condemnation, censure.*

commensurate (*SYN.*) keep,

celebrate, observe, honor, commend, extol, glorify, laud, praise, honor. (*ANT.*) *decry, disgrace, disregard, overlook, profane, dishonor.*

comment (*SYN.*) assertion, declaration, annotation, explanation, review, commentary, report, remark, observation, utterance, criticism, statement.

commerce (*SYN.*) business, engagement, employment, art, trade, marketing, enterprise, occupation. (*ANT.*) *hobby, pastime, avocation.*

commiseration (*SYN.*) condolence, empathy, pity. (*ANT.*) *hardness, brutality, inhumanity, cruelty.*

commission (*SYN.*) board, committee, command, permit, order, permission, delegate, authorize, deputize, entrust.

commit (*SYN.*) perpetrate, perform, obligate, do, commend, consign, relegate, bind, delegate, empower, pledge, entrust, authorize, trust. (*ANT.*) *neglect, mistrust, release, free, miscarry, fail.*

commitment (*SYN.*) duty, promise, responsibility, pledge.

committee (*SYN.*) commission, bureau, board, delegate, council.

commodious (*SYN.*) appropriate, accessible, adapted, favorable, handy, fitting, timely. (*ANT.*) *inconvenient, troublesome, awkward.*

commodity (*SYN.*) article, merchandise, wares, goods.

common (*SYN.*) ordinary, popular, familiar, mean, low, general, vulgar, communal, mutual, shared, natural, frequent, prevalent, joint, conventional, plain, usual, universal. (*ANT.*) *odd, exceptional, scarce, noble, extraordinary, different, separate, outstanding, rare, unusual, distinctive, refined.*

commonplace (*SYN.*) common, usual, frequent, ordinary, everyday. (*ANT.*) *distinctive, unusual, original.*

commonsense (*SYN.*) perceptible, alive, apprehensible, aware, awake, cognizant, conscious, comprehending, perceptible. (*ANT.*) *unaware, impalpable, imperceptible.*

commotion (*SYN.*) confusion, chaos, disarray, ferment, disorder, stir, tumult, agitation. (*ANT.*) *tranquillity, peace, order.*

communicable (*SYN.*)

infectious, virulent, catching, transferable, contagious. (*ANT.*) *hygienic, non-communicable.*

communicate (*SYN.*) convey, impart, inform, confer, disclose, reveal, relate, tell, advertise, publish, transmit, publicize, divulge. (*ANT.*) *withhold, hide, conceal.*

communication (*SYN.*) disclosure, transmission, declaration, announcement, notification, publication, message, report, news, information.

communicative (*SYN.*) unreserved, open, frank, free, straightforward, unrestrained. (*ANT.*) *close-mouthed, secretive.*

communion (*SYN.*) intercourse, fellowship, participation, association, sacrament, union. (*ANT.*) *nonparticipation, alienation.*

community (*SYN.*) public, society, city, town, village, township.

compact (*SYN.*) contracted, firm, narrow, snug, close, constricted, packed, vanity, treaty, agreement, tense, taut, tight, niggardly, close-fisted, parsimonious, compressed, stingy. (*ANT.*) *slack, open, loose, relaxed, unconfined, unfretted, sprawling, lax.*

companion (*SYN.*) attendant, comrade, consort, friend, colleague, partner, crony, mate, associate. (*ANT.*) *stranger, enemy, adversary.*

companionship (*SYN.*) familiarity, cognizance, acquaintance, fellowship, knowledge, intimacy. (*ANT.*) *unfamiliarity, inexperience, ignorance.*

company (*SYN.*) crew, group, band, party, throng, house, assemblage, troop, fellowship, association, business, concern, partnership, corporation, companionship, firm. (*ANT.*) *seclusion, individual, solitude.*

comparable (*SYN.*) allied, analogous, alike, akin, like, correspondent, correlative, parallel. (*ANT.*) *opposed, incongruous, dissimilar, unalike, different, divergent.*

compare (*SYN.*) discriminate, match, differentiate, contrast, oppose.

comparison (*SYN.*) likening, contrasting, judgment.

compartment (*SYN.*) division, section.

compassion (*SYN.*) mercy, sympathy, pity.

compassionate (*SYN.*)

sympathizing, benign, forbearing, good, tender, affable, humane, indulgent, kind, sympathetic, kindly. (*ANT.*) *inhuman, merciless, unkind, cold-hearted, unsympathetic, cruel.*

compatible (*SYN.*) consistent, agreeing, conforming, accordant, congruous, harmonious, cooperative, agreeable, constant, consonant, correspondent. (*ANT.*) *discrepant, paradoxical, disagreeable, contradictory.*

compel (*SYN.*) drive, enforce, coerce, constrain, force, oblige, impel. (*ANT.*) *induce, coax, wheedle, persuade, cajole, convince.*

compensate (*SYN.*) remunerate, repay, reimburse, recompense, balance.

compensation (*SYN.*) fee, earnings, pay, payment, recompense, allowance, remuneration, remittance, settlement, stipend, repayment, salary, wages. (*ANT.*) *present, gratuity, gift.*

compete (*SYN.*) rival, contest, oppose, vie. (*ANT.*) *reconcile, accord.*

competence (*SYN.*) skill, ability, capability.

competent (*SYN.*) efficient, clever, capable, able, apt, proficient, skillful, fitted, qualified. (*ANT.*) *inept, incapable, unfitted, awkward, incompetent, inadequate.*

competition (*SYN.*) contest, match, rivalry, tournament.

competitor (*SYN.*) rival, contestant, opponent. (*ANT.*) *ally, friend, colleague.*

complain (*SYN.*) lament, murmur, protest, grouch, grumble, regret, moan, remonstrate, whine, repine. (*ANT.*) *rejoice, praise, applaud, approve.*

complaint (*SYN.*) protest, objection, grievance.

complement (*SYN.*) supplement, complete. (*ANT.*) *clash, conflict.*

complete (*SYN.*) consummate, entire, ended, thorough, finished, full, whole, concluded, over, done, terminate, unbroken, total, undivided. (*ANT.*) *unfinished, imperfect, incomplete, start, partial, begin, commence, lacking.*

completion (*SYN.*) achievement, attainment, end, conclusion, close, finish, windup, accomplishment, realization. (*ANT.*) *omission, neglect, failure, defeat.*

complex (*SYN.*) sophisticated,

compound, intricate, involved, perplexing, elaborate, complicated. (*ANT.*) *basic, simple, rudimentary, uncompounded, uncomplicated, plain.*

complexion (*SYN.*) paint, pigment, hue, color, dye, stain, tincture, tinge, tint, shade. (*ANT.*) *paleness, transparency.*

compliant (*SYN.*) meek, modest, lowly, plain, submissive, simple, unostentatious, unassuming, unpretentious. (*ANT.*) *proud, vain, arrogant, haughty, boastful.*

complicated (*SYN.*) intricate, involved, complex, compound, perplexing. (*ANT.*) *simple, plain, uncompounded.*

compliment (*SYN.*) eulogy, flattery, praise, admiration, honor, adulation, flatter, commendation, tribute. (*ANT.*) *taunt, affront, aspersion, insult, disparage, criticism.*

complimentary (*SYN.*) gratis, free.

comply (*SYN.*) assent, consent, accede, acquiesce, coincide, conform, concur, tally. (*ANT.*) *differ, dissent, protest, disagree.*

component (*SYN.*) division, fragment, allotment, moiety, apportionment, scrap, portion, section, share, segment, ingredient, organ. (*ANT.*) *whole, entirety.*

comport (*SYN.*) carry, conduct, behave, act, deport, interact, operate, manage.

compose (*SYN.*) forge, fashion, mold, make, construct, create, produce, shape, form, constitute, arrange, organize, make up, write, invent, devise, frame. (*ANT.*) *misshape, dismantle, disfigure, destroy.*

composed (*SYN.*) calm, cool, imperturbable, placid, quiet, unmoved, sedate, peaceful, collected, tranquil. (*ANT.*) *aroused, violent, nervous, agitated, perturbed, excited.*

composer (*SYN.*) author, inventor, creator, maker, originator.

composition (*SYN.*) paper, theme, work, essay, compound, mixture, mix.

composure (*SYN.*) calmness, poise, control, self-control, self-possession. (*ANT.*) *anger, rage, turbulence, agitation.*

compound (*SYN.*) blend, confound, jumble, consort, aggregate, complicated, combination, combined, mixture, complex, join.

(ANT.) segregate, separate, divide, simple, sort.

comprehend *(SYN.)* apprehend, discern, learn, perceive, see, grasp, understand. *(ANT.)* mistake, misunderstand, ignore.

comprehension *(SYN.)* insight, perception, understanding, awareness, discernment. *(ANT.)* misconception, insensibility.

comprehensive *(SYN.)* wide, inclusive, complete, broad, full. *(ANT.)* fragmentary, partial, limited, incomplete.

compress *(SYN.)* press, compact, squeeze, pack, crowd. *(ANT.)* spread, stretch, expand.

comprise *(SYN.)* contain, hold, embrace. *(ANT.)* emit, encourage, yield, discharge.

compulsion *(SYN.)* might, energy, potency, strength, vigor. *(ANT.)* persuasion, impotence, frailty.

compulsory *(SYN.)* required, obligatory, necessary, unavoidable. *(ANT.)* elective, optional, free, unrestricted.

computation *(SYN.)* reckoning, record. *(ANT.)* misrepresentation.

compute *(SYN.)* count, calculate, determine, figure, reckon. *(ANT.)* conjecture, guess, miscalculate.

comrade *(SYN.)* attendant, companion, colleague, associate, friend. *(ANT.)* stranger, enemy, adversary.

conceal *(SYN.)* disguise, cover, hide, mask, screen, secrete, veil, withhold. *(ANT.)* reveal, show, disclose, expose.

concede *(SYN.)* permit, suffer, tolerate, grant, give, admit, acknowledge, allow, yield. *(ANT.)* forbid, contradict, protest, refuse, deny, negate, resist.

conceit *(SYN.)* pride, vanity, complacency, conception, idea, egotism, self-esteem, caprice, fancy, whim. *(ANT.)* humility, meekness, humbleness, modesty.

conceited *(SYN.)* proud, arrogant, vain, smug, egotistical. *(ANT.)* humble, modest, self-effacing.

conceive *(SYN.)* design, create, imagine, understand, devise, concoct, perceive, frame, grasp, invent. *(ANT.)* imitate, reproduce, copy.

concentrate *(SYN.)* localize, focus, condense, ponder, meditate, center, scrutinize. *(ANT.)* scatter, diffuse, dissipate, disperse.

concentrated *(SYN.)* compressed, thick, dense. *(ANT.)* sparse, quick, dispersed.

concept *(SYN.)* fancy, conception, image, notion, idea, sentiment, thought. *(ANT.)* thing, matter, substance, entity.

conception *(SYN.)* consideration, deliberation, fancy, idea, notion, regard, thought, view.

concern *(SYN.)* matter, anxiety, affair, disturb, care, business, solicitude, interest, affect, involve, touch, trouble, worry. *(ANT.)* unconcern, negligence, disinterest, tire, bore, calm, indifference.

concerning *(SYN.)* regarding, about, respecting.

concerted *(SYN.)* united, joint, combined. *(ANT.)* individual, unorganized, separate.

concession *(SYN.)* admission, yielding, granting. *(ANT.)* insistence, demand.

concise *(SYN.)* pity, neat, brief, compact, succinct, terse. *(ANT.)* wordy, lengthy, verbose, prolix.

conclude *(SYN.)* decide, achieve, close, end, finish, terminate, complete, arrange, determine, settle, perfect, perform. *(ANT.)* start, begin, commence.

concluding *(SYN.)* extreme, final, last, terminal, utmost. *(ANT.)* first, foremost, opening, initial.

conclusion *(SYN.)* end, finale, termination, deduction, close, settlement, decision, finish, resolution, determination, completion, issue, judgment. *(ANT.)* commencement, inception, opening, start, beginning.

conclusive *(SYN.)* decisive, eventual, final, terminal, ultimate. *(ANT.)* original, first, inaugural.

concord *(SYN.)* agreement, unison, understanding, accordance, stipulation. *(ANT.)* disagreement, discord, dissension.

concrete *(SYN.)* solid, firm, precise, definite, specific. *(ANT.)* undetermined, vague, general.

concur *(SYN.)* agree, assent, consent, accede. *(ANT.)* dissent, protest, differ.

condemn *(SYN.)* denounce, reproach, blame, upbraid, convict, rebuke, doom, judge, censure, reprehend, punish, reprobate, sentence. *(ANT.)* condone, forgive, absolve, praise, applaud, extol, approve, pardon, laud, excuse, commend.

condense *(SYN.)* shorten, reduce, abridge, abbreviate, concentrate, digest, compress, diminish. *(ANT.)* enlarge, increase, swell, expand.

condition *(SYN.)* circumstance, state, situation, case, plight, requirement, position, necessity, stipulation, predicament, provision, term.

conditional *(SYN.)* dependent, relying. *(ANT.)* casual, original, absolute.

condolence *(SYN.)* commiseration, concord, harmony, pity, sympathy, warmth. *(ANT.)* harshness, indifference, unconcern.

conduct *(SYN.)* control, supervise, manage, behavior, deed, actions, act, behave, manners, deportment.

confederate *(SYN.)* ally, abettor, assistant. *(ANT.)* enemy, rival, opponent, adversary.

confederation *(SYN.)* combination, league, union, marriage, treaty. *(ANT.)* separation, divorce.

confer *(SYN.)* gossip, grant, speak, tattle, blab, chat, deliberate, consult, award, give, bestow, talk. *(ANT.)* retrieve, withdraw.

confess *(SYN.)* avow, acknowledge, admit, concede, grant, divulge, reveal. *(ANT.)* disown, renounce, deny, conceal.

confession *(SYN.)* defense, justification, excuse, apology. *(ANT.)* dissimulation, denial, complaint.

confidence *(SYN.)* firmness, self-reliance, assurance, faith, trust, pledge, declaration, self-confidence, reliance, self-assurance, courage, statement. *(ANT.)* distrust, shyness, mistrust, bashfulness, diffidence, doubt, modesty, suspicion.

confident *(SYN.)* certain, sure, dauntless, self-assured. *(ANT.)* uncertain, timid, shy.

confine *(SYN.)* enclose, restrict, hinder, fence, limit, bound. *(ANT.)* release, expose, free, expand, open.

confirm *(SYN.)* acknowledge, establish, settle, substantiate, approve, fix, verify, assure, validate, ratify, corroborate, strengthen. *(ANT.)* disclaim, deny, disavow.

confirmation *(SYN.)* demonstration, experiment, test, trial, verification. *(ANT.)* fallacy, invalidity.

confirmed *(SYN.)* regular, established, habitual. *(ANT.)* occasional, infrequent.

confiscate *(SYN.)* capture, catch, gain, purloin, steal, take, clutch, grip, seize, get, obtain, bear.

conflagration *(SYN.)* flame, glow, heat, warmth, fervor, passion, vigor. *(ANT.)* apathy, cold, quiescence.

conflict *(SYN.)* duel, combat, fight, collision, discord, encounter, interference, inconsistency, contention, struggle, opposition, clash, oppose, battle, controversy, contend, engagement, contest, variance. *(ANT.)* consonance, harmony, amity.

conform *(SYN.)* adapt, comply, yield, submit, obey, adjust, agree, fit, suit. *(ANT.)* misapply, misfit, rebel, vary.

conformity *(SYN.)* congruence, accord, agreement, correspondence.

confound *(SYN.)* confuse, baffle, perplex, puzzle, bewilder.

confront *(SYN.)* defy, hinder, resist, thwart, withstand, bar. *(ANT.)* submit, agree, support, succumb.

confuse *(SYN.)* confound, perplex, mystify, dumbfound, baffle, puzzle, jumble, mislead, mix up, mistake, bewilder. *(ANT.)* explain, instruct, edify, illumine, enlighten, illuminate, solve.

confused *(SYN.)* deranged, indistinct, disordered, muddled, bewildered, disconcerted, disorganized, perplexed. *(ANT.)* organized, plain, clear, obvious.

confusion *(SYN.)* commotion, disarray, agitation, disorder, chaos, ferment, stir, perplexity, tumult, bewilderment, disarrangement, uncertainty, muss, mess, turmoil. *(ANT.)* order, tranquility, enlightenment, comprehension, understanding, tidiness, organization, peace.

congregate *(SYN.)* gather, foregather, meet, convene. *(ANT.)* scatter, dispel, disperse, dissipate.

congress *(SYN.)* parliament, legislature, assembly.

congruous *(SYN.)* agreeing, conforming, constant, correspondent. *(ANT.)* incongruous, inconsistent, discrepant.

conjecture *(SYN.)* law, supposition, theory. *(ANT.)* proof, fact, certainty.

conjunction *(SYN.)* combination, junction, connection, link. *(ANT.)* separation, disconnection, diversion.

connect *(SYN.)* adjoin, link, combine, relate, join, attach, unite, associate, attribute, affix. (*ANT.*) *detach, separate, disjoin, untie, dissociation, disconnect, disassociation, unfasten.*

connection (*SYN.*) conjunction, alliance, link, affinity, bond, tie, association, relationship, union. (*ANT.*) *isolation, dissociation, separation, disassociation, disunion.*

conquer (*SYN.*) master, beat, humble, defeat, overcome, rout, win, succeed, achieve, gain, overpower, quell, subdue, crush, vanquish. (*ANT.*) *cede, yield, retreat, surrender.*

conquest (*SYN.*) triumph, victory, achievement. (*ANT.*) *surrender, failure, defeat.*

conscientious (*SYN.*) upright, straight, honest, incorruptible, scrupulous. (*ANT.*) *careless, irresponsible, slovenly.*

conscious (*SYN.*) cognizant, informed, perceptive, aware, intentional, sensible, awake, purposeful, deliberate. (*ANT.*) *unaware, insensible, asleep, comatose, ignorant.*

consecrate (*SYN.*) exalt, extol, hallow, honor. (*ANT.*) *mock, degrade, debase, abuse.*

consecrated (*SYN.*) holy, divine, devout, spiritual. (*ANT.*) *evil, worldly, secular.*

consent (*SYN.*) permission, leave, agree, let, assent, agreement, license, permit. (*ANT.*) *refusal, opposition, denial, dissent, prohibition.*

consequence (*SYN.*) outcome, issue, result, effect, significance, importance. (*ANT.*) *impetus, cause.*

consequential (*SYN.*) significant, important, weighty. (*ANT.*) *trivial, unimportant, minor, insignificant.*

consequently (*SYN.*) hence, thence, therefore.

conservative (*SYN.*) conventional, reactionary, cautious, moderate, careful. (*ANT.*) *radical, liberal, foolhardy, reckless.*

conserve (*SYN.*) save, retain, reserve, guard, keep, support, sustain. (*ANT.*) *dismiss, neglect, waste, reject, discard.*

consider (*SYN.*) heed, ponder, contemplate, examine, study, weigh, reflect, think about, regard, deliberate, respect. (*ANT.*) *ignore, overlook, disdain, disregard, neglect.*

considerable (*SYN.*) much, noteworthy, worthwhile, significant, important.

considerate (*SYN.*) careful, heedful, prudent, kind, thoughtful, polite, introspective, reflective. (*ANT.*) *thoughtless, heedless, inconsiderate, selfish, rash.*

consideration (*SYN.*) kindness, care, heed, politeness, empathy, notice, watchfulness, kindliness, thoughtfulness, courtesy, concern, sympathy, thought, attention, reflection, fee, pay, study. (*ANT.*) *omission, oversight, negligence.*

consistent (*SYN.*) conforming, accordant, compatible, agreeing, faithful, constant, harmonious, expected, regular, congruous, correspondent. (*ANT.*) *paradoxical, discrepant, contrary, antagonistic, opposed, eccentric, inconsistent, incongruous.*

consolation (*SYN.*) enjoyment, sympathy, relief, ease, contentment, comfort, solace. (*ANT.*) *discomfort, suffering, discouragement, torture, burden, misery.*

console (*SYN.*) solace, comfort, sympathize with, assuage, soothe. (*ANT.*) *worry, annoy, upset, disturb, distress.*

consolidate (*SYN.*) blend, combine, conjoin, fuse, mix, merge, unite. (*ANT.*) *decompose, separate, analyze, disintegrate.*

consort (*SYN.*) companion, comrade, friend. (*ANT.*) *stranger, enemy, adversary.*

conspicuous (*SYN.*) distinguished, clear, manifest, salient, noticeable, striking, obvious, prominent, visible. (*ANT.*) *hidden, obscure, neutral, common, inconspicuous.*

conspiracy (*SYN.*) machination, combination, treason, intrigue, cabal, treachery, plot, collusion.

conspire (*SYN.*) plan, plot, scheme.

constancy (*SYN.*) devotion, faithfulness, accuracy, precision, exactness. (*ANT.*) *faithlessness, treachery, perfidy.*

constant (*SYN.*) continual, invariable, abiding, permanent, faithful, invariant, true, ceaseless, enduring, unchanging, steadfast, unchangeable, loyal, stable, immutable, staunch, steady, fixed. (*ANT.*) *fickle, irregular, wavering, off-and-on, infrequent, occasional, mutable.*

constantly (*SYN.*) eternally, ever, evermore, forever, unceasingly. (*ANT.*) *rarely, sometimes, never, occasionally.*

consternation (*SYN.*) apprehension, dismay, alarm, fear, fright, dread, horror, terror. (*ANT.*) *bravery, courage, boldness, assurance.*

constitute (*SYN.*) compose, found, form, establish, organize, create, appoint, delegate, authorize, commission.

constitution (*SYN.*) law, code, physique, health, vitality.

constrain (*SYN.*) necessity, indigence, need, want, poverty. (*ANT.*) *luxury, freedom, uncertainty.*

construct (*SYN.*) build, form, erect, make, fabricate, raise, frame. (*ANT.*) *raze, demolish, destroy.*

constructive (*SYN.*) useful, helpful, valuable. (*ANT.*) *ruinous, destructive.*

construe (*SYN.*) explain, interpret, solve, render, translate. (*ANT.*) *distort, confuse, misconstrue.*

consult (*SYN.*) discuss, chatter, discourse, gossip, confer, report, rumor, deliberate, speech, talk. (*ANT.*) *writing, correspondence, silence.*

consume (*SYN.*) engulf, absorb, use up, use, expend, exhaust, devour, devastate, destroy, engross. (*ANT.*) *emit, expel, exude, discharge.*

consumer (*SYN.*) user, buyer, purchaser.

consummate (*SYN.*) close, conclude, do, finish, perfect, terminate.

consummation (*SYN.*) climax, apex, culmination, peak. (*ANT.*) *depth, base, floor.*

contact (*SYN.*) meeting, touching.

contagious (*SYN.*) infectious, virulent, communicable, catching. (*ANT.*) *noncommunicable, healthful, hygienic.*

contain (*SYN.*) embody, hold, embrace, include, accommodate, repress, restrain. (*ANT.*) *emit, encourage, yield, discharge.*

contaminate (*SYN.*) corrupt, sully, taint, defile, soil, pollute, dirty, infect, poison. (*ANT.*) *purify.*

contemplate (*SYN.*) imagine, recollect, consider, study, reflect upon, observe, deliberate, muse, ponder, plan, intend, view, regard, think about, reflect, think, mean. (*ANT.*) *forget, guess, conjecture.*

contemplative (*SYN.*) meditative, thoughtful, pensive, studious. (*ANT.*) *inattentive, indifferent, thoughtless.*

contemporary (*SYN.*) modern, present, simultaneous, fashionable, coexisting, contemporaneous, up-to-date. (*ANT.*) *old, antecedent, past, ancient, succeeding, bygone.*

contempt (*SYN.*) detestation, malice, contumely, disdain, derision, scorn. (*ANT.*) *respect, reverence, admiration, esteem, awe.*

contemptible (*SYN.*) base, mean, vile, vulgar, nasty, low, detestable, selfish, miserable, offensive. (*ANT.*) *generous, honorable, noble, exalted, admirable.*

contemptuous (*SYN.*) disdainful, sneering, scornful, insolent. (*ANT.*) *modest, humble.*

contend (*SYN.*) dispute, combat, contest, assert, claim, argue, maintain.

content (*SYN.*) pleased, happy, contented, satisfied. (*ANT.*) *restless, dissatisfied, discontented.*

contented (*SYN.*) delighted, fortunate, gay, happy, joyous, lucky, merry. (*ANT.*) *gloomy, blue, depressed.*

contention (*SYN.*) combat, duel, struggle, discord, battle, variance. (*ANT.*) *concord, harmony, amity, consonance.*

contentment (*SYN.*) delight, happiness, gladness, pleasure, satisfaction. (*ANT.*) *misery, sorrow, grief, sadness, despair.*

contest (*SYN.*) dispute, debate, competition, tournament, oppose, discuss, quarrel, squabble. (*ANT.*) *allow, concede, agree, assent.*

continence (*SYN.*) forbearance, temperance. (*ANT.*) *self-indulgence, excess, intoxication.*

contingency (*SYN.*) likelihood, possibility, occasion, circumstance.

contingent (*SYN.*) depending, subject. (*ANT.*) *independent, original, casual.*

continual (*SYN.*) constant, unceasing, everlasting, unremitting, endless, continuous, uninterrupted, regular, connected, consecutive, ceaseless. (*ANT.*) *periodic, rare, irregular.*

continue (*SYN.*) proceed, extend, endure, persist, resume, renew, recommence, last, remain, prolong, pursue. (*ANT.*) *check, cease, discontinue, stop, suspend.*

continuous (*SYN.*) continuing, uninterrupted, ceaseless, unceasing, incessant, constant. (*ANT.*) *intermittent, irregular, sporadic.*

contract (*SYN.*) condense,

diminish, reduce, bargain, restrict, agreement, compact, pact, shrink, get, treaty, shorten. *(ANT.)* *lengthen, extend, swell, expand.*

contraction *(SYN.)* reduction, shortening. *(ANT.) enlargement, expansion, extension.*

contradict *(SYN.)* gainsay, counter, oppose, confute, dispute. *(ANT.) verify, confirm, agree, support.*

contradictory *(SYN.)* inconsistent, conflicting, incompatible, paradoxical, unsteady. *(ANT.) congruous, consistent, correspondent.*

contrary *(SYN.)* disagreeable, perverse, hostile, stubborn, opposite, opposing, opposed, disagreeing, disastrous, conflicting, headstrong, unlucky. *(ANT.) lucky, agreeable, propitious, favorable, like, obliging, similar, complementary, tractable.*

contrast *(SYN.)* differentiate, compare, distinction, disagreement, distinguish, differ, discriminate, difference, oppose. *(ANT.) agreement, similarity, likeness.*

contribute *(SYN.)* grant, give, donate, bestow, provide, offer. *(ANT.) deny, withhold.*

contribution *(SYN.)* grant, gift, offering, donation.

contrition *(SYN.)* grief, regret, self-reproach. *(ANT.) self-satisfaction, complacency.*

contrive *(SYN.)* devise, intend, plan, make, invent, plot, hatch, form, project, arrange, manage, maneuver, scheme, sketch.

control *(SYN.)* govern, regulate, rule, command, dominate, direct, manage, check, repress, curb, management, mastery, direction, restraint, superintend. *(ANT.) ignore, forsake, follow, submit, abandon.*

controversy *(SYN.)* disagreement, dispute, debate. *(ANT.) agreement, harmony, accord, concord, decision.*

convenience *(SYN.)* accessibility, aid, benefit, help, service, availability. *(ANT.) inconvenience.*

convenient *(SYN.)* adapted, appropriate, fitting, favorable, handy, suitable, accessible, nearby, ready, available, advantageous, timely. *(ANT.) inconvenient, troublesome, awkward.*

convention *(SYN.)* meeting, conference, assembly, practice, custom, rule.

conventional *(SYN.)* common, regular, usual, everyday, habitual, routine, accustomed. *(ANT.) exotic, unusual, bizarre, extraordinary.*

conversant *(SYN.)* aware, intimate, familiar, versed, close, friendly, sociable. *(ANT.) affected, distant, cold, reserved.*

conversation *(SYN.)* colloquy, dialogue, chat, parley, discussion, talk.

converse *(SYN.)* jabber, talk, argue, comment, harangue, plead, rant, spout, discuss, chat, speak, reason.

conversion *(SYN.)* alteration, change, mutation, modification, metamorphosis.

convert *(SYN.)* change, alter, turn, transform, shift, modify, exchange, win over, vary, veer. *(ANT.) establish, settle, retain.*

convey *(SYN.)* carry, bear, communicate, transport, transmit, support, sustain. *(ANT.) drop, abandon.*

conveyance *(SYN.)* van, car, train, truck, plane.

convict *(SYN.)* felon, offender, criminal.

conviction *(SYN.)* opinion, position, view, faith, belief, confidence, feeling, reliance, trust. *(ANT.) doubt, incredulity, denial.*

convince *(SYN.)* persuade, assure, exhort, induce, influence. *(ANT.) deter, compel, restrain, dissuade.*

convivial *(SYN.)* jolly, social, jovial, gregarious. *(ANT.) solemn, stern, unsociable.*

convoy *(SYN.)* with, attend, chaperone. *(ANT.) avoid, desert, quit, leave.*

cool *(SYN.)* frosty, chilly, icy, cold, wintry, quiet, composed, collected, distant, unfriendly, quiet, moderate. *(ANT.) hot, warm, heated, overwrought, excited, hysterical, friendly, outgoing.*

cooperate *(SYN.)* unite, combine, help, contribute, support.

coordinate *(SYN.)* attune, harmonize, adapt, match, balance.

copious *(SYN.)* ample, abundant, bountiful, overflowing, plentiful, profuse, rich. *(ANT.) scant, scarce, insufficient, meager, deficient.*

copy *(SYN.)* facsimile, exemplar, imitation, duplicate, reproduction, likeness, print, carbon, transcript. *(ANT.) prototype, original.*

cordial *(SYN.)* polite, friendly, affable, genial, earnest, gracious, warm, ardent, warmhearted, hearty, sincere. *(ANT.) unfriendly, cool, aloof, hostile, reserved.*

core *(SYN.)* midpoint, heart, kernel, center, middle. *(ANT.) outskirts, border, surface, outside, boundary, rim.*

corporation *(SYN.)* business, organization, crew, group, troop, society, company, conglomerate, firm. *(ANT.) individual, dispersion, seclusion.*

corpse *(SYN.)* cadaver, carcass, remains, body, form. *(ANT.) spirit, soul, mind, intellect.*

corpulent *(SYN.)* obese, portly, chubby, stout. *(ANT.) slim, thin, slender, lean.*

correct *(SYN.)* true, set right, faultless, impeccable, proper, accurate, precise, mend, right, rebuke, punish, amend, rectify, better, emend, caution, discipline, exact, strict. *(ANT.) condone, aggravate, false, inaccurate, wrong, untrue, faulty.*

correction *(SYN.)* order, improvement, regulation, instruction, amendment, emendation, remedy, rectification, repair, training, punishment. *(ANT.) confusion, turbulence, chaos.*

correlative *(SYN.)* allied, correspondent, like, similar, parallel. *(ANT.) different, opposed, divergent.*

correspond *(SYN.)* compare, coincide, match, agree, suit, fit, write. *(ANT.) differ, diverge, vary.*

correspondent *(SYN.)* allied, alike, comparable, like, parallel, similar. *(ANT.) different, opposed, divergent, dissimilar.*

corridor *(SYN.)* hallway, hall, foyer, passage, lobby, passageway.

corrode *(SYN.)* erode.

corrupt *(SYN.)* crooked, untrustworthy, treacherous, debased, unscrupulous, wicked, evil, low, contaminated, perverted, bribe, depraved, corrupted, demoralize, degrade, venal, putrid, tainted, dishonest, impure. *(ANT.) upright, honest, pure, sanctify, edify, purify, sanctified, scrupulous.*

corrupted *(SYN.)* crooked, dishonest, impure, spoiled, unsound.

cost *(SYN.)* price, value, damage, charge, loss, sacrifice, penalty, worth.

costly *(SYN.)* dear, expensive. *(ANT.) cheap, inexpensive.*

costume *(SYN.)* dress, clothes, apparel, clothing, garb.

couch *(SYN.)* davenport, sofa, loveseat.

council *(SYN.)* caution, instruction, committee, cabinet, board, suggestion.

counsel *(SYN.)* guidance, attorney, lawyer, counselor, hint, imply, opinion, advice, offer, advise. *(ANT.) declare, dictate, insist.*

count *(SYN.)* consider, number, enumerate, total, figure, compute, tally, estimate. *(ANT.) conjecture, guess, miscalculate.*

countenance *(SYN.)* visage, face, aspect, support, appearance, approval, encouragement, favor. *(ANT.) forbid, prohibit.*

counteract *(SYN.)* thwart, neutralize, offset, counterbalance, defeat.

counterfeit *(SYN.)* false, fraudulent, pretended, pretend, sham, imitate, forgery, artificial, bogus, fake, spurious, imitation, unreal. *(ANT.) authentic, natural, real, genuine, true.*

country *(SYN.)* state, nation, forest, farmland. *(ANT.) city.*

couple *(SYN.)* team, pair, accompany, associate, attach, combine, connect, brace, join, link, unite. *(ANT.) detach, separate, disjoin, disconnect.*

courage *(SYN.)* fearlessness, boldness, chivalry, fortitude, mettle, spirit, daring, bravery, prowess, intrepidity, valor, resolution. *(ANT.) fear, timidity, cowardice.*

courageous *(SYN.)* bold, dauntless, brave, daring, intrepid, valorous, plucky, fearless, heroic, valiant. *(ANT.) fearful, weak, timid, cowardly.*

course *(SYN.)* passage, advance, path, road, progress, way, direction, bearing, route, street, track, trail, way.

courteous *(SYN.)* civil, respectful, polite, genteel, well-mannered, gracious, refined. *(ANT.) discourteous, rude, uncivil, impolite.*

courtesy *(SYN.)* graciousness, politeness, respect. *(ANT.) discourtesy, rudeness.*

covenant *(SYN.)* agreement, concord, harmony, unison, compact, stipulation. *(ANT.) variance, discord, dissension, difference.*

cover *(SYN.)* clothe, conceal, disguise, curtain, guard, envelop, mask, cloak, shield, hide, screen, protect, embrace, top, lid, covering, stopper, protection, refuge, spread, overlay, include, veil. *(ANT.) bare, expose, reveal.*

covert *(SYN.)* potential, undeveloped, concealed, dormant. *(ANT.) explicit, visible, manifest.*

covetous *(SYN.)* grasping, greedy, acquisitive, avaricious. *(ANT.) generous.*

coward *(SYN.)* dastard, milquetoast, cad. *(ANT.) hero.*

cowardice *(SYN.)* dread, dismay, fright, dismay, panic, terror, timidity. *(ANT.) fearlessness, courage, bravery.*

cowardly *(SYN.)* fearful, timorous, afraid, faint-hearted, yellow, pusillanimous, spineless.

cower *(SYN.)* wince, flinch, cringe, quail, tremble.

coy *(SYN.)* embarrassed, sheepish, shy, timid. *(ANT.) fearless, outgoing, bold, adventurous, daring.*

crack *(SYN.)* snap, break, split.

cracker *(SYN.)* wafer, biscuit, saltine.

craft *(SYN.)* talent, skill, expertness, ability, cunning, guile, deceit, trade, profession, occupation.

crafty *(SYN.)* covert, clever, cunning, skillful, foxy, tricky, sly, underhand, shrewd. *(ANT.) frank, sincere, gullible, open, guileless, ingenuous.*

craggy *(SYN.)* rough, rugged, irregular, uneven. *(ANT.) level, sleek, smooth, fine, polished.*

crank *(SYN.)* cross, irritable, bad tempered, testy. *(ANT.) cheerful, happy.*

crash *(SYN.)* smash, shatter, dash.

crave *(SYN.)* want, desire, hunger for. *(ANT.) relinquish, renounce.*

craving *(SYN.)* relish, appetite, desire, liking, longing, passion. *(ANT.) renunciation, distaste, disgust.*

crazy *(SYN.)* delirious, deranged, idiotic, mad, insane, imbecilic, demented, foolish, maniacal. *(ANT.) sane, sensible, sound, rational, reasonable.*

creak *(SYN.)* squeak.

create *(SYN.)* fashion, form, generate, engender, formulate, make, originate, produce, cause, ordain, invent, beget, design, construct, constitute. *(ANT.) disband, abolish, terminate, destroy, demolish.*

creative *(SYN.)* imaginative, ingenious, original, resourceful, clever, inventive,

innovative, mystical. *(ANT.) unromantic, dull, literal.*

credence *(SYN.)* confidence, faith, feeling, opinion, trust. *(ANT.) doubt, incredulity, denial.*

credible *(SYN.)* conceivable, believable. *(ANT.) inconceivable, unbelievable.*

credit *(SYN.)* believe, accept, belief, trust, faith, merit, honor, apprehend, fancy, hold, support. *(ANT.) doubt, reject, question, distrust, debt.*

creditable *(SYN.)* worthy, praiseworthy. *(ANT.) dishonorable, discreditable, shameful.*

credulous *(SYN.)* trusting, naive, believing, gullible. *(ANT.) suspicious.*

creed *(SYN.)* belief, precept, credo, faith, teaching. *(ANT.) practice, deed, conduct, performance.*

creek *(SYN.)* brook, spring, stream, rivulet.

crime *(SYN.)* offense, insult, aggression, wrongdoing, wrong, misdeed. *(ANT.) right, gentleness, innocence, morality.*

criminal *(SYN.)* unlawful, crook, gangster, outlaw, illegal, convict, delinquent, offender, malefactor, culprit, felonious, felon, transgressor.

cripple *(SYN.)* hurt, maim, damage, injure.

crippled *(SYN.)* deformed, disabled, maimed, hobbling, limping, unconvincing, unsatisfactory. *(ANT.) robust, sound, vigorous, athletic.*

crisis *(SYN.)* conjuncture, emergency, pass, pinch, acme, climax, contingency, juncture, exigency, strait. *(ANT.) calm, normality, stability, equilibrium.*

crisp *(SYN.)* crumbling, delicate, frail, brittle. *(ANT.) calm, normality, stability.*

criterion *(SYN.)* measure, law, rule, principle, gauge, proof. *(ANT.) fancy, guess, chance, supposition.*

critic *(SYN.)* reviewer, judge, commentator, censor, defamer, slanderer, faultfinder.

critical *(SYN.)* exact, fastidious, faultfinding, accurate, condemning, reproachful, risky, dangerous, momentous, carping, acute, hazardous, hypercritical, perilous, decisive, important. *(ANT.) shallow, uncritical, approving, insignificant, trivial, unimportant.*

criticize *(SYN.)* examine, analyze, inspect, blame, censure, appraise, evaluate, scrutinize,

reprehend. *(ANT.) neglect, overlook, approve.*

critique *(SYN.)* criticism, inspection, review.

crony *(SYN.)* colleague, companion, chum, buddy, comrade, friend, mate. *(ANT.) stranger, enemy, adversary.*

crooked *(SYN.)* twisted, corrupt, hooked, curved, criminal, dishonest, degraded, bent, zigzag, impaired. *(ANT.) improved, raised, straight, honest, vitalized, upright, enhanced.*

crop *(SYN.)* fruit, produce, harvest, cut, mow, reaping, result, yield.

cross *(SYN.)* mix, mingle, traverse, interbreed, annoyed, irritable, cranky, testy, angry, mean, ill-natured. *(ANT.) cheerful.*

crouch *(SYN.)* duck, stoop.

crow *(SYN.)* boast, brag.

crowd *(SYN.)* masses, flock, host, squeeze, mob, multitude, populace, press, cramp, throng, swarm.

crown *(SYN.)* coronet, apex, crest, circlet, pinnacle, tiara, skull, head, top, zenith. *(ANT.) base, bottom, foundation, foot.*

crude *(SYN.)* rude, graceless, unpolished, green, harsh, rough, coarse, ill-prepared, unfinished, raw, boorish, unrefined, uncouth. *(ANT.) finished, refined, polished, cultured, genteel, cultivated.*

cruel *(SYN.)* ferocious, mean, heartless, unmerciful, malignant, savage, brutal, pitiless, inhuman, ruthless, merciless. *(ANT.) humane, forbearing, kind, compassionate, merciful, benevolent, kindhearted, gentle.*

cruelty *(SYN.)* harshness, meanness, savagery, brutality. *(ANT.) compassion, kindness.*

crumb *(SYN.)* jot, grain, mite, particle, shred. *(ANT.) mass, bulk, quantity.*

crunch *(SYN.)* champ, gnaw, nibble, pierce.

crush *(SYN.)* smash, break, crash.

cry *(SYN.)* yowl, yell, roar, shout, bellow, scream, wail, weep, bawl, sob.

cryptic *(SYN.)* puzzling, mysterious, enigmatic, hidden, secret, vague, obscure, occult, unclear.

cull *(SYN.)* elect, choose, pick, select. *(ANT.) reject, refuse.*

culpable *(SYN.)* guilty, blameworthy. *(ANT.) innocent.*

cultivate *(SYN.)* plant, seed, farm, till, refine, educate,

teach.

cultivation *(SYN.)* farming, horticulture, tillage, agriculture.

cultural *(SYN.)* civilizing, educational, elevating, instructive.

cumbersome *(SYN.)* bulky, clumsy, awkward, unmanageable. *(ANT.) handy.*

cunning *(SYN.)* clever, wily, crafty, foxy, skillful, tricky, ingenious, foxiness, ability, skill, wiliness, devious. *(ANT.) gullible, honest, naive, openness, straightforward, simple, direct.*

curb *(SYN.)* check, restraint, hinder, hold, limit, control, stop, suppress. *(ANT.) aid, loosen, incite, encourage.*

cure *(SYN.)* help, treatment, heal, medicine, restorative, relief, remedy.

curiosity *(SYN.)* marvel, rarity, phenomenon, admiration, amazement. *(ANT.) apathy, indifference, expectation.*

curious *(SYN.)* interrogative, interested, peculiar, queer, nosy, peeping, prying, inquisitive, snoopy, inquiring, unusual. *(ANT.) unconcerned, ordinary, indifferent, uninterested, common.*

current *(SYN.)* up-to-date, contemporary, present, new, tide, stream, modern. *(ANT.) antiquated, old, bygone, ancient, past.*

curse *(SYN.)* ban, oath, denounce, swear, condemn. *(ANT.) boon, blessing.*

cursory *(SYN.)* frivolous, shallow, slight. *(ANT.) complete, deep, profound, thorough.*

curt *(SYN.)* hasty, short, abrupt, brusque, brief, blunt, rude, harsh. *(ANT.) friendly, smooth, gradual, polite, courteous, generous.*

curtail *(SYN.)* condense, contract, diminish, reduce, limit, abbreviate. *(ANT.) lengthen, extend.*

curtain *(SYN.)* blind, drapery, drape, shade.

curve *(SYN.)* crook, deflect, bend, bow, incline, turn, twist. *(ANT.) resist, stiffen, straighten.*

cushion *(SYN.)* pillow, pad, absorb.

custodian *(SYN.)* guard, keeper, guardian, watchman.

custody *(SYN.)* guardianship, care. *(ANT.) neglect, disregard, indifference.*

custom *(SYN.)* fashion, rule, routine.

customary *(SYN.)* common, usual, regular, everyday,

general. *(ANT.)* exceptional, irregular, rare, unusual, abnormal.

customer *(SYN.)* patron, client, buyer.

cut *(SYN.)* slash, gash, prick, slit, sever, cleave, mow, incision, chop, lop, slice.

cutting *(SYN.)* bitter, stern, caustic, scathing, harsh, acerbic.

cylindrical *(SYN.)* circular, curved, plump, rotund, spherical, round.

D

dab *(SYN.)* coat, pat, smear.

dabble *(SYN.)* splatter, toy, splash, fiddle, putter.

dabbler *(SYN.)* amateur, dilettante, tinkerer, trifler. *(ANT.)* master, expert, scholar, specialist, authority.

daft *(SYN.)* crazy, foolish, insane.

dagger *(SYN.)* knife, dirk, blade.

daily *(SYN.)* every day, diurnal, regularly.

daily *(SYN.)* dawdle, linger, lag, delay. *(ANT.)* rush, hurry, dash, bustle.

dam *(SYN.)* dike, levee, barrier, slow, stop, check, obstruct, block. *(ANT.)* free, release, loose, unleash.

damage *(SYN.)* spoil, deface, impair, mar, hurt, injury, impairment, destruction. *(ANT.)* repair, benefit, mend, rebuild, improve, ameliorate.

dame *(SYN.)* woman, lady.

damn *(SYN.)* denounce, doom, curse, reprove, blame. *(ANT.)* bless, honor, glorify, praise, accept, applaud, commend, consecrate.

damp *(SYN.)* humid, dank, moisture, wetness, humidity. *(ANT.)* arid, dry.

dampen *(SYN.)* wet, depressed, moisten, dull, suppress, sprinkle, discouraged, retard, slow, inhibit, deaden, muffle. *(ANT.)* dehumidify, increase, encourage.

dance *(SYN.)* bounce, flit, skip, sway, prance, bob, glide, caper, cavort, frisk.

dandle *(SYN.)* jounce, joggle, bounce, jiggle, nestle, cuddle, caress.

dandy *(SYN.)* coxcomb, fop, swell, great, fine, wonderful, excellent. *(ANT.)* rotten, terrible, awful, miserable, slob.

danger *(SYN.)* jeopardy, risk, threat, hazard, uncertainty, peril. *(ANT.)* safety, immunity,

security, defense.

dangerous *(SYN.)* risky, insecure, threatening, critical, perilous, unsafe, uncertain, hazardous. *(ANT.)* secure, protected, safe.

dangle *(SYN.)* swing, flap, hang, sag.

dank *(SYN.)* moist, muggy, wet. *(ANT.)* dry.

dapper *(SYN.)* spruce, trim, natty, smart, well-tailored, dashing, neat. *(ANT.)* untidy, shabby, messy, unkempt.

dappled *(SYN.)* spotted, flecked, brindled, variegated, piebald, pied. *(ANT.)* uniform, solid, unvaried.

dare *(SYN.)* brave, call, question, defy, risk, challenge, summon.

daredevil *(SYN.)* lunatic, thrill-seeker, madcap, adventurer.

daring *(SYN.)* foolhardy, chivalrous, rash, fearless, courageous, intrepid, valiant, courage, bravery, brave, precipitate, bold. *(ANT.)* timid, cowardice, timidity, cautious.

dark *(SYN.)* somber, obscure, gloomy, black, unilluminated, dim, evil, hidden, secret, swarthy, murky, opaque, dismal, mournful, sable, sullen, shadowy, sinister, dusky, mystic, shadowy, unlit, sunless, shaded, wicked, occult. *(ANT.)* lucid, light, happy, cheerful, illuminated, pleasant.

darling *(SYN.)* dear, adored, sweetheart, favorite, cherished. *(ANT.)* uncherished, unlovable, disagreeable, rejected, forlorn.

darn *(SYN.)* repair, mend.

dart *(SYN.)* scurry, arrow, barb, hurry, dash, throw, missile, run, hasten, scamper, toss, rush, cast.

dash *(SYN.)* pound, thump, beat, smite, buffet, thrash, smash, break, scurry, run, dart, rush, scamper, hint, pinch, hit, strike. *(ANT.)* stroke, hearten, encourage, defend.

dashing *(SYN.)* swashbuckling, dapper, flamboyant, handsome. *(ANT.)* dull, colorless, shabby, lifeless.

dastardly *(SYN.)* mean-spirited, craven, cowardly, mean, rotten, villainous, dishonorable. *(ANT.)* heroic, brave, high-minded, courageous.

data *(SYN.)* information, statistics, proof, facts, evidence.

date *(SYN.)* interview, appointment, commitment, engagement, meeting,

rendezvous, regale, entertain.

dated *(SYN.)* out-of-date, old-fashioned, outmoded. *(ANT.)* latest, now, current, fashionable, hot.

daub *(SYN.)* coat, grease, soil, scribble, cover, stain, smear, scrawl.

daunt *(SYN.)* discourage, dishearten, intimidate, frighten, deter. *(ANT.)* enspirit, encourage.

dauntless *(SYN.)* fearless, brave, bold, courageous, intrepid, valiant. *(ANT.)* fearful, timid, cowardly.

dawn *(SYN.)* sunrise, start, outset, daybreak, origin, commencement. *(ANT.)* dusk, sunset, nightfall, end, conclusion, finish.

daydream *(SYN.)* woolgather, muse.

daze *(SYN.)* perplex, stun, puzzle, bewilder, upset, confuse, ruffle, confusion, stupor, bewilderment.

dazzle *(SYN.)* surprise, stun, astonish, impress, bewilder, stupefy.

dead *(SYN.)* departed, lifeless, deceased, insensible, inanimate, dull, defunct, gone, lifeless, unconscious, inoperative, inactive, inert, motionless, spiritless. *(ANT.)* animate, functioning, active, living, alive, stirring.

deaden *(SYN.)* anesthetize, numb, paralyze.

deadlock *(SYN.)* standstill, impasse, stalemate.

deadly *(SYN.)* lethal, mortal, fatal, deathly.

deaf *(SYN.)* unhearing, unheeding, unaware, unheedful, stubborn, oblivious, inattentive. *(ANT.)* aware, conscious.

deafening *(SYN.)* vociferous, noisy, stentorian, resounding, loud. *(ANT.)* soft, inaudible, subdued.

deal *(SYN.)* act, treat, attend, cope, barter, trade, bargain, apportion, give, distribute, deliver.

dear *(SYN.)* valued, esteemed, expensive, beloved, costly, darling, high-priced, loved, precious. *(ANT.)* hateful, reasonable, inexpensive, cheap, unwanted.

dearth *(SYN.)* shortage, lack, scarcity.

death *(SYN.)* decease, extinction, demise, passing. *(ANT.)* life.

debase *(SYN.)* lower, degrade, alloy, adulterate, defile, humiliate, depress, abase, pervert, corrupt. *(ANT.)* restore, improve, vitalize, enhance.

debate *(SYN.)* wrangle, discuss, plead, argue, discussion, contend, argument, controversy, dispute. *(ANT.)* agreement, accord, ignore, spurn.

debonair *(SYN.)* urbane, sophisticated, refined, dapper, well-bred.

debris *(SYN.)* rubbish, litter, junk, wreckage, refuse, detritus, ruins, trash, residue.

debt *(SYN.)* amount due, liability, obligation.

decay *(SYN.)* decrease, spoil, ebb, decline, waste, disintegrate, wane, dwindle, molder, deteriorate, perish, wither, rot, collapse, rottenness, putrefy, decompose. *(ANT.)* progress, rise, increase, grow, flourish.

deceased *(SYN.)* lifeless, departed, dead, insensible, defunct. *(ANT.)* living, alive.

deceit *(SYN.)* duplicity, cheat, fraud, chicanery, trick, cunning, deception, guile, beguilement, deceitfulness, dishonesty, wiliness. *(ANT.)* truthfulness, openness, forthrightness, honesty, candor.

deceitful *(SYN.)* false, fraudulent, insincere, dishonest, deceptive. *(ANT.)* sincere, honest.

deceive *(SYN.)* cheat, defraud, hoodwink, mislead, swindle.

decency *(SYN.)* decorum, dignity, propriety, respectability.

decent *(SYN.)* befitting, fit, suitable, becoming, respectable, adequate, seemly, fitting, comely, appropriate, proper, tolerable, decorous. *(ANT.)* vulgar, gross, improper, unsuitable, indecorous, reprehensible, indecent, coarse.

deception *(SYN.)* trick, cheat, sham, deceit, trickery, craftiness, treachery, beguilement, cunning. *(ANT.)* openness, frankness, candor, probity, truthfulness, honesty.

deceptive *(SYN.)* specious, fallacious, deceitful, false, delusive, unreliable, illusive, tricky, dishonest, deceiving, misleading, delusory. *(ANT.)* honest, real, genuine, true, truthful, authentic.

decide *(SYN.)* resolve, determine, terminate, conclude, close, settle, adjudicate, choose, end. *(ANT.)* waver, hesitate, vacillate, doubt, suspend.

decipher *(SYN.)* render, unravel, construe, solve, decode, translate, elucidate, determine. *(ANT.)* misconstrue, distort, *misinterpret, confuse.*

decision *(SYN.)* resolution, determination, settlement.

decisive *(SYN.)* determined, firm, decided, unhesitating, resolute.

declaration *(SYN.)* pronouncement, notice, affirmation, statement, announcement, assertion.

declare *(SYN.)* assert, promulgate, affirm, tell, broadcast, express, proclaim, aver, say, pronounce, profess, announce. *(ANT.) deny, withhold, conceal, suppress.*

decline *(SYN.)* descend, decay, dwindle, refuse, incline, wane, sink, depreciate, deny, diminish, weaken. *(ANT.) accept, ascend, ameliorate, increase.*

decompose *(SYN.)* rot, disintegrate, molder, decay, crumble.

decorate *(SYN.)* trim, paint, deck, enrich, color, beautify, enhance, furbish, furnish, adorn, ornament. *(ANT.) uncover, mar, deface, defame, debase.*

decoration *(SYN.)* ornamentation, embellishment, adornment, furnishing, award, citation, medal.

decoy *(SYN.)* lure, bait.

decrease *(SYN.)* lessen, wane, deduct, diminish, curtail, remove, lessening, decline. *(ANT.) expansion, increase, enlarge, expand, grow.*

decree *(SYN.)* order, edict, statute, declaration, announce, act.

decrepit *(SYN.)* feeble, puny, weakened, infirm, enfeebled, languid, rickety, weak, rundown, tumble-down, dilapidated, faint. *(ANT.) strong, forceful, vigorous, energetic, lusty.*

decry *(SYN.)* lower, belittle, derogate, minimize, undervalue. *(ANT.) praise, commend, magnify, aggrandize.*

dedicate *(SYN.)* sanctify, consecrate, hallow, devote, assign.

dedicated *(SYN.)* disposed, true, affectionate, fond, wedded. *(ANT.) indisposed, detached, untrammeled, disinclined.*

deduct *(SYN.)* lessen, shorten, abate, remove, eliminate, curtail, subtract. *(ANT.) grow, enlarge, add, increase, amplify, expand.*

deed *(SYN.)* feat, transaction, action, performance, act, operation, achievement, document, certificate, title, accomplishment. *(ANT.)*

intention, cessation, inactivity, deliberation.

deem *(SYN.)* hold, determine, believe, regard, reckon, judge, consider, account, expound, view.

deep *(SYN.)* bottomless, low, unplumbed, acute, obscure, involved, absorbed. *(ANT.) shallow.*

deface *(SYN.)* spoil, impair, damage, mar, hurt, scratch, mutilate, disfigure, injure, harm. *(ANT.) mend, benefit, repair.*

defamation *(SYN.)* invective, reproach, upbraiding, abuse, insult, outrage, reviling, desecration. *(ANT.) respect, approval, laudation, commendation.*

default *(SYN.)* loss, omission, lack, failure, want, dereliction. *(ANT.) victory, achievement, sufficiency, success.*

defeat *(SYN.)* quell, vanquish, beat, overcome, overthrow, subdue, frustrate, spoil, conquest. *(ANT.) submit, retreat, cede, yield, surrender, capitulate, lose.*

defect *(SYN.)* shortcoming, fault, omission, blemish, imperfection, forsake, leave, weakness, failure. *(ANT.) perfection, flawlessness, support, join, completeness.*

defective *(SYN.)* faulty, imperfect, inoperative, flawed, inoperable. *(ANT.) flawless, perfect, faultless.*

defend *(SYN.)* screen, espouse, justify, protect, vindicate, fortify, assert, guard, safeguard, shield. *(ANT.) oppose, assault, submit, attack, deny.*

defense *(SYN.)* resistance, protection, bulwark, fort, barricade, trench, rampart, fortress.

defer *(SYN.)* postpone, delay. *(ANT.) speed, hurry, expedite.*

deference *(SYN.)* fame, worship, adoration, reverence, admiration, respect, fame, dignity, homage. *(ANT.) dishonor, derision, reproach, contempt.*

defiant *(SYN.)* rebellious, antagonistic, obstinate. *(ANT.) yielding, submissive.*

deficient *(SYN.)* lacking, short, incomplete, defective, scanty, insufficient, inadequate. *(ANT.) enough, ample, sufficient, adequate.*

defile *(SYN.)* pollute, corrupt, dirty, debase, contaminate. *(ANT.) purify.*

define *(SYN.)* describe, fix, establish, label, designate, set,

name, explain.

definite *(SYN.)* fixed, prescribed, certain, specific, exact, determined, distinct, explicit, correct. *(ANT.) indefinite, confused, undetermined, equivocal.*

definitely *(SYN.)* certainly, assuredly, absolutely, positively, surely.

definition *(SYN.)* sense, interpretation, meaning, explanation.

deft *(SYN.)* handy, adroit, clever, adept, dexterous, skillful, skilled. *(ANT.) inept, clumsy, maladroit, awkward.*

defunct *(SYN.)* lifeless, dead, departed, expired, extinct, spiritless, inanimate. *(ANT.) living, alive, stirring.*

defy *(SYN.)* hinder, oppose, withstand, attack, resist, confront, challenge, flout, dare, thwart. *(ANT.) yield, allow, relent, surrender, submit, accede.*

degenerate *(SYN.)* dwindle, decline, weaken, deteriorate, decrease. *(ANT.) ascend, ameliorate, increase, appreciate.*

degrade *(SYN.)* crush, reduce, subdue, abash, humble, lower, shame, demote, downgrade, abase, mortify. *(ANT.) praise, elevate, honor.*

degree *(SYN.)* grade, amount, step, measure, rank, honor, extent.

deign *(SYN.)* condescend, stoop.

dejected *(SYN.)* depressed, downcast, sad, disheartened, blue, discouraged. *(ANT.) cheerful, happy, optimistic.*

delectable *(SYN.)* tasty, delicious, savory, delightful, sweet, luscious. *(ANT.) unsavory, distasteful, unpalatable, acrid.*

delegate *(SYN.)* emissary, envoy, ambassador, representative, commission, deputize, authorize.

delete *(SYN.)* erase, cancel, remove. *(ANT.) add.*

deleterious *(SYN.)* evil, unwholesome, base, sinful, bad, wicked, immoral, destructive, injurious, hurtful, damaging, detrimental, unsound. *(ANT.) moral, excellent, reputable, healthful, healthy, helpful, constructive, good.*

deliberate *(SYN.)* studied, willful, intended, contemplated, premeditated, planned, methodical, designed. *(ANT.) fortuitous, hasty, accidental.*

delicate *(SYN.)* frail, critical, slender, dainty, pleasing, fastidious, exquisite, precarious,

demanding, sensitive, savory, fragile, weak. *(ANT.) tough, strong, coarse, clumsy, hearty, hale, vulgar, rude.*

delicious *(SYN.)* tasty, luscious, delectable, sweet, savory. *(ANT.) unsavory, distasteful, unpalatable, unpleasant, acrid.*

delight *(SYN.)* joy, bliss, gladness, pleasure, ecstasy, happiness, rapture. *(ANT.) revolt, sorrow, annoyance, displeasure, disgust, displease, revulsion, misery.*

delightful *(SYN.)* pleasing, pleasant, charming, refreshing, pleasurable. *(ANT.) nasty, disagreeable, unpleasant.*

delirious *(SYN.)* raving, mad, giddy, frantic, hysterical, violent.

deliver *(SYN.)* impart, publish, rescue, commit, communicate, free, address, offer, save, give, liberate. *(ANT.) restrict, confine, capture, enslave, withhold, imprison.*

deluge *(SYN.)* overflow, flood.

delusion *(SYN.)* mirage, fantasy, phantasm, vision, dream, illusion, phantom, hallucination. *(ANT.) substance, actuality.*

delve *(SYN.)* dig, look, search, scoop, explore, hunt.

demand *(SYN.)* claim, inquire, ask, need, require, obligation, requirement, ask for, necessitate. *(ANT.) tender, give, present, waive, relinquish, offer.*

demean *(SYN.)* comport, bear, operate, carry, act, manage, deport.

demeanor *(SYN.)* manner, way, conduct, actions, behavior.

demented *(SYN.)* insane, crazy, mad, mental, psychotic, lunatic.

demolish *(SYN.)* ruin, devastate, ravage, annihilate, wreck, destroy, raze, exterminate, obliterate. *(ANT.) erect, make, save, construct, preserve, build, establish.*

demolition *(SYN.)* wrecking, destruction. *(ANT.) erection, construction.*

demon *(SYN.)* fiend, devil, ogre, spirit.

demonstrate *(SYN.)* evince, show, prove, display, illustrate, describe, explain, manifest, exhibit. *(ANT.) hide, conceal.*

demonstration *(SYN.)* exhibit, show, presentation, exhibition, display, rally.

demur *(SYN.)* waver, falter, delay, stutter, doubt, vacillate, hesitate, scruple. *(ANT.)*

proceed, decide, resolve.

demure *(SYN.)* meek, shy, modest, diffident, retiring, bashful, coy.

den *(SYN.)* cave, lair, cavern.

denial *(SYN.)* disallowance, proscription, refusal, prohibition.

denounce *(SYN.)* condemn, blame, reprove, reprehend, censure, reproach, upbraid, reprobate. *(ANT.) condone, approve, forgive, commend, praise.*

dense *(SYN.)* crowded, slow, close, obtuse, compact, dull, stupid, compressed, thick, concentrated, packed, solid. *(ANT.) sparse, quick, dispersed, clever, dissipated, empty, smart, bright.*

dent *(SYN.)* notch, impress, pit, nick.

deny *(SYN.)* refuse, withhold, dispute, disavow, forbid, refute, contradict, abjure, confute, gainsay. *(ANT.) confirm, affirm, admit, confess, permit, allow, concede, assert.*

depart *(SYN.)* quit, forsake, withdraw, renounce, desert, relinquish, die, perish, decease. *(ANT.) tarry, remain, come, abide, stay, arrive.*

departure *(SYN.)* valediction, farewell.

depend *(SYN.)* trust, rely, confide.

dependable *(SYN.)* secure, trustworthy, certain, safe, trusty, reliable, tried. *(ANT.) unreliable, fallible, dubious, uncertain.*

dependent *(SYN.)* relying, contingent, subordinate, conditional. *(ANT.) original, casual, absolute, independent.*

depict *(SYN.)* explain, recount, describe, portray, characterize, relate, narrate.

deplore *(SYN.)* repine, lament, bemoan, wail, bewail, weep, grieve, regret.

deport *(SYN.)* exile, eject, oust, banish, expel, dismiss, ostracize, dispel, exclude. *(ANT.) receive, admit, shelter, accept, harbor.*

deportment *(SYN.)* deed, behavior, manner, action, carriage, disposition, bearing, demeanor.

deposit *(SYN.)* place, put, bank, save, store, sediment, dregs, addition, entry. *(ANT.) withdraw, withdrawal.*

depreciate *(SYN.)* dwindle, decrease, belittle, disparage, weaken, minimize, descend, deteriorate. *(ANT.) ascend, ameliorate, praise, increase, applaud, appreciate.*

depress *(SYN.)* deject, dishearten, sadden, dampen, devaluate, devalue, lessen, lower, cheapen, reduce, dispirit, discourage, sink. *(ANT.) exalt, cheer, exhilarate.*

depression *(SYN.)* hopelessness, despondency, pessimism, dip, cavity, pothole, hole, despair, gloom, melancholy, sadness, sorrow, recession, decline, desperation, discouragement. *(ANT.) elation, optimism, happiness, confidence, elevation, hope.*

deprive *(SYN.)* bereave, deny, strip. *(ANT.) provision, supply, provide.*

derelict *(SYN.)* decrepit, shabby, dilapidated, neglected, forsaken, deserted, remiss, abandoned, lax.

dereliction *(SYN.)* want, lack, failure, miscarriage, loss, default, deficiency, omission, fiasco. *(ANT.) sufficiency, success, achievement, victory.*

derision *(SYN.)* irony, satire, banter, raillery, sneering, gibe, ridicule.

derivation *(SYN.)* source, birth, inception, start, beginning, spring, commencement, foundation, origin. *(ANT.) issue, end, outcome, harvest, product.*

derive *(SYN.)* obtain, acquire, get, receive.

descend *(SYN.)* wane, lower, move, slope, incline, decline, slant, sink. *(ANT.) increase, appreciate, ameliorate, ascend.*

descendant *(SYN.)* child, issue, progeny, offspring.

describe *(SYN.)* portray, picture, recount, depict, relate, characterize, represent.

description *(SYN.)* history, record, recital, account, computation, chronicle, reckoning, narration, detail, narrative. *(ANT.) misrepresentation, confusion, caricature.*

desecration *(SYN.)* profanation, insult, defamation, reviling, abuse, maltreatment, aspersion, perversion, dishonor. *(ANT.) respect, commendation, approval, laudation.*

desert *(SYN.)* forsake, wilderness, resign, abjure, abandon, wasteland, waste, leave, surrender, abdicate, quit, barren, uninhabited. *(ANT.) uphold, defend, stay, maintain, accompany, join, support.*

deserter *(SYN.)* runaway, renegade, fugitive, defector.

deserts *(SYN.)* right, compensation, due, reward, requital, condign.

deserve *(SYN.)* earn, warrant, merit.

design *(SYN.)* drawing, purpose, outline, devise, intend, draw, contrive, draft, cunning, plan, artfulness, delineation, scheming, sketch, intent, invent, objective, mean, contrivance, plotting, intention, create. *(ANT.) candor, accident, result, chance.*

designate *(SYN.)* manifest, indicate, show, specify, denote, reveal, name, appoint, select, assign, disclose, signify, imply, nominate, intimate. *(ANT.) divert, mislead, conceal, falsify, distract.*

desirable *(SYN.)* coveted, wanted.

desire *(SYN.)* longing, craving, yearning, appetite, lust, long for, crave, covet, want, request, ask, need, wish, aspiration, urge. *(ANT.) hate, aversion, loathing, abomination, detest, loathe, abhor, distaste.*

desist *(SYN.)* cork, stop, cease, hinder, terminate, abstain, halt, interrupt, seal, arrest, plug, bar. *(ANT.) promote, begin, speed, proceed, start.*

desolate *(SYN.)* forlorn, waste, bare, lonely, abandoned, wild, deserted, uninhabited, empty, sad, miserable, wretched, unhappy, bleak, forsaken. *(ANT.) crowded, teeming, populous, happy, cheerful, fertile.*

despair *(SYN.)* discouragement, pessimism, depression, hopelessness, despondency, desperation. *(ANT.) elation, optimism, hope, joy, confidence.*

desperado *(SYN.)* criminal, crook, thug, gangster, hoodlum.

desperate *(SYN.)* reckless, determined, despairing, wild, daring, hopeless, despondent, audacious. *(ANT.) optimistic, composed, hopeful, collected, calm, assured.*

despicable *(SYN.)* vulgar, offensive, base, vile, contemptible, selfish, low, mean, worthless, nasty. *(ANT.) noble, exalted, admirable, generous, worthy, dignified.*

despise *(SYN.)* hate, scorn, detest, loath, disdain, abhor, condemn, dislike, abominate. *(ANT.) love, approve, like, admire.*

despite *(SYN.)* notwithstanding.

despoil *(SYN.)* plunder, rob, loot.

despondent *(SYN.)* sad, dismal, depressed, somber, dejected, melancholy, doleful, sorrowful. *(ANT.) joyous, cheerful, merry, happy.*

despot *(SYN.)* tyrant, ruler, oppressor, dictator.

despotic *(SYN.)* authoritative, unconditional, absolute, tyrannous, entire, unrestricted. *(ANT.) dependent, conditional, qualified, accountable.*

destiny *(SYN.)* fate, portion, outcome, consequence, result, fortune, doom, lot.

destitute *(SYN.)* poor, penurious, needy, impecunious, poverty-stricken, impoverished, indigent. *(ANT.) opulent, wealthy, affluent, rich.*

destroy *(SYN.)* raze, devastate, ruin, end, demolish, wreck, extinguish, annihilate, exterminate, obliterate, waste, slay, kill, eradicate. *(ANT.) make, construct, start, create, save, establish.*

destroyed *(SYN.)* rent, smashed, interrupted, flattened, wrecked, broken, ruptured, crushed. *(ANT.) whole, repaired, integral, united.*

destruction *(SYN.)* ruin, devastation, extinction, demolition. *(ANT.) beginning, creation.*

destructive *(SYN.)* deadly, baneful, noxious, deleterious, injurious, pernicious, fatal, detrimental. *(ANT.) salutary, beneficial, creative.*

detach *(SYN.)* deduct, remove, subtract, curtail, divide, shorten, decrease, disengage, reduce, separate, diminish. *(ANT.) hitch, grow, enlarge, increase, connect, amplify, attack, expand.*

detail *(SYN.)* elaborate, commission, part, itemize, portion, division, fragment, assign, circumstance, segment.

detain *(SYN.)* impede, delay, hold back, retard, arrest, restrain, stay. *(ANT.) quicken, hasten, expedite, forward, precipitate.*

detect *(SYN.)* discover, reveal, find, ascertain, determine, learn, originate, devise. *(ANT.) hide, screen, lose, cover, mask.*

determinant *(SYN.)* reason, incentive, source, agent, principle, inducement. *(ANT.) result, effect, consequence, end.*

determine *(SYN.)* decide, settle, end, conclude, ascertain, induce, fix, verify, resolve, establish, necessitate.

detest *(SYN.)* loathe, hate, despise. *(ANT.) savor, appreciate, like, love.*

detriment *(SYN.)* injury, harm, disadvantage, damage.

(ANT.) benefit.

detrimental (SYN.) hurtful, mischievous, damaging, harmful. (ANT.) salutary, advantageous, profitable, beneficial.

develop (SYN.) evolve, unfold, enlarge, amplify, expand, create, grow, advance, reveal, unfold, mature, elaborate. (ANT.) wither, contract, degenerate, stunt, deteriorate, compress.

development (SYN.) growth, expansion, progress, unraveling, elaboration, evolution, maturing, unfolding. (ANT.) compression, abbreviation, curtailment.

deviate (SYN.) deflect, stray, divert, diverge, wander, sidetrack, digress. (ANT.) preserve, follow, remain, continue, persist.

device (SYN.) tool, utensil, means, channel, machine, agent, vehicle, gadget, apparatus, instrument, contrivance.

devilish (SYN.) diabolical, fiendish, diabolic, satanic, demonic.

devious (SYN.) tortuous, winding, distorted, circuitous, tricky, crooked, roundabout, cunning, erratic, indirect. (ANT.) straight, direct, straightforward, honest.

devise (SYN.) create, concoct, invent, originate.

devote (SYN.) assign, dedicate, give, apply. (ANT.) withhold, relinquish, ignore, withdraw.

devoted (SYN.) attached, dedicated, prone, wedded, addicted, ardent, earnest, loyal, disposed, inclined, fond, affectionate, faithful. (ANT.) untrammeled, disinclined, detached, indisposed.

devotion (SYN.) piety, zeal, ardor, loyalty, dedication, religiousness, consecration, affection, love, devoutness, fidelity, attachment. (ANT.) unfaithfulness, aversion, alienation, indifference.

devour (SYN.) consume, gulp, gorge, waste, eat, ruin, swallow, destroy.

devout (SYN.) sacred, religious, spiritual, holy, theological, pietistic, pious, sanctimonious, reverent. (ANT.) profane, skeptical, atheistic, secular, impious.

dexterity (SYN.) talent, capability, qualification, aptness, skill, ability. (ANT.) unreadiness, incapacity, disability, incompetency.

dexterous (SYN.) clever, adroit, handy, deft, facile, skillful, skilled, proficient. (ANT.) awkward, clumsy.

dialed (SYN.) slang, jargon, cant, speech, idiom, tongue, diction, vernacular. (ANT.) nonsense, drivel, babble, gibberish.

dialogue (SYN.) interview, chat, discussion, conference, exchange, talk, conversation.

diary (SYN.) memo, account, journal.

dicker (SYN.) haggle, bargain, negotiate.

dictate (SYN.) deliver, speak, record, command, order, direct.

dictator (SYN.) oppressor, tyrant, despot, persecutor, overlord, autocrat.

die (SYN.) fade, wane, cease, depart, wither, decay, decline, sink, expire, perish, decease, go, diminish, fail, languish, decrease. (ANT.) live, begin, grow, survive, flourish.

difference (SYN.) inequality, variety, disparity, discord, distinction, dissension, dissimilarity, disagreement, contrast, separation. (ANT.) harmony, similarity, identity, agreement, likeness, compatibility, kinship, resemblance.

different (SYN.) unlike, various, distinct, miscellaneous, divergent, contrary, differing, diverse, variant, incongruous, unalike, changed, dissimilar, opposite. (ANT.) similar, congruous, alike, identical.

differentiate (SYN.) separate, discriminate, distinguish, perceive, detect, recognize, discern. (ANT.) confuse, omit, mingle, confound, overlook.

difficult (SYN.) involved, demanding, arduous, trying, complicated, hard, laborious, perplexing, hard, intricate. (ANT.) simple, easy, facile, effortless.

difficulty (SYN.) trouble, hardship, fix, predicament, trouble. (ANT.) ease.

diffuse (SYN.) spread, sparse, scattered, scanty, dispersed, thin, rare. (ANT.) concentrated.

dig (SYN.) burrow, excavate, appreciate, understand.

digest (SYN.) consume, eat, reflect on, study, shorten, consider, summarize, abridge, abstract, abridgment, synopsis.

dignified (SYN.) serious, solemn, noble, stately, elegant.

dignify (SYN.) honor, elevate.

(ANT.) shame, degrade, humiliate.

dignity (SYN.) stateliness, distinction, bearing.

digress (SYN.) divert, wander, bend, stray, deflect, sidetrack, crook. (ANT.) preserve, continue, remain, follow, persist.

dilate (SYN.) increase, widen, amplify, enlarge, augment, expand. (ANT.) shrink, contract, restrict, abridge.

dilemma (SYN.) fix, strait, condition, scrape, difficulty, plight. (ANT.) ease, calmness, satisfaction, comfort.

diligent (SYN.) patient, busy, hardworking, active, perseverant, assiduous, industrious, careful. (ANT.) unconcerned, indifferent, apathetic, lethargic, careless.

dim (SYN.) pale, shadowy, faint, faded, unclear, vague, darken, dull, indistinct. (ANT.) brighten, brilliant, bright, illuminate, glaring.

dimension (SYN.) size, importance, measure, extent.

diminish (SYN.) suppress, lower, decrease, shrink, wane, abate, reduce, lessen, assuage. (ANT.) enlarge, revive, amplify, increase.

diminutive (SYN.) small, wee, tiny, little, minute. (ANT.) large, big, gigantic, huge.

din (SYN.) tumult, clamor, sound, babble, outcry, row, noise, racket. (ANT.) quiet, stillness, hush.

dine (SYN.) lunch, eat, sup, feed.

dingy (SYN.) dull, dark, dismal, dirty, drab, murky, gray. (ANT.) cheerful, bright.

dip (SYN.) immerse, plunge, submerge, wet, swim.

diplomacy (SYN.) knack, dexterity, skill, address, poise, tact, finesse. (ANT.) vulgarity, blunder, awkwardness, incompetence.

diplomatic (SYN.) politic, adroit, tactful, discreet, judicious, gracious, polite, discriminating. (ANT.) rude, churlish, gruff, boorish, impolite, coarse.

dire (SYN.) horrible, terrible, appalling, fearful, harrowing, grievous, ghastly, awful, horrid, terrifying, dreadful, frightful, horrifying, monstrous, horrendous, repulsive. (ANT.) lovely, enchanting, fascinating, beautiful, enjoyable.

direct (SYN.) rule, manage, bid, order, level, command, conduct, regulate, point, indicate, show, aim, control, sight,

guide, instruct, train, govern. (ANT.) swerving, untruthful, misguide, distract, indirect, crooked, deceive.

direction (SYN.) way, order, course, instruction, tendency, management, route, trend, guidance, administration, supervision, inclination.

directly (SYN.) immediately, straight.

dirt (SYN.) pollution, soil, filthiness, filth. (ANT.) cleanliness.

dirty (SYN.) muddy, base, pitiful, filthy, shabby, foul, soiled, nasty, mean, grimy, low, obscene, untidy, indecent, unclean, messy, squalid, contemptible, sloppy. (ANT.) pure, neat, wholesome, clean, presentable.

disability (SYN.) inability, weakness, handicap, incapacity, injury, unfitness, incompetence, impotence. (ANT.) power, ability, strength, capability.

disable (SYN.) weaken, incapacitate, cripple. (ANT.) strengthen.

disabled (SYN.) deformed, limping, weak, crippled, maimed, defective, unsatisfactory, halt, feeble. (ANT.) vigorous, athletic, sound, agile, robust.

disadvantage (SYN.) drawback, hindrance, handicap, inconvenience, obstacle. (ANT.) advantage, benefit, convenience.

disagree (SYN.) quarrel, dispute, differ, conflict. (ANT.) agree.

disagreement (SYN.) nonconformity, variance, difference, objection, challenge, remonstrance, dissent. (ANT.) assent, acceptance, compliance, agreement.

disappear (SYN.) end, fade out, vanish. (ANT.) emerge, appear.

disappoint (SYN.) fail, displease, mislead, dissatisfy. (ANT.) please, satisfy, gratify.

disappointment (SYN.) dissatisfaction, defeat, discouragement, failure. (ANT.) pleasure, satisfaction, gratification.

disapprove (SYN.) object to, disfavor, oppose. (ANT.) approve.

disarm (SYN.) paralyze, demilitarize.

disaster (SYN.) casualty, mishap, misfortune, catastrophe, accident, adversity, ruin, calamity. (ANT.) fortune, advantage.

disavow (SYN.) reject, revoke, disclaim, retract, disown. (ANT.) recognize, acknowledge.

disband (SYN.) scatter, split, dismiss, separate.

disbelief (SYN.) doubt, incredulity, skepticism. (ANT.) certainty, credulity.

discard (SYN.) scrap, reject.

discern (SYN.) distinguish, see, descry, separate, differentiate, perceive, discriminate, detect, observe, recognize. (ANT.) omit, confuse, overlook, mingle, confound.

discernment (SYN.) perception, sharpness, intelligence, perspicacity, acuity, keenness. (ANT.) dullness, stupidity.

discharge (SYN.) remove, relieve, dismiss, banish, unburden, shoot, fire, explosion, eject, detonation, liberation, release, unload, discard, send. (ANT.) retain, employ, enlist, hire, accept, recall, detain.

disciple (SYN.) learner, follower, student, adherent, supporter, scholar, pupil, votary, devotee. (ANT.) guide, leader.

discipline (SYN.) training, order, instruction, drill, restraint, regulation, practice, correction, control, self-control, train, teach, exercise. (ANT.) carelessness, sloppiness, confusion, negligence, messiness, chaos, turbulence.

disclaim (SYN.) retract, reject, deny, renounce, disavow, revoke. (ANT.) recognize, acknowledge.

disclose (SYN.) show, divulge, betray, uncover, discover, reveal, expose. (ANT.) hide, cloak, mask, cover, obscure, conceal.

discomfit (SYN.) malaise, concern, confuse, baffle, perplex, disconcert.

discomfort (SYN.) malaise, concern, anxiety, uneasiness.

disconcerted (SYN.) disturbed, agitated, upset.

disconnect (SYN.) divide, separate, unhook, disengage, detach. (ANT.) connect, bind, attach, unify, engage.

disconsolate (SYN.) depressed, downcast, sorrowful, dejected, dismal, sad, unhappy, wretched, somber, cheerless, morose, lugubrious, miserable, mournful. (ANT.) delightful, merry, glad, cheerful, happy.

discontent (SYN.) displeased, disgruntled, unhappy, dissatisfied, vexed.

discontinue (SYN.) postpone, delay, adjourn, stay, stop, defer, suspend, end, cease, interrupt. (ANT.) prolong, persist, continue, start, begin, proceed, maintain.

discord (SYN.) disagreement, conflict. (ANT.) concord, accord, agreement.

discourage (SYN.) hamper, obstruct, restrain, block, dishearten, retard, check, dispirit, thwart, depress, hinder, stop. (ANT.) expedite, inspire, encourage, promote, inspirit, assist, further.

discourteous (SYN.) gruff, rude, vulgar, blunt, impolite, saucy, uncivil, boorish, rough. (ANT.) stately, courtly, civil, dignified, genteel.

discover (SYN.) find out, invent, expose, ascertain, devise, reveal, learn, determine, detect. (ANT.) hide, screen, cover, conceal, lose.

discredit (SYN.) disbelieve, dishonor, doubt, disgrace, shame.

discreet (SYN.) politic, discriminating, judicious, adroit, prudent, cautious, wise, tactful, careful, diplomatic. (ANT.) incautious, rude, coarse, boorish, tactless, imprudent, indiscreet, careless, gruff.

discrepant (SYN.) incompatible, wavering, contrary, irreconcilable, unsteady, illogical, contradictory. (ANT.) correspondent, compatible, consistent.

discriminating (SYN.) exact, particular, critical, accurate, discerning. (ANT.) unimportant, shallow, insignificant, superficial.

discrimination (SYN.) perspicacity, discernment, racism, wisdom, bias, sagacity, intolerance, prejudice, intelligence, understanding. (ANT.) thoughtlessness, senselessness, arbitrariness.

discuss (SYN.) gossip, plead, discourse, blab, lecture, talk, chat, spout, mutter, deliberate, consider, reason, comment.

discussion (SYN.) speech, chatter, lecture, conference, talk, dialogue, conversation, rumor. (ANT.) silence, correspondence, writing.

disdain (SYN.) derision, hatred, contempt, scorn, contumely, reject, haughtiness, detestation. (ANT.) respect, esteem, reverence, admire, prize, honor, admiration, awe, regard.

disdainful (SYN.) haughty, scornful, arrogant, contemptuous. (ANT.) awed, admiring, regardful.

disease (SYN.) malady, disorder, ailment, illness, affliction, infirmity, complaint, sickness. (ANT.) soundness, health, vigor.

disentangle (SYN.) unwind, untie, clear, unravel, unknot, unsnarl, untangle.

disfigured (SYN.) deformed, marred, defaced, scarred.

disgrace (SYN.) odium, chagrin, shame, mortification, embarrassment, humiliate, scandal, dishonor, mortification. (ANT.) renown, glory, respect, praise, dignity, honor.

disgraceful (SYN.) ignominious, shameful, discreditable, disreputable, scandalous, dishonorable. (ANT.) renowned, esteemed, respectable, honorable.

disguise (SYN.) excuse, simulation, pretension, hide, camouflage, make-up, cover-up, mask, conceal, screen, affectation, pretext. (ANT.) show, reality, actuality, display, reveal, sincerity, fact.

disgust (SYN.) offend, repulse, nauseate, revolt, sicken. (ANT.) admiration, liking.

disgusting (SYN.) repulsive, nauseating, revolting, nauseous, repugnant.

dish (SYN.) serve, container, give, receptacle.

dishearten (SYN.) depress, sadden, discourage.

disheveled (SYN.) mussed, sloppy, rumpled, untidy.

dishonest (SYN.) crooked, impure, unsound, false, contaminated, venal, corrupt, putrid, thievish, vitiated, tainted. (ANT.) upright, honest, straightforward.

dishonor (SYN.) disrepute, scandal, indignity, chagrin, mortification, shame, obloquy, defamation, humiliation, disgrace, scandal. (ANT.) renown, glory, praise, honor, dignify.

disinclined (SYN.) unwilling, reluctant, loath.

disingenuous (SYN.) tricky, deceitful, scheming, dishonest, underhanded, cunning, artful, crafty, insidious.

disintegrate (SYN.) decompose, dwindle, spoil, decay, wane, ebb, decline, rot. (ANT.) increase, flourish, rise, grow.

disinterested (SYN.) unbiased, open-minded, neutral, impartial, unprejudiced.

dislike (SYN.) aversion, dread, reluctance, abhorrence, disinclination, hatred, repugnance. (ANT.) devotion, affection, enthusiasm, attachment.

disloyal (SYN.) false, treasonable, apostate, unfaithful, recreant, treacherous, untrue, traitorous, faithless. (ANT.) true, devoted, constant, loyal.

dismal (SYN.) dark, lonesome, somber, bleak, dull, sad, doleful, sorrowful, cheerless, depressing, dreary, funeral, gloomy, melancholy. (ANT.) lively, gay, happy, lighthearted, charming, cheerful.

dismantle (SYN.) take apart, wreck, disassemble.

dismay (SYN.) disturb, bother, dishearten, horror, alarm, bewilder, frighten, scare, discourage, confuse. (ANT.) encourage, hearten.

dismiss (SYN.) remove, discharge, discard, release, liberate, exile, banish, eject, oust. (ANT.) retain, detain, engage, hire, accept.

disobedient (SYN.) refractory, forward, unruly, insubordinate, defiant, rebellious, undutiful. (ANT.) submissive, complaint, obedient.

disobey (SYN.) invade, break, violate, infringe, defile.

disorder (SYN.) tumult, chaos, jumble, confusion, muddle, turmoil, anarchy. (ANT.) organization, neatness, system, order.

disorganization (SYN.) jumble, confusion, muddle, anarchy. (ANT.) system, order.

disorganized (SYN.) muddled, confused, indistinct, bewildered, mixed. (ANT.) organized, lucid, clear, plain.

disown (SYN.) deny, renounce, reject, repudiate, forsake, disinherit.

disparage (SYN.) undervalue, depreciate, lower, belittle, derogate, minimize, decry, discredit. (ANT.) exalting, praise, aggrandize, magnify, commend.

disparagement (SYN.) lowering, decrying, undervaluing, belittling, minimizing. (ANT.) praise, exalting, aggrandizement, magnification.

disparaging (SYN.) belittling, deprecatory, discrediting, deprecating.

dispassionate (SYN.) calm, cool, composed, controlled, unemotional, imperturbable.

dispatch (SYN.) throw, impel, transmit, emit, cast, finish, report, message, send, speed, achieve, conclude, communication, promptness, discharge. (ANT.) reluctance, get, redeem, bring, slowness, hold.

dispel (SYN.) disseminate, scatter, disperse, separate, diffuse. (ANT.) collect, accumulate, gather.

dispense (SYN.) deal, give, allot, assign, apportion, mete, distribute, grant, allocate, measure. (ANT.) refuse, withhold, confiscate, retain, keep.

disperse (SYN.) dissipate, scatter, disseminate, diffuse, separate, dispel. (ANT.) collect, amass, gather, assemble, accumulate.

dispirited (SYN.) downhearted, unhappy, dejected, disheartened, sad, depressed, melancholy. (ANT.) cheerful, happy, optimistic.

displace (SYN.) remove, transport, lodge, shift, move. (ANT.) retain, leave, stay, remain.

display (SYN.) parade, exhibit, show, cover, flaunt. (ANT.) hide, cover, conceal.

displeasure (SYN.) dislike, disapproval, dissatisfaction, distaste, discontentment.

disposal (SYN.) elimination, adjustment, removal, release, arrangement, administration, settlement.

dispose (SYN.) settle, adjust, arrange.

disposition (SYN.) behavior, character, deed, deportment, action, manner, bearing, temperament, nature, demeanor, personality, carriage.

dispossess (SYN.) eject, expel, evict, oust, dislodge.

disprove (SYN.) refute, deny, invalidate, controvert.

dispute (SYN.) squabble, debate, argument, controversy, contention, disagreement, bicker, contest, argue, contend, quarrel, contradict, discuss, deny, oppose, altercate. (ANT.) harmony, concord, agreement, allow, concur, agree, concede, decision.

disregard (SYN.) slight, omit, ignore, inattention, oversight, skip, neglect, overlook. (ANT.) regard, include.

disrepair (SYN.) ruin, decay, dilapidation, destruction.

disreputable (SYN.) dishonored, notorious, dishonorable, disgraced.

disrespectful (SYN.) fresh, impertinent, rude, impolite, impudent. (ANT.) polite, respectful, courteous.

dissect (SYN.) examine, cut, analyze.

disseminate (SYN.) publish, circulate, spread, publish, broadcast.

dissent (SYN.) objection, challenge, disagreement, protest, remonstrance, difference, nonconformity, variance, noncompliance. (ANT.) assent, acceptance, compliance, agreement.

dissertation (SYN.) thesis, treatise, disquisition.

dissimilar (SYN.) diverse, unlike, various, distinct, contrary, sundry, different, miscellaneous. (ANT.) same, alike, similar, congruous.

dissimulation (SYN.) pretense, deceit, sanctimony, hypocrisy, cant. (ANT.) honesty, condone, openness, frankness, truth.

dissipate (SYN.) misuse, squander, dwindle, consume, waste, lavish, diminish. (ANT.) save, conserve, preserve, accumulate, economize.

dissolve (SYN.) liquefy, end, cease, melt, fade, disappear.

distant (SYN.) stiff, cold, removed, far, afar, unfriendly, remote, faraway, separated, aloof, reserved. (ANT.) nigh, friendly, close, cordial, near.

distasteful (SYN.) disagreeable, unpleasant, objectionable.

distend (SYN.) swell, widen, magnify, expand, enlarge.

distinct (SYN.) plain, evident, lucid, visible, apparent, different, separate, individual, obvious, manifest, clear. (ANT.) vague, indistinct, uncertain, obscure, ambiguous.

distinction (SYN.) importance, peculiarity, trait, honor, fame, characteristic, repute, quality, renown, prominence, attribute, property. (ANT.) nature, substance, essence, being.

distinctive (SYN.) odd, exceptional, rare, individual, eccentric, special, strange. (ANT.) ordinary, general, common, normal.

distinguish (SYN.) recognize, differentiate, divide, classify, descry, discern, separate, perceive, detect. (ANT.) mingle, conjoin, blend, found, omit, confuse, overlook.

distinguished (SYN.) eminent, illustrious, renowned, celebrated, elevated, noted, important, famous, prominent. (ANT.) ordinary, common, obscure, unimportant.

distort (SYN.) contort, falsify, twist, misrepresent.

distract (SYN.) occupy, bewilder, disturb, divert, confuse. (ANT.) focus, concentrate.

distracted (SYN.) abstracted, preoccupied, absent. (ANT.) attentive, attending, watchful, present.

distraction (SYN.) entertainment, confusion, amusement, diversion.

distress (SYN.) torment, misery, trouble, worry, pain, agony, torture, anguish, anxiety, disaster, wretchedness, peril, danger, suffering. (ANT.) joy, solace, comfort, relief.

distribute (SYN.) deal, sort, allot, mete, classify, share, issue, dole, apportion, allocate, dispense, group.

district (SYN.) domain, place, territory, country, region, division, neighborhood, section, area, land.

distrust (SYN.) scruple, unbelief, suspect, mistrust, hesitation, suspense, uncertainty, doubt, suspicion, ambiguity. (ANT.) faith, conviction, trust, belief, determination.

disturb (SYN.) perturb, vex, confuse, worry, agitate, derange, unsettle, perplex, rouse, bother, trouble, annoy, interrupt, discompose. (ANT.) quiet, order, calm, settle, pacify, soothe.

disturbance (SYN.) disorder, commotion, confusion, riot, light, brawl. (ANT.) calm, tranquility, serenity.

disturbed (SYN.) neurotic, psychopathic, psychotic. (ANT.) normal.

diverge (SYN.) fork, separate. (ANT.) converge, join, merge.

diverse (SYN.) unlike, various, different, several.

diversify (SYN.) change, modify, alter.

diversion (SYN.) entertainment, sport, distraction, amusement, recreation.

divert (SYN.) detract, amuse, confuse, distract, deflect, entertain, tickle. (ANT.) tire, bore, weary.

divide (SYN.) share, split, detach, cleave, apportion, sunder, part, distribute, allocate, disunite, estrange, separate, allot, sever. (ANT.) merge, unite, convene, join, gather, combine.

divine (SYN.) holy, supernatural, godlike, transcendent, celestial, heavenly. (ANT.) mundane, wicked, blasphemous, profane.

division (SYN.) partition, separation, sharing, section, segment, part, portion. (ANT.) union, agreement.

divorce (SYN.) disjoin, disconnect, separate, divide.

divulge (SYN.) discover, release, expose, show, betray, reveal, admit, disclose, uncover. (ANT.) hide, conceal, cloak, cover.

dizzy (SYN.) staggering, unsteady, giddy, light-headed, confused. (ANT.) rational, clearheaded, unconfused.

do (SYN.) effect, conduct, perform, work, suffice, accomplish, finish, transact, serve, discharge, execute, complete, carry on, make, settle, conclude, fulfill, consummate, produce, terminate, practice.

docile (SYN.) pliant, tame, complaint, teachable, obedient, submissive, yielding. (ANT.) unruly, obstinate, ungovernable, mulish.

dock (SYN.) moor, clip, anchor, tie.

doctor (SYN.) heal, treat, medic, remedy, cure.

doctrinaire (SYN.) formal, dogmatic, overbearing, authoritarian, formal, arrogant, magisterial. (ANT.) skeptical, indecisive, fluctuating.

doctrine (SYN.) tenet, precept, belief, dogma, teaching, principle, creed. (ANT.) deed, practice, conduct, perform.

document (SYN.) report, minute, memorial, vestige, account, note, trace.

dodge (SYN.) equivocate, recoil, elude, evade, avoid, duck.

dogma (SYN.) tenet, doctrine, belief, teaching, creed. (ANT.) deed, practice, conduct, performance.

dogmatic (SYN.) formal, domineering, authoritarian, doctrinaire, opinionated, dictatorial, positive, arrogant, authoritative, overbearing, doctrinal, magisterial. (ANT.) skeptical, indecisive, fluctuating.

doing (SYN.) feat, performance, act, deed, action, accomplishment, transaction. (ANT.) intention, inactivity, cessation.

dole (SYN.) deal, spread, allot, relief, divide, apportion, alms, welfare, distribute, dispense.

doleful (SYN.) dark, depressed, sad, dismal, dejected, bleak, dull, blue, sorrowful, unhappy, morose, lonesome, mournful, somber. (ANT.) gay, lively, cheerful, joyous.

dolt (SYN.) blockhead, dunce.

domain (SYN.) place, division, region, territory, empire, country, charge, kingdom, realm, quarter, dominion, bailiwick, jurisdiction, land.

domestic (SYN.) family, tame, native, servant, home-made, household, internal. (ANT.) alien, foreign, outside.

domesticate (SYN.) train, tame, housebreak, teach.

domicile (SYN.) dwelling, residence, home, abode.

dominate (SYN.) control, manage, rule, influence, sub-jugate, command, govern, tyrannize, direct, regulate. (ANT.) follow, ignore, aban-don, submit, forsake.

domination (SYN.) mastery, sway, ascendancy, transcen-dence.

don (SYN.) wear, slip on.

donation (SYN.) gift, bequest, present, benefaction, grant, contribution, offering, largess, boon. (ANT.) earn-ings, purchase, deprivation, loss.

done (SYN.) complete, con-cluded, finished, over, termi-nated.

doom (SYN.) fortune, issue, result, destruction, destiny, consequence, fate, outcome, destine, ruin, death, lot.

doomed (SYN.) fated, predes-tined, destined, foreordained.

dormant (SYN.) unemployed, inert, lazy, unoccupied, idle, indolent. (ANT.) working, employed, occupied, active, industrious.

dose (SYN.) quantity, amount, portion.

dote (SYN.) indulge, treasure, coddle, pamper, spoil. (ANT.) ignore.

double (SYN.) copy, fold, duplicate.

doubt (SYN.) distrust, incredulity, suspicion, hesita-tion, uncertainty, question, scruple, ambiguity, skepti-cism, suspect, mistrust, unbe-lief. (ANT.) conviction, belief, determination, trust, certainty.

doubtful (SYN.) uncertain, unsettled, dubious, question-able, unsure.

doubtless (SYN.) certainly, undoubtedly, assuredly, posi-tively, unquestionably.

dour (SYN.) gloomy, sulky, crabbed, morose, fretful. (ANT.) joyous, pleasant, ami-able, merry.

douse (SYN.) immerse, quench, dip, dunk, extin-guish.

dowdy (SYN.) messy, unkempt, untidy, sloppy, shabby, frowzy.

downcast (SYN.) sad, dis-heartened, unhappy, down-hearted, dejected, dispirited, discourage, depressed, glum.

downfall (SYN.) destruction, comedown.

downgrade (SYN.) reduce, lower, diminish, decrease, depreciate. (ANT.) improve, upgrade, appreciate.

downhearted (SYN.) glum, discouraged, depressed, gloomy, downcast, sad, dejected. (ANT.) enthusiastic, cheerful, happy.

downpour (SYN.) cloud-burst, deluge, flood.

downright (SYN.) totally, positively, completely, defi-nitely.

dowry (SYN.) endowment, gift, settlement, talent, ability.

drab (SYN.) flat, dull, lifeless, unattractive.

draft (SYN.) air, induction, wind, enrollment, drawing, outline.

drag (SYN.) heave, pull, tug, crawl, draw, tarry, tow, haul, delay.

drain (SYN.) empty, deprive, dry, filter, spend, tap, exhaust, waste, sap, use. (ANT.) fulfill, fill.

drama (SYN.) show, play, pro-duction, piece.

dramatist (SYN.) playwright.

drape (SYN.) flow, cover, hang.

drastic (SYN.) severe, rough, extreme, violent, tough, intense.

draw (SYN.) tug, obtain, trace, lure, drag, attract, persuade, induce, haul, write, remove, extend, stretch, take out, allure, pull, prolong, extract, tow, draft, delineate, unsheathe, lure, depict, en-tice, sketch, infer. (ANT.) shorten, contract, propel, alien-ate, drive.

drawback (SYN.) snag, hitch, disadvantage, handicap, defi-ciency, difficulty, check, obstacle, hindrance, impedi-ment. (ANT.) gain, benefit, windfall, advantage.

drawing (SYN.) likeness, print, view, engraving, por-trait, sketch, illustration, pic-ture, resemblance, scene.

drawn (SYN.) tired, haggard, taut, strained, harrowed, weary, tense, sapped, spent. (ANT.) rested, relaxed, ener-getic, fresh.

draw out (SYN.) protract, extend, persist, prolong, lengthen, sustain, continue. (ANT.) reduce, curtail, shorten, abridge.

draw up (SYN.) draft, write out, prepare, compose, indite, formulate, wait, stay.

dread (SYN.) awe, horror, fear,

terror, alarm, apprehension, foreboding. (ANT.) courage, boldness, assurance, confidence.

dreadful (SYN.) dire, inspir-ing, ghastly, appalling, horrid, impressive, terrible, awful, frightful, horrible, bad, hideous, outrageous, repul-sive. (ANT.) fascinating, beau-tiful, enjoyable, enchanting, lovely.

dream (SYN.) fantasy, wish, hope, vision, daydream, rever-ie, imagine, fantasize, fancy, invent, muse.

dream up (SYN.) cook up, create, think up, concoct, contrive, originate, imagine, devise.

dreary (SYN.) dull, sad, bleak, lonesome, gloomy, chilling, somber, depressing, dismal, cheerless, dark. (ANT.) lively, hopeful, gay, cheerful, bright, joyous.

dregs (SYN.) riffraff, scum, outcasts, dross, leftovers, flot-sam.

drench (SYN.) wet, bathe, flood, soak, saturate.

dress (SYN.) garb, frock, gown, clothing, costume, apparel, attire, wardrobe, gar-ments, vesture, clothes, habit, wear, don, robe, raiment. (ANT.) undress, strip, divest, disrobe.

dresser (SYN.) dude, clother-horse, fop, dandy.

dressing (SYN.) bandage, seasoning, medicine, sauce.

dressy (SYN.) flashy, swank, showy, dapper. (ANT.) dowdy, drab, frumpy, shabby, tacky.

dribble (SYN.) fall, drip, leak, slaver, slobber.

drift (SYN.) roam, tendency, meander, sail, float, direction, wander, intention, stray.

drifter (SYN.) hobo, tramp, vagabond.

drill (SYN.) employment, les-son, task, use, activity, opera-tion, training. (ANT.) relax-ation, indolence, rest, idleness, repose.

drink (SYN.) gulp, swallow, imbibe, beverage, refresh-ment, potion.

drip (SYN.) dribble, drop, trickle.

drive (SYN.) impel, coerce, oblige, force, push, direct, constrain, journey, urge, enforce, trip, handle, ride, propel, control, run, compel.

drivel (SYN.) slaver, drool, spit, spittle, dribble, slobber, saliva, nonsense, twaddle, rubbish, babble, gibberish.

driver (SYN.) motorist, operator, teamster, trucker,

motorman, pilot, coachman.

droll (SYN.) laughable, funny, amusing, witty, comical. (ANT.) sober, sad, solemn, melancholy.

drone (SYN.) buzz, hum, loafer, idler, non-worker.

drool (SYN.) drivel, slaver, dribble, spit, gibber, jabber, twaddle, trickle, salivate.

droop (SYN.) dangle, weaken, hang, sink, fail, settle, sag, weary, languish, despond. (ANT.) stand, tower, extend, rise, straighten.

drop (SYN.) droop, dribble, topple, collapse, downward, drip, trickle, tumble, gob, droplet, reduction, slump, slip, decrease, fall, dismiss, decline. (ANT.) ascend, mount, steady, arise, soar.

drop out (SYN.) back out, withdraw, stop, forsake, aban-don, give up, leave, quit.

droppings (SYN.) feces, dung, waste, manure, excre-ment, ordure, guano.

dross (SYN.) dregs, impurity, leftovers, residue, debris, leav-ings, remains.

drove (SYN.) flock, herd.

drown (SYN.) sink, inundate, submerge, immerse.

drowse (SYN.) nap, doze, cat-nap, snooze, sleep, slumber, rest, drop off, repose.

drowsy (SYN.) dozing, tor-pid, soothing, dreamy, sleepy, comatose, sluggish, lulling, dull, calming, restful, lethar-gic. (ANT.) alert, awake, sharp, keen, acute.

drub (SYN.) wallop, thrash, beat, thump, cane, flog, rout, outclass, overcome, belabor, pummel, defeat, outplay.

drubbing (SYN.) walloping, flogging, beating, pounding, pummeling, thwacking, thrashing, rout, licking, clob-bering.

drudge (SYN.) work, labor, hack, slave, toil, grub, grind, toiler, flunky, menial, servant.

drudgery (SYN.) toil, travail, effort, task, work, endeavor, labor. (ANT.) recreation, indo-lence, leisure.

drug (SYN.) remedy, medicine, stupefy, anesthetize, numb, benumb.

drugged (SYN.) numb, doped, numbed, stupefied, dazed, groggy, benumbed.

druggist (SYN.) apothecary, chemist, pharmacist.

drunk (SYN.) tight, intoxicat-ed, soused, drunken, inebriat-ed, alcoholic, sozzled, besot-ted, sot, toper, boozer, wino, rummy, dipsomaniac, lush, tipsy.

drunkard *(SYN.)* sot, drunk, alcoholic, lush.

dry *(SYN.)* thirsty, dehydrated, vapid, plain and uninteresting, drained, parched, barren, waterless, dull, tedious, boring, desiccated, tiresome. *(ANT.)* fresh, wet, soaked, fascinating, attractive, lively, moist, interesting.

dub *(SYN.)* nickname, name, christen, call, style, term, confer, bestow, denominate, entitle, characterize, tag, label.

dubious *(SYN.)* unsure, uncertain, undecided, hesitant, spurious, unreliable, puzzling, untrustworthy, questionable, ambiguous. *(ANT.)* decided, fixed, irrefutable, definite, genuine, unquestionable, sound, authentic, trustworthy.

duct *(SYN.)* pipe, tube, passage, vein, funnel, gutter, main, trough, artery.

due *(SYN.)* payable, unpaid, owing, owed, imminent, expected.

duel *(SYN.)* competition, contest, engagement, rivalry, combat, strife, encounter.

dues *(SYN.)* assessment, fees, cost, levy, admission, fare, toll, contribution.

duffer *(SYN.)* bungler, slouch, blunderer, novice, incompetent, fumbler, lummox. *(ANT.)* master, expert, pro.

dull *(SYN.)* commonplace, slow, sad, dreary, boring, stupid, uninteresting. *(ANT.)* clear, animated, interesting, lively.

dullard *(SYN.)* dolt, dunce, moron, clod, blockhead, numskull.

dumb *(SYN.)* dull, witless, ignorant, mute, speechless, brainless, dense. *(ANT.)* bright, alert, clever, intelligent.

dump *(SYN.)* heap, fling down, drop, empty, unload, clear out, dispose of. *(ANT.)* store, fill, load, hoard, pack.

dunce *(SYN.)* deadhead, nitwit, booby, idiot, ignoramus, numskull, noddy, fool.

dungeon *(SYN.)* jail, prison, keep, cell.

dunk *(SYN.)* plunge, submerge, dip. *(ANT.)* uplift, elevate, recover.

dupe *(SYN.)* sucker, victim, gull, pushover, fool, cheat, deceive, defraud.

duplicate *(SYN.)* replica, replicate, facsimile, copy, reproduce, clone, double, twin, transcript. *(ANT.)* prototype.

duplicity *(SYN.)* dissimulation, deception, hypocrisy, deceitfulness, insincerity, artifice, cant, guile. *(ANT.)* openness, artlessness, candor, straightforwardness, genuineness.

durability *(SYN.)* might, strength, force, sturdiness, intensity, potency, vigor. *(ANT.)* weakness, frailty, feebleness.

durable *(SYN.)* constant, firm, fixed, unchangeable, enduring, abiding, lasting. *(ANT.)* unstable, temporary, perishable, transitory.

duration *(SYN.)* time, term, period, while, stage, era, epoch, interim.

duress *(SYN.)* force, demand, compulsion, emergency, pressure.

dusky *(SYN.)* sable, black, dark, darkish, swarthy, tawny, gloomy, overcast, misty, obscure, opaque, shadowy. *(ANT.)* light, fair, white, pale, shining, clear, bright.

dutiful *(SYN.)* docile, faithful, obedient. *(ANT.)* disobedient, willful, unruly.

duty *(SYN.)* bond, responsibility, accountability, faithfulness, function, obligation, assignment, engagement. *(ANT.)* freedom, choice.

dwarf *(SYN.)* midget, runt, reduce, stunt, minimize, tiny. *(ANT.)* mammoth, colossus, monster, giant.

dwell *(SYN.)* inhabit, roost, settle, abide, live, reside.

dwindle *(SYN.)* wane, decrease, diminish, fade, subside, ebb, shrivel, lessen. *(ANT.)* enlarge, increase, grow, gain.

dynamic *(SYN.)* active, forceful, kinetic, energetic, motive, mighty, vigorous. *(ANT.)* sleepy, stable, inert, fixed, dead, still, uninspiring, ineffectual, listless.

E

eager *(SYN.)* avid, hot, anxious, fervent, enthusiastic, impatient, ardent, impassioned, yearning. *(ANT.)* unconcerned, apathetic, dull, uninterested, indifferent.

early *(SYN.)* betimes, opportune, first, beforehand, advanced, soon, shortly. *(ANT.)* retarded, late, tardy, belated, overdue.

earmark *(SYN.)* peculiarity, characteristic, brand, sign, stamp, trademark.

earn *(SYN.)* attain, win, get, achieve, obtain, gain, deserve, realize, collect, net, acquire, merit. *(ANT.)* lose, waste, forfeit.

earnest *(SYN.)* sincere, decided, determined, intent, serious, eager, resolute. *(ANT.)* indifferent, frivolous, insincere.

earnings *(SYN.)* wages, pay, salary, income.

earth *(SYN.)* globe, dirt, land, world, turf, soil, sod, ground.

earthly *(SYN.)* mundane, everyday, worldly. *(ANT.)* heavenly.

earthy *(SYN.)* earthlike, coarse, earthen, crude, unrefined, vulgar. *(ANT.)* tasteful, elegant, polished, refined.

ease *(SYN.)* lighten, alleviate, pacify, soothe, allay, comfort, contentedness. *(ANT.)* worry, disturb, confound, trouble, intensify, distress.

easily *(SYN.)* readily, effortlessly, smoothly, naturally, facilely. *(ANT.)* hardly, arduously, painfully, laboriously.

easiness *(SYN.)* repose, comfort, satisfaction, contentment, liberty, leisure, facility, simplicity. *(ANT.)* unrest, torment, arduousness, difficulty, discomfort.

easy *(SYN.)* light, simple, facile, gentle, effortless, unhurried, comfortable. *(ANT.)* hard, demanding, awkward, strict, difficult, formal.

eat *(SYN.)* consume, swallow, dine, corrode, chew, lunch, devour, feast.

eavesdrop *(SYN.)* spy, listen, snoop, overhear.

ebb *(SYN.)* diminish, recede, decline, decrease, retreat, lessen. *(ANT.)* wax, grow, thrive, increase, swell.

ebullient *(SYN.)* vivacious, buoyant, exuberant. *(ANT.)* lethargic, sad, gloomy, depressed.

eccentric *(SYN.)* odd, irregular, unusual, abnormal, peculiar. *(ANT.)* ordinary, conventional, normal.

eccentricity *(SYN.)* kink, idiosyncrasy, whim, freak, caprice, foible, quirk, oddness, strangeness, aberration. *(ANT.)* conventionality, ordinariness.

ecclesiastical *(SYN.)* religious, churchly, clerical.

echelon *(SYN.)* rank, level, grade, status.

echo *(SYN.)* response, imitation, suggestion, trace, reaction, imitate, repeat.

eclectic *(SYN.)* selective, diverse, broad, liberal, comprehensive. *(ANT.)* limited, narrow, rigid, confined.

eclipse *(SYN.)* conceal, screen, hide, cover, obscure, overcast, veil.

economical *(SYN.)* saving, thrifty, careful, frugal, provident, sparing. *(ANT.)* wasteful, extravagant, lavish, improvident.

economy *(SYN.)* saving, thrift.

ecstasy *(SYN.)* frenzy, gladness, delight, madness, joy, glee, exaltation, pleasure, trance, rapture. *(ANT.)* misery, melancholy, sadness.

ecstatic *(SYN.)* overjoyed, thrilled, delighted, happy, elated.

edge *(SYN.)* margin, brim, verge, brink, border, keenness, extremity, boundary, trim, periphery, hem, rim, sting. *(ANT.)* dullness, center, bluntness.

edgy *(SYN.)* tense, touchy, nervous, irritable.

edict *(SYN.)* declaration, order, ruling, decree, pronouncement, command, law, proclamation.

edifice *(SYN.)* construction, building, establishment.

edit *(SYN.)* check, revise, correct, amend.

educate *(SYN.)* instruct, teach, school, train.

education *(SYN.)* training, development, knowledge, learning, cultivation, schooling, instruction, study.

eerie *(SYN.)* weird, fearful, ghastly, spooky, strange.

efface *(SYN.)* obliterate, erase.

effect *(SYN.)* produce, consequence, evoke, cause, make, complete, outcome, result, determine.

effective *(SYN.)* efficient, practical, productive. *(ANT.)* useless, wasteful, ineffective.

efficiency *(SYN.)* efficacy, capability, effectiveness, competency, ability. *(ANT.)* wastefulness, inability.

efficient *(SYN.)* efficacious, skillful, capable, adept, competent, useful, effectual, effective, apt, proficient. *(ANT.)* inefficient, unskilled, ineffectual, incompetent.

effort *(SYN.)* labor, endeavor, pains, essay, trial, exertion, struggle, strain.

egg *(SYN.)* stir, ovum, incite, urge, arouse, embryo, provoke.

egghead *(SYN.)* scholar, intellectual, pedant.

egoism *(SYN.)* self-interest, conceit, pride, selfishness, egotism. *(ANT.)* modesty, *generosity, selflessness.*

eject *(SYN.)* expel, remove, oust, eliminate. *(ANT.) include.*

elaborate *(SYN.)* detail, develop, decorated, decorative, ornate, complex. *(ANT.) simplify, simple, unadorned.*

elapse *(SYN.)* expire.

elastic *(SYN.)* yielding, flexible, adaptable, pliable.

elated *(SYN.)* delighted, rejoicing, overjoyed, jubilant. *(ANT.) sad, unhappy.*

elder *(SYN.)* senior. *(ANT.) younger.*

elderly *(SYN.)* aged, old. *(ANT.) young, youthful.*

elect *(SYN.)* pick, appoint, choose.

electrify *(SYN.)* shock, charge, stir, upset, generate, agitate.

elegant *(SYN.)* tasteful, refined, cultivated, choice, polished, superior, fine. *(ANT.) crude, coarse, unpolished, tasteless.*

elementary *(SYN.)* simple, primary, basic, uncomplicated, initial, beginning, fundamental. *(ANT.) involved, complex, sophisticated, complicated.*

elevate *(SYN.)* raise, lift. *(ANT.) lower, drop.*

elf *(SYN.)* devil, fairy, imp.

elicit *(SYN.)* summon.

eligible *(SYN.)* fit, suitable, qualified.

eliminate *(SYN.)* expel, eject, remove, dislodge, extirpate, erase, oust. *(ANT.) admit, involve.*

elite *(SYN.)* nobility, upperclass, aristocracy, gentry. *(ANT.) mob, proletariat.*

elongate *(SYN.)* extend, prolong, lengthen.

elope *(SYN.)* escape, flee.

eloquent *(SYN.)* expressive, fluent, articulate, glib, meaningful. *(ANT.) inarticulate.*

else *(SYN.)* different, another, other.

elude *(SYN.)* escape, miss, avoid, dodge. *(ANT.) odd, include.*

emaciated *(SYN.)* wasted, thin, starved, withered, shriveled, gaunt, shrunken, drawn, undernourished.

emancipate *(SYN.)* liberate, free, deliver, save. *(ANT.) restrain.*

embankment *(SYN.)* shore, dam, bank, fortification, buttress.

embargo *(SYN.)* prohibition, restriction, restraint.

embark *(SYN.)* board, depart.

embarrass *(SYN.)* discomfit, rattle, distress, hamper, fluster, entangle, abash, mortify, hinder, perplex, confuse, shame, trouble. *(ANT.) relieve, encourage, help.*

embassy *(SYN.)* ministry, legation, consulate.

embed *(SYN.)* root, inset, enclose, plant.

embellish *(SYN.)* adorn, decorate, ornament.

embezzle *(SYN.)* pilfer, misuse, rob, misappropriate, steal, take.

embitter *(SYN.)* provoke, arouse, alienate, anger, inflame.

emblem *(SYN.)* token, mark, symbol, badge.

embody *(SYN.)* comprise, cover, embrace, include.

embrace *(SYN.)* espouse, accept, receive, comprehend, contain, welcome, comprise, cover, clasp, include, adopt, hug. *(ANT.) spurn, reject, bar, exclude, repudiate.*

embroider *(SYN.)* decorate, adorn, stitch, trim, overstate, embellish, ornament, exaggerate, magnify.

emerge *(SYN.)* surface, show, appear.

emergency *(SYN.)* strait, pass, crisis, urgency, predicament, pinch.

eminent *(SYN.)* renowned, glorious, important, conspicuous, prominent, famous. *(ANT.) ordinary, commonplace, unknown, undistinguished, common.*

emissary *(SYN.)* envoy, minister, delegate, agent, spy.

emit *(SYN.)* expel, breathe, shoot, hurl, ooze, vent, belch, discharge.

emotion *(SYN.)* passion, turmoil, perturbation, affection, sentiment, feeling, trepidation, agitation. *(ANT.) dispassion, indifference, tranquillity, calm, restraint.*

emotional *(SYN.)* ardent, passionate, stirring, zealous, impetuous, overwrought, enthusiastic. *(ANT.) tranquil, calm, placid.*

emphasis *(SYN.)* accent, stress, insistence.

emphatic *(SYN.)* positive, definite, forceful, energetic, strong. *(ANT.) lax, quiet, unforceful.*

employ *(SYN.)* avail, use, devote, apply, utilize, engage, sign, hire, retain, service, contract. *(ANT.) reject, discard.*

employee *(SYN.)* laborer, worker, servant. *(ANT.) boss, employer.*

employer *(SYN.)* owner, boss, management, proprietor, manager, superintendent, supervisor. *(ANT.) employee, worker.*

employment *(SYN.)* occupation, work, business, position, job, service, engagement. *(ANT.) leisure, idleness, slothfulness.*

empower *(SYN.)* enable, sanction, permit, warrant.

empty *(SYN.)* void, devoid, unfilled, barren, senseless, unoccupied, unfurnished, vacant, blank, evacuate, unload, hollow. *(ANT.) supplied, full, occupied.*

emulate *(SYN.)* follow, imitate, copy.

enable *(SYN.)* authorize, empower, sanction, qualify.

enact *(SYN.)* legislate, portray, pass, stage.

enchant *(SYN.)* charm, titillate, fascinate, bewitch, delight, thrill, captivate. *(ANT.) tire, bore.*

encircle *(SYN.)* comprise, include, bound, encompass.

enclose *(SYN.)* envelop, confine, bound, surround, encompass, encircle, circumscribe. *(ANT.) open, exclude, distend, expose, develop.*

encompass *(SYN.)* include, surround, encircle.

encore *(SYN.)* repetition, repeat, again.

encounter *(SYN.)* battle, meet, oppose, run into, face, collide.

encourage *(SYN.)* incite, favor, cheer, impel, countenance, inspirit, exhilarate, animate, hearten, embolden, support. *(ANT.) deter, dispirit, deject, dissuade.*

encroach *(SYN.)* interfere, trespass, intrude, infringe.

encumber *(SYN.)* hamper, load, burden.

end *(SYN.)* completion, object, close, aim, result, conclusion, finish, extremity, intent, halt, stop, limit, purpose, cessation, expiration, termination. *(ANT.) opening, start, introduction, beginning, launch, inception.*

endanger *(SYN.)* imperil, hazard, risk. *(ANT.) secure.*

endear *(SYN.)* allure, charm.

endeavor *(SYN.)* strive, struggle, exertion, attempt, try, labor.

endless *(SYN.)* constant, nonstop, continuous, incessant, everlasting.

endorse *(SYN.)* approve, accept, sign, confirm, pass.

endow *(SYN.)* provide, furnish, bestow, give, contribute. *(ANT.) divest.*

endure *(SYN.)* experience, undergo, sustain, last, bear, continue, remain, undergo, persist, brook, tolerate, suffer. *(ANT.) wane, perish, succumb, fail.*

enemy *(SYN.)* foe, antagonist, rival, opponent, competitor, adversary, opposition. *(ANT.) colleague, ally, friend, accomplice.*

energy *(SYN.)* strength, vim, force, power, stamina, vigor, might. *(ANT.) feebleness, lethargy.*

enervate *(SYN.)* enfeeble, weaken, debilitate, exhaust, devitalize. *(ANT.) invigorate.*

enfold *(SYN.)* clasp, surround, wrap, embrace, hug.

enforce *(SYN.)* make, drive, compel, execute, force.

engage *(SYN.)* absorb, occupy, employ, hold, involve, hire, agree, engross, retain, promise, commit, entangle. *(ANT.) fire, disengage, discharge, dismiss.*

engaged *(SYN.)* affianced, betrothed, busy, occupied.

engaging *(SYN.)* fascinating, appealing, enticing, interesting, tempting, lovely, beguiling, charming, enchanting, engrossing, delightful, exquisite. *(ANT.) ordinary, boring.*

engender *(SYN.)* develop, breed, cause, generate, produce.

engineer *(SYN.)* direct, conduct, guide, lead, manage.

engrave *(SYN.)* print, cut, impress, inscribe, carve, sketch.

engross *(SYN.)* engage, enthrall, occupy, fascinate, absorb.

engulf *(SYN.)* flood, swallow.

enhance *(SYN.)* better, uplift, improve.

enigma *(SYN.)* mystery, stumper, riddle.

enigmatic *(SYN.)* perplexing, confusing, puzzling, baffling, mystifying.

enjoy *(SYN.)* savor, like, relish.

enjoyment *(SYN.)* pleasure, delight, gratification. *(ANT.) abhorrence, displeasure.*

enlarge *(SYN.)* widen, distend, amplify, broaden, extend, increase, augment, expand, dilate. *(ANT.) diminish, shrink, contract, decrease, wane, restrict.*

enlighten *(SYN.)* inform, illuminate, clarify, teach, instruct. *(ANT.) confuse.*

enlist *(SYN.)* enroll, prompt,

join, induce, enter, register, persuade. (ANT.) quit, leave, abandon.

enliven (SYN.) inspire, brighten, stimulate.

enmity (SYN.) antagonism, hatred, animosity, malignity, ill-will, antipathy, hostility, unfriendliness. (ANT.) love, like, friendliness.

enormity (SYN.) heinousness, wickedness, barbarity, atrociousness.

enormous (SYN.) vast, huge, colossal, immense, gargantuan, elephantine, gigantic, stupendous, large. (ANT.) small, slight, tiny, minute, infinitesimal, diminutive, little.

enough (SYN.) ample, adequate, sufficient, plenty. (ANT.) inadequate, insufficient.

enrage (SYN.) anger, provoke, madden, inflame. (ANT.) appease, soothe, calm.

enrich (SYN.) better, improve.

enroll (SYN.) record, list, recruit, register, enlist, write, induct. (ANT.) quit, leave, abandon.

enshrine (SYN.) bury, entomb.

ensign (SYN.) banner, colors, flag, officer.

enslave (SYN.) keep, hold, capture.

ensue (SYN.) arise, succeed, follow.

ensure (SYN.) guarantee, assure, protect, defend, cover.

entangle (SYN.) confuse, snare, involve, ravel, snarl, tangle, trap.

enter (SYN.) join, go inside.

enterprise (SYN.) fete, deed, venture, project, adventure, undertaking, ambition, business, exploit.

enterprising (SYN.) energetic, resourceful. (ANT.) lazy, indolent, sluggish, unresourceful.

entertain (SYN.) cheer, gladden, hold, consider, please, contemplate, divert, amuse, harbor, fascinate, interest. (ANT.) repulse, tire, bore, disgust, annoy.

enthrall (SYN.) captivate, fascinate, enchant, charm, thrill.

enthusiasm (SYN.) fervor, fanaticism, zeal, ardor, intensity, devotion, excitement, eagerness, fervency, earnestness. (ANT.) indifference, ennui, apathy, unconcern, detachment.

enthusiastic (SYN.) earnest, zealous, eager. (ANT.) aloof, indifferent, unconcerned.

entice (SYN.) lure, attract, seduce.

entire (SYN.) complete, intact, whole, undivided. (ANT.) divided, separated, incomplete, partial.

entirely (SYN.) altogether, thoroughly, wholly, solely.

entitle (SYN.) call, label, name, empower, allow, authorize, license, title.

entourage (SYN.) train, company, retinue, escort.

entrance (SYN.) inlet, portal, doorway, fascinate, entry, intrigue, door, thrill.

entreat (SYN.) implore, beg, plead.

entreaty (SYN.) plea, appeal.

entrust (SYN.) commit, charge, assign, delegate, consign, commission.

enumerate (SYN.) count, tally, list, number.

enunciate (SYN.) announce, express, speak, state.

envelop (SYN.) embrace, cover, conceal, surround, wrap.

environment (SYN.) neighborhood, habitat, surroundings, setting.

envision (SYN.) picture, imagine, visualize.

envoy (SYN.) delegate, emissary, representative, agent, messenger.

envy (SYN.) covetousness, jealousy, spitefulness, covet. (ANT.) indifference, generosity.

epicure (SYN.) gourmand, gourmet, connoisseur, gastronome, Epicurean, aesthete.

epidemic (SYN.) prevalent, scourge, plague, catching, widespread, pestilence, infectious.

episode (SYN.) happening, affair, occurrence, event, experience.

epoch (SYN.) age, era, period, time.

equal (SYN.) even, uniform, like, alike, equitable, same, identical, commensurate, equivalent, regular, parallel. (ANT.) different, unequal, irregular, uneven.

equilibrium (SYN.) stability, steadiness, balance, firmness.

equip (SYN.) fit, rig, provide, outfit, prepare, furnish.

equipment (SYN.) utensils, material, apparatus.

equitable (SYN.) square, rightful, fair, due, just, fit. (ANT.) partial, biased, unjust, uneven.

equity (SYN.) impartiality, fairness, justness, justice, fair-mindedness, evenhandedness.

equivalent (SYN.) match, rival, equal, like, replacement.

equivocal (SYN.) oblique, ambiguous, vague, indeterminate, uncertain, obscure. (ANT.) clear, precise, explicit, certain, clear-cut, definite.

equivocate (SYN.) temporize, evade, hedge, quibble, fudge, waffle, straddle.

era (SYN.) epoch, cycle, age, time, period.

eradicate (SYN.) remove, demolish, eliminate.

erase (SYN.) obliterate, remove, cancel. (ANT.) add, include.

erect (SYN.) upright, build, straight, raise, construct, vertical. (ANT.) flat, horizontal, raze, flatten, demolish.

erection (SYN.) building, construction, raising, fabrication.

erode (SYN.) rust, consume, disintegrate.

erotic (SYN.) carnal, sensual, amatory, prurient, lewd, wanton, passionate, lecherous.

err (SYN.) slip, misjudge.

errand (SYN.) chore, duty, task, exercise.

errant (SYN.) roving, rambling, wandering, vagrant.

erratic (SYN.) irregular, abnormal, uneven, occasional, sporadic, changeable, unsteady, odd, eccentric, strange, extraordinary, unconventional, bizarre, peculiar, uncertain, unusual, unstable. (ANT.) regular, steady, normal, ordinary.

erroneous (SYN.) wrong, mistaken, incorrect, inaccurate, false, untrue. (ANT.) true, right, correct, accurate.

error (SYN.) inaccuracy, fault, slip, oversight, fallacy, mistake, blunder.

erudite (SYN.) sage, wise, learned, deep, profound.

erupt (SYN.) vomit.

escapade (SYN.) caper, antic, stunt, trick, prank.

escape (SYN.) shun, avoid, flee, decamp, elude, flight, avert, departure, abscond, fly, evade. (ANT.) meet, confront, invite, catch.

escort (SYN.) conduct, lead, attend, accompany, protection, guard, guide, convoy, usher, squire.

especially (SYN.) unusually, principally, mainly, particularly, primarily.

essay (SYN.) test, thesis, undertake, paper, try.

essence (SYN.) substance, character, nature, principle, odor, meaning, basis, smell, perfume.

essential (SYN.) vital, intrinsic, basic, requisite, fundamental, indispensable, critical, requirement, necessity, necessary, important. (ANT.) dispensable, unimportant, inessential.

establish (SYN.) prove, fix, found, settle, institute, raise, verify, conform, form, sanction, ordain, begin, organize. (ANT.) upset, discontinue, scatter, disperse, refute, abolish, unsettle.

esteem (SYN.) revere, deem, appreciate, honor, value, think, admire, respect, hold, prize, reverence, regard. (ANT.) scorn, disdain, depreciate, disregard, contempt, abhor.

estimate (SYN.) calculate, gauge, judge, rate, evaluate, compute, value, figure.

estimation (SYN.) judgment, viewpoint, opinion.

etch (SYN.) stamp, engrave, impress.

eternal (SYN.) undying, immortal, ceaseless, infinite, everlasting, deathless, perpetual, endless, timeless. (ANT.) mortal, transient, finite, brief, temporary, passing.

etiquette (SYN.) decorum, formality.

evacuate (SYN.) withdraw, depart, leave, vacate.

evade (SYN.) miss, avoid, bypass. (ANT.) confront, meet, face.

evaluate (SYN.) value, appraise, assay.

evaporate (SYN.) disappear, vanish. (ANT.) condense, appear.

even (SYN.) smooth, level, still, square, same, flat, balanced, equal, parallel, identical. (ANT.) irregular, bumpy, unbalanced, unequal, divergent.

evening (SYN.) twilight, dusk, sunset. (ANT.) sunrise, dawn.

event (SYN.) issue, end, result, circumstance, occurrence, incident, consequence, happening, episode, outcome.

even-tempered (SYN.) composed, calm, cool. (ANT.) hotheaded.

eventual (SYN.) consequent, ultimate. (ANT.) present, current.

eventually (SYN.) ultimately.

ever (SYN.) continuously, always, constantly. (ANT.) never.

everlasting (SYN.) permanent, ceaseless, endless, continual.

evermore (SYN.) always.

everyday (SYN.) commonplace, common, usual, ordinary, customary. (ANT.) rare.

evict (SYN.) oust, put out, expel.

evidence (SYN.) grounds, clue, facts, testimony, data, sign, proof.

evident (SYN.) apparent, clear, obvious, indubitable, plain, conspicuous, patent, manifest, open, unmistakable. (ANT.) hidden, unclear, uncertain, obscure, concealed.

evil (SYN.) immoral, harmful, badness, sinful, injurious, woe, bad, wicked. (ANT.) goodness, moral, useful, upright, virtuous, beneficial, virtue, advantageous.

evoke (SYN.) summon, prompt.

evolve (SYN.) grow, advance, develop, result, emerge, unfold.

exact (SYN.) correct, faultless, errorless, detailed, accurate. (ANT.) inaccurate, inexact, faulty.

exaggerate (SYN.) stretch, expand, amplify, embroider, heighten, overstate, caricature, magnify, enlarge. (ANT.) understate, minimize, diminish, depreciate.

exalt (SYN.) erect, consecrate, raise, elevate, extol, dignify. (ANT.) humble, degrade, humiliate.

examination (SYN.) investigation, inspection, test, scrutiny.

examine (SYN.) assess, contemplate, question, review, audit, notice, inquire, analyze, check, investigate, dissect, inspect, survey. (ANT.) omit, disregard, overlook.

example (SYN.) pattern, archetype, specimen, illustration, model, instance, prototype, sample. (ANT.) rule, principle.

exasperate (SYN.) aggravate, anger, madden, irritate.

excavate (SYN.) unearth, dig, burrow.

exceed (SYN.) excel, beat, surpass, top.

exceedingly (SYN.) extremely, very, especially, unusually, surprisingly.

excel (SYN.) better, beat, surpass.

excellence (SYN.) distinction, superiority. (ANT.) poorness, inferiority, badness.

excellent (SYN.) wonderful, fine, marvelous, superior. (ANT.) poor, terrible, bad, inferior.

except (SYN.) omitting, but, reject, excluding, save, exclude.

exception (SYN.) affront, offense, exclusion, deviation, omission, anomaly.

exceptional (SYN.) different, irregular, strange, unusual, abnormal.

excerpt (SYN.) abstract, extract.

excess (SYN.) surplus, intemperance, extravagance, immoderation, profusion, abundant, profuse, superfluity. (ANT.) want, sparse, lack, dearth.

exchange (SYN.) barter, interchange, substitute, trade, change, swap.

excite (SYN.) arouse, incite, agitate, stimulate, awaken, disquiet. (ANT.) lull, quiet, bore, pacify.

exclaim (SYN.) vociferate, cry, call out, cry out, ejaculate, shout.

exclamation (SYN.) shout, outcry, clamor.

exclude (SYN.) omit, restrain, hinder, bar, except, prevent. (ANT.) welcome, involve, embrace, admit, accept, include.

exclusion (SYN.) exception, bar, rejection. (ANT.) inclusion.

exclusive (SYN.) restricted, limited, restrictive, choice, selective, fashionable. (ANT.) common, general, ordinary, unrestricted, unfashionable.

excursion (SYN.) voyage, tour, trip.

excuse (SYN.) exculpate, forgive, remit, acquit, free, pardon, condone, explanation, overlook, exempt, reason, justify, absolve. (ANT.) revenge, punish, convict.

execute (SYN.) complete, accomplish, do, achieve, kill, perform.

exemplify (SYN.) show, illustrate.

exempt (SYN.) excuse, free, except, release.

exercise (SYN.) drill, task, use, activity, lesson, training, exertion, application, gymnastics, operation, practice. (ANT.) rest, indolence, repose.

exertion (SYN.) attempt, effort, strain, endeavor.

exhale (SYN.) blow, breathe out.

exhaust (SYN.) drain, tire, empty, wear out, use, finish, fatigue. (ANT.) renew, refresh, replace.

exhaustive (SYN.) comprehensive, thorough, extensive, complete. (ANT.) incomplete.

exhibit (SYN.) demonstrate, display, present, reveal, betray, show, flaunt. (ANT.) hide, conceal, disguise.

exhilarate (SYN.) gladden, refresh, cheer, excite, stimulate.

exhort (SYN.) advise, coax, press, urge.

exile (SYN.) expulsion, proscription, deportation, ostracism, expatriation, deport, extradition, expel, banishment. (ANT.) retrieval, welcome, recall, admittance.

exist (SYN.) stand, live, occur, be.

exit (SYN.) leave, depart.

exodus (SYN.) leaving, exit, parting, departure.

exonerate (SYN.) acquit, clear.

exorbitant (SYN.) unreasonable, outrageous, overpriced, preposterous, excessive. (ANT.) normal, reasonable.

exotic (SYN.) strange, vivid, foreign, gay. (ANT.) dull, normal.

expand (SYN.) unfold, enlarge, broaden, spread, inflate, swell, grow. (ANT.) contract, shrivel, shrink.

expect (SYN.) await, think, hope, anticipate.

expedient (SYN.) helpful, desirable, rush, hasten, useful, fitting, sensible.

expedition (SYN.) trek, speed, trip, haste, voyage, journey, hurry.

expel (SYN.) exile, dislodge, discharge, excommunicate, oust, eject, dismiss, banish, disown. (ANT.) recall, invite, admit.

expend (SYN.) consume, waste, spend, exhaust. (ANT.) ration, reserve, conserve.

expense (SYN.) charge, cost, payment, price.

expensive (SYN.) costly, dear. (ANT.) modest, inexpensive, cheap.

experience (SYN.) occurrence, episode, sensation, happening, existence, background, feeling, living, encountering, knowledge.

experienced (SYN.) expert, qualified, accomplished, skilled, practiced. (ANT.) untutored, inexperienced, naive.

experiment (SYN.) trial, test, prove, research, examine, try, verify.

expert (SYN.) adept, handy, skillful, clever, specialist, authority, skilled, knowledgeable, ingenious. (ANT.) untrained, unskilled, inexperienced.

expire (SYN.) terminate, die, cease, perish, pass, end, disappear. (ANT.) commence, continue.

explain (SYN.) illustrate, decipher, expound, clarify, resolve, define, unravel, elucidate, unfold, justify, interpret. (ANT.) darken, baffle, obscure.

explanation (SYN.) definition, description, interpretation, account, reason, justification, excuse.

explicit (SYN.) lucid, definitive, specific, express, clear, manifest. (ANT.) vague, implicit, ambiguous.

exploit (SYN.) feat, deed, accomplishment, adventure.

explore (SYN.) research, hunt, probe, search, investigate, look, examine.

explosion (SYN.) bang, boom, blowup, flare-up, blast, detonation, outbreak, convulsion, furor, tantrum, paroxysm.

explosive (SYN.) fiery, rabid, eruptive, volcanic, fulminatory, inflammatory. (ANT.) stable, inert, peaceful, calm.

exponent (SYN.) explicator, spokesman, supporter, expounder, interpreter.

expose (SYN.) uncover, display, bare, open, unmask, reveal. (ANT.) hide, conceal, mask, covered.

exposition (SYN.) fair, bazaar, show, expo, exhibition.

expound (SYN.) clarify, present, explain, lecture, demonstrate.

express (SYN.) voice, tell, send, say, ship, declare, stale, precise, specific, swift, describe.

expression (SYN.) declaration, statement, look.

expressive (SYN.) suggestive, meaningful, telling, significant, thoughtful. (ANT.) unthinking, meaningless, nondescript.

expressly (SYN.) precisely, exactly, definitely, clearly. (ANT.) tentatively, vaguely, ambiguously.

expulsion (SYN.) ejection, discharge, removal, elimination.

expunge (SYN.) blot out, erase, cancel, obliterate, delete, efface, remove.

expurgate (SYN.) cleanse, purge, censor, edit, emasculate, abridge, blip.

exquisite (SYN.) delicate, delightful, attractive, dainty, beautiful, elegant, fine, superb, lovely, excellent, perfect. (ANT.) *vulgar, dull, ugly, unattractive.*

extant (SYN.) subsisting, remaining, surviving, present, existing. (ANT.) *lost, defunct, extinct, vanished.*

extemporize (SYN.) improvise, devise.

extend (SYN.) lengthen, stretch, increase, offer, give, grant, magnify, expand. (ANT.) *abbreviate, shorten, curtail.*

extension (SYN.) expansion, increase, stretching, enlargement.

extensive (SYN.) vast, wide, spacious. (ANT.) *cramped, confined, restricted.*

extent (SYN.) length, degree, range, amount, measure, size, compass, reach, magnitude, scope, expanse, area.

extenuating (SYN.) exculpating, excusable, qualifying, justifying, softening.

exterior (SYN.) surface, face, outside, covering, outer, external. (ANT.) *inside, interior, inner, internal.*

exterminate (SYN.) slay, kill, destroy.

external (SYN.) outer, exterior, outside. (ANT.) *inner, internal, inside, interior.*

externals (SYN.) images, effects, look, appearance, veneer, aspect.

extinct (SYN.) lost, dead, gone, vanished. (ANT.) *present, flourishing, alive, extant.*

extinction (SYN.) eclipse, annihilation, obliteration, death, extirpation.

extol (SYN.) laud, eulogize, exalt, praise. (ANT.) *denounce, discredit, disparage.*

extra (SYN.) surplus, spare, additional.

extract (SYN.) remove, essence. (ANT.) *penetrate, introduce.*

extraordinary (SYN.) unusual, wonderful, marvelous, peculiar, noteworthy. (ANT.) *commonplace, ordinary, usual.*

extravagant (SYN.) excessive, exaggerated, lavish, wasteful, extreme. (ANT.) *prudent, frugal, thrifty, economical.*

extreme (SYN.) excessive, overdone, outermost, limit, greatest, utmost, furthest. (ANT.) *reasonable, modest, moderate.*

extricate (SYN.) rescue, free, clear, release, liberate.

exuberant (SYN.) buoyant, ebullient, vivacious. (ANT.) *sad, depressed.*

exult (SYN.) rejoice, delight.
eye (SYN.) watch, view, stare, look, inspect, glance.

F

fable (SYN.) legend, parable, myth, fib, falsehood, fiction, tale, story.

fabled (SYN.) legendary, famous, tamed, historic.

fabric (SYN.) goods, textile, material, cloth, yard goods.

fabricate (SYN.) assemble, make, construct, produce, create, manufacture, form. (ANT.) *raze, destroy, demolish.*

fabrication (SYN.) deceit, lie, falsehood, untruth, forgery, prevarication, deception. (ANT.) *verity, reality, actuality, truth, fact.*

fabulous (SYN.) amazing, marvelous, unbelievable, fantastic, astounding, astonishing, striking. (ANT.) *ordinary, commonplace, credible, proven, factual.*

façade (SYN.) deception, mask, front, show, pose, veneer, guise, affectation.

face (SYN.) cover, mug, front, assurance, countenance, audacity, visage, expression, look, features, facade, encounter, meet, surface. (ANT.) *rear, shun, avoid, evade, back, timidity.*

facet (SYN.) perspective, view, side, phase.

facetious (SYN.) jocular, pungent, humorous, funny, clever, droll, witty, playful, jesting. (ANT.) *sober, serious, grave, weighty.*

face to face (SYN.) opposing, nose to nose, confronting.

facile (SYN.) simple, easy, quick, uncomplicated, clever, fluent, skillful. (ANT.) *complex, difficult, complicated, laborious, hard, ponderous, painstaking, arduous.*

facilitate (SYN.) help, speed, ease, promote, accelerate, expedite.

facilities (SYN.) aid, means, resources, conveniences.

facility (SYN.) ability, skill, ease, skillfulness, material. (ANT.) *effort, difficulty.*

facsimile (SYN.) reproduction, likeness, replica.

fact (SYN.) reality, deed, certainty, act, incident, circumstance, occurrence, event, truth, actuality. (ANT.) *falsehood, fiction, delusion.*

faction (SYN.) clique, party, sect.

factitious (SYN.) false, sham, artificial, spurious, unnatural, affected. (ANT.) *natural, real, genuine, artless.*

factor (SYN.) part, element, basis, cause.

factory (SYN.) installation, plant, mill, works.

factual (SYN.) true, correct, accurate, sure, genuine, authentic. (ANT.) *incorrect, erroneous, fabricated, invented.*

faculty (SYN.) power, capacity, talent, staff, gift, ability, qualification, ability, skill.

fad (SYN.) fashion, vogue, mania, rage.

faddish (SYN.) ephemeral, modish, temporary, passing, fleeting. (ANT.) *lasting, permanent, enduring, classic.*

fade (SYN.) pale, bleach, weaken, dim, decline, sink, discolor, fail, diminish, droop.

fagged (SYN.) exhausted, tired, weary, jaded, pooped, worn.

fail (SYN.) neglect, weaken, flunk, miss, decline, disappoint, fade. (ANT.) *succeed, achieve, accomplish.*

failing (SYN.) fault, foible, imperfection, frailty, defect, peccadillo, shortcoming. (ANT.) *steadiness, strength, integrity.*

failure (SYN.) miscarriage, omission, decline, deficiency, fiasco, lack, dereliction, failing, unsuccessfulness, loss, default, want, insufficiency, decay. (ANT.) *conquest, accomplishment, success, triumph, victory, hit, luck, achievement.*

faint (SYN.) timid, faded, languid, halfhearted, dim, pale, wearied, feeble, indistinct, weak. (ANT.) *strong, sharp, forceful, glaring, clear, distinct, conspicuous.*

fainthearted (SYN.) shy, cowardly, timid, bashful. (ANT.) *fearless, brave, stouthearted, courageous.*

fair (SYN.) pale, average, light, sunny, mediocre, just, clear, lovely, market, blond, honest, equitable, impartial, reasonable, comely, exposition. (ANT.) *ugly, fraudulent, foul, outstanding, dishonorable, unfair.*

fairly (SYN.) equally, evenly, rather, impartially, passably, justly, squarely, somewhat.

fair-minded (SYN.) reasonable, just, open-minded, honest, unprejudiced, impartial, evenhanded. (ANT.) *bigoted, narrow-minded, unjust, close-minded, partisan.*

fairness (SYN.) equity, justice, evenhandedness, honesty. (ANT.) *favoritism, partiality, bias, one-sidedness.*

fairy (SYN.) leprechaun, gnome, elf, pixie, sprite.

faith (SYN.) dependence, trust, reliance, creed, loyalty, doctrine, confidence, dogma, tenet, persuasion, constancy, credence, fidelity, religion, belief. (ANT.) *mistrust, disbelief, doubt, infidelity.*

faithful (SYN.) staunch, true, devoted, trusty, loyal, constant, credible, steadfast, strict, trust-worthy, accurate. (ANT.) *untrustworthy, faithless, inaccurate, wrong, false, disloyal, erroneous, treacherous.*

faithless (SYN.) treacherous, unfaithful, disloyal, perfidious, untrue. (ANT.) *loyal, true, unwavering, constant, faithful.*

fake (SYN.) falsify, distort, pretend, feign, fraud, counterfeit, cheat, false, artificial, phony, imitation, forgery, mock. (ANT.) *honest, pure, real, genuine, authentic.*

falderol (SYN.) foolery, jargon, nonsense, gibberish, blather, balderdash.

fall (SYN.) drop, decline, diminish, droop, topple, decrease, sink, hang, descend, subside, plunge, collapse. (ANT.) *soar, climb, steady, rise, ascend.*

fallacious (SYN.) untrue, false, wrong, erroneous, deceptive, illusory, delusive. (ANT.) *accurate, true, exact, real, factual.*

fallacy (SYN.) mistake, error, illusion, sophism, misconception, deception.

fall back (SYN.) retreat, recede, retire, withdraw, concede. (ANT.) *progress, advance, gain, prosper, proceed.*

fallow (SYN.) idle, unprepared, unproductive, inactive. (ANT.) *prepared, productive, cultivated.*

false (SYN.) incorrect, wrong, deceitful, fake, imitation, counterfeit. (ANT.) *genuine, loyal, true, honest.*

falsehood (SYN.) untruth, lie, fib, story. (ANT.) *truth.*

falsify (SYN.) misquote, distort, misstate, mislead, adulterate.

falter (SYN.) stumble, tremble, waver, hesitate, flounder.

fame (SYN.) distinction, glory, mane, eminence, credit, reputation, renown, acclaim, notoriety. (ANT.) *infamy, obscurity, anonymity, disrepute.*

famed (SYN.) known, renowned, famous. (ANT.)

obscure, unknown, anonymous.

familiar *(SYN.)* informal, intimate, close, acquainted, amicable, knowing, cognizant, well-acquainted, versed, unreserved, friendly, sociable, affable, aware, known, courteous, intimate. *(ANT.)* unfamiliar, distant, affected, reserved.

familiarity *(SYN.)* sociability, acquaintance, awareness, frankness, intimacy, understanding, knowledge, fellowship. *(ANT.)* distance, ignorance, reserve, presumption, constraint, haughtiness.

family *(SYN.)* kin, tribe, folks, group, relatives.

famine *(SYN.)* want, deficiency, starvation, need. *(ANT.)* excess, plenty.

famous *(SYN.)* distinguished, noted, illustrious, famed, celebrated, well-known, eminent, renowned, prominent, esteemed. *(ANT.)* obscure, hidden, unknown.

fan *(SYN.)* arouse, spread, admirer, enthusiast, devotee, stir, whip, follower.

fanatic *(SYN.)* bigot, enthusiast, zealot.

fancy *(SYN.)* love, dream, ornate, imagine, suppose, imagination, taste, fantasy, ornamented, elaborate, think. *(ANT.)* plain, undecorated, simple, unadorned.

fantastic *(SYN.)* strange, unusual, odd, wild, unimaginable, incredible, unbelievable, unreal, bizarre, capricious. *(ANT.)* mundane, ordinary, staid, humdrum.

fantasy *(SYN.)* illusion, dream, whim, hallucination, delusion, caprice, mirage, daydream, fancy. *(ANT.)* bore.

far *(SYN.)* removed, much, distant, remote, estranged, alienated. *(ANT.)* close, near.

fare *(SYN.)* prosper, eat, passenger, thrive, toll, progress, succeed.

farewell *(SYN.)* good-by, valediction, departure, leaving. *(ANT.)* welcome, greeting.

farm *(SYN.)* grow, harvest, cultivate, ranch, hire, charter, plantation.

fascinate *(SYN.)* charm, enchant, bewitch, attract, enthrall.

fashion *(SYN.)* create, shape, style, mode, make, custom, form, manner, method, way, vogue.

fashionable *(SYN.)* chic, smart, stylish, modish, elegant, voguish. *(ANT.)* dowdy, unfashionable.

fast *(SYN.)* fleet, firm, quick, swift, inflexible, stable, secure, expeditious, rapid, steady, solid, constant, speedy. *(ANT.)* insecure, sluggish, unstable, loose, slow, unsteady.

fasten *(SYN.)* secure, bind, tie, join, fix, connect, attach, unite. *(ANT.)* open, loose, free, loosen, release, separate.

fastidious *(SYN.)* choosy, selective, discriminating, picky, meticulous.

fat *(SYN.)* stout, plump, chubby, pudgy, obese, oily, fleshy, greasy, fatty, portly, corpulent, paunchy, wide, thick, rotund. *(ANT.)* slim, gaunt, emaciated, thin, slender.

fatal *(SYN.)* killing, lethal, doomed, disastrous, deadly, fateful, mortal. *(ANT.)* nonfatal.

fate *(SYN.)* end, fortune, doom, issue, destiny, necessity, portion, result, lot, chance, luck, outcome, consequence, kismet.

father *(SYN.)* cause, sire, breed, originate, founder, inventor.

fatherly *(SYN.)* protective, paternal, kind, paternalistic.

fathom *(SYN.)* penetrate, understand, interpret, comprehend.

fatigue *(SYN.)* weariness, lassitude, exhaustion, enervation, languor, tiredness. *(ANT.)* vivacity, rejuvenation, energy, vigor.

fault *(SYN.)* defect, flaw, mistake, imperfection, shortcoming, error, weakness, responsibility, omission, blemish, blame, failure. *(ANT.)* perfection, completeness.

faultfinding *(SYN.)* carping, censorious, critical, caviling, nitpicking.

faulty *(SYN.)* imperfect, broken, defective, damaged, impaired. *(ANT.)* flawless, perfect, whole.

favor *(SYN.)* resemble, liking, service, prefer, approval, like, support, patronize, benefit. *(ANT.)* deplore, disapprove.

favorite *(SYN.)* prized, pet, choice, darling, treasured, preferred.

favoritism *(SYN.)* prejudice, bias, partiality. *(ANT.)* fairness, impartiality.

fear *(SYN.)* horror, terror, fright, trepidation, alarm, consternation, dismay, cowardice, panic, anxiety, dread, scare, apprehension. *(ANT.)* fearlessness, boldness, courage, assurance.

fearless *(SYN.)* bold, brave, courageous, gallant, dauntless,

confident. *(ANT.)* timid, fearful, cowardly.

feast *(SYN.)* dinner, banquet, barbecue.

feat *(SYN.)* performance, act, operation, accomplishment, achievement, doing, transaction, deed. *(ANT.)* intention, deliberation, cessation.

feature *(SYN.)* trait, quality, characteristic, highlight, attribute.

fee *(SYN.)* payment, pay, remuneration, charge, recompense.

feeble *(SYN.)* faint, puny, exhausted, delicate, weak, enervated, frail, powerless, forceless, sickly, decrepit, ailing. *(ANT.)* strong, forceful, powerful, vigorous, stout.

feed *(SYN.)* satisfy, nourish, food, fodder, forage.

feel *(SYN.)* sense, experience, perceive.

feeling *(SYN.)* opinion, sensibility, tenderness, affection, impression, belief, sensation, sympathy, thought, passion, sentiment, attitude, emotion. *(ANT.)* fact, imperturbability, anesthesia, insensibility.

fellowship *(SYN.)* clan, society, brotherhood, fraternity, camaraderie, companionship, comradeship, association. *(ANT.)* dislike, discord, distrust, enmity, strife, acrimony.

felonious *(SYN.)* murderous, criminal, larcenous.

feminine *(SYN.)* womanly, girlish, ladylike, female, maidenly, womanish. *(ANT.)* masculine, male, virile.

ferocious *(SYN.)* savage, fierce, wild, blood-thirsty, brutal. *(ANT.)* playful, gentle, harmless, calm.

fertile *(SYN.)* rich, fruitful, teeming, plenteous, bountiful, prolific, luxuriant, productive, fecund. *(ANT.)* unproductive, barren, sterile.

festival *(SYN.)* feast, banquet, regalement, celebration.

festive *(SYN.)* joyful, gay, joyous, merry, gala, jovial, jubilant. *(ANT.)* sad, gloomy, mournful, morose.

fetching *(SYN.)* charming, attractive, pleasing, captivating, winsome.

feud *(SYN.)* dispute, quarrel, strife, argument, conflict, controversy. *(ANT.)* amity, understanding, harmony, peace.

fiber *(SYN.)* line, strand, thread, string.

fickle *(SYN.)* unstable, capricious, restless, changeable, inconstant, variable. *(ANT.)* stable, constant, steady, reliable,

dependable.

fiction *(SYN.)* fabrication, romance, falsehood, tale, allegory, narrative, fable, novel, story, invention. *(ANT.)* verity, reality, fact, truth.

fictitious *(SYN.)* invented, make-believe, imaginary, fabricated, unreal, counterfeit, feigned. *(ANT.)* real, true, genuine, actual.

fidelity *(SYN.)* fealty, devotion, precision, allegiance, exactness, constancy, accuracy, faithfulness, loyalty. *(ANT.)* treachery, disloyalty.

fidget *(SYN.)* squirm, twitch, wriggle.

fiendish *(SYN.)* devilish, demonic, diabolical, savage, satanic.

fierce *(SYN.)* furious, wild, savage, violent, ferocious, vehement. *(ANT.)* calm, meek, mild, gentle, placid.

fight *(SYN.)* contend, scuffle, struggle, battle, wrangle, combat, brawl, quarrel, dispute, war, skirmish, conflict.

figure *(SYN.)* design, pattern, mold, shape, form, frame, reckon, calculate, compute, determine.

fill *(SYN.)* glut, furnish, store, stuff, occupy, gorge, pervade, content, stock, fill up, supply, sate, replenish, satisfy. *(ANT.)* void, drain, exhaust, deplete, empty.

filter *(SYN.)* screen, strainer, sieve.

filth *(SYN.)* pollution, dirt, sewage, foulness. *(ANT.)* cleanliness, innocence, purity.

filthy *(SYN.)* foul, polluted, dirty, stained, unwashed, squalid. *(ANT.)* pure, clean, unspoiled.

final *(SYN.)* ultimate, decisive, concluding, ending, terminal, last, conclusive, eventual, latest. *(ANT.)* inaugural, rudimentary, beginning, initial, incipient, first, original.

finally *(SYN.)* at last, eventually, ultimately.

find *(SYN.)* observe, detect, discover, locate.

fine *(SYN.)* thin, pure, choice, small, elegant, dainty, splendid, handsome, delicate, nice, powdered, beautiful, minute, exquisite, subtle, pretty, refined. *(ANT.)* thick, coarse, rough, blunt, large.

finicky *(SYN.)* fussy, meticulous, finical, fastidious, prim.

finish *(SYN.)* consummate, close, get done, terminate, accomplish, conclude, execute, perform, complete, end, achieve, fulfill, do, perfect.

(ANT.) open, begin, start, beginning.

fire (SYN.) vigor, glow, combustion, passion, burning, conflagration, ardor, flame, blaze, intensity, fervor. (ANT.) apathy, cold.

firm (SYN.) solid, rigid, inflexible, stiff, unchanging, steadfast, dense, hard, unshakable, compact, business, company, corporation, partnership. (ANT.) weak, limp, soft, drooping.

first (SYN.) chief, primary, initial, pristine, beginning, foremost, primeval, earliest, prime, primitive, original. (ANT.) subordinate, last, least, hindmost, latest.

fishy (SYN.) suspicious, questionable, doubtful. (ANT.) believable, credible.

fit (SYN.) adjust, suit, suitable, accommodate, conform, robust, harmonize, belong, seizure, spasm, attack, suited, appropriate, healthy, agree, adapt. (ANT.) misfit, disturb, improper.

fitful (SYN.) variable, restless, fickle, capricious, unstable, changeable. (ANT.) trustworthy, stable, constant, steady.

fitting (SYN.) apt, due, suitable, proper. (ANT.) improper, unsuitable, inappropriate.

fix (SYN.) mend, regulate, affix, set, tie, repair, attach, settle, link, bind, determine, establish, define, place, rectify, stick, limit, adjust, fasten. (ANT.) damage, change, mistreat, displace, alter, disturb, mutilate.

fixation (SYN.) fetish, obsession, infatuation, compulsion.

flair (SYN.) style, dash, flamboyance, drama, gift, knack, aptitude.

flamboyant (SYN.) showy, flashy, gaudy, ostentatious.

flame (SYN.) blaze, fire.

flash (SYN.) flare, flame, wink, twinkling, instant, gleam.

flashy (SYN.) tawdry, tasteless, pretentious, garish, flamboyant.

flat (SYN.) vapid, stale, even, smooth, tasteless, horizontal, dull, level, insipid, uninteresting, lifeless, boring. (ANT.) tasty, racy, hilly, savory, stimulating, interesting, broken, sloping.

flattery (SYN.) compliment, praise, applause, blarney, acclaim.

flaunt (SYN.) exhibit, show off, display, parade. (ANT.) conceal, hide, disguise.

flavor (SYN.) tang, taste, savor, essence, quality, character, season, spice.

flaw (SYN.) spot, imperfection, blemish, fault, deformity, blotch.

flee (SYN.) fly, abscond, hasten, escape, run away, decamp, evade. (ANT.) remain, appear, stay, arrive.

fleece (SYN.) filch, rob, purloin, swindle, defraud, pilfer, cheat.

fleet (SYN.) rapid, swift, quick, fast. (ANT.) unhurried, sluggish, slow.

fleeting (SYN.) brief, swift, passing, temporary. (ANT.) stable, fixed, lasting, permanent.

fleshy (SYN.) overweight, chubby, stocky, plump, obese, stout. (ANT.) spare, underweight, skinny.

flexible (SYN.) lithe, resilient, pliable, tractable, complaint, elastic, yielding, adaptable, agreeable, supple, pliant, easy, ductile. (ANT.) hard, unbending, firm, brittle, inflexible, rigid, fired.

flighty (SYN.) giddy, lightheaded, frivolous, irresponsible. (ANT.) solid, responsible, steady.

flimsy (SYN.) wobbly, weak, frail, fragile, unsteady, delicate, thin. (ANT.) durable, stable, firm, strong.

fling (SYN.) pitch, throw, toss, fun, celebration, party.

flippant (SYN.) disrespectful, sassy, insolent, brazen, rude, impertinent. (ANT.) courteous, polite, mannerly.

flit (SYN.) flutter, scurry, hasten, dart, skim.

flock (SYN.) gathering, group, flight, swarm, herd, school.

flog (SYN.) thrash, lash, switch, strike, paddle.

flood (SYN.) overflow, deluge, inundate, cascade.

florid (SYN.) gaudy, fancy, ornate, embellished. (ANT.) spare, simple, plain.

flourish (SYN.) succeed, grow, prosper, wave, thrive, bloom. (ANT.) wither, wane, die, decline.

flout (SYN.) disdain, scorn, spurn, ignore, taunt, ridicule, mock.

flow (SYN.) proceed, abound, spout, come, stream, run, originate, emanate, result, pour, squirt, issue, gush, spurt.

fluctuate (SYN.) vary, oscillate, change, waver, hesitate, vacillate. (ANT.) persist, stick, adhere, resolve.

fluent (SYN.) graceful, glib, flowing.

fluid (SYN.) liquid, running, liquefied.

flush (SYN.) abundant, flat, even, level.

fluster (SYN.) rattle, flurry, agitate, upset, perturb, quiver, vibrate.

fly (SYN.) flee, mount, shoot, decamp, hover, soar, flit, flutter, sail, escape, rush, spring, glide, abscond, dart, float. (ANT.) sink, descend, plummet.

foam (SYN.) suds, froth, lather.

foe (SYN.) opponent, enemy, antagonist, adversary. (ANT.) associate, ally, friend, comrade.

fog (SYN.) haze, mist, cloud, daze, confusion, stupor, vapor, smog.

foible (SYN.) frailty, weakness, failing, shortcoming, kink.

foist (SYN.) misrepresent, insinuate, falsify.

fold (SYN.) lap, double, overlap, clasp, pleat, tuck.

follow (SYN.) trail, observe, succeed, ensue, obey, chase, comply, accompany, copy, result, imitate, heed, adopt. (ANT.) elude, cause, precede, avoid, flee.

follower (SYN.) supporter, devotee, henchman, adherent, partisan, votary, attendant, disciple, successor. (ANT.) master, head, chief, dissenter.

following (SYN.) public, disciples, supporters, clientele, customers.

folly (SYN.) silliness, foolishness, indiscretion, absurdity, imprudence, imbecility, stupidity, extravagance. (ANT.) reasonableness, judgment, sense, prudence, wisdom.

fond (SYN.) affectionate, loving, attached, tender, devoted. (ANT.) hostile, cool, distant, unfriendly.

fondness (SYN.) partiality, liking, affection. (ANT.) hostility, unfriendliness.

food (SYN.) viands, edibles, feed, repast, nutriment, sustenance, diet, bread, provisions, meal, rations, victuals, fare. (ANT.) want, hunger, drink, starvation.

fool (SYN.) dunce, jester, idiot, simpleton, buffoon, harlequin, dolt, blockhead, numskull, clown, dope, trick, deceive, nincompoop. (ANT.) scholar, genius, sage.

foolish (SYN.) senseless, irrational, crazy, silly, brainless, idiotic, simple, nonsensical, stupid, preposterous, asinine. (ANT.) sane, sound, sensible, rational, judicious, wise, reasonable, prudent.

footing (SYN.) base, basis, foundation.

footloose (SYN.) uncommitted, free, detached, independent. (ANT.) engaged, rooted, involved.

forbearance (SYN.) moderation, abstinence, abstention, continence. (ANT.) greed, excess, intoxication.

forbid (SYN.) disallow, prevent, ban, prohibit, taboo, outlaw. (ANT.) approve, let, allow, permit.

forbidding (SYN.) evil, hostile, unfriendly, sinister, scary, repulsive. (ANT.) pleasant, beneficent, friendly.

force (SYN.) energy, might, violence, vigor, intensity, dint, power, constraint, coercion, compel, compulsion, oblige, make, coerce, strength. (ANT.) weakness, frailty, persuasion, feebleness, impotence, ineffectiveness.

forceful (SYN.) dynamic, vigorous, energetic, potent, drastic, intense. (ANT.) lackadaisical, insipid, weak.

foreboding (SYN.) misgiving, suspicion, apprehension, presage, intuition.

forecast (SYN.) prophesy, predict.

foregoing (SYN.) above, former, preceding, previous, prior. (ANT.) later, coming, below, follow.

foreign (SYN.) alien, strange, exotic, different, unfamiliar. (ANT.) commonplace, ordinary, familiar.

foreigner (SYN.) outsider, alien, newcomer, stranger. (ANT.) native.

foreman (SYN.) super, boss, overseer, supervisor.

forerunner (SYN.) harbinger, proclaimer, informant.

foresee (SYN.) forecast, expect, anticipate, surmise, envisage.

forest (SYN.) grove, woodland, wood, copse, woods.

forestall (SYN.) hinder, thwart, prevent, obstruct, repel.

foretell (SYN.) soothsay, divine, predict.

forever (SYN.) evermore, always, everlasting, hereafter, endlessly. (ANT.) fleeting, temporarily.

forfeit (SYN.) yield, resign, lose, sacrifice.

forgive (SYN.) exonerate, clear, excuse, pardon. (ANT.) impeach, accuse, blame, censure.

forgo (SYN.) relinquish,

release, surrender, waive, abandon. (ANT.) *keep, retain.*

forlorn (SYN.) pitiable, desolate, dejected, woeful, wretched. (ANT.) *optimistic, cherished, cheerful.*

form (SYN.) frame, compose, fashion, arrange, construct, make up, devise, create, invent, mold, shape, forge, organize, produce, constitute, make. (ANT.) *wreck, dismantle, destroy, misshape.*

formal (SYN.) exact, stiff, correct, outward, conformist, conventional, affected, regular, proper, ceremonious, decorous, methodical, precise, solemn, external, perfunctory. (ANT.) *heartfelt, unconstrained, easy, unconventional.*

former (SYN.) earlier, previous, erstwhile, prior.

formidable (SYN.) alarming, frightful, imposing, terrible, terrifying, dire, fearful, forbidding. (ANT.) *weak, unimpressive, ordinary.*

forsake (SYN.) abandon, desert, forgo, quit, discard, neglect.

forte (SYN.) gift, capability, talent, specialty, aptitude, bulwark.

forth (SYN.) out, onward, forward.

forthright (SYN.) honest, direct, candid, outspoken, blunt, sincere, plain, explicit.

forthwith (SYN.) instantly, promptly, immediately. (ANT.) *afterward, later, ultimately, slowly.*

fortify (SYN.) bolster, strengthen, buttress, barricade, defend.

fortuitous (SYN.) successful, benign, lucky, advantageous, propitious, happy, favored, chance. (ANT.) *unlucky, condemned.*

fortunate (SYN.) happy, auspicious, fortuitous, successful, favored, advantageous, benign, charmed, lucky, felicitous, blessed, propitious, blissful. (ANT.) *ill-fated, cheerless, unlucky, unfortunate, cursed, condemned.*

fortune (SYN.) chance, fate, lot, luck, riches, wealth, kismet, destiny.

fortuneteller (SYN.) soothsayer, clairvoyant, forecaster, oracle, medium.

forward (SYN.) leading, front, promote, elevate, advance, first, ahead, onward, further, foremost, aggrandize. (ANT.) *withhold, retard, hinder, retreat,*

oppose.

foul (SYN.) base, soiled, dirty, mean, unclean, polluted, impure, vile, evil, muddy, wicked, rainy, stormy, despicable, filthy. (ANT.) *pure, neat, wholesome, clean.*

found (SYN.) organize, establish.

foundation (SYN.) support, root, base, underpinning, groundwork, bottom, establishment, substructure, basis. (ANT.) *top, cover, building.*

foxy (SYN.) cunning, sly, artful, crafty, wily, sharp, shrewd, slick.

fraction (SYN.) fragment, part, section, morsel, share, piece.

fracture (SYN.) crack, break, rupture.

fragile (SYN.) delicate, frail, weak, breakable, infirm, brittle, feeble. (ANT.) *tough, hardy, sturdy, strong, stout, durable.*

fragment (SYN.) scrap, piece, bit, remnant, part, splinter, segment.

fragrance (SYN.) odor, smell, scent, perfume, aroma.

fragrant (SYN.) aromatic, scented, perfumed.

frail (SYN.) feeble, weak, delicate, breakable, fragile. (ANT.) *sturdy, strong, powerful.*

frame (SYN.) support, framework, skeleton, molding, border, mount.

frank (SYN.) honest, candid, open, unreserved, direct, sincere, straight-forward. (ANT.) *tricky, dishonest.*

frantic (SYN.) frenzied, crazed, raving, panicky. (ANT.) *composed, stoic.*

fraud (SYN.) deception, guile, swindle, deceit, artifice, imposture, trick, cheat, imposition, duplicity, chicanery. (ANT.) *sincerity, fairness, integrity.*

fraudulent (SYN.) tricky, fake, dishonest, deceitful.

fray (SYN.) strife, fight, battle, struggle, tussle, combat, brawl, melee, skirmish. (ANT.) *truce, agreement, peace, concord.*

freak (SYN.) curiosity, abnormality, monster, oddity.

free (SYN.) munificent, clear, autonomous, immune, open, freed, bountiful, liberated, unfastened, emancipated, unconfined, unobstructed, easy, artless, loose, familiar, bounteous, unrestricted, liberal, independent,

careless, frank, exempt. (ANT.) *stingy, clogged, illiberal, confined, parsimonious.*

freedom (SYN.) independence, privilege, familiarity, unrestraint, liberty, exemption, liberation, immunity, license. (ANT.) *servitude, constraint, bondage, slavery, necessity.*

freely (SYN.) liberally, generously, unstintingly.

freight (SYN.) shipping, cargo, load, shipment.

frenzy (SYN.) craze, agitation, excitement.

frequent (SYN.) usual, habitual, common, often, customary, general. (ANT.) *unique, rare, solitary, uncommon, exceptional, infrequent, scanty.*

fresh (SYN.) recent, new, additional, modem, further, refreshing, natural, brisk, novel, inexperienced, late, current, sweet, pure, cool. (ANT.) *stagnant, decayed, musty, faded.*

fret (SYN.) torment, worry, grieve, anguish.

fretful (SYN.) testy, irritable, touchy, peevish, short-tempered. (ANT.) *calm.*

friend (SYN.) crony, supporter, ally, companion, intimate, associate, comrade, mate, patron, acquaintance, chum, defender. (ANT.) *stranger, adversary.*

friendly (SYN.) sociable, kindly, affable, genial, companionable, social, neighborly, amicable. (ANT.) *hostile, antagonistic, reserved.*

friendship (SYN.) knowledge, familiarity, fraternity, acquaintance, intimacy, fellowship, comradeship, cognizance. (ANT.) *unfamiliarity, ignorance.*

fright (SYN.) alarm, fear, panic, terror.

frighten (SYN.) scare, horrify, daunt, affright, appall, terrify, alarm, terrorize, astound, dismay, startle, panic. (ANT.) *soothe, embolden, compose, reassure.*

frigid (SYN.) cold, wintry, icy, glacial, arctic, freezing.

fringe (SYN.) hem, edge, border, trimming, edging.

frisky (SYN.) animated, lively, peppy, vivacious.

frolic (SYN.) play, cavort, romp, frisk.

front (SYN.) facade, face, start, beginning, border, head. (ANT.) *rear, back.*

frontier (SYN.) border, boundary.

frugal (SYN.) parsimonious,

saving, stingy, provident, temperate, economical, sparing. (ANT.) *extravagant, wasteful, self-indulgent, intemperate.*

fruitful (SYN.) fertile, rich, bountiful, teeming, fecund, productive, luxuriant. (ANT.) *lean, barren, sterile.*

fruitless (SYN.) barren, futile, vain, sterile, unproductive. (ANT.) *fertile, productive.*

frustrate (SYN.) hinder, defeat, thwart, circumvent, outwit, foil, baffle, disappoint, balk, discourage, prevent. (ANT.) *promote, accomplish, further.*

fulfill (SYN.) do, effect, complete, accomplish, realize.

full (SYN.) baggy, crammed, entire, satiated, flowing, perfect, gorged, soaked, complete, filled, packed, extensive. (ANT.) *lacking, partial, empty, depleted.*

full-grown (SYN.) ripe, adult, mature, developed, grown-up, complete. (ANT.) *green, young, unripe, adolescent.*

fulsome (SYN.) disgusting, repulsive, nauseating, repellent, revolting.

fume (SYN.) gas, steam, smoke, rage, rave, vapor.

fun (SYN.) merriment, pleasure, enjoyment, piety, sport, amusement.

function (SYN.) operation, activity, affair, ceremony, gathering, party.

fundamental (SYN.) basic, essential, primary, elementary.

funny (SYN.) odd, droll, ridiculous, farcical, laughable, comic, curious, amusing. (ANT.) *solemn, sad, sober, melancholy.*

furious (SYN.) angry, enraged. (ANT.) *serene, calm.*

furnish (SYN.) yield, give, endow, fit, produce, equip, afford, decorate, supply. (ANT.) *divest, denude, strip.*

furor (SYN.) commotion, tumult, turmoil.

furtive (SYN.) surreptitious, secret, hidden, clandestine. (ANT.) *honest, open.*

fury (SYN.) wrath, anger, frenzy, rage, violence, fierceness. (ANT.) *calmness, serenity.*

fuss (SYN.) commotion, bother, pester, annoy, irritate.

futile (SYN.) pointless, idle, vain, useless, worthless, minor. (ANT.) *weighty, important, worthwhile, serious, valuable.*

future (SYN.) approaching, imminent, coming,

impending. (ANT.) *former, past.*
fuzzy (SYN.) indistinct, blurred. (ANT.) *lucid, clear.*

G

gab (SYN.) jabber, babble, chatter, prattle, gossip.

gabble (SYN.) chatter, babble, jabber, blab, prate, gaggle, prattle, gibberish.

gabby (SYN.) chatty, talkative, wordy, verbose.

gad (SYN.) wander, roam, rove, ramble, meander, cruise.

gadget (SYN.) contrivance, device, doodad, jigger, thing, contraption.

gaffe (SYN.) blunder, boner, mistake, gaucherie, error, howler.

gag (SYN.) witticism, crack, jest, joke.

gaiety (SYN.) joyousness, cheerfulness, joyfulness, light-heartedness. (ANT.) *melancholy, sadness, depression.*

gain (SYN.) acquire, avail, account, good, interest, attain, favor, achieve, get, secure, advantage, earn, profit, procure. (ANT.) *trouble, lose, calamity, forfeit, handicap, lose, distress.*

gainful (SYN.) lucrative, rewarding, profitable, beneficial, payable, productive. (ANT.) *unprofitable, unrewarding.*

gainsay (SYN.) refute, contradict, controvert, deny, refuse, impugn, contravene, disavow, differ. (ANT.) *aver, affirm, asseverate.*

gait (SYN.) stride, walk, tread, step.

gala (SYN.) ball, party, carnival, festival.

gale (SYN.) burst, surge, outburst.

gall (SYN.) nerve, audacity, impudence, annoy, vex, anger, provoke, irritate.

gallant (SYN.) bold, brave, courageous, valorous, valiant, noble, polite, fearless, heroic, chivalrous.

gallantry (SYN.) valor, daring, courage, prowess, heroism, manliness, dauntlessness, graciousness, attentiveness. (ANT.) *poltroonery, timidity, cowardice, cravenness, cloddishness.*

gallery (SYN.) passageway, hall, aisle, hallway, passage, corridor.

galling (SYN.) vexing, irritating, annoying, distressful, irksome.

galore (SYN.) abounding, plentiful, profuse, rich, overflowing.

gamble (SYN.) game, wager, bet, hazard, risk, venture, chance.

gambol (SYN.) romp, dance, cavort, frolic.

game (SYN.) fun, contest, merriment, pastime, match, play, amusement, recreation, diversion, entertainment. (ANT.) *labor, hardship, work, business.*

gamut (SYN.) extent, scope, sweep, horizon, range.

gang (SYN.) group, troop, band, company, horde, crew.

gangling (SYN.) rangy, lean, skinny, tall, lanky.

gangster (SYN.) crook, hoodlum, gunman, criminal.

gap (SYN.) cavity, chasm, pore, gulf, aperture, abyss, interval, space, hole, void, pore, break, opening.

gape (SYN.) ogle, stare, gawk.

garb (SYN.) clothing, dress, vesture, array, attire, clothes, drapery, apparel, garments, costume, raiment.

garbage (SYN.) refuse, waste, trash, rubbish.

gargantuan (SYN.) colossal, monumental, giant, huge, large, enormous.

garments (SYN.) drapery, dress, garb, apparel, array, attire, clothes, vesture. (ANT.) *nakedness, nudity.*

garnish (SYN.) decorate, embellish, trim, adorn, enrich, beautify, deck, ornament. (ANT.) *expose, strip, debase, uncover, defame.*

garrulous (SYN.) chatty, glib, verbose, talkative, communicative, voluble. (ANT.) *silent, uncommunicative, laconic, reticent, taciturn.*

gash (SYN.) lacerate, slash, pierce, cut, hew, slice.

gasp (SYN.) pant, puff, wheeze.

gather (SYN.) assemble, collect, garner, harvest, reap, deduce, judge, amass, congregate, muster, cull, glean, accumulate, convene. (ANT.) *scatter, disperse, distribute, disband, separate.*

gathering (SYN.) meeting, crowd, throng, company, assembly.

gaudy (SYN.) showy, flashy, loud, bold, ostentatious.

gaunt (SYN.) lank, flimsy, gauzy, narrow, rare, scanty, meager, gossamer, emaciated, scrawny, tenuous, thin, fine, lean, skinny, spare, slim, slight, slender, diluted. (ANT.) *wide, fat, thick, broad, bulky.*

gay (SYN.) merry, lighthearted, joyful, cheerful, sprightly, jolly, happy, joyous, gleeful, jovial, colorful, bright, glad. (ANT.) *glum, mournful, sad, depressed, sorrowful, somber, sullen.*

gaze (SYN.) look, stare, view, watch, examine, observe, glance, behold, discern, seem, see, survey, witness, inspect, goggle, appear. (ANT.) *hide, overlook, avert, miss.*

geld (SYN.) neuter, alter, spay, castrate.

gem (SYN.) jewel, semi-precious stone.

general (SYN.) ordinary, universal, usual, common, customary, regular, vague, miscellaneous, indefinite, inexact. (ANT.) *definite, particular, exceptional, singular, rare, precise, exact, specific.*

generally (SYN.) ordinarily, usually, customarily, normally, mainly. (ANT.) *seldom, infrequently, rare.*

generate (SYN.) produce, bestow, impart, concede, permit, acquiesce, cede, relent, succumb, surrender, pay, supply, grant, bear, afford, submit, waive, allow, breed, accord, accede, abdicate, resign, relinquish, surrender, quit. (ANT.) *assert, refuse, smuggle, resist, dissent, oppose, deny, strive.*

generation (SYN.) age, date, era, period, seniority, senescence, senility, time, epoch, dotage. (ANT.) *infancy, youth, childhood.*

generosity (SYN.) magnanimity, benevolence, humanity, kindness, philanthropy, tenderness, altruism, liberality, charity, beneficence. (ANT.) *selfishness, malevolence, cruelty, inhumanity, unkindness.*

generous (SYN.) giving, liberal, unselfish, magnanimous, bountiful, munificent, charitable, big, noble, beneficent. (ANT.) *greedy, stingy, selfish, covetous, mew, miserly.*

genesis (SYN.) birth, root, creation, source, origin, beginning.

genius (SYN.) intellect, adept, intellectual, sagacity, proficient, creativity, ability, inspiration, faculty, originality, aptitude, brain, gift, prodigy, talent. (ANT.) *dullard, stupidity, dolt, shallowness, moron, ineptitude, obtuseness.*

genre (SYN.) chaste, order, set, elegance, class, excellence, kind, caste, denomination, grade.

genteel (SYN.) cultured, polished, polite, refined, elegant. (ANT.) *discourteous, churlish, common.*

gentle (SYN.) peaceful, placid, tame, serene, relaxed, docile, benign, soothing, calm, soft, mild, amiable, friendly, kindly, cultivated. (ANT.) *nasty, harsh, rough, fierce, mew, violent, savage.*

genuine (SYN.) real, true, unaffected, authentic, sincere, bona fide, unadulterated, legitimate, actual, veritable, definite, proven. (ANT.) *false, sham, artificial, fake, counterfeit, bogus, pretended, insincere.*

genus (SYN.) kind, race, species, type, variety, character, family, breed, sort.

germ (SYN.) pest, virus, contamination, disease, pollution, taint, infection, contagion, poison, ailment.

germinate (SYN.) vegetate, pullulate, sprout, develop, grow.

gesture (SYN.) omen, signal, symbol, emblem, indication, note, token, symptom, movement, sign, motion.

get (SYN.) obtain, receive, attain, gain, achieve, acquire, procure, earn, fetch, carry, remove, prepare, take, ready, urge, induce, secure. (ANT.) *lose, surrender, forfeit, leave, renounce.*

ghastly (SYN.) frightful, horrible, horrifying, frightening, grisly, hideous, dreadful.

ghost (SYN.) phantom, spook, apparition, specter, trace, hint, vestige, spirit.

ghoulish (SYN.) weird, eerie, horrifying, gruesome, sinister, scary.

giant (SYN.) monster, colossus, mammoth, superman, gigantic. (ANT.) *small, tiny, dwarf, runt, midget, infinitesimal.*

gibe (SYN.) sneer, jeer, mock, scoff, boo, hoot, hiss. (ANT.) *approve.*

giddy (SYN.) reeling, dizzy, flighty, silly, scatterbrained. (ANT.) *serious.*

gift (SYN.) endowment, favor, gratuity, bequest, talent, charity, present, largess, donation, grant, aptitude, boon, offering, faculty, genius, benefaction. (ANT.) *purchase, loss, ineptitude, deprivation, earnings.*

gigantic (SYN.) huge, colossal, immense, large, vast, elephantine, gargantuan, prodigious, mammoth, monumental, enormous. (ANT.) *small, tiny, minute, diminutive, little.*

giggle (SYN.) chuckle, jeer, laugh, roar, snicker, titter, cackle, guffaw, mock.

gild (SYN.) cover, coat, paint, embellish, sweeten, retouch, camouflage.

gingerly (SYN.) gentle, cautiously, carefully, gently. (ANT.) *roughly.*

gird (SYN.) wrap, tie, bind, belt, encircle, surround, get set, prepare.

girl (SYN.) female, lass, miss, maiden, damsel.

girth (SYN.) measure, size, width, dimensions, expanse, proportions.

gist (SYN.) connotation, explanation, purpose, significance, acceptation, implication, interpretation, meaning. (ANT.) *redundancy.*

give (SYN.) bestow, contribute, grant, impart, provide, donate, confer, deliver, present, furnish, yield, develop, offer, produce, hand over, award, allot, deal out, mete out, bend, sacrifice, supply. (ANT.) *withdraw, take, retain, keep, seize.*

given (SYN.) handed over, presented, supposed, stated, disposed, assumed, inclined.

glacier (SYN.) frigid, icy, iceberg.

glad (SYN.) happy, cheerful, gratified, delighted, joyous, merry, pleased, exulting, charmed, thrilled, satisfied, tickled, gay, bright. (ANT.) *sad, depressed, dejected, melancholy, unhappy, morose, somber, despondent.*

glade (SYN.) clearing.

gladiator (SYN.) battler, fighter, competitor, combatant, contender, contestant.

gladness (SYN.) bliss, contentment, happiness, pleasure, well-being, beatitude, delight, satisfaction, blessedness. (ANT.) *sadness, sorrow, despair, misery, grief.*

glamorous (SYN.) spellbinding, fascinating, alluring, charming, bewitching, entrancing, captivating, enchanting, attractive, appealing, enticing, enthralling.

glamour (SYN.) charm, allure, attraction, magnetism, fascination.

glance (SYN.) eye, gaze, survey, view, examine, inspect, discern, look, see, witness, peek, regard, skim, reflect, glimpse, behold, observe.

glare (SYN.) flash, dazzle, stare, glower, glow, shine, glaze, burn, brilliance, flare, blind, scowl.

glaring (SYN.) flagrant, obvious, blatant, prominent, dazzling.

glass (SYN.) cup, tumbler, goblet, pane, crystal.

glassy (SYN.) blank, empty, emotionless, vacant, fixed, expressionless.

glaze (SYN.) buff, luster, cover, wax, gloss, coat, polish, shellac.

gleam (SYN.) flash, glimmer, glisten, shimmer, sparkle, twinkle, glare, beam, glow, radiate, glimmering, shine, burn, reflection, blaze.

glean (SYN.) reap, gather, select, harvest, pick, separate, cull.

glee (SYN.) mirth, joy, gladness, enchantment, delight, cheer, bliss, elation, merriment. (ANT.) *depression, misery, dejection.*

glen (SYN.) ravine, valley.

glib (SYN.) smooth, suave, flat, plain, polished, sleek, urbane. (ANT.) *rough, rugged, blunt, harsh, bluff.*

glide (SYN.) sweep, sail, fly, flow, slip, coast, cruise, move easily, skim, slide.

glimmer (SYN.) blink, shimmer, flicker, indication, hint, clue, suggestion.

glimpse (SYN.) notice, glance, peek, see, impression, look, flash.

glint (SYN.) flash, gleam, peek, glance, glimpse, sparkle, glitter.

glisten (SYN.) shimmer, shine, glimmer, twinkle, glitter, glister, sparkle.

glitch (SYN.) mishap, snag, hitch, malfunction.

glitter (SYN.) glisten, glimmer, sparkle, shine, twinkle.

gloat (SYN.) triumph, exult, glory, rejoice, revel.

global (SYN.) universal, international, worldwide.

globe (SYN.) orb, ball, world, earth, map, universe, sphere.

gloom (SYN.) bleakness, despondency, misery, sadness, woe, darkness, dejection, obscurity, blackness, shadow, shade, dimness, shadows, melancholy. (ANT.) *joy, mirth, exultation, cheerfulness, light, happiness, brightness, frivolity.*

gloomy (SYN.) despondent, dismal, glum, somber, sorrowful, sad, dejected, disconsolate, dim, dark, morose,

dispirited, moody, grave, pensive. (ANT.) *happy, merry, cheerful, high-spirited, bright, sunny, joyous.*

glorify (SYN.) enthrone, exalt, honor, revere, adore, dignify, enshrine, consecrate, praise, worship, laud, venerate. (ANT.) *mock, dishonor, debase, abuse, degrade.*

glorious (SYN.) exalted, high, noble, splendid, supreme, elevated, lofty, raised, majestic, famous, noted, stately, distinguished, celebrated, renowned, famed, magnificent, grand, proud, impressive, elegant, sublime. (ANT.) *ridiculous, low, base, ignoble, terrible, ordinary.*

glory (SYN.) esteem, praise, respect, reverence, admiration, honor, dignity, worship, eminence, homage, deference. (ANT.) *dishonor, disgrace, contempt, reproach, derision.*

gloss (SYN.) luster, shine, glow, sheen.

glossary (SYN.) dictionary, thesaurus, wordbook, lexicon.

glossy (SYN.) smooth, glistening, shiny, sleek, polished. (ANT.) *matte, dull.*

glow (SYN.) beam, glisten, radiate, shimmer, sparkle, glare, blaze, scintillate, shine, light, gleam, burn, flare, flame, dazzle, blush, redden, heat, warmth, flicker.

glower (SYN.) scowl, stare, frown, glare. (ANT.) *beam, grin, smile.*

glowing (SYN.) fiery, intense, passionate, zealous, enthusiastic, ardent, eager, fervent, favorable, impassioned, keen, complimentary, vehement. (ANT.) *cool, indifferent, apathetic, nonchalant.*

glue (SYN.) bind, fasten, cement, paste.

glum (SYN.) morose, sulky, fretful, crabbed, sullen, dismal, dour, moody. (ANT.) *joyous, merry, amiable, gay, pleasant.*

glut (SYN.) gorge, sate, content, furnish, fill, pervade, satiate, stuff, replenish, fill up, satisfy, stock. (ANT.) *empty, exhaust, deplete, void, drain.*

glutton (SYN.) pig, hog, greedy eater.

gluttony (SYN.) ravenousness, piggishness, devouring, hoggishness, insatiability, voraciousness. (ANT.) *satisfaction, fullness.*

gnarled (SYN.) twisted, knotted, rugged, knobby, nodular.

gnash (SYN.) gnaw, crunch,

grind.

gnaw (SYN.) chew, eat, gnash, grind, erode.

go (SYN.) proceed, depart, flee, move, vanish, exit, walk, quit, fade, progress, travel, become, fit, agree, leave, suit, harmonize, pass, travel, function, operate, withdraw. (ANT.) *stay, arrive, enter, stand, come.*

goad (SYN.) incite, prod, drive, urge, push, shove, jab, provoke, stimulate.

goal (SYN.) craving, destination, desire, longing, objective, finish, end, passion, aim, object, aspiration.

gobble (SYN.) devour, eat fast, gorge, gulp, stuff.

goblet (SYN.) cup, glass.

goblin (SYN.) troll, elf, dwarf, spirit.

godlike (SYN.) holy, supernatural, heavenly, celestial, divine, transcendent. (ANT.) *profane, wicked, blasphemous, diabolical, mundane.*

godly (SYN.) pious, religious, holy, pure, divine, spiritual, righteous, saintly.

golden (SYN.) shining, metallic, bright, fine, superior, nice, excellent, valuable. (ANT.) *dull, inferior.*

gong (SYN.) chimes, bells.

good (SYN.) honest, sound, valid, cheerful, honorable, worthy, conscientious, moral, genuine, humane, kind, fair, useful, skilful, adequate, friendly, genial, proficient, pleasant, exemplary, admirable, virtuous, reliable, precious, benevolent, excellent, pure, agreeable, gracious, safe, commendable. (ANT.) *bad, imperfect, vicious, undesirable, unfriendly, unkind, evil.*

good-bye (SYN.) so long, farewell.

good-hearted (SYN.) good, kind, thoughtful, kindhearted, considerate. (ANT.) *evil-hearted.*

good-humored (SYN.) pleasant, good-natured, cheerful, sunny, amiable. (ANT.) *petulant, cranky.*

goodness (SYN.) good, honesty, integrity, virtue, righteousness. (ANT.) *sin, evil, dishonesty, corruption.*

goods (SYN.) property, belongings, holdings, possessions, merchandise, wares.

good will (SYN.) harmony, willingness, readiness.

gore (SYN.) impale, penetrate, puncture, gouge.

gorge (SYN.) ravine, devour, stuff, gobble, valley, defile, pass, cram, fill.

gorgeous (SYN.) grand, ravishing, glorious, stunning, brilliant, divine, splendid, dazzling, beautiful, magnificent. (ANT.) homely, ugly, squalid.

gory (SYN.) bloody.

gossamer (SYN.) dainty, fine, filmy, delicate, sheer, transparent.

gossip (SYN.) prate, rumor, prattle, hearsay, meddler, tattler, chatter, talk, chat, blabbermouth.

gouge (SYN.) scoop, dig, carve, burrow, excavate, chisel, notch.

gourmet (SYN.) gourmand, gastronome, connoisseur.

govern (SYN.) manage, oversee, reign, preside over, supervise, direct, command, sway, administer, control, regulate, determine, influence, guide, lead, head, rule. (ANT.) assent, submit, acquiesce, obey, yield.

government (SYN.) control, direction, rule, command, authority.

governor (SYN.) controller, administrator, director, leader, manager.

gown (SYN.) garment, robe, frock, dress, costume, attire.

grab (SYN.) snatch, grip, clutch, seize, grasp, capture, pluck.

grace (SYN.) charm, beauty, handsomeness, loveliness, dignify, fairness, honor, distinguish, sympathy, attractiveness, elegance, clemency, excuse, pardon, thanks, blessing, prayer, pulchritude. (ANT.) eyesore, homeliness, deformity, ugliness.

graceful (SYN.) elegant, fluid, natural, supple, beautiful, comely, flowing, lithe. (ANT.) clumsy, awkward, gawky, ungainly, deformed.

gracious (SYN.) warm-hearted, pleasing, friendly, engaging, agreeable, kind, amiable, kindly, nice, good, courteous, polite, generous, good-natured. (ANT.) surly, hateful, churlish, rude, disagreeable, impolite, thoughtless, discourteous, ill-natured.

grade (SYN.) kind, rank, elegance, denomination, sort, arrange, category, classify, rate, group, place, mark, incline, slope, excellence, caste, order.

gradual (SYN.) deliberate, sluggish, dawdling, laggard, slow, leisurely, moderate, easy, delaying. (ANT.) quick, swift,

fast, speedy, raid.

graduate (SYN.) pass, finish, advance.

graft (SYN.) fraud, theft, cheating, bribery, dishonesty, transplant, corruption.

grain (SYN.) speck, particle, plant, bit, seed, temper, fiber, character, texture, markings, nature, tendency.

grand (SYN.) great, elaborate, splendid, royal, stately, noble, considerable, outstanding, distinguished, impressive, prominent, majestic, fine, dignified, large, main, principal. (ANT.) unassuming, modest, insignificant, unimportant, humble.

grandeur (SYN.) resplendence, majesty, distinction, glory.

grandiose (SYN.) grand, lofty, magnificent, stately, noble, pompous, dignified, imposing, sublime, majestic. (ANT.) lowly, ordinary, common, undignified, humble.

grandstand (SYN.) bleachers, gallery.

granite (SYN.) stone, rock.

grant (SYN.) confer, allocate, deal, divide, mete, appropriation, assign, benefaction, distribute, allowance, donate, award, mete out, deal out, consent, bestow, give, measure. (ANT.) refuse, withhold, confiscate, keep, retain.

granular (SYN.) grainy, sandy, crumbly, rough, gritty.

graph (SYN.) design, plan, stratagem, draw up, chart, sketch, cabal, machination, outline, plot, scheme, diagram.

graphic (SYN.) vivid, lifelike, significant, meaningful, pictorial, descriptive, representative.

grapple (SYN.) grip, seize, clutch, clasp, grasp, fight, struggle.

grasp (SYN.) clutch, grip, seize, apprehend, capture, snare, hold, clasp, comprehend, reach, grab, understand, grapple, possession, control, domination, command, perceive, trap. (ANT.) release, lose, throw, liberate.

grasping (SYN.) possessive, greedy, selfish, acquisitive, mercenary. (ANT.) liberal, unselfish, generous.

grate (SYN.) file, pulverize, grind, scrape, scratch, annoy, irritate.

grateful (SYN.) beholden, obliged, appreciative, thankful, indebted. (ANT.) ungrateful,

unappreciative, grudging.

gratify (SYN.) charm, gladden, please, satisfy. (ANT.) frustrate.

gratifying (SYN.) contentment, solace, relief, comfort, ease, succor, consolation, enjoyment. (ANT.) suffering, torment, affliction, discomfort, torture, misery.

grating (SYN.) harsh, rugged, severe, stringent, coarse, gruff, jarring, rigorous, strict. (ANT.) smooth, melodious, mild, gentle, soft.

gratis (SYN.) complimentary, free.

gratitude (SYN.) gratefulness, thankfulness, appreciation. (ANT.) ungratefulness.

gratuity (SYN.) tip, bonus, gift, donation.

grave (SYN.) sober, grim, earnest, serious, important, momentous, sedate, solemn, somber, imposing, vital, essential, staid, consequential, thoughtful. (ANT.) light, flighty, trivial, insignificant, unimportant, trifling, merry, gay, cheery, frivolous.

gravel (SYN.) stones, pebbles, grain.

gravitate (SYN.) incline, tend, lean, approach, toward.

gravity (SYN.) concern, importance, seriousness, pull. (ANT.) triviality.

graze (SYN.) scrape, feed, rub, brush, contact, skim.

grease (SYN.) fat, oil, lubrication.

greasy (SYN.) messy, buttery, waxy, fatty.

great (SYN.) large, numerous, eminent, illustrious, big, gigantic, enormous, immense, vast, weighty, fine, important, countless, prominent, vital, huge, momentous, serious, famed, dignified, excellent, critical, renowned, majestic, august, elevated, noble, grand. (ANT.) minute, common, menial, ordinary, diminutive, small, paltry, unknown.

greed (SYN.) piggishness, lust, desire, greediness, avarice, covetousness. (ANT.) unselfishness, selflessness, generosity.

greedy (SYN.) selfish, devouring, ravenous, avaricious, covetous, rapacious, gluttonous, insatiable, voracious. (ANT.) full, generous, munificent, giving, satisfied.

green (SYN.) inexperienced, modern, novel, recent, further, naive, fresh, natural, raw, unsophisticated, immature,

undeveloped, unripe, additional, brisk, artless. (ANT.) hackneyed, musty, decayed, faded, stagnant.

greenhorn (SYN.) tenderfoot, beginner, apprentice, amateur, novice.

greenhouse (SYN.) hot-house.

greet (SYN.) hail, accost, meet, address, talk to, speak to, welcome, approach. (ANT.) pass by, avoid.

gregarious (SYN.) outgoing, civil, affable, communicative, hospitable, sociable. (ANT.) inhospitable, antisocial, disagreeable, hermitic.

grief (SYN.) misery, sadness, tribulation, affliction, heartache, woe, trial, anguish, mourning, distress, lamentation. (ANT.) happiness, solace, consolation, comfort, joy.

grief-stricken (SYN.) heartsick, ravaged, devastated, wretched, forlorn, desolate, wretched. (ANT.) joyous, blissful, content.

grievance (SYN.) injury, wrong, injustice, detriment, complaint, damage, prejudice, evil, objection, protest, accusation, harm. (ANT.) improvement, benefit, repair.

grieve (SYN.) lament, brood over, mourn, weep, wail, sorrow, distress, bemoan, hurt, deplore. (ANT.) revel, carouse, celebrate, rejoice, gladden, soothe.

grieved (SYN.) contrite, remorseful, beggarly, mean, pitiful, shabby, vile, sorrowful, pained, hurt, sorry, contemptible, worthless. (ANT.) splendid, delighted, cheerful, impenitent, unrepentant.

grievous (SYN.) gross, awful, outrageous, shameful, lamentable, regrettable. (ANT.) agreeable, comforting, pleasurable.

grill (SYN.) cook, broil, question, interrogate, barbecue, grating, gridiron, cross-examine.

grim (SYN.) severe, harsh, strict, merciless, fierce, horrible, inflexible, adamant, ghastly, frightful, unyielding, rigid, stern. (ANT.) pleasant, lenient, relaxed, amiable, congenial, smiling.

grimace (SYN.) expression, sneer, scowl.

grimy (SYN.) unclean, grubby, soiled.

grin (SYN.) beam, smile, smirk.

grind (SYN.) mill, mash, powder, crush, crumble, pulverize, smooth, grate, sharpen, even.

grip (SYN.) catch, clutch, apprehend, trap, arrest, grasp, hold, bag, suitcase, lay hold of, clench, command, control, possession, domination, comprehension, understanding, seize. (ANT.) release, liberate, lose, throw.

gripe (SYN.) protest, lament, complaint, grumbling.

grit (SYN.) rub, grind, grate, sand, gravel, pluck, courage, stamina.

groan (SYN.) sob, wail, howl, moan, whimper, wail, complain.

groggy (SYN.) dazed, dopey, stupefied, stunned, drugged, unsteady. (ANT.) alert.

groom (SYN.) tend, tidy, preen, curry, spouse, consort.

groove (SYN.) furrow, channel, track, routine, slot, scratch.

groovy (SYN.) marvelous, delightful, wonderful.

grope (SYN.) fumble, feel around.

gross (SYN.) glaring, coarse, indelicate, obscene, bulky, great, total, whole, brutal, grievous, aggregate, earthy, rude, vulgar, entire, enormous, plain, crass, rough, large. (ANT.) appealing, delicate, refined, proper, polite, cultivated, slight, comely, trivial, decent.

grotesque (SYN.) strange, weird, odd, incredible, fantastic, monstrous, absurd, freakish, bizarre, peculiar, deformed, disfigured, unnatural, queer.

grotto (SYN.) tunnel, cave, hole, cavern.

grouch (SYN.) protest, remonstrate, whine, complain, grumble, murmur, mope, mutter, repine. (ANT.) praise, applaud, rejoice.

grouchy (SYN.) cantankerous, grumpy, surly. (ANT.) cheerful, contented, agreeable, pleasant.

ground (SYN.) foundation, presumption, surface, principle, underpinning, premise, base, bottom, fix, basis, soil, land, earth, set, root, support, establish, dirt, presupposition. (ANT.) implication, superstructure, trimming, derivative.

groundless (SYN.) baseless, unfounded, unwarranted, needless.

grounds (SYN.) garden, lawns, dregs, foundation, leftovers, reason, sediment, cause, basis, premise, motive.

groundwork (SYN.) support, bottom, base, underpinning, premise, presupposition, principle, basis. (ANT.) trimming, implication, derivative, superstructure.

group (SYN.) crowd, clock, party, troupe, swarm, bunch, brook, assembly, herd, band, mob, brood, class, throng, cluster, flock, lot, collection, pack, horde, gathering, aggregation. (ANT.) disassemble.

grouse (SYN.) mutter, grumble, gripe, scold, growl, complain.

grovel (SYN.) creep, crawl, cower, cringe, slouch, stoop, scramble.

groveling (SYN.) dishonorable, lowly, sordid, vile, mean, abject, despicable, ignoble, menial, servile, vulgar, ignominious. (ANT.) lofty, noble, esteemed, exalted.

grow (SYN.) extend, swell, advance, develop, enlarge, germinate, mature, expand, flower, raise, become, cultivate, increase, distend. (ANT.) wane, shrink, atrophy, decay, diminish, contract.

growl (SYN.) complain, snarl, grumble, gnarl, roar, clamor, bellow.

grown-up (SYN.) full-grown, adult, of age, mature, big, senior. (ANT.) little, childish, budding, junior, juvenile.

growth (SYN.) expansion, development, unfolding, maturing, progress, elaboration, evolution. (ANT.) degeneration, deterioration, curtailment, abbreviation, compression.

grub (SYN.) gouge, dig, scoop out, burrow, tunnel, excavate, plod, toil, drudge.

grubby (SYN.) unkempt, grimy, slovenly, dirty. (ANT.) tidy, spruce, neat, clean, well-groomed.

grudge (SYN.) malevolence, malice, resentment, bitterness, spite, animosity, enmity, rancor, ill will. (ANT.) kindness, love, benevolence, affection, good will, friendliness, toleration.

grudgingly (SYN.) reluctantly, unwillingly, under protest, involuntarily.

grueling (SYN.) taxing, exhausting, excruciating, trying, arduous, grinding, crushing. (ANT.) effortless, easy, light, simple.

gruesome (SYN.) hideous, frightful, horrible, loathsome, ghastly, horrifying, grisly.

(ANT.) agreeable, soothing, delightful, charming.

gruff (SYN.) scratchy, crude, incomplete, unpolished, stormy, brusque, rude, rough, uncivil, churlish, violent, harsh, imperfect, craggy, irregular, deep, husky, approximate, tempestuous, blunt. (ANT.) civil, courteous, polished, calm, even, sleek, smooth, finished, gentle, placid, pleasant, tranquil.

grumble (SYN.) protest, mutter, complain.

grumpy (SYN.) ill-tempered, cranky, grouchy, surly, crossgained, crabbed, fractious, pettish, disgruntled, moody. (ANT.) winsome, amiable, pleasant, cheery.

guarantee (SYN.) bond, pledge, token, warrant, earnest, surety, bail, commitment, promise, secure, swear, assure, sponsor, certify, warranty, insure, endorse, security.

guarantor (SYN.) voucher, sponsor, warrantor, signatory, underwriter, surety.

guaranty (SYN.) warranty, token, deposit, earnest, pledge, gage, collateral, stake.

guard (SYN.) protect, shield, veil, cloak, conceal, disguise, envelop, preserve, hide, defend, cover, sentry, protector, shroud, curtain. (ANT.) unveil, expose, ignore, neglect, bare, reveal, disregard, divulge.

guarded (SYN.) discreet, cautious, careful. (ANT.) audacious, reckless, indiscreet, careless.

guardian (SYN.) curator, keeper, protector, custodian, patron, champion.

guess (SYN.) estimate, suppose, think, assume, reason, believe, reckon, speculate, notion, surmise, hypothesis, imagine, consider, opinion, conjecture. (ANT.) know.

guest (SYN.) caller, client, customer, patient, visitor, company. (ANT.) host.

guide (SYN.) manage, supervise, conduct, direct, lead, steer, escort, pilot, show, squire, usher, control, affect, influence, regulate. (ANT.) follower, follow.

guild (SYN.) association, union, society.

guile (SYN.) deceitfulness, fraud, wiliness, trick, deceit, chicanery, cunning, deception, craftiness, sham, sneakiness, cheat. (ANT.) sincerity, openness, honesty, truthfulness, candor, frankness.

guilt (SYN.) sin, blame, fault, offense.

guilty (SYN.) culpable, to blame, responsible, at fault, criminal, blameworthy. (ANT.) blameless, innocent, guileless.

guise (SYN.) aspect, pretense, mien, look, air, advent, apparition, appearance.

gulch (SYN.) gorge, valley, gully, ravine.

gullible (SYN.) trustful, naive, innocent, deceivable, unsuspicious, believing, (ANT.) skeptical, sophisticated.

gully (SYN.) ditch, gorge, ravine, valley, gulch, gulf.

gulp (SYN.) devour, swallow, gasp, repress, choke.

gun (SYN.) fire, shoot, weapon, discharge, pistol, firearm, revolver.

gust (SYN.) blast, wind, outbreak, outburst, eruption.

gutter (SYN.) ditch, groove, drain, channel, trench, sewer, trough.

gymnasium (SYN.) playground, arena, court, athletic field.

gymnastics (SYN.) drill, exercise, acrobatics, calisthenics.

gyp (SYN.) swindle, cheat, defraud.

gypsy (SYN.) nomad.

gyrate (SYN.) spin, whirl, rotate, revolve.

H

habit (SYN.) usage, routine, compulsion, use, wont, custom, disposition, practice, addiction, fashion.

habitation (SYN.) abode, domicile, lodgings, dwelling, home.

habitual (SYN.) general, usual, common, typical, frequent, persistent, customary, routine, regular, often. (ANT.) solitary, unique, exceptional, occasional, unusual, scanty, rare.

habituated (SYN.) used, accustomed, adapted, acclimated, comfortable, familiarized, addicted, settled.

hack (SYN.) cleave, chop, slash, hew, slice, pick, sever, mangle.

hag (SYN.) beldam, crone, vixen, granny, ogress, harridan, visage.

haggard (SYN.) drawn, careworn, debilitated, spent, gaunt, worn. (ANT.) bright, fresh, animated.

haggle (SYN.) dicker, bargain.

hail (SYN.) welcome, approach, accost, speak to, address, greet. (ANT.) pass by, avoid.

hair-do (SYN.) hairstyle, coiffure, haircut.

hairdresser (SYN.) beautician, barber.

hairless (SYN.) shorn, glabrous, bald, depilated. (ANT.) hirsute, hairy, unshaven.

hairy (SYN.) bearded, shaggy, hirsute, bewhiskered.

hale (SYN.) robust, well, wholesome, hearty, healthy, sound, strong, vigorous, salubrious. (ANT.) noxious, frail, diseased, delicate, infirm, injurious.

half-baked (SYN.) crude, premature, makeshift, illogical, shallow.

half-hearted (SYN.) uncaring, indifferent, unenthusiastic, cool. (ANT.) eager, enthusiastic, earnest.

half-wit (SYN.) dope, simpleton, nitwit, dunce, idiot, fool.

hall (SYN.) corridor, lobby, passage, hallway, vestibule, foyer.

hallow (SYN.) glorify, exalt, dignify, aggrandize, consecrate, elevate, ennoble, raise, erect. (ANT.) dishonor, humiliate, debase, degrade.

hallowed (SYN.) holy, sacred, sacrosanct, blessed, divine.

hallucination (SYN.) fantasy, mirage, dream, vision, phantasm, appearance, aberration, illusion.

halt (SYN.) impede, obstruct, terminate, stop, hinder, desist, check, arrest, abstain, discontinue, hold, end, cork, interrupt, bar, cease. (ANT.) start, begin, proceed, speed, beginning, promote.

halting (SYN.) imperfect, awkward, stuttering, faltering, hobbling, doubtful, limping, wavering. (ANT.) decisive, confident, smooth, graceful, facile.

hammer (SYN.) beat, bang, whack, pound, batter, drive, tap, cudgel.

hamper (SYN.) prevent, impede, thwart, restrain, hinder, obstruct. (ANT.) help, assist, expedite, encourage, facilitate.

hamstrung (SYN.) disabled, helpless, paralyzed.

hand (SYN.) assistant, helper, support, aid, farmhand, laborer.

handicap (SYN.) retribution, penalty, disadvantage, forfeiture, hindrance, chastisement.

(ANT.) reward, pardon, compensation, remuneration.

handily (SYN.) readily, skillfully, easily, dexterously, smoothly, adroitly, deftly.

handkerchief (SYN.) bandanna, kerchief.

handle (SYN.) hold, touch, finger, clutch, grip, manipulate, feel, grasp, control, oversee, direct, steer, supervise, run, regulate.

hand out (SYN.) disburse, distribute, deal, mete, circulate.

hand over (SYN.) release, surrender, deliver, yield, present, fork over.

handsome (SYN.) lovely, pretty, fair, comely, beautiful, charming, elegant, good-looking, large, generous, liberal, beauteous, fine. (ANT.) repulsive, ugly, unattractive, stingy, small, mean, petty, unsightly, meager, homely, foul, hideous.

handy (SYN.) suitable, adapted, appropriate, favorable, fitting, near, ready, close, nearby, clever, helpful, useful, timely, accessible. (ANT.) inopportune, troublesome, awkward, inconvenient.

hang (SYN.) drape, hover, dangle, suspend, kill, sag, execute, lynch.

hang in (SYN.) continue, endure, remain, persevere, resist, persist.

hang-up (SYN.) inhibition, difficulty, snag, hindrance, block.

hanker (SYN.) wish, yearn, long, desire, pine, thirst, covet.

haphazard (SYN.) aimless, random, purposeless, casual, indiscriminate, accidental. (ANT.) determined, planned, designed, deliberate.

hapless (SYN.) ill-fated, unfortunate, jinxed, luckless, wretched.

happen (SYN.) occur, take place, bechance, betide, transpire, come to pass, chance, befall.

happening (SYN.) episode, event, scene, incident, affair, experience, phenomenon, transaction.

happiness (SYN.) pleasure, gladness, delight, beatitude, bliss, contentment, satisfaction, joy, joyousness, blessedness, joyfulness, felicity, elation. (ANT.) sadness, sorrow, despair, misery, grief.

happy (SYN.) gay, joyous, cheerful, fortunate, glad, merry, contented, satisfied,

lucky, blessed, pleased, opportune, delighted. (ANT.) gloomy, morose, sad, sorrowful, miserable, inconvenient, unlucky, depressed, blue.

happy-go-lucky (SYN.) easygoing, carefree, unconcerned. (ANT.) prudent, responsible, concerned.

harangue (SYN.) oration, diatribe, lecture, tirade, exhortation.

harass (SYN.) badger, irritate, molest, pester, taunt, torment, provoke, tantalize, worry, aggravate, annoy, nag, plague, vex. (ANT.) please, soothe, comfort, delight, gratify.

harbinger (SYN.) sign, messenger, proclaim, forerunner, herald.

harbor (SYN.) haven, port, anchorage, cherish, entertain, protect, shelter.

hard (SYN.) difficult, burdensome, arduous, rigid, puzzling, cruel, strict, unfeeling, severe, stern, impenetrable, compact, tough, solid, onerous, rigorous, firm, intricate, harsh, perplexing. (ANT.) fluid, effortless, gentle, tender, easy, simple, plastic, soft, lenient, flabby, elastic.

hard-boiled (SYN.) unsympathetic, tough, harsh, unsentimental.

harden (SYN.) petrify, solidify. (ANT.) loose, soften.

hardheaded (SYN.) stubborn, obstinate, unyielding, headstrong.

hard-hearted (SYN.) merciless, hard, unmerciful, callous, pitiless, ruthless.

hardly (SYN.) barely, scarcely.

hard-nosed (SYN.) shrewd, tough, practical.

hardship (SYN.) ordeal, test, effort, affliction, misfortune, trouble, experiment, proof, essay, misery, examination, difficulty, tribulation.

hardy (SYN.) sturdy, strong, tough, vigorous. (ANT.) frail, decrepit, feeble, weak, fragile.

harm (SYN.) hurt, mischief, misfortune, mishap, damage, wickedness, cripple, injury, evil, detriment, ill, infliction, wrong. (ANT.) favor, kindness, benefit, boon.

harmful (SYN.) damaging, injurious, mischievous, detrimental, hurtful, deleterious. (ANT.) helpful, salutary, profitable, advantageous, beneficial.

harmless (SYN.) protected, secure, snag, dependable, certain, painless, innocent, trustworthy. (ANT.) perilous, hazardous, insecure,

dangerous, unsafe.

harmonious (SYN.) tuneful, melodious, congenial, amicable. (ANT.) dissonant, discordant, disagreeable.

harmony (SYN.) unison, bargain, contract, stipulation, pact, agreement, accordance, concord, accord, understanding, unity, coincidence. (ANT.) discord, dissension, difference, variance, disagreement.

harness (SYN.) control, yoke.

harry (SYN.) vex, pester, harass, bother, plague.

harsh (SYN.) jarring, gruff, rugged, severe, stringent, blunt, grating, unpleasant, tough, stern, strict, unkind, rigorous, cruel, coarse. (ANT.) smooth, soft, gentle, melodious, soothing, easy, mild.

harvest (SYN.) reap, gather, produce, yield, crop, gain, acquire, fruit, result, reaping, product, proceeds, glean, garner. (ANT.) plant, squander, lose, sow.

haste (SYN.) speed, hurry, rush, rapidity, flurry, scramble. (ANT.) sloth, sluggishness.

hasten (SYN.) hurry, sprint, quicken, rush, precipitate, accelerate, scurry, run, scamper, dispatch, press, urge, dash, expedite, speed. (ANT.) retard, tarry, detain, linger, dawdle, delay, hinder.

hasty (SYN.) quick, swift, irascible, lively, nimble, brisk, active, speedy, impatient, testy, sharp, fast, rapid. (ANT.) slow, dull, sluggish.

hat (SYN.) helmet, bonnet, cap.

hatch (SYN.) breed, incubate, brood.

hate (SYN.) loathe, detest, despise, disfavor, hatred, abhorrence, abominate, abhor, dislike. (ANT.) love, cherish, approve, admire, like.

hateful (SYN.) loathsome, detestable, offensive. (ANT.) likable, loving, admirable.

hatred (SYN.) detestation, dislike, malevolence, enmity, rancor, ill will, loathing, hate, hostility, abhorrence, aversion, animosity. (ANT.) friendship, love, affection, attraction.

haughty (SYN.) proud, stately, vainglorious, arrogant, disdainful, overbearing, supercilious, vain. (ANT.) meek, ashamed, lowly, humble.

haul (SYN.) draw, pull, drag, tow.

have (SYN.) own, possess, seize, hold, control, occupy,

47

havoc

acquire, undergo, maintain, experience, receive, gain, affect, include, contain, get, take, obtain. (*ANT.*) *surrender, abandon, renounce, lose.*

havoc (*SYN.*) devastation, ruin, destruction.

hazard (*SYN.*) peril, chance, dare, risk, offer, conjecture, jeopardy, danger. (*ANT.*) *safety, defense, protection, immunity.*

hazardous (*SYN.*) perilous, precarious, threatening, unsafe, dangerous, critical, menacing, risky. (*ANT.*) *protected, secure, safe.*

hazy (*SYN.*) uncertain, unclear, ambiguous, dim, obscure, undetermined, vague, unsettled, indefinite. (*ANT.*) *specific, clear, lucid, precise, explicit.*

head (*SYN.*) leader, summit, top, culmination, director, chief, master, commander, supervisor, start, source, crest, beginning, crisis. (*ANT.*) *foot, base, bottom, follower, subordinate, underling.*

headstrong (*SYN.*) obstinate, stubborn, willful. (*ANT.*) *easygoing, amenable.*

headway (*SYN.*) movement, progress.

heady (*SYN.*) thrilling, intoxicating, exciting, electrifying.

heal (*SYN.*) restore, cure.

healthy (*SYN.*) wholesome, hale, robust, sound, well, vigorous, strong, hearty, healthful, hygienic, salubrious, salutary. (*ANT.*) *noxious, diseased, unhealthy, delicate, frail, infirm, injurious.*

heap (*SYN.*) collection, mound, increase, store, stack, pile, gather, accumulate, amass, accrue, accumulation, collect. (*ANT.*) *dissipate, scatter, waste, disperse.*

hear (*SYN.*) heed, listen, detect, hearken, perceive, regard.

heart (*SYN.*) middle, center, sympathy, nucleus, midpoint, sentiment, core, feeling, midst. (*ANT.*) *outskirts, periphery, border, rim, boundary.*

heartache (*SYN.*) anguish, mourning, sadness, sorrow, affliction, distress, grief, lamentation, tribulation. (*ANT.*) *happiness, joy, solace, comfort, consolation.*

heartbroken (*SYN.*) distressed, forlorn, mean, paltry, worthless, contemptible, wretched, crestfallen, disconsolate, downhearted, comfortless, brokenhearted, low.

(*ANT.*) *noble, fortunate, contented, significant.*

hearten (*SYN.*) encourage, favor, impel, urge, promote, sanction, animate, cheer, exhilarate. (*ANT.*) *deter, dissuade, deject, discourage, dispirit.*

heartrending (*SYN.*) heartbreaking, depressing, agonizing.

hearty (*SYN.*) warm, earnest, ardent, cordial, sincere, gracious, sociable. (*ANT.*) *taciturn, aloof, cool, reserved.*

heat (*SYN.*) hotness, warmth, temperature, passion, ardor, zeal, inflame, cook, excitement, warm. (*ANT.*) *cool, chill, coolness, freeze, coldness, chilliness, iciness, cold.*

heated (*SYN.*) vehement, fiery, intense, passionate.

heave (*SYN.*) boost, hoist, raise.

heaven (*SYN.*) empyrean, paradise.

heavenly (*SYN.*) superhuman, godlike, blissful, saintly, holy, divine, celestial, angelic, blessed. (*ANT.*) *wicked, mundane, profane, blasphemous, diabolical.*

heavy (*SYN.*) weighty, massive, gloomy, serious, ponderous, cumbersome, trying, burdensome, harsh, grave, intense, dull, grievous, concentrated, severe, oppressive, sluggish. (*ANT.*) *brisk, light, animated.*

heckle (*SYN.*) torment, harass, tease, hector, harry.

heed (*SYN.*) care, alertness, circumspection, mindfulness, consider, watchfulness, reflection, study, attention, notice, regard, obey, ponder, respect, meditate, mind, observe, deliberate, examine, contemplate, weigh, esteem, application. (*ANT.*) *negligence, oversight, overlook, neglect, ignore, disregard, indifference, omission.*

heedless (*SYN.*) sightless, headlong, rash, unmindful, deaf, unseeing, oblivious, ignorant, inattentive, disregardful, blind. (*ANT.*) *perceiving, sensible, aware, calculated, discerning.*

height (*SYN.*) zenith, peak, summit, tallness, mountain, acme, apex, elevation, altitude, prominence, maximum, pinnacle, culmination. (*ANT.*) *base, depth.*

heighten (*SYN.*) increase, magnify, annoy, chafe, intensify, amplify, aggravate, provoke, irritate, concentrate,

nettle. (*ANT.*) *soothe, mitigate, palliate, soften, appease.*

heinous (*SYN.*) abominable, grievous, atrocious.

hello (*SYN.*) greeting, good evening, good afternoon, good morning. (*ANT.*) *farewell, good-bye, so long.*

help (*SYN.*) assist, support, promote, relieve, abet, succor, back, uphold, further, remedy, encourage, aid, facilitate, mitigate. (*ANT.*) *afflict, thwart, resist, hinder, impede.*

helper (*SYN.*) aide, assistant, supporter.

helpful (*SYN.*) beneficial, serviceable, wholesome, useful, profitable, advantageous, good, salutary. (*ANT.*) *harmful, injurious, useless, worthless, destructive, deleterious, detrimental.*

helpfulness (*SYN.*) assistance, cooperation, usefulness, serviceability, kindness, neighborliness, willingness, collaboration, supportiveness, readiness. (*ANT.*) *antagonism, hostility, opposition.*

helpless (*SYN.*) weak, feeble, dependent, disabled, inept, unresourceful, incapable, incompetent. (*ANT.*) *resourceful, competent, enterprising.*

helplessness (*SYN.*) impotence, feebleness, weakness, incapacity, ineptitude, invalidism, shiftless, awkwardness. (*ANT.*) *power, strength, might, potency.*

helter-skelter (*SYN.*) haphazardly, chaotically, irregularly.

hem (*SYN.*) bottom, border, edge, rim, margin, pale, verge, flounce, boundary, fringe, brim, fence, hedge, frame.

hem in (*SYN.*) enclose, shut in, confine, restrict, limit.

hence (*SYN.*) consequently, thence, therefore, so, accordingly.

herald (*SYN.*) harbinger, crier, envoy, forerunner, precursor, augury, forecast.

herculean (*SYN.*) demanding, heroic, titanic, mighty, prodigious, laborious, arduous, overwhelming, backbreaking.

herd (*SYN.*) group, pack, drove, crowd, flock, gather.

heretic (*SYN.*) nonconformist, sectarian, unbeliever, sectary, schismatic, apostate, dissenter.

heritage (*SYN.*) birthright, legacy, patrimony, inheritance.

hermit (*SYN.*) recluse, anchorite, eremite.

hero (*SYN.*) paladin, champion, idol.

heroic (*SYN.*) bold, courageous, fearless, gallant, valiant, valorous, brave, chivalrous, adventurous, dauntless, intrepid, magnanimous. (*ANT.*) *fearful, weak, cringing, timid, cowardly.*

heroism (*SYN.*) valor, bravery, gallant, dauntless, bold, courageous, fearless.

hesitant (*SYN.*) reluctant, unwilling, disinclined, loath, slow, averse. (*ANT.*) *willing, inclined, eager, ready, disposed.*

hesitate (*SYN.*) falter, waver, pause, doubt, demur, delay, vacillate, wait, stammer, stutter, scruple. (*ANT.*) *proceed, resolve, continue, decide, persevere.*

hesitation (*SYN.*) distrust, scruple, suspense, uncertainty, unbelief, doubt, incredulity, skepticism. (*ANT.*) *determination, belief, certainty, faith, conviction.*

hidden (*SYN.*) undeveloped, unseen, dormant, concealed, quiescent, latent, potential, inactive. (*ANT.*) *visible, explicit, conspicuous, evident.*

hide (*SYN.*) disguise, mask, suppress, withhold, veil, cloak, conceal, screen, camouflage, shroud, pelt, skin, leather, cover. (*ANT.*) *reveal, show, expose, disclose, uncover, divulge.*

hideous (*SYN.*) frightful, ugly, shocking, frightening, horrible, terrible, horrifying, terrifying, grisly, gross. (*ANT.*) *lovely, beautiful, beauteous.*

high (*SYN.*) tall, eminent, exalted, elevated, high-pitched, sharp, lofty, proud, shrill, raised, strident, prominent, important, powerful, expensive, dear, high-priced, costly, grave, serious, extreme, towering. (*ANT.*) *low, mean, tiny, short, base, lowly, deep, insignificant, unimportant, inexpensive, reasonable, trivial, petty, small.*

highly (*SYN.*) extremely, very, extraordinarily, exceedingly.

high-minded (*SYN.*) lofty, noble, honorable. (*ANT.*) *dishonorable, base.*

high-priced (*SYN.*) dear, expensive, costly. (*ANT.*) *economical, cheap.*

high-strung (*SYN.*) nervous, tense, wrought-up, intense. (*ANT.*) *calm.*

highway (*SYN.*) parkway, speedway, turnpike, superhighway, freeway.

hilarious (*SYN.*) funny,

side-splitting, hysterical. *(ANT.) depressing, sad.*

hinder *(SYN.)* hamper, impede, block, retard, stop, resist, thwart, obstruct, check, prevent, interrupt, delay, slow, restrain. *(ANT.) promote, further, assist, expedite, advance, facilitate.*

hindrance *(SYN.)* interruption, delay, interference, obstruction, obstacle, barrier.

hinge *(SYN.)* rely, depend, pivot.

hint *(SYN.)* reminder, allusion, suggestion, clue, tip, taste, whisper, implication, intimate, suspicion, mention, insinuation. *(ANT.) declaration, affirmation, statement.*

hire *(SYN.)* employ, occupy, devote, apply, enlist, lease, rent, charter, rental, busy, engage, utilize, retain, let, avail. *(ANT.) reject, banish, discard, fire, dismiss, discharge.*

history *(SYN.)* narration, relation, computation, record, account, chronicle, detail, description, narrative, annal, tale, recital. *(ANT.) confusion, misrepresentation, distortion, caricature.*

hit *(SYN.)* knock, pound, strike, hurt, pummel, beat, come upon, find, discover, blow, smite.

hitch *(SYN.)* tether, fasten, harness, interruption, hindrance, interference.

hoard *(SYN.)* amass, increase, accumulate, gather, save, secret, cache, store, accrue, heap. *(ANT.) dissipate, scatter, waste, diminish, squander, spend, disperse.*

hoarse *(SYN.)* deep, rough, husky, raucous, grating, harsh. *(ANT.) clear.*

hoax *(SYN.)* ploy, ruse, wile, device, cheat, deception, antic, imposture, stratagem, stunt, guile, fraud. *(ANT.) openness, sincerity, candor, exposure, honesty.*

hobbling *(SYN.)* deformed, crippled, lame, unconvincing, unsatisfactory, defective, feeble, disabled, maimed, weak. *(ANT.) robust, vigorous, agile, sound, athletic.*

hobby *(SYN.)* diversion, pastime, avocation. *(ANT.) vocation, profession.*

hobo *(SYN.)* derelict, vagrant, vagabond, tramp.

hoist *(SYN.)* heave, lift, elevate, raise, crane, elevator, derrick.

hold *(SYN.)* grasp, occupy, possess, curb, contain, stow, carry, adhere, have, clutch, keep, maintain, clasp, grip, retain, detain, accommodate, restrain, observe, conduct, check, support. *(ANT.) vacate, relinquish, surrender, abandon.*

holdup *(SYN.)* heist, robbery, stickup, delay, interruption, slowdown.

hole *(SYN.)* cavity, void, pore, opening, abyss, chasm, gulf, aperture, tear, pit, burrow, lair, den, gap.

hollow *(SYN.)* unfilled, vacant, vain, meaningless, flimsy, false, hole, cavity, depression, hypocritical, depressed, empty, pit, insincere. *(ANT.) sound, solid, genuine, sincere, full.*

holocaust *(SYN.)* fire, burning, extermination, butchery, disaster, massacre.

holy *(SYN.)* devout, divine, blessed, consecrated, sacred, spiritual, pious, sainted, religious, saintly, hallowed. *(ANT.) worldly, sacrilegious, unconsecrated, evil, profane, secular.*

homage *(SYN.)* reverence, honor, respect.

home *(SYN.)* dwelling, abode, residence, seat, quarters, hearth, domicile, family, house, habitat.

homely *(SYN.)* uncommonly, disagreeable, ill-natured, ugly, vicious, plain, hideous, unattractive, deformed, surly, repellent, spiteful. *(ANT.) fair, handsome, pretty, attractive, comely, beautiful.*

homesick *(SYN.)* lonely, nostalgic.

honest *(SYN.)* sincere, trustworthy, truthful, fair, ingenuous, candid, conscientious, moral, upright, open, frank, forthright, honorable, just, straightforward. *(ANT.) fraudulent, tricky, deceitful, dishonest, lying.*

honesty *(SYN.)* frankness, openness, fairness, sincerity, trustworthiness, justice, candor, honor, integrity, responsibility, uprightness. *(ANT.) deceit, dishonesty, trickery, fraud, cheating.*

honor *(SYN.)* esteem, praise, worship, admiration, homage, glory, respect, admire, heed, dignity, revere, value, deference, venerate, reverence, consider, distinction, character, principle, uprightness, honesty, adoration. *(ANT.) scorn, dishonor, despise, neglect, abuse, shame, reproach, disdain, contempt, derision, disgrace.*

honorable *(SYN.)* fair, noble, creditable, proper, reputable, honest, admirable, true, trusty, eminent, respectable, esteemed, just, famed, illustrious, noble, virtuous, upright. *(ANT.) infamous, disgraceful, shameful, dishonorable, ignominious.*

honorary *(SYN.)* gratuitous, complimentary.

hoodlum *(SYN.)* crook, gangster, criminal, hooligan, mobster.

hop *(SYN.)* jump, leap.

hope *(SYN.)* expectation, faith, optimism, anticipation, expectancy, confidence, desire, trust. *(ANT.) pessimism, despair, despondency.*

hopeful *(SYN.)* optimistic, confident. *(ANT.) despairing, hopeless.*

hopeless *(SYN.)* desperate, despairing, forlorn, fatal, incurable, disastrous. *(ANT.) promising, hopeful.*

hopelessness *(SYN.)* gloom, discouragement, depression, pessimism, despondency. *(ANT.) hope, optimism, confidence, elation.*

horde *(SYN.)* host, masses, press, rabble, swarm, throng, bevy, crush, mob, multitude, crowd, populace.

horizontal *(SYN.)* even, level, plane, flat, straight, sideways. *(ANT.) upright, vertical.*

horrendous *(SYN.)* awful, horrifying, terrible, dreadful, horrid, ghastly. *(ANT.) splendid, wonderful.*

horrible *(SYN.)* awful, dire, ghastly, horrid, terrible, repulsive, frightful, appalling, horrifying, dreadful, ghastly, fearful. *(ANT.) enjoyable, enchanting, beautiful, lovely, fascinating.*

horrid *(SYN.)* repulsive, terrible, appalling, dire, awful, frightful, fearful, shocking, horrible, horrifying, ghastly, dreadful, revolting, hideous. *(ANT.) fascinating, enchanting, enjoyable, lovely, beautiful.*

horror *(SYN.)* dread, awe, hatred, loathing, foreboding, alarm, apprehension, aversion, terror. *(ANT.) courage, boldness, assurance, confidence.*

horseplay *(SYN.)* tomfoolery, clowning, shenanigans.

hospital *(SYN.)* infirmary, clinic, sanatorium, rest home, sanitarium.

hospitality *(SYN.)* warmth, liberality, generosity, graciousness, welcome.

hostile *(SYN.)* unfriendly, opposed, antagonistic, inimical, adverse, warlike. *(ANT.) friendly, favorable, amicable, cordial.*

hostility *(SYN.)* grudge, hatred, rancor, spite, bitterness, enmity, malevolence. *(ANT.) love, friendliness, goodwill.*

hot *(SYN.)* scorching, fervent, hot-blooded, passionate, peppery, ardent, burning, fiery, impetuous, scalding, heated, sizzling, blazing, frying, roasting, warm, intense, torrid, pungent. *(ANT.) indifferent, apathetic, impassive, passionless, bland, frigid, cold, freezing, cool, phlegmatic.*

hot air *(SYN.)* bombast, blather, jabber, gabble.

hotbed *(SYN.)* sink, nest, well, den, nursery, cradle, source, incubator, seedbed.

hot-blooded *(SYN.)* passionate, ardent, excitable, wild, fervent, fiery, impetuous, rash, brash, intense, impulsive. *(ANT.) stolid, impassive, cold, staid.*

hotel *(SYN.)* hostel, motel, inn, hostelry.

hotheaded *(SYN.)* rash, touchy, short-tempered, reckless, unruly. *(ANT.) levelheaded, cool-headed, calm.*

hound *(SYN.)* harry, pursue, pester, harass.

hourly *(SYN.)* frequently, steadily, constantly, unfailingly, periodically, perpetually, ceaselessly, continually, incessantly. *(ANT.) occasionally, seldom.*

house *(SYN.)* building, residence, abode, dwelling.

housebreaker *(SYN.)* robber, thief, prowler, cracksman, burglar.

household *(SYN.)* manage, family, home.

householder *(SYN.)* homeowner, occupant.

housing *(SYN.)* lodgings, shelter, dwelling, lodgment, case, casing, quarters, domicile, enclosure, console, bracket.

hovel *(SYN.)* cabin, hut, sty, shack, hole, shed.

hover *(SYN.)* hang, drift, poise, stand by, linger, impend, waver, hand around.

however *(SYN.)* notwithstanding, still, nevertheless, but, yet.

howl *(SYN.)* bellow, yowl, wail, yell, cry.

hub *(SYN.)* pivot, center, core, heart, axis, basis, focus, nucleus.

hubbub *(SYN.)* uproar, tumult, commotion, clamor, bustle, turmoil, racket, confusion. *(ANT.)* *peacefulness, stillness, silence, quiet.*

huckster *(SYN.)* peddler, adman, hawker, salesman, pitchman.

huddle *(SYN.)* mass, herd, bunch, crowd, cram, gather, shove, pack, flock, ball, conglomeration, knot, clump, medley, scrum.

hue *(SYN.)* pigment, tint, shade, dye, complexion, paint, stain, color, tone, tincture. *(ANT.)* *transparency, achromatism, paleness.*

huffy *(SYN.)* sensitive, vulnerable, testy, offended, thin-skinned, touchy, irascible, cross, offended. *(ANT.)* *tough, placid, stolid, impassive.*

hug *(SYN.)* embrace, coddle, caress, kiss, pet, press, clasp, fondle, cuddle. *(ANT.)* *tease, vex, spurn, buffet, annoy.*

huge *(SYN.)* great, immense, vast, ample, big, capacious, extensive, gigantic, enormous, tremendous, large, wide, colossal. *(ANT.)* *short, small, mean, little, tiny.*

hulking *(SYN.)* massive, awkward, bulky, ponderous, unwieldy, overgrown, lumpish, oafish.

hullabaloo *(SYN.)* clamor, uproar, din, racket, tumult, hubbub, commotion, noise, blare. *(ANT.)* *calm, peace, silence.*

hum *(SYN.)* whir, buzz, whiz, purr, croon, murmur, intone, vibrate.

human *(SYN.)* manlike, hominid, mortal, fleshly, individual, person, tellurian.

humane *(SYN.)* lenient, tender, tolerant, compassionate, clement, forgiving, kind, forbearing, thoughtful, kindhearted, kindly, gentle, merciful. *(ANT.)* *remorseless, cruel, heartless, pitiless, unfeeling, brutal.*

humanist *(SYN.)* scholar, sage, classicist, savant.

humanitarian *(SYN.)* benefactor, philanthropist.

humanitarianism *(SYN.)* goodwill, beneficence, philanthropy, welfarism, humanism.

humanity *(SYN.)* generosity, magnanimity, tenderness, altruism, beneficence, kindness, charity, philanthropy. *(ANT.)* *selfishness, unkindness, cruelty, inhumanity.*

humble *(SYN.)* modest, crush, mortify, simple, shame, subdue, meek, abase, break, plain, submissive, compliant, unpretentious, unassuming, abash,

unostentatious, lowly, polite, courteous, unpretending, degrade. *(ANT.)* *praise, arrogant, exalt, illustrious, boastful, honor, elevate.*

humbly *(SYN.)* deferentially, meekly, respectfully, unassumingly, diffidently, modestly, subserviently, submissively. *(ANT.)* *insolently, proudly, grandly, arrogantly.*

humbug *(SYN.)* drivel, gammon, bosh, nonsense, rubbish, inanity.

humdrum *(SYN.)* commonplace, prosy, mundane, insipid, tedious, routine, dull, boring. *(ANT.)* *interesting, stimulating, arresting, striking, exciting.*

humid *(SYN.)* moist, damp, misty, muggy, wet, watery, vaporous. *(ANT.)* *parched, dry, desiccated.*

humiliate *(SYN.)* corrupt, defile, depress, pervert, abase, degrade, disgrace, adulterate, humble, shame, lower, impair, deprave, depress. *(ANT.)* *restore, raise, enhance, improve, vitalize.*

humiliation *(SYN.)* chagrin, dishonor, ignominy, scandal, abasement, mortification, disrepute, odium, disgrace, shame. *(ANT.)* *honor, praise, glory, dignity, renown.*

humor *(SYN.)* jocularity, wit, temperament, sarcasm, irony, joking, amusement, facetiousness, joke, disposition, waggery, fun, clowning, satire, mood. *(ANT.)* *sorrow, gravity, seriousness.*

humorous *(SYN.)* funny, ludicrous, witty, curious, queer, amusing, comical, farcical, laughable, droll. *(ANT.)* *sober, unfunny, melancholy, serious, sad, solemn.*

hunger *(SYN.)* desire, longing, inclination, relish, stomach, zest, craving, liking, passion. *(ANT.)* *satiety, repugnance, disgust, distaste, renunciation.*

hungry *(SYN.)* famished, thirsting, craving, avid, longing, starved, ravenous. *(ANT.)* *gorged, satisfied, full, sated.*

hunt *(SYN.)* pursuit, investigation, examination, inquiry, pursue, track. *(ANT.)* *cession, abandonment.*

hurl *(SYN.)* throw, cast, propel, fling, toss, pitch, thrust. *(ANT.)* *retain, pull, draw, haul, hold.*

hurried *(SYN.)* rushed, hasty, swift, headlong, slipshod, careless, impulsive, superficial. *(ANT.)* *deliberate, slow,

dilatory, thorough, prolonged.*

hurry *(SYN.)* quicken, speed, ado, rush, accelerate, run, hasten, race, urge, bustle, expedite, precipitate. *(ANT.)* *retard, tarry, hinder, linger, dawdle, delay.*

hurt *(SYN.)* damage, harm, grievance, detriment, pain, injustice, injure, abuse, distress, disfigured, mar, afflict, spoil, affront, insult. *(ANT.)* *improvement, repair, compliment, help, praise, benefit.*

hurtle *(SYN.)* charge, collide, rush, crash, lunge, bump, fling.

husband *(SYN.)* spouse, mate.

hush *(SYN.)* quiet, silence, still.

husk *(SYN.)* shell, hull, pod, skin, covering, crust, bark.

husky *(SYN.)* strong, brawny, strapping, muscular. *(ANT.)* *feeble, weak.*

hustle *(SYN.)* hasten, run, race, hurry, speed.

hut *(SYN.)* cottage, shanty, cabin, shed.

hutch *(SYN.)* box, chest, locker, trunk, coffer, bin.

hybrid *(SYN.)* mule, mixture, crossbreed, cross, mongrel, mutt.

hygiene *(SYN.)* cleanliness, sanitation, health, prophylaxis.

hygienic *(SYN.)* robust, strong, clean, well, wholesome, hale, healthy, sound. *(ANT.)* *frail, noxious, infirm, delicate, diseased.*

hyperbole *(SYN.)* puffery, exaggeration, embellishment, overstatement.

hypercritical *(SYN.)* faultfinding, captious, censorious, finicky, exacting, carping, querulous, nagging, finical, hairsplitting. *(ANT.)* *lax, easygoing, indulgent, lenient, tolerant.*

hypnotic *(SYN.)* soothing, opiate, sedative, soporific, entrancing, spellbinding, arresting, charming.

hypnotize *(SYN.)* entrance, dazzle, mesmerize, fascinate, spellbind.

hypocrisy *(SYN.)* pretense, deceit, dissembling, fakery, feigning, sanctimony, cant. *(ANT.)* *openness, candor, truth, directness, honesty, frankness.*

hypocrite *(SYN.)* cheat, deceiver, pretender, dissembler, fake, fraud.

hypothesis *(SYN.)* law, theory, supposition, conjecture. *(ANT.)* *proof, fact, certainty.*

hypothetical *(SYN.)*

conjectural, speculative, theoretical. *(ANT.)* *actual.*

I

idea *(SYN.)* conception, image, opinion, sentiment, concept, fancy, notion, thought, impression. *(ANT.)* *thing, matter, entity, object, substance.*

ideal *(SYN.)* imaginary, supreme, unreal, visionary, perfect, faultless, fancied, exemplary, utopian. *(ANT.)* *imperfect, actual, material, real, faulty.*

idealistic *(SYN.)* extravagant, dreamy, fantastic, fanciful, ideal, maudlin, imaginative, mawkish, sentimental, poetic, picturesque. *(ANT.)* *practical, literal, factual, prosaic.*

identify *(SYN.)* recollect, apprehend, perceive, remember, confess, acknowledge, name, describe, classify. *(ANT.)* *ignore, forget, overlook, renounce, disown, repudiate.*

identity *(SYN.)* uniqueness, personality, character, individuality.

ideology *(SYN.)* credo, principles, belief.

idiom *(SYN.)* language, speech, vernacular, lingo, dialect, jargon, slang, tongue. *(ANT.)* *babble, gibberish, drivel, nonsense.*

idiot *(SYN.)* buffoon, harlequin, dolt, jester, dunce, blockhead, imbecile, numbskull, simpleton, oaf, nincompoop, fool, moron. *(ANT.)* *philosopher, genius, scholar, sage.*

idiotic *(SYN.)* asinine, absurd, brainless, irrational, crazy, nonsensical, senseless, preposterous, silly, ridiculous, simple, stupid, foolish, inane, moronic, half-witted, simpleminded, dimwitted. *(ANT.)* *prudent, wise, sagacious, judicious, sane, intelligent, bright, brilliant, smart.*

idle *(SYN.)* unemployed, dormant, lazy, inactive, unoccupied, indolent, slothful, inert, unused. *(ANT.)* *occupied, working, employed, active, industrious, busy, engaged.*

idolize *(SYN.)* revere, worship, adore. *(ANT.)* *despise.*

ignoble *(SYN.)* dishonorable, ignominious, lowly, menial, vile, sordid, vulgar, abject, base, despicable, groveling, mean. *(ANT.)* *righteous, lofty, honored, esteemed, noble, exalted.*

imperative

ignominious *(SYN.)* contemptible, abject, despicable, groveling, dishonorable, ignoble, lowly, low, menial, mean, sordid, servile, vulgar, vile. *(ANT.)* lofty, noble, esteemed, righteous, exalted.

ignorant *(SYN.)* uneducated, untaught, uncultured, illiterate, uninformed, unlearned, unlettered, untrained, unaware, unmindful. *(ANT.)* cultured, literate, educated, erudite, informed, cultivated, schooled, learned, lettered.

ignore *(SYN.)* omit, slight, disregard, overlook, neglect, skip. *(ANT.)* notice, regard, include.

ill *(SYN.)* diseased, ailing, indisposed, morbid, infirm, unwell, sick, unhealthy. *(ANT.)* robust, healthy, well, sound, fit.

ill-advised *(SYN.)* injudicious, ill-considered, imprudent.

ill-at-ease *(SYN.)* nervous, uncomfortable, uneasy. *(ANT.)* comfortable.

illegal *(SYN.)* prohibited, unlawful, criminal, illicit, outlawed, illegitimate. *(ANT.)* permitted, lawful, honest, legal, legitimate.

illiberal *(SYN.)* fanatical, bigoted, intolerant, narrowminded, dogmatic, prejudiced. *(ANT.)* progressive, liberal, radical.

illicit *(SYN.)* illegitimate, criminal, outlawed, unlawful, prohibited, illegal, unauthorized. *(ANT.)* legal, honest, permitted, lawful, licit.

ill-natured *(SYN.)* crabby, cranky, grouchy, cross, irascible.

illness *(SYN.)* complaint, infirmity, ailment, disorder, malady, sickness. *(ANT.)* healthiness, health, soundness, vigor.

illogical *(SYN.)* absurd, irrational, preposterous.

ill-tempered *(SYN.)* crabby, cranky, cross, grouchy.

ill-treated *(SYN.)* harmed, mistreated, abused, maltreated.

illuminate *(SYN.)* enlighten, clarify, irradiate, illustrate, light, lighten, explain, interpret, elucidate, brighten, illumine. *(ANT.)* obscure, confuse, darken, obfuscate, shadow, complicate.

ill-use *(SYN.)* defame, revile, vilify, misemploy, disparage, abuse, traduce, asperse, misapply, misuse. *(ANT.)* protect, cherish, respect, honor, praise.

illusion *(SYN.)* hallucination, vision, phantom, delusion, fantasy, dream, mirage. *(ANT.)* substance, actuality, reality.

illusive *(SYN.)* fallacious, delusive, false, specious, misleading, deceptive, deceitful, delusory. *(ANT.)* real, truthful, authentic, genuine, honest.

illustrate *(SYN.)* decorate, illuminate, adorn, show, picture, embellish, demonstrate.

illustration *(SYN.)* likeness, painting, picture, print, scene, sketch, view, engraving, drawing, panorama, photograph, cinema, etching, effigy, film, appearance, portrayal, resemblance, image, portrait.

illustrator *(SYN.)* painter, artist.

illustrious *(SYN.)* prominent, eminent, renowned, famed, great, vital, elevated, majestic, noble, excellent, dignified, big, gigantic, enormous, immense, huge, vast, large, countless, numerous, celebrated, critical, momentous, august, weighty, grand, fine, magnificent, serious, important. *(ANT.)* menial, common, minute, diminutive, small, obscure, ordinary, little.

image *(SYN.)* reflection, likeness, idea, representation, notion, picture, conception.

imaginary *(SYN.)* fanciful, fantastic, unreal, whimsical. *(ANT.)* actual, real.

imagination *(SYN.)* creation, invention, fancy, notion, conception, fantasy, idea.

imaginative *(SYN.)* inventive, poetical, fanciful, clever, creative, mystical, visionary. *(ANT.)* prosaic, dull, unromantic, literal.

imagine *(SYN.)* assume, surmise, suppose, conceive, dream, pretend, conjecture, fancy, opine, envisage, think, envision, guess, picture.

imbecile *(SYN.)* idiot, numbskull, simpleton, blockhead, dolt, dunce, jester, buffoon, harlequin, nincompoop, clown, fool, oaf. *(ANT.)* scholar, genius, philosopher, sage.

imbibe *(SYN.)* absorb, consume, assimilate, engulf, engage, occupy, engross. *(ANT.)* dispense, discharge, emit.

imitate *(SYN.)* duplicate, mimic, follow, reproduce, mock, ape, counterfeit, copy, simulate, impersonate. *(ANT.)* invent, distort, alter, diverge.

imitation *(SYN.)* replica, reproduction, copy, duplicate, facsimile, transcript, exemplar. *(ANT.)* prototype, original.

immaculate *(SYN.)* clean, spotless, unblemished. *(ANT.)* dirty.

immature *(SYN.)* young, boyish, childish, youthful, childlike, puerile, girlish, juvenile, callow. *(ANT.)* old, senile, aged, elderly, mature.

immeasurable *(SYN.)* unlimited, endless, eternal, immense, interminable, unbounded, boundless, illimitable, infinite. *(ANT.)* limited, confined, bounded, finite, circumscribed.

immediate *(SYN.)* present, instant, instantaneous, near, close, next, prompt, direct. *(ANT.)* distant, future.

immediately *(SYN.)* now, presently, instantly, promptly, straightway, directly, instantaneously, forthwith. *(ANT.)* sometime, hereafter, later, shortly, distantly.

immense *(SYN.)* enormous, large, gigantic, huge, colossal, elephantine, great, gargantuan, vast. *(ANT.)* small, diminutive, little, minuscule, minute, petite, tiny.

immensity *(SYN.)* hugeness, enormousness, vastness.

immerse *(SYN.)* plunge, dip, dunk, sink, submerge, engage, absorb, engross, douse. *(ANT.)* uplift, elevate, recover.

immigration *(SYN.)* settlement, colonization. *(ANT.)* exodus, emigration.

imminent *(SYN.)* nigh, impending, overhanging, approaching, menacing, threatening. *(ANT.)* retreating, afar, distant, improbable, remote.

immoderation *(SYN.)* profusion, surplus, extravagance, excess, intemperance, superabundance. *(ANT.)* lack, want, deficiency, dearth, paucity.

immoral *(SYN.)* sinful, wicked, corrupt, bad, indecent, profligate, unprincipled, antisocial, dissolute. *(ANT.)* pure, high-minded, chaste, virtuous, noble.

immortal *(SYN.)* infinite, eternal, timeless, undying, perpetual, ceaseless, endless, deathless, everlasting. *(ANT.)* mortal, transient, finite, ephemeral, temporal.

immune *(SYN.)* easy, open, autonomous, unobstructed, free, emancipated, clear, independent, unrestricted, exempt, liberated, familiar, loose, unconfined, frank, unfastened, careless, freed. *(ANT.)* confined, impeded, restricted, subject.

immutable *(SYN.)* constant, faithful, invariant, persistent, unchanging, unalterable, continual, ceaseless, enduring, fixed, permanent, abiding, perpetual, unwavering. *(ANT.)* mutable, vacillating, wavering, fickle.

impact *(SYN.)* striking, contact, collision.

impair *(SYN.)* harm, injure, spoil, deface, destroy, hurt, damage, mar. *(ANT.)* repair, mend, ameliorate, enhance, benefit.

impart *(SYN.)* convey, disclose, inform, tell, reveal, transmit, notify, confer, divulge, communicate, relate. *(ANT.)* hide, withhold, conceal.

impartial *(SYN.)* unbiased, just, honest, fair, reasonable, equitable. *(ANT.)* fraudulent, dishonorable, partial.

impartiality *(SYN.)* indifference, unconcern, neutrality, disinterestedness, apathy, insensibility. *(ANT.)* passion, ardor, fervor.

impasse *(SYN.)* standstill, deadlock, stalemate.

impede *(SYN.)* hamper, hinder, retard, thwart, check, encumber, interrupt, bar, clog, delay, obstruct, block, frustrate, restrain, stop. *(ANT.)* assist, promote, help, advance, further.

impediment *(SYN.)* barrier, bar, block, difficulty, check, hindrance, snag, obstruction. *(ANT.)* assistance, help, aid.

impel *(SYN.)* oblige, enforce, drive, coerce, force, constrain. *(ANT.)* induce, prevent, convince, persuade.

impending *(SYN.)* imminent, nigh, threatening, overhanging, approaching, menacing. *(ANT.)* remote, improbable, afar, distant, retreating.

impenetrable *(SYN.)* rigid, tough, harsh, strict, unfeeling, rigorous, intricate, arduous, penetrable, cruel, difficult, severe, stem, firm, hard, compact. *(ANT.)* soft, simple, gentle, tender, brittle, fluid, flabby, elastic, lenient, easy, effortless.

imperative *(SYN.)* critical, instant, important, necessary, serious, urgent, cogent, compelling, crucial, pressing, impelling, importunate, exigent, insistent. *(ANT.)* trivial, insignificant, unimportant, petty.

51

imperceptible (SYN.) invisible, indiscernible, unseen, indistinguishable. (ANT.) seen, evident, visible, perceptible.

imperfection (SYN.) flaw, shortcoming, vice, defect, blemish, failure, mistake, omission, fault, error. (ANT.) correctness, perfection, completeness.

imperil (SYN.) jeopardize, risk, endanger, hazard, risk. (ANT.) guard, insure.

impersonal (SYN.) objective, detached, disinterested. (ANT.) personal.

impersonate (SYN.) mock, simulate, imitate, ape, counterfeit, mimic, copy, duplicate. (ANT.) alter, invent, diverge, distort.

impertinence (SYN.) impudence, presumption, sauciness, effrontery, audacity, rudeness, assurance, boldness, insolence. (ANT.) truckling, politeness, diffidence, subservience.

impertinent (SYN.) rude, offensive, insolent, disrespectful, arrogant, brazen, impudent, insulting, contemptuous, abusive. (ANT.) polite, respectful, considerate, courteous.

impetuous (SYN.) rash, heedless, quick, hasty, careless, passionate, impulsive. (ANT.) cautious, reasoning, careful, prudent, thoughtful, calculating.

implicate (SYN.) reproach, accuse, blame, involve, upbraid, condemn, incriminate, rebuke, censure. (ANT.) exonerate, absolve.

implore (SYN.) beg, pray, request, solicit, crave, entreat, beseech, ask, importune, supplicate, adjure, appeal, petition. (ANT.) give, cede, bestow, favor, grant.

imply (SYN.) mean, involve, suggest, connote, hint, mention, indicate, insinuate, signify. (ANT.) state, assert, declare, express.

impolite (SYN.) rude, unpolished, impudent, boorish, blunt, discourteous, rough, saucy, surly, savage, insolent, gruff, uncivil, coarse, ignorant, crude, illiterate, raw, primitive, vulgar, untaught. (ANT.) genteel, courteous, courtly, dignified, polite, stately, noble, civil.

import (SYN.) influence, significance, stress, emphasis, importance, value, weight. (ANT.) triviality, insignificance.

important (SYN.) critical, grave, influential, momentous, well-known, pressing, relevant, prominent, primary, essential, weighty, material, considerable, famous, principle, famed, sequential, notable, significant, illustrious, decisive. (ANT.) unimportant, trifling, petty, trivial, insignificant, secondary, anonymous, irrelevant.

impose (SYN.) levy, require, demand.

imposing (SYN.) lofty, noble, majestic, magnificent, august, dignified, grandiose, high, grand, impressive, pompous, stately. (ANT.) ordinary, undignified, humble, common, lowly.

imposition (SYN.) load, onus, burden.

impossible (SYN.) preposterous.

impregnable (SYN.) safe, invulnerable, secure, unassailable. (ANT.) vulnerable.

impress (SYN.) awe, emboss, affect, mark, imprint, indent, influence.

impression (SYN.) influence, indentation, feeling, opinion, mark, effect, depression, guess, thought, belief, dent, sensibility. (ANT.) fact, insensibility.

impressive (SYN.) arresting, moving, remarkable, splendid, thrilling, striking, majestic, grandiose, imposing, commanding, affecting, exciting, touching, stirring. (ANT.) regular, unimpressive, commonplace.

impromptu (SYN.) casual, unprepared, offhand, extemporaneous.

improper (SYN.) unfit, unsuitable, inappropriate, naughty, indecent, unbecoming. (ANT.) fitting, proper, appropriate.

improve (SYN.) better, reform, refine, ameliorate, amend, help, upgrade, rectify. (ANT.) debase, vitiate, impair, corrupt, damage.

improvement (SYN.) growth, advance, progress, betterment, development, advancement, progression. (ANT.) relapse, regression, decline, retrogression, delay.

imprudent (SYN.) indiscreet, thoughtless, desultory, lax, neglectful, remiss, careless, inattentive, heedless, inconsiderate, reckless, ill-advised, irresponsible. (ANT.) careful, meticulous, accurate.

impudence (SYN.) boldness, insolence, rudeness, sauciness, assurance, effrontery, impertinence, presumption, audacity. (ANT.) politeness, truckling, subservience, diffidence.

impudent (SYN.) forward, rude, abrupt, prominent, striking, bold, fresh, impertinent, insolent, pushy, insulting, brazen. (ANT.) bashful, flinching, polite, courteous, cowardly, retiring, timid.

impulse (SYN.) hunch, whim, fancy, urge, caprice, surge, pulse.

impulsive (SYN.) passionate, rash, spontaneous, heedless, careless, hasty, quick, impetuous. (ANT.) reasoning, calculating, careful, prudent, cautious.

impure (SYN.) dishonest, spoiled, tainted, contaminated, debased, corrupt, profligate, unsound, putrid, corrupted, crooked, depraved, vitiated, venal.

imputation (SYN.) diary, incrimination, arraignment, indictment. (ANT.) exoneration, pardon, exculpation.

inability (SYN.) incompetence, incapacity, handicap, disability, impotence, weakness. (ANT.) power, strength, ability, capability.

inaccurate (SYN.) false, incorrect, mistaken, untrue, askew, wrong, awry, erroneous, fallacious, imprecise, faulty, amiss. (ANT.) right, accurate, true, correct.

inactive (SYN.) lazy, unemployed, indolent, motionless, still, inert, dormant, idle, unoccupied. (ANT.) employed, working, active, industrious, occupied.

inadequate (SYN.) insufficient, lacking, short, incomplete, defective, scanty. (ANT.) satisfactory, enough, adequate, ample, sufficient.

inadvertent (SYN.) careless, negligent, unthinking, thoughtless.

inane (SYN.) trite, insipid, banal, absurd, silly, commonplace, vapid, foolish, stupid, hackneyed. (ANT.) stimulating, novel, fresh, original, striking.

inanimate (SYN.) deceased, spiritless, lifeless, gone, dull, mineral, departed, dead, insensible, vegetable, unconscious. (ANT.) living, stirring, alive, animate.

inattentive (SYN.) absentminded, distracted, abstracted, preoccupied. (ANT.) watchful, attending, attentive.

inaugurate (SYN.) commence, begin, open, originate, start, arise, launch, enter, initiate. (ANT.) end, terminate, close, complete, finish.

incense (SYN.) anger, enrage, infuriate.

incentive (SYN.) impulse, stimulus, inducement, encouragement. (ANT.) discouragement.

inception (SYN.) origin, start, source, opening, beginning, outset, commencement. (ANT.) end, termination, close, completion, consummation.

incessant (SYN.) perennial, uninterrupted, continual, ceaseless, continuous, unremitting, eternal, constant, unceasing, unending, perpetual, everlasting. (ANT.) rare, occasional, periodic, interrupted.

incident (SYN.) happening, situation, occurrence, circumstance, condition, event.

incidental (SYN.) casual, contingent, trivial, undesigned, chance, fortuitous, accidental, secondary, unimportant, unintended. (ANT.) intended, fundamental, planned, calculated, willed, decreed.

incidentally (SYN.) by the way.

incinerate (SYN.) sear, char, blaze, scald, singe, consume, scorch, burn. (ANT.) quench, put out, extinguish.

incisive (SYN.) neat, succinct, terse, brief, compact, condensed, neat, summary, concise. (ANT.) wordy, prolix, verbose, lengthy.

incite (SYN.) goad, provoke, urge, arouse, encourage, cause, stimulate, induce, instigate, foment. (ANT.) quiet, bore, pacify, soothe.

inclination (SYN.) bent, preference, desire, slope, affection, bent, bias, disposition, bending, penchant, incline, attachment, predisposition, predication, tendency, prejudice, slant, lean, leaning. (ANT.) nonchalance, apathy, distaste, aversion, reluctance, disinclination, uprightness, repugnance.

incline (SYN.) slope, nod, lean.

include (SYN.) contain, hold, accommodate, embody, encompass, involve, comprise, embrace. (ANT.) omit, exclude.

income (SYN.) earnings, salary, wages, revenue, pay,

return, receipts.

incomparable *(SYN.)* peerless, matchless, unequaled.

incompetency *(SYN.)* inability, weakness, handicap, impotence, disability, incapacity. *(ANT.) strength, ability, power, capability.*

incomprehensible *(SYN.)* unintelligible, indecipherable.

inconceivable *(SYN.)* unbelievable, unimaginable, impossible. *(ANT.) possible, believable.*

incongruous *(SYN.)* inconsistent, contrary, incompatible, irreconcilable, contradictory, unsteady, wavering, paradoxical, vacillating, discrepant, illogical. *(ANT.) consistent, compatible, correspondent.*

inconsiderate *(SYN.)* unthinking, careless, unthoughtful, unmindful. *(ANT.) thoughtful, considerate, kind.*

inconsistency *(SYN.)* discord, variance, contention, conflict, controversy, interference. *(ANT.) harmony, concord, amity, consonance.*

inconsistent *(SYN.)* fickle, wavering, variable, changeable, contrary, unstable, illogical, contradictory, irreconcilable, discrepant, paradoxical, incompatible, self-contradictory, incongruous, unsteady, fitful, shifting. *(ANT.) unchanging, steady, logical, stable, uniform, constant.*

inconspicuous *(SYN.)* retiring, unnoticed, unostentatious. *(ANT.) obvious, conspicuous.*

inconstant *(SYN.)* fickle, shifting, changeable, fitful, vacillating, unstable, wavering. *(ANT.) stable, constant, steady, uniform, unchanging.*

inconvenient *(SYN.)* awkward, inappropriate, untimely, troublesome. *(ANT.) handy, convenient.*

incorrect *(SYN.)* mistaken, wrong, erroneous, inaccurate. *(ANT.) proper, accurate, suitable.*

increase *(SYN.)* amplify, enlarge, grow, magnify, multiply, augment, enhance, expand, intensify, swell, raise, greaten, prolong, broaden, lengthen, expansion, accrue, extend, heighten. *(ANT.) diminish, reduce, atrophy, shrink, shrinkage, decrease, lessen, lessen, contract.*

incredible *(SYN.)* improbable, unbelievable. *(ANT.)* plausible, credible, believable.

incriminate *(SYN.)* charge, accuse, indict, arraign, censure. *(ANT.) release, exonerate, acquit, absolve, vindicate.*

incrimination *(SYN.)* imputation, indictment, accusation, charge, arraignment. *(ANT.) exoneration, pardon, exculpation.*

indebted *(SYN.)* obliged, grateful, beholden, thankful, appreciative. *(ANT.) unappreciative, thankless.*

indecent *(SYN.)* impure, obscene, pornographic, coarse, dirty, filthy, smutty, gross, disgusting. *(ANT.) modest, refined, decent.*

indeed *(SYN.)* truthfully, really, honestly, surely.

indefinite *(SYN.)* unsure, uncertain, vague, confused, unsettled, confusing. *(ANT.) decided, definite, equivocal.*

independence *(SYN.)* liberation, privilege, freedom, immunity, familiarity, liberty, exemption, license. *(ANT.) necessity, constraint, compulsion, reliance, dependence, bondage, servitude.*

independent *(SYN.)* free, unrestrained, voluntary, autonomous, self-reliant, uncontrolled, unrestricted. *(ANT.) enslaved, contingent, dependent, restricted.*

indestructible *(SYN.)* enduring, lasting, permanent, unchangeable, abiding, constant, fixed, stable, changeless. *(ANT.) unstable, temporary, transitory, ephemeral.*

indicate *(SYN.)* imply, denote, signify, specify, intimate, designate, symbolize, show, manifest, disclose, mean, reveal. *(ANT.) mislead, distract, conceal, falsify.*

indication *(SYN.)* proof, emblem, omen, sign, symbol, token, mark, portent, gesture, signal.

indict *(SYN.)* charge, accuse, incriminate, censure, arraign. *(ANT.) acquit, vindicate, absolve, exonerate.*

indictment *(SYN.)* incrimination, arraignment, imputation, charge. *(ANT.) pardon, exoneration, exculpation.*

indifference *(SYN.)* unconcern, apathy, impartiality, disinterestedness, insensibility, neutrality. *(ANT.) ardor, passion, affection, fervor.*

indifferent *(SYN.)* uncaring, insensitive, cool, unconcerned. *(ANT.) caring, concerned, earnest.*

indigence *(SYN.)* necessity, destitution, poverty, want, need, privation, penury. *(ANT.) wealth, abundance, plenty, riches, affluence.*

indigenous *(SYN.)* inborn, native, inherent, domestic, aboriginal, plenty, endemic, innate, natural.

indigent *(SYN.)* destitute, covetous, poor, lacking, requiring, wanting, needy, craving.

indignant *(SYN.)* irritated, irate, angry, aroused, exasperated. *(ANT.) calm, serene, content.*

indignation *(SYN.)* ire, petulance, passion, choler, anger, wrath, temper, irritation, exasperation, animosity, resentment, rage. *(ANT.) self-control, peace, forbearance, patience.*

indignity *(SYN.)* insolence, insult, abuse, affront, offense. *(ANT.) homage, apology.*

indirect *(SYN.)* winding, crooked, devious, roundabout, cunning, tricky, tortuous, circuitous, distorted, erratic, swerving. *(ANT.) straightforward, direct, straight, honest.*

indiscretion *(SYN.)* imprudence, folly, absurdity, extravagance. *(ANT.) prudence, sense, wisdom, reasonableness, judgment.*

indispensable *(SYN.)* necessary, fundamental, basic, essential, important, intrinsic, vital. *(ANT.) optional, expendable, peripheral, extrinsic.*

indistinct *(SYN.)* cloudy, dark, mysterious, vague, blurry, ambiguous, cryptic, dim, obscure, enigmatic, abstruse, hazy, blurred, unintelligible. *(ANT.) clear, lucid, bright, distinct.*

indistinguishable *(SYN.)* identical, like, coincident, equal, same, equivalent. *(ANT.) dissimilar, opposed, contrary, disparate, distinct.*

individual *(SYN.)* singular, specific, unique, distinctive, single, particular, undivided, human, apart, marked, person, different, special, separate. *(ANT.) universal, common, general, ordinary.*

individuality *(SYN.)* symbol, description, mark, kind, character, repute, class, standing, sort, nature, disposition, reputation, sign.

indolent *(SYN.)* slothful, lazy, idle, inactive, slow, sluggish, torpid, supine, inert. *(ANT.) diligent, active, assiduous, vigorous, zesty, alert.*

indomitable *(SYN.)* insurmountable, unconquerable, invulnerable, impregnable, unassailable. *(ANT.) weak, puny, powerless, vulnerable.*

induce *(SYN.)* evoke, cause, influence, persuade, effect, make, originate, prompt, incite, create.

inducement *(SYN.)* incentive, motive, purpose, stimulus, reason, impulse, cause, principle, spur, incitement. *(ANT.) result, attempt, action, effort, deed.*

induct *(SYN.)* instate, establish, install. *(ANT.) eject, oust.*

indulge *(SYN.)* humor, satisfy, gratify.

indulgent *(SYN.)* obliging, pampering, tolerant, easy.

indurate *(SYN.)* impenitent, hard, insensible, tough, obdurate, callous, unfeeling. *(ANT.) soft, compassionate, tender, sensitive.*

industrious *(SYN.)* hardworking, perseverant, busy, active, diligent, assiduous, careful, patient. *(ANT.) unconcerned, indifferent, lethargic, careless, apathetic, lazy, indolent, shiftless.*

inebriated *(SYN.)* drunk, tight, drunken, intoxicated, tipsy. *(ANT.) sober, clearheaded, temperate.*

ineffective *(SYN.)* pliant, tender, vague, wavering, defenseless, weak, inadequate, poor, irresolute, frail, decrepit, delicate, vacillating, assailable, exposed, vulnerable. *(ANT.) sturdy, robust, potent, powerful.*

inept *(SYN.)* clumsy, awkward, improper, inappropriate. *(ANT.) adroit, dexterous, adept, appropriate, proper, apt, fitting.*

inequity *(SYN.)* wrong, injustice, unfairness, grievance, injury. *(ANT.) righteousness, lawfulness, equity, justice.*

inert *(SYN.)* lazy, dormant, slothful, inactive, idle, indolent, motionless, unmoving, fixed, static. *(ANT.) working, active, industrious, occupied.*

inertia *(SYN.)* indolence, torpidity, idleness, slothfulness, sluggishness. *(ANT.) assiduousness, activity, alertness, diligence.*

inevitable *(SYN.)* definite, fixed, positive, sure, undeniable, indubitable, certain, assured, unquestionable, secure. *(ANT.) uncertain, probable, doubtful, questionable.*

inexpensive *(SYN.)* low-priced, cheap, inferior, mean,

beggarly, common, poor, shabby, modest, economical. (*ANT.*) *expensive, costly, dear.*

inexperienced (*SYN.*) naive, untrained, uninformed, green. (*ANT.*) *experienced, skilled, sophisticated, trained, seasoned.*

inexplicable (*SYN.*) hidden, mysterious, obscure, secret, dark, cryptic, enigmatical, incomprehensible, occult, recondite, inscrutable, dim. (*ANT.*) *plain, simple, clear, obvious, explained.*

infamous (*SYN.*) shocking, shameful, scandalous.

infantile (*SYN.*) babyish, naive, immature, childish. (*ANT.*) *mature, grownup, adult.*

infect (*SYN.*) pollute, poison, contaminate, defile, sully, taint. (*ANT.*) *purify, disinfect.*

infection (*SYN.*) virus, poison, ailment, disease, pollution, pest, germ, taint, contamination, contagion.

infectious (*SYN.*) contagious, virulent, catching, communicable, pestilential, transferable. (*ANT.*) *noncommunicable, hygienic, healthful.*

infer (*SYN.*) understand, deduce, extract.

inference (*SYN.*) consequence, result, conclusion, corollary, judgment, deduction. (*ANT.*) *preconception, foreknowledge, assumption, presupposition.*

inferior (*SYN.*) secondary, lower, poorer, minor, subordinate, mediocre. (*ANT.*) *greater, superior, better, higher.*

infinite (*SYN.*) immeasurable, interminable, unlimited, unbounded, eternal, boundless, illimitable, immense, endless, vast, innumerable, numberless, limitless. (*ANT.*) *confined, limited, bounded, circumscribed, finite.*

infinitesimal (*SYN.*) minute, microscopic, tiny, submicroscopic. (*ANT.*) *gigantic, huge, enormous.*

infirm (*SYN.*) feeble, impaired, decrepit, forceless, languid, puny, powerless, enervated, weak, exhausted. (*ANT.*) *stout, vigorous, forceful, lusty, strong.*

infirmity (*SYN.*) disease, illness, malady, ailment, sickness, disorder, complaint. (*ANT.*) *soundness, health, vigor, healthiness.*

inflame (*SYN.*) fire, incite, excite, arouse. (*ANT.*) *soothe, calm.*

inflammation (*SYN.*) infection, soreness, irritation.

inflammatory (*SYN.*) instigating, inciting, provocative.

inflate (*SYN.*) expand, swell, distend. (*ANT.*) *collapse, deflate.*

inflexible (*SYN.*) firm, stubborn, headstrong, immovable, uncompromising, dogged, contumacious, determined, obstinate, rigid, unbending, unyielding, steadfast. (*ANT.*) *submissive, compliant, docile, amenable, yielding, flexible, giving, elastic.*

inflict (*SYN.*) deliver, deal, give, impose, apply.

influence (*SYN.*) weight, control, effect, sway.

influenced (*SYN.*) sway, affect, bias, control, actuate, impel, stir, incite.

influential (*SYN.*) important, weighty, prominent, significant, critical, decisive, momentous, relevant, material, pressing, consequential, grave. (*ANT.*) *petty, irrelevant, mean, trivial, insignificant.*

inform (*SYN.*) apprise, instruct, tell, notify, advise, acquaint, enlighten, impart, warn, teach, advise, relate. (*ANT.*) *delude, mislead, distract, conceal.*

informal (*SYN.*) simple, easy, natural, unofficial, familiar. (*ANT.*) *formal, distant, reserved, proper.*

informality (*SYN.*) friendship, frankness, liberty, acquaintance, sociability, intimacy, unreserved. (*ANT.*) *presumption, constraint, reserve, distance, haughtiness.*

information (*SYN.*) knowledge, data, intelligence, facts.

informative (*SYN.*) educational, enlightening, instructive.

informer (*SYN.*) tattler, traitor, betrayer.

infrequent (*SYN.*) unusual, rare, occasional, strange. (*ANT.*) *commonplace, abundant, usual, ordinary, customary, frequent, numerous.*

ingenious (*SYN.*) clever, skillful, talented, adroit, dexterous, quick-witted, bright, smart, witty, sharp, apt, resourceful, imaginative, inventive, creative. (*ANT.*) *dull, slow, awkward, bungling, unskilled, stupid.*

ingenuity (*SYN.*) cunning, inventiveness, resourcefulness, aptitude, faculty, cleverness, ingenuousness. (*ANT.*) *ineptitude, clumsiness, dullness, stupidity.*

ingenuous (*SYN.*) open,

sincere, honest, candid, straightforward, plain, frank, truthful, free, naive, simple, innocent, unsophisticated. (*ANT.*) *scheming, sly, contrived, wily.*

ingredient (*SYN.*) component, element, constituent.

inhabit (*SYN.*) fill, possess, absorb, dwell, occupy, live. (*ANT.*) *relinquish, abandon, release.*

inherent (*SYN.*) innate, native, congenital, intrinsic, inborn, inbred, natural, real. (*ANT.*) *extraneous, acquired, external, extrinsic.*

inhibit (*SYN.*) curb, constrain, hold back, restrain, bridle, hinder, repress, suppress, stop, limit. (*ANT.*) *loosen, aid, incite, encourage.*

inhuman (*SYN.*) merciless, cruel, brutal, ferocious, savage, ruthless, malignant, barbarous, barbaric, bestial. (*ANT.*) *kind, benevolent, forbearing, gentle, compassionate, merciful, humane.*

inimical (*SYN.*) hostile, warlike, adverse, antagonistic, opposed, unfriendly. (*ANT.*) *favorable, amicable, cordial.*

iniquitous (*SYN.*) baleful, immoral, pernicious, sinful, wicked, base, bad, evil, noxious, unsound, villainous, unwholesome. (*ANT.*) *moral, good, excellent, honorable, reputable.*

iniquity (*SYN.*) injustice, wrong, grievance, unfairness, injury. (*ANT.*) *lawful, equity, righteousness, justice.*

initial (*SYN.*) original, first, prime, beginning, earliest, pristine, chief, primeval, primary, foremost, basic, elementary. (*ANT.*) *latest, subordinate, last, least, hindmost, final, terminal.*

initiate (*SYN.*) institute, enter, arise, inaugurate, commence, originate, start, open, begin. (*ANT.*) *terminate, complete, end, finish, close, stop.*

initiative (*SYN.*) enthusiasm, energy, vigor, enterprise.

injure (*SYN.*) harm, wound, abuse, dishonor, damage, hurt, impair, spoil, disfigure, affront, insult, mar. (*ANT.*) *praise, ameliorate, help, preserve, compliment, benefit.*

injurious (*SYN.*) detrimental, harmful, mischievous, damaging, hurtful, deleterious, harmful, destructive. (*ANT.*) *profitable, helpful, advantageous, salutary, beneficial, useful.*

injury (*SYN.*) harm, detriment, damage, injustice,

wrong, prejudice, grievance, mischief. (*ANT.*) *repair, benefit, improvement.*

injustice (*SYN.*) unfairness, grievance, iniquity, wrong, injury. (*ANT.*) *righteousness, justice, equity, lawfulness.*

inmate (*SYN.*) patient, prisoner.

inn (*SYN.*) motel, lodge, hotel.

innate (*SYN.*) native, inherent, congenital, real, inborn, natural, intrinsic, inbred. (*ANT.*) *extraneous, acquired, external, extrinsic.*

innocent (*SYN.*) pure, sinless, blameless, innocuous, lawful, naive, faultless, virtuous, not guilty. (*ANT.*) *guilty, corrupt, sinful, culpable, sophisticated, wise, worldly.*

innocuous (*SYN.*) naive, pure, innocent, blameless, virtuous, lawful, faultless, sinless. (*ANT.*) *sinful, corrupt, unrighteous, culpable, guilty.*

inquire (*SYN.*) ask, solicit, invite, demand, claim, entreat, interrogate, query, beg, request, question, investigate, examine. (*ANT.*) *dictate, insist, reply, command, order.*

inquiring (*SYN.*) prying, searching, curious, inquisitive, peering, snoopy, peeping, meddling, interrogative. (*ANT.*) *unconcerned, indifferent, uninterested, incurious.*

inquiry (*SYN.*) investigation, quest, research, examination, interrogation, exploration, query, question, scrutiny, study. (*ANT.*) *inattention, inactivity, disregard, negligence.*

inquisitive (*SYN.*) meddling, peeping, nosy, interrogative, peering, searching, prying, snoopy, inquiring, curious. (*ANT.*) *unconcerned, indifferent, uninterested.*

insane (*SYN.*) deranged, mad, foolish, idiotic, demented, crazy, delirious, maniacal, lunatic. (*ANT.*) *sane, rational, reasonable, sensible, coherent.*

insanity (*SYN.*) delirium, aberration, dementia, psychosis, lunacy, madness, frenzy, mania, craziness, derangement. (*ANT.*) *stability, rationality, sanity.*

insecure (*SYN.*) uneasy, nervous, uncertain, shaky. (*ANT.*) *secure.*

insensitive (*SYN.*) unfeeling, impenitent, callous, hard, indurate, obdurate, tough. (*ANT.*) *soft, compassionate, tender, sensitive.*

insight (*SYN.*) intuition,

acumen, penetration, discernment, perspicuity. (ANT.) obtuseness.

insignificant (SYN.) trivial, paltry, petty, small, frivolous, unimportant, insignificant, trifling. (ANT.) momentous, serious, important, weighty.

insincere (SYN.) false, dishonest, deceitful. (ANT.) honest, sincere.

insinuate (SYN.) imply, mean, suggest, connote, signify, involve. (ANT.) express, state, assert.

insipid (SYN.) tasteless, dull, stale, flat, vapid. (ANT.) racy, tasty, savory, exciting.

insist (SYN.) command, demand, require.

insolence (SYN.) boldness, presumption, sauciness, effrontery, audacity, assurance, impertinence, rudeness. (ANT.) politeness, truckling, diffidence, subservience.

insolent (SYN.) arrogant, impertinent, insulting, rude, brazen, contemptuous, abusive, offensive, disrespectful. (ANT.) respectful, courteous, polite, considerate.

inspect (SYN.) observe, discern, survey, view, watch, witness, examine, investigate. (ANT.) overlook, miss, ignore, skip.

inspection (SYN.) examination, retrospect, survey, revision, reconsideration, critique, criticism, review.

inspiration (SYN.) creativity, aptitude, genius, originality, ability, faculty, sagacity, talent, proficient, master, gift, adept, intellectual, thought, impulse, idea, notion, hunch. (ANT.) dullard, moron, shallowness, ineptitude, stupidity, obtuseness, dolt.

install (SYN.) establish.

instance (SYN.) occasion, illustration, occurrence, example, case.

instant (SYN.) flash, moment.

instantaneous (SYN.) hasty, sudden, unexpected, rapid, abrupt, immediate. (ANT.) slowly, anticipated, gradual.

instantly (SYN.) now, presently, directly, forthwith, immediately, rapidly, straight-away, at once, instantaneously. (ANT.) sometime, distantly, hereafter, later, shortly.

instinct (SYN.) intuition, feeling.

instinctive (SYN.) offhand, voluntary, willing, spontaneous, automatic, impulsive, extemporaneous. (ANT.)

rehearsed, planned, compulsory, prepared, forced.

institute (SYN.) ordain, establish, raise, form, organize, sanction, fix, found, launch, begin, initiate. (ANT.) overthrow, upset, demolish, abolish, unsettle.

instruct (SYN.) teach, tutor, educate, inform, school, instill, train, inculcate, drill. (ANT.) misinform, misguide.

instruction (SYN.) advise, warning, information, exhortation, notification, admonition, caution, recommendation, counsel, suggestion, teaching, training, education, command, order.

instrument (SYN.) channel, device, utensil, tool, agent, apparatus, means, vehicle, medium, agent, implement. (ANT.) obstruction, hindrance, preventive, impediment.

insubordinate (SYN.) rebellious, unruly, defiant, disorderly, disobedient, undutiful, refractory, intractable, mutinous. (ANT.) obedient, compliant, submissive, dutiful.

insufficient (SYN.) limited, lacking, deficient, short, inadequate. (ANT.) ample, protracted, abundant, big, extended.

insulation (SYN.) quarantine, segregation, seclusion, withdrawal, isolation, loneliness, alienation, solitude. (ANT.) union, communion, association, connection.

insult (SYN.) insolence, offense, abuse, dishonor, affront, indignity, offend, humiliate, outrage. (ANT.) compliment, homage, apology, salutation, flatter, praise.

integrated (SYN.) mingled, mixed, combined, interspersed, desegregated, nonsectarian, interracial. (ANT.) separated, divided, segregated.

integrity (SYN.) honesty, openness, trustworthiness, fairness, candor, justice, rectitude, sincerity, uprightness, soundness, wholeness, honor, principle, virtue. (ANT.) fraud, deceit, cheating, trickery, dishonesty.

intellect (SYN.) understanding, judgment.

intellectual (SYN.) intelligent.

intelligence (SYN.) reason, sense, intellect, understanding, mind, ability, skill, aptitude. (ANT.) feeling, passion, emotion.

intelligent (SYN.) clever, smart, knowledgeable,

well-informed, alert, discerning, astute, quick, enlightened, smart, bright, wise. (ANT.) insipid, obtuse, dull, stupid, slow, foolish, unintelligent, dumb.

intend (SYN.) plan, prepare, scheme, contrive, outline, design, sketch, plot, project.

intense (SYN.) brilliant, animated, graphic, lucid, bright, expressive, vivid, deep, profound, concentrated, serious, earnest. (ANT.) dull, vague, dusky, dim, dreary.

intensify (SYN.) accrue, augment, amplify, enlarge, enhance, extend, expand, heighten, grow, magnify, raise, multiply. (ANT.) reduce, decrease, contract, diminish.

intensity (SYN.) force, potency, power, toughness, activity, durability, fortitude, vigor, stamina. (ANT.) weakness, feebleness, infirmity, frailty.

intent (SYN.) purpose, design, objective, intention, aim. (ANT.) accidental, result, chance.

intention (SYN.) intent, purpose, objective, plan, expectation, aim, object. (ANT.) chance, accident.

intentional (SYN.) deliberate, intended, studied, willful, contemplated, premeditated, designed, voluntary, purposeful, planned. (ANT.) fortuitous, accidental, chance.

intentionally (SYN.) purposefully, deliberately, maliciously. (ANT.) accidentally.

interest (SYN.) attention, concern, care, advantage, benefit, profit, ownership, credit, attract, engage, amuse, entertain. (ANT.) apathy, weary, disinterest.

interested (SYN.) affected, concerned. (ANT.) unconcerned, indifferent, uninterested.

interesting (SYN.) engaging, inviting, fascinating, attractive. (ANT.) boring, tedious, uninteresting, wearisome.

interfere (SYN.) meddle, monkey, interpose, interrupt, tamper, butt in, intervene.

interference (SYN.) prying, intrusion, meddling, obstacle, obstruction.

interior (SYN.) internal, inmost, inner, inward, inside, center. (ANT.) outer, adjacent, exterior, external, outside.

interject (SYN.) intrude, introduce, insert, inject, interpose.

interminable (SYN.) immense, endless, immeasurable,

unlimited, vast, unbounded, boundless, eternal, infinite. (ANT.) limited, bounded, circumscribed, confined.

internal (SYN.) inner, interior, inside, intimate, private. (ANT.) outer, external, surface.

interpose (SYN.) arbitrate, inject, intervene, meddle, insert, interject, introduce, intercede, intrude, interfere. (ANT.) overlook, avoid, disregard.

interpret (SYN.) explain, solve, translate, construe, elucidate, decode, explicate, render, unravel, define, understand. (ANT.) misinterpret, falsify, confuse, distort, misconstrue.

interrogate (SYN.) quiz, analyze, inquire, audit, question, contemplate, assess, dissect, notice, scan, review, view, check, survey, scrutinize, examine. (ANT.) overlook, omit, neglect, disregard.

interrupt (SYN.) suspend, delay, postpone, defer, adjourn, stay, discontinue, intrude, interfere. (ANT.) prolong, persist, continue, maintain, proceed.

interval (SYN.) pause, gap.

intervene (SYN.) insert, intercede, meddle, inject, introduce, interpose, mediate, interfere, interrupt, intrude. (ANT.) overlook, avoid, disregard.

intimacy (SYN.) fellowship, friendship, acquaintance, frankness, familiarity, unreserved, liberty. (ANT.) presumption, distance, haughtiness, constraint, reserve.

intimate (SYN.) chummy, confidential, friendly, loving, affectionate, close, familiar, near, personal, private, secret. (ANT.) conventional, formal, ceremonious, distant.

intimation (SYN.) reminder, implication, allusion, hint, insinuation. (ANT.) declaration, statement, affirmation.

intolerant (SYN.) fanatical, narrow-minded, prejudiced, bigoted, illiberal, dogmatic, biased. (ANT.) tolerant, radical, liberal, progressive, broad-minded, fair.

intoxicated (SYN.) inebriated, tipsy, drunk, tight, drunken, high. (ANT.) sober, temperate, clearheaded.

intrepid (SYN.) brave, fearless, insolent, abrupt, rude, pushy, adventurous, daring, courageous, prominent, striking, forward, imprudent.

(ANT.) timid, bashful, flinching, cowardly, retiring.

intricate *(SYN.)* compound, perplexing, complex, involved, complicated. *(ANT.) simple, plain, uncompounded.*

intrigue *(SYN.)* design, plot, cabal, machination, stratagem, scheme, attract, charm, interest, captivate.

intrinsic *(SYN.)* natural, inherent, inbred, congenital, inborn, native. *(ANT.) extraneous, acquired, external, extrinsic.*

introduce *(SYN.)* acquaint, present, submit, present, offer, propose.

introduction *(SYN.)* preamble, prelude, beginning, prologue, start, preface. *(ANT.) finale, conclusion, end, epilogue, completion.*

intrude *(SYN.)* invade, attack, encroach, trespass, penetrate, infringe, interrupt. *(ANT.) vacate, evacuate, abandon.*

intruder *(SYN.)* trespasser, thief, prowler, robber.

intuition *(SYN.)* insight, acumen, perspicuity, penetration, discernment, instinct, clairvoyance.

invade *(SYN.)* intrude, violate, infringe, attack, penetrate, encroach, trespass. *(ANT.) vacate, abandon, evacuate, relinquish.*

invalidate *(SYN.)* annul, cancel, abolish, revoke, abrogate. *(ANT.) promote, restore, sustain, establish, continue.*

invaluable *(SYN.)* priceless, precious, valuable. *(ANT.) worthless.*

invasion *(SYN.)* assault, onslaught, aggression, attack, intrusion. *(ANT.) surrender, opposition, resistance, defense.*

invective *(SYN.)* insult, abuse, disparagement, upbraiding, reproach, defamation, aspersion. *(ANT.) laudation, plaudit, commendation.*

invent *(SYN.)* devise, fabricate, design, concoct, frame, conceive, contrive, create, originate, devise. *(ANT.) reproduce, copy, imitate.*

inventive *(SYN.)* fanciful, imaginative, visionary, poetical, clever, creative. *(ANT.) unromantic, literal, dull, prosaic.*

inventiveness *(SYN.)* cunning, cleverness, ingeniousness, aptitude. *(ANT.) ineptitude, clumsiness, dullness, stupidity.*

invert *(SYN.)* upset, turn about, transpose, countermand,

revoke, reverse. *(ANT.) maintain, stabilize, endorse.*

investigate *(SYN.)* look, probe, ransack, scrutinize, ferret, examine, seek, explore, search, scour, inspect, study.

investigation *(SYN.)* exploration, interrogation, quest, question, scrutiny, inquiry, query, examination, study, research. *(ANT.) inattention, disregard, inactivity, negligence.*

invigorating *(SYN.)* bracing, fortifying, vitalizing, stimulating.

invincible *(SYN.)* insurmountable, unconquerable, impregnable, indomitable, invulnerable, unassailable. *(ANT.) powerless, weak, vulnerable.*

invisible *(SYN.)* indistinguishable, unseen, imperceptible, indiscernible. *(ANT.) evident, visible, seen, perceptible.*

invite *(SYN.)* bid, ask, encourage, request, urge.

inviting *(SYN.)* appealing, attractive, tempting, luring, alluring. *(ANT.) unattractive, uninviting.*

involuntary *(SYN.)* reflex, uncontrolled, automatic, unintentional. *(ANT.) voluntary, willful.*

involve *(SYN.)* include, embrace, entangle, envelop, incriminate, embroil, implicate, contain, complicate, confuse. *(ANT.) separate, extricate, disengage.*

involved *(SYN.)* compound, intricate, complicated, complex, perplexing. *(ANT.) plain, uncompounded, simple.*

invulnerable *(SYN.)* indomitable, unassailable, invincible, unconquerable, insurmountable, impregnable. *(ANT.) weak, puny, powerless, vulnerable.*

irate *(SYN.)* incensed, enraged, angry.

ire *(SYN.)* indignation, irritation, wrath, anger, animosity, fury, passion, temper, exasperation, petulance, rage. *(ANT.) peace, patience, self-control, forbearance.*

irk *(SYN.)* irritate, bother, disturb, pester, trouble, vex, tease, chafe, annoy. *(ANT.) console, accommodate, gratify.*

irrational *(SYN.)* inconsistent, preposterous, unreasonable, absurd, foolish, nonsensical, ridiculous. *(ANT.) sensible, sound, rational, consistent, reasonable.*

irregular *(SYN.)* eccentric,

unusual, aberrant, devious, abnormal, unnatural. *(ANT.) regular, methodical, fixed, usual, ordinary, even.*

irrelevant *(SYN.)* foreign, unconnected, remote, alien, strange. *(ANT.) germane, relevant, akin, kindred.*

irresolute *(SYN.)* frail, pliant, vacillating, ineffective, wavering, weak, yielding, fragile, pliable. *(ANT.) robust, potent, sturdy, strong, powerful.*

irresponsible *(SYN.)* unreliable.

irritable *(SYN.)* hasty, hot, peevish, testy, irascible, fiery, snappish, petulant. *(ANT.) composed, tranquil, calm.*

irritate *(SYN.)* irk, molest, bother, annoy, tease, disturb, inconvenience, vex, trouble, pester, inflame, chafe. *(ANT.) console, gratify, accommodate, soothe, pacify, calm.*

irritation *(SYN.)* chagrin, mortification, vexation, annoyance, exasperation, pique. *(ANT.) pleasure, comfort, gratification, appeasement.*

isolate *(SYN.)* detach, segregate, separate, disconnect. *(ANT.) happy, cheerful.*

isolated *(SYN.)* lone, single, alone, desolate, secluded, solitary, deserted, sole. *(ANT.) surrounded, accompanied.*

isolation *(SYN.)* quarantine, seclusion, separation, solitude, alienation, retirement, segregation, detachment. *(ANT.) fellowship, union, association, communion, connection.*

issue *(SYN.)* flow, proceed, result, come, emanate, originate, abound, copy, number, edition, problem, question.

itemize *(SYN.)* register, detail, record. *(ANT.) generalize, include, summarize.*

J

jab *(SYN.)* thrust, poke, nudge, prod, shove, jolt, boost, tap, slap, rap, thwack, push.

jabber *(SYN.)* mumble, gossip, prattle, chatter, gab, palaver.

jacent *(SYN.)* level, flatness, plane, proneness, recline.

jacinth *(SYN.)* decoration, ornament, embellishment.

jack *(SYN.)* fellow, boy, toiler, guy, man, worker.

jackal *(SYN.)* puppet, drone, slave, legman, flunky, slavery, tool, servility, vassal.

jackass *(SYN.)* fool, idiot, dope, dunce, ignoramus,

imbecile, ninny, simpleton, blockhead.

jacket *(SYN.)* wrapper, envelope, coat, sheath, cover, casing, folder, enclosure.

jack-of-all-trades *(SYN.)* man friday, expert, proficient, amateur, adept, handyman, dab, master, specialist, mastermind, generalist.

jade *(SYN.)* hussy, wanton, trollop, harlot, common, whore, ignoble, wench, hag, shrew.

jaded *(SYN.)* exhausted, bored, tired, fatigued, satiated, weary, hardened.

jag *(SYN.)* notch, snag, protuberance, barb, dent, cut, nick, serration, indentation, point.

jagged *(SYN.)* crooked, bent, ragged, pointy, notched, aquiline, furcated, serrated. *(ANT.) smooth.*

jail *(SYN.)* stockade, prison, reformatory, penitentiary, keep, dungeon, brig, confine, lock up, detain, imprison, hold captive, coop, cage, house of detention, incarcerate.

jailbird *(SYN.)* convict, parolee, con, inmate, prisoner.

jailer *(SYN.)* guard, keeper, turnkey, warden.

jam *(SYN.)* force, pack, ram, crowd, push, wedge, squeeze, stuff, load, cram, press, crush, marmalade, jelly, conserve, preserve.

jamboree *(SYN.)* celebration, fete, spree, festival, festivity, carousal.

jangle *(SYN.)* rattle, vibrate, clank, clatter, dissonance, discord, quarrel, din, discord.

janitor *(SYN.)* custodian, doorkeeper, caretaker, superintendent, gatekeeper.

jape *(SYN.)* lampoon, banter, joke, jest, tease, ridicule.

jar *(SYN.)* rattle, shake, bounce, jolt.

jargon *(SYN.)* speech, idiom, dialect, vernacular, diction, argot, phraseology, language, patois, parlance, slang. *(ANT.) gibberish, babble, nonsense, drivel.*

jaundiced *(SYN.)* biased, prejudiced. *(ANT.) fair.*

jaunt *(SYN.)* journey, trip, tour, excursion, outing, voyage, expedition.

jaunty *(SYN.)* lively, vivacious, buoyant, winsome, frisky, showy, dapper, breezy.

jazzy *(SYN.)* garish, vivacious, loud, splashy, exaggerated, flashy.

jealous *(SYN.)* covetous, desirous of, envious.

jealousy *(SYN.)* suspicion, envy, resentfulness, greed, covetousness. *(ANT.)* tolerance, indifference, geniality, liberality.

jeer *(SYN.)* taunt, mock, scoff, deride, make fun of, gibe, sneer. *(ANT.)* flatter, praise, compliment, laud.

jeering *(SYN.)* mockery, sneering, derision, sarcasm, irony, ridicule.

jell *(SYN.)* finalize, congeal, set, solidify, shape up, take form.

jeopardize *(SYN.)* risk, dare, expose, imperil, chance, venture, conjecture, hazard, endanger. *(ANT.)* know, guard, determine.

jerk *(SYN.)* quiver, twitch, shake, spasm, jolt, yank, fool.

jerkwater *(SYN.)* remote, hick, backwoods, unimportant, one-horse.

jest *(SYN.)* mock, joke, tease, fun, witticism, quip.

jester *(SYN.)* fool, buffoon, harlequin, clown. *(ANT.)* sage, genius, scholar.

jet *(SYN.)* squirt, spurt, gush, inky, coalblack, nozzle.

jettison *(SYN.)* heave, discharge, throw, eject, cast off, dismiss.

jetty *(SYN.)* pier, breakwater, bulwark, buttress.

jewel *(SYN.)* ornament, gemstone, gem, bauble, stone.

jib *(SYN.)* shrink, shy, dodge, retreat, balk.

jig *(SYN.)* caper, prance, jiggle, leap, skip.

jiggle *(SYN.)* shimmy, agitate, jerk, twitch, wiggle.

jilt *(SYN.)* abandon, get rid of, reject, desert, forsake, leave.

jingle *(SYN.)* chime, ring, tinkle.

jinx *(SYN.)* hex, whammy, nemesis, curse, evil eye.

jittery *(SYN.)* jumpy, nervous, quivering, shaky, skittish.

job *(SYN.)* toil, business, occupation, post, chore, stint, career, duty, employment, profession, trade, work, situation, labor, assignment, position, undertaking, calling, task.

jobless *(SYN.)* idle, unoccupied, inactive, unemployed.

jocularity *(SYN.)* humor, wit, joke, facetiousness, waggery. *(ANT.)* sorrow, gravity.

jocund *(SYN.)* mirthful, elated, pleasant, cheerful, merry, gay, jovial, frolicsome.

jog *(SYN.)* gait, trot, sprint, run, lope.

join *(SYN.)* conjoin, unite, attach, accompany, associate,

assemble, fit, couple, combine, fasten, unite, clasp, put together, go with, adjoin, link, connect. *(ANT.)* separate, disconnect, split, sunder, part, divide, detach.

joint *(SYN.)* link, union, connection, junction, coupling, common, combined, mutual, connected. *(ANT.)* divided, separate.

joke *(SYN.)* game, jest, caper, prank, anecdote, quip, tease, antic, banter, laugh.

joker *(SYN.)* wisecracker, humorist, comedian, trickster, comic, jester, wit, punster.

jolly *(SYN.)* merry, joyful, gay, happy, sprightly, pleasant, jovial, gleeful, spirited, cheerful, glad. *(ANT.)* mournful, depressed, sullen, glum.

jolt *(SYN.)* sway, waver, startle, rock, jar, totter, jerk, bounce, quake, bump, shake.

josh *(SYN.)* poke fun at, kid, tease, ridicule.

jostle *(SYN.)* shove, push, bump, thrust, jar, shake.

jot *(SYN.)* note, write, record.

jounce *(SYN.)* bounce, jolt, bump, jostle.

journey *(SYN.)* tour, passage, cruise, voyage, pilgrimage, jaunt, trip, outing, expedition, junket, excursion, travel.

joust *(SYN.)* tournament, contest, skirmish, competition, fight.

jovial *(SYN.)* good-natured, kindly, merry, good-humored, good-hearted, joyful, jolly, gleeful. *(ANT.)* solemn, sad, serious, grim.

joy *(SYN.)* pleasure, glee, bliss, elation, mirth, felicity, rapture, delight, transport, exultation, gladness, happiness, festivity, satisfaction, merriment, ecstasy. *(ANT.)* grief, depression, unhappiness, sorrow, misery, gloom, sadness, affliction.

joyful *(SYN.)* gay, lucky, opportune, cheerful, happy, blissful, jovial, merry, gleeful, delighted, glad, contented, fortunate. *(ANT.)* gloomy, sad, blue, solemn, serious, grim, morose, glum, depressed.

joyous *(SYN.)* jolly, gay, blithe, merry, gleeful, cheerful, jovial. *(ANT.)* sad, gloomy, sorrowful, melancholy.

jubilant *(SYN.)* exulting, rejoicing, overjoyed, triumphant, gay, elated, delighted. *(ANT.)* dejected.

jubilee *(SYN.)* gala, holiday, celebration, festival, fete.

judge *(SYN.)* umpire, think, estimate, decide, arbitrator,

condemn, decree, critic, appreciate, adjudicator, determine, arbiter, magistrate, arbitrate, justice, consider, mediate, referee, evaluate.

judgment *(SYN.)* wisdom, perspicacity, discernment, decision, common sense, estimation, verdict, understanding, intelligence, discretion, opinion, sense, discrimination. *(ANT.)* thoughtlessness, senselessness, arbitrariness.

judicial *(SYN.)* legal, judicatory, forensic.

judicious *(SYN.)* sensible, wise, well-advised, thoughtful. *(ANT.)* ignorant.

jug *(SYN.)* bottle, jar, flask, flagon, pitcher.

juice *(SYN.)* broth, liquid, sap, distillation, serum, fluid.

jumble *(SYN.)* disarrangement, tumult, agitation, ferment, turmoil, commotion, confuse, mix, muddle, scramble, disorder. *(ANT.)* peace, arrange, compose, certainty, tranquillity.

jumbo *(SYN.)* huge, big, immense, enormous, giant, colossal, monstrous, mammoth, gigantic, tremendous. *(ANT.)* miniature, midget, dwarf, small, tiny.

jump *(SYN.)* leap, caper, skip, bound, jerk, vault, hop, spring.

jumpy *(SYN.)* touchy, excitable, nervous, sensitive. *(ANT.)* tranquil, calm, unruffled.

junction *(SYN.)* coupling, joining, union, crossroads, intersection, weld, connection, linking, meeting, tie-up, seam, joint. *(ANT.)* separation.

jungle *(SYN.)* woods, thicket, undergrowth, forest, bush.

junior *(SYN.)* secondary, inferior, minor, lower, younger.

junk *(SYN.)* rubbish, scraps, trash, waste, dump, discard, castoffs, debris.

junky *(SYN.)* tawdry, ramshackle, tattered, tacky, shoddy.

jurisdiction *(SYN.)* power, commission, warrant, authority, authorization, sovereignty.

just *(SYN.)* fair, trustworthy, precise, exact, candid, upright, honest, impartial, lawful, rightful, proper, legal, truthful, merely, only, conscientious. *(ANT.)* tricky, dishonest, unjust, corrupt, lying, deceitful.

justice *(SYN.)* justness, rectitude, equity, law, fairness, impartiality, right. *(ANT.)*

inequity, wrong, partiality.

justifiable *(SYN.)* allowable, tolerable, admissible, warranted. *(ANT.)* unsuitable, inadmissible.

justify *(SYN.)* uphold, excuse, defend, acquit, exonerate, absolve, clear, vindicate.

jut *(SYN.)* project, protrude, stick out.

juvenile *(SYN.)* puerile, youthful, childish, youngster, youth, young, child. *(ANT.)* old, aged, adult, mature.

K

kaiser *(SYN.)* czar, caesar, caliph, mogul, padishah, tycoon, khan.

kavass *(SYN.)* badel, macebearer, constable.

keck *(SYN.)* vomit, belch, retch.

keen *(SYN.)* clever, cunning, acute, penetrating, exact, severe, shrewd, wily, astute, sharp, bright, intelligent, smart, sharp-witted, witty, cutting, fine, quick. *(ANT.)* stupid, shallow, dull, blunted, slow, bland, gentle, obtuse, blunt.

keep *(SYN.)* maintain, retain, observe, protect, confine, sustain, continue, preserve, save, guard, restrain, reserve, obey, support, honor, execute, celebrate, conserve, have, tend, detain, commemorate, hold. *(ANT.)* abandon, disobey, dismiss, discard, ignore, neglect, lose, reject, relinquish.

keeper *(SYN.)* warden, jailer, ranger, guard, turnkey, watchman, escort, custodian.

keeping *(SYN.)* congeniality, uniformity, consentaneousness, conformance, congruity, union.

keepsake *(SYN.)* reminder, memorial, relic, souvenir, memento, hint, remembrance.

keg *(SYN.)* container, drum, tub, barrel, receptacle, reservatory, capsule, cask, tank.

kelpie *(SYN.)* sprite, nixie, naiad, pixy.

kelson *(SYN.)* bottom, sole, toe, foot, root, keel.

kempt *(SYN.)* neat, trim, tidy, spruce, cleaned.

ken *(SYN.)* field, view, vision, range, scope.

kennel *(SYN.)* swarm, flock, covy, drove, herd, pound, doghouse.

kerchief *(SYN.)* neckcloth, handkerchief, scarf, headpiece, babushka.

kern (SYN.) peasant, carle, serf, tike, tyke, countryman.

kernel (SYN.) marrow, pith, backbone, soul, heart, core, nucleus.

ketch (SYN.) lugger, cutter, clipper, ship, barge, sloop.

kettle (SYN.) pan, caldron, vat, pot, teapot, vessel, receptacle, receiver, tureen.

key (SYN.) opener, explanation, tone, lead, cause, source, note, pitch, answer, clue.

keynote (SYN.) core, model, theme, pattern, standard, gist.

keystone (SYN.) backbone, support.

khan (SYN.) master, czar, kaiser, padishah, caesar.

kick (SYN.) punt, remonstrate, boot.

kickback (SYN.) repercussion, backfire, rebound.

kickoff (SYN.) beginning, opening, commencement, outset, start.

kid (SYN.) joke, tease, fool, jest, tot, child.

kidnap (SYN.) abduct, snatch, shanghai.

kill (SYN.) execute, put to death, slay, butcher, assassinate, murder, cancel, destroy, slaughter, finish, end, annihilate, massacre. (ANT.) save, protect, animate, resuscitate, vivify.

killing (SYN.) massacre, genocide, slaughter, carnage, butchery, bloodshed.

killjoy (SYN.) wet blanket, sourpuss, party-pooper.

kin (SYN.) relatives, family, folks, relations.

kind (SYN.) humane, affable, compassionate, benevolent, merciful, tender, sympathetic, breed, indulgent, forbearing, kindly, race, good, thoughtful, character, benign, family, sort, species, variety, class, type, gentle. (ANT.) unkind, cruel, merciless, severe, mean, inhuman.

kindle (SYN.) fire, ignite, light, arouse, excite, set afire, stir up, trigger, move, provoke, inflame. (ANT.) extinguish, calm.

kindly (SYN.) warm, kindhearted, kind, warm-hearted. (ANT.) mean, cruel.

kindred (SYN.) family, relations, relatives, consanguinity, kinsfolk, affinity. (ANT.) strangers, disconnection.

kinetic (SYN.) vigorous, active, dynamic, energetic, mobile, forceful.

king (SYN.) sovereign, ruler, chief, monarch, potentate.

kingdom (SYN.) realm, empire, monarchy, domain.

kingly (SYN.) kinglike, imperial, regal, royal, majestic.

kink (SYN.) twist, curl, quirk, complication.

kinship (SYN.) lineage, blood, family, stock, relationship.

kismet (SYN.) fate, end, fortune, destiny.

kiss (SYN.) pet, caress, fondle, cuddle, osculate, embrace. (ANT.) vex, spurn, annoy, tease, buffet.

kit (SYN.) outfit, collection, furnishings, equipment, rig, gear, set.

knack (SYN.) cleverness, readiness, deftness, ability, ingenuity, skill, talent, aptitude, know-how, art, adroitness, skillfulness. (ANT.) inability, clumsiness, awkwardness, ineptitude.

knave (SYN.) rogue, rascal, villain, scoundrel.

knead (SYN.) combine, massage, blend.

knickknack (SYN.) trinket, bric-a-brac, trifle.

knife (SYN.) sword, blade.

knightly (SYN.) valiant, courageous, gallant, chivalrous, noble.

knit (SYN.) unite, join, mend, fasten, connect, combine, heal.

knob (SYN.) doorknob, handle, protuberance, bump.

knock (SYN.) thump, tap, rap, strike, hit, jab, punch, beat, pound, bang, hammer.

knoll (SYN.) hill, elevation, hump, mound, butte.

knot (SYN.) cluster, gathering, collection, group, crowd, twist, snarl, tangle.

know (SYN.) perceive, comprehend, apprehend, recognize, understand, discern, discriminate, ascertain, identify, be aware, distinguish. (ANT.) doubt, suspect, dispute.

knowing (SYN.) sage, smart, wise, clever, sagacious, shrewd.

knowledge (SYN.) information, wisdom, erudition, learning, apprehension, scholarship, lore, cognizance. (ANT.) misunderstanding, ignorance, stupidity, illiteracy.

knurl (SYN.) gnarl, knot, projection, burl, node, lump.

kosher (SYN.) permitted, okay, fit, proper, acceptable.

kowtow (SYN.) stoop, bend, kneel, genuflect, bow.

kudos (SYN.) acclaim, praise, approbation, approval.

L

label (SYN.) mark, tag, title, name, marker, stamp, sticker, ticket, docket, identity.

labor (SYN.) toil, travail, effort, task, childbirth, work, parturition, striving, workers, effort, industry, workingmen, strive, exertion, employment, drudgery, endeavor. (ANT.) recreation, indolence, idleness, leisure.

laboratory (SYN.) lab, workroom, workshop.

laborer (SYN.) wage earner, helper, worker, toiler, coolie, blue-collar worker.

laborious (SYN.) tiring, difficult, hard, burdensome, industrious, painstaking. (ANT.) simple, easy, relaxing, restful.

labyrinth (SYN.) complex, maze, tangle.

lace (SYN.) openwork, fancywork, embroidery, edging.

lacerate (SYN.) mangle, tear roughly.

laceration (SYN.) cut, wound, puncture, gash, lesion, injury.

lack (SYN.) want, need, shortage, dearth, scarcity, require. (ANT.) profusion, quantity, plentifulness.

lackey (SYN.) yes-man, stooge, flatterer, flunky.

lacking (SYN.) insufficient, short, deficient, incomplete, defective, scanty. (ANT.) satisfactory, enough, ample, sufficient, adequate.

lackluster (SYN.) dull, pallid, flat, lifeless, drab, dim.

laconic (SYN.) short, terse, compact, brief, curt, succinct, concise.

lacquer (SYN.) polish, varnish, gild.

lad (SYN.) youth, boy, fellow, stripling.

laden (SYN.) burdened, loaded, weighted.

ladle (SYN.) scoop, dipper.

lady (SYN.) matron, woman, dame, gentlewoman.

ladylike (SYN.) feminine, womanly, maidenly, womanish, female. (ANT.) masculine, male, virile, mannish, manly.

lag (SYN.) dawdle, loiter, linger, poke, dilly-dally, straggle, delay, tarry, slowdown.

laggard (SYN.) idler, lingerer, slowpoke, dawdler.

lair (SYN.) retreat, burrow, den, nest, mew, hole.

lambaste (SYN.) berate, castigate, scold, censure.

lame (SYN.) feeble, maimed, disabled, crippled, deformed, hobbling, unconvincing, weak, poor, inadequate, halt, defective, limping. (ANT.) vigorous, convincing, plausible, athletic, robust, agile, sound.

lament (SYN.) deplore, wail, bemoan, bewail, regret, grieve, mourning, lamentation, moaning, wailing, weep, mourn, sorrow. (ANT.) celebrate, rejoice.

lamentable (SYN.) unfortunate, deplorable.

lamp (SYN.) light, beam, illumination, shine, insight, knowledge, understanding, radiance, luminosity, incandescence. (ANT.) shadow, darkness, obscurity, gloom.

lampoon (SYN.) skit, tirade, burlesque, parody, satire.

lance (SYN.) cut, pierce, perforate, stab, puncture, impale, knife.

land (SYN.) earth, continent, ground, soil, domain, estate, field, realm, plain, surface, arrive, descend, country, island, region, alight, shore, sod, tract, farm.

landlord (SYN.) owner, landholder, landowner, proprietor.

landmark (SYN.) keystone, monument, milestone, point, cornerstone.

landscape (SYN.) panorama, environs, countryside, scenery, scene.

landslide (SYN.) rockfall, glissade, avalanche.

lane (SYN.) alley, way, road, path, aisle, pass, channel, avenue, artery, passage.

language (SYN.) dialect, tongue, speech, lingo, jargon, cant, diction, idiom, patter, phraseology, vernacular, words, lingo, talk, slang. (ANT.) gibberish, nonsense, babble, drivel.

languid (SYN.) feeble, drooping, irresolute, debilitated, dull, lethargic, weak, faint, listless, wearied. (ANT.) forceful, strong, vigorous.

languish (SYN.) decline, sink, droop, wither, waste, fail, wilt, weaken. (ANT.) revive, rejuvenate, refresh, renew.

languor (SYN.) weariness, depression, torpor, inertia, apathy.

lanky (SYN.) skinny, gaunt, lean, scrawny, slender, thin. (ANT.) chunky, stocky, obese.

lantern (SYN.) torch, light, lamp, flashlight.

lap (SYN.) drink, lick, fold over.

lapse (SYN.) decline, sink, go down, slump.

larceny (SYN.) pillage, robbery,

stealing, theft, burglary, plunder.

lard *(SYN.)* grease, fat.

large *(SYN.)* great, vast, colossal, ample, extensive, capacious, sizable, broad, massive, grand, immense, big, enormous, huge, giant, mammoth, wide. *(ANT.) tiny, little, short, small.*

largely *(SYN.)* chiefly, mainly, principally, mostly.

lariat *(SYN.)* lasso, rope.

lark *(SYN.)* fling, frolic, play, fun, spree, joke, revel, celebration.

lascivious *(SYN.)* lecherous, raunchy, lustful, wanton, lewd.

lash *(SYN.)* thong, whip, rod, cane, blow, strike, hit, beat, knout.

lass *(SYN.)* maiden, girl, damsel. *(ANT.) woman, lad.*

lasso *(SYN.)* lariat, rope, noose, snare.

last *(SYN.)* terminal, final, ultimate, remain, endure, concluding, latest, utmost, end, conclusive, hindmost, continue, extreme. *(ANT.) first, initial, beginning, opening, starring, foremost.*

latch *(SYN.)* clasp, hook, fastener, lock, closing, seal, catch.

late *(SYN.)* overdue, tardy, behind, advanced, delayed, new, slow, recent. *(ANT.) timely, early.*

lately *(SYN.)* recently, yesterday.

latent *(SYN.)* potential, undeveloped, unseen, dormant, secret, concealed, inactive, hidden, obscured, covered, quiescent. *(ANT.) visible, evident, conspicuous, explicit, manifest.*

lateral *(SYN.)* sideways, glancing, tangential, marginal, skirting, side.

lather *(SYN.)* suds, foam, froth.

latitude *(SYN.)* range, scope, freedom, extent.

latter *(SYN.)* more recent, later.

lattice *(SYN.)* grating, screen, frame, trellis, openwork, framework, grid.

laud *(SYN.)* commend, praise, extol, glorify, compliment. *(ANT.) criticize, belittle.*

laudable *(SYN.)* creditable, praiseworthy, commendable, admirable.

laudation *(SYN.)* applause, compliment, flattery, praise, commendation, acclaim, extolling, glorification. *(ANT.) criticizing, condemnation,* reproach, disparagement, censure.

laugh *(SYN.)* chuckle, giggle, snicker, cackle, titter, grin, smile, roar, guffaw, jeer, mock.

laughable *(SYN.)* funny, amusing, comical, humorous, ridiculous.

launch *(SYN.)* drive, fire, propel, start, begin, originate, set afloat, initiate. *(ANT.) finish, stop, terminate.*

launder *(SYN.)* bathe, wash, scrub, scour.

laurels *(SYN.)* glory, distinction, recognition, award, commendation, reward, honor.

lavatory *(SYN.)* toilet, washroom, bathroom, latrine.

lavish *(SYN.)* squander, waste, dissipate, scatter, abundant, free, plentiful, liberal, extravagant, ample, wear out, prodigal, generous, spend. *(ANT.) economize, save, conserve, accumulate, sparing, stingy, preserve.*

law *(SYN.)* decree, formula, statute, act, rule, ruling, standard, principle, ordinance, proclamation, regulation, order, edict.

lawful *(SYN.)* legal, permissible, allowable, legitimate, authorized, constitutional, rightful. *(ANT.) prohibited, criminal, illicit, illegal, illegitimate.*

lawless *(SYN.)* uncivilized, uncontrolled, wild, savage, untamed, violent. *(ANT.) obedient, law-abiding, tame.*

lawlessness *(SYN.)* chaos, anarchy.

lawn *(SYN.)* grass, meadow, turf.

lawyer *(SYN.)* counsel, attorney, counselor.

lax *(SYN.)* slack, loose, careless, vague, lenient, lazy. *(ANT.) firm, rigid.*

lay *(SYN.)* mundane, worldly, temporal, place, dispose, bet, wager, hazard, risk, stake, site, earthly, profane, laic, arrange, location, put, set, ballad, deposit, position, song, secular. *(ANT.) spiritual, unworldly, remove, misplace, disturb, mislay, disarrange, ecclesiastical, religious.*

lay off *(SYN.)* discharge, bounce, fire, dismiss.

layout *(SYN.)* plan, arrangement, design.

lazy *(SYN.)* slothful, supine, idle, inactive, sluggish, inert, indolent, torpid. *(ANT.) alert, ambitious, forceful, diligent, active, assiduous.*

lea *(SYN.)* pasture, meadow.

leach *(SYN.)* remove, extract, seep, dilute, wash out.

lead *(SYN.)* regulate, conduct, guide, escort, direct, supervise, command, come first, steer, control. *(ANT.) follow.*

leader *(SYN.)* master, ruler, captain, chief, commander, principal, director, head, chieftain. *(ANT.) follower, servant, disciple, subordinate, attendant.*

leading *(SYN.)* dominant, foremost, principal, first, main, primary.

league *(SYN.)* entente, partnership, association, confederacy, coalition, society, alliance, federation, union. *(ANT.) separation, schism.*

leak *(SYN.)* dribble, flow, drip, opening, perforation.

lean *(SYN.)* rely, tilt, slim, slender, slope, incline, tend, trust, bend, tendency, slant, depend, spare, scant, lanky, thin, meager, inclination, narrow, sag. *(ANT.) rise, heavy, fat, erect, straighten, portly, raise.*

leaning *(SYN.)* trend, proclivity, bias, tendency, bent, predisposition, proneness. *(ANT.) disinclination, aversion.*

leap *(SYN.)* vault, skip, caper, dive, hurdle, jump, bound, start, hop, plunge, spring.

learn *(SYN.)* gain, find out, memorize, acquire, determine.

learned *(SYN.)* erudite, knowing, enlightened, deep, wise, discerning, scholarly, intelligent, educated, sagacious. *(ANT.) simple, uneducated, ignorant, illiterate, unlettered, foolish.*

learning *(SYN.)* science, education, lore, apprehension, wisdom, knowledge, scholarship, erudition. *(ANT.) misunderstanding, ignorance, stupidity.*

lease *(SYN.)* charter, let, rent, engage.

leash *(SYN.)* chain, strap, shackle, collar.

least *(SYN.)* minutest, smallest, tiniest, minimum, fewest, slightest. *(ANT.) most.*

leave *(SYN.)* give up, retire, desert, abandon, withdraw, relinquish, will, depart, quit, liberty, renounce, go, bequeath, consent, allowance, permission, freedom, forsake. *(ANT.) come, stay, arrive, tarry, remain, abide.*

lecherous *(SYN.)* lustful, sensual, carnal, lascivious.

lecture *(SYN.)* talk, discussion, lesson, instruct, speech, conference, sermon, report, recitation, address, oration, discourse. *(ANT.) writing, meditation, correspondence.*

ledge *(SYN.)* eaves, ridge, shelf, rim, edge.

lee *(SYN.)* shelter, asylum, sanctuary, haven.

leech *(SYN.)* barnacle, bloodsucker, parasite.

leer *(SYN.)* eye, grimace, ogle, wink, squint.

leeway *(SYN.)* reserve, allowance, elbowroom, slack, clearance.

leftovers *(SYN.)* scraps, remains, residue, remainder.

legacy *(SYN.)* bequest, inheritance, heirloom.

legal *(SYN.)* legitimate, rightful, honest, allowable, allowed, permissible, lawful, permitted, authorized. *(ANT.) illicit, illegal, prohibited, illegitimate.*

legalize *(SYN.)* authorize, ordain, approve, sanction.

legate *(SYN.)* envoy, agent, representative, emissary.

legend *(SYN.)* saga, fable, allegory, myth, parable, tale, story, folklore, fiction, chronicle. *(ANT.) history, facts.*

legendary *(SYN.)* fictitious, traditional, mythical, imaginary, fanciful.

legible *(SYN.)* plain, readable, clear, distinct. *(ANT.) illegible.*

legion *(SYN.)* outfit, unit, troop, regiment, company, battalion, force, army, team, division.

legislation *(SYN.)* resolution, ruling, lawmaking, regulation, enactment, statute, decree.

legislator *(SYN.)* statesman, congressman, senator, politician, lawmaker.

legitimate *(SYN.)* true, real, bonafide, lawful, proper, right, valid, correct, unadulterated, authentic, rightful, legal, sincere. *(ANT.) sham, counterfeit, artificial, false.*

leisure *(SYN.)* respite, intermission, ease, relaxation, rest, calm, tranquillity, recreation, peace, pause. *(ANT.) motion, commotion, tumult, agitation, disturbance.*

leisurely *(SYN.)* sluggish, laggard, unhurried, relaxed, casual, dawdling, slow, deliberate. *(ANT.) hurried, swift, pressed, rushed, forced, fast, speedy, quick.*

lend *(SYN.)* entrust, advance, confer.

length *(SYN.)* reach, measure,

extent, distance, span, longness, stretch.

lengthen *(SYN.)* stretch, prolong, draw, reach, increase, grow, protract, extend. *(ANT.)* shrink, contract, shorten.

leniency *(SYN.)* grace, pity, compassion, mildness, charity, mercy, clemency. *(ANT.)* vengeance, punishment, cruelty.

lenient *(SYN.)* tender, humane, clement, tolerant, compassionate, merciful, relaxed, forgiving, gentle, mild, lax, kind. *(ANT.)* unfeeling, pitiless, brutal, remorseless.

leprechaun *(SYN.)* gnome, imp, goblin, fairy, elf, sprite, banshee.

lesion *(SYN.)* wound, blemish, sore, trauma, injury.

less *(SYN.)* fewer, smaller, reduced, negative, stinted. *(ANT.)* more.

lessen *(SYN.)* shorten, reduce, deduct, subtract, curtail, diminish, shrink, dwindle, decline, instruction, teaching, remove, decrease. *(ANT.)* swell, grow, enlarge, increase, expand, multiply, amplify.

lesson *(SYN.)* exercise, session, class, assignment, section, recitation.

let *(SYN.)* admit, hire out, contract, allow, permit, consent, leave, grant, rent. *(ANT.)* deny.

letdown *(SYN.)* disillusionment, disappointment.

lethal *(SYN.)* mortal, dangerous, deadly, fatal, devastating.

lethargic *(SYN.)* sluggish, logy, slow, listless, phlegmatic, lazy. *(ANT.)* vivacious, energetic.

lethargy *(SYN.)* numbness, stupor, daze, insensibility, torpor. *(ANT.)* wakefulness, liveliness, activity, readiness.

letter *(SYN.)* note, mark, message, character, symbol, sign, memorandum.

letup *(SYN.)* slowdown, slackening, lessening, abatement, reduction.

levee *(SYN.)* dike, breakwater, dam, embankment.

level *(SYN.)* smooth, even, plane, equivalent, uniform, horizontal, equal, flatten, equalize, raze, demolish, flat. *(ANT.)* uneven, sloping, hilly, broken.

level-headed *(SYN.)* reasonable, sensible, calm, collected, cool.

leverage *(SYN.)* clout, power, influence, weight, rank.

levity *(SYN.)* humor, triviality, giddiness, hilarity, fun, frivolity.

levy *(SYN.)* tax, duty, tribute, rate, assessment, exaction, charge, custom. *(ANT.)* wages, remuneration, gift.

lewd *(SYN.)* indecent, smutty, course, gross, disgusting, impure. *(ANT.)* pure, decent, refined.

liability *(SYN.)* indebtedness, answerability, obligation, vulnerability.

liable *(SYN.)* answerable, responsible, likely, exposed to, subject, amenable, probable, accountable. *(ANT.)* immune, exempt, independent.

liaison *(SYN.)* union, coupling, link, connection, alliance.

liar *(SYN.)* fibber, falsifier, storyteller, fabricator, prevaricator.

libel *(SYN.)* slander, calumny, vilification, aspersion, defamation. *(ANT.)* defense, praise, applause, flattery.

liberal *(SYN.)* large, generous, unselfish, openhanded, broad, tolerant, kind, unprejudiced, open-minded, lavish, plentiful, ample, abundant, extravagant, extensive. *(ANT.)* restricted, conservative, stingy.

liberality *(SYN.)* kindness, philanthropy, beneficence, humanity, altruism, benevolence, generosity, charity. *(ANT.)* selfishness, cruelty, malevolence.

liberate *(SYN.)* emancipate, loose, release, let go, deliver, free, discharge. *(ANT.)* subjugate, oppress, jail, confine, restrict, imprison.

liberated *(SYN.)* loose, frank, emancipated, careless, liberal, freed, autonomous, exempt, familiar. *(ANT.)* subject, clogged, restricted, impeded.

liberty *(SYN.)* permission, independence, autonomy, license, privilege, emancipation, self-government, freedom. *(ANT.)* constraint, imprisonment, bondage, captivity.

license *(SYN.)* liberty, freedom, liberation, permission, exemption, authorization, warrant, allow, consent, permit, sanction, approval, unrestraint. *(ANT.)* servitude, constraint, bondage, necessity.

lick *(SYN.)* taste, lap, lave.

lid *(SYN.)* top, cover, cap, plug, cork, stopper.

lie *(SYN.)* untruth, fib, illusion, delusion, falsehood, fiction, equivocation, prevarication, repose, location, perjury, misinform, site, recline, similitude. *(ANT.)* variance, truth, difference.

life *(SYN.)* sparkle, being, spirit, vivacity, animation, buoyancy, vitality, existence, biography, energy, liveliness, vigor. *(ANT.)* demise, lethargy, death, languor.

lift *(SYN.)* hoist, pick up, elevate, raise, heft.

light *(SYN.)* brightness, illumination, beam, gleam, lamp, knowledge, brilliance, fixture, bulb, candle, fire, ignite, burn, dawn, incandescence, flame, airy, unsubstantial, dainty, luminosity, shine, radiance, giddy, weightless. *(ANT.)* darkness, gloom, shadow, extinguish, darken.

lighten *(SYN.)* diminish, unburden, reduce, brighten.

light-headed *(SYN.)* giddy, silly, dizzy, frivolous. *(ANT.)* sober, clear-headed, rational.

lighthearted *(SYN.)* carefree, merry, gay, cheerful, happy, glad. *(ANT.)* somber, sad, serious, melancholy.

like *(SYN.)* fancy, esteem, adore, love, admire, care for, prefer, cherish. *(ANT.)* disapprove, loathes, hate, dislike.

likely *(SYN.)* liable, reasonable, probable, possible.

likeness *(SYN.)* similarity, resemblance, representation, image, portrait. *(ANT.)* difference.

likewise *(SYN.)* besides, as well, also, too, similarly.

liking *(SYN.)* fondness, affection, partiality. *(ANT.)* antipathy, dislike.

limb *(SYN.)* arm, leg, member, appendage, part, bough.

limber *(SYN.)* bending, flexible, elastic, pliable. *(ANT.)* inflexible, stiff.

limbo *(SYN.)* exile, banishment, purgatory.

limelight *(SYN.)* spotlight, notice, notoriety, fame, prominence.

limerick *(SYN.)* jingle, rhyme.

limit *(SYN.)* terminus, bound, extent, confine, border, restriction, boundary, restraint, edge, frontier, check, end, limitation. *(ANT.)* endlessness, vastness, boundlessness.

limn *(SYN.)* depict, portray, sketch, paint, illustrate.

limp *(SYN.)* soft, flabby, drooping, walk, limber, supple, flexible, hobble, stagger. *(ANT.)* stiff.

limpid *(SYN.)* clear, open, transparent, unobstructed. *(ANT.)* cloudy.

line *(SYN.)* row, file, series, array, sequence, wire, seam, wrinkle, crease, boundary, arrangement, kind, type, division.

lineage *(SYN.)* race, family, tribe, nation, strain, folk, people, ancestry, clan.

linger *(SYN.)* wait, rest, bide, delay, dawdle, stay, loiter, remain, dilly-dally, tarry. *(ANT.)* leave, expedite.

lingo *(SYN.)* vernacular, dialect, language, jargon, speech.

link *(SYN.)* unite, connector, loop, couple, attach, connective, connection, coupling, juncture, bond. *(ANT.)* separate, disconnect, split.

lip *(SYN.)* edge, brim, rim.

liquid *(SYN.)* watery, fluent, fluid, flowing. *(ANT.)* solid, congealed.

liquidate *(SYN.)* pay off, settle, defray.

liquor *(SYN.)* spirits, alcohol, drink, booze.

lissome *(SYN.)* nimble, quick, lively, flexible, agile.

list *(SYN.)* roll, register, slate, series.

listen *(SYN.)* overhear, attend to, heed, hear, list, hearken. *(ANT.)* ignore, scorn, disregard, reject.

listless *(SYN.)* uninterested, tired, lethargic, unconcerned, apathetic. *(ANT.)* active.

literal *(SYN.)* exact, verbatim, precise, strict, faithful.

literally *(SYN.)* actually, exactly, really.

literate *(SYN.)* informed, educated, learned, intelligent, versed, knowledgeable. *(ANT.)* unread, illiterate, ignorant, unlettered.

literature *(SYN.)* books, writings, publications.

lithe *(SYN.)* supple, flexible, bending, limber, pliable. *(ANT.)* stiff.

litigious *(SYN.)* quarrelsome, disputatious, argumentative.

litter *(SYN.)* rubbish, trash, scatter, clutter, strew, debris, rubble, disorder.

little *(SYN.)* tiny, petty, miniature, diminutive, puny, wee, significant, small, short, brief, bit, trivial. *(ANT.)* huge, large, big, long, immense.

liturgy *(SYN.)* ritual, sacrament, worship, service.

live *(SYN.)* dwell, reside, abide, survive, exist, alive, occupy, stay, active, surviving. *(ANT.)* die.

livelihood *(SYN.)* keep, sustenance, support, subsistence, job, trade, profession, vocation.

lively *(SYN.)* blithe,

vivaciousness, clear, vivid, active, frolicsome, brisk, fresh, animated, energetic, live, spry, vigorous, quick, nimble, bright, exciting, supple. (ANT.) *stale, dull, listless, slow, vapid.*

livestock (SYN.) animals, cattle.

livid (SYN.) grayish, furious, pale, enraged.

living (SYN.) support, livelihood, existent, alive.

load (SYN.) oppress, trouble, burden, weight, freight, afflict, encumber, pack, shipment, cargo, lade, tax. (ANT.) *lighten, console, unload, mitigate, empty, ease.*

loafer (SYN.) loiterer, bum, idler, sponger, deadbeat.

loan (SYN.) credit, advance, lend.

loath (SYN.) reluctant, unwilling, opposed.

loathe (SYN.) dislike, despise, hate, abhor, detest, abominate. (ANT.) *love, approve, like, admire.*

loathsome (SYN.) foul, vile, detestable, revolting, abominable, atrocious, offensive, odious. (ANT.) *pleasant, commendable, alluring, agreeable, delightful.*

lob (SYN.) toss, hurl, pitch, throw, heave.

lobby (SYN.) foyer, entry, entrance, vestibule, passageway, entryway.

local (SYN.) limited, regional, restricted.

locality (SYN.) nearness, neighborhood, district, vicinity. (ANT.) *remoteness.*

locate (SYN.) discover, find, unearth, site, situate, place.

located (SYN.) found, residing, positioned, situated, placed.

location (SYN.) spot, locale, station, locality, situation, place, area, site, vicinity, position, zone, region.

lock (SYN.) curl, hook, bolt, braid, ringlet, plait, close, latch, tuft, fastening, bar, hasp, fasten, tress. (ANT.) *open.*

locker (SYN.) wardrobe, closet, cabinet, chest.

locket (SYN.) case, lavaliere, pendant.

locomotion (SYN.) movement, travel, transit, motion.

locution (SYN.) discourse, cadence, manner, accent.

lodge (SYN.) cabin, cottage, hut, club, chalet, society, room, reside, dwell, live, occupy, inhabit, abide, board, fix, settle.

lodger (SYN.) guest, tenant, boarder, occupant.

lofty (SYN.) high, stately, grandiose, towering, elevated, exalted, sublime, majestic, proud, grand, tall, pompous. (ANT.) *undignified, lowly, common, ordinary.*

log (SYN.) lumber, wood, board, register, record, album, account, journal, timber.

logical (SYN.) strong, effective, telling, convincing, reasonable, sensible, rational, sane, sound, cogent. (ANT.) *crazy, illogical, irrational, unreasonable, weak.*

logy (SYN.) tired, inactive, lethargic, sleepy, weary.

loiter (SYN.) idle, linger, wait, stay, tarry, dilly-dally, dawdle.

loll (SYN.) hang, droop, recline, repose, relax.

lone (SYN.) lonely, sole, unaided, single, deserted, isolated, secluded, apart, alone, solitary. (ANT.) *surrounded, accompanied.*

loneliness (SYN.) solitude, isolation, seclusion, alienation.

lonely (SYN.) unaided, isolated, single, solitary, lonesome, unaccompanied, deserted, alone, desolate. (ANT.) *surrounded, attended.*

loner (SYN.) recluse, maverick, outsider, hermit.

lonesome (SYN.) secluded, remote, unpopulated, barren, empty, desolate.

long (SYN.) lengthy, prolonged, wordy, elongated, lingering, drawn out, lasting, protracted, extensive, length, prolix, far-reaching, extended. (ANT.) *terse, concise, abridged, short.*

long-standing (SYN.) persistent, established.

long-winded (SYN.) boring, dull, wordy. (ANT.) *curt, terse.*

look (SYN.) gaze, witness, seem, eye, behold, see, watch, scan, view, appear, stare, discern, glance, examine, examination, peep, expression, appearance, regard, study, contemplation, survey. (ANT.) *overlook, hide, avert, miss.*

loom (SYN.) emerge, appear, show up.

loop (SYN.) ringlet, noose, spiral, fastener.

loose (SYN.) untied, unbound, lax, vague, unrestrained, dissolute, limp, undone, baggy, disengaged, indefinite, slack, careless, heedless, unfastened, free, wanton. (ANT.) *restrained, steady, fastened, secure, tied, firm, fast, definite,*
inhibited.

loosen (SYN.) untie, undo, loose, unchain. (ANT.) *tie, tighten, secure.*

loot (SYN.) booty, plunder, take, steal, rob, sack, rifle, pillage, ravage, devastate.

lope (SYN.) run, race, bound, gallop.

lopsided (SYN.) unequal, twisted, uneven, askew, distorted.

loquacious (SYN.) garrulous, wordy, profuse, chatty, verbose.

lord (SYN.) peer, ruler, proprietor, nobleman, master, owner, boss, governor.

lore (SYN.) learning, knowledge, wisdom, stories, legends, beliefs, teachings.

lose (SYN.) misplace, flop, fail, sacrifice, forfeit, mislay, vanish, surrender. (ANT.) *succeed, locate, place, win, discover, find.*

loss (SYN.) injury, damage, want, hurt, need, bereavement, trouble, death, failure, deficiency.

lost (SYN.) dazed, wasted, astray, forfeited, preoccupied, used, adrift, bewildered, missing, distracted, consumed, misspent, absorbed, confused, mislaid, gone, destroyed. (ANT.) *found, anchored.*

lot (SYN.) result, destiny, bunch, many, amount, fate, cluster, group, sum, portion, outcome, number, doom, issue.

lotion (SYN.) cosmetic, salve, balm, cream.

lottery (SYN.) wager, chance, drawing, raffle.

loud (SYN.) vociferous, noisy, resounding, stentorian, clamorous, sonorous, thunderous, shrill, blaring, roaring, deafening. (ANT.) *soft, inaudible, murmuring, subdued, quiet, dulcet.*

lounge (SYN.) idle, loaf, laze, sofa, couch, davenport, relax, rest, lobby, salon, divan.

louse (SYN.) scoundrel, knave, cad, rat.

lousy (SYN.) revolting, grimy, rotten, dirty, disgusting.

lovable (SYN.) charming, attractive, delightful, amiable, sweet, cuddly, likeable.

love (SYN.) attachment, endearment, affection, adoration, liking, devotion, warmth, tenderness, friendliness, adore, worship, like, cherish, fondness. (ANT.) *loathing, detest, indifference, dislike, hate, hatred.*

loveliness (SYN.) grace, pulchritude, elegance, charm,
attractiveness, comeliness, fairness, beauty. (ANT.) *ugliness, eyesore, disfigurement, deformity.*

lovely (SYN.) handsome, fair, charming, pretty, attractive, delightful, beautiful, beauteous, exquisite, comely. (ANT.) *ugly, unsightly, homely, foul, hideous, repulsive.*

lover (SYN.) fiancé, suitor, courter, sweetheart, beau.

loving (SYN.) close, intimate, confidential, affectionate, friendly. (ANT.) *formal, conventional, ceremonious, distant.*

low (SYN.) mean, vile, despicable, vulgar, abject, groveling, contemptible, lesser, menial. (ANT.) *righteous, lofty, esteemed, noble.*

lower (SYN.) subordinate, minor, secondary, quiet, soften, disgrace, degrade, decrease, reduce, diminish, inferior. (ANT.) *greater, superior, increase, better.*

loyal (SYN.) earnest, ardent, addicted, inclined, faithful, devoted, affectionate, prone, fond, patriotic, dependable, true. (ANT.) *indisposed, detached, disloyal, traitorous, untrammeled.*

loyalty (SYN.) devotion, steadfastness, constancy, faithfulness, fidelity, patriotism, allegiance. (ANT.) *treachery, falseness, disloyalty.*

lubricate (SYN.) oil, grease, anoint.

lucent (SYN.) radiant, beaming, vivid, illuminated, lustrous.

lucid (SYN.) plain, visible, clear, intelligible, unmistakable, transparent, limpid, translucent, open, shining, light. (ANT.) *unclear, vague, obscure.*

luck (SYN.) chance, fortunate, fortune, lot, fate, fluke, destiny, karma. (ANT.) *misfortune.*

lucrative (SYN.) well-paying, profitable, high-paying, productive, beneficial.

ludicrous (SYN.) absurd, ridiculous, preposterous.

lug (SYN.) pull, haul, drag, tug.

luggage (SYN.) bags, valises, baggage, suitcases, trunks.

lugubrious (SYN.) mournful, sad, gloomy, somber, melancholy.

lukewarm (SYN.) unenthusiastic, tepid, spiritless, detached, apathetic, mild.

lull (SYN.) quiet, calm, soothe, rest, hush, stillness, pause, break, intermission.

lumber (SYN.) logs, timber,

wood.

luminous (SYN.) beaming, lustrous, shining, glowing, gleaming, bright, light. (ANT.) murky, dull, dark.

lummox (SYN.) yokel, oaf, bumpkin, clown, klutz.

lump (SYN.) swelling, protuberance, mass, chunk, hunk, bump.

lunacy (SYN.) derangement, madness, aberration, psychosis, craziness. (ANT.) stability, rationality.

lunge (SYN.) charge, stab, attack, thrust, push.

lurch (SYN.) topple, sway, toss, roll, rock, tip, pitch.

lure (SYN.) draw, tug, drag, entice, attraction, haul, attract, temptation, persuade, pull, draw on, allure. (ANT.) drive, alienate, propel.

lurid (SYN.) sensational, terrible, melodramatic, startling.

lurk (SYN.) sneak, hide, prowl, slink, creep.

luscious (SYN.) savory, delightful, juicy, sweet, pleasing, delectable, palatable, delicious, tasty. (ANT.) unsavory, nauseous, acrid.

lush (SYN.) tender, succulent, ripe, juicy. (ANT.) dry, arrid, barren.

lust (SYN.) longing, desire, passion, appetite, craving, aspiration, urge.

lusty (SYN.) healthy, strong, mighty, powerful, sturdy, strapping, hale, hardy. (ANT.) weak.

luxuriant (SYN.) abundant, flourishing, dense, lush, rich.

luxurious (SYN.) rich, lavish, deluxe, elaborate, fancy, opulent, splendid. (ANT.) simple, crude, sparse.

luxury (SYN.) frills, comfort, extravagance, elegance, splendor. (ANT.) poverty.

lyric (SYN.) musical, text, words, libretto.

lyrical (SYN.) poetic, musical.

luster (SYN.) shine, gleam, gloss, sparkle, reflection.

macabre (SYN.) ghastly, grim, horrible, gruesome.

macala (SYN.) mole, patch, freckle, spot.

maceration (SYN.) dilution, washing.

machination (SYN.) hoax, swindle, cardsharking, cunning, plot, cabal, conspiracy.

machinator (SYN.) strategist, schemer.

machine (SYN.) motor, mechanism, device, contrivance.

machinist (SYN.) engineer.

macilent (SYN.) gaunt, lean, lank, meager, emaciated.

mactation (SYN.) immolation, self-immolation, infanticide.

maculate (SYN.) bespot, stipple.

maculation (SYN.) irritation, striae, iridescence, spottiness.

mad (SYN.) incensed, crazy, insane, angry, furious, delirious, provoked, enraged, demented, maniacal, exasperated, wrathful, crazy, deranged. (ANT.) sane, calm, healthy, rational, lucid, cheerful, happy.

madam (SYN.) dame, woman, lady, matron, mistress.

madden (SYN.) anger, annoy, infuriate, enrage, provoke, aspirate, outrage. (ANT.) please, mollify, calm.

madness (SYN.) derangement, delirium, aberration, mania, insanity, craziness, frenzy, psychosis.

maelstrom (SYN.) surge, rapids, eddy, white water, riptide.

magazine (SYN.) journal, periodical, arsenal, armory.

magic (SYN.) sorcery, wizardry, charm, legerdemain, enchantment, black art, necromancy, conjuring.

magical (SYN.) mystical, marvelous, magic, miraculous, bewitching, spellbinding.

magician (SYN.) conjuror, sorcerer, wizard, witch, artist, trickster.

magistrate (SYN.) judge, adjudicator.

magnanimous (SYN.) giving, bountiful, beneficent, unselfish. (ANT.) stingy, greedy, selfish.

magnate (SYN.) leader, bigwig, tycoon, chief, giant.

magnet (SYN.) enticer, enticement, lure, temptation.

magnetic (SYN.) pulling, attractive, alluring, drawing, enthralling, seductive.

magnetism (SYN.) allure, irresistibility, attraction, appeal.

magnificence (SYN.) luxury, grandeur, splendor, majesty, dynamic, mesmerizing.

magnificent (SYN.) rich, lavish, luxurious, splendid, wonderful, extraordinary, impressive. (ANT.) simple, plain.

magnify (SYN.) heighten, exaggerate, amplify, expand, stretch, caricature, increase, enhance. (ANT.) compress, understate, depreciate, belittle.

magnitude (SYN.) mass, bigness, size, area, volume, dimensions, greatness, extent, measure, importance, consequence, significance.

maid (SYN.) chambermaid, servant, maidservant.

maiden (SYN.) original, foremost, first, damsel, lass, miss.

mail (SYN.) dispatch, send, letters, post, correspondence.

maim (SYN.) disable, cripple, hurt, wound, injure, mangle, mutilate, incapacitate.

main (SYN.) essential, chief, highest, principal, first, leading, cardinal, supreme, foremost. (ANT.) supplemental, subordinate, auxiliary.

mainstay (SYN.) buttress, pillar, refuge, reinforcement, support, backbone.

maintain (SYN.) claim, support, uphold, defend, vindicate, sustain, continue, allege, contend, preserve, affirm, keep, justify, keep up. (ANT.) neglect, oppose, discontinue, resist, deny.

maintenance (SYN.) subsistence, livelihood, living, support, preservation, upkeep.

majestic (SYN.) magnificent, stately, noble, august, grand, imposing, sublime, lofty, high, grandiose, dignified, royal, kingly, princely, regal. (ANT.) humble, lowly, undignified, common, ordinary.

majesty (SYN.) grandeur, dignity, nobility, splendor, distinction, eminence.

major (SYN.) important, superior, larger, chief, greater, uppermost. (ANT.) inconsequential, minor.

make (SYN.) execute, cause, produce, establish, assemble, create, shape, compel, fashion, construct, build, fabricate, manufacture, form, become. (ANT.) unmake, break, undo, demolish.

make-believe (SYN.) pretend, imagined, simulated, false, fake, unreal.

maker (SYN.) inventor, creator, producer, builder, manufacturer, originator.

makeshift (SYN.) proxy, deputy, understudy, expedient, agent, lieutenant, alternate, substitute, equivalent. (ANT.) sovereign, head, principal.

make-up (SYN.) composition, formation, structure, cosmetics.

malady (SYN.) disease, illness, sickness, ailment, infirmity, disorder, affliction. (ANT.) vigor, healthiness, health.

malaise (SYN.) anxiety, apprehension, dissatisfaction, uneasiness, nervousness, disquiet, discontent.

malcontent (SYN.) displeased, ill-humored, querulous, discontented, quarrelsome.

male (SYN.) masculine, virile. (ANT.) female, womanly, feminine.

malefactor (SYN.) perpetrator, gangster, hoodlum, wrongdoer, troublemaker, criminal, scoundrel, evildoer, lawbreaker.

malevolence (SYN.) spite, malice, enmity, rancor, animosity. (ANT.) love, affection, toleration, kindness.

malfunction (SYN.) flaw, breakdown, snag, glitch, failure.

malice (SYN.) spite, grudge, enmity, ill will, malignity, animosity, rancor, resentment, viciousness, grudge, bitterness. (ANT.) love, affection, toleration, benevolence, charity.

malicious (SYN.) hostile, malignant, virulent, bitter, rancorous, evil-minded, malevolent, spiteful, wicked. (ANT.) kind, benevolent, affectionate.

malign (SYN.) misuse, defame, revile, abuse, traduce, asperse, misapply, disparage. (ANT.) praise, cherish, protect, minor.

malignant (SYN.) harmful, deadly, killing, lethal, mortal, destructive, hurtful, malicious. (ANT.) benign, harmless.

malingerer (SYN.) quitter, idler, goldbrick.

malleable (SYN.) meek, tender, soft, lenient, flexible, mild, compassionate, supple. (ANT.) tough, rigid, unyielding, hard.

malodorous (SYN.) reeking, fetid, smelly, noxious, vile, rancid, offensive.

malpractice (SYN.) wrongdoing, misdeed, abuse, malfeasance, error, mismanagement, dereliction, fault, sin, misconduct.

maltreat (SYN.) mistreat, ill-treatment, abuse.

maltreatment (SYN.) disparagement, perversion, aspersion, invective, defamation, profanation. (ANT.) respect, approval, laudation, commendation.

mammoth (SYN.) enormous,

immense, huge, colossal, gigantic, gargantuan, ponderous. (*ANT.*) minuscule, tiny, small.

man (*SYN.*) person, human being, society, folk, soul, individual, mortal, fellow, male, gentleman. (*ANT.*) woman.

manacle (*SYN.*) chain, shackle, cuff, handcuff, bond.

manage (*SYN.*) curb, govern, direct, bridle, command, regulate, repress, check, restrain, dominate, guide, lead, supervise, superintend, control, rule. (*ANT.*) forsake, submit, abandon, mismanage, bungle.

manageable (*SYN.*) willing, obedient, docile, controllable, tractable, submissive, governable, wieldy, untroublesome. (*ANT.*) recalcitrant, unmanageable, wild.

management (*SYN.*) regulation, administration, supervision, direction, control.

manager (*SYN.*) overseer, superintendent, supervisor, director, boss, executive.

mandate (*SYN.*) order, injunction, command, referendum, dictate, writ, directive, commission.

mandatory (*SYN.*) compulsory, required, obligatory, imperative, necessary. (*ANT.*) optional.

maneuver (*SYN.*) execution, effort, proceeding, enterprise, working, action, operation, agency, instrumentality. (*ANT.*) rest, inaction, cessation.

mangle (*SYN.*) tear apart, cut, maim, wound, mutilate, injure, break, demolish.

mangy (*SYN.*) shoddy, frazzled, seedy, threadbare, shabby, ragged, sordid.

manhandle (*SYN.*) maltreat, maul, abuse, ill-treat.

manhood (*SYN.*) maturity, manliness. (*ANT.*) youth.

mania (*SYN.*) insanity, enthusiasm, craze, desire, madness.

manic (*SYN.*) excited, hyped up, agitated.

manifest (*SYN.*) open, evident, lucid, clear, distinct, unobstructed, cloudless, apparent, intelligible, apparent. (*ANT.*) vague, overcast, unclear, cloudy, hidden, concealed.

manifesto (*SYN.*) pronouncement, edict, proclamation, statement, declaration.

manifold (*SYN.*) various, many, multiple, numerous, abundant, copious, profuse. (*ANT.*) few.

manipulate (*SYN.*) manage, feel, work, operate, handle, touch, maneuver.

manly (*SYN.*) strong, brave, masculine, manful, courageous, stalwart.

man-made (*SYN.*) artificial. (*ANT.*) natural.

manner (*SYN.*) air, demeanor, custom, style, method, deportment, mode, habit, practice, way, behavior, fashion.

mannerism (*SYN.*) eccentricity, quirk, habit, peculiarity, idiosyncrasy, trait.

mannerly (*SYN.*) well-bred, gentlemanly, courteous, suave, polite, genteel.

manor (*SYN.*) land, mansion, estate, domain, villa, castle, property, palace.

manslaughter (*SYN.*) murder, killing, assassination, homicide, elimination.

mantle (*SYN.*) serape, garment, overgarment, cover, cloak, wrap.

manual (*SYN.*) directory, guidebook, handbook, physical, laborious, menial.

manufacture (*SYN.*) construct, make, assemble, fabricate, produce, fashion, build.

manure (*SYN.*) fertilizer, droppings, waste, compost.

manuscript (*SYN.*) copy, writing, work, paper, composition, document.

many (*SYN.*) numerous, various, diverse, multitudinous, sundry, multifarious, manifold, abundant, plentiful. (*ANT.*) infrequent, meager, few, scanty.

map (*SYN.*) sketch, plan, chart, graph.

mar (*SYN.*) spoil, hurt, damage, impair, harm, deface, injure. (*ANT.*) repair, benefit, mend.

marathon (*SYN.*) relay, race, contest.

maraud (*SYN.*) invade, plunder, loot, ransack, ravage, raid.

march (*SYN.*) promenade, parade, pace, hike, walk, tramp.

margin (*SYN.*) boundary, border, rim, edge.

marginal (*SYN.*) unnecessary, nonessential, borderline, noncritical. (*ANT.*) essential.

marine (*SYN.*) naval, oceanic, nautical, ocean, maritime.

mariner (*SYN.*) seafarer, gob, seaman, sailor.

marionette (*SYN.*) doll, puppet.

maritime (*SYN.*) shore, coastal, nautical.

mark (*SYN.*) stain, badge, stigma, vestige, sign, feature, label, characteristic, trace,

brand, trait, scar, indication, impression, effect, imprint, stamp, brand.

marked (*SYN.*) plain, apparent, noticeable, evident, decided, noted, special, noteworthy.

market (*SYN.*) supermarket, store, bazaar, mart, stall, marketplace, plaza, emporium.

maroon (*SYN.*) desert, leave behind, forsake, abandon, jettison.

marriage (*SYN.*) wedding, matrimony, nuptials, espousal, union, alliance, association. (*ANT.*) divorce, celibacy, separation.

marrow (*SYN.*) center, core, gist, essential.

marry (*SYN.*) wed, espouse, betroth.

marsh (*SYN.*) bog, swamp, mire, everglade, estuary.

marshal (*SYN.*) adjutant, officer, order, arrange, rank.

mart (*SYN.*) shop, market, store.

martial (*SYN.*) warlike, combative, militant, belligerent. (*ANT.*) peaceful.

martyr (*SYN.*) victim, sufferer, tortured, torment, plague, harass, persecute.

marvel (*SYN.*) phenomenon, wonder, miracle, astonishment, sensation.

marvelous (*SYN.*) rare, wonderful, extraordinary, unusual, exceptional, miraculous, wondrous, amazing, astonishing, astounding. (*ANT.*) usual, common, ordinary.

mascot (*SYN.*) pet, amulet, charm.

masculine (*SYN.*) robust, manly, virile, strong, bold, male, lusty, vigorous, hardy, mannish. (*ANT.*) weak, emasculated, feminine, effeminate, womanish, female.

mash (*SYN.*) mix, pulverize, crush, grind, crumble, granulate.

mask (*SYN.*) veil, disguise, cloak, secrete, withhold, hide, cover, protection, protector, camouflage, conceal, screen. (*ANT.*) uncover, reveal, disclose, show, expose.

masquerade (*SYN.*) pretend, disguise, pose, impersonate, costume party.

mass (*SYN.*) society, torso, body, remains, association, carcass, bulk, company, pile, heap, quantity, aggregation. (*ANT.*) spirit, mind, intellect.

massacre (*SYN.*) butcher, murder, carnage, slaughter, execute, slay, genocide, killing, butchery, extermination.

(*ANT.*) save, protect, vivify, animate.

massage (*SYN.*) knead, rub, stroke.

masses (*SYN.*) populace, crowd, multitude, people.

massive (*SYN.*) grave, cumbersome, heavy, sluggish, ponderous, serious, burdensome, huge, immense, tremendous, gigantic. (*ANT.*) light, animated, small, tiny, little.

mast (*SYN.*) pole, post.

master (*SYN.*) owner, employer, leader, ruler, chief, head, lord, teacher, manager, holder, commander, overseer, expert, maestro, genius, captain, director, boss. (*ANT.*) slave, servant.

masterful (*SYN.*) commanding, bossy, domineering, dictatorial, cunning, wise, accomplished, skillful, sharp.

masterly (*SYN.*) adroit, superb, skillful, expert. (*ANT.*) awkward, clumsy.

mastermind (*SYN.*) prodigy, sage, guru.

masterpiece (*SYN.*) prizewinner, classic, perfection, model.

mastery (*SYN.*) sway, sovereignty, domination, transcendence, ascendancy, influence, jurisdiction, prestige.

masticate (*SYN.*) chew.

mat (*SYN.*) cover, rug, pallet, bedding, pad.

match (*SYN.*) equivalent, equal, contest, balance, resemble, peer, mate.

matchless (*SYN.*) peerless, incomparable, unequaled, unrivaled, excellent. (*ANT.*) ordinary, unimpressive.

mate (*SYN.*) friend, colleague, associate, partner, companion, comrade. (*ANT.*) stranger, adversary.

material (*SYN.*) sensible, momentous, germane, bodily, palpable, important, physical, essential, corporeal, tangible, substance, matter, fabric. (*ANT.*) metaphysical, spiritual, insignificant, mental, immaterial, irrelevant, intangible.

materialize (*SYN.*) take shape, finalize, embody, incarnate, emerge, appear.

maternal (*SYN.*) motherly. (*ANT.*) fatherly.

mathematics (*SYN.*) measurements, computations, numbers, calculation, figures.

matrimony (*SYN.*) marriage, wedding, espousal, union. (*ANT.*) virginity, divorce.

matrix (*SYN.*) template, stamp, negative, stencil,

mold, form, die, cutout.

matron (SYN.) lady.

matted (SYN.) tangled, clustered, rumpled, shaggy, knotted, gnarled, tousled.

matter (SYN.) cause, thing, substance, occasion, material, moment, topic, stuff, concern, theme, subject, consequence, affair, business, interest. (ANT.) spirit, immateriality.

mature (SYN.) ready, matured, complete, ripe, consummate, mellow, aged, seasoned, full-grown. (ANT.) raw, crude, undeveloped, young, immature, innocent.

maudlin (SYN.) emotional, mushy, sentimental, mawkish.

maul (SYN.) pummel, mistreat, manhandle, beat, batter, bruise, abuse.

mausoleum (SYN.) shrine, tomb, vault.

maverick (SYN.) nonconformist, oddball, outsider, dissenter, loner.

mawkish (SYN.) sentimental, emotional, nostalgic.

maxim (SYN.) rule, code, law, proverb, principle, saying, adage, motto.

maximum (SYN.) highest, largest, head, greatest, climax. (ANT.) minimum.

may (SYN.) can, be able.

maybe (SYN.) feasibly, perchance, perhaps, possibly. (ANT.) definitely.

mayhem (SYN.) brutality, viciousness, ruthlessness.

maze (SYN.) complex, labyrinth, network, muddle, confusion, snarl, tangle.

meadow (SYN.) field, pasture, lea, range, grassland.

meager (SYN.) sparse, scanty, mean, frugal, slight, paltry, inadequate. (ANT.) ample, plentiful, abundant, bountiful.

meal (SYN.) refreshment, dinner, lunch, repast, breakfast.

mean (SYN.) sordid, base, intend, plan, propose, expect, indicate, denote, say, signify, suggest, express, average, nasty, middle, contemptible, offensive, vulgar, unkind, cruel, despicable, vile, low, medium. (ANT.) dignified, noble, exalted, thoughtful, gentle, openhanded, kind, generous, admirable.

meander (SYN.) wind, stray, wander, twist.

meaning (SYN.) gist, connotation, intent, purport, drift, acceptance, implication, sense, import, interpretation, denotation, signification, explanation, purpose, significance.

meaningful (SYN.) profound, deep, expressive, important, crucial.

meaningless (SYN.) nonsensical, senseless, unreasonable, preposterous.

means (SYN.) utensil, channel, agent, money, riches, vehicle, apparatus, device, wealth, support, medium, instrument. (ANT.) preventive, impediment, hindrance.

measly (SYN.) scanty, puny, skimpy, meager, petty.

measure (SYN.) law, bulk, rule, criterion, size, volume, weight, standard, dimension, breadth, depth, test, touchstone, trial, length, extent, gauge.

measureless (SYN.) immeasurable, immense, boundless, limitless, infinite, vast. (ANT.) figurable, ascertainable, measurable.

meat (SYN.) lean, flesh, food.

mecca (SYN.) target, shrine, goal, sanctuary, destination.

mechanic (SYN.) repairman, machinist.

mechanism (SYN.) device, contrivance, tool, machine, machinery.

medal (SYN.) decoration, award, badge, medallion, reward, ribbon, prize, honor.

meddle (SYN.) tamper, interpose, pry, snoop, intrude, interrupt, interfere, monkey.

meddlesome (SYN.) forward, bothersome, intrusive, obtrusive.

mediate (SYN.) settle, intercede, umpire, intervene, negotiate, arbitrate, referee.

medicinal (SYN.) helping, healing, remedial, therapeutic, corrective.

medicine (SYN.) drug, medication, remedy, cure, prescription, potion.

mediocre (SYN.) medium, mean, average, moderate, fair, ordinary. (ANT.) outstanding, exceptional.

meditate (SYN.) remember, muse, think, judge, mean, conceive, contemplate, deem, suppose, purpose, consider, picture, reflect, believe, plan, reckon.

medium (SYN.) modicum, average, middling, median. (ANT.) extreme.

medley (SYN.) hodgepodge, mixture, assortment, conglomeration, mishmash, miscellany.

meek (SYN.) subdued, dull, tedious, flat, docile, domesticated, tame, insipid, domestic. (ANT.) spirited, exciting, savage, wild.

meet (SYN.) fulfill, suffer, find, collide, gratify, engage, connect, converge, encounter, unite, join, satisfy, settle, greet, answer, undergo, meeting, contest, match, assemble, discharge, gather, convene, congregate, confront, intersect. (ANT.) scatter, disperse, separate, cleave.

melancholy (SYN.) disconsolate, dejected, despondent, glum, somber, pensive, moody, dispirited, depressed, gloomy, dismal, doleful, depression, downcast, gloom, sadness, sad, grave, downhearted, sorrowful. (ANT.) happy, cheerful, merry.

meld (SYN.) unite, mix, combine, fuse, merge, blend, commingle, amalgamate.

melee (SYN.) battle royal, fight, brawl, free-for-all, fracas.

mellow (SYN.) mature, ripe, aged, cured, full-flavored, sweet, smooth, melodious, develop, soften. (ANT.) unripened, immature.

melodious (SYN.) lilting, musical, lyric, dulcet, mellifluous, tuneful, melodic.

melodramatic (SYN.) dramatic, ceremonious, affected, stagy, histrionic, overwrought, sensational, stagy. (ANT.) unemotional, subdued, modest.

melody (SYN.) strand, concord, music, air, song, tune, harmony.

melt (SYN.) dissolve, liquefy, blend, fade out, vanish, dwindle, disappear, thaw. (ANT.) freeze, harden, solidify.

member (SYN.) share, part, allotment, moiety, element, concern, interest, lines, faction, role, apportionment.

membrane (SYN.) layer, sheath, tissue, covering.

memento (SYN.) keepsake, token, reminder, trophy, sign, souvenir, remembrance.

memoirs (SYN.) diary, reflections, experiences, autobiography, journal, confessions.

memorable (SYN.) important, historic, significant, unforgettable, noteworthy, momentous, crucial, impressive. (ANT.) passing, forgettable, transitory, commonplace.

memorandum (SYN.) letter, mark, token, note, indication, remark, message.

memorial (SYN.) monument, souvenir, memento, remembrance, commemoration, reminiscent, ritual, testimonial.

memorize (SYN.) study, remember.

memory (SYN.) renown, remembrance, reminiscence, fame, retrospection, recollection, reputation. (ANT.) oblivion.

menace (SYN.) warning, threat, intimidation, warn, threaten, imperil, forebode.

menagerie (SYN.) collection, zoo, kennel.

mend (SYN.) restore, better, refit, sew, remedy, patch, correct, repair, rectify, ameliorate, improve, reform, recover, fix. (ANT.) hurt, deface, rend, destroy.

mendacious (SYN.) dishonest, false, lying, deceitful, deceptive, tricky. (ANT.) honest, truthful, sincere, creditable.

mendicant (SYN.) ragamuffin, vagabond, beggar.

menial (SYN.) unskilled, lowly, degrading, tedious, humble, routine.

mental (SYN.) reasoning, intellectual, rational, thinking, conscious, reflective, thoughtful. (ANT.) physical.

mentality (SYN.) intellect, reason, understanding, liking, disposition, judgment, brain, inclination, faculties, outlook. (ANT.) materiality, corporeality.

mention (SYN.) introduce, refer to, reference, allude, enumerate, speak of.

mentor (SYN.) advisor, tutor, sponsor, guru, teacher, counselor, master, coach.

mercenary (SYN.) sordid, corrupt, venal, covetous, grasping, avaricious, greedy. (ANT.) liberal, generous.

merchandise (SYN.) stock, wares, goods, sell, commodities, promote, staples, products.

merchant (SYN.) retailer, dealer, trader, storekeeper, salesman, businessman.

merciful (SYN.) humane, kindhearted, tender, clement, sympathetic, forgiving, tolerant, forbearing, lenient, compassionate, tenderhearted, kind. (ANT.) remorseless, cruel, unjust, mean, harsh, unforgiving, vengeful, brutal, unfeeling, pitiless.

merciless (SYN.) carnal, ferocious, brute, barbarous, gross, ruthless, cruel, remorseless, bestial, savage, rough, pitiless, inhuman. (ANT.) humane, courteous, merciful, openhearted, kind, civilized.

mercurial (SYN.) fickle,

unstable, volatile, changeable, inconstant, capricious, flighty.

mercy (SYN.) grace, consideration, kindness, clemency, mildness, forgiveness, pity, charity, sympathy, leniency, compassion. (ANT.) punishment, retribution, ruthlessness, cruelty, vengeance.

mere (SYN.) only, simple, scant, bare. (ANT.) substantial, considerable.

merely (SYN.) only, barely, simply, hardly.

meretricious (SYN.) gaudy, sham, bogus, tawdry, flashy.

merge (SYN.) unify, fuse, combine, amalgamate, unite, blend, commingle. (ANT.) separate, decompose, analyze.

merger (SYN.) cartel, union, conglomerate, trust, incorporation, combine, pool.

meridian (SYN.) climax, summit, pinnacle, zenith, peak, acme, apex, culmination.

merit (SYN.) worthiness, earn, goodness, effectiveness, power, value, virtue, goodness, quality, deserve, excellence, worth. (ANT.) sin, fault, lose, consume.

merited (SYN.) proper, deserved, suitable, adequate, earned. (ANT.) unmerited, improper.

meritorious (SYN.) laudable, excellent, commendable, good, praiseworthy, deserving.

merry (SYN.) hilarious, lively, festive, joyous, sprightly, mirthful, blithe, gay, cheery, joyful, jolly, happy, gleeful, jovial, cheerful. (ANT.) sorrowful, doleful, morose, gloomy, sad, melancholy.

mesh (SYN.) grid, screen, net, complex.

mesmerize (SYN.) enthrall, transfix, spellbind, bewitch, charm, fascinate, hypnotize.

mess (SYN.) dirtiness, untidiness, disorder, confusion, muddle, trouble, jumble, difficulty, predicament, confuse, dirty.

message (SYN.) letter, annotation, memo, symbol, indication, sign, note, communication, memorandum, observation, token.

messenger (SYN.) bearer, agent, runner, courier, liaison, delegate, page.

messy (SYN.) disorderly, dirty, confusing, confused, disordered, sloppy, untidy, slovenly. (ANT.) orderly, neat, tidy.

metallic (SYN.) grating, harsh, clanging, brassy, brazen.

metamorphosis (SYN.) transfiguration, change, alteration, rebirth, mutation.

mete (SYN.) deal, assign, apportion, divide, give, allocate, allot, measure. (ANT.) withhold, keep, retain.

meteoric (SYN.) flashing, blazing, swift, brilliant, spectacular, remarkable.

meter (SYN.) record, measure, gauge.

method (SYN.) order, manner, plan, way, mode, technique, fashion, approach, design, procedure. (ANT.) disorder.

methodical (SYN.) exact, definite, ceremonious, stiff, accurate, distinct, unequivocal. (ANT.) easy, loose, informal.

meticulous (SYN.) precise, careful, exacting, fastidious, fussy, perfectionist.

metropolitan (SYN.) civic, city, municipal.

mettle (SYN.) intrepidity, resolution, boldness, prowess, bravery, fearlessness. (ANT.) fear, timidity, cowardice.

microscopic (SYN.) tiny, precise, fine, detailed, minute, infinitesimal, minimal. (ANT.) general, huge, enormous.

middle (SYN.) midpoint, nucleus, center, midst, median, central, intermediate, core. (ANT.) end, rim, outskirts, beginning, border, periphery.

middleman (SYN.) dealer, agent, distributor, broker, representative, intermediary.

midget (SYN.) gnome, shrimp, pygmy, runt, dwarf. (ANT.) giant.

midst (SYN.) center, heart, middle, thick.

midway (SYN.) halfway, midmost, inside, central, middle.

mien (SYN.) way, semblance, manner, behavior, demeanor, expression, deportment.

miff (SYN.) provoke, rile, chagrin, irk, irritate, affront, offend, annoy, exasperate.

might (SYN.) force, power, vigor, potency, ability, strength. (ANT.) frailty, vulnerability, weakness.

mighty (SYN.) firm, fortified, powerful, athletic, potent, muscular, robust, strong, cogent. (ANT.) feeble, weak, brittle, insipid, frail, delicate.

migrant (SYN.) traveling, roaming, straying, roving, rambling, transient, meandering.

(ANT.) stationary.

migrate (SYN.) resettle, move, emigrate, immigrate, relocate, journey. (ANT.) stay, remain, settle.

migratory (SYN.) itinerant, roving, mobile, vagabond, unsettled, nomadic, wandering.

mild (SYN.) soothing, moderate, gentle, tender, bland, pleasant, kind, meek, calm, amiable, compassionate, temperate, peaceful, soft. (ANT.) severe, turbulent, stormy, excitable, violent, harsh, bitter.

milieu (SYN.) environment, background, locale, setting, scene, circumstances.

militant (SYN.) warlike, belligerent, hostile, fighting, pugnacious, aggressive, combative. (ANT.) peaceful.

military (SYN.) troops, army, service, soldiers.

milksop (SYN.) namby-pamby, weakling, sissy, coward.

mill (SYN.) foundry, shop, plant, factory, manufactory.

millstone (SYN.) load, impediment, burden, encumbrance, hindrance.

mimic (SYN.) simulate, duplicate, copy, imitate, mock, counterfeit, simulate. (ANT.) invent, distort, alter.

mince (SYN.) shatter, fragment, chop, smash.

mind (SYN.) intelligence, psyche, disposition, intention, understanding, intellect, spirit, brain, inclination, mentality, soul, wit, liking, brain, sense, watch, faculties, judgment, reason.

mindful (SYN.) alert, aware, cognizant, watchful, sensible, heedful.

mine (SYN.) shaft, lode, pit, excavation, drill, dig, quarry, source.

mingle (SYN.) unite, coalesce, fuse, merge, combine, amalgamate, unify, conjoin, mix, blend, commingle. (ANT.) separate, analyze, sort, disintegrate.

miniature (SYN.) small, little, tiny, midget, minute, minuscule, wee, petite, diminutive. (ANT.) outsize.

minimize (SYN.) shorten, deduct, belittle, decrease, reduce, curtail, lessen, diminish, subtract. (ANT.) enlarge, increase, amplify.

minimum (SYN.) lowest, least, smallest, slightest. (ANT.) maximum.

minister (SYN.) pastor, clergyman, vicar, parson, curate,

preacher, prelate, chaplain, cleric, deacon, reverend.

minor (SYN.) poorer, lesser, petty, youth, inferior, secondary, smaller, unimportant, lower. (ANT.) higher, superior, major, greater.

minority (SYN.) youth, childhood, immaturity.

minstrel (SYN.) bard, musician.

mint (SYN.) stamp, coin, strike, punch.

minus (SYN.) lacking, missing, less, absent, without.

minute (SYN.) tiny, particular, fine, precise, jiffy, instant, moment, wee, exact, detailed, microscopic. (ANT.) large, huge, enormous.

miraculous (SYN.) spiritual, supernatural, wonderful, marvelous, incredible, preternatural. (ANT.) commonplace, natural, common, plain, everyday, human.

mirage (SYN.) vision, illusion, fantasy, dream, phantom. (ANT.) reality, actuality.

mire (SYN.) marsh, slush, slime, mud.

mirror (SYN.) glass, reflector, reflect.

mirth (SYN.) joy, glee, jollity, joyousness, gaiety, joyfulness, laughter, merriment. (ANT.) sadness, gloom, seriousness.

misadventure (SYN.) accident, adversity, reverse, calamity, catastrophe, hardship, mischance, setback.

misappropriate (SYN.) embezzle, steal, purloin, plunder, cheat, filch, defraud.

misbehave (SYN.) trespass, act badly. (ANT.) behave.

miscalculate (SYN.) miscount, blunder, confuse, err, mistake, misconstrue.

miscarriage (SYN.) omission, want, decay, fiasco, default, deficiency, loss, abortion, prematurity. (ANT.) success, sufficiency, achievement.

miscarry (SYN.) flounder, fall short, falter, go wrong, fail. (ANT.) succeed.

miscellaneous (SYN.) diverse, motley, indiscriminate, assorted, sundry, heterogeneous, mixed, varied. (ANT.) classified, selected, homogeneous, alike, ordered.

miscellany (SYN.) medley, gallimaufry, jumble, potpourri, mixture, collection.

mischief (SYN.) injury, harm, damage, evil, prankishness, rascality, roguishness, playfulness, wrong, detriment, hurt. (ANT.) kindness, boon, benefit.

mischievous (SYN.) roguish, prankish, naughty, playful.

(ANT.) well-behaved, good.

misconduct (SYN.) transgression, delinquency, wrongdoing, negligence.

miscreant (SYN.) rascal, wretch, rogue, sinner, criminal, villain, scoundrel.

miscue (SYN.) blunder, fluff, mistake, error, lapse.

misdemeanor (SYN.) infringement, transgression, violation, offense, wrong.

miser (SYN.) cheapskate, tightwad, skinflint. (ANT.) philanthropist.

miserable (SYN.) abject, forlorn, comfortless, low, worthless, pitiable, distressed, heartbroken, disconsolate, despicable, wretched, uncomfortable, unhappy, poor, unlucky, paltry, contemptible, mean. (ANT.) fortunate, happy, contented, joyful, content, wealthy, honorable, lucky, noble.

miserly (SYN.) stingy, greedy, acquisitive, tight, tightfisted, cheap, mean, parsimonious, avaricious. (ANT.) bountiful, generous, spendthrift, munificent, extravagant, openhanded, altruistic.

misery (SYN.) suffering, woe, evil, agony, torment, trouble, distress, anguish, grief, unhappiness, tribulation, calamity, sorrow. (ANT.) fun, pleasure, delight, joy.

misfit (SYN.) crank, loner, deviate, fifth wheel, individualist.

misfortune (SYN.) adversity, distress, mishap, calamity, accident, catastrophe, hardship, ruin, disaster, affliction. (ANT.) success, blessing, prosperity.

misgiving (SYN.) suspicion, doubt, mistrust, hesitation, uncertainty.

misguided (SYN.) misdirected, misled.

misinformed (SYN.) wrong, unwise, foolish, erroneous, unwarranted, ill-advised, misguided.

mishap (SYN.) misfortune, casualty, accident, disaster, adversity, reverse. (ANT.) intention, calculation, purpose.

mishmash (SYN.) medley, muddle, gallimaufry, hodgepodge, hash.

misjudge (SYN.) err, mistake, miscalculate.

mislay (SYN.) misplace, lose. (ANT.) discover, find.

mislead (SYN.) misdirect, misinform, deceive, delude.

misleading (SYN.) fallacious, delusive, deceitful, false, deceptive, illusive. (ANT.) real, genuine, truthful, honest.

mismatched (SYN.) unfit, unsuitable, incompatible, unsuited.

misplace (SYN.) lose, mislay, miss. (ANT.) find.

misrepresent (SYN.) misstate, distort, falsify, twist, belie, garble, disguise.

miss (SYN.) lose, want, crave, yearn for, fumble, drop, error, slip, default, omit, lack, need, desire, fail. (ANT.) suffice, have, achieve, succeed.

misshapen (SYN.) disfigured, deformed, grotesque, malformed, ungainly, gnarled, contorted.

missile (SYN.) grenade, shot, projectile.

missing (SYN.) wanting, lacking, absent, lost, gone, vanished.

mission (SYN.) business, task, job, stint, work, errand, assignment, delegation.

missionary (SYN.) publicist, evangelist, propagandist.

mist (SYN.) cloud, fog, haze, steam, haze.

mistake (SYN.) slip, misjudge, fault, blunder, misunderstand, confuse, inaccuracy, misinterpret, error. (ANT.) truth, accuracy.

mistaken (SYN.) false, amiss, incorrect, awry, wrong, misinformed, confused, inaccurate, askew. (ANT.) true, correct, suitable, right.

mister (SYN.) young man, gentleman, esquire, fellow, buddy.

mistreat (SYN.) wrong, pervert, oppress, harm, maltreat, abuse.

mistrust (SYN.) suspect, doubt, distrust, dispute, question, skepticism, apprehension. (ANT.) trust.

misunderstand (SYN.) misjudge, misinterpret, jumble, confuse, mistake. (ANT.) perceive, comprehend.

misunderstanding (SYN.) clash, disagreement, dispute, conflict, misinterpretation.

misuse (SYN.) defame, malign, abuse, misapply, traduce, asperse, revile, vilify. (ANT.) protect, honor, respect, cherish.

mite (SYN.) particle, mote, smidgen, trifle, iota, corpuscle.

mitigate (SYN.) soften, soothe, abate, assuage, relieve, allay, diminish. (ANT.) irritate, agitate, increase.

mix (SYN.) mingle, blend, consort, fuse, alloy, combine, jumble, fraternize, associate, concoct, commingle, amalgamate, confound, compound, join. (ANT.) divide, sort, segregate, dissociate, separate.

mixture (SYN.) diversity, variety, strain, change, kind, confusion, heterogeneity, jumble, mess, assortment, breed, mix, hodge-podge, subspecies. (ANT.) likeness, sameness, homogeneity, monotony.

moan (SYN.) wail, groan, cry, lament.

moat (SYN.) fortification, ditch, trench, entrenchment.

mob (SYN.) crowd, host, populace, swarm, rot, bevy, horde, rabble, throng, multitude.

mobile (SYN.) free, movable, portable. (ANT.) stationary, immobile, fixed.

mock (SYN.) taunt, jeer, deride, scoff, scorn, ridicule, tease, fake, imitation, sham, gibe, sneer, fraudulent, flout. (ANT.) praise, applaud, real, genuine, honor, authentic, compliment.

mockery (SYN.) gibe, ridicule, satire, derision, sham, banter, irony, sneering, scorn, travesty, jeering. (ANT.) admiration, praise.

mode (SYN.) method, fashion, procedure, design, manner, technique, way, style, practice, plan. (ANT.) disorder, confusion.

model (SYN.) copy, prototype, type, example, ideal, imitation, version, facsimile, design, style, archetype, pattern, standard, mold. (ANT.) reproduction, imitation.

moderate (SYN.) lower, decrease, average, fair, reasonable, abate, medium, conservative, referee, umpire, suppress, judge, lessen, assuage. (ANT.) intensify, enlarge, amplify.

moderation (SYN.) sobriety, forbearance, self-control, restraint, continence, temperance. (ANT.) greed, excess, intoxication.

moderator (SYN.) referee, leader, arbitrator, chairman, chairperson, master of ceremonies, emcee.

modern (SYN.) modish, current, recent, novel, fresh, contemporary, new. (ANT.) old, antiquated, past, bygone, ancient.

modernize (SYN.) refurnish, refurbish, improve, rebuild, renew, renovate.

modest (SYN.) unassuming, virtuous, bashful, meek, shy, humble, decent, demure, unpretentious, prudish, moderate, reserved. (ANT.) forward, bold, ostentatious, conceited, immodest, arrogant.

modesty (SYN.) decency, humility, propriety, simplicity, shyness. (ANT.) conceit, vanity, pride.

modicum (SYN.) particle, fragment, grain, trifle, smidgen, bit.

modification (SYN.) alternation, substitution, variety, change, alteration. (ANT.) uniformity, monotony.

modify (SYN.) shift, vary, alter, change, convert, adjust, temper, moderate, curb, exchange, transform, veer. (ANT.) settle, establish, retain, stabilize.

modish (SYN.) current, fashionable, chick, stylish, voguish.

modulate (SYN.) temper, align, balance, correct, regulate, adjust, modify.

module (SYN.) unit, measure, norm, dimension, component, gauge.

modus operandi (SYN.) method, technique, system, means, process, workings, procedure.

mogul (SYN.) bigwig, personage, figure, tycoon, magnate, potentate.

moiety (SYN.) part, scrap, share, allotment, piece, division, portion.

moist (SYN.) damp, humid, dank, muggy, clammy.

moisten (SYN.) wet, dampen, sponge. (ANT.) dry.

moisture (SYN.) wetness, mist, dampness, condensation, evaporation, vapor, humidity. (ANT.) aridity, dryness.

mold (SYN.) make, fashion, organize, produce, forge, constitute, create, combine, construct, form, pattern, format. (ANT.) wreck, dismantle, destroy, misshape.

moldy (SYN.) dusty, crumbling, dank, old, deteriorating.

molest (SYN.) irk, disturb, trouble, annoy, pester, bother, vex, inconvenience. (ANT.) console, accommodate.

mollify (SYN.) soothe, compose, quiet, humor, appease, tranquilize, pacify.

molt (SYN.) slough off, shed, cast off.

molten (SYN.) fusible, melted, smelted, redhot.

moment (SYN.) flash, jiffy, instant, twinkling, gravity, importance, consequence, seriousness.

momentary *(SYN.)* concise, pithy, brief, curt, terse, laconic, compendious. *(ANT.) long, extended, prolonged.*

momentous *(SYN.)* critical, serious, essential, grave, material, weighty, consequential, decisive, important. *(ANT.) unimportant, trifling, mean, trivial, insignificant.*

momentum *(SYN.)* impetus, push, thrust, force, impulse, drive, vigor, propulsion, energy.

monarch *(SYN.)* ruler, king, queen, empress, emperor, sovereign.

monastery *(SYN.)* convent, priory, abbey, hermitage, cloister.

monastic *(SYN.)* withdrawn, dedicated, austere, unworldly, celibate, abstinent, ascetic.

money *(SYN.)* cash, bills, coin, notes, currency, funds, specie, capital.

monger *(SYN.)* seller, hawker, huckster, trader, merchant, shopkeeper, retailer, vendor.

mongrel *(SYN.)* mixed-breed, hybrid, mutt.

monitor *(SYN.)* director, supervisor, advisor, observe, watch, control.

monkey *(SYN.)* tamper, interfere, interrupt, interpose.

monogram *(SYN.)* mark, stamp, signature.

monograph *(SYN.)* publication, report, thesis, biography, treatise, paper, dissertation.

monologue *(SYN.)* discourse, lecture, sermon, talk, speech, address, soliloquy, oration.

monomania *(SYN.)* obsessiveness, passion, single-mindedness, extremism.

monopoly *(SYN.)* corner, control, possession.

monotonous *(SYN.)* dull, slow, tiresome, boring, humdrum, dilatory, tiring, irksome, tedious, burdensome, wearisome. *(ANT.) interesting, riveting, quick, fascinating, exciting, amusing.*

monsoon *(SYN.)* storm, rains.

monster *(SYN.)* brute, beast, villain, demon, fiend, wretch.

monstrous *(SYN.)* tremendous, huge, gigantic, immense, enormous, revolting, repulsive, shocking, horrible, hideous, terrible. *(ANT.) diminutive, tiny, miniature, small.*

monument *(SYN.)* remembrance, memento, commemoration, souvenir, statue, shrine.

monumental *(SYN.)* enormous, huge, colossal, immense, gigantic, important, significant. *(ANT.) trivial, insignificant, tiny, miniature.*

mood *(SYN.)* joke, irony, waggery, temper, disposition, temperament, sarcasm. *(ANT.) sorrow, gravity.*

moody *(SYN.)* morose, fretful, crabbed, changeable, sulky, dour, short-tempered, testy, temperamental, irritable, peevish, glum. *(ANT.) good-natured, even-tempered, merry, gay, pleasant, joyous.*

moor *(SYN.)* tether, fasten, tie, dock, anchor, bind.

moorings *(SYN.)* marina, slip, harbor, basin, landing, dock, wharf, pier, anchorage.

moot *(SYN.)* unsettled, questionable, problematical, controversial, contestable.

mop *(SYN.)* wash, wipe, swab, scrub.

mope *(SYN.)* gloom, pout, whine, grumble, grieve, sulk, fret. *(ANT.) rejoice.*

moral *(SYN.)* just, right, chaste, good, virtuous, pure, decent, honest, upright, ethical, righteous, honorable, scrupulous. *(ANT.) libertine, immoral, unethical, licentious, amoral, sinful.*

morale *(SYN.)* confidence, spirit, assurance.

morality *(SYN.)* virtue, strength, worth, chastity, probity, force, merit. *(ANT.) fault, sin, corruption, vice.*

morals *(SYN.)* conduct, scruples, guidelines, behavior, life style, standards.

morass *(SYN.)* fen, march, swamp, mire.

morbid *(SYN.)* sickly, unwholesome, unhealthy, ghastly, awful, horrible, shocking. *(ANT.) pleasant, healthy.*

more *(SYN.)* further, greater, farther, extra, another. *(ANT.) less.*

moreover *(SYN.)* further, in addition, also, furthermore, besides.

mores *(SYN.)* standards, rituals, rules, customs, conventions, traditions.

moron *(SYN.)* subnormal, dunce, blockhead, imbecile, retardate, simpleton.

morose *(SYN.)* gloomy, moody, fretful, crabbed, sulky, glum, dour, surly, downcast, sad, unhappy. *(ANT.) merry, gay, amiable, joyous, pleasant.*

morsel *(SYN.)* portion, fragment, bite, bit, scrap, amount, piece, taste, tidbit. *(ANT.) whole, all, sum.*

mortal *(SYN.)* fatal, destructive, human, perishable, deadly, temporary, momentary, final. *(ANT.) superficial, immortal.*

mortgage *(SYN.)* stake, post, promise, pledge.

mortician *(SYN.)* funeral director, embalmer.

mortified *(SYN.)* embarrassed, humiliated, abashed, ashamed.

mortify *(SYN.)* humiliate, crush, subdue, abase, degrade, shame. *(ANT.) praise, exalt, elevate.*

mortuary *(SYN.)* morgue, crematory, funeral parlor.

most *(SYN.)* extreme, highest, supreme, greatest, majority. *(ANT.) least.*

mostly *(SYN.)* chiefly, generally, largely, mainly, principally, especially, primarily.

mother *(SYN.)* bring about, produce, breed, mom, mama, watch, foster, mind, nurse, originate, nurture. *(ANT.) father.*

motif *(SYN.)* keynote, topic, subject, theme.

motion *(SYN.)* change, activity, movement, proposition, action, signal, gesture, move, proposal. *(ANT.) stability, immobility, equilibrium, stillness.*

motionless *(SYN.)* still, undisturbed, rigid, fixed, stationary, unresponsive, immobilized.

motivate *(SYN.)* move, prompt, stimulate, induce, activate, propel, arouse.

motive *(SYN.)* inducement, purpose, cause, incentive, reason, incitement, idea, ground, principle, stimulus, impulse, spur. *(ANT.) deed, result, attempt, effort.*

motley *(SYN.)* heterogeneous, mixed, assorted, sundry, diverse, miscellaneous. *(ANT.) ordered, classified.*

motor *(SYN.)* engine, generator, machine.

mottled *(SYN.)* streaked, flecked, dappled, spotted, speckled.

motto *(SYN.)* proverb, saying, adage, byword, saw, slogan, catchword, aphorism.

mound *(SYN.)* hillock, hill, heap, pile, stack, knoll, accumulation, dune.

mount *(SYN.)* scale, climb, increase, rise, prepare, ready, steed, horse, tower. *(ANT.) sink, descend.*

mountain *(SYN.)* alp, mount, pike, peak, ridge, height, range.

mountebank *(SYN.)* faker, rascal, swindler, cheat, fraud.

mounting *(SYN.)* backing, pedestal, easel, support, framework, background.

mourn *(SYN.)* suffer, grieve, bemoan, sorrow, lament, weep, bewail. *(ANT.) revel, celebrate, carouse.*

mournful *(SYN.)* gloomy, sorrowful, sad, melancholy, woeful, disconsolate. *(ANT.) joyful, cheerful, happy.*

mourning *(SYN.)* misery, trial, distress, affliction, tribulation, sorrow, woe. *(ANT.) happiness, solace, comfort, joy.*

mousy *(SYN.)* quiet, reserved, dull, colorless, withdrawn, shy, bashful.

move *(SYN.)* impel, agitate, persuade, induce, push, instigate, advance, stir, progress, propel, shift, drive, retreat, proceed, stir, transfer, budge, actuate. *(ANT.) halt, stop, deter, rest.*

moving *(SYN.)* stirring, touching.

mow *(SYN.)* prune, cut, shave, crop, clip.

much *(SYN.)* abundance, quantity, mass, ample, plenty, sufficient, substantial.

mucilage *(SYN.)* adhesive, glue, paste.

muck *(SYN.)* filth, mire, dirt, rot, sludge.

muddle *(SYN.)* disorder, chaos, mess.

muddled *(SYN.)* disconcerted, confused, mixed, bewildered, perplexed. *(ANT.) plain, lucid, organized.*

muff *(SYN.)* blunder, spoil, mess, fumble.

muffle *(SYN.)* soften, deaden, mute, quiet, drape, shroud, veil, cover. *(ANT.) louden, amplify.*

mug *(SYN.)* cup, stein, goblet, tankard.

muggy *(SYN.)* damp, warm, humid, stuffy, sticky, dank.

mulct *(SYN.)* amerce, punish, penalize.

mulish *(SYN.)* obstinate, stubborn, headstrong, rigid, tenacious, willful.

multifarious *(SYN.)* various, many, numerous, diversified, several, manifold. *(ANT.) scanty, infrequent, scarce, few.*

multiply *(SYN.)* double, treble, increase, triple, propagate, spread, expand. *(ANT.) lessen, decrease.*

multitude *(SYN.)* crowd, throng, mass, swarm, host,

mob, army, legion. (ANT.) scarcity, handful.

mumble (SYN.) stammer, whisper, hesitate, mutter. (ANT.) shout, yell.

mundane (SYN.) temporal, earthly, profane, worldly, lay, secular, common. (ANT.) unworldly, religious.

municipal (SYN.) urban, metropolitan.

munificent (SYN.) bountiful, full, generous, forthcoming, satisfied. (ANT.) voracious, insatiable, grasping, ravenous.

murder (SYN.) homicide, kill, slay, slaughter, butcher, killing, massacre, assassinate, execute. (ANT.) save, protect, vivify, animate.

murky (SYN.) gloomy, dark, obscure, unclear, impenetrable. (ANT.) cheerful, light.

murmur (SYN.) mumble, whine, grumble, whimper, lament, mutter. (ANT.) praise, applaud, rejoice.

muscle (SYN.) brawn, strength, power, fitness, vigor, vim, stamina, robustness.

muse (SYN.) ponder, brood, think, meditate, ruminate, reflect.

museum (SYN.) exhibit hall, treasure house, gallery, repository.

mushroom (SYN.) multiply, proliferate, flourish, spread, grow, pullulate.

musical (SYN.) tuneful, melodious, dulcet, lyrical, harmonious.

muss (SYN.) mess, disarray, rumple, litter, clutter, disarrange. (ANT.) fix, arrange.

must (SYN.) ought to, should, duty, obligation, ultimatum.

muster (SYN.) cull, pick, collect, harvest, accumulate, garner, reap, deduce. (ANT.) separate, disband, scatter.

musty (SYN.) mildewed, rancid, airless, dank, stale, decayed, rotten, funky.

mute (SYN.) quiet, noiseless, dumb, taciturn, hushed, peaceful, speechless, uncommunicative, silent. (ANT.) raucous, clamorous, noisy.

mutilate (SYN.) tear, cut, clip, amputate, lacerate, dismember, deform, castrate.

mutinous (SYN.) revolutionary, rebellious, unruly, turbulent, riotous. (ANT.) dutiful, obedient, complaint.

mutiny (SYN.) revolt, overthrow, rebellion, rebel, coup, uprising, insurrection.

mutter (SYN.) complain, mumble, whisper, grumble, murmur.

mutual (SYN.) correlative, interchangeable, shared, alternate, joint, common. (ANT.) unshared, unrequited, separate, dissociated.

muzzle (SYN.) restrain, silence, bridle, bind, curb, suppress, gag, stifle, censor.

myopia (SYN.) incomprehension, folly, shortsightedness, obtuseness.

myriad (SYN.) considerable, many.

mysterious (SYN.) hidden, mystical, secret, cryptic, incomprehensible, occult, dim, dark, inexplicable, enigmatical. (ANT.) simple, obvious, clear, plain.

mystery (SYN.) riddle, difficulty, enigma, puzzle, strangeness, conundrum. (ANT.) solution, key, answer, resolution.

mystical (SYN.) secret, cryptic, hidden, dim, obscure, dark, cabalistic. (ANT.) simple, explained, plain, clear.

mystify (SYN.) puzzle, confound, bewilder, stick, get, bamboozle.

myth (SYN.) fable, parable, allegory, fiction, tradition, lie, saga, legend. (ANT.) history.

N

nag (SYN.) badger, harry, provoke, tease, bother, annoy, molest, taunt, vex, torment, worry, annoy, pester, irritate, pick on, horse. (ANT.) please, comfort, soothe.

nail (SYN.) hold, fasten, secure, fix, seize, catch, snare, hook, capture. (ANT.) release.

naive (SYN.) frank, unsophisticated, natural, artless, ingenuous, simple, candid, open, innocent. (ANT.) worldly, cunning, crafty.

naked (SYN.) uncovered, unfinished, nude, bare, open, unclad, stripped, exposed, plain, mere, simple, barren, unprotected, bald, defenseless, unclothed. (ANT.) covered, protected, dressed, clothed, concealed.

name (SYN.) title, reputation, appellation, style, fame, repute, renown, denomination, appoint, character, designation, surname, distinction, christen, denominate, mention, specify, epithet, entitle, call, label. (ANT.) anonymity, hint, misname.

nap (SYN.) nod, doze, sleep, snooze, catnap, slumber, drowse.

narcissistic (SYN.) egotistical, egocentric, self-centered, egotistic.

narcotics (SYN.) opiates, drugs, sedatives, tranquilizers, barbiturates.

narrate (SYN.) recite, relate, declaim, detail, rehearse, deliver, review, tell, describe, recount.

narrative (SYN.) history, relation, account, record, chronicle, detail, recital, description, story, tale. (ANT.) distortion, caricature, misrepresentation.

narrow (SYN.) narrow-minded, illiberal, bigoted, fanatical, prejudiced, close, restricted, slender, cramped, confined, meager, thin, tapering, tight. (ANT.) progressive, liberal, wide.

narrow-minded (SYN.) close-minded, intolerant, partisan, arbitrary, bigoted. (ANT.) tolerant, liberal, broadminded.

nascent (SYN.) prime, introductory, emerging, elementary.

nasty (SYN.) offensive, malicious, selfish, mean, disagreeable, unpleasant, foul, dirty, filthy, loathsome, disgusting, polluted, obscene, indecent, sickening, nauseating, obnoxious, revolting. (ANT.) generous, dignified, noble, admirable, pleasant.

nation (SYN.) state, community, realm, nationality, commonwealth, kingdom, country, republic, land, society, tribe.

native (SYN.) domestic, inborn, inherent, natural, aboriginal, endemic, innate, inbred, indigenous, hereditary. (ANT.) alien, stranger, foreigner, outsider, foreign.

natty (SYN.) chic, well-dressed, sharp, dapper.

natural (SYN.) innate, genuine, real, unaffected, characteristic, native, normal, regular, inherent, original, simple, inbred, inborn, hereditary, typical, authentic, honest, legitimate, pure, customary. (ANT.) irregular, false, unnatural, formal, abnormal.

naturally (SYN.) typically, ordinarily, usually, indeed, normally, plainly, of course, surely, certainly. (ANT.) artificially.

nature (SYN.) kind, disposition, reputation, character, repute, world, quality, universe, essence, variety, features, traits.

naught (SYN.) zero, nothing.

naughty (SYN.) unmanageable, insubordinate, disobedient, mischievous, unruly, bad, misbehaving, disorderly, wrong, evil, rude, improper, indecent. (ANT.) obedient, good, well-behaved.

nausea (SYN.) sickness, vomiting, upset, queasiness, seasickness.

nauseated (SYN.) unwell, sick, queasy, squeamish.

nautical (SYN.) naval, oceanic, marine.

naval (SYN.) oceanic, marine, nautical, maritime.

navigate (SYN.) sail, cruise, pilot, guide, steer.

near (SYN.) close, nigh, dear, adjacent, familiar, at hand, neighboring, approaching, impending, proximate, imminent, bordering. (ANT.) removed, distant, far, remote.

nearly (SYN.) practically, close to, approximately, almost.

neat (SYN.) trim, orderly, precise, clear, spruce, nice, clean, well-kept, clever, skillful, adept, apt, dapper, smart, proficient, expert, handy, well-done, shipshape, elegant, well-organized. (ANT.) unkempt, sloppy, dirty, slovenly, messy, sloppy, disorganized.

nebulous (SYN.) fuzzy, indistinct, indefinite, clouded, hazy. (ANT.) definite, distinct, clear.

necessary (SYN.) needed, expedient, unavoidable, required, essential, indispensable, urgent, imperative, inevitable, compelling, compulsory, obligatory, needed, exigent. (ANT.) optional, nonessential, contingent, casual, accidental, unnecessary, dispensable, unneeded.

necessity (SYN.) requirement, fate, destiny, constraint, requisite, poverty, exigency, compulsion, want, essential, prerequisite. (ANT.) option, luxury, freedom, choice, uncertainty.

necromancy (SYN.) witchcraft, charm, sorcery, conjuring, wizardry.

need (SYN.) crave, want, demand, claim, desire, covet, wish, lack, necessity, requirement, poverty, require, pennilessness.

needed (SYN.) necessary, indispensable, essential, requisite. (ANT.) optional, contingent.

needle (SYN.) goad, badger, tease, nag, prod, provoke.

needless (SYN.) nonessential, unnecessary, superfluous, useless, purposeless.

needy (SYN.) poor, indigent, impoverished, penniless, destitute. (ANT.) affluent, well-off, wealthy, well-to-do.

nefarious (SYN.) detestable, vicious, wicked, atrocious, horrible, vile.

negate (SYN.) revoke, void, cancel, nullify.

neglect (SYN.) omission, default, heedlessness, carelessness, thoughtlessness, disregard, negligence, oversight, omission, ignore, slight, failure, overlook, omit, skip, pass over, be inattentive, miss. (ANT.) diligence, do, protect, watchfulness, care, attention, careful, attend, regard, concern.

negligent (SYN.) imprudent, thoughtless, lax, careless, inattentive, indifferent, remiss, neglectful. (ANT.) careful, nice, accurate, meticulous.

negligible (SYN.) trifling, insignificant, trivial, inconsiderable. (ANT.) major, vital, important.

negotiate (SYN.) intervene, talk over, mediate, transact, umpire, referee, arbitrate, arrange, settle, bargain.

neighborhood (SYN.) environs, nearness, district, vicinity, area, section, locality. (ANT.) remoteness.

neighboring (SYN.) bordering, near, adjacent, next to, surrounding, adjoining.

neighborly (SYN.) friendly, sociable, amiable, affable, companionable, congenial, kind, cordial, amicable. (ANT.) distant, reserved, cool, unfriendly, hostile.

neophyte (SYN.) greenhorn, rookie, amateur, beginner, apprentice, tyro, student.

nepotism (SYN.) bias, prejudice, patronage, favoritism.

nerve (SYN.) bravery, spirit, courage, boldness, rudeness, strength, stamina, bravado, daring, impudence, mettle, impertinence. (ANT.) frailty, cowardice, weakness.

nervous (SYN.) agitated, restless, excited shy, timid, upset, disturbed, shaken, rattle, high-strung, flustered, tense, jittery, strained, edgy, perturbed, fearful. (ANT.) placid, courageous, confident, calm, tranquil, composed, bold.

nest (SYN.) den, refuge, hideaway.

nestle (SYN.) cuddle, snuggle.

net (SYN.) snare, trap, mesh, earn, gain, web, get, acquire, secure, obtain.

nettle (SYN.) irritate, vex, provoke, annoy, disturb, irk, needle, pester.

neurotic (SYN.) disturbed, psychoneurotic.

neutral (SYN.) nonpartisan, uninvolved, detached, impartial, cool, unprejudiced, indifferent, inactive. (ANT.) involved, biased, partisan.

neutralize (SYN.) offset, counteract, nullify, negate.

nevertheless (SYN.) notwithstanding, however, although, anyway, but, regardless.

new (SYN.) modern, original, newfangled, late, recent, novel, young, firsthand, fresh, unique, unusual. (ANT.) antiquated, old, ancient, obsolete, outmoded.

newborn (SYN.) baby, infant, cub, suckling.

news (SYN.) report, intelligence, information, copy, message, advice, tidings, knowledge, word, story, data.

next (SYN.) nearest, following, closest, successive, succeeding, subsequent.

nibble (SYN.) munch, chew, bit.

nice (SYN.) pleasing, pleasant, agreeable, thoughtful, satisfactory, friendly, enjoyable, gratifying, desirable, fine, good, cordial. (ANT.) nasty, unpleasant, disagreeable, unkind, inexact, careless, thoughtless.

niche (SYN.) corner, nook, alcove, cranny, recess.

nick (SYN.) cut, notch, indentation, dash, score, mark.

nickname (SYN.) byname, sobriquet.

nigh (SYN.) close, imminent, near, adjacent, approaching, bordering, neighboring, impending. (ANT.) removed, distant.

nightmare (SYN.) calamity, horror, torment, bad dream.

nil (SYN.) zero, none, naught, nothing.

nimble (SYN.) brisk, quick, active, supple, alert, lively, spry, light, fast, speedy, swift, agile. (ANT.) slow, heavy, sluggish, clumsy.

nincompoop (SYN.) nitwit, idiot, fool, moron, blockhead, ninny, idiot, simpleton.

nip (SYN.) bite, pinch, chill, cold, squeeze, crispness, sip, small.

nippy (SYN.) chilly, sharp, bitter, cold, penetrating.

nit-picker (SYN.) fussbudget, precise, purist, perfectionist.

nitty-gritty (SYN.) essentials, substance, essence.

noble (SYN.) illustrious, exalted, dignified, stately, eminent, lofty, grand, elevated, honorable, honest, virtuous, great, distinguished, majestic, important, prominent, magnificent, grandiose, aristocratic, upright, well-born. (ANT.) vile, low, base, mean, dishonest, common, ignoble.

nod (SYN.) bob, bow, bend, tip, signal.

node (SYN.) protuberance, growth, nodule, cyst, lump, wen.

noise (SYN.) cry, sound, din, babel, racket, uproar, clamor, outcry, tumult, sounds, hubbub, bedlam, commotion, rumpus, clatter. (ANT.) quiet, stillness, hush, silence, peace.

noisome (SYN.) repulsive, disgusting, revolting, obnoxious, malodorous, rotten, rancid.

noisy (SYN.) resounding, loud, clamorous, vociferous, stentorian, tumultuous. (ANT.) soft, dulcet, subdued, quiet, silent, peaceful.

nomad (SYN.) gypsy, rover, traveler, roamer, migrant, vagrant, wanderer.

nominate (SYN.) propose, choose, select.

nomination (SYN.) appointment, naming, choice, selection, designation.

nominee (SYN.) contestant, candidate.

nonbeliever (SYN.) skeptic, infidel, atheist, heathen.

nonchalant (SYN.) unconcerned, indifferent, cool, casual, easygoing.

noncommittal (SYN.) neutral, tepid, undecided, cautious, guarded, uncommunicative.

nonconformist (SYN.) protester, rebel, radical, dissenter, renegade, dissident, eccentric.

nondescript (SYN.) unclassifiable, indescribable, indefinite.

nonentity (SYN.) nothing, menial, nullity.

nonessential (SYN.) needless, unnecessary.

nonpareil (SYN.) unsurpassed, exceptional, paramount, unrivaled.

nonplus (SYN.) confuse, perplex, dumfound, mystify, confound, puzzle, baffle, bewilder. (ANT.) illumine, clarify, salve, explain.

nonsense (SYN.) balderdash, rubbish, foolishness, folly, ridiculousness, stupidity, absurdity, poppycock, trash.

nonsensical (SYN.) silly, preposterous, absurd, unreasonable, foolish, irrational, ridiculous, stupid, senseless. (ANT.) sound, consistent, reasonable.

nonstop (SYN.) constant, continuous, unceasing, endless.

nook (SYN.) niche, corner, recess, cranny.

noose (SYN.) snare, rope, lasso, loop.

normal (SYN.) ordinary, uniform, natural, unvaried, customary, regular, healthy, sound, whole, usual, typical, characteristic, routine, standard. (ANT.) rare, erratic, unusual, abnormal.

normally (SYN.) regularly, frequently, usually, customarily.

nosy (SYN.) inquisitive, meddling, peering, searching, prying, snooping. (ANT.) unconcerned, incurious, uninterested.

notable (SYN.) noted, unusual, uncommon, noteworthy, remarkable, conspicuous, distinguished, distinctive, celebrity, starts, important, striking, special, memorable, extraordinary, rare, exceptional, personality. (ANT.) commonplace, ordinary, usual.

notch (SYN.) cut, nick, indentation, gash.

note (SYN.) sign, annotation, letter, indication, observation, mark, symbol, comment, remark, token, message, memorandum, record, memo, write, list, inscribe, notice.

noted (SYN.) renowned, glorious, celebrated, famous, illustrious, well-known, distinguished, famed, notable. (ANT.) unknown, hidden, infamous, ignominious.

noteworthy (SYN.) consequential, celebrated, exceptional, prominent.

notice (SYN.) heed, perceive, hold, mark, behold, descry, recognize, observe, attend to, remark, note, regard, see, sign, announcement, poster, advertisement, observation, warning. (ANT.) overlook, disregard, skip.

notify (SYN.) apprise, acquaint, instruct, tell, advise, warn, teach, inform, report, remind, announce, mention, reveal. (ANT.) mislead, delude, conceal.

notion (SYN.) image, conception, sentiment, abstraction, thought, idea, impression, fancy, understanding, view, opinion, concept. (*ANT.*) *thing, matter, substance, entity.*

notorious (*SYN.*) celebrated, renowned, famous, well-known, popular, infamous.

nourish (*SYN.*) strengthen, nurse, feed, supply, nurture, sustain, support.

nourishment (*SYN.*) nutriment, food, sustenance, support. (*ANT.*) *starvation, deprivation.*

novel (*SYN.*) fiction, narrative, allegory, tale, fable, story, romance, invention, different, unusual, strange, original. (*ANT.*) *verity, history, truth, fact.*

novice (*SYN.*) beginner, amateur, newcomer, greenhorn, learner, apprentice, freshman, dilettante. (*ANT.*) *expert, professional, adept, master.*

now (*SYN.*) today, at once, right away, immediately, at this time, present. (*ANT.*) *later.*

noxious (*SYN.*) poisonous, harmful, damaging, toxic, detrimental. (*ANT.*) *harmless.*

nucleus (*SYN.*) core, middle, heart, focus, hub, kernel.

nude (*SYN.*) naked, unclad, plain, open, defenseless, mere, bare, exposed, unprotected, simple, stripped, uncovered. (*ANT.*) *dressed, protected, clothed, covered.*

nudge (*SYN.*) prod, push, jab, shove, poke, prompt.

nugget (*SYN.*) clump, mass, lump, wad, chunk, hunk.

nuisance (*SYN.*) annoyance, bother, irritation, pest.

nullify (*SYN.*) abolish, cross out, delete, invalidate, obliterate, cancel, expunge, repeal, annul, revoke, quash, rescind. (*ANT.*) *perpetuate, confirm, enforce.*

numb (*SYN.*) unfeeling, dull, insensitive, deadened, anesthetized, stupefied.

numeral (*SYN.*) figure, symbol, digit.

numerous (*SYN.*) many, several, manifold, multifarious, various, multitudinous, diverse, abundant, sundry. (*ANT.*) *infrequent, meager, few, scarce.*

nuptials (*SYN.*) marriage, wedding, espousal, wedlock, matrimony. (*ANT.*) *virginity, divorce, celibacy.*

nurse (*SYN.*) tend, care for, nourish, nurture, feed, train, mind, attend.

nurture (*SYN.*) hold dear, foster, sustain, appreciate, prize, rear, value, treasure. (*ANT.*) *dislike, disregard, abandon.*

nutriment (*SYN.*) food, diet, sustenance, repast, meal, fare, edibles. (*ANT.*) *hunger, want, starvation.*

nutrition (*SYN.*) nourishment, sustenance, food, nutriment.

O

oaf (*SYN.*) boor, clod, clown, lummox, fool, lout, dunce, bogtrotter.

oasis (*SYN.*) shelter, haven, retreat, refuge.

oath (*SYN.*) promise, pledge, vow, profanity, curse, agreement, commitment.

obdurate (*SYN.*) insensible, callous, hard, rough, unfeeling, insensitive. (*ANT.*) *soft, compassionate, tender.*

obedience (*SYN.*) docility, submission, subservience, compliance. (*ANT.*) *rebelliousness, disobedience.*

obedient (*SYN.*) dutiful, yielding, tractable, compliant, submissive. (*ANT.*) *rebellious, intractable, insubordinate, obstinate.*

obese (*SYN.*) portly, fat, pudgy, chubby, plump, rotund, stout, thickset, corpulent, stocky. (*ANT.*) *slim, lean, thin, slender.*

obey (*SYN.*) submit, yield, mind, comply, listen to, conform. (*ANT.*) *resist, disobey.*

obfuscate (*SYN.*) bewilder, complicate, fluster, confuse.

object (*SYN.*) thing, aim, intention, design, end, objective, particular, mark, purpose, goal, target, article. (*ANT.*) *assent, agree, concur, approve, acquiesce.*

objection (*SYN.*) disagreement, protest, rejection, dissent, challenge, noncompliance, difference, nonconformity, recusancy, disapproval, criticism. (*ANT.*) *acceptance, compliance, agreement, assent.*

objectionable (*SYN.*) improper, offensive, unbecoming, deplorable.

objective (*SYN.*) aspiration, goal, passion, desire, aim, hope, purpose, drift, design, ambition, end, object, intention, intent, longing, craving. (*ANT.*) *biased, subjective.*

objectivity (*SYN.*) disinterest, neutrality, impartiality.

obligate (*SYN.*) oblige, require, pledge, bind, force, compel.

obligation (*SYN.*) duty, bond, engagement, compulsion, account, contract, ability, debt. (*ANT.*) *freedom, choice, exemption.*

oblige (*SYN.*) constrain, force, impel, enforce, coerce, drive, gratify. (*ANT.*) *persuade, convince, allure, free, induce, disoblige, prevent.*

obliging (*SYN.*) considerate, helpful, thoughtful, well-meaning, accommodating. (*ANT.*) *discourteous.*

obliterate (*SYN.*) terminate, destroy, eradicate, raze, extinguish, exterminate, annihilate, devastate, wipe out, ravage. (*ANT.*) *make, save, construct, establish, preserve.*

oblivious (*SYN.*) sightless, unmindful, headlong, rash, blind, senseless, ignorant, forgetful, undiscerning, preoccupied, unconscious, heedless. (*ANT.*) *sensible, aware, calculated, perceiving, discerning.*

obloquy (*SYN.*) defamation, rebuke, censure.

obnoxious (*SYN.*) hateful, offensive, nasty, disagreeable, repulsive, loathsome, vile, disgusting, detestable, wretched, terrible, despicable, dreadful.

obscene (*SYN.*) indecent, filthy, impure, dirty, gross, lewd, pornographic, coarse, disgusting, bawdy, offensive, smutty. (*ANT.*) *modest, pure, decent, refined.*

obscure *SYN.*) cloudy, enigmatic, mysterious, abstruse, cryptic, dim, dusky, ambiguous, dark, indistinct, unintelligible, unclear, shadowy, fuzzy, blurred, vague. (*ANT.*) *clear, famous, distinguished, noted, illumined, lucid, bright, distinct.*

obsequious (*SYN.*) fawning, flattering.

observance (*SYN.*) protocol, ritual, ceremony, rite, parade, pomp, solemnity. (*ANT.*) *omission.*

observant (*SYN.*) aware, alert, mindful, watchful, heedful, considerate, attentive, anxious, circumspect, cautious, wary. (*ANT.*) *unaware, indifferent, oblivious.*

observation (*SYN.*) attention, watching, comment, opinion, remark, notice.

observe (*SYN.*) note, behold, discover, notice, perceive, eye, detect, inspect, keep, commemorate, mention, utter, watch, examine, mark, view, express, see, celebrate. (*ANT.*) *neglect, overlook, disregard, ignore.*

observer (*SYN.*) examiner, overseer, lookout, spectator, bystander, witness, watcher.

obsession (*SYN.*) preoccupation, mania, compulsion, passion, fetish, infatuation.

obsolete (*SYN.*) old, out-of-date, ancient, archaic, extinct, old-fashioned, discontinued, obsolescent, venerable, dated, antiquated. (*ANT.*) *modern, stylish, current, recent, fashionable, extant.*

obstacle (*SYN.*) block, hindrance, barrier, impediment, snag, check, deterrent, stoppage, hitch, bar, difficulty, obstruction. (*ANT.*) *help, aid, assistance, encouragement.*

obstinate (*SYN.*) firm, headstrong, immovable, stubborn, determined, dogged, intractable, uncompromising, inflexible, willful, bullheaded, contumacious, obdurate, unbending, unyielding, pertinacious. (*ANT.*) *yielding, docile, amenable, submissive, pliable, flexible, compliant.*

obstruct (*SYN.*) clog, barricade, impede, block, delay, hinder, stop, close, bar. (*ANT.*) *promote, clear, aid, help, open, further.*

obstruction (*SYN.*) block, obstacle, barrier, blockage, interference.

obtain (*SYN.*) get, acquire, secure, win, procure, attain, earn, gain, receive, assimilate. (*ANT.*) *surrender, forfeit, lose, forego, miss.*

obtrusive (*SYN.*) blatant, garish, conspicuous.

obtuse (*SYN.*) blunt, dull, slow-witted, unsharpened, stupid, dense, slow. (*ANT.*) *clear, interesting, lively, bright, animated, sharp.*

obviate (*SYN.*) prevent, obstruct, forestall, preclude, intercept, avert, evade.

obvious (*SYN.*) plain, clear, evident, palpable, patent, self-evident, apparent, distinct, understandable, manifest, unmistakable. (*ANT.*) *concealed, hidden, abstruse, obscure.*

obviously (*SYN.*) plainly, clearly, surely, evidently, certainly.

occasion (*SYN.*) occurrence, time, happening, excuse, opportunity, chance.

occasional (*SYN.*) random, irregular, sporadic, infrequent, periodically, spasmodic. (*ANT.*) *chronic, regular, constant.*

occasionally (*SYN.*) seldom, now and then, infrequently, sometimes, irregularly.

(ANT.) *regularly, often.*

occlude (SYN.) clog, obstruct, choke, throttle.

occupant (SYN.) tenant, lodger, boarder, dweller, resident, inhabitant.

occupation (SYN.) employment, business, enterprise, job, trade, vocation, work, profession, matter, interest, concern, affair, activity, commerce, trading, engagement. (ANT.) *hobby, pastime, avocation.*

occupy (SYN.) dwell, have, inhabit, absorb, hold, possess, fill, busy, keep. (ANT.) *relinquish, abandon, release.*

occur (SYN.) take place, bechance, come about, befall, chance, transpire, betide, happen.

occurrence (SYN.) episode, event, issue, end, result, consequence, happening, circumstance, outcome.

ocean (SYN.) deep, sea, main, briny.

odd (SYN.) strange, bizarre, eccentric, unusual, single, uneven, unique, queer, quaint, peculiar, curious, unmatched, remaining, singular. (ANT.) *matched, common, typical, normal, familiar, even, usual.*

odious (SYN.) obscene, depraved, vulgar, despicable, mean, wicked, sordid, foul, base, loathsome, vicious, displeasing, hateful, revolting, offensive, repulsive, horrible, obnoxious, vile. (ANT.) *decent, upright, laudable, attractive, honorable.*

odor (SYN.) fume, aroma, fragrance, redolence, smell, stink, scent, essence, stench.

odorous (SYN.) scented, aromatic, fragrant.

odyssey (SYN.) crusade, quest, journey, voyage.

offbeat (SYN.) uncommon, eccentric, strange, unconventional, peculiar.

off-color (SYN.) rude, improper, earthy, suggestive, salty.

offend (SYN.) annoy, anger, vex, irritate, displease, provoke, hurt, grieve, pain, disgust, wound, horrify, stricken, insult, outrage. (ANT.) *flatter, please, delight.*

offender (SYN.) criminal, culprit, lawbreaker, miscreant.

offense (SYN.) indignity, injustice, transgression, affront, outrage, misdeed, sin, insult, atrocity, aggression, crime. (ANT.) *morality, gentleness, innocence, right.*

offensive (SYN.) attacking, aggressive, unpleasant, revolting, disagreeable, nauseous, disgusting. (ANT.) *pleasing, defending, defensive, pleasant, attractive, agreeable.*

offer (SYN.) suggestion, overture, proposal, present, suggest, propose, try, submit, attempt, tender. (ANT.) *withdrawal, denial, rejection.*

offhand (SYN.) informal, unprepared, casual, impromptu, spontaneous. (ANT.) *considered, planned, calculated.*

office (SYN.) position, job, situation, studio, berth, incumbency, capacity, headquarters, duty, task, function, work, post.

officiate (SYN.) regulate, administer, superintend, oversee, emcee.

offset (SYN.) compensate, counterbalance, cushion, counteract, neutralize, soften, balance.

offshoot (SYN.) outgrowth, addition, byproduct, supplement, appendage, accessory, branch.

offspring (SYN.) issue, children, progeny, descendants.

often (SYN.) frequently, repeatedly, commonly, generally, many times, recurrently. (ANT.) *seldom, infrequently, rarely, occasionally, sporadically.*

ogle (SYN.) gaze, stare, eye, leer.

ogre (SYN.) fiend, monster, devil, demon.

ointment (SYN.) lotion, pomade, balm, emollient.

old (SYN.) antique, senile, ancient, archaic, old-fashioned, superannuated, obsolete, venerable, antiquated, elderly, discontinued, abandoned, aged. (ANT.) *new, youthful, recent, modern, young.*

old-fashioned (SYN.) outmoded, old, dated, ancient. (ANT.) *modern, fashionable, current, new.*

olio (SYN.) potpourri, variety, mixture, jumble.

omen (SYN.) sign, gesture, indication, proof, portent, symbol, token, emblem, signal.

ominous (SYN.) unfavorable, threatening, sinister, menacing.

omission (SYN.) failure, neglect, oversight, default. (ANT.) *inclusion, notice, insertion.*

omit (SYN.) exclude, delete, cancel, eliminate, ignore, neglect, skip, leave out, drop, miss, bar, overlook, disregard.

(ANT.) *insert, notice, enter, include, introduce.*

omnipotent (SYN.) all-powerful, almighty, divine.

oncoming (SYN.) imminent, approaching, arriving, nearing.

onerous (SYN.) intricate, arduous, hard, perplexing, difficult, burdensome, puzzling. (ANT.) *simple, easy, facile, effortless.*

one-sided (SYN.) unfair, partial, biased, prejudiced. (ANT.) *impartial, neutral.*

ongoing (SYN.) advancing, developing, continuing, progressive.

onlooker (SYN.) witness, spectator, observer, bystander.

only (SYN.) lone, sole, solitary, single, merely, but, just.

onset (SYN.) commencement, beginning, opening, start, assault, attack, charge, offense, onslaught. (ANT.) *end.*

onslaught (SYN.) invasion, aggression, attack, assault, offense, drive, criticism, onset, charge, denunciation. (ANT.) *vindication, defense, surrender, opposition, resistance.*

onus (SYN.) load, weight, burden, duty.

onward (SYN.) ahead, forward, frontward. (ANT.) *backward.*

ooze (SYN.) seep, leak, drip, flow, filter.

opacity (SYN.) obscurity, thickness, imperviousness.

opaque (SYN.) murky, dull, cloudy, filmy, unilluminated, dim, obtuse, indistinct, shadowy, dark, obscure. (ANT.) *light, clear, bright.*

open (SYN.) uncovered, overt, agape, unlocked, passable, accessible, unrestricted, candid, plain, clear, exposed, unclosed, unobstructed, free, disengaged, frank, unoccupied, public, honest, ajar, available.

open (SYN.) unbar, unfold, exhibit, spread, unseal, expand, unfasten. (ANT.) *close, shut, conceal, hide.*

open-handed (SYN.) kind, generous, charitable, lavish, extravagant, bountiful. (ANT.) *mean, stingy.*

openhearted (SYN.) frank, honest, candid, sincere, ingenuous, straightforward. (ANT.) *insincere, devious.*

opening (SYN.) cavity, hole, void, abyss, aperture, chasm, pore, gap, loophole.

openly (SYN.) sincerely, frankly, freely. (ANT.) *secretly.*

open-minded (SYN.) tolerant, fair, just, liberal, impartial, reasonable, unprejudiced. (ANT.) *prejudiced, bigoted.*

operate (SYN.) comport, avail, behave, interact, apply, manage, utilize, demean, run, manipulate, employ, act, exploit, exert, exercise, practice, conduct. (ANT.) *neglect, waste.*

operation (SYN.) effort, enterprise, mentality, maneuver, action, instrumentality, performance, working, proceeding, agency. (ANT.) *inaction, cessation, rest, inactivity.*

operative (SYN.) busy, active, industrious, working, effective, functional. (ANT.) *inactive, dormant.*

opiate (SYN.) hypnotic, tranquilizer, narcotic.

opinion (SYN.) decision, feeling, notion, view, idea, conviction, belief, judgment, sentiment, persuasion, impression. (ANT.) *knowledge, fact, misgiving, skepticism.*

opinionated (SYN.) domineering, overbearing, arrogant, dogmatic, positive, magisterial, obstinate, pertinacious. (ANT.) *questioning, fluctuating, indecisive, skeptical, open-minded, indecisive.*

opponent (SYN.) competitor, foe, adversary, contestant, enemy, rival, contender, combatant, antagonist. (ANT.) *comrade, team, ally, confederate.*

opportune (SYN.) fitting, suitable, appropriate, proper, favorable, felicitous.

opportunity (SYN.) possibility, chance, occasion, time, contingency, opening. (ANT.) *obstacle, disadvantage, hindrance.*

oppose (SYN.) defy, resist, withstand, combat, bar, counteract, confront, thwart, struggle, fight, contradict, hinder, obstruct. (ANT.) *submit, support, agree, cooperate, succumb.*

opposed (SYN.) opposite, contrary, hostile, adverse, counteractive, unlucky, antagonistic, unfavorable, disastrous. (ANT.) *lucky, benign, propitious, fortunate, favorable.*

opposite (SYN.) reverse, contrary, different, unlike, opposed. (ANT.) *like, same, similar.*

opposition (SYN.) combat, struggle, discord, collision, conflict, battle, fight, encounter, discord, controversy, inconsistency, variance. (ANT.) *harmony, amity,* concord, consonance.

oppress (SYN.) harass, torment, vex, afflict, annoy, harry, pester, hound, worry, persecute. (ANT.) encourage, support, comfort, assist, aid.

oppression (SYN.) cruelty, tyranny, persecution, injustice, despotism, brutality, abuse. (ANT.) liberty, freedom.

oppressive (SYN.) difficult, stifling, burdensome, severe, domineering, harsh, unjust, overbearing, overwhelming.

oppressor (SYN.) bully, scourge, slave-driver.

opprobrium (SYN.) disgrace, contempt, reproach, shame, discredit.

opt (SYN.) choose, prefer, pick, select.

optical (SYN.) seeing, visual.

optimism (SYN.) faith, expectation, optimism, anticipation, trust, expectancy, confidence, hope. (ANT.) despair, pessimism, despondency.

optimistic (SYN.) happy, cheerful, bright, glad, pleasant, radiant, lighthearted. (ANT.) pessimistic.

option (SYN.) preference, choice, selection, alternative, election, self-determination.

optional (SYN.) selective, elective, voluntary. (ANT.) required.

opulence (SYN.) luxury, abundance, fortune, riches, wealth, plenty, affluence. (ANT.) need, indigence, want, poverty.

opulent (SYN.) wealthy, rich, prosperous, well-off, affluent, well-heeled.

oracle (SYN.) authority, forecaster, wizard, seer, mastermind, clairvoyant.

oral (SYN.) voiced, sounded, vocalized, said, uttered, verbal, vocal, spoken. (ANT.) recorded, written, documentary.

orate (SYN.) preach, lecture, sermonize.

oration (SYN.) address, lecture, speech, sermon, discourse, recital, declamation.

orb (SYN.) globe, sphere, ball, moon.

orbit (SYN.) path, lap, course, circuit, revolution, revolve, circle.

orchestra (SYN.) ensemble, band.

orchestrate (SYN.) coordinate, direct, synchronize, organize.

ordain (SYN.) constitute, create, order, decree, decide, dictate, command, rule, bid, sanction, appoint. (ANT.) terminate, disband.

ordeal (SYN.) hardship, suffering, test, affliction, trouble, fortune, proof, examination, trial, experiment, tribulation, misery. (ANT.) consolation, alleviation.

order (SYN.) plan, series, decree, instruction, command, system, method, aim, arrangement, class, injunction, mandate, instruct, requirement, dictate, guide, rule, direct, govern, manage, regulate, bid, conduct (ANT.) consent, license, confusion, disarray, irregularity, permission.

orderly (SYN.) regulated, neat, well-organized, disciplined, methodical, shipshape. (ANT.) sloppy, messy, haphazard, disorganized.

ordinarily (SYN.) commonly, usually, generally, mostly, customarily, normally.

ordinary (SYN.) common, habitual, normal, typical, usual, conventional, familiar, accustomed, customary, average, standard, everyday, inferior, mediocre, regular, vulgar, plain. (ANT.) uncommon, marvelous, extraordinary, remarkable, strange.

ordnance (SYN.) munitions, artillery.

organ (SYN.) instrument, journal, voice.

organic (SYN.) living, biological, animate.

organism (SYN.) creature, plant, microorganism.

organization (SYN.) order, rule, system, arrangement, method, plan, regularity, scheme, mode, process. (ANT.) irregularity, chaos, disarrangement, chance, disorder.

organize (SYN.) assort, arrange, plan, regulate, systematize, devise, categorize, classify, prepare. (ANT.) jumble, disorder, disturb, confuse, scatter.

organized (SYN.) planned, neat, orderly, arranged.

orient (SYN.) align, fit, accustom, adjust.

orifice (SYN.) vent, slot, opening, hole.

origin (SYN.) birth, foundation, source, start, commencement, inception, beginning, derivation, infancy, parentage, spring, cradle. (ANT.) product, issue, outcome, end.

original (SYN.) primary, fresh, new, initial, pristine, creative, first, primordial, inventive, primeval, novel, introductory.

(ANT.) banal, trite, subsequent, derivative, later, modern, terminal.

originality (SYN.) unconventionality, genius, novelty, creativity, imagination.

originate (SYN.) fashion, invent, cause, create, make, initiate, inaugurate, organize, institute, produce, engender, commence, found, establish, form, begin, arise, generate, formulate. (ANT.) demolish, terminate, annihilate, disband, destroy.

originator (SYN.) creator, inventor, discoverer. (ANT.) follower, imitator.

ornament (SYN.) decoration, ornamentation, adornment, embellishment, trimming, garnish.

ornamental (SYN.) ornate, decorative.

ornate (SYN.) florid, overdone, elaborate, showy, flowery, pretentious.

ornery (SYN.) disobedient, firm, unruly, stiff, rebellious, stubborn, headstrong, willful, contrary, rigid, mean, difficult, malicious, cross, disagreeable. (ANT.) pleasant.

orthodox (SYN.) customary, usual, conventional, correct, proper, accepted. (ANT.) different, unorthodox.

oscillate (SYN.) vary, change, hesitate, waver, undulate, fluctuate, vacillate. (ANT.) persist, resolve, adhere, stick, decide.

ostentation (SYN.) parade, show, boasting, pageantry, vaunting, pomp, display, flourish. (ANT.) reserve, humility, unobtrusiveness, modesty.

ostentatious (SYN.) flashy, showy, overdone, fancy, pretentious, garish.

ostracize (SYN.) hinder, omit, bar, exclude, blackball, expel, prohibit, shout out, prevent, except. (ANT.) welcome, accept, include, admit.

other (SYN.) distinct, different, extra, further, new, additional, supplementary.

ought (SYN.) must, should, be obliged.

oust (SYN.) eject, banish, exclude, expatriate, ostracize, dismiss, exile, expel. (ANT.) shelter, accept, receive, admit, harbor.

ouster (SYN.) expulsion, banishment, ejection, overthrow.

outbreak (SYN.) riot, revolt, uprising, disturbance, torrent, eruption, outburst.

outburst (SYN.) outbreak, eruption, torrent, ejection, discharge.

outcast (SYN.) friendless, homeless, deserted, abandoned, forsaken, disowned, derelict, forlorn, rejected.

outclass (SYN.) outshine, surpass.

outcome (SYN.) fate, destiny, necessity, doom, portion, consequence, result, end, fortune, effect, issue, aftermath.

outcry (SYN.) scream, protest, clamor, noise, uproar.

outdated (SYN.) old-fashioned, unfashionable, old, outmoded. (ANT.) stylish.

outdo (SYN.) outshine, defeat, excel, beat, surpass.

outer (SYN.) remote, exterior, external.

outfit (SYN.) garb, kit, gear, furnish, equip, rig, clothing, provisions.

outgoing (SYN.) leaving, departing, friendly, congenial, amicable. (ANT.) unfriendly, incoming.

outgrowth (SYN.) effect, outcome, upshot, fruit, result, consequence, product.

outing (SYN.) journey, trip, excursion, jaunt, expedition, junket.

outlandish (SYN.) peculiar, odd, weird, curious, strange, queer, exotic, bazaar. (ANT.) ordinary, common.

outlast (SYN.) survive, endure, outlive.

outlaw (SYN.) exile, bandit, outcast, bad-man, convict, criminal, fugitive, desperado.

outlay (SYN.) expense, costs, spending, disbursement, expenditure, charge.

outlet (SYN.) spout, opening, passage.

outline (SYN.) form, sketch, brief, draft, figure, profile, contour, chart, diagram, skeleton, delineation, plan, silhouette.

outlook (SYN.) viewpoint, view, prospect, opportunity, position, attitude, future.

outlying (SYN.) external, remote, outer, out-of-the-way, suburban, rural.

outmoded (SYN.) unfashionable, old-fashioned. (ANT.) up-to-date, modern.

outnumber (SYN.) exceed.

output (SYN.) yield, crop, harvest, proceeds, productivity, production.

outrage (SYN.) aggression, transgression, vice, affront, offense, insult, indignity, atrocity, misdeed, trespass, wrong. (ANT.) morality, right, gentleness, innocence.

outrageous (SYN.) shameful, shocking, disgraceful, insulting, nonsensical, absurd, foolish, crazy, excessive, ridiculous, bizarre, preposterous, offensive. (ANT.) *prudent, reasonable, sensible.*

outright (SYN.) entirely, altogether, completely, quite, fully, thoroughly.

outset (SYN.) inception, origin, start, commencement, opening, source. (ANT.) *end, completion, termination, consummation, close.*

outside (SYN.) covering, exterior, surface, facade, externals, appearance. (ANT.) *intimate, insider.*

outsider (SYN.) immigrant, stranger, foreigner, alien, newcomer, bystander. (ANT.) *countryman, friend, acquaintance, neighbor, associate.*

outsmart (SYN.) outmaneuver, outwit.

outspoken (SYN.) rude, impolite, unceremonious, brusque, unrestrained, vocal, open, straight-forward, blunt, unreserved, frank, forthright, rough. (ANT.) *suave, tactful, shy, polished, polite, subtle.*

outstanding (SYN.) well-known, important, prominent, leading, eminent, distinguished, significant, conspicuous. (ANT.) *insignificant, unimportant.*

outward (SYN.) apparent, outside, exterior, visible.

outweigh (SYN.) predominate, supersede, counteract, dwarf.

outwit (SYN.) baffle, trick, outsmart, bewilder, outdo, outmaneuver, confuse.

oval (SYN.) egg-shaped, elliptical, ovular.

ovation (SYN.) fanfare, homage, applause, tribute, cheers, acclamation.

overall (SYN.) comprehensive, complete, general, extensive, wide-spread, entire.

overbearing (SYN.) domineering, masterful, autocratic, dictatorial, arrogant, bossy, imperious, haughty. (ANT.) *humble.*

overcast (SYN.) dim, shadowy, cloudy, murky, dark, mysterious, gloomy, somber, dismal, hazy, indistinct. (ANT.) *sunny, bright, limpid, clear.*

overcome (SYN.) quell, beat, crush, surmount, rout, humble, conquer, subjugate, defeat, subdue, upset, vanquish. (ANT.) *retreat, surrender, capitulate, cede, lose.*

overconfident (SYN.) egotistical, presumptuous, arrogant, conceited.

overdo (SYN.) stretch, exaggerate, enlarge, magnify, exhaust, overexert.

overdue (SYN.) tardy, advanced, slow, delayed, new. (ANT.) *timely, early, beforehand.*

overflow (SYN.) run over, flood, spill, cascade, inundate.

overflowing (SYN.) ample, plentiful, teeming, abundant, copious, profuse. (ANT.) *insufficient, deficient, scarce.*

overhang (SYN.) protrude, extend.

overhaul (SYN.) recondition, rebuild, service, repair, condition, revamp.

overhead (SYN.) high, above, aloft, expenses, costs.

overjoyed (SYN.) enchanted, delighted, ecstatic, enraptured, elated, blissful. (ANT.) *depressed.*

overlap (SYN.) overhang, extend, superimpose.

overload (SYN.) burden, weight, oppress, afflict, weigh, trouble, encumber, tax. (ANT.) *ease, lighten, console, alleviate.*

overlook (SYN.) miss, disregard, exclude, cancel, omit, skip, ignore, drop, delete, neglect, exclude, watch, eliminate. (ANT.) *notice, include, introduce, inset.*

overly (SYN.) exceedingly, unreasonably.

overpass (SYN.) span, bridge, viaduct.

overpower (SYN.) overcome, conquer, defeat, surmount, vanquish, overwhelm. (ANT.) *surrender.*

overrule (SYN.) disallow, nullify, cancel, override, repeal, revoke.

overrun (SYN.) spread, exceed, beset, infest, flood, abound.

oversee (SYN.) direct, run, operate, administer, boss, manage, supervise.

overseer (SYN.) leader, ruler, master, teacher, chief, commander, lord, employer, manager, head. (ANT.) *slave, servant.*

overshadow (SYN.) dominate, control, outclass, surpass, domineer.

oversight (SYN.) omission, charge, superintendence, surveillance, inattention, error, inadvertence, neglect, mistake, inspection, control, slip, management. (ANT.) *scrutiny, attention, observation.*

overstep (SYN.) surpass, exceed, trespass, transcend, impinge, violate, intrude.

overt (SYN.) honest, candid, frank, plain, open, apparent, straightforward.

overtake (SYN.) outdistance, reach, catch, pass.

overthrow (SYN.) defeat, demolish, overcome, destroy, ruin, rout, vanquish, subvert, reverse, supplant, overturn, overpower, upset. (ANT.) *revive, restore, construct, regenerate, reinstate.*

overturn (SYN.) demolish, overcome, vanquish, upset, supplant, destroy. (ANT.) *uphold, construct, build, preserve, conserve.*

overweight (SYN.) pudgy, stout, heavy, obese, fat.

overwhelm (SYN.) crush, surmount, vanquish, conquer, astonish, surprise, bewilder, astound, startle, overcome.

overwrought (SYN.) distraught, hysterical.

owe (SYN.) be liable, be indebted.

own (SYN.) monopolize, hold, possess, maintain, have.

owner (SYN.) landholder, partner, proprietor, possessor.

P

pace (SYN.) rate, gait, step.

pacify (SYN.) appease, lull, relieve, quell, soothe, allay, assuage, calm, satisfy, compose, placate, alleviate. (ANT.) *incense, inflame, arouse, excite.*

pack (SYN.) prepare, stow, crowd, stuff, bundle, parcel, load, crowd, gang, mob.

package (SYN.) parcel, packet, load, bundle, box, bottle, crate.

packed (SYN.) filled, complete, plentiful, crammed, fall, replete, gorged, satiated. (ANT.) *lacking, depleted, devoid, vacant, insufficient, partial, empty.*

pageant (SYN.) show, display, spectacle.

pain (SYN.) twinge, ache, pang, agony, distress, grief, anguish, throe, paroxysm. (ANT.) *happiness, pleasure, comfort, relief, solace, ease, delight, joy.*

painful (SYN.) hurting, galling, poignant, bitter, grievous, agonizing, aching. (ANT.) *sweet, pleasant, soothing.*

painting (SYN.) image, picture, portrayal, scene, view, sketch, illustration, panorama, likeness, representation.

pair (SYN.) team, couple, mate, match.

palatial (SYN.) majestic, magnificent, sumptuous, luxurious.

pale (SYN.) colorless, white, pallid, dim, faint, whiten, blanch. (ANT.) *flushed, ruddy, bright, dark.*

pamphlet (SYN.) leaflet, brochure.

pang (SYN.) throb, pain, hurt.

panic (SYN.) fear, terror, fright, alarm, apprehension, trembling, horror, dread. (ANT.) *tranquillity, composure, calmness, serenity, calm, soothe.*

pant (SYN.) wheeze, puff, gasp.

pantry (SYN.) cupboard, storeroom.

paper (SYN.) journal, newspaper, document, article, essay.

parable (SYN.) fable, saga, legend, myth, allegory, chronicle, fiction.

parade (SYN.) procession, cavalcade, succession, train, file, cortege, retinue, sequence, march, review, pageant, strut.

paradise (SYN.) utopia, heaven.

paradoxical (SYN.) unsteady, contradictory, discrepant, incompatible, inconsistent, vacillating, wavering, illogical. (ANT.) *correspondent, compatible, congruous, consistent.*

parallel (SYN.) allied, analogous, comparable, corresponding, akin, similar, correlative, alike, like, resembling, equal, counterpart, likeness, correspondence, resemble, equal, match. (ANT.) *opposed, different, incongruous.*

paralyze (SYN.) numb, deaden.

paraphernalia (SYN.) effect, gear, belonging, equipment.

parcel (SYN.) packet, package, bundle.

parched (SYN.) dry, arid, thirsty, drained, dehydrated, desiccated. (ANT.) *moist, damp.*

pardon (SYN.) absolution, amnesty, excuse, exoneration, forgive, acquit, condone, overlook, absolve, remit. (ANT.) *punish, chastise, accuse, sentence, penalty, conviction, condemn, convict.*

pare (SYN.) skin, peel, reduce, trim, shave.

parley (SYN.) interview, talk, conference, chat, dialogue, colloquy.

paroxysm (SYN.) twinge, pang, ache, pain. (ANT.) ease, relief, comfort.

parsimonious (SYN.) avaricious, miserly, penurious, stingy, acquisitive, greedy. (ANT.) munificent, extravagant, bountiful, altruistic, generous.

part (SYN.) piece, section, allotment, portion, segment, element, member, concern, side, interest, lines, role, apportionment, division, share, fragment, ingredient, organ, party, moiety, section, fraction, participation, divide, separate, sever, sunder. (ANT.) whole, entirety, join, combine, unite, convene.

partake (SYN.) dispense, parcel, allot, assign, distribute, partition, appropriate, divide, portion, share. (ANT.) condense, aggregate, combine.

partial (SYN.) unfinished, undone, incomplete, prejudiced, unfair. (ANT.) comprehensive, complete.

partiality (SYN.) preconception, bias, predisposition, bigotry. (ANT.) reason, fairness, impartiality.

participant (SYN.) associate, colleague, partner, shareholder.

participate (SYN.) join, share, partake.

participation (SYN.) communion, sacrament, union, intercourse, association, fellowship. (ANT.) nonparticipation, alienation.

particle (SYN.) mite, crumb, scrap, atom, corpuscle, grain, iota, shred, smidgen, grain, speck, bit, spot. (ANT.) quantity, bulk, mass.

particular (SYN.) peculiar, unusual, detailed, specific, fastidious, individual, distinctive, singular, circumstantial, exact, careful, squeamish, special. (ANT.) general, rough, universal, comprehensive, undiscriminating.

partisan (SYN.) follower, successor, adherent, attendant, henchman, devotee, disciple, votary. (ANT.) leader, chief, master, head.

partition (SYN.) distribution, division, separation, screen, barrier, separator, divider, wall. (ANT.) unification, joining.

partly (SYN.) comparatively, partially, somewhat.

partner (SYN.) colleague, comrade, friend, crony, consort, associate, companion,

mate, participant. (ANT.) stranger, enemy, adversary.

party (SYN.) company, gathering, crowd, group.

pass (SYN.) proceed, continue, move, go, disregard, ignore, exceed, gap, permit, permission, admission, throw, toss. (ANT.) note, consider, notice.

passable (SYN.) fair, average, mediocre, acceptable, adequate, satisfactory. (ANT.) worst, excellent, first-rate, exceptional, extraordinary, superior.

passage (SYN.) section, passageway, corridor, section, voyage, tour, crossing.

passenger (SYN.) traveler, tourist, rider, voyager, commuter.

passion (SYN.) feeling, affection, turmoil, sentiment, perturbation, agitation, emotion, trepidation, zeal, rapture, excitement, desire, love, liking, fondness, enthusiasm. (ANT.) tranquillity, indifference, calm, restraint, dispassion, apathy, coolness.

passionate (SYN.) fiery, ardent, burning, glowing, irascible, fervid, excitable, hot, impetuous, emotional, impulsive, excited, zealous, enthusiastic, earnest, sincere. (ANT.) calm, cool, apathetic, deliberate.

passive (SYN.) relaxed, idle, stoical, enduring, inert, inactive, patient, submissive. (ANT.) dynamic, active, aggressive.

password (SYN.) code word.

past (SYN.) done, finished, gone, over, former. (ANT.) future, present, ahead.

pastime (SYN.) match, amusement, diversion, fun, play, sport, contest, merriment, recreation, entertainment, hobby. (ANT.) quiescence, labor, apathy, business.

patch (SYN.) restore, fix, repair, ameliorate, correct, rectify, remedy, sew, mend, better. (ANT.) rend, deface, destroy, hurt, injure.

patent (SYN.) conspicuous, apparent, obvious, clear, evident, unmistakable, open, overt, manifest, indubitable, protection, control, copyright, permit. (ANT.) hidden, concealed, obscure, coven.

path (SYN.) avenue, street, trail, walk, course, route, thoroughfare, channel, way, track, lane, footpath, pathway, walkway.

pathetic (SYN.) piteous, sad,

affecting, moving, poignant, pitiable, touching, pitiful, touching. (ANT.) funny, comical.

patience (SYN.) perseverance, composure, endurance, fortitude, long-suffering, forbearance, calmness, passiveness, serenity, courage, persistence. (ANT.) restlessness, nervousness, impatience, impetuosity.

patient (SYN.) indulgent, stoical, forbearing, composed, assiduous, passive, uncomplaining, resigned, persistent, untiring, persevering, submissive, resigned, serene, calm, quiet, unexcited, unruffled. (ANT.) turbulent, high-strung, chafing, clamorous, hysterical.

patrol (SYN.) inspect, watch, guard.

patron (SYN.) purchaser, buyer, client, customer.

patronize (SYN.) support.

pattern (SYN.) guide, example, original, model, design, figure, decoration.

paunchy (SYN.) fat, pudgy, stout, plump, portly, rotund, corpulent, obese, stocky. (ANT.) slim, slender, gaunt, lean, thin.

pause (SYN.) falter, hesitate, waver, demur, doubt, scruple, delay, vacillate, hesitation, rest, interruption, break, delay, intermission, recess. (ANT.) proceed, continue, decide, resolve, persevere, continuity.

pawn (SYN.) tool, puppet, stooge.

pay (SYN.) earnings, salary, allowance, stipend, wages, payment, compensation, recompense. (ANT.) gratuity, present, gift.

payable (SYN.) unpaid, due, owed, owing.

peace (SYN.) hush, repose, serenity, tranquillity, silence, stillness, calmness, quiescence, calm, quietude, rest, quiet, peacefulness, pact. (ANT.) noise, tumult, agitation, disturbance, excitement.

peaceable (SYN.) mild, calm, friendly, peaceful, amiable, gentle, pacific. (ANT.) aggressive, hostile, warlike.

peaceful (SYN.) pacific, calm, undisturbed, quiet, serene, mild, placid, gentle, tranquil, peaceable. (ANT.) noisy, violent, agitated, turbulent, disturbed, disrupted, riotous.

peak (SYN.) climax, culmination, summit, zenith, height, acme, consummation, apex, top, point, crest. (ANT.)

depth, floor, base, anticlimax, base, bottom.

peculiar (SYN.) odd, eccentric, extraordinary, unusual, individual, particular, striking, rare, exceptional, distinctive, strange, unfamiliar, uncommon, queer, curious, outlandish. (ANT.) ordinary, common, normal, general, regular.

peculiarity (SYN.) characteristic, feature, mark, trait, quality, attribute, property, distinctiveness.

pedantic (SYN.) formal, scholastic, erudite, academic, learned, bookish, theoretical, scholarly. (ANT.) simple, commonsense, ignorant, practical, unlearned.

peddle (SYN.) sell, vend, hawk.

pedestrian (SYN.) stroller, walker.

pedigree (SYN.) descent, line, parentage, lineage, ancestry, family.

peek (SYN.) glimpse, look, peer, peep.

peel (SYN.) rind, skin, peeling.

peep (SYN.) squeak, cheep, chirp.

peer (SYN.) match, rival, equal, parallel, peep, glimpse, examine, peek, scrutinize.

peeve (SYN.) nettle, irk, irritate, annoy.

peevish (SYN.) ill-natured, irritable, waspish, touchy, petulant, snappish, fractious, ill-tempered, fretful. (ANT.) pleasant, affable, good-tempered, genial, good-natured.

pen (SYN.) coop, enclosure, cage.

penalize (SYN.) dock, punish.

penalty (SYN.) fine, retribution, handicap, punishment, chastisement, disadvantage, forfeiture, forfeit. (ANT.) remuneration, compensation, reward, pardon.

penchant (SYN.) disposition, propensity, tendency, partiality, inclination, bent, tendency, slant, bias. (ANT.) justice, fairness, equity, impartiality.

penetrate (SYN.) bore, hole, pierce, enter.

penetrating (SYN.) profound, recondite, abstruse, deep, solemn, piercing, puncturing, boring, sharp, acute. (ANT.) superficial, trivial, shallow, slight.

peninsula (SYN.) spit, headland, neck, point.

penitent (SYN.) remorseful, sorrowful, regretful, contrite, sorry, repentant. (ANT.) remorseless, objurgate.

penniless (SYN.) poor, destitute, impecunious, poverty-stricken, needy. (ANT.) rich, wealthy, affluent, opulent, prosperous, well-off.

pensive (SYN.) dreamy, meditative, thoughtful, introspective, reflective, contemplative. (ANT.) thoughtless, heedless, inconsiderate, precipitous, rash.

penurious (SYN.) avaricious, greedy, parsimonious, miserly, stingy, acquisitive, tight. (ANT.) munificent, extravagant, bountiful, generous, altruistic.

penury (SYN.) poverty, want, destitution, necessity, indigence, need, privation. (ANT.) riches, affluence, abundance, plenty.

people (SYN.) humans, person.

perceive (SYN.) note, conceive, see, comprehend, understand, discern, recognize, apprehend, notice, observe, distinguish, grasp. (ANT.) overlook, ignore, miss.

perceptible (SYN.) sensible, appreciable, apprehensible. (ANT.) imperceptible, absurd, impalpable.

perception (SYN.) understanding, apprehension, conception, insight, comprehension, discernment. (ANT.) misconception, ignorance, misapprehension.

perceptive (SYN.) informed, observant, apprised, cognizant, aware, conscious, sensible, mindful, discerning, sharp, acute, observant. (ANT.) unaware, ignorant, oblivious, insensible.

perfect (SYN.) ideal, whole, faultless, immaculate, complete, superlative, absolute, unqualified, utter, sinless, holy, finished, blameless, entire, excellent, pure, flawless, ideal. (ANT.) incomplete, defective, imperfect, deficient, blemished, lacking, faulty, flawed.

perfectionist (SYN.) purist, pedant.

perform (SYN.) impersonate, pretend, act, play, do, accomplish, achieve, complete.

performance (SYN.) parade, entertainment, demonstration, movie, show, production, ostentation, spectacle, presentation, offering.

performer (SYN.) entertainer, actress, actor.

perfume (SYN.) cologne, scent, essence.

perfunctory (SYN.) decorous, exact, formal, external, correct, affected, methodical, precise, stiff, outward, proper, solemn. (ANT.) unconventional, easy, unconstrained, natural, heartfelt.

perhaps (SYN.) conceivable, possible, maybe. (ANT.) absolutely, definitely.

peril (SYN.) jeopardy, risk, danger, hazard. (ANT.) safety, protection, defense, security.

perilous (SYN.) menacing, risky, hazardous, critical, dangerous, precarious, unsafe, insecure, threatening. (ANT.) safe, firm, protected, secure.

period (SYN.) era, age, interval, span, tempo, time, epoch, duration, spell, date.

periodical (SYN.) uniform, customary, orderly, systematic, regular, steady. (ANT.) exceptional, unusual, abnormal, rare, erratic.

perish (SYN.) die, sink, cease, decline, decay, depart, wane, wither, languish, expire, cease, pass away. (ANT.) grow, survive, flourish, begin, live.

perishable (SYN.) decomposable.

permanent (SYN.) constant, durable, enduring, abiding, fixed, changeless, unchangeable, lasting, indestructible, stable, continuing, long-lived, persistent, persisting, everlasting, unchanging, unaltered. (ANT.) unstable, transient, ephemeral, temporary, transitory, passing, inconstant, fluctuating.

permeate (SYN.) penetrate, pervade, run through, diffuse, fill, saturate, infiltrate.

permissible (SYN.) allowable, fair, tolerable, admissible, justifiable, probable, warranted. (ANT.) unsuitable, inadmissible.

permission (SYN.) authorization, liberty, permit, authority, consent, leave, license, freedom. (ANT.) refusal, prohibition, denial, opposition.

permissive (SYN.) easy, tolerant, open-minded. (ANT.) restrictive.

permit (SYN.) let, tolerate, authorize, sanction, allow, grant, give. (ANT.) refuse, resist, forbid, protest, object, prohibit, disallow.

perpendicular (SYN.) standing, upright, vertical. (ANT.) horizontal.

perpetrate (SYN.) commit, perform, do. (ANT.) neglect, fail, miscarry.

perpetual (SYN.) everlasting, immortal, ceaseless, endless, timeless, undying, infinite, eternal, unceasing, continuing, continual, continuous, permanent, constant, eternal. (ANT.) transient, mortal, finite, temporal, ephemeral, inconstant, intermittent, fluctuating.

perpetually (SYN.) continually, ever, incessantly, eternally, forever, always, constantly. (ANT.) rarely, sometimes, never, occasionally, fitfully.

perplex (SYN.) confuse, dumbfound, mystify, puzzle, bewilder, confound, nonplus. (ANT.) solve, explain, illumine, instruct, clarify.

perplexed (SYN.) confused, disorganized, mixed, bewildered, deranged, disordered, muddled, disconcerted. (ANT.) plain, obvious, clear, lucid, organized.

perplexing (SYN.) intricate, complex, involved, compound, complicated. (ANT.) uncompounded, plain, simple.

persecute (SYN.) harass, hound, torment, worry, vex, torture, harry, afflict, annoy, oppress, pester, ill-treat, victimize, maltreat. (ANT.) support, comfort, assist, encourage, aid.

persevere (SYN.) remain, abide, endure, last, persist, continue. (ANT.) vacillate, desist, discontinue, cease, waver, lapse.

perseverance (SYN.) persistency, constancy, pertinacity, steadfastness, tenacity, industry. (ANT.) sloth, cessation, laziness, idleness, rest.

persist (SYN.) endure, remain, abide, persevere, continue, last. (ANT.) vacillate, waver, desist, cease, discontinue, stop.

persistence (SYN.) persistency, constancy, perseverance, steadfastness, tenacity. (ANT.) cessation, rest, sloth, idleness.

persistent (SYN.) lasting, steady, obstinate, stubborn, fixed, enduring, immovable, constant, indefatigable, dogged. (ANT.) wavering, unsure, hesitant.

person (SYN.) human, individual, somebody, someone.

personal (SYN.) secret, private. (ANT.) general, public.

personality (SYN.) make-up, nature, disposition, character.

perspicacity (SYN.) intelligence, understanding, discernment, judgment, wisdom, sagacity. (ANT.) thoughtlessness, stupidity, arbitrariness, senselessness.

persuade (SYN.) entice, coax, exhort, prevail upon, urge, allure, induce, influence, win over, convince. (ANT.) restrain, deter, compel, dissuade, coerce, discourage.

persuasion (SYN.) decision, feeling, notion, view, sentiment, conviction, belief, opinion. (ANT.) knowledge, skepticism, fact, misgiving.

persuasive (SYN.) winning, alluring, compelling, convincing, stimulating, influential. (ANT.) dubious, unconvincing.

pertain (SYN.) refer, relate, apply.

pertinacious (SYN.) firm, obstinate, contumacious, head-strong, dogged, inflexible, obdurate, uncompromising, determined, immovable, unyielding. (ANT.) yielding, docile, amenable, submissive, compliant.

pertinent (SYN.) apt, material, relevant, relating, applicable, to the point, germane, apropos, apposite, appropriate. (ANT.) unrelated, foreign, alien, extraneous.

perturbed (SYN.) agitated, disturbed, upset, flustered.

pervade (SYN.) penetrate, saturate, fill, diffuse, infiltrate, run through, permeate.

perverse (SYN.) obstinate, ungovernable, sinful, contrary, fractious, peevish, forward, disobedient, wicked, intractable, petulant. (ANT.) docile, agreeable, tractable.

perversion (SYN.) maltreatment, outrage, desecration, abuse, profanation, misuse, reviling. (ANT.) respect.

pervert (SYN.) deprave, humiliate, impair, debase, corrupt, degrade, abase, defile. (ANT.) improve, raise, enhance.

perverted (SYN.) wicked, perverse, sinful.

pest (SYN.) annoyance, bother, nuisance, bother, irritant, irritation.

pester (SYN.) disturb, annoy, irritate, tease, bother, chafe, inconvenience, molest, trouble, vex, harass, torment, worry. (ANT.) console, soothe, accommodate, gratify.

pet (SYN.) darling, favorite, caress.

petition (SYN.) invocation, prayer, request, appeal, entreaty, supplication, suit, plea, application, solicitation, entreaty.

petty (SYN.) paltry, trivial, frivolous, small, unimportant, trifling, insignificant. *(ANT.) important, serious, weighty, momentous, grand, vital, significant, generous.*

petulant *(SYN.)* irritable, ill-natured, fretful, snappish, peevish, ill-tempered, waspish, touchy. *(ANT.) pleasant, affable, good-tempered, genial, good-natured.*

phantom *(SYN.)* apparition, ghost, specter.

phase *(SYN.)* period, stage, view, condition.

phenomenon *(SYN.)* occurrence, fact, happening, incident.

philanthropy *(SYN.)* kindness, benevolence, charity, generosity, tenderness, liberality, humanity, magnanimity, altruism. *(ANT.) unkindness, inhumanity, cruelty, malevolence, selfishness.*

phlegmatic *(SYN.)* unfeeling, passionless, listless, cold, lethargic, sluggish, slow, lazy. *(ANT.) passionate, ardent, energetic.*

phony *(SYN.)* counterfeit, artificial, ersatz, fake, synthetic, unreal, spurious, feigned, assumed, bogus, sham, false, forged. *(ANT.) real, genuine, natural, true.*

phrase *(SYN.)* expression, term, word, name.

physical *(SYN.)* material, bodily, carnal, corporeal, natural, somatic, corporal. *(ANT.) spiritual, mental.*

pick *(SYN.)* cull, opt, select, elect, choose. *(ANT.) reject, refuse.*

picture *(SYN.)* etching, image, painting, portrait, print, representation, sketch, appearance, cinema, effigy, engraving, scene, view, illustration, panorama, resemblance, likeness, drawing, photograph.

piece *(SYN.)* portion, bit, fraction, morsel, scrap, fragment, amount, part, quantity, unit, section, portion. *(ANT.) sum, whole, entirety, all, total.*

piecemeal *(SYN.)* gradually, partially. *(ANT.) whole, complete, entire.*

pierce *(SYN.)* puncture, perforate.

pigheaded *(SYN.)* inflexible, stubborn, obstinate.

pigment *(SYN.)* shade, tint, color, dye, hue, complexion, tincture, stain, tinge. *(ANT.) transparency, paleness.*

pile *(SYN.)* accumulation, heap, collection.

pilgrim *(SYN.)* wanderer, traveler.

pilgrimage *(SYN.)* trip, journey, tour, expedition.

pillar *(SYN.)* support, prop, column, shaft.

pillow *(SYN.)* bolster, cushion, pad.

pilot *(SYN.)* helmsman, aviator, steersman.

pin *(SYN.)* clip, fastening, peg, fastener.

pinch *(SYN.)* squeeze, nip.

pinnacle *(SYN.)* crown, zenith, head, summit, chief, apex, crest, top. *(ANT.) bottom, foundation, base, foot.*

pioneer *(SYN.)* guide, pilgrim, pathfinder, explorer.

pious *(SYN.)* devout, religious, spiritual, consecrated, divine, hallowed, holy, saintly, reverent. *(ANT.) worldly, sacrilegious, evil, secular, profane, irreligious, impious.*

pirate *(SYN.)* plunderer, buccaneer, privateer.

pistol *(SYN.)* gun, revolver, weapon, handgun.

pit *(SYN.)* well, cavity, hole, excavation.

pitch *(SYN.)* throw, cast, toss, propel, hurl, fling, thrust, establish. *(ANT.) retain, draw, hold, pull, haul.*

pitcher *(SYN.)* jug.

piteous *(SYN.)* poignant, touching, affecting, moving, pitiable, sad, pathetic. *(ANT.) funny, ludicrous, comical.*

pitfall *(SYN.)* lure, snare, wile, ambush, bait, intrigue, trick, trap, artifice, net, snare.

pitiable *(SYN.)* poignant, touching, moving, affecting, sad. *(ANT.) ludicrous, funny, comical.*

pitiful *(SYN.)* distressing, pathetic, pitiable.

pitiless *(SYN.)* unmerciful, mean, unpitying, merciless, cruel. *(ANT.) gentle, kind.*

pity *(SYN.)* sympathy, commiseration, condolence, mercy, compassion, charity, mercy. *(ANT.) ruthlessness, hardness, cruelty, inhumanity, brutality, vindictiveness.*

pivotal *(SYN.)* crucial, critical, essential, central. *(ANT.) peripheral, unimportant.*

place *(SYN.)* lay, arrange, dispose, put, deposit, space, region, location, plot, area, spot. *(ANT.) mislay, remove, disarrange, disturb, misplace.*

placid *(SYN.)* pacific, serene, tranquil, calm, imperturbable, composed, peaceful, quiet, still, undisturbed, unruffled. *(ANT.) wild, frantic, turbulent, stormy, excited.*

plagiarize *(SYN.)* recite, adduce, cite, quote, paraphrase, repeat, extract. *(ANT.)* retort, contradict, misquote, refute.

plague *(SYN.)* hound, pester, worry, harass, annoy, persecute, torment, vex, afflict, badger, torture, epidemic, trouble. *(ANT.) encourage, aid, comfort, assist, support.*

plain *(SYN.)* candid, simple, flat, smooth, clear, evident, sincere, unpretentious, level, distinct, absolute, visible, open, frank, palpable, undecorated, ordinary, unembellished, unadorned. *(ANT.) embellished, abstruse, abrupt, rough, insincere, adorned, fancy, elaborate, beautiful, ornamented.*

plan *(SYN.)* design, purpose, sketch, devise, invent, contrive, intend, draw, create, scheme, plot, method, procedure.

plane *(SYN.)* level, airplane.

plastic *(SYN.)* pliable, moldable, supple, flexible, synthetic.

platform *(SYN.)* stage, pulpit.

plausible *(SYN.)* likely, practical, credible, feasible, possible, probable. *(ANT.) impracticable, impossible, visionary.*

play *(SYN.)* entertainment, amusement, pastime, sport, game, fun, diversion, recreation, show, performance, drama, theatrical. *(ANT.) work, labor, boredom, toil.*

playful *(SYN.)* sportive, frolicsome, frisky.

plaything *(SYN.)* game, trinket, toy, gadget.

playwright *(SYN.)* scriptwriter, dramatist.

plea *(SYN.)* invocation, request, appeal, entreaty, supplication, petition, suit.

plead *(SYN.)* beseech, defend, rejoin, supplicate, discuss, beg, appeal, ask, implore, argue, entreat. *(ANT.) deny, refuse.*

pleasant *(SYN.)* agreeable, welcome, suitable, charming, pleasing, amiable, gratifying, acceptable, pleasurable, enjoyable, nice, satisfying, satisfactory, acceptable, affable, mild, friendly. *(ANT.) offensive, disagreeable, obnoxious, unpleasant, horrid, sour, difficult, nasty.*

please *(SYN.)* satisfy, suffice, fulfill, content, appease, gratify, satiate, compensate, remunerate. *(ANT.) dissatisfy, annoy, tantalize, frustrate, displease, vex.*

pleasing *(SYN.)* luscious, melodious, sugary, delightful, agreeable, honeyed, mellifluous, engaging, pleasant, charming, engaging. *(ANT.) repulsive, sour, acrid, bitter, offensive, irritating, annoying.*

pleasure *(SYN.)* felicity, delight, amusement, enjoyment, gratification, happiness, joy, satisfaction, gladness, well-being. *(ANT.) suffering, pain, vexation, trouble, affliction, discomfort, torment.*

pledge *(SYN.)* promise, statement, assertion, declaration, assurance, agreement, oath, commitment, agree, vow, swear; bind, obligate, commit. *(ANT.) renounce, release, neglect, mistrust.*

plentiful *(SYN.)* ample, profuse, replete, bountiful, abundant, plenteous, luxurious, fullness, fruitful, copious. *(ANT.) rare, scanty, deficient, scarce, insufficient.*

plenty *(SYN.)* fruitfulness, bounty, fullness, abundance. *(ANT.) want, scarcity, need.*

pliable *(SYN.)* elastic, supple, flexible, compliant, pliant, resilient, ductile. *(ANT.) rigid, unbending, hard, brittle, stiff.*

plight *(SYN.)* dilemma, situation, difficulty, condition, predicament, fix, scrape, state. *(ANT.) satisfaction, ease, comfort, calmness.*

plot *(SYN.)* design, plan, scheme, cabal, conspiracy, diagram, sketch, graph, chart, machination, intrigue.

plotting *(SYN.)* cunning, scheming, objective, artfulness, contrivance, purpose, intent, design. *(ANT.) accident, chance, result, candor, sincerity.*

ploy *(SYN.)* ruse, guile, antic, deception, hoax, subterfuge, wile, cheat, artifice, fraud, trick. *(ANT.) honesty, sincerity, openness, exposure, candor.*

pluck *(SYN.)* yank, snatch, jerk, pull.

plug *(SYN.)* cork, stopper.

plump *(SYN.)* obese, portly, stout, thickset, rotund, chubby, fat, paunchy, stocky, corpulent, pudgy, fleshy. *(ANT.) slim, thin, gaunt, lean, slender, skinny.*

plunder *(SYN.)* ravage, strip, sack, rob, pillage, raid, loot.

plunge *(SYN.)* immerse, dip, submerge.

pocketbook *(SYN.)* purse, handbag.

poem *(SYN.)* lyric, verse, poetry, rhyme.

pogrom *(SYN.)* massacre, carnage, slaughter, butchery.

poignant *(SYN.)* pitiable,

touching, affecting, impressive, sad, tender, moving, heart-rending.

point *(SYN.)* direct, level, train, aim, locality, position, spot, location. *(ANT.)* distract, misguide, deceive, misdirect.

pointed *(SYN.)* keen, sharp, shrewd, witty, quick, acute, penetrating, cutting, piercing, astute, severe. *(ANT.)* shallow, stupid, bland, blunt, gentle.

pointless *(SYN.)* vain, purposeless.

poise *(SYN.)* composure, self-possession, equanimity, equilibrium, carriage, calmness, balance, self-control, assurance, control, dignity. *(ANT.)* rage, turbulence, agitation, anger, excitement.

poison *(SYN.)* corrupt, sully, taint, infect, befoul, defile, contaminate, venom, toxin, virus. *(ANT.)* purify, disinfect.

poke *(SYN.)* punch, stab, thrust, jab.

policy *(SYN.)* procedure, system, rule, approach, tactic.

polish *(SYN.)* brighten, shine, finish, brightness, gloss. *(ANT.)* tarnish, dull.

polished *(SYN.)* glib, diplomatic, urbane, refined, sleek, suave, slick. *(ANT.)* rough, blunt, bluff, harsh, rugged.

polite *(SYN.)* civil, refined, well-mannered, accomplished, courteous, genteel, urbane, well-bred, cultivated, considerate, thoughtful, mannerly, respectful. *(ANT.)* uncouth, impertinent, rude, boorish, uncivil, discourteous.

pollute *(SYN.)* contaminate, poison, taint, sully, infect, befoul, defile, dirty. *(ANT.)* purify, disinfect, clean, clarify.

pomp *(SYN.)* flourish, pageantry, vaunting, show, boasting, ostentation, parade, display. *(ANT.)* reserve, humility, modesty.

pompous *(SYN.)* high, magnificent, stately, august, dignified, grandiose, noble, majestic, lofty, imposing, arrogant, vain, pretentious. *(ANT.)* lowly, undignified, humble, common, ordinary.

ponder *(SYN.)* examined, study, contemplate, investigate, meditate, muse, scrutinize, cogitate, reflect, weigh, deliberate, consider.

ponderous *(SYN.)* burdensome, trying, gloomy, serious, sluggish, massive, heavy, cumbersome, grievous, grave, dull, weighty. *(ANT.)* light, animated, brisk.

poor *(SYN.)* penniless, bad, deficient, destitute, inferior, shabby, wrong, scanty, indigent, needy, poverty-stricken, unfavorable, impoverished. *(ANT.)* wealthy, prosperous, rich, fortunate, good, excellent.

poppycock *(SYN.)* rubbish, babble, twaddle, nonsense.

popular *(SYN.)* favorite, general, common, familiar, prevalent, liked, prevailing, well-liked, approved, accepted, celebrated, admired, ordinary. *(ANT.)* unpopular, esoteric, restricted, exclusive.

populous *(SYN.)* dense, thronged, crowded.

porch *(SYN.)* patio, veranda.

pornographic *(SYN.)* impure, indecent, obscene, coarse, dirty, filthy, lewd, smutty, offensive, disgusting. *(ANT.)* refined, modest, pure, decent.

port *(SYN.)* harbor, refuge, anchorage.

portable *(SYN.)* transportable, movable.

portal *(SYN.)* entry, doorway, opening, inlet, entrance. *(ANT.)* exit, departure.

portend *(SYN.)* foreshadow, presage, foretoken.

portentous *(SYN.)* significant, critical, momentous. *(ANT.)* trivial.

portion *(SYN.)* share, bit, parcel, part, piece, section, fragment, division, quota, segment, allotment. *(ANT.)* whole, bulk.

portly *(SYN.)* majestic, grand, impressive, dignified, stout, fat, heavy, obese. *(ANT.)* slender, thin, slim.

portrait *(SYN.)* painting, representation, picture, likeness.

portray *(SYN.)* depict, picture, represent, sketch, describe, delineate, paint. *(ANT.)* misrepresent, caricature, suggest.

position *(SYN.)* caste, site, locality, situation, condition, standing, incumbency, office, bearing, posture, berth, place, job, pose, rank, attitude, location, spot, station, situation, occupation.

positive *(SYN.)* sure, definite, fixed, inevitable, undeniable, indubitable, assured, certain, unquestionable, unmistakable. *(ANT.)* uncertain, doubtful, questionable, unsure, dubious, confused, negative, adverse.

positively *(SYN.)* unquestionably, surely, certainly, absolutely.

possess *(SYN.)* own, obtain, have, seize, hold, occupy, affect, control. *(ANT.)*

surrender, abandon, lose, renounce.

possessed *(SYN.)* entranced, obsessed, consumed, haunted, enchanted.

possession *(SYN.)* custody, ownership, occupancy.

possessions *(SYN.)* commodities, effects, goods, property, merchandise, wares, wealth, belongings, stock.

possible *(SYN.)* likely, practical, probable, achievable, feasible, plausible, credible, practicable. *(ANT.)* implausible, impossible, improbable.

possibility *(SYN.)* opportunity, chance, contingency, occasion. *(ANT.)* obstacle, disadvantage, hindrance.

possibly *(SYN.)* perchance, perhaps, maybe.

post *(SYN.)* position, job, berth, incumbency, situation, shaft, pole, fort, base, station.

postpone *(SYN.)* delay, stay, suspend, discontinue, defer, adjourn, interrupt, put off. *(ANT.)* persist, maintain, continue, proceed.

postulate *(SYN.)* principle, adage, saying, proverb, truism, byword, aphorism, axiom, fundamental, maxim.

potency *(SYN.)* effectiveness, capability, skillfulness, efficiency, competency, ability. *(ANT.)* wastefulness, inability, ineptitude.

potent *(SYN.)* mighty, influential, convincing, effective. *(ANT.)* feeble, weak, powerless, impotent.

potential *(SYN.)* likely, possible, dormant, hidden, latent.

pouch *(SYN.)* container, bag, sack.

pound *(SYN.)* buffet, beat, punch, strike, thrash, defeat, subdue, pulse, smite, belabor, knock, thump, overpower, palpitate, rout, vanquish. *(ANT.)* fail, surrender, stroke, defend, shield.

pour *(SYN.)* flow.

pout *(SYN.)* brood, sulk, mope.

poverty *(SYN.)* necessity, need, want, destitution, privation, indigence, distress. *(ANT.)* plenty, abundance, wealth, riches, affluence, richness, comfort.

power *(SYN.)* potency, might, authority, control, predominance, capability, faculty, validity, force, vigor, command, influence, talent, ability, dominion, competency. *(ANT.)* incapacity, fatigue, weakness, disablement, impotence, ineptitude.

powerful *(SYN.)* firm, strong, concentrated, enduring, forcible, robust, sturdy, tough, athletic, forceful, hale, impregnable, hardy, mighty, potent. *(ANT.)* feeble, insipid, brittle, delicate, fragile, weak, ineffectual, powerless.

practical *(SYN.)* sensible, wise, prudent, reasonable, sagacious, sober, sound, workable, attainable. *(ANT.)* stupid, unaware, impalpable, absurd, impractical.

practically *(SYN.)* almost, nearly.

practice *(SYN.)* exercise, habit, custom, manner, wont, usage, drill, tradition, performance, action, repetition. *(ANT.)* inexperience, theory, disuse, idleness, speculation.

practiced *(SYN.)* able, expert, skilled, adept. *(ANT.)* inept.

prairie *(SYN.)* plain, grassland.

praise *(SYN.)* applaud, compliment, extol, laud, glorify, commend, acclaim, eulogize, flatter, admire, celebrate, commendation, approval. *(ANT.)* criticize, censure, reprove, condemn, disparage, disapprove, criticism.

pray *(SYN.)* supplicate, importune, beseech, beg.

prayer *(SYN.)* plea, suit, appeal, invocation, supplication, petition, entreaty, request.

preach *(SYN.)* teach, moralize, lecture.

preamble *(SYN.)* overture, prologue, beginning, introduction, prelude, start, foreword, preface. *(ANT.)* end, finale, completion, conclusion, epilogue.

precarious *(SYN.)* dangerous, perilous, threatening, menacing, critical, risky, unsafe, hazardous. *(ANT.)* secure, firm, protected, safe.

precaution *(SYN.)* foresight, forethought, care.

precedence *(SYN.)* preference, priority.

precedent *(SYN.)* model, example.

precept *(SYN.)* doctrine, tenet, belief, creed, teaching, dogma. *(ANT.)* practice, conduct, performance, deed.

precious *(SYN.)* dear, useful, valuable, costly, esteemed, profitable, expensive, priceless, dear. *(ANT.)* poor, worthless, cheap, mean, trashy.

precipice *(SYN.)* bluff, cliff.

precipitate *(SYN.)* speedy, swift, hasty, sudden.

precipitous *(SYN.)* unannounced, sudden, harsh,

rough, unexpected, sharp, abrupt, hasty, craggy, steep, precipitate. (*ANT.*) *expected, smooth, anticipated, gradual.*

precise (*SYN.*) strict, exact, formal, rigid, definite, unequivocal, prim, ceremonious, distinct, accurate, correct. (*ANT.*) *loose, easy, vague, informal, careless, erroneous.*

precisely (*SYN.*) specifically, exactly.

precision (*SYN.*) correction, accuracy, exactness.

preclude (*SYN.*) hinder, prevent, obstruct, forestall, obviate, thwart, impede. (*ANT.*) *permit, aid, expedite, encourage, promote.*

preclusion (*SYN.*) omission, exception, exclusion. (*ANT.*) *standard, rule, inclusion.*

predicament (*SYN.*) dilemma, plight, situation, condition, fix, difficulty, strait, scrape. (*ANT.*) *satisfaction, comfort, ease.*

predict (*SYN.*) forecast, foretell.

prediction (*SYN.*) forecast, prophecy.

predilection (*SYN.*) attachment, inclination, affection, bent, desire, penchant, disposition, preference. (*ANT.*) *repugnance, aversion, apathy, distaste, nonchalance.*

predominant (*SYN.*) highest, paramount, cardinal, foremost, main, first, leading, supreme, principal, essential, prevalent, dominant, prevailing. (*ANT.*) *subsidiary, auxiliary, supplemental, minor, subordinate.*

predominate (*SYN.*) prevail, outweigh, rule.

preface (*SYN.*) foreword, introduction, preliminary, prelude, prologue, preamble.

prefer (*SYN.*) select, favor, elect, fancy.

preference (*SYN.*) election, choice, selection, alternative, option.

prejudice (*SYN.*) bias, favoritism, unfairness, partiality.

prejudiced (*SYN.*) fanatical, narrow-minded, dogmatic, bigoted, illiberal, intolerant. (*ANT.*) *radical, liberal, tolerant, progressive.*

preliminary (*SYN.*) introductory, preparatory, prelude, preface.

premature (*SYN.*) early, untimely, unexpected. (*ANT.*) *timely.*

premeditated (*SYN.*) intended, voluntary, contemplated, designed, intentional, willful, deliberate, studied. (*ANT.*) *fortuitous, accidental.*

premeditation (*SYN.*) intention, deliberation, forethought, forecast. (*ANT.*) *hazard, accident, impromptu, extemporization.*

premise (*SYN.*) basis, presupposition, assumption, postulate, principle, presumption. (*ANT.*) *superstructure, derivative, trimming, implication.*

preoccupied (*SYN.*) abstracted, distracted, absorbed, meditative, inattentive, absent, absent-minded. (*ANT.*) *attentive, alert, conscious, present, attending, watchful.*

prepare (*SYN.*) contrive, furnish, ready, predispose, condition, fit, arrange, plan, qualify, make ready, get ready.

preposterous (*SYN.*) foolish, nonsensical, silly, contradictory, unreasonable, absurd, inconsistent, irrational, self-contradictory. (*ANT.*) *sensible, rational, consistent, sound.*

prerequisite (*SYN.*) essential, requirement, necessity, condition, demand.

prerogative (*SYN.*) grant, right, license, authority, privilege. (*ANT.*) *violation, encroachment, wrong, injustice.*

prescribe (*SYN.*) order, direct, designate.

presence (*SYN.*) nearness, attendance, closeness, vicinity, appearance, bearing, personality.

present (*SYN.*) donation, gift, today, now, existing, current, largess, donate, acquaint, introduce, being, give, gratuity, boon, grant. (*ANT.*) *reject, spurn, accept, retain, receive.*

presentable (*SYN.*) polite, well-bred, respectable, well-mannered.

presently (*SYN.*) shortly, soon, directly, immediately.

preserve (*SYN.*) protect, save, conserve, maintain, secure, rescue, uphold, spare, keep, can, safeguard, defend, rescue. (*ANT.*) *impair, abolish, destroy, abandon, squander, injure.*

preside (*SYN.*) officiate, direct, administrate.

press (*SYN.*) impel, shove, urge, hasten, push, compress, squeeze, hug, crowd, propel, force, drive, embrace, smooth, iron, insist on, pressure, promote, urgency, jostle. (*ANT.*) *oppose, pull, falter, drag, retreat.*

pressing (*SYN.*) impelling, insistent, necessary, urgent, compelling, imperative, instant, serious, important, cogent, exigent, importunate. (*ANT.*) *unimportant, trifling, insignificant, petty, trivial.*

pressure (*SYN.*) force, influence, stress, press, compulsion, urgency, constraint, compression. (*ANT.*) *relaxation, leniency, ease, recreation.*

prestige (*SYN.*) importance, reputation, influence, renown, fame, distinction.

presume (*SYN.*) guess, speculate, surmise, imagine, conjecture, apprehend, believe, think, assume, suppose, deduce. (*ANT.*) *prove, ascertain, demonstrate, know.*

presumption (*SYN.*) boldness, impertinence, insolence, rudeness, assurance, effrontery, impudence, assumption, audacity, supposition, sauciness. (*ANT.*) *politeness, diffidence.*

presumptuous (*SYN.*) bold, impertinent, fresh, imprudent, rude, forward, arrogant.

presupposition (*SYN.*) basis, principle, premise, assumption, postulate. (*ANT.*) *superstructure, derivative, implication.*

pretend (*SYN.*) feign, simulate, act, profess, make believe, imagine, fake, sham, affect. (*ANT.*) *expose, reveal, display.*

pretense (*SYN.*) mask, pretext, show, affection, disguise, garb, semblance, simulation, fabrication, lie, excuse, falsification, deceit, subterfuge. (*ANT.*) *sincerity, actuality, truth, fact, reality.*

pretentious (*SYN.*) gaudy, ostentatious. (*ANT.*) *simple, humble.*

pretty (*SYN.*) charming, handsome, lovely, beauteous, fair, comely, attractive, beautiful, elegant. (*ANT.*) *repulsive, foul, unsightly, homely, plain, hideous.*

prevail (*SYN.*) win, succeed, predominate, triumph. (*ANT.*) *yield, lose.*

prevailing (*SYN.*) common, current, general, habitual, steady, regular, universal.

prevalent (*SYN.*) ordinary, usual, common, general, familiar, popular, prevailing, widespread, universal, frequent. (*ANT.*) *odd, scarce, exceptional, extraordinary.*

prevent (*SYN.*) impede, preclude, forestall, stop, block, check, halt, interrupt, deter, slow, obviate, hinder, obstruct, thwart. (*ANT.*) *expedite, help, allow, abet, aid, permit, encourage, promote.*

previous (*SYN.*) former, anterior, preceding, prior, antecedent, earlier, aforesaid, foregoing. (*ANT.*) *subsequent, following, consequent, succeeding, later.*

prey (*SYN.*) raid, seize, victimize.

price (*SYN.*) worth, cost, expense, charge, value.

pride (*SYN.*) self-respect, vanity, glory, superciliousness, haughtiness, conceit, arrogance, self-importance, pretension, egotism, satisfaction, fulfillment, enjoyment, self-esteem. (*ANT.*) *modesty, shame, humbleness, lowliness, meekness, humility.*

prim (*SYN.*) formal, puritanical, priggish, prudish.

primarily (*SYN.*) mainly, chiefly, firstly, essentially, originally. (*ANT.*) *secondarily.*

primary (*SYN.*) first, principal, primeval, pristine, beginning, original, initial, fundamental, elementary, chief, foremost, earliest, main, prime. (*ANT.*) *subordinate, last, secondary, least, hindmost, latest.*

prime (*SYN.*) first, primary, chief, excellent, best, superior, ready.

primeval (*SYN.*) fresh, primary, novel, inventive, creative, primordial, original, first, new, initial. (*ANT.*) *modern, subsequent, banal, later, terminal, derivative.*

primitive (*SYN.*) antiquated, early, primeval, prehistoric, uncivilized, uncultured, simple, pristine, old, aboriginal, unsophisticated, rude, rough, primary. (*ANT.*) *sophisticated, modish, civilized, cultured, cultivated, late.*

primordial (*SYN.*) pristine, inventive, novel, creative, original, first, initial, new, primary. (*ANT.*) *trite, terminal, banal, modern, derivative, subsequent, later.*

principal (*SYN.*) first, leading, main, supreme, predominant, chief, foremost, highest, prime, primary, leader, headmaster, paramount, essential, cardinal. (*ANT.*) *supplemental, secondary, auxiliary, subsidiary, accessory, minor, subordinate.*

principle (*SYN.*) law, method, axiom, rule, propriety, regulation, maxim, formula, order, statute. (*ANT.*) *exception, hazard, chance, deviation.*

print (*SYN.*) issue, reprint, publish, letter, sign, fingerprint, mark, picture, lithograph, engraving, etching.

prior (SYN.) previous, aforesaid, antecedent, sooner, earlier, preceding, former, foregoing. (ANT.) succeeding, following, later, consequent, subsequent.

prison (SYN.) brig, jail, stockade, penitentiary.

pristine (SYN.) primordial, creative, first, original, fresh, inventive, novel, primary, initial. (ANT.) trite, terminal, derivative, modem, banal, subsequent, plagiarized, later.

private (SYN.) concealed, hidden, secret, clandestine, unknown, personal, surreptitious, covert, individual, particular, special, latent. (ANT.) exposed, known, closed, general, public, conspicuous, disclosed.

privation (SYN.) necessity, penury, destitution, need, poverty, want. (ANT.) wealth, affluence, abundance, plenty, riches.

privilege (SYN.) liberty, right, advantage, immunity, freedom, license, favor, sanction. (ANT.) restriction, inhibition, prohibition, disallowance.

prize (SYN.) compensation, bonus, award, premium, remuneration, reward, bounty, esteem, value, rate, recompense, requital. (ANT.) charge, punishment, wages, earnings, assessment.

probable (SYN.) presumable, likely.

probe (SYN.) stretch, reach, investigate, examine, examination, scrutiny, scrutinize, inquire, explore, inquiry, investigation, extend. (ANT.) miss, short.

problem (SYN.) dilemma, question, predicament, riddle, difficulty, puzzle.

procedure (SYN.) process, way, fashion, form, mode, conduct, practice, manner, habit, system, operation, management, plan.

proceed (SYN.) progress, continue, issue, result, spring, thrive, improve, advance, emanate, rise. (ANT.) retard, withhold, withdraw, hinder, retreat, oppose.

proceeding (SYN.) occurrence, business, affair, deal, negotiation, transaction, deed.

proceedings (SYN.) account, record, document.

proceeds (SYN.) result, produce, income, reward, intake, fruit, profit, store, yield,

product, return, harvest, crop.

process (SYN.) method, course, system, procedure, operation, prepare, treat.

procession (SYN.) cortege, parade, sequence, train, cavalcade, file, retinue, succession.

proclaim (SYN.) declare, assert, make known, promulgate, state, assert, broadcast, express, announce, aver, advertise, tell, publish, profess.

proclamation (SYN.) declaration, announcement, promulgation.

procrastinate (SYN.) waver, vacillate, defer, hesitate, delay, postpone.

procreate (SYN.) generate, produce, beget, engender, originate, propagate, sire, create, father. (ANT.) murder, destroy, abort, kill, extinguish.

procure (SYN.) secure, gain, win, attain, obtain, get, acquire, earn. (ANT.) lose.

prod (SYN.) goad, nudge, jab, push.

prodigious (SYN.) astonishing, enormous, immense, monstrous, remarkable, marvelous, huge, amazing, astounding, stupendous, monumental. (ANT.) insignificant, commonplace, small.

produce (SYN.) harvest, reaping, bear, result, originate, bring about, store, supply, make, create, crop, proceeds, bring forth, occasion, breed, generate, cause, exhibit, show, demonstrate, fabricate, hatch, display, manufacture, exhibit, give, yield. (ANT.) conceal, reduce, destroy, consume, waste, hide.

product (SYN.) outcome, result, output, produce, goods, commodity, stock, merchandise.

productive (SYN.) fertile, luxuriant, rich, bountiful, fruitful, creative, fecund, teeming, plenteous, prolific. (ANT.) wasteful, unproductive, barren, useless, sterile.

profanation (SYN.) dishonor, insult, outrage, aspersion, defamation, invective, misuse, abuse, reviling, maltreatment, desecration, perversion. (ANT.) plaudit, commendation, laudation, respect, approval.

profane (SYN.) deflower, violate, desecrate, pollute, dishonor, ravish, debauch.

profess (SYN.) declare, assert, make known, state, protest, announce, aver, express,

broadcast, avow, tell. (ANT.) suppress, conceal, repress, withhold.

profession (SYN.) calling, occupation, vocation, employment. (ANT.) hobby, avocation, pastime.

proffer (SYN.) extend, tender, volunteer, propose, advance. (ANT.) reject, spurn, accept, receive, retain.

proficient (SYN.) competent, adept, clever, able, cunning, practiced, skilled, versed, ingenious, accomplished, skillful, expert. (ANT.) untrained, inexpert, bungling, awkward, clumsy.

profit (SYN.) gain, service, advantage, return, earnings, emolument, improvement, benefit, better, improve, use, avail. (ANT.) waste, loss, detriment, debit, lose, damage, mum.

profitable (SYN.) beneficial, advantageous, helpful, wholesome, useful, gainful, favorable, beneficial, serviceable, salutary, productive, good. (ANT.) harmful, destructive, injurious, deleterious, detrimental.

profligate (SYN.) corrupt, debased, tainted, unsound, vitiated, contaminated, crooked, depraved, impure, venal.

profound (SYN.) deep, serious, knowing, wise, intelligent, knowledgeable, recondite, solemn, abstruse, penetrating. (ANT.) trivial, slight, shallow, superficial.

profuse (SYN.) lavish, excessive, extravagant, improvident, luxuriant, prodigal, wasteful, exuberant, immoderate, plentiful. (ANT.) meager, poor, economical, sparse, skimpy.

profusion (SYN.) immoderation, superabundance, surplus, extravagance, intemperance, superfluity. (ANT.) lack, paucity, death, want, deficiency.

program (SYN.) record, schedule, plan, agenda, calendar.

progress (SYN.) advancement, improvement, development, betterment, advance, movement, improve, progression. (ANT.) regression, relapse, retrogression, decline.

progression (SYN.) gradation, string, train, chain, arrangement, following, arrangement, order.

prohibit (SYN.) hinder, forbid, disallow, obstruct, prevent, stop, ban, interdict,

debar. (ANT.) help, tolerate, allow, sanction, encourage, permit.

prohibition (SYN.) prevention, ban, embargo, restriction. (ANT.) allowance, permission.

prohibitive (SYN.) forbidding, restrictive.

project (SYN.) design, proposal, scheme, contrivance, outline, homework, activity, purpose, bulge, protrude, throw, cast, device, plan. (ANT.) production, accomplishment, performance.

prolific (SYN.) fertile, rich, fruitful, teeming, fecund, bountiful, luxuriant, productive, plenteous. (ANT.) unproductive, barren, sterile, impotent.

prolong (SYN.) extend, increase, protract, draw, stretch, lengthen. (ANT.) shorten.

prominent (SYN.) distinguished, illustrious, outstanding, renowned, influential, famous, well-known, noted, notable, important, conspicuous, eminent, leading, celebrated. (ANT.) low, vulgar, ordinary, common.

promise (SYN.) assurance, guarantee, pledge, undertaking, agreement, bestowal, word, contract, oath, vow.

promote (SYN.) advance, foster, encourage, assist, support, further, aid, help, elevate, raise, facilitate, forward. (ANT.) obstruct, demote, hinder, impede.

prompt (SYN.) punctual, timely, exact, arouse, evoke, occasion, induce, urge, effect, cite, suggest, hint, cause, mention, propose, make, precise, originate. (ANT.) laggardly, slow, tardy, dilatory.

promptly (SYN.) immediately, instantly, straightaway, forthwith, directly, instantaneously, presently. (ANT.) later, sometime, hereafter, distantly, shortly.

promulgate (SYN.) declare, known, protest, affirm, broadcast, profess, assert, proclaim, state, aver, tell. (ANT.) repress, conceal, withhold.

prone (SYN.) apt, inclined, disposed, likely, predisposed.

pronounce (SYN.) proclaim, utter, announce, articulate, enunciate.

pronounced (SYN.) clear, definite. (ANT.) minor, unnoticeable.

proof (SYN.) evidence, verification, confirmation,

experiment, demonstration, testimony, trial, protected, impenetrable, corroboration, test. *(ANT.) fallacy, invalidity, failure.*

propagate *(SYN.)* create, procreate, sire, beget, breed, father, originate, produce. *(ANT.) extinguish, kill, abort, destroy.*

propel *(SYN.)* drive, push, transfer, actuate, induce, shift, persuade, move. *(ANT.) stay, deter, halt, rest, stop.*

propensity *(SYN.)* leaning, proneness, trend, drift, aim, inclination, bias, proclivity, tendency, predisposition. *(ANT.) disinclination, aversion.*

proper *(SYN.)* correct, suitable, decent, peculiar, legitimate, right, conventional.

property *(SYN.)* real estate, effects, possessions, quality, characteristic, merchandise, stock, possession, land. *(ANT.) poverty, destitution, want, deprivation.*

prophecy *(SYN.)* augury, prediction.

prophesy *(SYN.)* foretell, predict, augur.

prophet *(SYN.)* fortuneteller, oracle, seer, soothsayer, clairvoyant.

propitious *(SYN.)* lucky, opportune, advantageous, favorable, fortunate, promising, happy.

proportion *(SYN.)* steadiness, poise, composure, relation, balance, equilibrium. *(ANT.) unsteadiness, imbalance, fall.*

proposal *(SYN.)* plan, proposition, tender, scheme, program, offer, suggestion, overture. *(ANT.) rejection, acceptance, denial.*

propose *(SYN.)* offer, proffer, recommend, plan, mean, expect, move, design, propound, present, tender. *(ANT.) fulfill, perform, effect.*

proposition *(SYN.)* proposal, motion.

propound *(SYN.)* bring forward, offer, advance, allege, propose, assign. *(ANT.) retreat, hinder, withhold, retard.*

proprietor *(SYN.)* master, owner. *(ANT.) slave, servant.*

prosaic *(SYN.)* commonplace, common, everyday, ordinary, routine. *(ANT.) exciting, different, extraordinary.*

proscribe *(SYN.)* forbid, ban, prohibit. *(ANT.) permit, allow.*

prospect *(SYN.)* anticipation, expectation, candidate, buyer,

explore, search.

prospective *(SYN.)* planned, proposed.

prosper *(SYN.)* succeed, win, achieve, gain, rise, prevail, flourish, thrive. *(ANT.) miscarry, wane, miss, fail.*

prosperous *(SYN.)* rich, wealthy, affluent, well-to-do, sumptuous, well-off, flourishing, thriving, opulent, luxurious. *(ANT.) impoverished, indigent, beggarly, needy, destitute, poor.*

prostrate *(SYN.)* prone, supine, overcome, recumbent, crushed.

protect *(SYN.)* defend, preserve, save, keep, conserve, safeguard, maintain, guard, shield, secure. *(ANT.) impair, abandon, destroy, abolish, injure.*

protest *(SYN.)* dissent, noncompliance, disagree, objection, disagreement, challenge, difference, complaint, nonconformity, variance, opposition. *(ANT.) acquiesce, assent, compliance, concur, comply, acceptance, approval.*

prototype *(SYN.)* model, archetype, specimen, instance, illustration, example, pattern, sample. *(ANT.) rule, concept, precept.*

protract *(SYN.)* extend, strain, distend, expand, spread, stretch, elongate, distort, lengthen. *(ANT.) tighten, contract, loosen.*

protuberance *(SYN.)* prominence, projection, bulge, protrusion, swelling.

proud *(SYN.)* overbearing, vain, arrogant, haughty, stately, vain, glorious, disdainful, prideful, conceited, egotistical, self-important, supercilious. *(ANT.) humble, meek, ashamed, lowly.*

prove *(SYN.)* manifest, verify, confirm, demonstrate, establish, show, affirm, examine, corroborate, try, test. *(ANT.) contradict, refute, disprove.*

proverb *(SYN.)* maxim, byword, saying, adage, saw, motto, apothegm.

proverbial *(SYN.)* common, well-known.

provide *(SYN.)* supply, endow, afford, produce, yield, give, fit, equip, furnish. *(ANT.) strip, denude, divest, despoil.*

provident *(SYN.)* saving, thrifty, economical, frugal, sparing. *(ANT.) wasteful, lavish, extravagant.*

provision *(SYN.)* supply, fund, condition, arrangement, accumulation, reserve, store.

provisions *(SYN.)* stock, supplies, store.

provoke *(SYN.)* excite, stimulate, agitate, arouse, incite, stir up, vex, bother, disquiet, excite, irritate, annoy, anger. *(ANT.) quell, allay, pacify, calm, quiet.*

prowess *(SYN.)* fortitude, mettle, boldness, fearlessness, courage, chivalry, bravery. *(ANT.) fear, cowardice, timidity.*

prowl *(SYN.)* sneak, slink, lurk.

proximate *(SYN.)* nigh, imminent, adjacent, neighboring, bordering, close. *(ANT.) removed, distant, far.*

proximity *(SYN.)* vicinity, nearness.

proxy *(SYN.)* representative, equivalent, makeshift, alternate, deputy, substitute. *(ANT.) sovereign, head, principal, master.*

prudence *(SYN.)* watchfulness, care, heed, vigilance, wariness, carefulness, tact, judgment, wisdom, common, foresight, caution. *(ANT.) rashness, recklessness, abandon, foolishness, carelessness.*

prudent *(SYN.)* reasonable, sensible, sound, discreet, practical, judicious. *(ANT.) stupid, unaware, absurd.*

pry *(SYN.)* peer, peep, meddle, peek.

prying *(SYN.)* inquisitive, meddling, curious, inquiring, nosy, peering, searching, interrogative, snoopy. *(ANT.) unconcerned, incurious, indifferent, uninterested.*

psyche *(SYN.)* judgment, reason, understanding, brain, intellect, mentality, soul, mind, faculties, spirit. *(ANT.) materiality, body, matter, corporeality.*

psychosis *(SYN.)* derangement, insanity, madness, delirium, dementia, frenzy, lunacy, mania, aberration. *(ANT.) stability, rationality, sanity.*

public *(SYN.)* common, civil, governmental, federal, unrestricted, people, society, open.

publish *(SYN.)* distribute, issue, declare, announce, reveal, proclaim, publicize.

pull *(SYN.)* attract, induce, prolong, draw, tow, drag, remove, take out, persuade, allure, entice, extract. *(ANT.) shorten, alienate, drive, propel.*

pulsate *(SYN.)* beat, throb, palpitate.

pummel *(SYN.)* punish, correct, castigate, discipline,

chastise, strike. *(ANT.) release, acquit, free, exonerate.*

pump *(SYN.)* interrogate, question, ask, inquire, quiz, examine, query. *(ANT.) state, answer, respond, reply.*

punctual *(SYN.)* timely, prompt, exact, ready, precise. *(ANT.) laggardly, tardy, dilatory, late.*

punish *(SYN.)* correct, pummel, chasten, reprove, strike, castigate, chastise. *(ANT.) release, exonerate, reward, pardon, acquit, free.*

puny *(SYN.)* feeble, impaired, exhausted, infirm, unimportant, weak, decrepit. *(ANT.) strong, forceful, lusty, vigorous.*

purchase *(SYN.)* get, procure, buy, acquire, obtain. *(ANT.) sell, dispose of, vend.*

pure *(SYN.)* chaste, absolute, clean, immaculate, untainted, spotless, guiltless, modest, virgin, bare, unmixed, simple. *(ANT.) corrupt, mixed, defiled, foul, tainted, adulterated, polluted, tarnished.*

puritanical *(SYN.)* prim, stiff. *(ANT.) permissive.*

purport *(SYN.)* import, meaning, explanation, acceptation, drift, sense, significance, purpose, intent, gist.

purpose *(SYN.)* intention, end, goal, aim, objective, application, use, drift, object. *(ANT.) hazard, accident, fate.*

pursue *(SYN.)* persist, track, follow, hunt, hound, chase, trail. *(ANT.) evade, abandon, flee, elude.*

pursuit *(SYN.)* hunt, chase.

push *(SYN.)* jostle, urge, press, thrust, force, drive, crowd, hasten, shove, propel, promote. *(ANT.) ignore, falter, halt, drag, oppose.*

pushy *(SYN.)* impudent, abrupt, prominent, insolent, forward, brazen, conspicuous, bold, striking. *(ANT.) retiring, timid, cowardly, bashful.*

put *(SYN.)* set, place, state, express, say, assign, attach, establish.

putrefy *(SYN.)* disintegrate, decay, rot, waste, spoil, decompose. *(ANT.) grow, increase, luxuriate.*

putrid *(SYN.)* decayed, rotten, moldy, decomposed.

puzzle *(SYN.)* mystery, mystify, confound, perplex, riddle, conundrum, confusion, bewilder, enigma, dilemma. *(ANT.) key, solution, solve, explain, answer, resolution, illumine, clue.*

quack *(SYN.)* faker, fake, fraud, gaggle, clack, gabble, bluffer, cackle, dissembler, charlatan, impostor.

quackery *(SYN.)* charlatanism, deceit, make-believe, fakery, duplicity, dissimulation, pretense, fraudulence, sham, counterfeiting, show. *(ANT.)* integrity, probity, veracity, sincerity, honesty.

quaff *(SYN.)* swig, swill, swallow, lap up, sip, drink, ingurgitate, guzzle, imbibe.

quagmire *(SYN.)* swamp, bog, fen, ooze, morass, slough, marsh, plight, predicament, dilemma, impasse, fix, entanglement, quicksand, hole, quandary.

quail *(SYN.)* recoil, cower, flinch, blench, wince, falter, shrink, shake, hesitate, faint, droop. *(ANT.)* brave, resist, defy, withstand.

quaint *(SYN.)* odd, uncommon, old-fashioned, antique, antiquated, queer, unusual, curious, eccentric, peculiar, picturesque, singular, whimsical, droll, charming, fanciful, strange. *(ANT.)* usual, normal, common, navel, ordinary, modern, current, commonplace, familiar.

quake *(SYN.)* shake, tremble, shudder, quiver, pulsate, stagger, shiver, temblor, vibrate, quaver, throb, earthquake.

qualification *(SYN.)* efficiency, adaptation, restriction, aptness, skill, ability, faculty, talent, power, aptitude, competence, suitability, capability, fitness, condition, dexterity. *(ANT.)* unreadiness, incapacity, disability.

qualified *(SYN.)* clever, skillful, efficient, suitable, able, capable, fit, fitted, suited, bounded, limited, contingent, eligible, delimited, adept, circumscribed, equipped, modified, competent. *(ANT.)* deficient, inept, impotent, categorical, unlimited, unfitted, unfit, incapable, unsuitable, inadequate.

qualify *(SYN.)* fit, suit, befit, ready, prepare, empower, lessen, moderate, soften, capacitate, condition, adapt, label, designate, name, call, equip, train, restrict, limit, change. *(ANT.)* unfit, incapacitate, disable, disqualify, enlarge, reinforce, aggravate.

quality *(SYN.)* trait, feature, attribute, value, peculiarity, grade, caliber, character, distinction, rank, condition, status, characteristic, kind, nature, constitution, mark, type, property. *(ANT.)* nature, inferiority, mediocrity, triviality, indifference, inferior, shoddy, second-rate, being, substance, essence.

qualm *(SYN.)* doubt, uneasiness, anxiety, suspicion, skepticism, question, pang, compunction, twinge, regret, uncertainty, demur, fear, remorse, misgiving. *(ANT.)* security, comfort, confidence, easiness, invulnerability, firmness.

quandary *(SYN.)* predicament, perplexity, confusion, uncertainty, puzzle, plight, bewilderment, fix, difficulty, entanglement, impasse, doubt, dilemma. *(ANT.)* ease, relief, certainty, assurance.

quantity *(SYN.)* sum, measure, volume, content, aggregate, bulk, mass, portion, amount, number, multitude, extent. *(ANT.)* zero, nothing.

quarantine *(SYN.)* segregate, separate, confine, isolate, seclude.

quarrel *(SYN.)* contention, argument, affray, dispute, altercation, squabble, feud, difference, disagree, bicker, differ, spar, fight, bickering, tiff, argue, disagreement, spat. *(ANT.)* peace, friendliness, reconciliation, amity, agreement, sympathy, accord, concur, support, agree, unity, harmony.

quarrelsome *(SYN.)* testy, contentious, edgy, peevish, irritable, snappish, argumentative, disputatious, cranky, belligerent, combative, disagreeable. *(ANT.)* genial, friendly, peaceful, easygoing, peaceable, tempered.

quarry *(SYN.)* prey, quest, game, victim, goal, aim, prize, objective.

quarter *(SYN.)* place, source, fount, well, origin, mainspring, mercy, pity, compassion, clemency, spring, benevolence, forbearance. *(ANT.)* ruthlessness, brutality, cruelty, barbarity, harshness, ferocity.

quarters *(SYN.)* residence, rooms, lodgings, dwelling, flat, billets, chambers, accommodations.

quash *(SYN.)* void, annul, overthrow, nullify, suppress, cancel, quench, quell, repress, invalidate. *(ANT.)* reinforce, sustain, authorize, sanction, validate, incite.

quasi *(SYN.)* would-be, partial, synthetic, nominal, imitation, bogus, counterfeit, mock. *(ANT.)* certified, real, legitimate.

quaver *(SYN.)* tremble, shake, hesitate, trill, oscillate, waver, vibrate, shiver, quiver, falter, quake.

quay *(SYN.)* dock, wharf, pier, jetty, bank.

queasy *(SYN.)* sick, squeamish, nauseated, uneasy, queer, restless, nauseous, uncomfortable. *(ANT.)* untroubled, comfortable, easy, relaxed.

queen *(SYN.)* empress, diva, goddess, star.

queer *(SYN.)* odd, quaint, curious, unusual, droll, strange, peculiar, extraordinary, singular, uncommon, eccentric, weird, funny, nutty, screwy, wacky, deviant, whimsical. *(ANT.)* familiar, usual, normal, common, commonplace, plain, patent, ordinary.

queerness *(SYN.)* oddity, oddness, freakishness, strangeness, singularity, outlandishness, weirdness. *(ANT.)* normality, familiarity, commonness, standardization.

quell *(SYN.)* subdue, calm, pacify, quiet, cool, hush, appease, lull, mollify, reduce, crush, smother, suppress, stifle, extinguish. *(ANT.)* foment, arouse, foster, incite.

quench *(SYN.)* extinguish, stop, suppress, sate, allay, abate, stifle, slacken, put out, slake, satisfy *(ANT.)* set, light, begin, start, kindle.

querulous *(SYN.)* faultfinding, fretful, carping, critical, complaining, censorious, captious, petulant. *(ANT.)* pleased, easygoing, contented, carefree.

query *(SYN.)* inquire, interrogate, demand, investigate, probe, examine, question, inquiry, ask. *(ANT.)* answer.

quest *(SYN.)* investigation, interrogation, research, examination, search, question, exploration, seek, pursue, journey, hunt, pursuit, explore, query. *(ANT.)* negligence, inactivity, disregard.

question *(SYN.)* interrogate, quiz, doubt, ask, pump, challenge, inquiry, uncertainty, interview, suspect, inquire, dispute, demand, examine, query. *(ANT.)* accept, solution, reply, assurance, rejoinder, state, answer, result, response, attest, avow, confidence, respond.

questionable *(SYN.)* uncertain, doubtful, dubious, implausible, debatable, hypothetical, unlikely. *(ANT.)* obvious, assured, indubitable, proper, unimpeachable, seemly, conventional, sure, certain.

queue *(SYN.)* file, row, line, series, chain, tier, sequence, string.

quibble *(SYN.)* cavil, shift, evasion, equivocation, dodge, sophism, prevaricate.

quick *(SYN.)* rapid, touchy, shrewd, active, hasty, testy, nimble, irascible, discerning, fast, swift, precipitate, excitable, speedy, sharp, impatient, acute, abrupt, curt, brisk, clever, keen, sensitive, lively. *(ANT.)* inattentive, dull, gradual, patient, slow, unhurried, backward, deliberate, sluggish.

quicken *(SYN.)* expedite, forward, rush, hurry, accelerate, push, hasten, dispatch, facilitate, speed. *(ANT.)* slow, impede, hinder, hamper, delay, kill, deaden, retard, block.

quickly *(SYN.)* soon, rapidly, fast, at once, promptly, presently, swiftly, hastily, fleetly, headlong. *(ANT.)* deliberately, gradually.

quickness *(SYN.)* energy, vigor, intensity, action, movement, briskness, exercise, motion, rapidity, agility, enterprise. *(ANT.)* sloth, idleness, inertia, dullness.

quick-witted *(SYN.)* astute, shrewd, alert, keen, penetrating, quick, intelligent. *(ANT.)* slow, dull, unintelligent, plodding.

quiescent *(SYN.)* latent, resting, silent, tranquil, undeveloped, still, quiet, dormant, secret, unseen, inactive. *(ANT.)* visible, aroused, evident, active, patent, astir, manifest.

quiet *(SYN.)* meek, passive, hushed, peaceful, calm, patient, quiescent, motionless, tranquil, gentle, undisturbed, mild, peace, silent, quiescence, hush, modest, quietude, rest, tranquillity. *(ANT.)* disturbed, agitation, excitement, loud, disturbance, restless, noisy, boisterous, perturbed, noise, agitated.

quietness *(SYN.)* tranquillity, repose, calm, silence, quietude, stillness. *(ANT.)* flurry, disturbance, fuss, turbulence, agitation, uproar, tumult.

quintessence *(SYN.)* heart, soul, extract, essence, distillation, core. *(ANT.)* contingency, adjunct, excrescence, nonessential.

quip *(SYN.)* jest, sally, wisecrack,

witticism, joke, jibe, pleasantry.

quirk *(SYN.)* mannerism, idiosyncrasy, foible, peculiarity, oddity, quiddity, vagary, habit, trait, eccentricity.

quirky *(SYN.)* odd, weird, whimsical, peculiar, pixilated, erratic, kinky. *(ANT.) normal, conventional, steady.*

quisling *(SYN.)* collaborationist, traitor, subversive, betrayer. *(ANT.) partisan, loyalist.*

quit *(SYN.)* leave, stop, desist, depart, abandon, resign, withdraw, refrain, retreat, cease, vacate, end, relinquish, discontinue, halt, lay off, surrender. *(ANT.) persevere, remain, stay, endure, persist, abide, continue.*

quite *(SYN.)* somewhat, rather, completely, truly, absolutely, really, entirely. *(ANT.) hardly, merely, barely, somewhat.*

quitter *(SYN.)* shirker, dropout, defeatist, piker, loser, malingerer.

quiver *(SYN.)* quake, shake, shudder, tremble, vibrate, shiver.

quixotic *(SYN.)* unrealistic, romantic, visionary, impractical, idealistic, chimerical, lofty, fantastic, fey. *(ANT.) pragmatic, realistic, practical.*

quiz *(SYN.)* challenge, interrogate, inquire, pump, doubt, question, ask, dispute, test, query, examine. *(ANT.) reply, say, inform, respond, accept, answer, state.*

quizzical *(SYN.)* teasing, coy, mocking, derisive, insolent, arch, bantering, puzzled, questioning, baffled. *(ANT.) respectful, obsequious, uninterested, normal, usual, serious, attentive.*

quota *(SYN.)* share, portion, apportionment, ratio, proportion, allotment.

quotation *(SYN.)* quote, selection, excerpt, repetition, cutting, reference.

quote *(SYN.)* refer to, recite, paraphrase, adduce, repeat, illustrate, cite, echo. *(ANT.) retort, contradict, refute.*

R

rabble *(SYN.)* throng, mob, horde, crowd.

rabid *(SYN.)* frantic, frenzied, violent, raging, raving, zealous, fanatical. *(ANT.) normal, sound, sober, moderate.*

race *(SYN.)* meet, run, clan, stock, lineage, strain, match, course, stream, hasten, compete, folk, competition. *(ANT.) linger, dawdle, dwell.*

rack *(SYN.)* frame, framework, bracket, scaffold, skeleton.

racket *(SYN.)* sound, cry, babel, noise, uproar, hubbub, clamor, fuss, disturbance, din, tumult, fracas, clatter. *(ANT.) stillness, hush, silence, quiet, tranquillity, peace.*

racy *(SYN.)* interesting, vigorous, lively, bawdy, lewd, shameless, spirited, animated, entertaining.

radiance *(SYN.)* luster, brilliancy, brightness, splendor, effulgence, glowing. *(ANT.) gloom, darkness, obscurity.*

radiant *(SYN.)* showy, superb, brilliant, illustrious, dazzling, grand, shining, bright, effulgent, beaming, sumptuous. *(ANT.) dark, unimpressive, dull, dim, lusterless, ordinary.*

radiate *(SYN.)* spread, emit, diffuse, shed, irradiate, shine, gleam, illuminate.

radical *(SYN.)* ultra, innate, essential, organic, complete, revolutionary, insurgent, natural, total, fundamental, extreme, basic, original, thorough. *(ANT.) extraneous, moderate, conservative, superficial, shallow, established.*

radius *(SYN.)* orbit, reach, extent, scope, sphere, range, sweep.

raft *(SYN.)* pontoon, platform, float.

rag *(SYN.)* dishcloth, dishrag, cloth.

rage *(SYN.)* passion, ire, exasperation, fashion, fad, vogue, craze, anger, temper, fury, irritation, mania, rave, rant, storm, fume, wrath. *(ANT.) peace, forbearance, patience.*

ragged *(SYN.)* tattered, torn, worn, shredded, seedy, threadbare, shabby.

raging *(SYN.)* raving, severe, boisterous, violent, fierce, wild, passionate, acute, intense, powerful. *(ANT.) feeble, soft, calm, quiet.*

raid *(SYN.)* assault, attack, invasion, arrest, invade, seizure, maraud, foray.

rail *(SYN.)* railing, fence, bar.

railing *(SYN.)* balustrade, banister, barrier, fence.

rain *(SYN.)* shower, drizzle, rainstorm, sprinkle, deluge, downpour.

raise *(SYN.)* grow, muster, elevate, heave, cultivate, awake, rouse, excite, enlarge, increase, rise, breed, hoist, bring up. *(ANT.) destroy, decrease, lessen, cut, depreciate, lower, abase, debase, drop, demolish.*

rakish *(SYN.)* dapper, dashing, smart, debonair, natty, swanky, showy.

rally *(SYN.)* muster, convoke, summon, convene, convention, assemblage.

ramble *(SYN.)* amble, wander, roam, saunter, walk, deviate. *(ANT.) stop, linger, stay, halt, settle.*

rambling *(SYN.)* incoherent, erratic. *(ANT.) straightforward, coherent.*

rambunctious *(SYN.)* stubborn, defiant, unruly, aggressive, contrary.

ramification *(SYN.)* aftermath, extension, branch, offshoot, result, consequence.

rampage *(SYN.)* tumult, outbreak, uproar, rage, frenzy, ebullition, storm.

rampant *(SYN.)* excessive, flagrant, boisterous, menacing. *(ANT.) bland, calm, mild.*

ramshackle *(SYN.)* rickety, decrepit, flimsy, dilapidated, shaky.

rancid *(SYN.)* spoiled, rank, tainted, sour, musty, putrid, rotten, putrescent. *(ANT.) pure, fresh, wholesome, fragrant.*

rancor *(SYN.)* spite, grudge, malice, animosity, malevolence, hostility. *(ANT.) kindness, toleration, affection.*

random *(SYN.)* haphazard, chance, unscheduled, unplanned, casual. *(ANT.) intentional, specific, particular.*

range *(SYN.)* expanse, extent, limit, area, grassland, pasture, plain, change, wander, roam, travel, rove.

ransack *(SYN.)* pillage, loot, rummage, plunder, despoil, ravish, search.

ransom *(SYN.)* release, deliverance, compensation, redeem.

rant *(SYN.)* declaim, rave, harangue.

rap *(SYN.)* thump, knock, blow, whack.

rapacious *(SYN.)* greedy, wolfish, avaricious, ravenous, grasping, predatory.

rapid *(SYN.)* speedy, quick, swift, fast. *(ANT.) deliberate, halting, sluggish, slow.*

rapine *(SYN.)* destruction, pillage, robbery, marauding, spoiling.

rapport *(SYN.)* harmony, fellowship, agreement, mutuality, accord, empathy.

rapture *(SYN.)* joy, gladness, ecstasy, bliss, transport, exultation, delight, happiness, enchantment, ravishment. *(ANT.) woe, misery, wretch, depression.*

rare *(SYN.)* unique, strange, precious, uncommon, infrequent, choice, singular, occasional, unusual, fine, matchless. *(ANT.) worthless, common, commonplace, usual, everyday, customary.*

rarely *(SYN.)* scarcely, hardly, infrequently, occasionally, sparingly, barely. *(ANT.) usually, continually, often.*

rascal *(SYN.)* scoundrel, villain, trickster, rogue, scamp, swindler, imp, prankster.

rash *(SYN.)* quick, careless, passionate, thoughtless, hotheaded, reckless, foolhardy, eruption, dermatitis, heedless. *(ANT.) thoughtful, considered, prudent, reasoning, calculating, careful.*

raspy *(SYN.)* gruff, harsh, dissonant, grinding, hoarse, grating, strident.

rate *(SYN.)* try, adjudicate, consider, decide, condemn, decree, estimate, speed, pace, measure, judge, arbitrate.

ratify *(SYN.)* validate, certify, confirm, establish, support, endorse, uphold.

rating *(SYN.)* assessment, position, assignment, status, classification.

ration *(SYN.)* portion, allowance, distribute, measure, allotment, share, percentage.

rational *(SYN.)* sound, wise, sane, intelligent, sober, sensible, judicious, sober. *(ANT.) irrational, absurd, insane.*

rationality *(SYN.)* cause, aim, intelligence, reason, basis, understanding, ground, argument, mind, sense.

raucous *(SYN.)* raspy, harsh, grating, hoarse, discordant, rowdy. *(ANT.) pleasant, sweet.*

ravage *(SYN.)* ruin, despoil, strip, waste, destroy, pillage, plunder, sack, havoc. *(ANT.) conserve, save, accumulate.*

rave *(SYN.)* rage, storm, laud, praise.

ravenous *(SYN.)* hungry, voracious, craving, starved,

gluttonous, famished. (*ANT.*) *replete, gorged, satiated, full.*

ravine (*SYN.*) chasm, gorge, crevasse, canyon, abyss.

ravish (*SYN.*) violate, debauch.

ravishing (*SYN.*) enchanting, captivating, bewitching, fascinating, alluring. (*ANT.*) *loathsome, disgusting, repulsive.*

raw (*SYN.*) harsh, rough, coarse, unrefined, undone, uncooked, unprocessed, crude, unpolished, natural. (*ANT.*) *finished, refined, processed.*

ray (*SYN.*) beam.

raze (*SYN.*) ravage, wreck, destroy, flatten, annihilate, obliterate, demolish. (*ANT.*) *erect, construct, preserve, establish, save.*

reach (*SYN.*) overtake, arrive at, extent, distance, scope, range, extend, attain, stretch. (*ANT.*) *fail, miss.*

react (*SYN.*) result, reply, respond. (*ANT.*) *overlook, disregard.*

reaction (*SYN.*) result, response, reception, repercussion.

readable (*SYN.*) understandable, distinct, legible, plain, clear, comprehensible. (*ANT.*) *obliterated, illegible, defaced.*

readily (*SYN.*) quickly, promptly, easily.

ready (*SYN.*) mature, ripe, complete, seasonable, done, arrange, prompt, prepared, completed, quick, mellow. (*ANT.*) *undeveloped, immature, green.*

real (*SYN.*) true, actual, positive, authentic, genuine, veritable. (*ANT.*) *counterfeit, unreal, fictitious, false, sham, supposed.*

realization (*SYN.*) completion, achievement, performance, accomplishment, comprehension, insight. (*ANT.*) *failure.*

realize (*SYN.*) discern, learn, comprehend, appreciate, perfect, actualize, understand, apprehend, know, see. (*ANT.*) *misunderstand, misapprehend.*

really (*SYN.*) truly, actually, honestly, undoubtedly, positively, genuinely. (*ANT.*) *questionably, possibly, doubtfully.*

realm (*SYN.*) land, domain, farm, kingdom, sphere, department, estate, world.

reap (*SYN.*) gather, harvest, gain, glean, produce, cut, pick, acquire, garner. (*ANT.*) *plant, seed, sow, lose, squander.*

reaping (*SYN.*) proceeds, result, crop, yield, fruit, produce.

rear (*SYN.*) posterior, raise, lift, train, nurture, rump, back, elevate, construct, build.

reason (*SYN.*) intelligence, objective, understanding, mind, aim, argument, cause, judgment, common sense, sanity, gather, assume, sake, motive.

reasonable (*SYN.*) prudent, rational, logical, sage, sound, moderate, intelligent, sensible, discreet. (*ANT.*) *unaware, insane, absurd, stupid, illogical, irrational.*

rebel (*SYN.*) revolutionary, traitor, mutineer, mutiny, revolt, disobey.

rebellion (*SYN.*) revolt, uprising, coup, overthrow, insurrection, revolution. (*ANT.*) *submission, obedience, repression, peace.*

rebellious (*SYN.*) unruly, forward, defiant, undutiful, disobedient. (*ANT.*) *obedient, compliant, submissive.*

rebirth (*SYN.*) renascence, renaissance, revival.

rebuff (*SYN.*) snub, oppose, resist, reject, refuse, slight, opposition. (*ANT.*) *welcome, encourage, support.*

rebuild (*SYN.*) restore, renew, refresh, reconstruct, renovate.

rebuke (*SYN.*) chide, scold, reproach, censure, upbraid, scolding, condemn. (*ANT.*) *praise, exonerate, absolve.*

rebuttal (*SYN.*) contradiction, defense, answer. (*ANT.*) *argument, validation, corroboration.*

recall (*SYN.*) recollect, remembrance, withdraw, retract, remember, recollection. reminisce, mind, memory, remind. (*ANT.*) *forget, overlook, ignore.*

recede (*SYN.*) withdraw, ebb, retire, retreat.

receive (*SYN.*) entertain, acquire, admit, accept, shelter, greet, obtain, welcome. (*ANT.*) *reject, offer, give, bestow, discharge.*

recent (*SYN.*) novel, original, late, new, newfangled, fresh, modern, current. (*ANT.*) *old, antiquated, ancient.*

reception (*SYN.*) gathering, party.

recess (*SYN.*) hollow, opening, nook, cranny, dent, respite, rest, break, pause. (*ANT.*) *gather, convene.*

recession (*SYN.*) slump, depression.

recipe (*SYN.*) instructions, formula, prescriptions, procedure, method.

recital (*SYN.*) history,

account, relation, chronicle, narrative, detail, narration. (*ANT.*) *distortion, confusion, misrepresentation.*

recite (*SYN.*) describe, narrate, declaim, rehearse, tell, mention, repeat, detail, recapitulate, report, list, relate, deliver.

reckless (*SYN.*) thoughtless, inconsiderate, careless, imprudent, rash, indiscreet, unconcerned. (*ANT.*) *careful, nice, accurate.*

reclaim (*SYN.*) reform, rescue, reinstate, regenerate, recycle.

recline (*SYN.*) stretch, sprawl, repose, rest, lounge, loll, incline.

recluse (*SYN.*) hermit, eremite, loner, anchorite.

recognize (*SYN.*) remember, avow, own, know, admit, apprehend, recollect, recall, concede, acknowledge, confess. (*ANT.*) *disown, ignore, renounce.*

recollect (*SYN.*) recall, remember, memory, reflect, call to mind, reminisce. (*ANT.*) *forget.*

recollection (*SYN.*) remembrance, retrospection, impression, recall. (*ANT.*) *forgetfulness, oblivion.*

recommend (*SYN.*) hind, refer, advise, commend, suggest, counsel, allude, praise, approve, intimate, advocate. (*ANT.*) *disapprove, declare, insist.*

recommendation (*SYN.*) instruction, justice, trustworthiness, counsel, admonition, caution, integrity, uprightness. (*ANT.*) *fraud, deceit, trickery, cheating.*

reconcile (*SYN.*) meditate, unite, adapt, adjust, settle, reunite, appease.

recondition (*SYN.*) rebuild, overhaul, restore, service.

reconsider (*SYN.*) ponder, reevaluate, mull over, reflect, reassess.

record (*SYN.*) enter, write, register, chronicle, history, account, document.

recount (*SYN.*) report, convey, narrate, tell, detail, recite, describe, repeat.

recoup (*SYN.*) regain, recover, repay, retrieve.

recover (*SYN.*) regain, redeem, recapture, retrieve, salvage, better, improve, mend, heal. (*ANT.*) *debilitate, succumb, worsen.*

recreation (*SYN.*) entertainment, amusement, enjoyment, diversion, fun.

recrimination (*SYN.*) vindication, reproach, dissension,

accusation, countercharge.

recruit (*SYN.*) trainee, beginner, volunteer, draftee, select, enlist, novice.

recuperate (*SYN.*) regain, retrieve, cure, recapture, redeem, rally, convalesce, recover, repossess, restore. (*ANT.*) *sicker, weaken, lose, regress, forfeit.*

redeem (*SYN.*) claim, recover, repossess, regain, reclaim, cash in, retrieve.

reduce (*SYN.*) lessen, decrease, lower, downgrade, degrade, suppress, abate, diminish. (*ANT.*) *enlarge, swell, raise, elevate, revive, increase, amplify.*

reduction (*SYN.*) shortening, abridgment, abbreviation. (*ANT.*) *amplification, extension, enlargement.*

reek (*SYN.*) odor, stench, stink, smell.

refer (*SYN.*) recommend, direct, commend, regard, concern, relate, suggest, mention.

referee (*SYN.*) judge, arbitrator, umpire, arbiter, moderator, mediator.

reference (*SYN.*) allusion, direction, mention, concern, respect, referral.

refine (*SYN.*) purify, clarify, improve, clean. (*ANT.*) *pollute, debase, muddy, downgrade.*

refined (*SYN.*) purified, cultured, cultivated, courteous, courtly. (*ANT.*) *rude, coarse, crude, vulgar.*

refinement (*SYN.*) culture, enlightenment, education, civilization. (*ANT.*) *vulgarity, ignorance, boorishness.*

reflect (*SYN.*) muse, mirror, deliberate, cogitate, think, reproduce, ponder, consider, reason, meditate, contemplate.

reflection (*SYN.*) warning, conception, intelligence, appearance, likeness, image, cogitation, notification.

reform (*SYN.*) right, improve, correction, change, amend, improvement, better, betterment, correct, rectify. (*ANT.*) *spoil, damage, aggravate, vitiate.*

refresh (*SYN.*) exhilarate, renew, invigorate. (*ANT.*) *exhaust, tire.*

refreshing (*SYN.*) bracing, cool, brisk, fresh.

refreshment (*SYN.*) food, snack, drink, nourishment, exhilaration, stimulation.

refuge (*SYN.*) safety, retreat, shelter, asylum, sanctuary, harbor. (*ANT.*) *peril,* *exposure, jeopardy, danger.*

refuse *(SYN.)* spurn, rebuff, decline, reject, trash, rubbish, withhold, disallow, waste, garbage, deny, demur. *(ANT.) allow, accept, welcome, grant.*

refute *(SYN.)* rebut, disprove, confute, falsify, controvert, contradict. *(ANT.) prove, confirm, accept, establish.*

regain *(SYN.)* redeem, retrieve, recover, repossess, recapture. *(ANT.) lose.*

regalement *(SYN.)* feast, dinner, celebration, entertainment.

regard *(SYN.)* estimate, value, honor, affection, notice, care, consideration, consider, relation, respect, attend, thought, reference, care, attention, esteem, concern, liking. *(ANT.) neglect, disgust, antipathy.*

regards *(SYN.)* salutation, greetings, good wishes, respects, remembrances.

regenerate *(SYN.)* improve, reconstruct, remedy, reestablish, rebuild.

regime *(SYN.)* direction, government, administration, management, dynasty, command, leadership.

regimented *(SYN.)* ordered, directed, controlled, orderly, rigid, disciplined. *(ANT.) loose, free, unstructured.*

region *(SYN.)* belt, place, spot, territory, climate, area, zone, locality, station, locale.

register *(SYN.)* catalog, record, book, list, roll, enter, roster, chronicle.

regressive *(SYN.)* revisionist, retrograde. *(ANT.) progressive, civilized, advanced.*

regret *(SYN.)* sorrow, qualm, lament, grief, compunction, bemoan, concern, scruple, misgiving, remorse, contrition. *(ANT.) obduracy, complacency.*

regular *(SYN.)* steady, orderly, natural, normal, customary, usual, habitual, even, uniform, systematic, unvaried, methodical, symmetrical. *(ANT.) odd, exceptional, unusual, irregular, abnormal, rare.*

regulate *(SYN.)* control, manage, govern, direct, legislate, set, adjust, systematize.

regulation *(SYN.)* method, rule, axiom, guide, control, standard, canon, precept, restraint, requirement. *(ANT.) chaos, deviation, hazard, turbulence, confusion.*

rehabilitate *(SYN.)* renew, restore, rebuild, reestablish,

repair, reconstruct.

rehearse *(SYN.)* repeat, practice, train, learn, coach, prepare, perfect, direct.

reign *(SYN.)* dominion, power, rule, sovereignty, govern, domination.

reimburse *(SYN.)* recompense, remunerate, compensate, remit.

rein *(SYN.)* restriction, bridle, check, deterrent, curb, restraint, barrier, control.

reinforce *(SYN.)* brace, strengthen, fortify, intensify, support.

reiterate *(SYN.)* reproduce, recapitulate, duplicate, repeat, rephrase.

reject *(SYN.)* spurn, rebuff, decline, renounce, expel, discard, deny, refuse. *(ANT.) endorse, grant, welcome, accept.*

rejection *(SYN.)* dissent, nonconformity, variance, challenge, remonstrance, difference, noncompliance. *(ANT.) assent, acceptance, compliance.*

rejoice *(SYN.)* celebrate, delight, enjoy, revel, exhilarate, elate.

rejuvenate *(SYN.)* refresh, rekindle, overhaul, revitalize, animate, invigorate. *(ANT.) deplete, weaken, exhaust.*

relapse *(SYN.)* worsen, deteriorate, regress, weaken, fade, sink, fail. *(ANT.) strengthen, progress, advance, get well.*

relate *(SYN.)* refer, beat, report, describe, tell, correlate, narrate, recount, compare, connect.

relation *(SYN.)* entente, compact, coalition, alliance, connection, relationship, association, partnership, similarity, kinsman, treaty, marriage. *(ANT.) separation, divorce.*

relationship *(SYN.)* link, tie, alliance, connection, union, bond, affinity, conjunction. *(ANT.) separation, disunion.*

relative *(SYN.)* dependent, proportional, about, pertinent, regarding.

relax *(SYN.)* slacken, loosen, repose, rest, recline, unwind. *(ANT.) increase, tighten, intensify.*

relaxation *(SYN.)* comfort, ease, rest, enjoyment, lull, recess, breather, loafing.

relaxed *(SYN.)* welcome, pleasing, casual, acceptable, informal, restful, agreeable. *(ANT.) formal, planned, wretched, distressing, troubling.*

release *(SYN.)* liberate, emancipate, relinquish, proclaim, publish, liberation, announce,

deliver, free, discharge. *(ANT.) restrict, imprison, subjugate.*

relegate *(SYN.)* entrust, authorize, remand, refer, assign.

relent *(SYN.)* cede, yield, surrender, give, relax, abdicate, relinquish, waive. *(ANT.) strive, assert, struggle.*

relentless *(SYN.)* eternal, stubborn, tenacious, dogged, ceaseless, incessant, persistent, determined.

relevant *(SYN.)* related, material, apt, applicable, fit, relating, germane. *(ANT.) foreign, alien, unrelated.*

reliable *(SYN.)* trusty, tried, certain, secure, trustworthy, dependable. *(ANT.) unreliable, eccentric, questionable, erratic, dubious.*

reliance *(SYN.)* faith, confidence, trust. *(ANT.) mistrust, doubt, skepticism.*

relic *(SYN.)* remains, fossil, throwback, souvenir, keepsake, heirloom.

relief *(SYN.)* help, aid, comfort, ease, backing, patronage, alms, support. *(ANT.) hostility, defiance, antagonism, resistance.*

relieve *(SYN.)* diminish, soothe, calm, abate, pacify, ease, lessen, replace, spell, lighten, comfort, alleviate. *(ANT.) disturb, irritate, agitate, trouble, aggravate, worry.*

religion *(SYN.)* tenet, belief, dogma, faith, creed, persuasion.

religious *(SYN.)* godly, reverent, faithful, devout, zeal, pious, divine, holy, devoted, sacred, theological. *(ANT.) profane, irreligious, skeptical, impious, lax, atheistic.*

religiousness *(SYN.)* love, zeal, affection, devoutness, fidelity, ardor. *(ANT.) indifference, apathy, unfaithfulness.*

relinquish *(SYN.)* capitulate, submit, yield, abandon, cede, sacrifice, disclaim. *(ANT.) overcome, conquer, rout, resist.*

relish *(SYN.)* enjoyment, satisfaction, delight, gusto, appreciation, condiment, like, enjoy, enthusiasm. *(ANT.) distaste, antipathy, disfavor, dislike.*

reluctance *(SYN.)* disgust, hatred, repulsion, abhorrence, distaste, repugnance, aversion. *(ANT.) enthusiasm, affection.*

reluctant *(SYN.)* slow, averse, hesitant, unwilling, loath,

disinclined, balky. *(ANT.) ready, eager, willing, disposed.*

rely *(SYN.)* confide, trust, lean, depend. *(ANT.) mistrust, disbelieve, question, distrust.*

remain *(SYN.)* survive, rest, stay, abide, halt, endure, dwell, tarry, continue, linger. *(ANT.) finish, leave, terminate, dissipate.*

remainder *(SYN.)* leftover, residue, rest, surplus, balance, excess.

remains *(SYN.)* residue, balance, rest, remnants, relics, discards, waste, junk.

remark *(SYN.)* comment, state, utterance, mention, note, observe, observation, annotation, declaration, statement.

remarkable *(SYN.)* exciting, impressive, overpowering, unusual, affecting, thrilling, splendid, special, noteworthy, extraordinary, touching, august. *(ANT.) ordinary, unimpressive, commonplace, average.*

remedy *(SYN.)* redress, help, cure, relief, medicine, restorative, rectify, alleviate, medication, correct, reparation.

remember *(SYN.)* recollect, reminisce, recall, memorize, mind, retain, remind. *(ANT.) forget, overlook, disregard.*

remembrance *(SYN.)* monument, memory, recollection, memento, recall, keepsake, souvenir, retrospection.

remiss *(SYN.)* delinquent, lax, careless, negligent, oblivious, forgetful, absentminded, sloppy, irresponsible.

remit *(SYN.)* send, pay, forward, forgive, pardon, overlook, excuse, reimburse.

remittance *(SYN.)* payment.

remnant *(SYN.)* remains, remainder, rest, residue, trace, relic.

remodel *(SYN.)* remake, reshape, rebuild, redecorate, renovate, modify, change, alter, convert, refurbish, update.

remonstrate *(SYN.)* grouch, protest, complain, grumble, murmur, repine, dispute. *(ANT.) rejoice, applaud, praise.*

remorse *(SYN.)* sorrow, qualm, contrition, regret, compunction, repentance. *(ANT.) obduracy, complacency.*

remorseless *(SYN.)* savage, unrelenting, crude, barbaric, merciless, cruel, fiendish, brutal, callous. *(ANT.) kind, refined, polite, civilized.*

remote *(SYN.)* inconsiderable, removed, slight, far,

unlikely, distant, inaccessible, unreachable, isolated, sequestered. (*ANT.*) *visible, nearby, current, near, close.*

remove (*SYN.*) transport, eject, move, vacate, withdraw, dislodge, transfer, doff, displace, eliminate, murder, kill, oust, extract. (*ANT.*) *insert, retain, stay, keep.*

removed (*SYN.*) aloof, distant, cool, remote.

remuneration (*SYN.*) wages, pay, salary, compensation, reimbursement, reward.

render (*SYN.*) become, make, perform, do, offer, present, give, submit.

rendition (*SYN.*) interpretation, version, depiction, expression, characterization.

renegade (*SYN.*) defector, insurgent, dissenter, rebel, maverick, mutineer, betrayer.

renege (*SYN.*) let down, doublecross, deceive.

renew (*SYN.*) restore, renovate, overhaul, revise, modernize, reshape, redo.

renounce (*SYN.*) resign, disown, revoke, abandon, quit, retract, forgo, leave, forsake, abdicate, reject, relinquish, deny. (*ANT.*) *assert, uphold, recognize, maintain.*

renovate (*SYN.*) restore, rehabilitate, rebuild, refresh, renew, overhaul, redesign.

renown (*SYN.*) honor, reputation, eminence, acclaim, glory, repute, luster, fame, notability. (*ANT.*) *obscurity, anonymity.*

renowned (*SYN.*) noted, famous, distinguished, well-known, glorious, celebrated. (*ANT.*) *unknown, infamous, hidden, obscure.*

rent (*SYN.*) payment, rental, let, lease, hire.

repair (*SYN.*) rebuilding, mend, renew, linker, correct, patch, restore, adjust, reconstruction, remedy, amend, rehabilitation, retrieve. (*ANT.*) *harm, break.*

repartee (*SYN.*) badinage, banter.

repast (*SYN.*) feast, banquet, meal, refreshment, snack.

repeal (*SYN.*) end, cancel, nullify, annul, quash, abolish, cancellation, rescind, abolition, abrogate.

repeat (*SYN.*) reiterate, restate, redo, rehearse, quote, remake, relate, iterate, reproduce.

repel (*SYN.*) check, repulse, rebuff, reject, decline, discourage. (*ANT.*) *lure, attract.*

repellent (*SYN.*) sickening,

offensive, disgusting, nauseating, repugnant, obnoxious.

repent (*SYN.*) deplore, regret, rue, lament.

repentance (*SYN.*) penitence, remorse, sorrow, compunction, qualm, grief. (*ANT.*) *obduracy, complacency.*

repentant (*SYN.*) regretful, sorrowful, contrite, sorry, penitent. (*ANT.*) *remorseless, obdurate.*

repented (*SYN.*) continuous, frequent, recurrent, continual.

repetitious (*SYN.*) repeated, monotonous, boring, tiresome, humdrum.

repine (*SYN.*) protest, lament, complain, whine, regret, grouch, murmur, grumble. (*ANT.*) *rejoice, applaud, praise.*

replace (*SYN.*) alternate, return, reinstate.

replacement (*SYN.*) understudy, proxy, second, alternate, substitute, replica, surrogate.

replenish (*SYN.*) store, pervade, fill, stock, occupy, supply. (*ANT.*) *empty, void, deplete, exhaust.*

replica (*SYN.*) reproduction, copy, exemplar, imitation, duplicate, facsimile. (*ANT.*) *prototype.*

reply (*SYN.*) retort, rejoinder, answer, retaliate, respond, confirmation. (*ANT.*) *summoning, inquiry.*

report (*SYN.*) declare, herald, publish, announce, summary, publish, advertise. (*ANT.*) *suppress, conceal, withhold, bury.*

reporter (*SYN.*) journalist.

repose (*SYN.*) hush, quiet, tranquillity, rest, peace, slumber, calm, stillness, sleep, calmness. (*ANT.*) *tumult, excitement, agitation.*

reprehensible (*SYN.*) criminal, immoral, damnable, culpable, wrong, wicked.

represent (*SYN.*) picture, draw, delineate, portray, depict, denote, symbolize. (*ANT.*) *misrepresent, caricature.*

representation (*SYN.*) effigy, film, likeness, portrait, print, scene, appearance, drawing, scene, view, cinema.

representative (*SYN.*) delegate, agent, substitute, surrogate.

repress (*SYN.*) limit, stop, check, bridle, curb, restrain, constrain, suppress. (*ANT.*) *loosen, aid, incite, liberate, encourage.*

reprimand (*SYN.*) rate, scold, vituperate, berate, lecture,

blame, admonish, upbraid. (*ANT.*) *praise, approve.*

reproach (*SYN.*) defamation, dishonor, insult, profanation, abuse, disparagement, misuse, reviling. (*ANT.*) *respect, laudation, approval, plaudit.*

reproduction (*SYN.*) replica, copy, exemplar, transcript, duplicate, photocopy.

reproof (*SYN.*) rebuke, punishment, blame, censure, disapproval, scorn, disdain, admonition.

repugnance (*SYN.*) disgust, hatred, reluctance, abhorrence, aversion, loathing, antipathy, distaste, repulsion. (*ANT.*) *devotion, affection, enthusiasm, attachment.*

repulsive (*SYN.*) repellent, ugly, homely, deformed, horrid, offensive, plain, uncomely. (*ANT.*) *fair, pretty, attractive.*

reputable (*SYN.*) honest, upstanding, trustworthy, straightforward, upright, reliable. (*ANT.*) *notorious, corrupt, disreputable.*

reputation (*SYN.*) class, nature, standing, name, fame, kind, renown, prominence, character, distinction, disposition, repute.

repute (*SYN.*) class, nature, standing, kind, character, reputation, disposition, sort.

request (*SYN.*) sue, implore, petition, desire, appeal, question, entreaty, beseech, ask, pray, supplicate. (*ANT.*) *require.*

require (*SYN.*) exact, need, order, command, order, lack, claim, demand, want.

requirement (*SYN.*) demand, need, necessity, condition, provision, prerequisite.

requisite (*SYN.*) vital, necessary, basic, fundamental, indispensable, essential, needed. (*ANT.*) *casual, nonessential, peripheral.*

rescind (*SYN.*) annul, quash, revoke, abolish, invalidate, abrogate, withdraw.

rescue (*SYN.*) liberate, ransom, release, deliver, deliverance, liberation.

research (*SYN.*) exploration, quest, scrutiny, exploration, interrogation, query, examination, study, investigation. (*ANT.*) *inattention, disregard, negligence.*

resemblance (*SYN.*) parity, similitude, analogy, likeness, correspondence. (*ANT.*) *distinction, difference.*

resemble (*SYN.*) duplicate, mirror, look like.

resentfulness (*SYN.*) envy, jealousy, covetousness, suspicion. (*ANT.*) *liberality, geniality, tolerance, difference.*

resentment (*SYN.*) displeasure, bitterness, indignation, rancor, outrage, hostility. (*ANT.*) *complacency, understanding, good will.*

reservation (*SYN.*) skepticism, restriction, objection, limitation, doubt.

reserve (*SYN.*) fund, hold, keep, store, accumulation, save, stock, maintain, supply. (*ANT.*) *waste, squander.*

reserved (*SYN.*) cautious, fearful, timorous, wary, aloof, chary, sheepish, restrained, proper, unfriendly, bashful, diffident. (*ANT.*) *forward, bold, wild, immodest, brazen, abandoned, friendly.*

reside (*SYN.*) inhabit, dwell, abide, live, lie.

residence (*SYN.*) home, dwelling, stay, seat, abode, quarters, domicile, living quarters.

residue (*SYN.*) balance, remainder, rest, ashes, remnants, dregs, leftovers, ends.

resign (*SYN.*) vacate, withdraw, leave, surrender, quit.

resignation (*SYN.*) withdrawal, surrender, quitting, abdication, acquiescence. (*ANT.*) *recalcitrance, defiance, resistance.*

resigned (*SYN.*) forbearing, stoical, assiduous, passive, accepting, composed, uncomplaining, (*ANT.*) *turbulent, chafing.*

resilience (*SYN.*) rubbery, springy, buoyant, elasticity. (*ANT.*) *unresponsive, fixed, stolid.*

resist (*SYN.*) defy, attack, withstand, hinder, confront, oppose. (*ANT.*) *relent, allow, yield, accede.*

resolute (*SYN.*) firm, resolved, set, determined, decided. (*ANT.*) *irresolute, wavering, vacillating.*

resolution (*SYN.*) resolve, courage, determination, persistence, statement, verdict, recommendation, decision, steadfastness, dedication, perseverance. (*ANT.*) *indecision, inconstancy.*

resolve (*SYN.*) determination, resolution, courage, settle, decide, persistence, determine, confirm, decision, steadfastness. (*ANT.*) *integrate, indecision, inconstancy.*

resort (*SYN.*) motel, lodge, hotel, solve.

resound (*SYN.*) echo, ring,

reverberate.

resource (SYN.) store, source, supply, reserve.

resourceful (SYN.) inventive, ingenious, creative, clever, imaginative, skillful.

respect (SYN.) honor, approval, revere, heed, value, admire, esteem, point, detail, admiration, reverence, regard, feature, particular, venerate, consider. (ANT.) neglect, abuse, scorn, disregard, despise.

respectable (SYN.) becoming, respected, proper, seemly, tolerable, decent, acceptable, fair, adequate, passable, suitable, honorable, valuable. (ANT.) unsavory, vulgar, gross, disputable, reprehensible.

respectful (SYN.) courteous, polite, well-behaved, well-bred, compliant, submissive. (ANT.) disobedient, impertinent, rude.

respite (SYN.) deferment, adjournment, suspension.

respond (SYN.) rejoin, answer, reply, acknowledge, retort. (ANT.) overlook, disregard.

response (SYN.) reply, acknowledgment, answer, retort, rejoinder. (ANT.) summoning, inquiry.

responsibility (SYN.) duty, obligation, accountability, trustworthiness, trust, liability, commitment.

responsible (SYN.) answerable, chargeable, trustworthy, liable, accountable, able, capable, upstanding, reliable, solid, indebted, creditable. (ANT.) careless, free, negligent.

rest (SYN.) ease, intermission, calm, quiet, balance, surplus, repose, lounge, inactivity, motionlessness, immobility, standstill, relax, remainder, excess, relaxation, slumber, peace, tranquillity, leisure. (ANT.) tumult, commotion, motion, agitation.

restful (SYN.) peaceful, quiet, tranquil, calm. (ANT.) tumultuous, upsetting, agitated, disturbed.

restitution (SYN.) recompense, satisfaction, refund, amends, retrieval.

restive (SYN.) balky, disobedient, fractious, impatient, unruly, fidgety, uneasy.

restless (SYN.) sleepless, unquiet, transient, active, agitated, disturbed, jumpy, nervous, uneasy, disquieted, irresolute. (ANT.) quiet, tranquil, calm, peaceable.

restore (SYN.) repair, recover, rebuild, reestablish, renovate,

return, renew, mend, reinstall, revive, rehabilitate, replace.

restrain (SYN.) limit, curb, constraint, stop, bridle, control, constrain, repress, check, suppress, hinder. (ANT.) incite, aid, loosen.

restraint (SYN.) order, self-control, reserve, control, regulation, limitation, confinement. (ANT.) freedom, liberty.

restrict (SYN.) fetter, restrain, confine, limit, engage, attach, connect, link, tie, bind. (ANT.) broaden, enlarge, untie, loose, free.

restriction (SYN.) curb, handicap, check, boundary, ban, limitation, control, deterrent.

result (SYN.) effect, issue, outcome, resolve, end, consequence, happen, determination, conclusion, reward, aftermath. (ANT.) cause, beginning, origin.

resume (SYN.) restart, continue, recommence, reassume.

resurgence (SYN.) rebirth, comeback, recovery, revival, resuscitation, rejuvenation, renewal.

resuscitate (SYN.) restore, revive.

retain (SYN.) keep, hold, recall, remember, employ, hire, engage.

retainer (SYN.) aide, assistant, lackey, attendant, servant.

retaliate (SYN.) repay, revenge, return, avenge. (ANT.) condone, forgive, overlook, excuse, forget.

retard (SYN.) detain, slacken, defer, impede, hold back, delay, postpone. (ANT.) accelerate, speed, hasten, rush.

retention (SYN.) reservation, acquisition, holding, tenacity, possession.

reticent (SYN.) reserved, subdued, quiet, shy, withdrawn, restrained, bashful, silent. (ANT.) outspoken, forward, opinionated.

retire (SYN.) resign, quit, abdicate, depart, vacate.

retiring (SYN.) timid, bashful, withdrawn, modest, reticent, quiet, reserved. (ANT.) gregarious, assertive, bold.

retort (SYN.) reply, answer, response, respond, rejoin, rejoinder, retaliate. (ANT.) summoning, inquiry.

retreat (SYN.) leave, depart, retire, withdraw, retirement, withdrawal, departure, shelter, refuge. (ANT.) advanced.

retrench (SYN.) reduce, scrape, curtail.

retribution (SYN.) justice,

vengeance, reprisal, punishment, comeuppance, vindictiveness, revenge, retaliation.

retrieve (SYN.) regain, recover, recapture, repossess, reclaim, salvage, recoup.

retrograde (SYN.) regressive, backward, declining, deteriorating, worsening. (ANT.) onward, progression, advanced.

return (SYN.) restoration, replace, revert, recur, restore, retreat. (ANT.) keep, take, retain.

reveal (SYN.) discover, publish, communicate, impart, uncover, tell, betray, divulge, disclose. (ANT.) conceal, cover, obscure, cloak, hide.

revel (SYN.) rejoice, wallow, bask, enjoy, delight, savor, gloat, luxuriate, relish.

revelation (SYN.) hallucination, dream, prophecy, apparition, ghost, mirage, discovery, daydream, surprise, shocker.

revelry (SYN.) merriment, merry-making, carousal, feasting, gala, festival.

revenge (SYN.) vindictiveness, reprisal, requital, vengeance, repayment, repay, retribution, reparation. (ANT.) reconcile, forgive, pity.

revenue (SYN.) take, proceeds, income, profit, return.

revere (SYN.) admire, honor, worship, respect, venerate, adore. (ANT.) ignore, despise.

reverence (SYN.) glory, worship, homage, admiration, dignity, renown, respect, esteem, veneration, adoration, honor. (ANT.) dishonor, derision, reproach.

reverent (SYN.) honoring, respectful, adoring, pious, devout, humble. (ANT.) silent, disrespectful.

reverse (SYN.) overthrow, unmake, rescind, opposite, invert, contrary, rear, back, misfortune, defeat, upset, countermand, revoke. (ANT.) vouch, stabilize, endorse, affirm.

revert (SYN.) return, relapse, backslide, reverse, retreat, recur, go back. (ANT.) keep, take, appropriate.

review (SYN.) reconsideration, examination, commentary, retrospection, restudy, journal, synopsis, study, reexamine, critique, inspection.

revile (SYN.) defame, malign, vilify, abuse, traduce, asperse, scandalize, smear. (ANT.) honor, respect, cherish, protect.

revise (SYN.) change, alter, improve, correct, amend,

update, rewrite, polish.

revision (SYN.) inspection, survey, retrospection, commentary, critique.

revival (SYN.) renaissance, exhumation, resurgence, renewal, revitalization.

revive (SYN.) refresh, lessen, decrease, renew, reduce, lower, abate, reanimate, diminish, reawaken, rejuvenate, suppress. (ANT.) increase, amplify, intensify.

revoke (SYN.) nullify, cancel, abolish, quash, rescind, abrogate.

revolt (SYN.) mutiny, rebel, disgust, revolution, uprising, rebellion, upheaval, takeover, insurgence, abolish.

revolting (SYN.) hateful, odious, abominable, foul, vile, detestable, loathsome, repugnant, obnoxious, sickening. (ANT.) delightful, agreeable, pleasant.

revolution (SYN.) rebellion, mutiny, turn, coup, revolt, overthrow, cycle, spin, uprising.

revolutionary (SYN.) insurgent, extremist, radical, subversive, mutinous.

revolve (SYN.) spin, wheel, rotate, circle, turn, whirl, gyrate.

revolver (SYN.) gun, pistol.

revulsion (SYN.) dislike, distaste, aversion, repugnance, disgust. (ANT.) attraction, desire, fondness, preference.

reward (SYN.) bounty, premium, award, compensation, prize, recompense, bonus, remuneration, accolade. (ANT.) punishment, penalty, chastisement.

rewarding (SYN.) pleasing, productive, fruitful, profitable, favorable, satisfying, gratifying, fulfilling.

rhetoric (SYN.) style, verbosity, expressiveness, eloquence, fluency, flamboyance.

rhyme (SYN.) poem, verse, poetry, ballad, ditty, rhapsody, sonnet.

ribald (SYN.) suggestive, off-color, indecent, spicy, rude, vulgar.

rich (SYN.) ample, costly, wealthy, fruitful, prolific, abundant, well-off, affluent, plentiful, fertile, bountiful, luxuriant. (ANT.) poor, unfruitful, beggarly, barren, impoverished, scarce, scanty, unproductive, destitute.

rickety (SYN.) unsound, unsteady, flimsy, unstable, shaky, decrepit, wobbly. (ANT.) steady, solid, sturdy.

ricochet (SYN.) recoil, backfire,

rebound, bounce, deviate, boomerang.

rid *(SYN.)* free, clear, shed, delivered, eliminate, disperse, unload, purge.

riddle *(SYN.)* puzzle, mystery, conundrum, problem, question, enigma. *(ANT.) key, solution, answer, resolution.*

ride *(SYN.)* tour, journey, motor, manage, drive, control, guide.

ridge *(SYN.)* hillock, backbone, spine, crest, mound, hump.

ridicule *(SYN.)* gibe, banter, mock, jeering, deride, tease, taunt, satire, mockery, derision. *(ANT.) praise.*

ridiculous *(SYN.)* silly, nonsensical, absurd, accurate, inconsistent, farcical, proper, laughable, apt, preposterous, foolish. *(ANT.) sound, reasonable, consistent.*

rife *(SYN.)* widespread, abundant, innumerable, rampant, teeming.

rifle *(SYN.)* plunder, pillage, rummage, ransack, rob, steal.

rift *(SYN.)* crevice, fault, crack, flaw, fissure, split, breach, opening.

right *(SYN.)* correct, appropriate, suitable, ethical, fit, real, legitimate, justice, factual, just, directly, virtue, true, definite, straight, honorably, seemly. *(ANT.) immoral, unfair, wrong, bad, improper.*

righteous *(SYN.)* ethical, chaste, honorable, good, virtuous, noble. *(ANT.) sinful, libertine, amoral, licentious.*

rigid *(SYN.)* strict, unyielding, stiff, stern, austere, rigorous, inflexible, stringent, unbendable, severe, harsh, unbending. *(ANT.) supple, flexible, mild, compassionate, pliable, limp, relaxed.*

rigorous *(SYN.)* unfeeling, rough, strict, blunt, cruel, hard, severe, grating, coarse, jarring, stern, stringent. *(ANT.) soft, mild, tender, gentle, smooth.*

rile *(SYN.)* irritate, nettle, hector, exasperate, provoke, gripe.

rim *(SYN.)* verge, frontier, border, outskirts, edge, brink, lip, limit, termination, boundary, fringe, brim, margin. *(ANT.) core, mainland, center.*

rind *(SYN.)* layer, cover, skin, hide, peel, crust, bark.

ring *(SYN.)* fillet, band, loop, circlet, circle, surround, encircle, peal, sound, resound, jingle, tinkle.

ringleader *(SYN.)* provoker,

troublemaker, leader, instigator, chief, inciter, agitator.

rinse *(SYN.)* launder, cleanse, wash, soak, immerse, laundering, rinsing, bathe, clean.

riot *(SYN.)* disturbance, disorder, outburst, commotion, insurgence, uproar, panic, boisterousness, lark, hoot, sensation, caper, roister, frolic, eruption, confusion, tumult, revolt.

riotous *(SYN.)* boisterous, wild, rambunctious, tumultuous, turbulent, noisy, loud, rowdy, rollicking,

rip *(SYN.)* tear, rend, wound, rive, cleave, cut, slit, slash, lacerate, shred, scramble, dart, dash, split, disunite. *(ANT.) mend, join, repair.*

ripe *(SYN.)* ready, finished, mature, complete, full-grown, develop, mellow, seasonable, full-fledged, primed, disposed, keen, avid, consummate. *(ANT.) raw, crude, undeveloped, premature, unprepared, unripe.*

ripen *(SYN.)* grow, season, age, mature, mellow, develop, progress, maturate.

rip into *(SYN.)* assail, lash out at, attack, charge.

rip-off *(SYN.)* fraud, dishonesty, gyp, racket, swindle, exploitation, heist, theft, extortion, thievery, larceny, shakedown.

riposte *(SYN.)* rejoinder, comeback, quip, retort, response, reply, wisecrack.

ripple *(SYN.)* wave, ruffle, wavelet, gurgle, undulate, corrugation, rumple, crumple, dribble, bubble.

rise *(SYN.)* thrive, awaken, ascend, climb, mount, tower, arise, wake, scale, flourish, prosper, advance, proceed, soar. *(ANT.) fail, drop, plunge, fade, slump, decline, sinking, depression, waning, comedown, setback, retrogression, descend.*

risk *(SYN.)* hazard, peril, danger, endanger, chance, jeopardy, threat, vulnerability, contingency, precariousness, shakiness. *(ANT.) protection, safety, immunity, defense.*

risky *(SYN.)* menacing, chancy, threatening, critical, perilous, insecure, unsafe, dicey, unsound, dangerous. *(ANT.) guarded, safe, certain, firm, secure.*

rite *(SYN.)* pomp, solemnity, ceremony, observance, ceremonial, formality.

ritual *(SYN.)* pomp, solemnity, ceremony, parade, rite, ritualism, prescription, routine.

custom, tradition.

rival *(SYN.)* enemy, opponent, contestant, compete, foe, adversary, oppose, competitor, contest, antagonist. *(ANT.) colleague, confederate, allay, collaborator, helpmate, teammate.*

rivalry *(SYN.)* contest, struggle, duel, race, vying, opposition, contention, competition. *(ANT.) alliance, collaboration, partnership, teamwork, coalition.*

river *(SYN.)* brook, stream, headstream, watercourse, tributary, creek.

rivet *(SYN.)* weld, bolt, fasten, attach, secure, bind, join, staple, nail, couple.

road *(SYN.)* street, way, highway, pike, drive, expressway, boulevard.

roam *(SYN.)* err, saunter, deviate, rove, range, wander, digress, ramble, stroll. *(ANT.) stop, linger, stay, halt, settle.*

roar *(SYN.)* cry, bellow, yell, shout, yowl, howl, bawl, hoot, bang, boom, blast, blare, scream, whoop, holler, yelp.

roast *(SYN.)* deride, ridicule, kid, ride, mock, tease, twit, parody, burlesque.

rob *(SYN.)* fleece, steal, despoil, pilfer, pillage, sack, loot, plunder, burglarize, ransack, hold up, rip off, thieve.

robbery *(SYN.)* larceny, plundering, thievery, stealing, theft, pillage, swiping, caper, snatching, burglary, plunder.

robe *(SYN.)* housecoat, bathrobe, dressing gown, caftan, muumuu, smock, cape.

robot *(SYN.)* computer, android, automaton, pawn, workhorse, drudge, laborer.

robust *(SYN.)* well, hearty, hale, sound, healthy, strong, able-bodied, stalwart. *(ANT.) fragile, feeble, debilitated, reserved, refined, puny, frail, delicate, infirm.*

rock *(SYN.)* pebble, boulder, stone, gravel, granite, roll, sway, swagger, limestone.

rocky *(SYN.)* unstable, faint, rock-like, stony, pebbly, gravelly, rough, bumpy, formidable, quavering, challenging, unsteady, dizzy. *(ANT.) effortless, easy, slight, simple, sound, rugged, stout, hardy, strong, robust.*

rod *(SYN.)* bar, pole, wand, stick, pike, staff, billy, baton.

rogue *(SYN.)* criminal, rascal, outlaw, scoundrel, scamp, good-for-nothing, villain.

roguish *(SYN.)* prankish, playful, mischievous, elfish,

waggish, devilish, tricky. *(ANT.) grave, humorless, solemn, staid.*

roil *(SYN.)* muddy, rile, mire, disturb.

roister *(SYN.)* bluster, swagger, swashbuckle, vaunt, bluff, flourish, rollick.

role *(SYN.)* task, part, function, characterization, portrayal, face, character.

roll *(SYN.)* revolve, rotate, whirl, swing, rock, waver, reel, lumber, swagger, stagger, progress, proceed, turn, spin.

rollicking *(SYN.)* spirited, animated, frolicsome, exuberant, lighthearted, carefree.

roll up *(SYN.)* amass, collect, accumulate, gather.

romance *(SYN.)* affair, enchantment, novel, tale, adventure, enterprise, story.

romantic *(SYN.)* poetic, mental, dreamy, fanciful, imaginative, extravagant, impractical, exaggerated, wild, idealistic, mawkish, ideal, maudlin. *(ANT.) homely, faint-hearted, familiar, unromantic, pessimistic, unemotional, cynical, literal, prosaic.*

romp *(SYN.)* caper, gambol, frolic, play, conquer, triumph, horseplay, frisk. *(ANT.) defeat, rout.*

room *(SYN.)* enclosure, cell, chamber, space, stay, lodge, cubicle, reside.

roomy *(SYN.)* broad, large, wide, sizable, generous, capacious, ample, spacious, extensive, commodious, vast. *(ANT.) tight, limited, crowded, confined, narrow.*

roost *(SYN.)* coop, hen house, perch, hutch, residence, abode, hearth, lodgings.

root *(SYN.)* reason, bottom, groundwork, cause, support, base, underpinning, beginning, mainspring, source, basis. *(ANT.) cover, top, building.*

rooted *(SYN.)* fixed, fast, firm, steadfast, immovable, stationary.

root for *(SYN.)* back, support, boost, promote, bolster, encourage, hail, cheer.

root out *(SYN.)* dispose of, uproot, cut out, pluck out.

rope *(SYN.)* string, wire, cord, cable, line, strand, rigging, ropework, cordage.

ropy *(SYN.)* wiry, stringy, viscous, threadlike, viscoid.

roster *(SYN.)* list, census, muster, enrollment, listing, register.

rosy *(SYN.)* reddish, pink, healthy, fresh, cheerful,

bright, happy, glowing, flushed, promising, favorable. (ANT.) *pale, pallid, gray, wan, disheartening, ashen, unfavorable, gloomy.*

rot (SYN.) putrefy, waste, decay, mold, decompose, dwindle, spoil, decline, decomposition, wane, rotting, ebb. (ANT.) *increase, rise, grow.*

rotary (SYN.) axial, rotating, turning, gyrate, revolving, rolling, whirling, rotational.

rotate (SYN.) spin, twirl, wheel, circle, twist, orbit, invert, swivel, gyrate, wind, alternate, recur, intermit, pivot. (ANT.) *stop, arrest, stand.*

rote (SYN.) repetition, system, convention, routine, mechanization, habitude, habit, custom.

rough (SYN.) jagged, scratchy, crude, incomplete, severe, craggy, stormy, rugged, unpolished, approximate, uneven, irregular, bumpy, coarse. (ANT.) *calm, polished, civil, mild, refined, placid, gentle, smooth, sleek, sophisticated, suave.*

round (SYN.) rotund, chubby, curved, bulbous, entire, complete, spherical, circular, bowed. (ANT.) *slender, trim, slim, thin, lean.*

rouse (SYN.) waken, awaken, stimulate, excite, summon, arise, stir. (ANT.) *rest, calm, sleep, restrain, sedate.*

rousing (SYN.) exciting, galvanic, stimulating, electric, moving, exhilarating, stirring, breathtaking, inciting. (ANT.) *flat, uninteresting, drab, monotonous, boring, tiresome, slow, dull.*

rout (SYN.) defeat, beat, quell, vanquish, conquer, humble, subdue, scatter. (ANT.) *cede, retreat, surrender.*

route (SYN.) street, course, trail, way, avenue, passage, thoroughfare, track.

routine (SYN.) way, habit, use, custom, practice, fashion, method, system. (ANT.) *unusual, rate, uncommon.*

rover (SYN.) traveler, adventurer, wanderer, voyager.

row (SYN.) file, order, series, rank, progression, sequence, arrangement.

rowdy (SYN.) disorderly, unruly, brawling, roughneck, scrapper.

royal (SYN.) lordly, regal, noble, courtly, ruling, stately, dignified, supreme, majestic, sovereign, imperial, kingly.

(ANT.) *servile, common, low, humble, vulgar.*

rub (SYN.) shine, polish, scour, scrape.

rubbish (SYN.) debris, garbage, trash, waste, junk, clutter.

ruddy (SYN.) rosy, reddish, healthy, robust, blushing, sanguine.

rude (SYN.) gruff, impudent, blunt, impolite, boorish, insolent, saucy, rough, crude, unmannerly, coarse, impertinent. (ANT.) *courtly, civil, stately, calm, dignified, polished, courteous, cultivated, polite.*

rudimentary (SYN.) essential, primary, fundamental, original, imperfect.

rue (SYN.) lament, repine, sorrow, deplore, regret, bemoan.

ruffian (SYN.) crook, hoodlum, thug.

ruffle (SYN.) rumple, disarrange, disorder, disturb, trimming, frill.

rug (SYN.) floorcovering, carpet.

rugged (SYN.) jagged, craw, scratchy, irregular, uneven, harsh, severe, tough. (ANT.) *smooth, level, even.*

ruin (SYN.) wreck, exterminate, devastate, annihilate, raze, demolish, spoil. (ANT.) *save, establish, preserve.*

rule (SYN.) law, guide, order, regulation, dominion, sovereignty, control.

ruler (SYN.) commander, chief, leader, governor, yardstick.

ruling (SYN.) judgment, decision, decree.

ruminate (SYN.) brood, reflect, meditate, ponder, consider, speculate.

rummage (SYN.) root, scour, ransack.

rumor (SYN.) innuendo, hearsay, gossip.

rumple (SYN.) tousle, furrow, crease, wrinkle, dishevel.

run (SYN.) race, hurry, speed, hasten, sprint, dart, scamper, dash.

runaway (SYN.) refugee, deserter, fugitive.

run-down (SYN.) ramshackle, dilapidated, tumble-down, weakened.

rupture (SYN.) fracture, fissure, cleft, break, split, gash.

rural (SYN.) country, farm, rustic, backwoods. (ANT.) *citified, urban.*

rush (SYN.) dash, speed, hurry, hasten, run, scoot, hustle, scurry. (ANT.) *tarry, linger.*

rut (SYN.) routine, habit, groove, track.

S

sabotage (SYN.) subversion, undermine, treason, treachery, damage, disable, subvert.

sack (SYN.) pouch, bag.

sacrament (SYN.) communion, fellowship, rite, association, participation, union. (ANT.) *nonparticipation, alienation.*

sacred (SYN.) consecrated, blessed, devout, divine, holy, hallowed, pious, religious, spiritual, saintly. (ANT.) *profane, evil, sacrilegious, worldly, secular, blasphemous, impious.*

sad (SYN.) dejected, cheerless, despondent, depressed, disconsolate, doleful, downhearted, downcast, dismal, melancholy, somber, glum, saddening. (ANT.) *happy, cheerful, glad, merry.*

safe (SYN.) dependable, certain, harmless, secure, snug, trustworthy. (ANT.) *hazardous, dangerous, unsafe, insecure, perilous.*

sag (SYN.) incline, bend, lean, slant, tend, depend, rely, trust, fail. (ANT.) *rise, raise, erect, straighten.*

sagacity (SYN.) erudition, discretion, foresight, insight, information, judgment, intelligence, knowledge, learning. (ANT.) *foolishness, imprudence, stupidity, nonsense.*

sage (SYN.) intellectual, disciple, learner, savant, scholar, pupil, student, wise, judicious, sagacious, rational, logical. (ANT.) *dunce, fool, dolt, idiot.*

saintly (SYN.) virtuous, moral, holy, devout, righteous, good.

sake (SYN.) motive, reason, purpose, benefit, advantage, welfare.

salary (SYN.) compensation, allowance, earnings, pay, fee, payment, recompense, wages. (ANT.) *gratuity, present, gift.*

saloon (SYN.) pub, bar.

salubrious (SYN.) healthy, hale, sound, robust, strong, well, hygienic, wholesome, salutary. (ANT.) *diseased, delicate, frail, injurious.*

salutary (SYN.) beneficial, advantageous, profitable, useful, wholesome. (ANT.) *destructive, deleterious, detrimental, injurious, harmful.*

salute (SYN.) receive, greet.

salvage (SYN.) retrieve, rescue, recover.

salvation (SYN.) release, rescue, deliverance.

same (SYN.) equal, coincident, equivalent, like, indistinguishable. (ANT.) *disparate, contrary, dissimilar, opposed, distinct.*

sample (SYN.) example, case, illustration, model, instance, pattern, prototype, specimen, token.

sanction (SYN.) approval, approbation, authorization, authority, let, permit. (ANT.) *reproach, reprimand, stricture, censure, object, forbid, refuse, resist.*

sanctuary (SYN.) harbor, haven, asylum, refuge, retreat, shelter. (ANT.) *danger, hazard, exposure, jeopardy, peril.*

sane (SYN.) balanced, rational, normal, sound, reasonable. (ANT.) *crazy, insane, irrational.*

sanitary (SYN.) purified, clean, hygienic, disinfected. (ANT.) *soiled, fouled, unclean, dirty.*

sap (SYN.) exhausted, drain, weaken.

sarcastic (SYN.) biting, acrimonious, cutting, caustic, derisive, sardonic, satirical, ironic, sneering. (ANT.) *agreeable, affable, pleasant.*

sardonic (SYN.) bitter, caustic, acrimonious, severe, harsh. (ANT.) *mellow, pleasant, sweet.*

satanic (SYN.) demonic, fiendish, diabolic.

sate (SYN.) fill up, fill, occupy, furnish, pervade, stock, replenish, store, supply, content, gorge, satiate, stuff, satisfy. (ANT.) *empty, drain, deplete, void.*

satire (SYN.) cleverness, fun, banter, humor, irony, raillery, pleasantry. (ANT.) *platitude, sobriety, commonplace, solemnity.*

satirical (SYN.) biting, caustic, acrimonious, cutting, ironic, derisive, sarcastic, sneering, sardonic, taunting. (ANT.) *agreeable, affable, pleasant.*

satisfactory (SYN.) ample, capable, adequate, commensurate, enough, sufficient, fitting, suitable, okay. (ANT.) *scant, lacking, deficient, unsatisfactory, poor.*

satisfy (SYN.) compensate, appease, content, gratify, fulfill, suitable. (ANT.) *displease, dissatisfy, annoy, tantalize.*

saturate (SYN.) fill, diffuse, infiltrate, penetrate, permeate, run through.

saucy *(SYN.)* insolent, bold, impudent, impertinent. *(ANT.)* shy, demure.

savage *(SYN.)* brutal, cruel, barbarous, ferocious, inhuman, merciless. *(ANT.) compassionate, gentle, humane, kind, merciful, tame, cultivated.*

save *(SYN.)* defend, conserve, keep, maintain, guard, preserve, protect, safeguard, rescue, secure, uphold, spare. *(ANT.) abolish, destroy, abandon, impale, injure.*

savory *(SYN.)* delectable, delightful, delicious, palatable, luscious, tasty. *(ANT.) distasteful, nauseous, acrid, unpalatable, unsavory.*

say *(SYN.)* converse, articulate, declare, express, discourse, harangue, talk, speak, tell, utter, remark, state. *(ANT.) hush, refrain, be silent.*

saying *(SYN.)* aphorism, adage, byword, maxim, proverb, motto.

scalding *(SYN.)* hot, scorching, burning, torrid, warm, fervent, ardent, fiery. *(ANT.) cool, cold, freezing, passionless, frigid, bland.*

scale *(SYN.)* balance, proportion, ration, range, climb, mount.

scamp *(SYN.)* troublemaker, rascal.

scan *(SYN.)* examine, study.

scandal *(SYN.)* chagrin, humiliation, abashment, mortification, dishonor, disgrace, disrepute, odium. *(ANT.) glory, honor, dignity, praise.*

scandalize *(SYN.)* asperse, defame, abuse, disparage, revile, vilify, traduce. *(ANT.) honor, respect, cherish.*

scandalous *(SYN.)* disgraceful, discreditable, dishonorable, ignominious, disreputable, shameful. *(ANT.) honorable, renowned, esteemed.*

scant *(SYN.)* succinct, concise, terse, inadequate, deficient, insufficient. *(ANT.) ample, big, extended, abundant, protracted.*

scarce *(SYN.)* occasional, choice, infrequent, exceptional, incomparable, precious, singular, rare, uncommon. *(ANT.) frequent, ordinary, usual, customary, abundant, numerous, worthless.*

scarcely *(SYN.)* barely, hardly.

scarcity *(SYN.)* want, insufficiency, lack, need, dearth. *(ANT.) abundance.*

scare *(SYN.)* alarm, papal, affright, astound, dismay,

daunt, frighten, intimidate, horrify, terrorize, shock. *(ANT.) compose, reassure, soothe.*

scared *(SYN.)* apprehensive, afraid, faint-hearted, frightened, fearful, timid. *(ANT.) bold, assured, courageous, composed, sanguine.*

scarf *(SYN.)* kerchief.

scatter *(SYN.)* dispel, disperse, diffuse, disseminate, separate, dissipate, spread. *(ANT.) assemble, accumulate, amass, gather, collect.*

scene *(SYN.)* exhibition, view, display.

scent *(SYN.)* fragrance, fume, aroma, incense, perfume, odor, redolence, stench, stink, smell.

schedule *(SYN.)* program, timetable.

scheme *(SYN.)* conspiracy, cabal, design, machination, intrigue, plot, plan, chart.

scholar *(SYN.)* intellectual, pupil, learner, disciple, sage, student, savant, teacher. *(ANT.) dunce, idiot, fool, ignoramus.*

scholarly *(SYN.)* bookish, erudite, formal, academic, learned, pedantic, theoretical, scholastic. *(ANT.) practical, simple.*

scholarship *(SYN.)* cognizance, erudition, apprehension, information, learning, knowledge, science, wisdom. *(ANT.) illiteracy, stupidity, ignorance, misunderstanding.*

science *(SYN.)* enlightenment, discipline, knowledge, scholarship. *(ANT.) superstition, ignorance.*

scoff *(SYN.)* ridicule, belittle, mock.

scold *(SYN.)* berate, blame, lecture, rebuke, censure, admonish, reprehend, upbraid, reprimand, criticize. *(ANT.) commend, praise, approve.*

scope *(SYN.)* area, compass, expanse, amount, extent, magnitude, degree, measure, reach, size, range.

scorch *(SYN.)* burn, char, consume, blaze, incinerate, sear, singe, scald. *(ANT.) put out, quench, extinguish.*

score *(SYN.)* reckoning, tally, record, mark, rating.

scorn *(SYN.)* contumely, derision, contempt, detestation, hatred, disdain, despise, hate, spurn, refuse, reject. *(ANT.) esteem, respect, awe.*

scornful *(SYN.)* disdainful, contemptuous.

scoundrel *(SYN.)* rogue, villain,

cad.

scour *(SYN.)* wash, clean, scrub.

scourge *(SYN.)* affliction, lash, whip.

scowl *(SYN.)* glower, frown, glare.

scramble *(SYN.)* combine, mix, blend, hasten, clamber, climb.

scrap *(SYN.)* fragment, rag, apportionment, part, portion, piece, section, share, segment, crumb, junk. *(ANT.) whole, entirety.*

scrape *(SYN.)* difficulty, dilemma, condition, fix, predicament, plight, situation, strait, scour, rub, scratch. *(ANT.) comfort, ease, calmness.*

scratch *(SYN.)* scrape, scar.

scrawny *(SYN.)* gaunt, skinny, spindly. *(ANT.) husky, burly.*

scream *(SYN.)* screech, shriek, yell.

screech *(SYN.)* yell, cry, scream, shriek.

screen *(SYN.)* partition, cover, separation, protection.

scrimp *(SYN.)* skimp, save, economize, conserve.

script *(SYN.)* penmanship, hand, handwriting, text, lines.

scrounge *(SYN.)* sponge, borrow.

scrub *(SYN.)* cleanse, mop, purify, clean, sweep, wash, scour. *(ANT.) pollute, dirty, stain, sully.*

scrupulous *(SYN.)* conscientious, candid, honest, honorable, fair, just, sincere, truthful, upright, painstaking, critical. *(ANT.) dishonest, fraudulent, lying, deceitful, tricky.*

scrutinize *(SYN.)* criticize, appraise, evaluate, examine, inspect, analyze. *(ANT.) neglect, overlook, approve.*

scurrilous *(SYN.)* insulting, outrageous.

scurry *(SYN.)* scamper, scramble, hasten, hustle, hurry.

scuttle *(SYN.)* swamp, ditch, sink.

seal *(SYN.)* emblem, stamp, symbol, crest, signet.

search *(SYN.)* exploration, examination, investigation, inquiry, pursuit, quest, explore, scrutinize, investigate, hunt, probe, rummage, ransack, seek, scour. *(ANT.) resignation, abandonment.*

searching *(SYN.)* inquiring, inquisitive, interrogative, nosy, curious, peeping, peering, snoopy, prying. *(ANT.) indifferent, unconcerned, incurious, uninterested.*

season *(SYN.)* mature, perfect,

ripen, develop, age.

seasoned *(SYN.)* veteran, skilled.

secede *(SYN.)* quit, withdraw, resign.

secluded *(SYN.)* deserted, desolate, isolated, alone, lonely, lone, unaided, only, sole, solitary, single, separate, sheltered, hidden, secret. *(ANT.) surrounded, accompanied.*

seclusion *(SYN.)* insulation, isolation, loneliness, alienation, quarantine, segregation, separation, retirement. *(ANT.) fellowship, union, connection, association, communion.*

secondary *(SYN.)* minor, poorer, inferior, lower, subordinate. *(ANT.) greater, higher, superior.*

secret *(SYN.)* concealed, hidden, latent, covert, private, surreptitious, unknown. *(ANT.) disclosed, exposed, known, obvious, conspicuous, open, public.*

secrete *(SYN.)* clothe, conceal, cover, cloak, curtain, envelop, disguise, hide, mask, guard, protect, shroud, veil. *(ANT.) divulge, reveal, expose, unveil.*

sect *(SYN.)* segment, denomination, faction, group.

section *(SYN.)* district, country, domain, dominion, division, land, place, province, territory, subdivision.

secular *(SYN.)* lay, earthly, laic, mundane, temporal, profane, worldly, temporal. *(ANT.) religious, spiritual, unworldly, ecclesiastical.*

secure *(SYN.)* certain, definite, fixed, assured, indubitable, positive, inevitable, undeniable, sure, unquestionable, firm, *(ANT.) probable, questionable, uncertain, doubtful, loose, endangered, free.*

security *(SYN.)* bond, earnest, pawn, bail, guaranty, pledge, token, surety.

sedate *(SYN.)* controlled, serene, calm, composed, unruffled.

sediment *(SYN.)* residue, lees, dregs, grounds.

see *(SYN.)* contemplate, descry, behold, discern, espy, distinguish, glimpse, inspect, look at, observe, perceive, scan, watch, view, witness, regard, examine, study, notice, eye.

seek *(SYN.)* explore, hunt, examine, look, investigate, probe, ransack, search, scour, rummage, scrutinize.

seem *(SYN.)* look, appear,

segment

assume, suggest, resemble, pretend. (ANT.) exist, be, disappear, withdraw, vanish.

segment (SYN.) apportionment, division, fragment, moiety, allotment, part, portion, piece, scrap, share, section, element, faction, ingredient, interest, side. (ANT.) whole, entirety.

segregate (SYN.) exclude, separate. (ANT.) include, combine.

seize (SYN.) check, detain, hinder, apprehend, arrest, obstruct, stop, restrain, withhold, grab, grasp, clutch. (ANT.) free, liberate, release, activate, discharge, loosen.

seldom (SYN.) infrequently, scarcely, rarely.

select (SYN.) cull, opt, pick, choose, elect, prefer. (ANT.) reject, refuse.

selection (SYN.) election, choice, alternative, option, preference.

self-denial (SYN.) abstinence, continence, abstention, forbearance, fasting, sobriety, moderation, temperance. (ANT.) gluttony, excess, greed, intoxication, self-indulgence.

self-important (SYN.) egotistical, proud, conceited, egocentric.

self-indulgence (SYN.) egotism, narrowness, self-centeredness, self-seeking, stinginess. (ANT.) charity, magnanimity, altruism, liberality.

selfish (SYN.) narrow, self-centered, self-seeking, mercenary, stingy, ungenerous, greedy, mean, miserly. (ANT.) charitable.

self-satisfied (SYN.) smug, complacent.

sell (SYN.) market, retail, merchandise, vend, trade, barter.

send (SYN.) discharge, emit, dispatch, cast, propel, impel, throw, transmit, forward, ship, convey, mail. (ANT.) get, hold, retain, receive, bring.

senescence (SYN.) dotage, senility, age, seniority. (ANT.) infancy, youth, childhood.

senile (SYN.) antiquated, antique, aged, ancient, archaic, obsolete, old, elderly, old-fashioned, venerable. (ANT.) new, youthful, young, modern.

senior (SYN.) superior, older, elder. (ANT.) minor, junior.

sensation (SYN.) feeling, image, impression, apprehension, sense, sensibility, perception, sensitiveness. (ANT.) insensibility, torpor, stupor, apathy.

sensational (SYN.) exciting, marvelous, superb, thrilling, startling, spectacular.

sense (SYN.) drift, connotation, explanation, gist, implication, intent, import, interpretation, purport, meaning, purpose, signification, significance, sensation, perception, feeling, awareness, insight, consciousness, appreciate, discern, perceive.

senseless (SYN.) dense, dull, crass, brainless, dumb, obtuse, foolish, stupid. (ANT.) discerning, intelligent, alert, clever, bright.

sensibility (SYN.) sensation, emotion, feeling, passion, tenderness, sentiment. (ANT.) coldness, imperturbability, anesthesia, insensibility, fact.

sensible (SYN.) apprehensible, perceptible, appreciable, alive, aware, awake, cognizant, comprehending, perceiving, conscious, sentient, intelligent, discreet, practical, judicious, prudent, sagacious, reasonable, sage, sober, wise, sound. (ANT.) impalpable, imperceptible, absurd, stupid, unaware, foolish.

sensitive (SYN.) perceptive, prone, impressionable, responsive, susceptible, sentient, tender, sore, delicate, tender, tense, touchy, nervous, keen. (ANT.) dull, hard, callous, insensitive.

sensual (SYN.) lascivious, earthy, lecherous, carnal, sensory, voluptuous, wanton, erotic, lustful, sexual, indecent. (ANT.) chaste, ascetic, abstemious, virtuous, continent.

sentence (SYN.) convict, condemn. (ANT.) acquit, pardon, absolve.

sentiment (SYN.) affection, emotion, sensation, feeling, sensibility, passion, tenderness, impression, opinion, attitude. (ANT.) coldness, imperturbability, insensibility, fact.

sentimental (SYN.) extravagant, fanciful, fantastic, dreamy, fictitious, idealistic, ideal, maudlin, imaginative, mawkish, poetic, romantic, picturesque. (ANT.) literal, practical, prosaic.

separate (SYN.) part, sever, sunder, divide, allot, dispense, share, distribute, disconnect, split, isolate, segregate, different, distinct, independent. (ANT.) convene, join, gather, combine.

separation (SYN.) insulation,

isolation, loneliness, alienation, quarantine, seclusion, retirement, solitude, segregation, withdrawal. (ANT.) communion, fellowship, union, association, connection.

sequence (SYN.) chain, graduation, order, progression, arrangement, following, series, succession, train, string.

serene (SYN.) composed, imperturbable, calm, dispassionate, pacific, placid, peaceful, quiet, tranquil, still, undisturbed, unruffled. (ANT.) frantic, turbulent, wild, excited, stormy, agitated, turbulent.

serenity (SYN.) calmness, hush, calm, quiet, peace, quiescence, quietude, rest, repose, stillness, silence, tranquillity. (ANT.) tumult, excitement, noise, agitation.

series (SYN.) following, chain, arrangement, graduation, progression, order, sequence, train, string.

serious (SYN.) important, momentous, great, earnest, grave, sedate, sober, staid, alarming, solemn, critical, dangerous, risky, solemn. (ANT.) trivial, informal, relaxed, small.

servant (SYN.) attendant, butler, domestic, valet, manservant, maid.

serve (SYN.) assist, attend, help, succor, advance, benefit, forward, answer, promote, content, satisfy, suffice, supply, distribute, wait on, aid. (ANT.) command, direct, dictate, mule.

service (SYN.) advantage, account, avail, benefit, behalf, favor, good, gain, profit, interest. (ANT.) distress, calamity, trouble, handicap.

serviceable (SYN.) beneficial, good, helpful, advantageous, profitable, salutary, wholesome, useful. (ANT.) destructive, deleterious, detrimental, injurious, harmful.

servile (SYN.) base, contemptible, despicable, abject, groveling, dishonorable, ignominious, ignoble, lowly, low, menial, mean, sordid, vulgar, vile. (ANT.) honored, exalted, lofty, esteemed, righteous, noble.

servitude (SYN.) confinement, captivity, bondage, imprisonment, slavery. (ANT.) liberation, freedom.

set (SYN.) deposit, dispose, lay, arrange, place, put,

position, pose, station, appoint, fix, assign, settle, establish. (ANT.) mislay, misplace, disturb, remove, disarrange.

settle (SYN.) close, conclude, adjudicate, decide, end, resolve, agree upon, establish, satisfy, pay, lodge, locate, reside, determine, abide, terminate. (ANT.) suspend, hesitate, doubt, vacillate, waver.

settlement (SYN.) completion, close, end, finale, issue, conclusion, termination, deduction, decision, inference. (ANT.) commencement, prelude, start, inception, beginning.

sever (SYN.) part, divide, sunder, split, cut, separate. (ANT.) convene, connect, gather, join, unite, combine.

several (SYN.) some, few, a handful.

severe (SYN.) arduous, distressing, acute, exacting, hard, harsh, intense, relentless, rigorous, sharp, stem, rigid, stringent, strict, cruel, firm, unyielding, unmitigated, difficult, unpleasant, dangerous, violent. (ANT.) genial, indulgent, lenient, yielding, merciful, considerate.

sew (SYN.) mend, patch, fix, stitch, refit, restore, repair.

shabby (SYN.) indigent, impecunious, needy, penniless, worn, ragged, destitute, poor, threadbare, deficient, inferior, scanty. (ANT.) rich, wealthy, ample, affluent, opulent, right, sufficient, good.

shack (SYN.) hovel, hut, shanty, shed.

shackle (SYN.) chain, fetter, handcuff.

shade (SYN.) complexion, dye, hue, paint, color, stain, pigment, darkness, shadow, tincture, dusk, gloom, blacken, darken, conceal, screen, tint, tinge. (ANT.) transparency, paleness.

shadowy (SYN.) dark, dim, gloomy, murky, black, obscure, dusky, unilluminated, dismal, evil, gloomy, sinister, indistinct, hidden, vague, undefined, wicked, indefinite, mystic, secret, occult. (ANT.) bright, clear, light, pleasant, lucid.

shady (SYN.) shifty, shaded, questionable, doubtful, devious.

shaggy (SYN.) hairy, unkempt, uncombed, woolly.

shake (SYN.) flutter, jar, jolt, quake, agitate, quiver, shiver, shudder, rock, totter, sway, tremble, vibrate, waver.

silence

shaky (SYN.) questionable, uncertain, iffy, faltering, unsteady. (ANT.) sure, definite, positive, certain.

shallow (SYN.) exterior, cursory, flimsy, frivolous, slight, imperfect, superficial. (ANT.) complete, deep, abstruse, profound, thorough.

sham (SYN.) affect, act, feign, assume, pretend, simulate, profess. (ANT.) exhibit, display, reveal, expose.

shame (SYN.) chagrin, humiliation, abashment, disgrace, mortification, dishonor, ignominy, embarrassment, disrepute, odium, mortify, humiliate, abash, humble, opprobrium, scandal. (ANT.) pride, glory, praise, honor.

shameful (SYN.) disgraceful, dishonorable, disreputable, discreditable, humiliating, ignominious, scandalous. (ANT.) honorable, renowned, respectable, esteemed.

shameless (SYN.) unembarrassed, unashamed, brazen, bold, impudent. (ANT.) demure, modest.

shape (SYN.) create, construct, forge, fashion, form, make, produce, mold, constitute, compose, arrange, combine, organize, frame, outline, figure, invent, appearance, pattern, cast, model, devise. (ANT.) disfigure, misshape, dismantle, wreck.

shapeless (SYN.) rough, amorphous, vague.

shapely (SYN.) attractive, well-formed, curvy, alluring. (ANT.) shapeless.

share (SYN.) parcel, bit, part, division, portion, ration, piece, fragment, allotment, partake, apportion, participate, divide, section. (ANT.) whole.

shared (SYN.) joint, common, reciprocal, correlative, mutual.

sharp (SYN.) biting, pointed, cunning, acute, keen, rough, fine, cutting, shrill, pungent, witty, acrid, blunt, steep, shrewd. (ANT.) gentle, bland, shallow, smooth, blunt.

sharpen (SYN.) whet, hone, strop.

shatter (SYN.) crack, rend, break, pound, smash, burst, demolish, shiver, infringe. (ANT.) renovate, join, repair, mend.

shattered (SYN.) fractured, destroyed, reduced, separated, broken, smashed, flattened, rent, wrecked. (ANT.) united, integral, whole.

shawl (SYN.) stole, scarf.

sheepish (SYN.) coy, embarrassed, shy, humble, abashed, diffident, timid, modest, timorous. (ANT.) daring, outgoing, adventurous, gregarious.

sheer (SYN.) thin, transparent, clear, simple, utter, absolute, abrupt, steep, see-through.

sheet (SYN.) leaf, layer, coating, film.

shelter (SYN.) retreat, safety, cover, asylum, protection, sanctuary, harbor, guard, haven, security. (ANT.) unveil, expose, bare.

shield (SYN.) envelop, cover, clothe, curtain, protest, protection, cloak, guard, conceal, defense, shelter, hide, screen, veil, shroud. (ANT.) unveil, divulge, reveal, bare.

shift (SYN.) move, modify, transfer, substitute, vary, change, alter, spell, turn, transfigure. (ANT.) settle, establish.

shifting (SYN.) wavering, inconstant, changeable, fitful, variable, fickle. (ANT.) uniform, stable, unchanging.

shiftless (SYN.) idle, lazy, slothful. (ANT.) energetic.

shifty (SYN.) shrewd, crafty, tricky.

shilly-shally (SYN.) fluctuate, waver, hesitate, vacillate.

shimmer (SYN.) glimmer, shine, gleam. (ANT.) dull.

shine (SYN.) flicker, glisten, glow, blaze, glare, flash, beam, shimmer, glimmer, radiate, brush, polish, twinkle, buff, luster, gloss, scintillate, radiance, gleam.

shining (SYN.) dazzling, illustrious, showy, superb, brilliant, effulgent, magnificent, splendid, bright. (ANT.) ordinary, dull.

shiny (SYN.) bright, glossy, polished, glistening. (ANT.) lusterless, dull.

shipshape (SYN.) clean, neat. (ANT.) sloppy, messy.

shiver (SYN.) quiver, quake, quaver, tremble, shudder, shake, break, shatter.

shock (SYN.) disconcert, astonish, surprise, astound, amaze, clash, disturbance, bewilder, outrage, horrify, revolt, agitation, stagger, blow, impact, collision, surprise, startle, upset, stun.

shocking (SYN.) hideous, frightful, severe, appalling, horrible, awful, terrible, dire, fearful. (ANT.) safe, happy, secure, joyous.

shore (SYN.) seaside, beach, coast. (ANT.) inland.

short (SYN.) abrupt, squat, concise, brief, low, curtailed, dumpy, terse, inadequate, succinct, dwarfed, small, abbreviated, lacking, abridge, condensed, undersized, slight, little. (ANT.) extended, protracted.

shortage (SYN.) deficiency, deficit, shortfall. (ANT.) surplus, enough.

shortcoming (SYN.) error, vice, blemish, failure, flaw, omission, failing. (ANT.) perfection, completeness.

shorten (SYN.) curtail, limit, cut, abbreviate, reduce, abridge, lessen, restrict. (ANT.) lengthen, elongate.

shortening (SYN.) reduction, abridgment, abbreviation. (ANT.) enlargement, amplification.

short-handed (SYN.) understaffed.

shortly (SYN.) soon, directly, presently.

shortsighted (SYN.) myopic, nearsighted, unimaginative, unthinking, thoughtless.

shout (SYN.) ejaculate, cry, yell, roar, vociferate, bellow, exclaim. (ANT.) whisper.

shove (SYN.) propel, drive, urge, crowd, jostle, force, push, promote. (ANT.) retreat, falter, oppose, drag, halt.

shovel (SYN.) spade.

show (SYN.) flourish, parade, point, reveal, explain, array, movie, production, display, exhibit, note, spectacle, demonstrate, entertainment, tell, usher, guide, prove, indicate, present, lead, demonstration.

showy (SYN.) ceremonious, stagy, affected, theatrical, artificial. (ANT.) unaffected, modest, unemotional, subdued.

shred (SYN.) particle, speck, iota, mite, bit, smidgen, tear, slit, cleave, rip, disunite, wound, rend, mince, tatter, lacerate. (ANT.) bulk, unite, quantity, mend, aggregate, repair.

shrewd (SYN.) cunning, covert, artful, stealthy, foxy, astute, ingenious, guileful, crafty, sly, surreptitious, wily, tricky, clever, intelligent, clandestine. (ANT.) frank, sincere, candid, open.

shriek (SYN.) screech, scream, howl, yell.

shrill (SYN.) keen, penetrating, sharp, acute, piercing, severe. (ANT.) gentle, bland, shallow.

shrink (SYN.) diminish, shrivel, dwindle.

shrivel (SYN.) wizen, waste, droop, decline, sink, dry, languish, wither. (ANT.) renew, refresh, revive, rejuvenate.

shun (SYN.) escape, avert, forestall, avoid, forbear, evade, ward, elude, dodge, free. (ANT.) encounter, confront, meet.

shut (SYN.) seal, finish, stop, close, terminate, conclude, clog, end, obstruct. (ANT.) begin, open, start, unbar, inaugurate, unlock, commence.

shy (SYN.) reserved, fearful, bashful, retiring, cautious, demure, timid, shrinking, wary, chary. (ANT.) brazen, bold, immodest, self-confident, audacious.

sick (SYN.) ill, morbid, ailing, unhealthy, diseased, unwell, infirm. (ANT.) sound, well, robust, strong.

sickness (SYN.) illness, ailment, disease, complaint, disorder. (ANT.) soundness, healthiness, vigor.

side (SYN.) surface, face, foe, opponent, rival, indirect, secondary, unimportant.

siege (SYN.) blockade.

sieve (SYN.) screen, strainer, colander.

sight (SYN.) eyesight, vision, scene, view, display, spectacle, eyesore.

sightless (SYN.) unmindful, oblivious, blind, unseeing, heedless, ignorant. (ANT.) sensible, discerning, aware, perceiving.

sign (SYN.) omen, mark, emblem, token, suggestion, indication, clue, hint, approve, authorize, signal, gesture, symbol, portent.

signal (SYN.) beacon, sign, alarm.

significance (SYN.) connotation, drift, acceptation, explanation, implication, gist, importance, interpretation, intent, weight, meaning, purpose, purport, sense.

significant (SYN.) grave, important, critical, material, indicative, meaningful, crucial, momentous, telling, vital, weighty. (ANT.) irrelevant, insignificant, meaningless, unimportant, negligible.

signify (SYN.) designate, imply, denote, intimate, reveal, indicate, manifest, mean, communicate, show, specify. (ANT.) distract, divert, mislead, conceal.

silence (SYN.) motionless, peaceful, placid, hushed, stillness, quiescent, still,

91

soundlessness, quiet, tranquil, noiselessness, hush, muteness, undisturbed. (*ANT.*) *strident, loud, racket, disturbed, clamor, agitated.*

silent (*SYN.*) dumb, hushed, mute, calm, noiseless, quiet, peaceful, still, soundless, speechless, tranquil, uncommunicative, taciturn. (*ANT.*) *communicative, loud, noisy, raucous, talkative, clamorous.*

silhouette (*SYN.*) contour, delineation, brief, draft, form, figure, outline, profile, plan, sketch.

silly (*SYN.*) asinine, brainless, crazy, absurd, foolish, irrational, witless, nonsensical, simple, ridiculous, stupid. (*ANT.*) *sane, wise, judicious, prudent.*

similar (*SYN.*) alike, akin, allied, comparable, analogous, correlative, corresponding, correspondent, parallel, resembling, like. (*ANT.*) *dissimilar, divergent, opposed, different, incongruous.*

similarity (*SYN.*) likeness, parity, analogy, correspondence, resemblance, similitude. (*ANT.*) *distinction, variance, difference.*

simple (*SYN.*) effortless, elementary, pure, easy, facile, mere, single, uncompounded, homely, humble, unmixed, plain, artless, naive, frank, natural, unsophisticated, open, asinine, foolish, credulous, silly. (*ANT.*) *artful, complex, intricate, adorned.*

simpleton (*SYN.*) idiot, fool, ignoramus.

simulate (*SYN.*) copy, counterfeit, duplicate, ape, imitate, impersonate, mock, mimic. (*ANT.*) *distort, diverge, alter, invent.*

sin (*SYN.*) evil, crime, iniquity, transgress, guilt, offense, ungodliness, trespass, vice, transgression, wickedness, wrong. (*ANT.*) *goodness, purity, virtue, righteousness.*

sincere (*SYN.*) earnest, frank, heartfelt, genuine, candid, honest, open, true, straightforward, faithful, truthful, upright, trustworthy, unfeigned. (*ANT.*) *hypocritical, insincere, affected, dishonest, untruthful.*

sincerity (*SYN.*) fairness, frankness, honesty, justice, candor, integrity, openness, responsibility, rectitude, uprightness. (*ANT.*) *deceit, dishonesty, cheating.*

sinful (*SYN.*) bad, corrupt,

dissolute, antisocial, immoral, licentious, profligate, evil, indecent, unprincipled, vicious. (*ANT.*) *pure, noble, virtuous.*

sing (*SYN.*) chant, croon, hum, carol, intone, lilt, warble.

singe (*SYN.*) burn, char, consume, blaze, incinerate, scorch, sear, scald. (*ANT.*) *put out, quench, extinguish.*

single (*SYN.*) individual, marked, particular, distinctive, separate, special, specific, lone, one, solitary, sole, unwed, unmarried, singular, unique. (*ANT.*) *ordinary, universal, general.*

singular (*SYN.*) exceptional, eccentric, odd, peculiar, rate, extraordinary, strange, unusual, striking, characteristic, remarkable, rare, individual, distinctive, uncommon, special. (*ANT.*) *normal, ordinary.*

sink (*SYN.*) diminish, droop, subside, hang, decline, fall, extend, downward, drop, descend. (*ANT.*) *mount, climb, soar, arise.*

sinless (*SYN.*) faultless, holy, immaculate, perfect, blameless, holy, consummate, ideal, excellent, superlative, supreme. (*ANT.*) *defective, faulty, imperfect.*

sip (*SYN.*) drink, taste, swallow.

sire (*SYN.*) breed, create, father, engender, beget, generate, procreate, originate, produce, propagate. (*ANT.*) *destroy, ill, extinguish, murder, abort.*

site (*SYN.*) place, position, location, situation, station, locality.

situation (*SYN.*) circumstance, plight, state, site, location, placement, locale, predicament, position, state, condition.

size (*SYN.*) bigness, bulk, dimensions, expanse, amplitude, measurement, area, extent, largeness, magnitude, mass, greatness, volume.

skeptic (*SYN.*) doubter, infidel, agnostic, deist, questioner, unbeliever. (*ANT.*) *believer, worshiper, adorer.*

skepticism (*SYN.*) hesitation, questioning, wavering, doubting, distrust, mistrust, suspicion. (*ANT.*) *confidence, reliance, trust.*

sketch (*SYN.*) draft, figure, form, outline, contour, delineation, drawing, picture, represent, silhouette, draw, profile.

sketchy (*SYN.*) indefinite, vague, incomplete, indistinct. (*ANT.*) *definite, detailed, complete.*

skill (*SYN.*) cunning, deftness, dexterity, ability, adroitness, cleverness, talent, readiness, skillfulness. (*ANT.*) *ineptitude, inability.*

skillful (*SYN.*) adept, clever, able, accomplished, competent, expert, ingenious, cunning, proficient, practiced, versed, skilled. (*ANT.*) *untrained, inept, clumsy, inexpert, bungling, awkward.*

skimpy (*SYN.*) cheap, scanty, meager. (*ANT.*) *abundant, generous.*

skin (*SYN.*) outside, covering, peel, rind, shell, pare.

skinny (*SYN.*) gaunt, thin, raw-boned. (*ANT.*) *fat, hefty, heavy.*

skip (*SYN.*) drop, eliminate, ignore, exclude, cancel, delete, disregard, omit, overlook, neglect, miss. (*ANT.*) *notice, introduce, include, insert.*

skirmish (*SYN.*) brawl, battle, conflict, combat, dispute, encounter, contend, quarrel, squabble, scuffle, wrangle.

slack (*SYN.*) lax, limp, indefinite, free, disengaged, unbound, untied, unfastened, vague, dissolute, heedless, careless, unrestrained, limp, lazy, loose, inactive, sluggish, wanton. (*ANT.*) *restrained, tied, right, stiff, taunt, rigid, fast, inhibited.*

slander (*SYN.*) libel, calumny, backbiting, aspersion, scandal, vilification. (*ANT.*) *praise, flattery, commendation, defense.*

slang (*SYN.*) jargon, dialect.

slant (*SYN.*) disposition, inclination, bias, bent, partiality, slope, tilt, pitch, penchant, prejudice, proneness, proclivity, turn, incline, lean, tendency. (*ANT.*) *justice, fairness, impartiality, equity.*

slash (*SYN.*) gash, cut, slit, lower, reduce.

slaughter (*SYN.*) butcher, kill, massacre, slay, butchering, killing.

slave (*SYN.*) bondservant, serf.

slavery (*SYN.*) captivity, imprisonment, serfdom, confinement, bondage, thralldom, servitude, enslavement. (*ANT.*) *freedom, liberation.*

slay (*SYN.*) assassinate, kill, murder.

sleek (*SYN.*) smooth, polished, slick. (*ANT.*) *blunt,*

harsh, rough, rugged.

sleep (*SYN.*) drowse, nap, nod, catnap, repose, doze, rest, slumber, snooze.

sleepy (*SYN.*) tired, drowsy, nodding.

slender (*SYN.*) lank, lean, meager, emaciated, gaunt, scanty, rare, skinny, scrawny, slight, spare, trim, slim, tenuous, thin. (*ANT.*) *fat, broad, overweight, thick, wide, bulky.*

slide (*SYN.*) glide, slip, skim, skid.

slight (*SYN.*) lank, lean, meager, emaciated, gaunt, fine, narrow, scanty, scrawny, skinny, sparse, small, rare, slender, spare, insignificant, tenuous, unimportant, slim, thin. (*ANT.*) *regarded, notice, enormous, large, major, huge, include.*

slim (*SYN.*) thin, slender, lank, slight, weak, insignificant, unimportant.

slip (*SYN.*) error, fault, inaccuracy, shift, err, slide, mistake, glide, blunder. (*ANT.*) *precision, truth, accuracy.*

slipshod (*SYN.*) sloppy, careless. (*ANT.*) *careful.*

slit (*SYN.*) slash, cut, tear, slot.

slogan (*SYN.*) catchword, motto.

slope (*SYN.*) incline, leaning, inclination, bending, slant.

sloth (*SYN.*) indolence, idleness, inactivity, inertia, sluggishness, torpidity. (*ANT.*) *alertness, assiduousness, diligence, activity.*

slothful (*SYN.*) indolent, idle, inactive, lazy, inert, supine, sluggish, torpid. (*ANT.*) *alert, diligent, active, assiduous.*

slovenly (*SYN.*) sloppy, bedraggled, unkempt, messy. (*ANT.*) *meticulous, neat.*

slow (*SYN.*) deliberate, dull, delaying, dawdling, gradual, leisurely, tired, sluggish, unhurried, behindhand, delayed. (*ANT.*) *rapid, quick, swift, speedy, fast.*

sluggish (*SYN.*) dull, deliberate, dawdling, delaying, laggard, gradual, leisurely, tired, slow, lethargic. (*ANT.*) *quick, raid, fast, speedy, swift, energetic, vivacious.*

slumber (*SYN.*) drowse, catnap, nod, doze, repose, sleep, rest, snooze.

slump (*SYN.*) drop, decline, descent.

sly (*SYN.*) covert, artful, astute, crafty, clandestine, foxy, furtive, cunning, insidious, guileful, stealthy, subtle, shrewd, tricky, surreptitious, underhand, wily, secretive.

(ANT.) *sincere, ingenuous, open, candid.*

small (SYN.) little, minute, petty, diminutive, puny, wee, tiny, trivial, slight, miniature. (ANT.) *immense, enormous, large, huge.*

smart (SYN.) dexterous, quick, skillful, adroit, apt, clever, bright, witty, ingenious, sharp, intelligent. (ANT.) *foolish, stupid, unskilled, awkward, clumsy, bungling, slow, dumb.*

smash (SYN.) burst, crush, demolish, destroy, break, crack, fracture, pound, fringe, rack, rupture, shatter, rend. (ANT.) *mend, renovate, restore, repair.*

smear (SYN.) wipe, rub, spread.

smell (SYN.) fragrance, fume, odor, perfume, incense, aroma, fetidness, stench, stink, scent, sniff, detect, bouquet.

smidgen (SYN.) crumb, mite, small, bit, particle, shred, speck, scrap. (ANT.) *bulk, mass, quantity, aggregate.*

smile (SYN.) grin. (ANT.) *frown.*

smite (SYN.) knock, hit, dash, beat, belabor, buffet, pound, punch, pummel, thrash, thump, defeat, overthrow, overpower, subdue, vanquish, rout. (ANT.) *surrender, fail, defend, shield, stroke.*

smooth (SYN.) polished, sleek, slick, glib, diplomatic, flat, level, plain, suave, urbane, even, unwrinkled. (ANT.) *rugged, harsh, rough, blunt, bluff, uneven.*

smother (SYN.) suffocate, asphyxiate, stifle.

smutty (SYN.) disgusting, filthy, impure, coarse, dirty, lewd, offensive, obscene, pornographic. (ANT.) *modest, refined, decent, pure.*

snag (SYN.) difficulty, bar, barrier, check, hindrance, obstruction. (ANT.) *assistance, help, encouragement.*

snappish (SYN.) ill-natured, ill-tempered, fractious, irritable, fretful, peevish, testy, touchy, petulant. (ANT.) *good-tempered, pleasant, good-natured, affable, genial.*

snappy (SYN.) quick, stylish, chic.

snare (SYN.) capture, catch, arrest, clutch, grasp, grip, lay, apprehend, seize, trap, net. (ANT.) *throw, release, lose, liberate.*

snarl (SYN.) growl.

snatch (SYN.) grasp, seize, grab.

sneak (SYN.) steal, skulk, slink.

sneer (SYN.) flout, jeer, mock, gibe, deride, taunt, scoff, scorn. (ANT.) *laud, flatter, praise, compliment.*

sneering (SYN.) derision, gibe, banter, jeering, mockery, raillery, sarcasm, ridicule, satire.

sniveling (SYN.) whimpering, sniffling, weepy, whining, blubbering.

snobbish (SYN.) uppity, conceited, snobby, snotty.

snoopy (SYN.) inquisitive, interrogative, curious, inquiring, meddling, peeping, prying, peering. (ANT.) *uninterested, incurious, unconcerned, indifferent.*

snub (SYN.) rebuke, insult, slight.

snug (SYN.) constricted, close, contracted, compact, firm, narrow, taut, tense, stretched, tight, cozy, comfortable, sheltered. (ANT.) *loose, lax, slack, relaxed, open.*

soak (SYN.) saturate, drench, steep, wet.

soar (SYN.) flutter, fly, flit, float, glide, sail, hover. (ANT.) *plummet, sink, fall, descend.*

sob (SYN.) weep, cry, lament.

sober (SYN.) sedate, serious, staid, earnest, grave, solemn, moderate. (ANT.) *ordinary, joyful, informal, boisterous, drunk, fuddled, inebriated.*

sobriety (SYN.) forbearance, abstinence, abstention, self-denial, moderation, temperance. (ANT.) *self-indulgence, excess, intoxication.*

social (SYN.) friendly, civil, gregarious, affable, communicative, hospitable, sociable, group, common, genial, polite. (ANT.) *inhospitable, hermitic, antisocial, disagreeable.*

society (SYN.) nation, community, civilization, organization, club, association, fraternity, circle, association, company, companionship.

soft (SYN.) gentle, lenient, flexible, compassionate, malleable, meek, mellow, subdued, mild, tender, supple, yielding, pliable, elastic, pliant. (ANT.) *unyielding, rough, hard, tough, rigid.*

soften (SYN.) assuage, diminish, abate, allay, alleviate, mitigate, relieve, soothe. (ANT.) *irritate, increase, aggravate, agitate.*

soil (SYN.) defile, discolor,

spot, befoul, blemish, blight, stain, sully, earth, dirt, loam, dirty. (ANT.) *purify, honor, cleanse, bleach, decorate.*

solace (SYN.) contentment, ease, enjoyment, comfort, consolation, relief, succor. (ANT.) *torture, torment, misery, affliction, discomfort.*

sole (SYN.) isolated, desolate, deserted, secluded, unaided, lone, alone, only, single, solitary. (ANT.) *surrounded, accompanied, attended.*

solemn (SYN.) ceremonious, imposing, formal, impressive, reverential, ritualistic, grave, sedate, earnest, sober, staid, serious, dignified. (ANT.) *ordinary, joyful, informal, boisterous, cheerful, gay, happy.*

solicit (SYN.) beg, beseech, request, seek, pray.

solicitous (SYN.) anxious, concerned.

solicitude (SYN.) concern, worry, anxiety, care, attention, regard, vigilance, caution, wariness. (ANT.) *indifference, disregard, neglect, negligence.*

solid (SYN.) hard, dense, compact, firm. (ANT.) *loose.*

solitary (SYN.) isolated, alone, lonely, deserted, unaided, secluded, only, single, lone, sole. (ANT.) *surrounded, attended, accompanied.*

solitude (SYN.) loneliness, privacy, refuge, retirement, seclusion, retreat, alienation, asylum, concealment. (ANT.) *publicity, exposure, notoriety.*

solution (SYN.) explanation, answer.

solve (SYN.) explain, answer, unravel.

somatic (SYN.) corporeal, corporal, natural, material, bodily, physical. (ANT.) *spiritual, mental.*

somber (SYN.) dismal, dark, bleak, doleful, cheerless, natural, physical, serious, sober, gloomy, grave. (ANT.) *lively, joyous, cheerful, happy.*

sometimes (SYN.) occasionally. (ANT.) *invariably, always.*

soon (SYN.) shortly, early, betimes, beforehand. (ANT.) *tardy, late, overdue, belated.*

soothe (SYN.) encourage, console, solace, comfort, cheer, gladden, sympathize, calm, pacify. (ANT.) *dishearten, depress, antagonize, aggravate, disquiet, upset, unnerve.*

soothing (SYN.) gentle, benign, docile, calm, mild, placid, peaceful, serene, soft, relaxed, tractable, tame. (ANT.) *violent, savage, fierce,*

harsh.

sophisticated (SYN.) cultured, worldly, blase, cultivated, urbane, cosmopolitan, suave, intricate, complex, advanced. (ANT.) *uncouth, ingenuous, simple, naive, crude.*

sorcery (SYN.) enchantment, conjuring, art, charm, black magic, voodoo, witchcraft, wizardry.

sordid (SYN.) vicious, odious, revolting, obscene, foul, loathsome, base, depraved, debased, vile, vulgar, abject, wicked, ignoble, despicable, mean, low, worthless, wretched, dirty, unclean. (ANT.) *upright, decent, honorable.*

sore (SYN.) tender, sensitive, aching, hurting, painful.

sorrow (SYN.) grief, distress, heartache, anguish, misery, sadness, mourning, trial, tribulation, gloom, depression. (ANT.) *consolation, solace, joy, happiness, comfort.*

sorrowful (SYN.) dismal, doleful, dejected, despondent, depressed, disconsolate, gloomy, melancholy, glum, moody, somber, sad, grave, aggrieved. (ANT.) *merry, happy, cheerful, joyous.*

sorry (SYN.) hurt, pained, sorrowful, afflicted, grieved, contrite, repentant, paltry, poor, wretched, remorseful, mean, shabby, contemptible, worthless, vile, regretful, apologetic. (ANT.) *delighted, impenitent, cheerful, unrepentant, splendid.*

sort (SYN.) class, stamp, category, description, nature, character, kind, type, variety. (ANT.) *peculiarity, deviation.*

sound (SYN.) effective, logical, telling, binding, powerful, weighty, legal, strong, conclusive, valid. (ANT.) *weak, null, counterfeit.*

sour (SYN.) glum, sullen, bitter, peevish, acid, rancid, tart, acrimonious, sharp, bad-tempered, unpleasant, cranky. (ANT.) *wholesome, kindly, genial, benevolent, sweet.*

source (SYN.) birth, foundation, agent, determinant, reason, origin, cause, start, incentive, motive, spring, inducement, principle, beginning. (ANT.) *product, harvest, outcome, issue, consequence, end.*

souvenir (SYN.) memento, monument, commemoration, remembrance.

sovereign (SYN.) monarch, king, emperor, queen.

sovereignty (SYN.) command, influence, authority,

predominance, control, sway. (ANT.) debility, incapacity, disablement, ineptitude, impotence.

space (SYN.) room, area, location.

spacious (SYN.) capacious, large, vast, ample, extensive, wide, roomy, large. (ANT.) limited, narrow, small, cramped.

span (SYN.) spread, extent.

spare (SYN.) preserve, safeguard, uphold, conserve, protect, defend, rescue, reserve, additional, unoccupied. (ANT.) impair, abolish, injure, abandon.

sparing (SYN.) economical, thrifty, frugal. (ANT.) lavish.

sparkle (SYN.) gleam, glitter, twinkle, beam, glisten, radiate, shine, blaze.

spat (SYN.) quarrel, dispute, affray, wrangle, altercation. (ANT.) peace, friendliness, agreement, reconciliation.

spawn (SYN.) yield, bear.

speak (SYN.) declare, express, say, articulate, harangue, converse, talk, utter. (ANT.) refrain, hush, quiet.

special (SYN.) individual, uncommon, distinctive, peculiar, exceptional, unusual, extraordinary, different, particular. (ANT.) general, widespread, broad, prevailing, average, ordinary.

specialist (SYN.) authority, expert.

species (SYN.) variety, type, kind, class, sort.

specific (SYN.) limited, characteristic, definite, peculiar, explicit, categorical, particular, distinct, precise. (ANT.) generic, general, nonspecific.

specify (SYN.) name, call, mention, appoint, denominate, designate, define. (ANT.) miscall, hint.

specimen (SYN.) prototype, example, sample, model, pattern, type.

speck (SYN.) scrap, jot, bit, mite, smidgen, crumb, iota, particle, spot. (ANT.) quantity, bulk, aggregate.

spectacle (SYN.) demonstration, ostentation, movie, array, exhibition, show, display, performance, parade, splurge.

spectator (SYN.) viewer, observer.

speculate (SYN.) assume, deduce, surmise, apprehend, imagine, consider, view, think, guess, suppose, conjecture. (ANT.) prove, demonstrate, conclude.

speech (SYN.) gossip, discourse, talk, chatter, lecture, conference, discussion, address, dialogue, articulation, accent. (ANT.) silence, correspondence, writing, meditation.

speed (SYN.) forward, push, accelerate, hasten, rapidity, dispatch, swiftness. (ANT.) impede, slow, block, retard.

spellbound (SYN.) fascinated, entranced, hypnotized, mesmerized, rapt.

spend (SYN.) pay, disburse, consume. (ANT.) hoard, save.

spendthrift (SYN.) squanderer, profligate.

sphere (SYN.) globe, orb, ball, environment, area, domain.

spherical (SYN.) round, curved, globular.

spicy (SYN.) hot, indecent, off-color, suggestive, indelicate.

spin (SYN.) revolve, turn, rotate, whirl, twirl, tell, narrate, relate.

spine (SYN.) vertebrae, backbone.

spineless (SYN.) weak, limp, cowardly. (ANT.) brave, strong, courageous.

spirit (SYN.) courage, phantom, verve, fortitude, apparition, mood, soul, ghost. (ANT.) listlessness, substance, languor.

spirited (SYN.) excited, animated, lively, active, vigorous, energetic. (ANT.) indolent, lazy, sleepy.

spiritless (SYN.) gone, lifeless, departed, dead, insensible, deceased, unconscious. (ANT.) stirring, alive, living.

spiritual (SYN.) sacred, unearthly, holy, divine, immaterial, supernatural. (ANT.) material, physical, corporeal.

spite (SYN.) grudge, rancor, malice, animosity, malevolence, malignity. (ANT.) kindness, toleration, affection.

spiteful (SYN.) vicious, disagreeable, surly, ill-natured. (ANT.) pretty, beautiful, attractive, fair.

splendid (SYN.) glorious, illustrious, radiant, brilliant, showy, superb, bright. (ANT.) ordinary, mediocre, dull.

splendor (SYN.) effulgence, radiance, brightness, luster, magnificence, display. (ANT.) darkness, obscurity, dullness.

splinter (SYN.) fragment, piece, sliver, chip, shiver.

split (SYN.) rend, shred, cleave, disunite, sever, break, divide, opening, lacerate. (ANT.) repair, unite, join, sew.

spoil (SYN.) rot, disintegrate, waste, decay, ruin, damage, mold, destroy. (ANT.) luxuriate, grow, flourish.

spoken (SYN.) verbal, pronounced, articulated, vocal, uttered, oral. (ANT.) written, documentary.

spokesman (SYN.) agent, representative.

spontaneous (SYN.) impulsive, voluntary, automatic, instinctive, willing, extemporaneous, natural, unconscious. (ANT.) planned, rehearsed, forced, studied, prepared.

sport (SYN.) match, play, amusement, fun, pastime, entertainment, athletics.

sporting (SYN.) considerate, fair, sportsmanlike.

spot (SYN.) blemish, mark, stain, flaw, blot, location, place, site, splatter.

spotty (SYN.) erratic, uneven, irregular, inconsistent. (ANT.) regular, even.

spout (SYN.) spurt, squirt, tube, nozzle.

spray (SYN.) splash, spatter, sprinkle.

spread (SYN.) unfold, distribute, open, disperse, unroll, unfurl, scatter, jelly. (ANT.) shut, close, hide, conceal.

sprightly (SYN.) blithe, hopeful, vivacious, buoyant, lively, light, nimble. (ANT.) hopeless, depressed, sullen, dejected, despondent.

spring (SYN.) commencement, foundation, start, beginning, inception, jump, cradle, begin, birth, bound, originate. (ANT.) issue, product, end.

sprinkle (SYN.) strew, spread, scatter, rain.

spruce (SYN.) orderly, neat, trim, clear, nice. (ANT.) unkempt, sloppy, dirty.

spry (SYN.) brisk, quick, agile, nimble, energetic, supple, alert, active, lively. (ANT.) heavy, sluggish, inert, clumsy.

spur (SYN.) inducement, purpose, cause, motive, impulse, reason, incitement. (ANT.) effort, action, result, attempt.

squabble (SYN.) bicker, debate, altercate, contend, discuss, argue, quarrel. (ANT.) concede, agree, assent.

squalid (SYN.) base, indecent, grimy, dirty, pitiful, filthy, muddy, nasty. (ANT.) wholesome, clean, pure.

squander (SYN.) scatter, lavish, consume, dissipate, misuse. (ANT.) preserve, conserve, save, accumulate.

squeamish (SYN.) particular, careful.

stab (SYN.) stick, gore, pierce, knife, spear, bayonet.

stability (SYN.) steadiness, balance, proportion, composure, symmetry. (ANT.) imbalance, fall, unsteadiness.

stable (SYN.) firm, enduring, constant, fixed, unwavering, steadfast, steady. (ANT.) irresolute, variable, changeable.

stack (SYN.) mass, pile, mound, heap, accumulate.

staff (SYN.) pole, stick, club, personnel, crew, employees.

stage (SYN.) frame, platform, boards, theater, scaffold, period, phase, step, direct, produce, present.

stagger (SYN.) totter, sway, reel, vary, falter, alternate.

staid (SYN.) solemn, sedate, earnest, sober, grave. (ANT.) joyful, informal, ordinary.

stain (SYN.) blight, dye, tint, befoul, spot, defile, mark, dishonor, disgrace, smirch, blot, tint, blemish, discolor, color, tinge. (ANT.) honor, bleach, decorate, purify.

stair (SYN.) staircase, stairway, steps.

stake (SYN.) rod, pole, picket, post, pale, bet, wager, concern, interest.

stale (SYN.) tasteless, spoiled, old, inedible, dry, uninteresting, trite, flat, dull, vapid, insipid. (ANT.) new, fresh, tasty.

stalk (SYN.) dog, follow, track, shadow, hunt.

stall (SYN.) hesitate, stop, delay, postpone.

stammer (SYN.) falter, stutter.

stamp (SYN.) crush, trample, imprint, mark, brand, block, seal, die.

stand (SYN.) tolerate, suffer, stay, stand up, endure, bear, abide, halt, arise, rise, remain, sustain, rest. (ANT.) run, yield, advance.

standard (SYN.) law, proof, pennant, emblem, touchstone, measure, example, gauge, model, banner, symbol, test. (ANT.) guess, chance, irregular, unusual, supposition.

standing (SYN.) rank, position, station, status.

standpoint (SYN.) position, viewpoint, attitude.

staple (SYN.) main, principal, chief, essential, necessary.

stare (SYN.) gaze.

stark (SYN.) utter, absolute, sheer, complete, rough, severe, harsh, grim.

start (SYN.) opening, source,

commence, onset, surprise, shock, beginning, origin, begin, initiate, jerk, jump, advantage, lead, commencement, outset. (ANT.) end, completion, termination, close.

startle (SYN.) astonish, disconcert, aback, alarm, shock, agitate, surprise, astound, amaze, stun. (ANT.) caution, prepare, admonish, forewarn.

starved (SYN.) longing, voracious, hungry, craving, avid, famished. (ANT.) satisfied, sated, gouged, full.

state (SYN.) circumstance, predicament, case, situation, condition, affirm, declare, express, nation, country, status, assert, recite, tell, recount. (ANT.) imply, conceal, retract.

stately (SYN.) lordly, elegant, regal, sovereign, impressive, magnificent, courtly, grand, imposing, majestic, noble, supreme, dignified. (ANT.) low, common, mean, servile, humble, vulgar.

statement (SYN.) announcement, mention, allegation, declaration, thesis, assertion, report.

station (SYN.) post, depot, terminal, position, place.

statuesque (SYN.) imposing, stately, regal, majestic, dignified.

status (SYN.) place, caste, standing, condition, state, rank, position.

statute (SYN.) law, ruling, decree, rule. (ANT.) intention, deliberation.

staunch (SYN.) faithful, true, constant, reliable, loyal, devoted. (ANT.) treacherous, untrustworthy.

stay (SYN.) delay, continue, hinder, check, hold, hindrance, support, brace, line, rope, linger, sojourn, abide, halt, stand, rest, remain, tarry, arrest, wait. (ANT.) hasten, progress, go, depart, advance, leave.

stead (SYN.) place.

steadfast (SYN.) solid, inflexible, constant, stable, unyielding, secure. (ANT.) unstable, insecure, unsteady.

steadfastness (SYN.) persistence, industry, tenacity, constancy, persistency. (ANT.) laziness, sloth, cessation.

steady (SYN.) regular, even, unremitting, stable, steadfast, firm, reliable, solid.

steal (SYN.) rob, swipe, burglarize, pilfer, shoplift, embezzle, snitch. (ANT.) restore, buy, return, refund.

stealthy (SYN.) sly, secret, furtive. (ANT.) direct, open, obvious.

steep (SYN.) sharp, hilly, sheer, abrupt, perpendicular, precipitous. (ANT.) gradual, level, flat.

steer (SYN.) manage, guide, conduct, lead, supervise, navigate, drive, control, direct.

stem (SYN.) stalk, trunk, arise, check, stop, originate, hinder.

stench (SYN.) odor, fetor, fetidness, stink, aroma, smell, fume, scent.

step (SYN.) stride, pace, stage, move, action, measure, come, go, walk.

stern (SYN.) harsh, rigid, exacting, rigorous, sharp, severe, strict, hard, unyielding, unmitigated, stringent. (ANT.) indulgent, forgiving, yielding, lenient, considerate.

stew (SYN.) ragout, goulash, boil, simmer.

stick (SYN.) stalk, twig, rod, staff, pole, pierce, spear, stab, puncture, gore, cling, adhere, hold, catch, abide, remain, persist.

stickler (SYN.) nitpicker, perfectionist, disciplinarian.

sticky (SYN.) tricky, delicate, awkward.

stiff (SYN.) severe, unbendable, unyielding, harsh, inflexible, unbending, rigid, firm, hard, solid, rigorous. (ANT.) supple, yielding, compassionate, mild, lenient, resilient.

stifle (SYN.) choke, strangle, suffocate.

stigma (SYN.) trace, scar, blot, stain, mark, vestige.

still (SYN.) peaceful, undisturbed, but, mild, hushed, calm, patient, modest, nevertheless, motionless, meek, quiescent, stationary, besides, however, quiet, hush, tranquil, serene, placid. (ANT.) agitated, loud.

stimulate (SYN.) irritate, excite, arouse, disquiet, rouse, activate, urge, invigorate, animate, provoke. (ANT.) quell, calm, quiet.

stimulus (SYN.) motive, goad, arousal, provocation, encouragement. (ANT.) discouragement, depressant.

stingy (SYN.) greedy, penurious, avaricious, mean, penny-pinching, cheap, selfish, miserly, tight, tightfisted. (ANT.) munificent, generous, giving, extravagant, open-handed, bountiful.

stipend (SYN.) payment, earnings, salary, allowance, pay, compensation, wages. (ANT.) gratuity, gift.

stipulate (SYN.) require, demand.

stir (SYN.) instigate, impel, push, agitate, induce, mix, rouse, move, propel. (ANT.) halt, stop, deter.

stock (SYN.) hoard, store, strain, accumulation, supply, carry, keep, provision, fund, breed, sort. (ANT.) sameness, likeness, homogeneity, uniformity.

stoical (SYN.) passive, forbearing, uncomplaining, composed, patient. (ANT.) turbulent, chafing, hysterical.

stolid (SYN.) obtuse, unsharpened, dull, blunt, edgeless. (ANT.) suave, tactful, polished, subtle.

stone (SYN.) pebble, gravel, rock.

stony (SYN.) insensitive, unsentimental, cold.

stoop (SYN.) bow, bend, lean, crouch.

stop (SYN.) terminate, check, abstain, hinder, arrest, close, bar, cork, halt, end, conclude, obstruct, finish, quit, pause, discontinue, stay, impede, cease. (ANT.) start, proceed, speed, begin.

store (SYN.) amass, hoard, collect, market, shop, reserve, supply, deposit, bank, save, accrue, increase, stock. (ANT.) dissipate, waste, disperse.

storm (SYN.) gale, tempest, tornado, thunderstorm, hurricane, rage, rant, assault, besiege.

stormy (SYN.) rough, inclement, windy, blustery, roaring, tempestuous. (ANT.) quiet, calm, tranquil, peaceful.

story (SYN.) yarn, novel, history, tale, falsehood, account, fable, anecdote, narrative, fabrication, lie, level, floor, fiction, report.

stout (SYN.) plump, obese, chubby, fat, paunchy, overweight, portly, heavy, sturdy, strong, pudgy, thickset. (ANT.) thin, slender, flimsy, gaunt, slim.

straight (SYN.) erect, honorable, square, just, direct, undeviating, unbent, right, upright, honest, uncurving, directly, moral, correct, orderly, vertical. (ANT.) dishonest, bent, circuitous, twisted, crooked.

straightforward (SYN.) forthright, direct, open, candid, aboveboard. (ANT.) devious.

strain (SYN.) stock, kind, variety, stretch, breed, tighten, harm, injure, screen, filter, sprain, sort.

strainer (SYN.) colander, sieve, filter.

strait (SYN.) fix, situation, passage, condition, dilemma, channel, trouble, predicament, difficulty, distress, crisis. (ANT.) ease, calmness, satisfaction, comfort.

strange (SYN.) bizarre, peculiar, odd, abnormal, irregular, unusual, curious, uncommon, singular, extraordinary, foreign, eccentric, unfamiliar, queer. (ANT.) regular, common, familiar, conventional.

stranger (SYN.) foreigner, outsider, newcomer, alien, outlander, immigrant. (ANT.) friend, associate, acquaintance.

strap (SYN.) strip, belt, thong, band.

stratagem (SYN.) design, ruse, cabal, plot, machination, subterfuge, trick, wile, conspiracy.

strategy (SYN.) technique, management, tactics, approach.

stray (SYN.) ramble, rove, deviate, lost, strayed, wander, digress, roam, stroll. (ANT.) linger, stop, halt, settle.

stream (SYN.) issue, proceed, flow, come, abound, spout, run, brook.

street (SYN.) way, road, boulevard, avenue.

strength (SYN.) power, might, toughness, durability, soundness, vigor, potency. (ANT.) weakness, frailty, feebleness.

strengthen (SYN.) verify, assure, confirm, fix, sanction, ratify, substantiate.

strenuous (SYN.) forceful, energetic, active, vigorous, determined.

stress (SYN.) urgency, press, emphasize, accentuate, accent, weight, strain, importance, compulsion, pressure. (ANT.) relaxation, lenience, ease.

stretch (SYN.) strain, expand, elongate, extend, lengthen, spread, distend, protract, distort. (ANT.) tighten, loosen, slacken, contract.

strict (SYN.) rough, stiff, stringent, harsh, unbending, severe, rigorous. (ANT.) easygoing, lenient, mild.

strife (SYN.) disagreement, conflict, discord, quarrel, difference, unrest. (ANT.) tranquillity, peace, concord.

strike (SYN.) pound, hit, smite, beat, assault, attack, affect, impress, overwhelm, sit down, walkout, slowdown.

striking (SYN.) arresting, imposing, splendid, august, impressive, thrilling, stirring, awesome, awe-inspiring. (ANT.) ordinary, unimpressive, commonplace, regular.

stringent (SYN.) harsh, rugged, grating, severe, gruff.

strip (SYN.) disrobe, undress, remove, uncover, peel, ribbon, band, piece.

stripped (SYN.) open, simple, bare, nude, uncovered, exposed, bald, plain, naked, barren, defenseless. (ANT.) protected, dressed, concealed.

strive (SYN.) aim, struggle, attempt, undertake, design, endeavor, try. (ANT.) omit, abandon, neglect, decline.

stroke (SYN.) rap, blow, tap, knock, feat, achievement, accomplishment, caress.

stroll (SYN.) amble, walk, ramble.

strong (SYN.) potent, hale, athletic, mighty, sturdy, impregnable, resistant. (ANT.) feeble, insipid, brittle, weak, bland, fragile.

structure (SYN.) construction, framework, arrangement.

struggle (SYN.) fray, strive, fight, contest, battle, skirmish, oppose, clash. (ANT.) peace, agreement, truce.

stubborn (SYN.) obstinate, firm, determined, inflexible, obdurate, uncompromising, pigheaded, contumacious, rigid, unbending, intractable. (ANT.) docile, yielding, amenable, submissive.

student (SYN.) pupil, observer, disciple, scholar, learner.

studio (SYN.) workroom, workshop.

study (SYN.) weigh, muse, master, contemplate, reflect, examination, examine.

stuff (SYN.) thing, subject, material, theme, matter, substance, fill, ram, cram, pack, textile, cloth, topic.

stumble (SYN.) sink, collapse, tumble, drop, topple, lurch, trip, fall. (ANT.) steady, climb, soar, arise.

stun (SYN.) shock, knock out, dumbfound, take, amaze, alarm. (ANT.) forewarn, caution, prepare.

stunning (SYN.) brilliant, dazzling, exquisite, ravishing. (ANT.) drab, ugly.

stunt (SYN.) check, restrict, hinder.

stupid (SYN.) dull, obtuse, half-witted, brainless, foolish, dumb, witless, idiotic. (ANT.) smart, intelligent, clever, quick, bright, alert, discerning.

stupor (SYN.) lethargy, torpor, daze, languor, drowsiness, numbness. (ANT.) wakefulness, liveliness, activity.

sturdy (SYN.) hale, strong, rugged, stout, mighty, enduring, hardy, well-built. (ANT.) fragile, brittle, insipid, delicate.

style (SYN.) sort, type, kind, chic, smartness, elegance.

subdue (SYN.) crush, overcome, rout, beat, reduce, lower, defeat, vanquish. (ANT.) retreat, cede, surrender.

subject (SYN.) subordinate, theme, case, topic, dependent, citizen, matter.

sublime (SYN.) lofty, raised, elevated, supreme, exalted, splendid, grand. (ANT.) ordinary, vase, low, ridiculous.

submerge (SYN.) submerse, dunk, sink, dip, immerse, engage, douse, engross. (ANT.) surface, rise, uplift, elevate.

submissive (SYN.) deferential, yielding, dutiful, compliant. (ANT.) rebellious, intractable, insubordinate.

submit (SYN.) quit, resign, waive, yield, tender, offer, abdicate, cede, surrender. (ANT.) fight, oppose, resist, struggle, deny.

subordinate (SYN.) demean, reduce, inferior, assistant, citizen. (ANT.) superior.

subsequent (SYN.) later, following. (ANT.) preceding, previous.

subside (SYN.) decrease, lower, sink, droop, hang, collapse, downward. (ANT.) mount, steady, arise, climb.

subsidy (SYN.) support, aid, grant.

substance (SYN.) stuff, essence, importance, material, moment, matter. (ANT.) spirit, immaterial.

substantial (SYN.) large, considerable, sizable, actual, real, tangible, influential. (ANT.) unimportant, trivial.

substantiate (SYN.) strengthen, corroborate, confirm.

substitute (SYN.) proxy, expedient, deputy, makeshift, replacement, alternate, lieutenant, representative, surrogate, displace, exchange, equivalent. (ANT.) sovereign, master, head.

substitution (SYN.) change, mutation, vicissitude, alteration,

modification. (ANT.) uniformity, monotony.

subterfuge (SYN.) pretext, excuse, cloak, simulation, disguise, garb, pretension. (ANT.) reality, truth, actuality, sincerity.

subtle (SYN.) suggestive, indirect. (ANT.) overt, obvious.

subtract (SYN.) decrease, reduce, curtail, deduct, diminish, remove, lessen. (ANT.) expand, increase, add, enlarge, grow.

succeed (SYN.) thrive, follow, replace, achieve, win, flourish, prevail, inherit. (ANT.) flop, miscarry, anticipate, fail, precede.

success (SYN.) advance, prosperity, luck. (ANT.) failure.

successful (SYN.) fortunate, favorable, lucky, triumphant.

succession (SYN.) chain, course, series, order, string, arrangement, progression, train, following.

successive (SYN.) serial, sequential.

succinct (SYN.) pithy, curt, brief, short, compendious, terse. (ANT.) prolonged, extended, long, protracted.

succor (SYN.) ease, solace, comfort, enjoyment, consolation. (ANT.) suffering, discomfort, torture, affliction, torment.

sudden (SYN.) rapid, swift, immediate, abrupt, unexpected, unforeseen, hasty. (ANT.) slowly, anticipated.

suffer (SYN.) stand, experience, endure, bear, feel, allow, let, permit, sustain. (ANT.) exclude, banish, overcome.

suffering (SYN.) distress, ache, anguish, pain, woe, misery, torment. (ANT.) ease, relief, comfort.

sufficient (SYN.) fitting, enough, adequate, satisfactory. (ANT.) scant, deficient.

suffix (SYN.) ending. (ANT.) prefix.

suggest (SYN.) propose, offer, refer, advise, hint, insinuate, recommend, allude. (ANT.) dictate, declare, insist.

suggestion (SYN.) exhortation, recommendation, intelligence, caution, admonition, warning, advice.

suit (SYN.) conform, accommodate, fit. (ANT.) misapply, disturb.

suitable (SYN.) welcome, agreeable, acceptable, gratifying. (ANT.) offensive, disagreeable.

sullen (SYN.) fretful, morose, dismal, silent, sulky, bitter,

sad, somber, glum, gloomy, dour, moody. (ANT.) pleasant, joyous, merry.

sultry (SYN.) close, hot, stifling.

sum (SYN.) amount, total, aggregate, whole, increase, append, add. (ANT.) sample, fraction, reduce, deduct.

summarize (SYN.) abstract, abridge. (ANT.) restore, add, unite, return.

summary (SYN.) digest, outline, abstract, synopsis, concise, brief, short, compact.

summit (SYN.) peak, top, head, crest, zenith, apex, crown, pinnacle. (ANT.) bottom, foundation, base, foot.

summon (SYN.) invoke, call, invite. (ANT.) dismiss.

sundry (SYN.) miscellaneous, several, different, various, divers. (ANT.) similar, identical, alike, same, congruous.

sunny (SYN.) cheery, cheerful, fair, joyful, happy, cloudless. (ANT.) overcast, cloudy.

superannuated (SYN.) old, archaic, aged, senile, ancient, venerable, elderly. (ANT.) youthful, modern, young.

superb (SYN.) splendid, wonderful, extraordinary, marvelous.

supercilious (SYN.) contemptuous, snobbish, overbearing, vainglorious, arrogant, haughty. (ANT.) meek, ashamed, lowly.

superficial (SYN.) flimsy, shallow, cursory, slight, exterior. (ANT.) thorough, deep, abstruse, profound.

superintend (SYN.) control, govern, rule, command, manage, direct, regulate. (ANT.) ignore, follow, submit, abandon.

superintendence (SYN.) control, oversight, surveillance, management.

superintendent (SYN.) manager, supervisor, overseer, director, administrator.

superiority (SYN.) profit, mastery, advantage, good, service, edge, utility. (ANT.) harm, detriment, impediment.

superlative (SYN.) pure, consummate, sinless, blameless, holy, perfect, faultless, ideal, unqualified, immaculate. (ANT.) lacking, defective, imperfect, deficient.

supernatural (SYN.) unearthly, preternatural, marvelous, miraculous. (ANT.) plain, human, physical, common.

supervise (SYN.) rule, oversee, govern, command, direct, superintend, manage. (*ANT.*) *submit, forsake, abandon.*

supervision (*SYN.*) oversight, inspection, surveillance, charge, management.

supervisor (*SYN.*) manager, boss, foreman, director.

supplant (*SYN.*) overturn, overcome. (*ANT.*) *uphold, conserve.*

supple (*SYN.*) lithe, pliant, flexible, limber, elastic, pliable. (*ANT.*) *stiff, brittle, rigid.*

supplement (*SYN.*) extension, complement, addition, extend, add.

supplicate (*SYN.*) beg, petition, solicit, adjure, beseech, entreat, ask, pray, crave. (*ANT.*) *cede, give, bestow, grant.*

supplication (*SYN.*) invocation, plea, appeal, request, entreaty.

supply (*SYN.*) provide, inventory, hoard, reserve, store, accumulation, stock, furnish, endow, give.

support (*SYN.*) groundwork, aid, favor, base, prop, assistance, comfort, basis, succor, living, subsistence, encouragement, backing, livelihood, help. (*ANT.*) *discourage, abandon, oppose, opposition, attack.*

supporter (*SYN.*) follower, devotee, adherent, henchman, attendant, disciple, votary. (*ANT.*) *master, head, chief.*

suppose (*SYN.*) believe, presume, deduce, apprehend, think, assume, imagine, speculate, guess, conjecture. (*ANT.*) *prove, demonstrate, ascertain.*

supposition (*SYN.*) theory, conjecture. (*ANT.*) *proof, fact.*

suppress (*SYN.*) diminish, reduce, overpower, abate, lessen, decrease, subdue. (*ANT.*) *revive, amplify, intensify, enlarge.*

supremacy (*SYN.*) domination, predominance, ascendancy, sovereignty.

supreme (*SYN.*) greatest, best, highest, main, principal, cardinal, first, chief, foremost, paramount. (*ANT.*) *supplemental, minor, subsidiary, auxiliary.*

sure (*SYN.*) confident, fixed, inevitable, certain, positive, trustworthy, reliable, unquestionable, convinced, steady. (*ANT.*) *probable, uncertain, doubtful.*

surface (*SYN.*) outside, exterior, cover, covering.

surge (*SYN.*) heave, swell, grow. (*ANT.*) *wane, ebb, diminish.*

surly (*SYN.*) disagreeable, hostile, unfriendly, ugly, antagonistic.

surmise (*SYN.*) judge, think, believe, assume, suppose, presume, guess.

surpass (*SYN.*) pass, exceed, excel, outstrip, outdo.

surplus (*SYN.*) extravagance, intemperance, superabundance, excess, immoderation, remainder, extra, profusion, superfluity. (*ANT.*) *want, lack, dearth.*

surprise (*SYN.*) miracle, prodigy, wonder, awe, phenomenon, marvel, bewilderment, wonderment, rarity. (*ANT.*) *expectation, triviality, indifference, familiarity.*

surrender (*SYN.*) relinquish, resign, yield, abandon, sacrifice, submit, cede. (*ANT.*) *overcome, rout, conquer.*

surreptitious (*SYN.*) sneaky, sneaking, underhand, sly, furtive. (*ANT.*) *openhanded, open, straightforward.*

surround (*SYN.*) confine, encompass, circle, encircle, girdle, fence, circumscribe, limit, envelop. (*ANT.*) *open, distend, expose, enlarge.*

surveillance (*SYN.*) inspection, oversight, supervision, management, control.

survey (*SYN.*) scan, inspect, view, examine, inspection, examination.

survive (*SYN.*) live, remain, continue, persist. (*ANT.*) *die, fail, succumb.*

suspect (*SYN.*) waver, disbelieve, presume, suppose, mistrust, distrust.

suspend (*SYN.*) delay, hang, withhold, interrupt, postpone, dangle, adjourn, poise. (*ANT.*) *persist, proceed, maintain.*

suspicion (*SYN.*) unbelief, distrust, suspense, uncertainty, doubt. (*ANT.*) *determination, conviction, faith, belief.*

sustain (*SYN.*) bear, carry, undergo, foster, keep, prop, help, advocate, back. (*ANT.*) *discourage, oppose, destroy.*

sustenance (*SYN.*) fare, food, diet, rations, nutriment, edibles, victuals. (*ANT.*) *hunger, want, drink.*

swallow (*SYN.*) gorge, eat, mouthful.

swallow up (*SYN.*) consume, absorb, engulf, assimilate. (*ANT.*) *exude, dispense, expel, discharge.*

swarm (*SYN.*) throng, horde, crowd.

swarthy (*SYN.*) sable, dark. (*ANT.*) *bright, light.*

swear (*SYN.*) declare, state, affirm, vouchsafe, curse, maintain. (*ANT.*) *demur, oppose, deny, contradict.*

sweat (*SYN.*) perspiration, perspire.

sweeping (*SYN.*) extensive, wide, general, broad, tolerant, comprehensive, vast. (*ANT.*) *restricted, confined.*

sweet (*SYN.*) engaging, luscious, pure, clean, fresh, melodious, pleasant. (*ANT.*) *bitter, harsh, nasty, irascible, discordant, irritable, acrid.*

swell (*SYN.*) increase, grow, expand, enlarge. (*ANT.*) *diminish, shrink.*

swift (*SYN.*) quick, fast, fleet, speedy, rapid, expeditious.

swindle (*SYN.*) bilk, defraud, con, deceive, cheat, guile, deception, deceit. (*ANT.*) *sincerity, honesty, fairness.*

swing (*SYN.*) rock, sway, wave.

switch (*SYN.*) shift, change, turn.

swoon (*SYN.*) faint.

symbol (*SYN.*) sign, character.

sympathetic (*SYN.*) considerate, compassionate, gentle, benevolent, good, tender, affable, merciful, thoughtful. (*ANT.*) *unkind, merciless, unsympathetic, indifferent, intolerant, cruel.*

sympathy (*SYN.*) compassion, agreement, tenderness, commiseration, pity. (*ANT.*) *indifference, unconcern, antipathy.*

symptom (*SYN.*) indication, sign.

synopsis (*SYN.*) outline, digest.

synthetic (*SYN.*) counterfeit, artificial, phony, unreal, bogus, sham. (*ANT.*) *natural, true, genuine.*

system (*SYN.*) organization, procedure, regularity, arrangement, mode, order. (*ANT.*) *confusion, chance, disorder.*

systematic (SYN.) orderly, organized. (*ANT.*) *irregular, random.*

T

table (*SYN.*) catalog, list, schedule, postpone, chart, index, shelve, delay, put off.

tablet (*SYN.*) pad, notebook, capsule, sketchpad, pill, lozenge.

taboo (*SYN.*) banned, prohibited, forbidden, restriction. (*ANT.*) *accepted, allowed.*

tacit (*SYN.*) understood, assumed, implied.

taciturn (*SYN.*) quiet, withdrawn, reserved.

tack (*SYN.*) add, join, attach, clasp, fasten.

tackle (*SYN.*) rigging, gear, apparatus, equipment, grab, seize, catch, down, throw, try, undertake.

tacky (*SYN.*) gummy, sticky, gooey.

tact (*SYN.*) dexterity, poise, diplomacy, judgment, saviorfaire, skill, finesse, sense, prudence, adroitness, address. (*ANT.*) *incompetence, vulgarity, blunder, rudeness, insensitivity, grossness.*

tactical (*SYN.*) foxy, cunning, proficient, deft, adroit, clever, expert. (*ANT.*) *blundering, gauche, clumsy, inept.*

tactics (*SYN.*) plan, strategy, approach, maneuver, course, scheme.

tag (*SYN.*) sticker, label, mark, identification, marker, name.

tail (*SYN.*) rear, back, follow, end, shadow, pursue, trail, heel.

tailor (*SYN.*) modest, couturier, modify, redo, shape, fashion.

taint (*SYN.*) spot, stain, tarnish, soil, mark, discolor. (*ANT.*) *cleanse, disinfect, clean.*

tainted (*SYN.*) crooked, impure, vitiated, profligate, debased, spoiled, corrupted, depraved, dishonest, contaminated, putrid, unsound.

take (*SYN.*) accept, grasp, catch, confiscate, clutch, adopt, assume, receive, bring, attract, claim, necessitate, steal, ensnare, capture, demand, select, appropriate, obtain, captivate, hold, seize, win, escort, note, record, rob, shoplift, get, remove, gain, choose.

taking (*SYN.*) charming, captivating, winning, attractive.

takeover (*SYN.*) revolution, merger, usurpation, confiscation.

tale (*SYN.*) falsehood, history, yarn, chronicle, account, fable, fiction, narration, story, narrative, anecdote.

talent (*SYN.*) capability, knack, skill, endowment, gift, cleverness, aptitude, ability, genius. (*ANT.*) *ineptitude, incompetence.*

talented (*SYN.*) skillful, smart, adroit, dexterous, clever, apt, quick-witted, witty, ingenious. (*ANT.*) *dull, clumsy, awkward, unskilled,* *stupid, slow.*

talk *(SYN.)* conversation, gossip, report, speech, communicate, discuss, confer, chatter, conference, preach, dialogue, reason, jabber, discourse, lecture, communication, consul, plead, argue, converse, rant, chat, mutter, speak, rumor, deliberate, discussion. *(ANT.) silence, correspondence, meditation, writing.*

talkative *(SYN.)* glib, communicative, chattering, loquacious, voluble, garrulous, chatty. *(ANT.) uncommunicative, laconic, reticent, silent.*

tall *(SYN.)* elevated, high, towering, big, lofty, imposing, gigantic. *(ANT.) tiny, low, short, small, stunted.*

tally *(SYN.)* score, count, compute, reckon, calculate, estimate, list, figure, correspond, agree, match, check.

tame *(SYN.)* domesticated, dull, insipid, docile, broken, uninteresting, gentle, subdued, insipid, flat, unexciting, boring, break, domesticate, mild, tedious, domestic, submissive. *(ANT.) spirited, savage, wild, exciting, animated, undomesticated.*

tamper *(SYN.)* mix in, interrupt, interfere, meddle, interpose.

tang *(SYN.)* zest, sharpness, tartness, taste.

tangible *(SYN.)* material, sensible, palpable, corporeal, bodily. *(ANT.) metaphysical, mental, spiritual.*

tangle *(SYN.)* confuse, knot, snarl, twist, ensnare, embroil, implicate.

tangy *(SYN.)* pungent, peppery, seasoned, sharp, tart.

tantalize *(SYN.)* lease, tempt, entice, titillate, stimulate, frustrate.

tantrum *(SYN.)* outburst, fit, fury, flare-up, conniption, rampage.

tap *(SYN.)* pat, rap, hit, strike, blow, faucet, spout, spigot, bunghole.

tape *(SYN.)* ribbon, strip, fasten, bandage, bind, record, tie.

taper *(SYN.)* narrow, candle, decrease.

tardy *(SYN.)* slow, delayed, overdue, late, belated. *(ANT.) prompt, timely, punctual, early.*

target *(SYN.)* aim, goal, object, objective.

tariff *(SYN.)* duty, tax, levy, rate.

tarnish *(SYN.)* discolor, blight, defile, sully, spot, befoul, disgrace, stain. *(ANT.) honor, purify, cleanse, bleach, shine, gleam, sparkle.*

tarry *(SYN.)* dawdle, loiter, linger, dally, remain, delay, procrastinate.

tart *(SYN.)* sour, acrid, pungent, acid, sharp, distasteful, bitter. *(ANT.) mellow, sweet, delicious, pleasant.*

task *(SYN.)* work, job, undertaking, labor, chore, duty, stint.

taste *(SYN.)* tang, inclination, liking, sensibility, flavor, savor, try, sip, sample, zest, experience, undergo, appreciation, relish, discrimination, discernment, judgment. *(ANT.) indelicacy, disinclination, antipathy.*

tasteful *(SYN.)* elegant, choice, refined, suitable, artistic. *(ANT.) offensive, unbecoming.*

tasteless *(SYN.)* flavorless, insipid, unpalatable, rude, unrefined, uncultivated, boorish, uninteresting.

tasty *(SYN.)* delectable, delicious, luscious, palatable, tempting.

tattered *(SYN.)* ragged, torn, shoddy, shabby, frazzled, frayed, tacky, seedy.

tattle *(SYN.)* inform, divulge, disclose, blab, reveal.

taunt *(SYN.)* tease, deride, flout, scoff, sneer, mock, annoy, pester, bother, ridicule, jeer. *(ANT.) praise, compliment, laud, flatter.*

taunting *(SYN.)* ironic, caustic, cutting, sardonic, derisive, biting, acrimonious, sarcastic, satirical, sneering. *(ANT.) pleasant, agreeable, affable, amiable.*

taut *(SYN.)* tight, constricted, firm, stretched, snug, tense, extended. *(ANT.) slack, loose, relaxed, open, lax.*

tavern *(SYN.)* pub, bar, cocktail lounge.

tawdry *(SYN.)* pretentious, showy, vulgar, tasteless, sordid, garish.

tax *(SYN.)* duty, assessment, excise, levy, toll, burden, strain, tribute, tariff, assess, encumber, overload, impost, custom, exaction, rate. *(ANT.) reward, gift, remuneration, wages.*

taxi *(SYN.)* cab, taxicab.

teach *(SYN.)* inform, school, educate, train, inculcate, instruct, instill, tutor. *(ANT.) misinform, misguide.*

teacher *(SYN.)* tutor, instructor, professor, lecturer.

team *(SYN.)* company, band, party, crew, gang, group.

teamwork *(SYN.)* collaboration, cooperation.

tear *(SYN.)* rend, shred, sunder, cleave, rip, lacerate, teardrop, disunite, divide, drop, wound, split, slit, sever. *(ANT.) mend, repair, join, unite, sew.*

tearful *(SYN.)* sad, weeping, crying, sobbing, weepy, lachrymose.

tease *(SYN.)* badger, harry, bother, irritate, nag, pester, taunt, vex, annoy, disturb, harass, worry, tantalize, plague, aggravate, provoke, torment. *(ANT.) please, delight, soothe, comfort, gratify.*

technical *(SYN.)* industrial, technological, specialized, mechanical.

technique *(SYN.)* system, method, routine, approach, procedure.

tedious *(SYN.)* boring, dilatory, humdrum, sluggish, monotonous, irksome, dreary, dull, tiring, burdensome, tiresome, wearisome, tardy. *(ANT.) interesting, entertaining, engaging, exciting, amusing, quick.*

teem *(SYN.)* abound, swarm.

teeming *(SYN.)* overflowing, bountiful, abundant, ample, profuse, plenteous, rich, copious. *(ANT.) scant, scarce, deficient, insufficient.*

teeter *(SYN.)* sway, hesitate, hem and haw, waver.

telecast *(SYN.)* broadcast.

televise *(SYN.)* telecast.

tell *(SYN.)* report, mention, state, betray, announce, recount, relate, narrate, rehearse, mention, utter, confess, disclose, direct, request, acquaint, instruct, notify, inform, determine, reveal, divulge.

telling *(SYN.)* persuasive, convincing, forceful, effective.

telltale *(SYN.)* revealing, informative, suggestive, meaningful.

temerity *(SYN.)* rashness, foolhardiness, audacity, boldness, recklessness, precipitancy. *(ANT.) prudence, wariness, caution, hesitation, timidity.*

temper *(SYN.)* fury, choler, exasperation, anger, passion, petulance, disposition, nature, rage, soothe, soften, wrath, indignation, irritation, pacify, animosity, mood, resentment. *(ANT.) peace, self-control, forbearance, conciliation.*

temperament *(SYN.)* humor, mood, temper, nature, disposition.

temperamental *(SYN.)* testy, moody, touchy, sensitive, irritable. *(ANT.) calm, unruffled, serene.*

temperance *(SYN.)* abstinence, sobriety, self-denial, forbearance, abstention. *(ANT.) intoxication, excess, self-indulgence, gluttony, wantonness.*

temperate *(SYN.)* controlled, moderate, cool, calm, restrained. *(ANT.) excessive, extreme, prodigal.*

tempest *(SYN.)* draft, squall, wind, blast, gust, storm, hurricane, commotion, tumult, zephyr. *(ANT.) calm, tranquility.*

tempo *(SYN.)* measure, beat, cadence, rhythm.

temporal *(SYN.)* mundane, earthly, lay, profane, worldly, terrestrial, laic. *(ANT.) spiritual, ecclesiastical, unworldly, religious, heavenly.*

temporary *(SYN.)* brief, momentary, short-lived, fleeting, ephemeral, passing, short, transient. *(ANT.) lasting, permanent, immortal, everlasting, timeless, abiding.*

tempt *(SYN.)* entice, allure, lure, attract, seduce, invite, magnetize.

tenacious *(SYN.)* persistent, determined, unchanging, unyielding.

tenable *(SYN.)* correct, practical, rational, reasonable, sensible, defensible.

tenacity *(SYN.)* perseverance, steadfastness, industry, constancy, persistence, pertinacity. *(ANT.) laziness, rest, cessation, idleness, sloth.*

tenant *(SYN.)* renter, lessee, lodger, lease-holder, dweller, resident.

tend *(SYN.)* escort, follow, care for, lackey, watch, protect, take care of, attend, guard, serve.

tendency *(SYN.)* drift, inclination, proneness, leaning, bias, aim, disposition, predisposition, propensity, trend, impulse. *(ANT.) disinclination, aversion, deviation.*

tender *(SYN.)* sympathetic, sore, sensitive, painful, gentle, meek, delicate, fragile, proffer, bland, mild, loving, offer, affectionate, soothing, propose, moderate, soft. *(ANT.) rough, severe, fierce, chewy, tough, cruel, unfeeling, harsh.*

tenderfoot *(SYN.)* novice, apprentice, beginner, amateur.

tenderhearted *(SYN.)* kind, sympathetic, merciful, softhearted, understanding, sentimental, affectionate, gentle, sensitive.

tenderness *(SYN.)* attachment, kindness, love, affection, endearment. *(ANT.) repugnance, indifference, aversion, hatred.*

tenet *(SYN.)* dogma, belief, precept, doctrine, creed, opinion. *(ANT.) deed, conduct, practice, performance.*

tense *(SYN.)* strained, stretched, excited, tight, nervous. *(ANT.) loose, placid, lax, relaxed.*

tension *(SYN.)* stress, strain, pressure, anxiety, apprehension, distress.

tentative *(SYN.)* hypothetical, indefinite, probationary, conditional.

tenure *(SYN.)* administration, time, regime, term.

tepid *(SYN.)* temperate, mild, lukewarm. *(ANT.) boiling, scalding, passionate, hot.*

term *(SYN.)* period, limit, time, boundary, duration, name, phrase, interval, session, semester, expression, word.

terminal *(SYN.)* eventual, final, concluding, decisive, ending, fatal, latest, last, ultimate, conclusive. *(ANT.) original, first, rudimentary, incipient, inaugural.*

terminate *(SYN.)* close, end, finish, abolish, complete, cease, stop, conclude, expire, culminate. *(ANT.) establish, begin, initiate, start, commence.*

terminology *(SYN.)* vocabulary, nomenclature, terms, phraseology.

terms *(SYN.)* stipulations, agreement, conditions, provisions.

terrible *(SYN.)* frightful, dire, awful, gruesome, horrible, shocking, horrifying, terrifying, horrid, hideous, appalling. *(ANT.) secure, happy, joyous, pleasing, safe.*

terrific *(SYN.)* superb, wonderful, glorious, great, magnificent, divine, colossal, sensational, marvelous.

terrify *(SYN.)* dismay, intimidate, startle, terrorize, appall, frighten, petrify, astound, alarm, affright, horrify, scare. *(ANT.) soothe, allay, reassure, compose, embolden.*

territory *(SYN.)* dominion, province, quarter, section, country, division, region, domain, area, place, district.

terror *(SYN.)* fear, alarm, dismay, horror, dread, consternation, fright, panic. *(ANT.) calm, security, assurance, peace.*

terse *(SYN.)* concise, incisive, succinct, summary, condensed, compact, neat, pithy, summary. *(ANT.) verbose, wordy, lengthy, prolix.*

test *(SYN.)* exam, examination, trial, quiz, analyze, verify, validate.

testify *(SYN.)* depose, warrant, witness, state, attest, swear.

testimony *(SYN.)* evidence, attestation, declaration, proof, witness, confirmation. *(ANT.) refutation, argument, disproof, contradiction.*

testy *(SYN.)* ill-natured, irritable, snappish, waspish, fractious, fretful, touchy, ill-tempered, peevish, petulant. *(ANT.) pleasant, affable, good-tempered, genial, good-natured.*

tether *(SYN.)* tie, hamper, restraint, bridle.

text *(SYN.)* textbook, book, manual.

textile *(SYN.)* material, cloth, goods, fabric.

texture *(SYN.)* construction, structure, make-up, composition, grain, finish.

thankful *(SYN.)* obliged, grateful, appreciative. *(ANT.) thankless, ungrateful, resenting.*

thaw *(SYN.)* liquefy, melt, dissolve. *(ANT.) solidify, freeze.*

theater *(SYN.)* arena, playhouse, battlefield, stadium, hall.

theatrical *(SYN.)* ceremonious, melodramatic, stagy, artificial, affected, dramatic, showy, compelling. *(ANT.) unemotional, subdued, unaffected.*

theft *(SYN.)* larceny, robbery, stealing, plunder, burglary, pillage, thievery.

theme *(SYN.)* motive, topic, argument, subject, thesis, text, point, paper, essay, composition.

theoretical *(SYN.)* bookish, learned, scholarly, pedantic, academic, formal, erudite, scholastic. *(ANT.) practical, ignorant, commonsense, simple.*

theory *(SYN.)* doctrine, guess, presupposition, postulate, assumption, hypothesis, speculation. *(ANT.) practice, verity, fact, proof.*

therefore *(SYN.)* consequently, thence so, accordingly, hence, then.

thick *(SYN.)* compressed, heavy, compact, viscous, close, concentrated, crowded, syrupy, dense. *(ANT.) watery, slim, thin, sparse, dispersed, dissipated.*

thief *(SYN.)* burglar, robber,

criminal.

thin *(SYN.)* diluted, flimsy, lean, narrow, spare, emaciated, diaphanous, gauzy, meager, slender, tenuous, slim, rare, sparse, scanty, lank, gossamer, slight. *(ANT.) fat, wide, broad, thick, bulky.*

think *(SYN.)* picture, contemplate, ponder, esteem, intend, mean, imagine, deliberate, recall, speculate, recollect, deem, apprehend, consider, devise, plan, judge, reflect, suppose, assume, meditate, muse. *(ANT.) forget, conjecture, guess.*

thirst *(SYN.)* appetite, desire, craving.

thirsty *(SYN.)* arid, dry, dehydrated, parched, craving, desirous. *(ANT.) satisfied.*

thorn *(SYN.)* spine, barb, prickle, nettle, bramble.

thorough *(SYN.)* entire, complete, perfect, total, finished, unbroken, careful, thoroughgoing, consummate, undivided. *(ANT.) unfinished, careless, slapdash, imperfect, haphazard, lacking.*

thoroughfare *(SYN.)* avenue, street, parkway, highway, boulevard. *(ANT.) byway.*

though *(SYN.)* in any case, notwithstanding, however, nevertheless.

thought *(SYN.)* consideration, pensive, attentive, heedful, prudent, dreamy, reflective, introspective, meditation, notion, view, deliberation, sentiment, fancy, idea, impression, reasoning, contemplation, judgment, regard. *(ANT.) thoughtlessness.*

thoughtful *(SYN.)* considerate, attentive, dreamy, pensive, provident, introspective, meditative, cautious, heedful, kind, courteous, friendly. *(ANT.) thoughtless, heedless, inconsiderate, rash, precipitous, selfish.*

thoughtless *(SYN.)* inattentive, unconcerned, negligent, lax, desultory, inconsiderate, careless, imprudent, inaccurate, neglectful, indiscreet, remiss. *(ANT.) meticulous, accurate, nice, careful.*

thrash *(SYN.)* whip, beat, defeat, flog, punish, strap, thresh.

thread *(SYN.)* yarn, strand, filament, fiber, string, cord.

threadbare *(SYN.)* shabby, tacky, worn, ragged, frayed.

threat *(SYN.)* menace, warning, danger, hazard, jeopardy, omen.

threaten *(SYN.)* caution,

warning, forewarn, menace, intimidate, loom.

threatening *(SYN.)* imminent, nigh, approaching, impending, overhanging, sinister, foreboding. *(ANT.) improbable, retreating, afar, distant, remote.*

threshold *(SYN.)* edge, verge, start, beginning, doorsill, commencement.

thrift *(SYN.)* prudence, conservation, saving, economy.

thrifty *(SYN.)* saving, economical, sparing, frugal, provident, stingy, saving, parsimonious. *(ANT.) wasteful, spendthrift, intemperate, self-indulgent, extravagant.*

thrill *(SYN.)* arouse, rouse, excite, stimulation, excitement, tingle. *(ANT.) bore.*

thrive *(SYN.)* succeed, flourish, grow, prosper. *(ANT.) expire, fade, shrivel, die, fail.*

throb *(SYN.)* pound, pulsate, palpitate, beat, pulse.

throe *(SYN.)* pang, twinge, distress, suffering, pain, ache, grief, agony. *(ANT.) pleasure, relief, ease, solace, comfort.*

throng *(SYN.)* masses, press, crowd, bevy, populace, swarm, rabble, horde, host, mass, teem, mob, multitude.

throttle *(SYN.)* smother, choke, strangle.

through *(SYN.)* completed, done, finished, over.

throughout *(SYN.)* all over, everywhere, during.

throw *(SYN.)* propel, cast, pitch, toss, hurl, send, thrust, fling. *(ANT.) retain, pull, draw, haul, hold.*

thrust *(SYN.)* jostle, push, promote, crowd, force, drive, hasten, press, shove, urge. *(ANT.) ignore, falter, retreat, drag, oppose, halt.*

thug *(SYN.)* mobster, hoodlum, mugger, gangster, assassin, gunman.

thump *(SYN.)* blow, strike, knock, jab, poke, pound, beat, clout, bat, rap, bang.

thunderstruck *(SYN.)* amazed, astounded, astonished, awed, flabbergasted, surprised, dumbfounded, bewildered, spellbound.

thus *(SYN.)* hence, therefore, accordingly, so, consequently.

thwart *(SYN.)* defeat, frustrate, prevent, foil, stop, baffle, circumvent, hinder, obstruct, disappoint, balk, outwit. *(ANT.) promote, accomplish, fulfill, help, further.*

ticket *(SYN.)* stamp, label, tag, seal, token, pass, summons, certificate, ballot, sticker, slate, citation.

tickle *(SYN.)* delight, entertain, thrill, amuse, titillate, excite.

ticklish *(SYN.)* fragile, delicate, tough, difficult.

tidings *(SYN.)* message, report, information, word, intelligence, news.

tidy *(SYN.)* trim, clear, neat, precise, spruce, orderly, shipshape. *(ANT.) disheveled, unkempt, sloppy, dirty, slovenly.*

tie *(SYN.)* bond, join, relationship, bind, restrict, fetter, connect, conjunction, association, alliance, union, fasten, engage, attach, restrain, oblige, link, affinity. *(ANT.) separation, disunion, unfasten, open, loose, untie, free, isolation.*

tier *(SYN.)* line, row, level, deck, layer.

tiff *(SYN.)* bicker, squabble, argue, row, clash, dispute, altercation.

tight *(SYN.)* firm, taut, pennypinching, constricted, snug, taut, parsimonious, secure, fast, strong, sealed, fastened, watertight, locked, close, compact, stingy. *(ANT.) slack, lax, open, relaxed, loose.*

till *(SYN.)* plow, work, moneybox, depository, cultivate, vault.

tilt *(SYN.)* slant, slope, incline, tip, lean.

timber *(SYN.)* lumber, wood, logs.

time *(SYN.)* epoch, span, term, age, duration, interim, period, tempo, interval, space, spell, season.

timeless *(SYN.)* unending, lasting, perpetual, endless, immemorial. *(ANT.) temporary, mortal, temporal.*

timely *(SYN.)* prompt, exact, punctual, ready, precise. *(ANT.) slow, tardy, late.*

timepiece *(SYN.)* clock, watch.

timetable *(SYN.)* list, schedule.

timid *(SYN.)* coy, humble, sheepish, abashed, embarrassed, modest, bashful, diffident, shamefaced, retiring, fearful, faint-hearted, shy, timorous. *(ANT.) gregarious, bold, daring, adventurous, fearless.*

tinge *(SYN.)* color, tint, dye, stain, flavor, imbue, season, impregnate.

tingle *(SYN.)* shiver, chime, prickle.

tinker *(SYN.)* potter, putter, fiddle with, dawdle, dally, dabble.

tinkle *(SYN.)* sound, peal,

ring, jingle, chime, toll.

tint *(SYN.)* color, tinge, dye, stain, hue, tone, shade.

tiny *(SYN.)* minute, little, petty, wee, slight, diminutive, miniature, small, insignificant, trivial, puny. *(ANT.) huge, large, immense, big, enormous.*

tip *(SYN.)* point, end, top, peak, upset, tilt, reward, gift, gratuity, clue, hint, suggestion, inkling.

tirade *(SYN.)* outburst, harangue, scolding.

tire *(SYN.)* jade, tucker, bore, weary, exhaust, weaken, wear out, fatigue. *(ANT.) restore, revive, exhilarate, invigorate, refresh.*

tired *(SYN.)* weary, exhausted, fatigued, run-down, sleepy, faint, spent, wearied, worn, jaded. *(ANT.) rested, fresh, hearty, invigorated, energetic, tireless, eager.*

tireless *(SYN.)* active, enthusiastic, energetic, strenuous. *(ANT.) exhausted, wearied, fatigued.*

tiresome *(SYN.)* dull, boring, monotonous, tedious. *(ANT.) interesting.*

titan *(SYN.)* colossus, powerhouse, mammoth.

title *(SYN.)* epithet, privilege, name, appellation, claim, denomination, due, heading, ownership, right, deed, designation.

toast *(SYN.)* salutation, pledge, celebration.

toddle *(SYN.)* stumble, wobble, shuffle.

toil *(SYN.)* labor, drudgery, work, travail, performance, business, achievement, employment, occupation, slave, sweat, effort. *(ANT.) recreation, ease, vacation, relax, loll, play, leisure, repose.*

token *(SYN.)* mark, sign, sample, indication, evidence, symbol.

tolerant *(SYN.)* extensive, vast, considerate, broad, patient, large, sweeping, liberal, wide. *(ANT.) intolerant, bigoted, biased, restricted, narrow, confined.*

tolerate *(SYN.)* endure, allow, bear, authorize, permit, brook, stand, abide. *(ANT.) forbid, protest, prohibit, discriminating.*

toll *(SYN.)* impost, burden, rate, assessment, duty, custom, excise, tribute, levy, burden, strain. *(ANT.) reward, wages, gift, remuneration.*

tomb *(SYN.)* vault, monument, catacomb, grave,

mausoleum.

tone *(SYN.)* noise, sound, mood, manner, expression, cadence.

tongs *(SYN.)* tweezers, hook, grapnel, forceps.

tongue *(SYN.)* diction, lingo, cant, jargon, vernacular, dialect, idiom, speech, phraseology. *(ANT.) nonsense, drivel, babble.*

too *(SYN.)* furthermore, moreover, similarly, also, in addition, besides, likewise.

tool *(SYN.)* devise, medium, apparatus, agent, implement, utensil, agent, vehicle, instrument. *(ANT.) preventive, hindrance, impediment, obstruction.*

top *(SYN.)* crown, pinnacle, peak, tip, cover, cap, zenith, apex, crest, chief, head, summit. *(ANT.) bottom, foundation, base, foot.*

topic *(SYN.)* subject, thesis, issue, argument, matter, theme, point.

topple *(SYN.)* collapse, sink, fall, tumble.

torrent *(SYN.)* pain, woe, pester, ache, distress, misery, harass, throe, annoy, vex, torture, anguish, suffering, misery. *(ANT.) relief, comfort, ease, gratify, delight.*

torpid *(SYN.)* sluggish, idle, lazy, inert, inactive, supine, slothful, indolent, motionless, lethargic. *(ANT.) alert, assiduous, diligent, active.*

torpor *(SYN.)* lethargy, daze, numbness, stupor, drowsiness, insensibility, languor. *(ANT.) wakefulness, liveliness, activity, alertness, readiness.*

torrent *(SYN.)* flood, downpour, deluge.

torrid *(SYN.)* scorching, ardent, impetuous, passionate, scalding, warm, fiery, hot-blooded, sultry, tropical, intense, sweltering, burning, hot. *(ANT.) passionless, impassive, cold, frigid, apathetic, freezing, phlegmatic, indifferent, temperate.*

torso *(SYN.)* form, frame, body. *(ANT.) soul, mind, spirit, intellect.*

torture *(SYN.)* anguish, badger, plague, distress, ache, torment, pester, pain, hound, agony, woe, worry, vex, persecute, suffering, throe, afflict, misery. *(ANT.) aid, relief, comfort, ease, support, encourage, mitigation.*

toss *(SYN.)* throw, cast, hurl, pitch, tumble, thrust, fling, propel. *(ANT.) retain, pull, draw, haul, hold.*

total *(SYN.)* entire, complete, concluded, finished, thorough, whole, entirely, collection, aggregate, conglomeration, unbroken, perfect, undivided, consummate, full. *(ANT.) part, element, imperfect, unfinished, ingredient, particular, lacking.*

tote *(SYN.)* move, transfer, convey, drag, carry.

totter *(SYN.)* falter, stagger, reel, sway, waver, stumble, wobble.

touch *(SYN.)* finger, feel, handle, move, affect, concern, mention, hint, trace, suggestion, knack, skill, ability, talent.

touch-and-go *(SYN.)* dangerous, risky, perilous, hazardous.

touching *(SYN.)* pitiable, affecting, moving, sad, adjunct, bordering, tangent, poignant, tender, effective, impressive, adjacent. *(ANT.) removed, enlivening, animated, exhilarating.*

touchy *(SYN.)* snappish, irritable, fiery, choleric, testy, hot, irascible, nervous, excitable, petulant, sensitive, short-tempered, jumpy, peevish. *(ANT.) composed, agreeable, tranquil, calm, serene, stolid, cool.*

tough *(SYN.)* sturdy, difficult, trying, incorrigible, troublesome, hard, stout, leathery, strong, laborious, inedible, sinewy, cohesive, firm, callous, obdurate, vicious. *(ANT.) vulnerable, submissive, easy, brittle, facile, weak, fragile, compliant, tender, frail.*

toughness *(SYN.)* stamina, fortitude, durability, intensity, force, might, stoutness, power, sturdiness, vigor. *(ANT.) weakness, feebleness, infirmity, frailty.*

tour *(SYN.)* rove, travel, go, visit, excursion, ramble, journey, roam. *(ANT.) stop, stay.*

tourist *(SYN.)* traveler, sightseer, vagabond, voyager.

tournament *(SYN.)* tourney, match, contest, competition.

tout *(SYN.)* vend, importune, peddle, solicit, sell, hawk.

tow *(SYN.)* tug, take out, unsheathe, haul, draw, remove, extract, pull, drag. *(ANT.) propel, drive.*

towering *(SYN.)* elevated, exalted, high, lofty, tall, proud, eminent. *(ANT.) base, mean, stunted, small, tiny, low.*

town *(SYN.)* hamlet, village, community, municipality.

toxic *(SYN.)* deadly, poisonous,

fatal, lethal, harmful. (ANT.) *beneficial.*

toy (SYN.) play, romp, frolic, gamble, stake, caper, plaything, wager, revel.

trace (SYN.) stigma, feature, indication, trait, mark, stain, scar, sign, trial, trace, suggestion, characteristic, vestige.

track (SYN.) persist, pursue, follow, sign, mark, spoor, trace, path, route, road, carry, hunt, chase. (ANT.) *escape, evade, abandon, flee, elude.*

tract (SYN.) area, region, territory, district, expanse, domain.

tractable (SYN.) yielding, deferential, submissive, dutiful, compliant, obedient. (ANT.) *rebellious, intractable, insubordinate.*

trade (SYN.) business, traffic, commerce, dealing, craft, occupation, profession, livelihood, swap, barter, exchange.

trademark (SYN.) logo, brand name, identification, emblem, insignia, monogram.

tradition (SYN.) custom, legend, folklore, belief, rite, practice.

traduce (SYN.) defame, malign, vilify, revile, abuse, asperse, scandalize, disparage. (ANT.) *protect, honor, cherish, praise, respect, support, extol.*

tragedy (SYN.) unhappiness, misfortune, misery, adversity, catastrophe.

tragic (SYN.) miserable, unfortunate, depressing, melancholy, mournful. (ANT.) *happy, cheerful, comic.*

trail (SYN.) persist, pursue, chase, follow, drag, draw, hunt, track. (ANT.) *evade, flee, abandon, elude, escape.*

train (SYN.) direct, prepare, aim, point, level, teach, drill, tutor, bid, instruct, order, command. (ANT.) *distract, deceive, misguide, misdirect.*

traipse (SYN.) roam, wander, saunter, meander.

trait (SYN.) characteristic, feature, attribute, peculiarity, mark, quality, property.

traitor (SYN.) turncoat, betrayer, spy, double-dealer, conspirator.

traitorous (SYN.) disloyal, faithless, apostate, false, recreant, perfidious, treasonable, treacherous. (ANT.) *devoted, trite, loyal, constant.*

tramp (SYN.) bum, beggar, rover, hobo, march, stamp, stomp, vagabond, wanderer, vagrant. (ANT.) *laborer, worker, gentleman.*

trample (SYN.) crush, stomp,

squash.

tranquil (SYN.) composed, calm, dispassionate, imperturbable, peaceful, pacific, placid, quiet, still, serene, undisturbed, unruffled. (ANT.) *frantic, stormy, excited, disturbed, upset, turbulent, wild.*

tranquillity (SYN.) calmness, calm, hush, peace, quiet, quiescence, quietude, repose, serenity, rest, stillness, silence, placid. (ANT.) *disturbance, agitation, excitement, tumult, noise.*

transact (SYN.) conduct, manage, execute, treat, perform.

transaction (SYN.) business, deal, affair, deed, settlement, occurrence, negotiation, proceeding.

transcend (SYN.) overstep, overshadow, exceed.

transcribe (SYN.) write, copy, rewrite, record.

transfer (SYN.) dispatch, send, transmit, remove, transport, transplant, consign, move, shift, reassign, assign, relegate.

transform (SYN.) change, convert, alter, modify, transfigure, shift, vary, veer. (ANT.) *continue, settle, preserve, stabilize.*

transgression (SYN.) atrocity, indignity, offense, insult, outrage, aggression, injustice, crime, misdeed, trespass, sin, wrong, vice. (ANT.) *innocence, morality, gentleness, right.*

transient (SYN.) ephemeral, evanescent, brief, fleeting, momentary, temporary, short-lived. (ANT.) *immortal, abiding, permanent, lasting, timeless, established.*

transition (SYN.) change, variation, modification.

translate (SYN.) decipher, construe, decode, elucidate, explicate, explain, interpret, solve, render, unravel. (ANT.) *distort, falsify, misinterpret, misconstrue.*

transmit (SYN.) confer, convey, communicate, divulge, disclose, impart, send, inform, relate, notify, reveal, dispatch, tell. (ANT.) *withhold, hide, conceal.*

transparent (SYN.) crystalline, clear, limpid, lucid, translucent, thin, evident, manifest, plain, evident, explicit, obvious, open. (ANT.) *opaque, muddy, turbid, thick, questionable, ambiguous.*

transpire (SYN.) befall, bechance, betide, happen,

chance, occur.

transport (SYN.) carry, bear, convey, remove, move, shift, enrapture, transfer, lift, entrance, ravish, stimulate.

transpose (SYN.) change, switch, reverse.

trap (SYN.) artifice, bait, ambush, intrigue, net, lure, pitfall, ensnare, deadfall, snare, ruse, entrap, bag, trick, stratagem, wile.

trash (SYN.) refuse, garbage, rubbish, waste.

trashy (SYN.) insignificant, worthless.

trauma (SYN.) ordeal, upheaval, jolt, shock, disturbance.

travail (SYN.) suffering, torment, anxiety, distress, anguish, misery, ordeal.

travel (SYN.) journey, go, touring, ramble, rove, voyage, cruise, tour, roam. (ANT.) *stop, stay, remain, hibernate.*

travesty (SYN.) farce, joke, misrepresentation, counterfeit, mimicry.

treachery (SYN.) collusion, cabal, combination, intrigue, conspiracy, machination, disloyalty, betrayal, treason, plot. (ANT.) *allegiance, steadfastness, loyalty.*

treason (SYN.) cabal, combination, betrayal, sedition, collusion, intrigue, conspiracy, machination, disloyalty, treachery, plot.

treasure (SYN.) cherish, hold dear, abundance, guard, prize, appreciate, value, riches, wealth, foster, sustain, nurture. (ANT.) *disregard, neglect, dislike, abandon, reject.*

treat (SYN.) employ, avail, manipulate, exploit, operate, utilize, exert, act, exercise, practice, handle, manage, deal, entertain, indulge, host, negotiate, tend, attend, heal, use. (ANT.) *neglect, overlook, ignore, waste.*

treaty (SYN.) compact, agreement, pact, bargain, covenant, alliance, marriage. (ANT.) *schism, separation, divorce.*

trek (SYN.) tramp, hike, plod, trudge.

tremble (SYN.) flutter, jolt, jar, agitate, quake, quiver, quaver, rock, shake, shudder, shiver, totter, sway, vibrate, waver.

trembling (SYN.) apprehension, alarm, dread, fright, fear, horror, terror, panic. (ANT.) *composure, calmness, tranquillity.*

tremendous (SYN.) enormous, huge, colossal, gigantic,

great, large.

tremor (SYN.) flutter, vibration, palpitation.

trench (SYN.) gully, gorge, ditch, gulch, moat, dugout, trough.

trenchant (SYN.) clear, emphatic, forceful, impressive, meaningful.

trend (SYN.) inclination, drift, course, tendency, direction.

trendy (SYN.) modish, faddish, stylish, voguish, popular, current.

trepidation (SYN.) apprehension, alarm, dread, fright, fear, horror, panic, terror. (ANT.) *boldness, bravery, fearlessness, courage, assurance.*

trespass (SYN.) atrocity, indignity, affront, insult, outrage, offense, aggression, crime, misdeed, injustice, vice, wrong, sin. (ANT.) *evacuate, vacate, relinquish, abandon.*

trespasser (SYN.) invader, intruder, encroacher.

trial (SYN.) experiment, ordeal, proof, test, examination, attempt, effort, endeavor, essay, affliction, misery, hardship, suffering, difficulty, misfortune, tribulation, trouble. (ANT.) *consolation, alleviation.*

tribe (SYN.) group, race, clan, bunch.

tribulation (SYN.) anguish, distress, agony, grief, misery, sorrow, torment, suffering, woe, disaster, calamity, evil, trouble, misfortune. (ANT.) *elation, delight, joy, fun.*

tribunal (SYN.) arbitrators, judges, decision makers, judiciary.

trick (SYN.) artifice, antic, deception, device, cheat, fraud, hoax, guile, imposture, ruse, ploy, stratagem, trickery, deceit, jest, joke, prank, defraud, subterfuge, wile, stunt. (ANT.) *exposure, candor, openness, honesty, sincerity.*

trickle (SYN.) drip, drop, dribble, leak, seep.

tricky (SYN.) artifice, antic, covert, cunning, foxy, crafty, furtive, guileful, insidious, sly, shrews, stealthy, surreptitious, subtle, underhand, wily. (ANT.) *frank, candid, ingenuous, sincere, open.*

trifling (SYN.) insignificant, frivolous, paltry, petty, trivial, small, unimportant. (ANT.) *momentous, serious, important.*

trigger (SYN.) generate, provoke, prompt, motivate, activate.

trim (SYN.) nice, clear, orderly,

precise, tidy, spruce, adorn, bedeck, clip, shave, prune, cut, shear, compact, neat, decorate, embellish, garnish. (ANT.) deface, deform, spoil, mar, serious, momentous.

trimmings (SYN.) accessories, adornments, decorations, garnish, ornaments.

trinket (SYN.) bead, token, memento, bauble, charm, knickknack.

trio (SYN.) threesome, triad, triple.

trip (SYN.) expedition, cruise, stumble, err, journey, jaunt, passage, blunder, bungle, slip, excursion, tour, pilgrimage, voyage, travel.

trite (SYN.) common, banal, hackneyed, ordinary, stereotyped, stale. (ANT.) modern, fresh, momentous, stimulating, novel, new.

triumph (SYN.) conquest, achievement, success, prevail, win, jubilation, victory, ovation. (ANT.) succumb, failure, defeat.

triumphant (SYN.) celebrating, exultant, joyful, exhilarated, smug.

trivial (SYN.) insignificant, frivolous, paltry, petty, trifling, small, unimportant. (ANT.) momentous, important, weighty, serious.

troops (SYN.) militia, troopers, recruits, soldiers, enlisted men.

trophy (SYN.) award, memento, honor, testimonial, prize.

tropical (SYN.) sultry, sweltering, humid, torrid.

trouble (SYN.) anxiety, affliction, calamity, distress, hardship, grief, pain, misery, sorrow, woe, bother, annoyance, care, embarrassment, irritation, torment, pains, worry, disorder, problem, disturbance, effort, exertion, toil, inconvenience, misfortune, labor. (ANT.) console, accommodate, gratify, soothe, joy, peace.

troublemaker (SYN.) rebel, scamp, agitator, demon, devil, ruffian.

troublesome (SYN.) bothersome, annoying, distressing, irksome, disturbing, trying, arduous, vexatious, arduous, difficult, burdensome, laborious, tedious. (ANT.) accommodating, gratifying, easy, pleasant.

trounce (SYN.) lash, flog, switch, whack, punish, whip, stomp.

truant (SYN.) delinquent, absentee, vagrant, malingerer.

truce (SYN.) armistice,

cease-fire, interval, break, intermission, respite.

trudge (SYN.) march, trek, lumber, hike.

true (SYN.) actual, authentic, accurate, correct, exact, genuine, real, veracious, veritable, constant, honest, faithful, loyal, reliable, valid, legitimate, steadfast, sincere. (ANT.) erroneous, counterfeit, false, spurious, fictitious, faithless, inconstant, fickle.

truly (SYN.) indeed, actually, precisely, literally, really, factually.

truncate (SYN.) prune, clip, pare, shorten.

truss (SYN.) girder, brace, framework, shoring.

trust (SYN.) credence, confidence, dependence, reliance, faith, trust, depend on, rely on, reckon on, believe, hope, credit, commit, entrust, confide. (ANT.) incredulity, doubt, skepticism, mistrust.

trusted (SYN.) trustworthy, reliable, true, loyal, staunch, devoted.

trustworthy (SYN.) dependable, certain, reliable, secure, safe, sure, tried, trust. (ANT.) fallible, dubious, questionable, unreliable, uncertain.

truth (SYN.) actuality, authenticity, accuracy, correctness, exactness, honesty, fact, rightness, truthfulness, veracity, verisimilitude, verity. (ANT.) falsity, fiction, lie, untruth.

truthful (SYN.) frank, candid, honest, sincere, open, veracious, accurate, correct. (ANT.) misleading, sly, deceitful.

try (SYN.) endeavor, attempt, strive, struggle, undertake, afflict, test, prove, torment, trouble, essay, examine, analyze, investigate, effort, aim, design, aspire, intend, mean. (ANT.) decline, ignore, abandon, omit, neglect, comfort, console.

trying (SYN.) bothersome, annoying, distressing, disturbing, troublesome, arduous, vexatious, difficult, tedious. (ANT.) easy, accommodating, pleasant, gratifying.

tryout (SYN.) audition, trial, chance, test.

tryst (SYN.) rendezvous, meeting, appointment.

tub (SYN.) basin, vessel, sink, bowl.

tube (SYN.) hose, pipe, reed.

tubular (SYN.) hollow, cylindrical.

tuck (SYN.) crease, fold, gather, bend.

tuft (SYN.) bunch, group, cluster.

tug (SYN.) pull, wrench, tow, haul, jerk.

tuition (SYN.) instruction, schooling, teaching, education.

tumble (SYN.) toss, trip, fall, sprawl, wallow, lurch, flounder, plunge, topple.

tumult (SYN.) chaos, agitation, commotion, confusion, disarray, disarrangement, disorder, noise, hubbub, ferment. (ANT.) peacefulness, order, peace, tranquillity.

tune (SYN.) song, concord, harmony, air, melody, strain. (ANT.) aversion, discord.

tunnel (SYN.) passage, grotto, cave.

turbid (SYN.) dark, cloudy, thick, muddy, murky.

turf (SYN.) lawn, grassland, sod, grass.

turmoil (SYN.) chaos, agitation, commotion, confusion, disarray, disorder. (ANT.) order, peace, certainty, quiet, tranquillity.

turn (SYN.) circulate, circle, invert, rotate, revolve, spin, twist, twirl, whirl, wheel, avert, reverse, become, sour. (ANT.) fix, stand, arrest, stop, continue, endure, proceed.

turncoat (SYN.) renegade, defector, deserter, rat, betrayer, traitor. (ANT.) loyalist.

turret (SYN.) watchtower, belfry, steeple, tower, cupola, lookout.

tussle (SYN.) wrestle, struggle, contend, battle, fight, scuffle.

tutor (SYN.) instruct, prime, school, teach, train, prepare, drill.

tweak (SYN.) squeeze, pinch, nip.

twig (SYN.) sprig, branch, shoot, stem.

twilight (SYN.) sunset, sundown, nightfall, eventide, dusk.

twin (SYN.) lookalike, imitation, copy, double, replica.

twine (SYN.) string, cordage, rope, cord.

twinge (SYN.) smart, pang, pain.

twinkle (SYN.) shine, gleam, glisten, sparkle, glitter, shimmer, scintillate.

twirl (SYN.) rotate, spin, wind, turn, pivot, wheel, swivel, whirl.

twist (SYN.) bow, bend, crook, intertwine, curve, incline, deflect, lean, braid, distort, contort, warp, interweave, stoop, turn. (ANT.) resist,

break, straighten, stiffen.

twitch (SYN.) fidget, shudder, jerk.

two-faced (SYN.) deceitful, insincere, hypocritical, false, untrustworthy. (ANT.) straightforward, honest.

tycoon (SYN.) millionaire, industrialist, businessman.

tyke (SYN.) rascal, urchin, brat, ragamuffin, imp.

typhoon (SYN.) hurricane, cyclone, storm, tornado, whirlwind, twister.

typical (SYN.) common, accustomed, conventional, familiar, customary. (ANT.) marvelous, extraordinary, odd, atypical, uncommon, strange.

typify (SYN.) symbolize, illustrate, signify, represent, incarnate, indicate.

tyrannize (SYN.) oppress, victimize, threaten, brutalize, coerce.

tyrannous (SYN.) arbitrary, absolute, authoritative, despotic. (ANT.) conditional, accountable, contingent, qualified, dependent.

tyrant (SYN.) dictator, autocrat, despot, oppressor, slave driver, martinet, disciplinarian, persecutor.

U

ugly (SYN.) hideous, homely, plain, deformed, repellent, uncomely, repulsive, ill-natured, unsightly, nasty, unpleasant, wicked, disagreeable, spiteful, surly, vicious. (ANT.) beautiful, fair, pretty, attractive, handsome, comely, good.

ultimate (SYN.) extreme, latest, final, concluding, decisive, hindmost, last, terminal, utmost, greatest, maximum. (ANT.) foremost, opening, first, beginning, initial.

umbrage (SYN.) anger, displeasure.

umpire (SYN.) judge, referee, arbitrator.

unadulterated (SYN.) genuine, clear, clean, immaculate, spotless, pure, absolute, untainted, sheer, bare. (ANT.) foul, sullied, corrupt, tainted, polluted, tarnished, defiled.

unalterable (SYN.) fixed, unchangeable, steadfast, inflexible.

unanimity (SYN.) accord, unity, agreement.

unannounced (SYN.) hasty, precipitate, abrupt, unexpected. (ANT.) courteous, expected, anticipated.

unassuming (SYN.) humble, lowly, compliant, modest, plain, meek, simple, unostentatious, retiring, submissive, unpretentious. (ANT.) *haughty, showy, pompous, proud, vain, arrogant, boastful.*

unattached (SYN.) apart, separate, unmarried, single, free, independent. (ANT.) *committed, involved, entangled.*

unavoidable (SYN.) inescapable, certain, inevitable, unpreventible.

unawares (SYN.) abruptly, suddenly, unexpectedly, off guard.

unbalanced (SYN.) crazy, mad, insane, deranged.

unbearable (SYN.) insufferable, intolerable. (ANT.) *tolerable, acceptable.*

unbeliever (SYN.) dissenter, apostate, heretic, schismatic, nonconformist, sectary, sectarian.

unbending (SYN.) firm, inflexible, determined, obstinate. (ANT.) *flexible.*

unbiased (SYN.) honest, equitable, fair, impartial, reasonable, unprejudiced, just. (ANT.) *partial, fraudulent, dishonorable.*

unbroken (SYN.) complete, uninterrupted, continuous, whole.

unburden (SYN.) clear, disentangle, divest, free.

uncanny (SYN.) amazing, remarkable, extraordinary, strange.

uncertain (SYN.) dim, hazy, indefinite, obscure, indistinct, unclear, undetermined, unsettled, ambiguous, unsure, doubtful, questionable, dubious, vague. (ANT.) *explicit, lucid, specific, certain, unmistakable, precise, clear.*

uncertainty (SYN.) distrust, doubt, hesitation, incredulity, scruple, ambiguity, skepticism, suspense, suspicion, unbelief. (ANT.) *faith, belief, certainty, conviction, determination.*

uncivil (SYN.) impolite, rude, discourteous. (ANT.) *polite.*

uncivilized (SYN.) barbaric, barbarous, barbarian, brutal, crude, inhuman, cruel, merciless, rude, remorseless, uncultured, savage, unrelenting. (ANT.) *humane, kind, polite, civilized, refined.*

unclad (SYN.) exposed, nude, naked, bare, stripped, defenseless, uncovered, open, unprotected. (ANT.) *concealed, protected, clothed, covered, dressed.*

uncommon (SYN.) unusual, rare, odd, scarce, strange, peculiar, queer, exceptional, remarkable. (ANT.) *ordinary, usual.*

uncompromising (SYN.) determined, dogged, firm, immovable, contumacious, headstrong, inflexible, obdurate, intractable, obstinate, pertinacious, stubborn, unyielding. (ANT.) *docile, compliant, amenable, yielding, submissive, pliable.*

unconcern (SYN.) disinterestedness, impartiality, indifference, apathy, insensibility, neutrality. (ANT.) *affection, fervor, passion, ardor.*

unconditional (SYN.) unqualified, unrestricted, arbitrary, absolute, pure, complete, actual, authoritative, perfect, entire, ultimate, tyrannous. (ANT.) *conditional, contingent, accountable, dependent, qualified.*

unconscious (SYN.) lethargic, numb, comatose.

uncouth (SYN.) green, harsh, crude, coarse, ill-prepared, rough, raw, unfinished, unrefined, vulgar, rude, impolite, discourteous, unpolished, ill-mannered, crass. (ANT.) *well-prepared, cultivated, refined, civilized, finished.*

uncover (SYN.) disclose, discover, betray, divulge, expose, reveal, impart, show. (ANT.) *conceal, hide, cover, obscure, cloak.*

undependable (SYN.) changeable, unstable, uncertain, shifty, irresponsible. (ANT.) *stable, dependable, trustworthy.*

under (SYN.) beneath, underneath, following, below, lower, downward. (ANT.) *over, above, up, higher.*

undercover (SYN.) hidden, secret.

undergo (SYN.) endure, feel, stand, bear, indulge, suffer, sustain, experience, let, allow, permit, tolerate. (ANT.) *overcome, discard, exclude, banish.*

underhand (SYN.) sly, secret, sneaky, secretive, stealthy, crafty. (ANT.) *honest, open, direct, frank.*

undermine (SYN.) demoralize, thwart, erode, weaken, subvert, sabotage.

underscore (SYN.) emphasize, stress.

undersigned (SYN.) casual, chance, contingent, accidental, fortuitous, incidental, unintended. (ANT.) *decreed, planned, willed, calculated.*

understand (SYN.) apprehend, comprehend, appreciate, conceive, discern, know, grasp, hear, learn, realize, see, perceive. (ANT.) *misunderstand, mistake, misapprehend, ignore.*

understanding (SYN.) agreement, coincidence, concord, accordance, concurrence, harmony, unison, compact, contract, arrangement, bargain, covenant, stipulation. (ANT.) *variance, difference, discord, dissension, disagreement.*

understudy (SYN.) deputy, agent, proxy, representative, agent, alternate, lieutenant, substitute. (ANT.) *head, principal, sovereign, master.*

undertake (SYN.) venture, attempt.

undertaking (SYN.) effort, endeavor, attempt, experiment, trial, essay. (ANT.) *laziness, neglect, inaction.*

undesirable (SYN.) obnoxious, distasteful, objectionable, repugnant. (ANT.) *appealing, inviting, attractive.*

undivided (SYN.) complete, intact, entire, integral, total, perfect, unimpaired, whole. (ANT.) *partial, incomplete.*

undoing (SYN.) ruin, downfall, destruction, failure, disgrace.

undying (SYN.) endless, deathless, eternal, everlasting, ceaseless, immortal, infinite, perpetual, timeless. (ANT.) *transient, mortal, temporal, ephemeral, impermanent.*

unearthly (SYN.) metaphysical, ghostly, miraculous, marvelous, preternatural, superhuman, spiritual, foreign, strange, weird, supernatural. (ANT.) *physical, plain, human, natural, common, mundane.*

uneducated (SYN.) uncultured, ignorant, illiterate, uninformed, unlearned, untaught, unlettered. (ANT.) *erudite, cultured, educated, literate, formed.*

unemployed (SYN.) inert, inactive, idle, jobless, unoccupied. (ANT.) *working, occupied, active, industrious, employed.*

uneven (SYN.) remaining, single, odd, unmatched, rugged, gnarled, irregular. (ANT.) *matched, even, flat, smooth.*

unexceptional (SYN.) commonplace, trivial, customary.

unexpected (SYN.) immediate, hasty, surprising, instantaneous, unforeseen, abrupt, rapid, startling, sudden. (ANT.) *expected, gradual, predicted, anticipated, planned.*

unfaithful (SYN.) treacherous, disloyal, deceitful, capricious. (ANT.) *true, loyal, steadfast, faithful.*

unfasten (SYN.) open, expand, spread, exhibit, unbar, unlock, unfold, unseal. (ANT.) *shut, hide, conceal, close.*

unfavorable (SYN.) antagonistic, contrary, adverse, opposed, opposite, disastrous, counteractive, unlucky. (ANT.) *benign, fortunate, lucky, propitious.*

unfeeling (SYN.) hard, rigorous, cruel, stern, callous, numb, strict, unsympathetic, severe. (ANT.) *tender, gentle, lenient, humane.*

unfold (SYN.) develop, create, elaborate, amplify, evolve, mature, expand. (ANT.) *wither, restrict, contract, stunt, compress.*

unfurnished (SYN.) naked, mere, bare, exposed, stripped, plain, open, simple. (ANT.) *concealed, protected, covered.*

ungainly (SYN.) clumsy, awkward, bungling, clownish, gawky. (ANT.) *dexterous, graceful, elegant.*

unhappy (SYN.) sad, miserable, wretched, melancholy, distressed, depressed. (ANT.) *joyful, happy, cheerful.*

unhealthy (SYN.) infirm, sick, diseased, sickly. (ANT.) *vigorous, well, healthy, hale.*

uniform (SYN.) methodical, natural, customary, orderly, normal, consistent, ordinary, regular, unvarying, unchanging, systematic, steady, unvaried. (ANT.) *rare, unusual, erratic, abnormal, exceptional.*

unimportant (SYN.) petty, trivial, paltry, trifling, insignificant, indifferent, minor.

uninformed (SYN.) illiterate, uncultured, uneducated, ignorant, unlearned, untaught, unlettered. (ANT.) *informed, literate, erudite, cultured, educated.*

uninhibited (SYN.) loose, open, liberated, free. (ANT.) *constrained, tense, suppressed.*

unintelligible (SYN.) ambiguous, cryptic, dark, cloudy, abstruse, dusky, mysterious, indistinct, obscure, vague. (ANT.) *lucid, distinct, bright, clear.*

uninteresting (SYN.) burdensome, dilatory, dreary, dull, boring, slow, humdrum, monotonous, sluggish, tedious, tardy, wearisome, tiresome. (*ANT.*) *entertaining, exciting, quick, amusing.*

union (*SYN.*) fusion, incorporation, combination, joining, concurrence, solidarity, agreement, unification, concord, harmony, alliance, unanimity, coalition, confederacy, amalgamation, league, concert, marriage. (*ANT.*) *disagreement, separation, discord.*

unique (*SYN.*) exceptional, matchless, distinctive, choice, peculiar, singular, rare, sole, single, incomparable, uncommon, solitary, unequaled. (*ANT.*) *typical, ordinary, commonplace, frequent, common.*

unison (*SYN.*) harmony, concurrence, understanding, accordance, concord, agreeable, coincidence. (*ANT.*) *disagreement, difference, discord, variance.*

unite (*SYN.*) attach, blend, amalgamate, combine, conjoin, associate, connect, embody, consolidate, join, link, fuse, unify, merge. (*ANT.*) *sever, divide, separate, disrupt, disconnect.*

universal (*SYN.*) frequent, general, popular, common, familiar, prevailing, prevalent, usual. (*ANT.*) *scarce, odd, regional, local, extraordinary, exceptional.*

unkempt (*SYN.*) sloppy, rumpled, untidy, messy, bedraggled. (*ANT.*) *presentable, well-groomed, tidy, neat.*

unkind (*SYN.*) unfeeling, unsympathetic, unpleasant, cruel, harsh. (*ANT.*) *considerate, sympathetic, amiable, kind.*

unlawful (*SYN.*) illegitimate, illicit, illegal, outlawed, criminal, prohibited. (*ANT.*) *permitted, honest, legal, legitimate.*

unlike (*SYN.*) dissimilar, different, distinct, contrary, diverse, divergent, opposite, incongruous, variant, miscellaneous, divers. (*ANT.*) *conditional, accountable, contingent, qualified, dependent.*

unlucky (*SYN.*) cursed, inauspicious, unfortunate. (*ANT.*) *fortunate, blessed.*

unmerciful (*SYN.*) cruel, merciless, heartless, brutal.

unmistakable (*SYN.*) clear, patent, plain, visible, obvious.

unnecessary (*SYN.*) pointless, needless, superfluous, purposeless.

unoccupied (*SYN.*) empty, vacant, uninhabited.

unparalleled (*SYN.*) peerless, unequaled, rare, unique, unmatched.

unpleasant (*SYN.*) offensive, disagreeable, repulsive, obnoxious, unpleasing.

unqualified (*SYN.*) inept, unfit, incapable, incompetent, unquestioned, absolute.

unreasonable (*SYN.*) foolish, absurd, irrational, inconsistent, nonsensical, ridiculous, silly. (*ANT.*) *reasonable, sensible, sound, consistent, rational.*

unruffled (*SYN.*) calm, smooth, serene, unperturbed.

unruly (*SYN.*) unmanageable, disorganized, disorderly, disobedient. (*ANT.*) *orderly.*

unsafe (*SYN.*) hazardous, insecure, critical, dangerous, perilous, menacing, risky, precarious, threatening, (*ANT.*) *protected, secure, firm, safe.*

unselfish (*SYN.*) bountiful, generous, liberal, giving, beneficent, magnanimous, openhanded, munificent. (*ANT.*) *miserly, stingy, greedy, selfish, covetous.*

unsightly (*SYN.*) ugly, unattractive, hideous.

unsophisticated (*SYN.*) frank, candid, artless, ingenuous, naive, open, simple, natural. (*ANT.*) *sophisticated, worldly, cunning, crafty.*

unsound (*SYN.*) feeble, flimsy, weak, fragile, sick, unhealthy, diseased, invalid, faulty, false.

unstable (*SYN.*) fickle, fitful, inconstant, capricious, changeable, restless, variable. (*ANT.*) *steady, stable, trustworthy, constant.*

unswerving (*SYN.*) fast, firm, inflexible, constant, secure, stable, solid, steady, steadfast, unyielding. (*ANT.*) *sluggish, insecure, unsteady, unstable, loose, slow.*

untainted (*SYN.*) genuine, pure, spotless, clean, clear, unadulterated, guiltless, innocent, chaste, modest, undefiled, sincere, virgin. (*ANT.*) *polluted, tainted, sullied, tarnished, defiled, corrupt, foul.*

untamed (*SYN.*) fierce, savage, uncivilized, barbarous, outlandish, rude, undomesticated, wild, frenzied, mad, turbulent, impetuous, wanton, boisterous, wayward, stormy, extravagant, tempestuous, foolish, rash, giddy, reckless. (*ANT.*) *quiet, gentle, calm, civilized, placid.*

untidy (*SYN.*) messy, sloppy, disorderly, slovenly.

untoward (*SYN.*) disobedient, contrary, peevish, fractious, forward, petulant, obstinate, intractable, stubborn, perverse, ungovernable. (*ANT.*) *docile, tractable, obliging, agreeable.*

unusual (*SYN.*) capricious, abnormal, devious, eccentric, aberrant, irregular, variable, remarkable, extraordinary, odd, peculiar, uncommon, strange, exceptional, unnatural. (*ANT.*) *regular, usual, fixed, ordinary.*

unyielding (*SYN.*) fast, firm, inflexible, constant, solid, secure, stable, steadfast, unswerving, steady. (*ANT.*) *sluggish, slow, insecure, loose, unsteady, unstable.*

upbraid (*SYN.*) blame, censure, berate, admonish, rate, lecture, rebuke, reprimand, reprehend, scold, vituperate. (*ANT.*) *praise, commend, approve.*

uphold (*SYN.*) justify, espouse, assert, defend, maintain, vindicate. (*ANT.*) *oppose, submit, assault, deny, attack.*

upright (*SYN.*) undeviating, right, unswerving, direct, erect, unbent, straight, fair, vertical. (*ANT.*) *bent, dishonest, crooked, circuitous, winding.*

uprising (*SYN.*) revolution, mutiny, revolt, rebellion.

uproar (*SYN.*) noise, disorder, commotion, tumult, disturbance.

upset (*SYN.*) disturb, harass, bother, annoy, haunt, molest, inconvenience, perplex, pester, tease, plague, trouble, worry, overturn, topple, upend, capsize, fluster, agitate. (*ANT.*) *soothe, relieve, gratify.*

urbane (*SYN.*) civil, considerate, cultivated, courteous, genteel, polite, accomplished, refined, well-mannered. (*ANT.*) *rude, uncouth, boorish, uncivil.*

urge (*SYN.*) craving, desire, longing, lust, appetite, aspiration, yearning, incite, coax, entice, force, drive, prod, press, plead, coerce, persuade, implore, beg, recommend, advise. (*ANT.*) *loathing, hate, distaste, aversion, deter, dissuade, discourage.*

urgency (*SYN.*) emergency, exigency, pass, pinch, strait, crisis.

urgent (*SYN.*) critical, crucial, exigent, imperative, impelling, insistent, necessary, instant, serious, pressing, cogent, important, importunate, immediate. (*ANT.*) *trivial, unimportant, insignificant.*

usage (*SYN.*) use, treatment, custom, practice, tradition.

use (*SYN.*) custom, practice, habit, training, usage, manner, apply, avail, employ, operate, utilize, exert, exhaust, handle, manage, accustom, inure, exploit, manipulate, spend, expend, consume. (*ANT.*) *disuse, neglect, waste, ignore, overlook, idleness.*

useful (*SYN.*) beneficial, helpful, good, serviceable, wholesome, advantageous. (*ANT.*) *harmful, injurious, deleterious, destructive, detrimental.*

usefulness (*SYN.*) price, merit, utility, excellence, virtue, worth, worthiness. (*ANT.*) *cheapness, valueless, uselessness.*

useless (*SYN.*) bootless, empty, idle, pointless, vain, valueless, worthless, abortive, fruitless, unavailing, ineffectual, vapid. (*ANT.*) *profitable, potent, effective.*

usher (*SYN.*) guide, lead.

usual (*SYN.*) customary, common, familiar, general, normal, habitual, accustomed, everyday, ordinary, regular. (*ANT.*) *irregular, exceptional, rare, extraordinary, abnormal.*

utensil (*SYN.*) instrument, tool, vehicle, apparatus, device, implement. (*ANT.*) *preventive, obstruction.*

utilize (*SYN.*) use, apply, devote, busy, employ, occupy, avail. (*ANT.*) *reject, banish, discharge, discard.*

utopian (*SYN.*) perfect, ideal, faultless, exemplary, supreme, visionary, unreal. (*ANT.*) *real, imperfect, actual, faulty.*

utter (*SYN.*) full, perfect, whole, finished, entire, speak, say, complete, superlative. (*ANT.*) *imperfect, deficient, lacking, faulty, incomplete.*

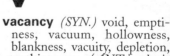

vacancy (*SYN.*) void, emptiness, vacuum, hollowness, blankness, vacuity, depletion, nothingness. (*ANT.*) *plenitude, fullness, profusion, completeness.*

vacant (*SYN.*) barren, empty, blank, bare, unoccupied, void, vacuous. (*ANT.*) *filled, packed, employed, full, replete, busy, engaged.*

vacate (*SYN.*) abjure, relinquish, abdicate, renounce, abandon, resign, surrender, desert, waive, quit, leave.

(ANT.) *stay, support, uphold, maintain.*

vacation (SYN.) rest, holiday, recess, break. (ANT.) *labor, work, routine.*

vacillate (SYN.) hesitate, oscillate, undulate, change, fluctuate, vary, waver. (ANT.) *adhere, persist, stick, decide.*

vacillating (SYN.) contrary, illogical, contradictory, inconsistent, incongruous, incompatible, paradoxical, irreconcilable, unsteady, wavering. (ANT.) *correspondent, congruous, consistent, compatible.*

vacuity (SYN.) space, emptiness, vacuum, void, blank, nothingness, ignorance, unawareness, senselessness, mindlessness, chatter, nonsense, froth, absurdity. (ANT.) *matter, fullness, content, substance, knowledge, intelligence.*

vacuous (SYN.) dull, blank, uncomprehending, imbecilic, foolish, thoughtless, distracted, absent-minded. (ANT.) *responsive, alert, attentive, bright, intelligent, aware.*

vacuum (SYN.) void, gap, emptiness, hole, chasm, nothingness, abyss.

vagabond (SYN.) pauper, ragamuffin, scrub, beggar, mendicant, starveling, wretch, tatterdemalion, hobo, tramp. (ANT.) *responsible, established, rooted, installed, reliable.*

vagary (SYN.) notion, whim, fantasy, fancy, daydream, caprice, conceit, quirk, whimsy, impulse.

vagrant (SYN.) hobo, rover, tramp, beggar, bum, wanderer, vagabond. (ANT.) *settled, worker, laborer, rooted, ambitious, gentleman.*

vague (SYN.) indefinite, hazy, dim, indistinct, ambiguous, obscure, undetermined, unclear, unsure, unsettled. (ANT.) *certain, spelled out, specific, lucid, clear, definite, distinct, explicit, precise, unequivocal.*

vain (SYN.) fruitless, empty, bootless, futile, idle, abortive, ineffectual, unavailing, vapid, pointless, valueless, useless, trivial, unfruitful, worthless, unsuccessful, proud, conceited. (ANT.) *meek, modest, potent, rewarding, self-effacing, diffident, profitable, effective, humble.*

vainglory (SYN.) conceit, pride, self-esteem, arrogance, self-respect, superciliousness, haughtiness, vanity. (ANT.)

shame, modesty, meekness, humility, lowliness.

valet (SYN.) groom, dresser, attendant, manservant.

valiant (SYN.) bold, brave, courageous, adventurous, audacious, chivalrous, daring, fearless, heroic, gallant, magnanimous, intrepid, unafraid, valorous, dauntless. (ANT.) *weak, fearful, cowardly, timid.*

valid (SYN.) cogent, conclusive, effective, convincing, binding, efficacious, logical, powerful, legal, sound, weighty, well-founded, real, genuine, actual, true, trustworthy, strong, telling, authentic. (ANT.) *weak, unconvincing, void, unproved, null, spurious, counterfeit.*

validate (SYN.) corroborate, substantiate, support, confirm, prove, uphold, sustain, authenticate. (ANT.) *disprove, contradict, cancel.*

valise (SYN.) satchel, bag, baggage.

valley (SYN.) dale, dell, lowland, basin, gully, vale, ravine. (ANT.) *highland, hill, upland, headland.*

valor (SYN.) courage, heroism, bravery, boldness, intrepidity, fearlessness.

valuable (SYN.) profitable, useful, costly, precious, dear, expensive, worthy, important, high-priced, esteemed. (ANT.) *trashy, poor, cheap, worthless.*

value (SYN.) price, merit, usefulness, value, virtue, utility, appreciate, prize, hold dear, treasure, excellence, benefit, cost, rate, evaluate, appraise, esteem, importance, worth, worthiness. (ANT.) *valueless, uselessness, cheapness.*

vanish (SYN.) evaporate, disappear. (ANT.) *appear.*

vanity (SYN.) complacency, egotism, pride, self-esteem, conceit, caprice, fancy, idea, conception, notion, haughtiness, self-respect, whim, smugness, vainglory, arrogance, imagination. (ANT.) *meekness, humility, diffidence.*

vanquish (SYN.) defeat, crush, humble, surmount, master, beat, conquer, overcome, rout, quell, subjugate, subdue. (ANT.) *surrender, cede, lose, retreat, capitulate.*

vapid (SYN.) hackneyed, inane, insipid, trite, banal, commonplace. (ANT.) *striking, novel, fresh, original, stimulating.*

vapor (SYN.) steam, fog, mist, smog, haze, steam.

variable (SYN.) fickle, fitful, inconstant, unstable, shifting, changeable, unsteady, wavering, vacillating. (ANT.) *unchanging, uniform, stable, unwavering, steady, constant.*

variant (SYN.) dissimilar, different, distinct, contrary, diverse, divergent, opposite, unlike, incongruous, divers, sundry, various, miscellaneous. (ANT.) *similar, same, congruous, identical, alike.*

variation (SYN.) change, alternation, alteration, substitution, variety, substitute, mutation, exchange, vicissitude. (ANT.) *uniformity, stability, monotony.*

variety (SYN.) dissimilarity, diversity, heterogeneity, assortment, change, difference, medley, mixture, miscellany, form, type, class, breed, sort, kind, strain, stock. (ANT.) *likeness, monotony, uniformity, sameness, homogeneity.*

various (SYN.) miscellaneous, sundry, divers, several, contrary, distinct, dissimilar, divergent, unlike, incongruous, opposite, different. (ANT.) *identical, similar, same, alike, congruous.*

vary (SYN.) exchange, substitute, alter, change, modify, shift, convert, transform, transfigure, diversify, veer. (ANT.) *settle, stabilize, continue, establish, preserve.*

vassalage (SYN.) confinement, captivity, imprisonment, slavery, thralldom. (ANT.) *liberation, freedom.*

vast (SYN.) big, capacious, extensive, huge, great, ample, immense, wide, unlimited, enormous, measureless, large. (ANT.) *tiny, small, short, little.*

vault (SYN.) caper, jerk, jump, leap, bound, crypt, sepulcher, hop, spring, safe, start, tomb, grave, catacomb, skip.

vaunt (SYN.) crow, flaunt, glory, boast. (ANT.) *minimize, humble, deprecate, apologize.*

vaunting (SYN.) flourish, display, ostentation, parade, show, pomp. (ANT.) *modesty, reserve, humility.*

vehement (SYN.) excitable, fervent, ardent, burning, fiery, glowing, impetuous, hot, irascible, passionate. (ANT.) *calm, quiet, cool, apathetic, deliberate.*

veil (SYN.) clothe, conceal, cover, cloak, web, hide, curtain, disguise, gauze, envelop, screen, mask, shield, film. (ANT.) *reveal, unveil, bare,*

divulge.

velocity (SYN.) quickness, rapidity, speed, swiftness.

venal (SYN.) greedy, mercenary, sordid, corrupt. (ANT.) *liberal, honorable, generous.*

venerable (SYN.) antiquated, aged, antique, ancient, elderly, old, superannuated, old-fashion. (ANT.) *young, new, youthful, modern.*

venerate (SYN.) approve, esteem, admire, appreciate, wonder, respect. (ANT.) *dislike, despise.*

vengeance (SYN.) requital, reprisal, reparation, retribution, revenge. (ANT.) *forgiveness, remission, pardon, mercy.*

venom (SYN.) toxin, poison, bitterness, spite, hate.

vent (SYN.) eject, emit, expel, shoot, spurt, emanate, hurl, shed, belch, discharge, breathe.

venture (SYN.) speculate, attempt, test, dare, hazard, gamble, chance, risk. (ANT.) *insure, secure, protect.*

verbal (SYN.) oral, spoken, literal, unwritten, vocal. (ANT.) *printed, written, recorded.*

verbose (SYN.) communicative, glib, chattering, chatty, garrulous, loquacious, talkative. (ANT.) *uncommunicative, silent.*

verbosity (SYN.) long-windedness, verboseness, redundancy, wordiness. (ANT.) *terseness, laconic, conciseness.*

verdict (SYN.) judgment, finding, opinion, decision.

verge (SYN.) lip, rim, edge, margin, brink, brim.

verification (SYN.) confirmation, demonstration, evidence, proof, test, experiment, testimony, trial.

verify (SYN.) confirm, substantiate, acknowledge, determine, assure, establish, approve, fix, settle, ratify, strengthen, corroborate, affirm, sanction.

veritable (SYN.) authentic, correct, genuine, real, true, accurate, actual. (ANT.) *false, fictitious, spurious, erroneous, counterfeit.*

versed (SYN.) conversant, familiar, intimate, knowing, acquainted, aware. (ANT.) *untrained, unaccomplished.*

version (SYN.) interpretation, rendition.

vertical (SYN.) erect, perpendicular, upright. (ANT.) *horizontal.*

very (SYN.) exceedingly, extremely, greatly, considerably.

vessel (SYN.) craft, boat, ship.

vestige *(SYN.)* stain, scar, mark, brand, stigma, characteristic, trace, feature, trait, symptom, hint, token, suggestion, indication.

veto *(SYN.)* refusal, denial, refuse, deny, negate, forbid, prohibit. *(ANT.)* approve, approval.

vex *(SYN.)* embitter, exasperate, aggravate, annoy, chafe, bother, provoke, pester, plague, anger, nettle. *(ANT.) soften, soothe, palliate, mitigate.*

vexation *(SYN.)* chagrin, irritation, annoyance, mortification, irritation, pique. *(ANT.) comfort, pleasure, appeasement, gratification.*

vibrate *(SYN.)* flutter, jar, quake, jolt, quaver, agitate, transgression, wickedness, ungodliness, tremble.

vice *(SYN.)* iniquity, crime, offense, evil, guilt, sin, ungodliness, wickedness, depravity, corruption, wrong. *(ANT.) righteousness, virtue, goodness, innocence, purity.*

vicinity *(SYN.)* district, area, locality, neighborhood, environs, proximity, nearness, adjacency. *(ANT.) remoteness, distance.*

vicious *(SYN.)* bad, evil, wicked, sinful, corrupt, cruel, savage, dangerous.

victimize *(SYN.)* cheat, dupe, swindle, deceive, take advantage of.

victor *(SYN.)* champion, winner. *(ANT.) loser.*

victory *(SYN.)* conquest, jubilation, triumph, success, achievement, ovation. *(ANT.) defeat, failure.*

view *(SYN.)* discern, gaze, glance, behold, eye, stare, watch, examine, witness, prospect, vision, vista, sight, look, panorama, opinion, judgment, belief, impression, perspective, range, regard, thought, observation, survey, scene, conception, outlook, inspect, observe. *(ANT.) miss, overlook, avert, hide.*

viewpoint *(SYN.)* attitude, standpoint, aspect, pose, disposition, position, stand, posture.

vigilant *(SYN.)* anxious, attentive, careful, alert, circumspect, cautious, observant, wary, watchful, wakeful. *(ANT.) inattentive, neglectful, careless.*

vigor *(SYN.)* spirit, verve, energy, zeal, fortitude, vitality, strength, liveliness. *(ANT.) listlessness.*

vigorous *(SYN.)* brisk, energetic, active, blithe, animated, frolicsome, strong, spirited, lively, forceful, sprightly, vivacious, powerful, supple. *(ANT.) vapid, dull, listless, insipid.*

vile *(SYN.)* foul, loathsome, base, depraved, debased, sordid, vulgar, wicked, abject, ignoble, mean, worthless, sinful, bad, low, wretched, evil, offensive, objectionable, disgusting. *(ANT.) honorable, upright, decent, laudable, attractive.*

vilify *(SYN.)* asperse, defame, disparage, abuse, malign, revile, scandalize. *(ANT.) protect, honor, praise, cherish.*

village *(SYN.)* hamlet, town. *(ANT.) metropolis, city.*

villain *(SYN.)* rascal, rogue, cad, brute, scoundrel, devil, scamp.

villainous *(SYN.)* deleterious, evil, bad, base, iniquitous, unsound, sinful, unwholesome, wicked. *(ANT.) honorable, reputable, moral, good, excellent.*

vindicate *(SYN.)* clear, assert, defend, absolve, excuse, acquit, uphold, support. *(ANT.) accuse, convict, abandon.*

violate *(SYN.)* disobey, invade, defile, break, desecrate, pollute, dishonor, debauch, profane, deflower, ravish.

violence *(SYN.)* constraint, force, compulsion, coercion. *(ANT.) weakness, persuasion, feebleness, impotence, frailty.*

violent *(SYN.)* strong, forceful, powerful, forcible, angry, fierce, savage, passionate, furious. *(ANT.) gentle.*

virgin *(SYN.)* immaculate, genuine, spotless, clean, clear, unadulterated, chaste, untainted, innocent, guiltless, untouched, modest, maid, maiden, sincere, unused, undefiled, pure. *(ANT.) foul, tainted, defiled, sullied, polluted, corrupt.*

virile *(SYN.)* hardy, male, mannish, lusty, bold, masculine, strong, vigorous. *(ANT.) feminine, unmanly, weak, effeminate, womanish, emasculated.*

virtue *(SYN.)* integrity, probity, purity, chastity, goodness, rectitude, effectiveness, force, honor, power, efficacy, quality, strength, merit, righteousness. *(ANT.) fault, vice, lewdness, corruption.*

virtuous *(SYN.)* good, ethical, chaste, honorable, moral, just, pure, righteous, upstanding, upright, scrupulous. *(ANT.) licentious, unethical, amoral, sinful, libertine, immoral.*

virulent *(SYN.)* hostile, malevolent, malignant, bitter, spiteful, wicked. *(ANT.) kind, affectionate, benevolent.*

vision *(SYN.)* dream, hallucination, mirage, eyesight, sight, fantasy, illusion, specter, revelation, phantom, spook. *(ANT.) verity, reality.*

visionary *(SYN.)* faultless, ideal, perfect, unreal, supreme. *(ANT.) real, actual, imperfect, faulty.*

visit *(SYN.)* attend, see, appointment.

visitor *(SYN.)* caller, guest.

vista *(SYN.)* view, scene, aspect.

vital *(SYN.)* cardinal, living, paramount, alive, essential, critical, basic, indispensable, urgent, life-and-death. *(ANT.) lifeless, unimportant, inanimate, nonessential.*

vitality *(SYN.)* buoyancy, being, life, liveliness, existence, spirit, vigor. *(ANT.) death, lethargy, dullness, demise.*

vitiate *(SYN.)* allay, abase, corrupt, adulterate, debase, defile, depress, deprave, degrade, impair, humiliate, pervert.

vivacious *(SYN.)* lively, spirited.

vivid *(SYN.)* brilliant, striking, clear, bright, intense, lively, strong, graphic. *(ANT.) dim, dusky, vague, dull, dreary.*

vocal *(SYN.)* said, uttered, oral, spoken, definite, outspoken, specific.

vocation *(SYN.)* commerce, employment, business, art, job, profession, trade, occupation, career, calling, work, trading. *(ANT.) pastime, hobby, avocation.*

void *(SYN.)* barren, emptiness, space, annul, cancel, empty, bare, unoccupied, meaningless, invalid, useless, invalidate, worthless, vacant, barren. *(ANT.) employed, full, replete, engaged.*

volatile *(SYN.)* effervescent, resilient, buoyant, animated, cheerful, hopeful, lively, sprightly, spirited, vivacious. *(ANT.) depressed, sullen, hopeless, dejected, despondent.*

volition *(SYN.)* desire, intention, pleasure, preference, choice, decision, resolution, testament, wish, will. *(ANT.) disinterest, compulsion, indifference.*

voluble *(SYN.)* glib, communicative, verbose, loquacious, chatty, chattering. *(ANT.) uncommunicative, laconic, taciturn, silent.*

volume *(SYN.)* capacity, loudness, sound, magnitude, mass, book, dimensions, quantity, amount, size.

voluntary *(SYN.)* extemporaneous, free, automatic, spontaneous, offhand. *(ANT.) forced, planned, required, rehearsed, compulsory, prepared.*

volunteer *(SYN.)* extend, offer, present, advance, propose, tender, sacrifice. *(ANT.) receive, spurn, reject, accept, retain.*

voracious *(SYN.)* insatiable, ravenous.

vow *(SYN.)* oath, pledge, swear, promise.

voyage *(SYN.)* tour, journey, excursion.

vulgar *(SYN.)* ordinary, popular, common, general, crude, coarse, low, rude. *(ANT.) polite, refined, select, aristocratic.*

vulnerable *(SYN.)* unguarded, defenseless, unprotected.

wacky *(SYN.)* strange, crazy, peculiar.

wad *(SYN.)* hunk, clump, chunk.

wafer *(SYN.)* cracker, lozenge.

waft *(SYN.)* convey, glide, sail, float.

wage *(SYN.)* conduct, pursue, make.

wager *(SYN.)* stake, bet, play, gamble, speculate, risk, chance.

wages *(SYN.)* payment, compensation, fee, allowance, pay, salary, earnings, rate, recompense.

wagon *(SYN.)* carriage, buggy, cart, surrey, stagecoach.

waif *(SYN.)* guttersnipe, ragamuffin, tramp, vagrant, urchin.

wail *(SYN.)* mourn, moan, cry, bewail, lament, bemoan, sorrow.

wait *(SYN.)* linger, tarry, attend, bide, watch, delay, await, abide, stay, serve, pause, remain, rest, minister, expect. *(ANT.) hasten, act, leave, expedite.*

waive *(SYN.)* renounce, abandon, surrender, relinquish, forgo. *(ANT.) uphold, maintain.*

wake *(SYN.)* awaken, rouse,

waken, arouse, stimulate, activate. (ANT.) doze, sleep.

waken (SYN.) wake, arouse, rouse, awaken, stimulate, activate. (ANT.) doze, sleep.

walk (SYN.) step, stroll, march, amble, saunter, hike, lane, path, passage.

wall (SYN.) barricade, divider, partition, panel, stockade.

wallow (SYN.) plunge, roll, flounder, grovel.

wan (SYN.) colorless, haggard, gaunt, pallid, pasty, pale.

wander (SYN.) rove, stroll, deviate, ramble, digress, roam, traipse, range, err, meander, saunter. (ANT.) linger, stop, settle.

wane (SYN.) abate, weaken, fade, ebb, decrease, wither, subside.

want (SYN.) penury, destitution, crave, desire, requirement, poverty, wish, require, need, privation. (ANT.) wealth, plenty, abundance.

wanton (SYN.) lecherous, immoral, loose, lewd, salacious, lustful.

war (SYN.) battle, hostility, combat, fight, strife, contention. (ANT.) peace, calm, friendship, harmony.

warble (SYN.) sing, trill, chirp.

ward (SYN.) annex, wing, section.

warden (SYN.) custodian, guard, guardian, keeper, turnkey, jailer, curator.

wares (SYN.) merchandise, staples, inventory, commodities, goods.

wariness (SYN.) heed, care, watchfulness, caution, vigilance. (ANT.) carelessness, abandon.

warlike (SYN.) hostile, unfriendly, combative, belligerent, antagonistic, pugnacious, bellicose, opposed, aggressive. (ANT.) cordial, peaceful, amicable.

warm (SYN.) sincere, cordial, hearty, earnest, sympathetic, ardent, heated, gracious, temperate, enthusiastic, lukewarm, tepid, eager, sociable. (ANT.) cool, aloof, taciturn, brisk, indifferent.

warmhearted (SYN.) loving, kind, kindhearted, friendly, generous.

warmth (SYN.) friendliness, cordiality, geniality, understanding, compassion.

warn (SYN.) apprise, notify, admonish, caution, advise, inform.

warning (SYN.) advice, information, caution, portent, admonition, indication, notice, sign.

warp (SYN.) turn, bend, twist, distort, deprave.

warrant (SYN.) pledge, assurance, warranty, guarantee, authorize, approve, mandate, sanction.

warrior (SYN.) combatant, fighter, soldier, mercenary, guerrilla.

wary (SYN.) careful, awake, watchful, heedful, attentive, alive, mindful, cautious, thoughtful. (ANT.) unaware, indifferent, careless, apathetic.

wash (SYN.) launder, cleanse, rub, wet, clean, scrub, bathe. (ANT.) soil, dirty, stain.

washed-out (SYN.) bleached, dull, faded, pale, discolored, pallid.

waspish (SYN.) irritable, petulant, fractious, ill-tempered, testy, snappish, touchy. (ANT.) pleasant, genial.

waste (SYN.) forlorn, bleak, wild, solitary, dissipate, abandoned, spend, deserted, bare, consume, dwindle, decay, misspend, decrease, wither, wear, effluent, useless, unused, garbage, rubbish, refuse, trash, squander, uninhabited. (ANT.) cultivated, attended.

wasteful (SYN.) wanton, costly, lavish, extravagant.

watch (SYN.) inspect, descry, behold, distinguish, guard, attend, observe, contemplate, espy, perceive, look at, protect, chronometer, timepiece, patrol, vigil, duty, shift, regard, note, view, scan, sentinel, watchman, sentry, discern.

watchdog (SYN.) lookout, guard, sentinel, sentry.

watchful (SYN.) alert, careful, attentive, vigilant, wary, cautious.

waterfall (SYN.) cascade, cataract.

watertight (SYN.) impregnable, firm, solid.

wave (SYN.) ripple, whitecap, undulation, breaker, surf, swell, sea, surge, tide, flow, roll.

waver (SYN.) question, suspect, flicker, deliberate, doubt, distrust, hesitate, falter, stagger. (ANT.) confide, trust, believe, decide.

wavering (SYN.) fickle, shifting, variable, changeable, vacillating, fitful. (ANT.) unchanging, constant, uniform.

wavy (SYN.) rippling, serpentine, curly.

wax (SYN.) raise, heighten, expand, accrue, enhance, extend, multiply, enlarge, augment, amplify. (ANT.) contract, reduce, atrophy, diminish.

way (SYN.) habit, road, course, avenue, route, mode, system, channel, track, fashion, method, walk, approach, manner, technique, means, procedure, trail, proceed, progress, path, style.

waylay (SYN.) surprise, accost, ambush, attack, pounce, intercept.

wayward (SYN.) stubborn, headstrong, contrary, obstinate, naughty, disobedient, rebellious, refractory.

weak (SYN.) frail, debilitated, delicate, poor, wavering, infirm, bending, lame, defenseless, vulnerable, fragile, pliant, feeble, watery, diluted, undecided, assailable, irresolute, unsteady, yielding, tender. (ANT.) strong, potent, sturdy, powerful.

weaken (SYN.) exhaust, sap, disable, devitalize.

weakling (SYN.) sissy, namby-pamby, milksop, milquetoast.

weakness (SYN.) incompetence, inability, impotence, handicap, fondness, liking, affection, disability, incapacity, feebleness. (ANT.) strength, ability, power.

wealth (SYN.) fortune, money, riches, possessions, means, abundance, opulence, affluence, property, quantity, profession, luxury. (ANT.) want, need.

wealthy (SYN.) rich, exorbitant, prosperous, affluent, successful. (ANT.) poverty-stricken, poor, indigent, impoverished, beggarly, destitute, needy.

wear (SYN.) erode, fray, grind, apparel, clothes, garb, attire.

wearied (SYN.) weak, languid, faint, irresolute, feeble, timid. (ANT.) brave, vigorous.

weary (SYN.) faint, spent, worn, tired, fatigued, exhausted, tiresome, bored, wearied, tedious, jaded. (ANT.) rested, hearty, fresh.

weasel (SYN.) cheat, traitor, betrayer.

weave (SYN.) lace, interlace, plait, intertwine, braid, knit.

web (SYN.) netting, network, net, cobweb, trap, entanglement.

wed (SYN.) espouse, marry.

wedge (SYN.) chock, jam, lodge.

wedlock (SYN.) marriage, union, espousal, wedding, matrimony.

wee (SYN.) small, tiny, miniature, petite, microscopic, minute.

weep (SYN.) mourn, sob, bemoan, cry, lament, whimper, wail.

weigh (SYN.) heed, deliberate, consider, study, ponder, contemplate, reflect, evaluate. (ANT.) neglect, ignore.

weight (SYN.) importance, emphasis, load, burden, import, stress, influence, heaviness, pressure, value, gravity, significance. (ANT.) triviality, levity, insignificance, lightness, buoyancy.

weird (SYN.) odd, eerie, strange, unnatural, peculiar, spooky.

welcome (SYN.) entertain, greet, accept, receive, reception, gain, greeting, shelter. (ANT.) reject, bestow, impart, discharge.

weld (SYN.) solder, connect, fuse, bond.

welfare (SYN.) good, well-being, prosperity.

well (SYN.) hearty, happy, sound, hale, beneficial, good, convenient, expedient, healthy, favorably, fully, thoroughly, surely, adequately, satisfactorily, competently, certainly, completely, trim, undoubtedly, fit, profitable. (ANT.) infirm, depressed, weak.

well-being (SYN.) delight, happiness, satisfaction, contentment, gladness. (ANT.) sorrow, grief, sadness, despair.

well-bred (SYN.) cultured, polite, genteel, courtly, refined, cultivated. (ANT.) crude, vulgar, boorish, rude.

well-known (SYN.) famous, illustrious, celebrated, noted, eminent, renowned. (ANT.) unknown, ignominious, obscure, hidden.

wet (SYN.) moist, dank, soaked, damp, drenched, dampen, moisten. (ANT.) arid, dry, parched.

wharf (SYN.) pier, dock.

wheedle (SYN.) coax, cajole, persuade.

whim (SYN.) fancy, notion, humor, quirk, caprice, whimsy, inclination, vagary.

whimsical (SYN.) quaint, strange, curious, odd, unusual, droll, queer, eccentric, peculiar. (ANT.) normal, common, usual, familiar.

whine (SYN.) whimper, cry, moan, complain.

whip (SYN.) scourge, thrash, beat, lash.

whirl (SYN.) rotate, twirl, spin, revolve, reel.

whole (SYN.) total, sound, all, intact, complete, well, hale, integral, unimpaired, healed, entire, uncut, undivided, unbroken, undamaged, perfect. (ANT.) partial, defective, imperfect, deficient.

wholesome (SYN.) robust, well, hale, healthy, sound, salubrious, good, hygienic, salutary, nourishing, healthful, strong, nutritious, hearty. (ANT.) frail, noxious, infirm, delicate, injurious, diseased.

wicked (SYN.) deleterious, iniquitous, immoral, bad, evil, base, ungodly, unsound, sinful, bitter, blasphemous, malicious, evil-minded, profane, baleful, hostile, rancorous, unwholesome. (ANT.) moral, good, reputable, honorable.

wide (SYN.) large, broad, sweeping, extensive, vast, expanded. (ANT.) restricted, narrow.

width (SYN.) wideness, extensiveness, breadth.

wield (SYN.) handle, brandish.

wild (SYN.) outlandish, uncivilized, untamed, irregular, wanton, foolish, mad, barbarous, rough, waste, desert, uncultivated, boisterous, unruly, savage, primitive, giddy, unrestrained, silly, wayward, uncontrolled, impetuous, crazy, ferocious, undomesticated, desolate. (ANT.) quiet, gentle, placid, tame, restrained, civilized.

will (SYN.) intention, desire, volition, decision, resolution, wish, resoluteness, choice, determination, pleasure. (ANT.) disinterest, coercion, indifference.

willful (SYN.) intentional, designed, contemplated, studied, premeditated. (ANT.) fortuitous.

willing (SYN.) agreeing, energetic, enthusiastic, consenting, agreeable, eager.

wilt (SYN.) sag, droop, weaken.

wily (SYN.) cunning, foxy, sly, crafty.

win (SYN.) gain, succeed, prevail, achieve, thrive, obtain, get, acquire, earn, flourish. (ANT.) lose, miss, forfeit, fail.

wind (SYN.) gale, breeze, storm, gust, blast, air, breath, flurry, puff, blow, hurricane, typhoon, cyclone, tornado, suggestion, hint, clue, zephyr,

squall, coil, crank, screw, meander, wander, twist, weave, draft.

winsome (SYN.) winning, charming, agreeable.

wisdom (SYN.) insight, judgment, learning, sense, discretion, reason, prudence, erudition, foresight, intelligence, knowledge, information, sagacity. (ANT.) nonsense, foolishness, stupidity, ignorance.

wise (SYN.) informed, sagacious, learned, penetrating, enlightened, advisable, prudent, profound, deep, erudite, scholarly, knowing, sound, intelligent, expedient, discerning. (ANT.) simple, shallow, foolish.

wish (SYN.) crave, hanker, long, hunger, yearning, lust, craving, yearn, want, appetite, covet, longing, desire, urge. (ANT.) hate, aversion, loathing, distaste.

wit (SYN.) sense, humor, pleasantry, satire, intelligence, comprehension, understanding, banter, mind, wisdom, intellect, wittiness, fun, drollery, humorist, wag, comedian, raillery, irony, witticism. (ANT.) solemnity, commonplace, sobriety.

witch (SYN.) magician, sorcerer, enchanter, sorceress, enchantress, warlock.

witchcraft (SYN.) enchantment, magic, wizardry, conjuring, voodoo.

withdraw (SYN.) renounce, leave, abandon, recall, retreat, go, secede, desert, quit, retire, depart, retract, remove, forsake. (ANT.) enter, tarry, abide, place, stay.

wither (SYN.) wilt, languish, dry, shrivel, decline, fade, decay, sear, waste, wizen, weaken, droop, sink, fail, shrink. (ANT.) renew, refresh, revive.

withhold (SYN.) forbear, abstain, repress, check, refrain. (ANT.) persist, continue.

witness (SYN.) perceive, proof, spectator, confirmation, see, attestation, watch, observe, eyewitness, notice, testimony. (ANT.) refutation, contradiction, argument.

witty (SYN.) funny, talented, apt, bright, adroit, sharp, clever. (ANT.) foolish, slow, dull, clumsy, awkward.

wizard (SYN.) magician, conjuror, sorcerer.

wizardry (SYN.) voodoo, legerdemain, conjuring, witchcraft, charm.

woe (SYN.) sorrow, disaster, trouble, evil, agony, suffering, anguish, sadness, grief, distress, misery, torment, misfortune. (ANT.) pleasure, delight, fun.

womanly (SYN.) girlish, womanish, female, ladylike. (ANT.) mannish, virile, male, masculine.

wonder (SYN.) awe, curiosity, miracle, admiration, surprise, wonderment. (ANT.) expectation, familiarity, indifference, apathy, triviality.

wonderful (SYN.) extraordinary, marvelous, astonishing, amazing, remarkable, astounding.

wont (SYN.) practice, use, custom, training, habit, usage, manner. (ANT.) inexperience, disuse.

word (SYN.) phrase, term, utterance, expression, articulate.

wordy (SYN.) talkative, verbose, garrulous.

work (SYN.) opus, employment, achievement, performance, toil, business, exertion, occupation, labor, job, product. (ANT.) recreation, leisure, vacation, ease.

working (SYN.) busy, active, industrious. (ANT.) lazy, dormant, passive, inactive.

world (SYN.) globe, earth, universe.

worn (SYN.) tired, jaded, exhausted, wearied, faint, weary. (ANT.) invigorated, fresh, rested.

worry (SYN.) concern, trouble, disquiet, anxiety, fear, pain, harry, gall, grieve. (ANT.) console, comfort, contentment, satisfaction, peace.

worship (SYN.) honor, revere, adore, idolize, reverence, glorify, respect. (ANT.) curse, scorn, blaspheme, despise.

worth (SYN.) value, price, deserving, excellence, usefulness, utility, worthiness. (ANT.) uselessness, valueless, cheapness.

worthless (SYN.) empty, idle, abortive, ineffectual, bootless, vain, unavailing. (ANT.) effective, valuable, potent.

wound (SYN.) mar, harm, damage, hurt, dishonor, injure, injury, spoil, wrong. (ANT.) compliment, preserve, help.

wrap (SYN.) cover, protect, shield, cloak, mask, clothe, curtain, guard, conceal. (ANT.) reveal, bare, unveil, expose.

wrath (SYN.) fury, anger,

irritation, rage, animosity, passion, temper, petulance. (ANT.) patience, conciliation, peace.

wreck (SYN.) ravage, devastation, extinguish, destroy, annihilate, damage, raze. (ANT.) construct, preserve, establish.

wrench (SYN.) tug, jerk, twist.

wrestle (SYN.) fight, tussle, grapple.

wretch (SYN.) cad, scoundrel, rogue.

wretched (SYN.) forlorn, miserable, comfortless, despicable, paltry, low. (ANT.) contented, happy, significant.

wring (SYN.) twist, extract.

writer (SYN.) creator, maker, author, composer.

writhe (SYN.) twist, squirm.

wrong (SYN.) awry, incorrect, improper, amiss, naughty, inappropriate, criminal, faulty, erroneous, bad, evil, imprecise. (ANT.) proper, true, correct, suitable.

wry (SYN.) amusing, witty, dry, droll.

Y

yacht (SYN.) sailboat, boat, cruiser.

yank (SYN.) pull, wrest, draw, haul, tug, jerk, wrench, heave, extract.

yap (SYN.) howl, bark.

yard (SYN.) pen, confine, court, enclosure, compound, garden.

yardstick (SYN.) measure, criterion, gauge.

yarn (SYN.) wool, tale, narrative, thread, story, fiber, anecdote.

yaw (SYN.) tack, change course, pitch, toss, roll.

yawn (SYN.) open, gape.

yearly (SYN.) annually.

yearn (SYN.) pine, long for, want, desire, crave, wish.

yearning (SYN.) hungering, craving, desire, longing, appetite, lust, urge, aspiration, wish. (ANT.) distaste, loathing, abomination, hate.

yell (SYN.) call, scream, shout, whoop, howl, roar, holler, wail, bawl.

yellow (SYN.) fearful, cowardly, chicken. (ANT.) bold, brave.

yelp (SYN.) screech, squeal, howl, bark.

yen (SYN.) longing, craving, fancy, appetite, desire, lust, hunger.

yet (SYN.) moreover, also,

additionally, besides.

yield *(SYN.)* produce, afford, breed, grant, accord, cede, relent, succumb, bestow, allow, permit, give way, submit, bear, surrender, supply, fruits, give up, abdicate, return, impart, harvest, permit, accede, acquiesce, crop, capitulate, pay, concede, generate, relinquish. *(ANT.) assert, deny, refuse, resist, struggle, oppose, strive.*

yielding *(SYN.)* dutiful, submissive, compliant, obedient, tractable. *(ANT.) rebellious, intractable, insubordinate.*

yoke *(SYN.)* tether, leash, bridle, harness.

yokel *(SYN.)* hick, peasant, hayseed, innocent.

young *(SYN.)* immature, undeveloped, youthful, underdeveloped, juvenile, junior, underage. *(ANT.) old, mature, elderly.*

youngster *(SYN.)* kid, lad, stripling, minor, youth, child, fledgling. *(ANT.) adult, elder.*

youthful *(SYN.)* childish, immature, young, boyish, childlike, callow, girlish, puerile. *(ANT.) old, elderly, senile, aged, mature.*

yowl *(SYN.)* yell, shriek, cry, wail, whoop, howl, scream.

Z

zany *(SYN.)* clownish, comical, foolish, silly, scatterbrained.

zap *(SYN.)* drive, vim, pep, determination.

zeal *(SYN.)* fervor, eagerness, passion, vehemence, devotion, intensity, excitement, earnestness, inspiration, warmth, ardor, fanaticism, enthusiasm. *(ANT.) unconcern, ennui, apathy, indifference.*

zealot *(SYN.)* champion, crank, fanatic, bigot.

zealous *(SYN.)* enthusiastic, fiery, keen, eager, fervid, ardent, intense, vehement, fervent, glowing, hot, impassioned, passionate. *(ANT.) cool, nonchalant, apathetic.*

zenith *(SYN.)* culmination, apex, height, acme, consummation, top, summit, pinnacle, climax, peak. *(ANT.) floor, nadir, depth, anticlimax.*

zero *(SYN.)* nonexistent, nil, nothing, none.

zest *(SYN.)* enjoyment, savor, eagerness, relish, satisfaction, gusto, spice, tang, pleasure, exhilaration.

zestful *(SYN.)* delightful, thrilling, exciting, stimulating, enjoyable.

zip *(SYN.)* vigor, vim, energy, vitality, spirited, animation, provocative.

zone *(SYN.)* region, climate, tract, belt, sector, section, district, locality, precinct, territory.

zoo *(SYN.)* menagerie.

zoom *(SYN.)* zip, fly, speed, whiz, roar, race.

VOCABULARY

This vocabulary section is designed to help you read and write better. In the reader's vocabulary, you'll find tips on homonyms, root and base words, prefixes, and suffixes. Knowing about these types of words will help you build your vocabulary. The writer's vocabulary has information on figurative language and many ideas that you can use to improve your fiction writing.

Just remember that to correctly use vocabulary, you must understand the parts of speech and how they are used. For example, the word excruciating is an excellent adjective to describe great pain. "My toothache was *excruciating*." However, if you use the word as a verb, "My toothache *excruciating* me," or as a noun, "The *excruciating* made me cry," your sentence will be incorrect. When in doubt about how to use a word, look it up in the dictionary.

READER'S VOCABULARY

Homonyms

Homonyms are words that sound the same but have different meanings and spellings. Homonyms can cause writers big problems. Read the following sentences.

> One mourning while weighting four the school bus, I felt a pane in my heal. It seams I had a whole inn my shoe and a peace of glass was cot inside.

See all the mistakes? The writer didn't pay attention to the spelling and meaning of those misused homonyms. The following sentences are correct.

> One morning while waiting for the school bus, I felt a pain in my heel. It seems I had a hole in my shoe and a piece of glass was caught inside.

Here is a list of commonly misused homonyms.

their/there/they're	aunt/ant	stationary/stationery	pail/pale
too/to/two	plane/plain	kernel/colonel	hi/high
your/you're	fare/fair	straight/strait	serial/cereal
its/it's	hall/haul	sight/site/cite	cell/sell
who's/whose	write/right/rite	piece/peace	weak/week
know/no	pear/pair/pare	would/wood	maid/made
feat/feet	rows/rose	steel/steal	main/mane
dew/do/due	toe/tow	grown/groan	lone/loan
week/weak	rowed/road/rode	meet/meat	hear/heard
ate/eight	sow/so/sew	through/threw	break/brake
flower/flour	knew/new	by/bye/buy	great/grate
scent/cent/sent	in/inn	heel/heal	bear/bare
weather/whether	see/sea	deer/dear	cheep/cheap
	sun/son	principal/principle	pair/pare/pear
	blew/blue	where/wear/ware	whole/hole

Homographs

The word *homograph* has two roots: *homo*, which means "the same," and *graph*, which means "write." **Homographs** are words that are written the same, having the same spelling. Homographs are even pronounced the same way sometimes, but they have different meanings. That's because each meaning comes from a different root. Take the word *hatch* for example. *Hatch* can be used to describe a chick coming out of its egg, markings someone has carved on a wall, or a door leading to a ship's cargo area.

     hatch—bring forth young

     hatch—to draw, cut, or engrave fine lines

     hatch—an opening in a ship's deck

Watch out for homographs in your writing. Look them up in a dictionary to be sure you have used these tricky words correctly.

Context Clues

Often you can guess what a word means from the clues given by other words in the sentence. For example, you may never have heard the word *illegible*. But if your teacher says, "I cannot read this paper because your handwriting is illegible," you could guess without the help of a dictionary that *illegible* means "impossible to read." Discovering the meaning of a word by looking at the other words in a sentence is called learning from context. This skill plays an important role in developing a good vocabulary.

Context clues can also help you write a report that any reader will be able to clearly understand. When you use new vocabulary that you have learned while researching your report, be sure to use context clues to define any new concept words you used. For example:

> Many submarines of the Civil War did not have *periscopes*, which allow the drivers
> to look above the water while the submarine is submerged. As a result, the drivers
> had to rely on other instruments to figure out where they were going.

Your readers may not know exactly what a *periscope* is, but by using context clues in the sentence, you can help them figure out that it is something used to look above the water.

Concept Words

A **concept word** is a word that has to do with a certain topic or idea. When you write about baseball, you may use the words *base, home run*, and *strike*. These are all baseball concept words. When you write about playing music, you may use the words *key, sharp*, and *time signature*. These are music concept words.

When you write a report about a topic that's new to you, be sure to learn the concept words that will help you explain your topic clearly. When you are researching your topic, look up words you don't know in the dictionary. You can also use the glossary of a book to help you find definitions.

Synonyms and Connotation

Synonyms are words that mean the same thing. *Big* and *large* are synonyms. Sometimes words that are synonyms have different shades of meaning. For example, *slim, skinny, slender*, and *scrawny* are synonyms. But while *slim* and *slender* are positive adjectives, *skinny* and *scrawny* give a negative sense of being too thin or ugly. A word's shade of meaning is called its *connotation*.

Connotation can also be defined as the "feeling" meaning rather than the literal dictionary definition that you get from a word. *Denotation* is the exact dictionary meaning of a word. Pay attention to the connotation, or feeling, of words that you use. When describing a dark and stormy night, you would not use the adjective *fluffy* to describe the clouds. *Fluffy* has a positive connotation. Instead, you could describe the clouds as *jagged, racing*, or *monstrous*. These words have the dark connotation you want.

You can use synonyms to improve your writing. A thesaurus is an excellent source of synonyms. While describing a perfect day, if you find yourself using *beautiful* too many times, a thesaurus will remind you of words like *dazzling* and *sparkling*—words that are more exact and descriptive. When using a thesaurus, beware of choosing a word whose exact meaning you do not understand. For example, *remark* and *yell* are both synonyms for *say*, but they have very different meanings.

Antonyms
Antonyms are words that have opposite meanings. *Tiny* and *huge* are antonyms. Use antonyms in your writing to help you stress an important point. When two things you are describing are very different, use antonyms to describe them. You can find antonyms at the end of thesaurus entries. To find words meaning *unhappy*, you could look up *happy* and find several antonyms such as *sad, melancholy*, or *miserable*.

Sensory Words
Sensory words are words that describe the senses. They explain and describe what a character sees, tastes, hears, smells, or touches. Sensory words are mostly adjectives, adverbs, and verbs. Add sensory words throughout your writing to make scenes more exciting and feelings stronger. Some words are used so often or can have so many different meanings that they do not give exact descriptions. These words usually can be replaced with synonyms that are more exact. When you see overused words in your writing, use a thesaurus to help you replace them with sensory words that are stronger and clearer.

Overused Words

nice	bad	happy	pretty
cute	said	sad	went
good	scary	great	came

Vivid Verbs

absorb	glare	rattle	smack
bolt	inspect	rip	swoop
decline	laud	sandbag	zoom
ebb	peek	scream	
glance	praise	screech	

Adjectives

beaming	deceitful	intriguing	quizzical
beefy	enchanting	inviting	sinister
bulky	engrossing	lustrous	vast
curious	glossy	magnificent	wicked
dark	immense	moldy	

Onomatopoeia

Onomatopoeia is a word that sounds like the sound it describes. Onomatopoeia words are excellent sensory words that add color and interest to your writing. Here is a list of useful onomatopoeia words.

ruff	bark	cluck	clop
clip	drip	murmur	rustle
chirp	clack	oink	howl
neigh	clang	crash	honk
cluck	clatter	snap	hiss
cock-a-doodle-doo	bong	swish	sizzle
moo	blink	smack	burp
baa	zip	smash	buzz
sigh	zoom	squeak	crack
giggle	meow	squeal	
drop	purr	roar	

Prefixes

A **prefix** is one or more syllables added to the beginning of a word to change the word's meaning. Many words have prefixes. By learning the meaning of the most common prefixes, you will be able to add many new words to your vocabulary. Here is list of common prefixes and their meanings.

Prefix	Meaning	Example
pre	before	prefix, preview
post	after	postpone, postgame
de	from	decide, debate
re	again	recreate, recharge
col	with	collect, collage
com	with	combine, comfort
con	with	concert, connect
mis	wrong	misbehave, misspell
un	not	unclear, untrue
im	not	improper, impossible
in	not, into	inactive, infects
mid	middle	midway, midnight
sub	beneath	submarine, subway
under	below	underneath, underline
semi	half, partly	semicircle, semifinal

super	more than	supernatural, superpower
auto	self	automobile, autobiography
un	not	unhappy, unpleasant
uni	one	unicycle, unicorn
bi	two	bicycle, bilingual
tri	three	tricycle, triangle
quadr	four	quarter, quadrant
pent	five	pentagon
quint	five	quintet
cent	hundred	century, cent

Suffixes

A **suffix** is a syllable, group of syllables, or a word added to the end of a word to change its meaning or part of speech. Here is a list of common suffixes and their meanings.

Suffix	Definition	Example
ist	person who does, makes, or practices	scientist, dentist
less	without or lacking	homeless, jobless
ness	state of quality of being	kindness, likeness
ly	when, how, like, or in the manner of	quietly, calmly
fy	to make or cause to be or become	beautify, purify
ize	to cause to be or become	hypnotize, realize
ion	state or quality of	nation, hibernation
ry	state or quality of	bravery, forgery
ry	place	bakery, grocery
ment	thing	ornament, instrument
ism	state or quality of	heroism, sexism
logy	study or science of	biology, zoology

Root and Base Words

Many words consist of one or more Greek or Latin roots. For example, the Greek root *tele* means "far." When it is combined with *vis*, the Latin root for "see," we get *television*—an invention that lets us *see* pictures coming from *far* away.

Here is a list of Greek and Latin roots. Use this list as a reference to help you use words correctly in your writing.

Greek Number Prefixes

Number	Prefix	Number	Prefix	Number	Prefix
one	mon	six	hexa	eleven	hendeca
two	di, bi	seven	hepta	twelve	dodeca
three	tri	eight	octa	hundred	hecta
four	tetra	nine	ennea		
five	penta	ten	deca		

Greek Prefixes

A–, AN–: without, not:
  agnostic, anarchy
ACRO–: a point, topmost, at the tip:
  acrobat, acrophobia
ANA–: back, again, according to:
  anabolism, anachronism
ANTI–: against:
  antibacterial, antidote
APO–: off, away from:
  Apocrypha, apostle
AUTO–: self:
  autobiography, autocracy
CAT–, CATA–: down, against, mind, remember:
  cataclysm, catacomb
DIA–: through, across, over:
  diabolic, diagonal
DYS–: ill, bad:
  dyslexia, dystopia
ECTO–: without, on the outside:
  ectoderm, ectopic (pregnancy)
EN–: in:
  encapsulate, endemic
ENDO–: within, internal:
  endocrine, endometrium
EPI–: upon, over, at, near:
  epicenter, epidermis
ESO–: inward:
  esoteric, esotery
EU–: good, well:
  eulogy, euphoria
EXO–: outside, external:
  exoskeleton, exothermic

HYPER–: over:
  hyperactive, hyperbole
HYPO–: under:
  hypocritical, hypodermic
MACRO–: large:
  macrocosm,
  macroglobulin
META–: among, between, changed:
  metabolic, metaphysics
MICRO–: small:
  microphone, microwave
MISO–, MISA–: hate:
  misogyny, misanthrope
PALIN–: back, again:
  palindrome, palingenesis
PAN–: all:
  panacea, pandemic
PARA–: beside, beyond:
  parabolic, parallel
PERI–: around:
  perimeter, periphery
POLY–: many:
  polygamy, polygon
PSEUD–: false:
  pseudepigrapha, pseudonym
SYM–, SYN–: together:
  sympathy, synonym
TELE–: at a distance:
  telegram, telephone
XENO–: foreign, strange:
  xenon, xenophobia

Greek Roots

ANGEL: messenger:
  angel, archangel, evangelist
ARCH: to rule, begin:
  archangel, monarch, anarchy
ARCH: ancient, old:
  archaeology, archaic, archetype
ASTRO, ASTER: star:
  astronaut, asterisk, disaster
ATHL: a prize, contest:
  athlete, decathlon

BIBLI: book, papyrus, scroll:
  bibliography, biblist
  (bible)
BIO: life:
  biological, autobiography
BLEM, BOL, PARL: to throw:
  problem, symbol, diabolic,
  parliament
CHROM: color:
  chromatic, chromolithography

ATMO: vapor, gas:
   atmometer, atmosphere
COSM: earth, world:
   cosmic, cosmopolitan
CYCL: cycle, wheel:
   cyclone, bicycle, recyclable
DEM, DEMO, PLEB: the people:
   demagogue, endemic, democracy,
   plebeian
DERM: skin:
   dermatosis, epidermis
DEUTERO: second:
   Deuteronomy, deuteropathy
DICHO: in two parts:
   dichogamous, dichotomy
DIPLO: double:
   diploid, diplopod
DOX: to praise, worship:
   doxology, orthodox
   (dogma)
DROME: to run:
   dromedary, palindrome
DYNA: force, power, strength:
   dynamic, dynasty
ECO: ecology:
   ecosystem, ecotype
ELECTRO: electric:
   electrolyte, electromagnetic
ERG, URG: work:
   energy, surgeon
ETHNO: race, nation:
   ethnocentrism, ethnography
GAM, GAMY: marriage:
   bigamist, polygamy
GEO: earth:
   geographic, geology
GNOS: to know:
   Gnosticism, agnostic, diagnosis
   (physiognomy)
GRAM, GRAPH: write:
   gramophone, telegram, graphic,
   autograph, autobiography
HELIO: sun:
   heliocentric, heliotrope
   (helium)

CHRON: time:
   chronology, anachronism
HOMO, HOMEO: same:
   homosapien, homeopathic
HYDR: water:
   hydrate, hydraulic
IDO: form, shape:
   idol, kaleidoscope
   (idyll)
LEXI, LOG, LOGUE: word, to speak:
   lexicographer, dyslexia, catalog,
   dialogue
LITH: stone:
   lithography, Paleolithic
LOG, LOGY: word, study of:
   logic, biological,
   chronology
MAT, METRO: mother:
   matrimony, metropolitan
METRO: measure:
   metrology, metronome
NAU: ship:
   nausea, astronaut
NECRO: corpse:
   necrophilia, necropsy
OD: way, journey:
   period, episode
ONYM: a name:
   acronym, patronymic
   (onomatopoeia)
OSTEO: bone:
   osteopath, osteoporosis
PALEO: ancient, old:
   Paleolithic, paleontology
PATH: to suffer:
   pathology, sociopath,
   homeopathic
PATRO: father:
   patronize, patronymic
PED: child:
   pediatrics, orthopedic
PHIL: love:
   philosopher, necrophilia
PHOB: fear:
   phobia, acrophobia

HETERO: different:
    heterogeneous, heterologous
PHOTO: light:
    photocopy, photography
PHYS: nature:
    physics, physiology
POD: foot:
    podiatry, tripod
POLI: city:
    police, politics, cosmopolitan,
    metropolis
PSYCH: mind:
    psychology, psychosis
PYR: fire:
    pyre, pyromaniac
SCHIZO: split:
    schizoid, schizophrenia
SCOPE: see, look at:
    horoscope, microscope
    (bishop)
    (episcopal)

PHON: sound:
    phonics, microphone
SOPH: wisdom:
    sophisticate, philosopher
THE: a god:
    theology, atheism, pantheon
THERM: heat:
    thermoelectric, thermostat
THES: to put, place:
    thesis, antithesis
    (apothecary)
TOM, TOMY: to cut:
    atom, appendectomy
TOP: a place:
    topic, utopia
TRI: three:
    triangle, tripod
ZOO: animal:
    zoo, zoology

Greek Suffixes

−AST: one associated with:
    enthusiast, gymnast
−IA: pathological condition, territory,
    pertaining to:
    malaria, Romania
−ICS: thing having to do with:
    ethics, politics
−ISM: action, condition, doctrine:
    barbarism, criticism

−IST: makes, advocates:
    apologist, socialist
−ITE: native, adherent, a part of
    a body, rock/mineral:
    Israelite, sulfite
−OID: resembling:
    factoid, humanoid

Latin Numbers

Number	Prefix	Number	Prefix	Number	Prefix
zero	nihil	five	quinque	ten	decem
one	una	six	sex	hundred	centum
two	duo	seven	septem	thousand	mille
three	tres	eight	octo		
four	quattuor	nine	novem		

Latin Prefixes

AB−: from, by:
    abdicate, abduct
AMBI−: around, about:
    ambidextrous, ambiguous

BENE−, BENI−: good, well:
    benediction, benign
CIRCUM−: around:
    circumcise, circumference

ANTE–: before:
  antebellum, antecedent
CONTRA–: against, facing:
  contraband, contradict
DE–: down, away, off, utterly:
  debase, descendant
DIS–: otherwise, apart:
  disable, disconnect
EX–: out, off, away, thoroughly:
  example, expatriate
EXTRA–: outside:
  extracurricular, extradite
IN–, IM–, EN–: in, into, on:
  inquest, important, enchant
IN–, IL–, IM–, IR–: not:
  infinite, illogical, impartial, irreverent
INFRA–: below, beneath, inferior to:
  infrasonic, infrastructure
INTER–: between:
  interact, intermural
INTRA–: within:
  intramural, intravenous
JUXTA–: near, beside:
  juxtapose, juxtaposit
MAGNI–: great, large:
  magnificent, magnify
MULTI–: many:
  multicultural, multifaceted
NE–, NON–: not:
  negate, nonchalant

CO–, COM–: together:
  coalition, communist
OB–: toward, across, opposite:
  object, obverse
PER–: through, by means of:
  percent, perennial
POST–: after:
  postdate, postpartum
PRE–: before:
  prejudice, president
PRO–: in favor of, forward, instead of, before:
  prodemocracy, prologue
RE–: again, back:
  reactor, realign
RETRO–: backward:
  retroactive, retrograde
  (retreat)
SE–: aside, apart:
  seclude, secret
SEMI–: half:
  semiannual, semicolon
SUB–: beneath, secretly:
  subterfuge, subterranean
SUPER–: above:
  superfluous, superior
TRANS–: across, over:
  transcend, transfer

Latin Roots

ACT, GATE, GEN, GI, GU: to act, do, drive:
  actual, enact, reactor, fumigate,
  agenda, agitate, ambiguous
AERO: air, gas:
  aerodynamics, aerosol
AL: to feed, nourish, grow:
  alimentary, coalition
  (adolescence)
  (adulthood)
AMA, AMO: to love:
  amateur, amorous, enamored
ANIM: mind, soul:
  animate, equanimity

BAT: to beat:
  battery, acrobat, debate
CAD, CAS, CID: to fall:
  cadaver, decadence, casualty,
  occasion, accident, coincide
CAL, CHA: to be warm, hot:
  calorie, scalding, nonchalant
CANT, CHANT: to sing:
  cantata, descant, incantation,
  chant, enchant
  (accent)
  (incentive)
CAP, CAPT, CAS, CHAS, CEIT, CEIV,

ANNI, ANNU, ENNI: year:
    anniversary, annual, semiannual, perennial
    conceit, deceive, accept, anticipate, occupy

CENTRI: center:
    centrifuge, centripetal (force)

CIT, CIV: citizen:
    city, civil

CLOS, CLUDE, CLUS: to shut, close:
    closet, conclude, exclusive
    (claustrophobia)
    (cloister)   **FLU**: to flow:

COGN, GNOR, NOTI: to get to know:
    cognitive, recognize, ignore, notice
    (acquaintance)

CRED: to believe, trust:
    credible, accredited
    (creed)
    (grant)
    (miscreant)

DAT, DIT: to give:
    data, edit, tradition
    (traitor)
    (rendezvous)
    (vendor)

DEXT: on the right, skillful:
    dexterity, ambidextrous

DIC: to tell, to say:
    dictator, benediction, contradict, judicial
    (judge)

DISCI: to learn:
    disciple, discipline

DOC: to teach:
    doctor, document

DON: to give:
    donate, pardon, condone

DOU, DUB, DUO, DUP: two:
    doubt, indubitably, duo, duplicate
    (dual)
    (duet)

EAS, JAC, JECT, JET: to lie, throw:
    easy, adjacent, reject, trajectory, jettisoned

EGO: I:

CEPT, CIP, CUP: to seize, lay hold of, contain:
    capable, captive, case, chase,

EV: age:
    longevity, medieval

FAC, FACE, FACT, FEAS, FEAT, FECT, FEIT, FIT, FIC, FICE: to make, do:
    faculty, surface, fact, feasible, feature, refectory, forfeit, profit, artificial, sacrifice

FER: to bear, bring, carry:
    fertile, transfer, circumference

    fluorescent, influenza

FORM: form, shape:
    formula, conform, reformatory

GEN: race, kind:
    gender, general

GRAC, GRAT, GREE: beloved, dear, pleasing:
    grace, gratuity, agree

GRAD, GRESS: to go, step, walk:
    grade, biodegradable, congress, aggression

IT: to go:
    itinerate, circuit, ambitious
    (ambience)
    (errant)
    (perishable)

JUR, JUS: to swear:
    jury, perjure, justice

LAT: carried, borne:
    latitude, legislator

LEG: law:
    legislator, privilege

LEV: to lighten, lift, raise:
    lever, elevate

LITER: letter of the alphabet:
    literature, alliterate

LONG: long:
    longevity, prolong, elongated

MAN: hand:
    manipulate, manual

MAN: to remain:
    mansion, permanent
    (remain)

egocentric, egotistic

ERR: to wander:
erratic, aberrant

MISE, MISS, MIT, MITT: to send:
compromise, mission, dismiss,
admit, permitted

NOM: name:
nomenclature, denomination

OMNI: all:
omnipotent, omnivore

PAR, EQU: equal, peer:
par, comparison, equanimity

PAR: to give birth to, come in sight:
parent, postpartum

PATRI: father:
patriarch, patriot
(paternoster)

PED: foot:
pedigree, biped, centipede
(impeach)

PEL, PUL: to drive:
pelt, propel, pulse, compulsive

PEN, PEND, PENS, POND: to weigh, hang, pay:
pensive, pendant, depend,
pension, dispense, ponder

PORT: to carry:
report, transport, important

PUN, PUNC: to point, stab:
pun, punctuate, compunction
(poignant)
(point)

QUEST, QUIR, QUIS: to seek:
quest, inquest, inquire, prerequisite

QUI: quiet, rest:
quit, requiem

ROG: to ask:
rogue, derogatory, interrogate

SAL, SULT/XULT: to leap, spring forward:
salmon, result, exultation

SCEN, SCEND: to climb, leap:
descendant, ascend, condescend
(scan)

SCI: to know:
science, conscious, omniscient

SCRI: to write:
scripture, describe, postscript

MED: middle:
median, medieval
(mean)
(middle)

SECU/XECU, SEQU, SUIT: to follow:
consecutive, execute, sequel,
pursuit
(sect)
(segue)
(intrinsic)

SED, SESS, SID: to sit, settle:
sediment, session, possess,
president, reside
(hostage)

SEMBL, SIMIL, SIMUL: like, at the same time:
assemble, similar, simulate

SEN: old, old man:
senate, senile

SEN, SENT: to be, exist:
absence, present

SIGN: a mark, seal, sign:
signature, assign, designate

SOL: alone:
solo, desolate

SOL: sun:
solar, insolate

SON, SOUND: to sound:
sonar, resound

TEMP: time:
temporary, extemporaneous

TERR, TERRA: earth, land:
territory, terrarium, mediterranean

ULT: last, beyond, extremely:
ultimate, penultimate
(outrageous)

USE, UTI: to use:
use, abuse, utilize

VIT, VIV: to live:
vitamin, vivid, survive
(viable)

VOC, VOK: to call, voice:
vocation, advocate, invoke

VOR: to devour:
voracious, carnivorous

Latin Suffixes

–ACIOUS: tending to:
  audacious, bodacious
–CLE, –CULUM: means, instrument, place:
  particle, curriculum
–ILE: relating to, capable of:
  docile, fragile
–ION: the act or result of, state or process:
  hydration, oxidation

–IUM: the act, something connected
  with the act:
  equilibrium, solarium
–MENT: result or means of an act:
  adornment, advancement
–OR: act or condition of, one who
  performs an action:
  accelerator, squalor

Imported Words

Imported words are English words that come from other languages, such as French, Arabic, or Japanese. Like Latin and Greek roots, many imported words have been used in the English language for a very long time. Many dictionaries give an etymology, or short word history, to tell what language a word comes from originally. Here is a list of commonly used imported words.

catalogue	toboggan	July	museum
carrousel	Texas	August	hypnosis
boulevard	Michigan	September	panic
question	pecan	October	jovial
bouquet	Alabama	November	titanic
budget	hickory	December	comrade
crayon	Alaska	Sunday	caravan
menu	raccoon	Monday	bungalow
lieu	moccasin	Tuesday	scant
bandage	January	Wednesday	solo
rare	February	Thursday	clan
cinema	March	Friday	asphalt
tepee	April	Saturday	
opossum	May	cereal	
Canada	June	geology	

Compound Words

Compound words are words made up of two or more base words. They can be written as one word, two words, or with a hyphen to connect them. Compound words can take the place of a long explanation and make a statement clearer.

  Ben was happy to meet his *mom's new husband's son* for the first time.
  Ben was happy to meet his *stepbrother* for the first time.

WRITER'S VOCABULARY

Literal v. Figurative Speech

When people say something that you know is untrue but is being said to make a point, you say they are using a **figure of speech**. Authors use figurative language to make their writing more interesting.

> I was so hungry I could have eaten an elephant.

When people say something true, they are speaking **literally**. They are saying exactly what they mean.

> I was so hungry I ate a bowl of hot soup and a cheese sandwich.

Idioms

An **idiom** is a phrase that has a non-literal, or figurative, meaning. Non-literal means that the words in the phrase, when understood by their dictionary meanings, do not literally mean what the phrase says. For example, *caught a cold* is an idiom. The speaker did not literally run around with a net until he or she caught the cold. The speaker means he or she got a cold.

It is fine to use idioms in your informal or fiction writing. But avoid idioms in your formal, non-fiction writing. People who speak English as their second language do not know idioms as well as native speakers, and idioms can be hard to learn. In formal writing, you want everyone who picks up your paper to be able to read it. Your reader may have trouble if you've used a lot of idioms. Here is a list of common idioms to avoid.

pull a fast one	get away with it	burn up
do the honors	get the picture	blow out
for the birds	get up on the wrong side	get lost
cost an arm and a leg	of the bed	pull through
caught a cold	really opened my eyes	hang out
ahead of time	the writing's on the wall	keep your head up
drop me a line	make ends meet	go back on your word
in the same boat	give your right arm	turn the tables
take the rap	see eye to eye	
lose your temper	on the ball	

Clichés

A **cliché** is an overused phrase or idea, such as "early to bed, early to rise makes a man healthy, wealthy, and wise." Avoid clichés at all cost. These phrases are old and tired and because they've been around so long, they make your writing unclear. Replace clichés with words that say what you really mean. Here is a list of clichés to avoid.

If you can't beat them, join them.
Actions speak louder than words.
Absence makes the heart grow fonder.
Don't count your chickens before they've hatched.
The early bird catches the worm.
Waste not, want not.

Beggars can't be choosers.
Look before you leap.
You can't have your cake and eat it too.
Like father, like son.
A rolling stone gathers no moss.
A picture is worth a thousand words.
Every cloud has a silver lining.

Imagery

Once you understand the idea behind figurative language, you will be able to understand
imagery as well. *Imagery* comes from the root word *image*, which means *picture*—something you
can see. When you write using the device of imagery, you write so vividly and creatively that
readers can see what you are writing in their imaginations.

Simile and Metaphor

Metaphors and **similes** are comparisons that are made for color or emphasis. Similes use *like*
or *as* to compare two unrelated things. Metaphors do not use *like* or *as* but make a direct
comparison.

> **simile:** The cat looked like a carved statue.
>
> **metaphor:** The fog was a gray blanket that lay over the town.

Symbolism

A **symbol** is a literal thing, place, or happening in writing that has a figurative meaning.

> Leaving the bright daylight of the May afternoon, he entered the gloomy
> darkness of the piano teacher's parlor. Another week had passed, and Bob
> still hadn't been practicing.

In the first sentence, *light* can symbolize peace of mind, while the *darkness* and *gloom* can
symbolize the uncertainty and anxiousness Bob feels because he hasn't prepared for his lesson.
Writers use symbolism to add depth to their writing. Instead of telling you that Bob feels
anxious or uncertain, the writer shows you by using symbolism.

Personification

Personification is exactly what it sounds like—giving an inanimate object, like a rock or a chair,
human qualities.

> Dressed in its best, glowing from head to toe, and standing perfectly straight
> and tall, the old house seemed brand new as it welcomed Susan in from the cold.

Sound Devices

Because there are fewer words in a poem than in a story, every word in poetry is
important. By writing or arranging words in a certain way, the author makes words and phrases
sound a certain way to set the tone of the poem.

Onomatopoeia is a term for words that sound like the sound they describe. *Buzz, pop, snap*, and
fizz are all words displaying onomatopoeia.

Alliteration is a sound device, too. Starting every word in a phrase with the same letter is alliteration. Using a soft sound like *s* makes a poem feel gentle. Using harsher tones like *k* or *r* make a poem sound tougher.

> Shining sun shone down on Susan as she sowed her sapling seed.

Assonance is like alliteration. Every word in a phrase starts with a similar vowel sound.

> The always awful authors often arrive on time.

Comparison and Contrast

To set two objects or ideas apart, compare or contrast them. To compare, list reasons why the two things are the same. Choose the strongest connection and circle it. To contrast, list reasons why the two things are different. Choose the strongest contrast and circle it. Then use these comparisons and contrasts in your writing.

An **oxymoron** is a figure of speech in which contrasting terms are put next to each other.

> There was a *deafening silence*.
> The party was a *sad celebration*.
> Jake was a *cold* person with a *warm* heart.

Comparison and contrast can be especially helpful in developing characters. When two characters are very different, show that difference with a point of contrast. When they are very similar, use a comparison to draw your reader's attention to this fact.

Rhyme Schemes

The word *scheme* means *pattern*, so a **rhyme scheme** is a pattern of rhyme used in a poem. How to use rhyme is up to the poet. For that reason, there are many different types of rhyme schemes.

When two lines that appear back to back rhyme, they are called a **couplet**.

> The light of sunset on the bay
> Always takes my cares away.

When there are four lines, and the first line rhymes with the third and the second rhymes with the fourth, it is an **a-b-a-b** pattern rhyme.

> One day in May
> While by the sea
> I ran away
> When you looked at me

Poetry can also be written in **free verse**. Free verse is poetry that doesn't rhyme or follow a specific rhyme scheme. The author writes freely.

> This is a free verse
> So it doesn't have to rhyme
> I can say what I want
> Without worrying about it.

GETTING STARTED WITH THE WRITING PROCESS

The writing process can be considered as five parts: **select, connect, draft, revise**, and **proofread**. These parts are constantly flowing into and influencing one another without any clear line between them. Writing does not proceed in nice, neat steps. As the writer, you might get an idea for the conclusion while writing the introduction.

The more you use the writing process, the more it becomes automatic to you. It is like riding a bike. When you first learn to ride, you are a little unsteady and unsure of yourself. With practice, riding a bike becomes more and more automatic. The writing process becomes automatic in the same way.

To begin the writing process, look through your writing folder for topics. You may get topics from television or the newspaper. Then, decide if your purpose will be to explain, describe, or convince your reader before you narrow your general topic. If your topic covers too much ground, pick the part that interests you most. You can select a narrower form of the topic by clustering.

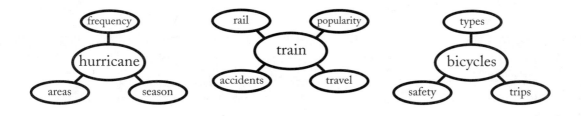

Write your clusters. Add all ideas that come to mind. Choose two or three ideas that interest you the most or that you want to learn more about. Create a new word cluster for each one. Review your new clusters. Select one to write about, and save the others for other projects. Now connect all ideas that go together. Draw lines from one circle to another within your cluster. Draft your ideas into paragraphs. Most likely, this will be the body of your writing. Next, write an introduction or beginning, and add a conclusion or ending. Remember, while you are writing the body of your paper, you might have an idea for an introduction or conclusion. Your writing evolves. Your revision stage can be part of your drafting stage. Read your paper aloud to yourself. Check for spelling and mechanics. Have another student read your work during the revision phase. Proofread your paper, make corrections, and write your final copy.

Tips for Your Own Writing
- Know whether your purpose is to explain, describe, or convince.
- Select a topic; it may help to cluster ideas you get from reading, observing, or watching television.
- Connect ideas and details within a cluster. If you need to, read about the topic for further details.
- Draft the ideas in your cluster by writing them as sentences and paragraphs.
- Revise with the help of a friend; proofread, revise, and proofread again.

Writer's Handbook

GETTING IDEAS

The best source of ideas comes from you. However, you may need a *push* to get you started. Look for ideas and then revert back to what **you** like best or are most interested in. When you write, always consider your resources.

There are many resources to consider when you write; however, your own experiences can bring an outlook to your topic unmatched by any other resource. The key is to choose a topic that you know or would like to know more about. When you know the subject well, you can focus your writing and describe details more distinctly. Brainstorm or cluster special hobbies, talents or skills, travel or other experiences, and people you know. They are good subjects for writing. Experiences, impressions, and perceptions that you have had are the best material for writing.

Imagine a story you would like to write. If you need more information, go to the library or glance through newspapers or magazines. As you preview the information, make a list of topics that interest you. Go through books. Pay attention to the table of contents. Watch information channels on television. The news is a good source of ideas. Again, take notes. Eventually, write down all the ideas and information you gained from previewing the different resources.

Think about your purpose, explore your topic, come up with a narrowed topic, gather material for the details, and decide on who your audience will be and how to appeal to that audience. Develop some sort of method for organizing your information.

Getting ideas involves deciding upon a general topic, and then limiting, or narrowing, that general topic. Then you need to gather details. Go to the library. Brainstorm or cluster by yourself or with others. Make a list of ideas. Group your ideas under related headings. Drop ideas that don't seem to fit in anywhere. Not only do you have ideas, but you now have details that are somewhat organized.

Tips for Your Own Writing
- Tap your greatest resource by imagining what might happen if . . ., or by thinking about special hobbies, talents or skills, travel or other experiences, and people you know.
- Go to the library and read books, magazines, and newspapers, or watch television for ideas.

WRITING A PARAGRAPH

A sentence is a group of words that has a subject and a verb. The verb indicates past, present, or future tense. A paragraph is a group of sentences that belongs together. When you begin a new idea or paragraph, start on a new line and indent the first word several spaces from the left margin like the first word in this paragraph you are reading. A composition is a group of paragraphs about one topic. Sometimes a composition is so short that it is only one paragraph long. No matter how many paragraphs you write, you develop them in the same way unless you are writing dialogue in a story. Remember, all sentences in the paragraph have a close relationship to each other.

First, determine whether your purpose is to entertain, explain, describe, or convince. Second, develop your main idea according to a specific order. Your sentences may be written according to **time, space,** or **order of importance**. Words used to show order include *first, last, second, next, finally, then, tomorrow, before, after, least, smallest,* or *most importantly.*

A paragraph may consist of an introductory sentence that tells the main idea. Supporting sentences add details. The concluding sentence of a composition usually draws together the supporting details and restates the main idea.

Once you know your purpose and order, write smooth-flowing, supporting sentences. They give details, reasons, examples, or likenesses and/or differences.

Details help the reader form a clearer picture. See how the details help you picture Robin's skateboard:

Robin enjoys her new skateboard.

Robin enjoys her shiny red skateboard with the turned-up, pointed front.

Reasons are used when the writer wants to persuade the reader. Sometimes writers show how their topic is like something the reader knows. Vocabulary used to show likenesses includes *also, just as, in the same manner, resembles,* and *similarly.* To develop a paragraph that shows differences, you might include words like *by contrast, on the other hand, unlike, on the contrary,* and *but.*

Tips for Your Own Writing
- Know your purpose and make your writing fit that purpose.
- Organize sentences or paragraphs by using some type of order.
- Support the topic with details, reasons, or examples.

Writer's Handbook

STAYING ON TOP

If you narrow your subject by clustering, it will not be difficult to stay on topic. Cluster, cluster, cluster! Cluster to find your general topic; cluster to find your narrowed topic; cluster to find the details. This will help your writing be more focused. Once you have a specific subject in mind, decide whether your purpose is to describe, inform, persuade, or entertain. That type of planning helps you stick with your topic. Determining the audience you are writing for will also help you remain on topic.

To stay on topic, think in terms of the whole picture and then parts of that picture. In a one-paragraph composition, the whole picture is the one main idea. The parts of that picture are the sentences that support that one idea. The final sentence completes or ends your piece.

The whole picture of a composition is its subject or main idea. The parts of that picture include the paragraphs that support that one idea. Each paragraph contains reasons, examples, details, or facts. The sentences in the paragraphs are also parts of the bigger picture. Clustering will help you come up with the details for those sentences. Don't forget to eliminate and add details to that cluster. Connect ideas that relate to each other. An introduction and a conclusion will help your subject be even more unified and organized.

One test to determine whether you have stayed on topic is to ask yourself, "What is the main idea of this paragraph?" Read each sentence and ask yourself, "Does this sentence give a reason, example, detail, or fact that directly relates to the main idea of the paragraph?"

Another test to help you stay on topic involves remembering the Ws of writing: *who, what, where, when,* and *why.* Answering those questions will help you identify some very basic information related only to your topic. It will help even more if you add *how* to that list.

Tips for Your Own Writing
- Narrow your general subject by clustering.
- Select the purpose and audience for your writing.
- Continue to cluster to support the different areas of your topic with details.
- Ask yourself *who, what, where, when, why,* and *how,* and you will identify very basic information that relates only to your subject.
- Ask yourself *why* about your subject until you completely run out of answers.

PROOFREADING CHECKLIST

Sometimes you think you wrote one thing but actually did not. This makes it difficult for you to find mistakes in your own writing. You read what you meant to say rather than the actual words on the page. It helps to put the writing away overnight. This gives your brain time to forget what you wrote. Later, you will be able to see the words that are actually on the page. It helps to read your work aloud, word for word. Listen to see whether it makes sense. Try to identify missing or extra words. Read your work again, silently. Look carefully for mistakes in punctuation, spelling, and grammar. Find punctuation mistakes by reading the sentences aloud and backwards. Start with the last sentence, then read the next-to-last sentence, and so on. If what you read doesn't sound like a sentence, check the punctuation. Page 3 of this thesaurus lists the basic proofreading marks you can use to mark mistakes.

Proofread for mistakes in spelling, punctuation, capitalization, and verb usage. It is best to check your work for no more than two items at a time. Be sure that your composition is clear, unified, and complete.

The paragraph below shows how to use these proofreading marks.

Would I make the team or word the coach pick someone else? that was the question. I knew that Ben, Lamar, and Carlos had already been chosen. Was I next? Just then Jana came, and stood in the doorway of the Gym. she seemed to be looking for someone. I hopped she was looking for me, but I didn't want her to see me me fail. What pressure!

Tips for Your Own Writing
Your proofreading checklist:
I. Mechanics
  A. Spelling
  B. Capitalization
    1. Start all sentences with a capital letter including sentences inside dialogue.
    2. Capitalize specific names of people, places, and things.
  C. Punctuation
    1. Punctuate the end of each sentence properly.
    2. Place commas in compound sentences and in items listed in a series.
    3. Punctuate dialogue or conversation with quotation marks and commas.
II. Usage
  A. Verify your use of commonly misused words.
  B. Check for correct usage of verbs and plurals.
Read your writing to make sure the meaning is clear, unified, and complete.

Writer's Handbook

STORIES

Every story needs a problem to be met and dealt with or solved, a setting, and interesting characters. It should also have a beginning, a middle, and an end. Actually, the most important part of many stories is the characters. You want readers to care about your characters or people (or sometimes animals). You write about characters in three ways: by what the character says and does; by what other characters say about the character; and by what you, the writer, show us about the character.

Good writers show; they don't tell. See the difference below in *telling* what a character is like and *showing* what a character is like.

How a character—	Telling	Showing
Looked:	He was strong.	Muscles bulged under his shirt.
Felt:	He felt sad.	A dark cloud seemed to have settled over him.
Acted:	She was friendly.	She smiled and waved every time she saw me.
Talked:	She said a car was coming.	She screamed, "Watch out for that car!"

Write so your reader knows what the characters look like, say, do, think, and feel. The best way to do this is to include sensory details that draw upon any of the five senses—sight, sound, smell, touch, and even taste. Help the reader experience the situation just as the   character did. Bring your characters to life. "The outside of the spacecraft looked bad" is not as descriptive as "The outside of the spacecraft was scorched and scratched."

The setting of a story is the time (the "when") and place (the "where") of the story. The reader can visualize the setting when you describe it well.

What happens in a story is the plot, or plan. Most likely, the beginning contains a problem of some kind, and the ending has a solution. The solution may be that there is no solution, but at least the character or characters have gained a new insight about the situation. The plot is the heart of the story. Think of an interesting or funny problem, then think of a solution. Don't forget to explain and develop the events or episodes of the story in the proper sequence. That would be the middle of your story. It helps to show the reader a clear connection between the problem, the main character, and the character's feelings.

Tips for Your Own Writing
- Each story has characters, setting (time and place), and plan, or plot.
- The plan, or plot, of the story has a beginning, a middle, and an end.
- Develop a character by what the character says and does, what other characters say about the character, and/or what you, the writer, tell us about the character.

EXPOSITORY WRITING – PLANNING A REPORT

Expository reports give information about a subject using description, facts, or examples. Reports inform and explain. In a report that informs, the writer gives information about a topic. In a report that explains, the writer explains how to do something. Once you have chosen a narrowed topic and decided whether you need to inform or explain, make a K-W-L chart.

K- What I **K**now	W- What I **W**ant to Know	L- What I Have Learned

First, list all the things you know about your topic in the **K** column. Next, list all the questions you have about your topic under the **W** column. Then, research the topic. List the most important things you learned about your topic in the **L** column.

Take notes regarding the subject. If you want, you may use note cards. Put one fact or detail on a card with a note as to the source of the information. Add as much information as necessary in case you need to find the source again.

Review all your note cards once again. Choose the fact or detail that you find most interesting, and use that as your main idea. Go through your note cards again, and choose the facts and details that support your main idea. Eliminate unnecessary notes.

Sort your cards into three or four categories. Those categories will be the main points of your report. If your teacher requires an outline, these main points may be used as the main headings of your outline. Write each main point on a different sheet of paper with one main point at the top of each sheet. Each main point should support your main topic. Arrange the note cards in some sort of logical order. Next, write under each main point all the notes from the cards that support the main idea on the top of the paper. Write each note in the proper order. Work with one paper and one stack of note cards at a time. The discussion on the next page will show you how to draft or shape the details and facts from each sheet of paper into paragraphs. You have done most of the difficult work in the planning stage of your report.

Tips for Your Own Writing
- Choose a topic and narrow it according to the first two topics in the *Writer's Handbook* on pages 125 and 126.
- Gather facts and details by reading and taking notes about your topic.
- Choose the most interesting fact as your main point.
- Arrange notes in a logical order to support your main idea.
- Draft details and facts into paragraphs.

Writer's Handbook

EXPOSITORY WRITING – WRITING A REPORT

In the previous lesson, you were asked to organize your notes in some logical order and then to write them on one of three or four sheets of paper with one main idea at the top of each sheet of paper. Next, look at the notes on that paper and decide how to organize the information. Here are three possible choices:

1. **Time order:** Use this approach if you are writing about something that happened over time, such as a war, a famous person's life, the life cycle of an animal, or changes in climate. You will describe the events in the order they happened.

2. **Order of importance:** This is a good approach if you are writing about the causes of something (such as allergies), the uses of something (such as gold), or a scientist's inventions. Start with the most important item and proceed to the least important items.

3. **Problem-cause-solution:** This approach is helpful for topics such as ways to avoid skin cancer, better ways to distribute the world's food, ways to save energy, or ways to solve another problem. Describe the problem, explain the cause, and conclude with the solution.

Work with one sheet of paper at a time. That is, work with one main idea at a time. Organize the notes in the order of your choice, and draft sentences and paragraphs with the examples, facts, or details from those notes. After writing all the paragraphs, draft an introduction and a conclusion. Remember, this is merely a draft; it can be revised at any time. Go through your paper to determine whether any part of it needs more development. If so, add more details, facts, or examples in the margins. You may decide to use carets (∧) where you want to insert new information and write it at the bottom of the page. Delete parts that do not support or relate to the main idea or the main points. Add charts or illustrations if needed. Use your proofreading list from page 114 to proofread your paper, and ask someone to review your paper. Make revisions again before writing your final copy. Proofread one more time, and your report is finished.

Tips for Your Own Writing
- Decide whether to organize your report by **time, importance, problem-cause-solution,** or some other type of order, and arrange your notes accordingly.
- Keep in mind the main idea listed at the top of each paper, and draft sentences and paragraph(s) using the examples, facts, or details from your notes.
- Draft an introduction and conclusion for your report.
- Revise the paper by deleting or adding information.
- Proofread, revise, write your final copy, and proofread again.

WRITING A PERSUASIVE COMPOSITION

When you write a composition, you are putting together a written message. The message in a *persuasive* composition is that you want to *coax* or talk someone into believing or acting a certain way. Write a letter to that person asking him or her to let you do something. Your letter is a form of persuasive writing.

In a persuasive composition, first decide *what* you want to talk someone into doing or believing. Narrow your topic as you have learned to do in earlier in this handbook. Next, think *who* your audience or readers will be. Will your composition be read only by your peers or by adults?

Gather evidence to support your belief, or gather evidence and then formulate an opinion. Evidence includes *facts and information*. A *fact* can be proved and checked. On the other hand, an *opinion* is a belief or feeling. It cannot be proved or checked.

Fact: Northville city government plans to tear down the old school.
(If you check with city officials, they will tell you that they do plan to tear down the school.)

Opinion: The old school is very beautiful, and it should be preserved.
(That is your opinion as a writer. Not everyone would agree with you.)

You need to learn about your subject to make a convincing argument. Go to the library and read, interview people, or write for information to gather evidence. Determine *why* you believe what you do about your subject. Make note of your source if necessary. Sometimes noting your source strengthens your argument. It backs up your opinion with the opinions of authorities.

Organize your notes or ideas in a specific order. Write a conclusion and include a general statement that can be logically drawn from the information you have collected. Your conclusion needs to be supported by the evidence you have gathered.

Now draft the remainder of the composition. The introduction needs to present your position with a strong statement about your stand on the issue. The body of the composition simply supports your position with clear reasons, facts, and examples as to *why* you believe as you do.

You have completed your first draft. Revise and edit your paper. Ask someone to help you edit it. Revise as many times as necessary. Proofread your final copy.

Tips for Your Own Writing

- Decide *what* you want someone else to believe or do and *who* you want to convince.
- Gather evidence and learn more about your topic.
- Ideas are organized as to how they support your position.
- The introduction presents your position with a strong statement on the issue.
- The conclusion makes a general statement that is supported by the evidence.

Writer's Handbook

WORD LISTS

Verbs: **Forms of some irregular verbs.**

Present Today I...	Past Yesterday I...	Past Participle I have...
★be	★was/were	★been
become/becomes	became	become
begin/begins	began	begun
burn/burns	burned/burnt	burned/burnt
burst	burst	burst
dive/dives	dived/dove	dived
drink/drinks	drank	drunk
forget/forgets	forgot	forgotten/forgot
lay/lays	laid	laid
lead/leads	led	led
lend/lends	lent	lent
lie (recline)/lies	lay	lain
lose/loses	lost	lost
rise/rises	rose	risen
see/sees	saw	seen
shake/shakes	shook	shaken
strike/strikes	struck	struck/stricken
swim/swims	swam	swum

★conjugation of *to be*:	Singular	Plural
	I **am**	we **are**
	you **are**	you **are**
	he, she, *or* it **is**	they **are**

Vivid Verbs

absorb	ebb	inspect	praise	sandbag	smack
bolt	glance	laud	rattle	scream	swoop
decline	glare	peek	rip	screech	zoom

Adjectives

beaming	dark	featherbrained	inviting	quizzical
beefy	deceitful	glossy	lustrous	sinister
bulky	enchanting	immense	magnificent	vast
curious	engrossing	intriguing	moldy	wicked

Prepositions: **Below is a partial list of some common prepositions.**

aboard	considering	from between	in regard to	outside
alongside	despite	from under	inside	over to
away from	down from	in addition to	instead of	regarding
behind	except for	in front of	on account of	underneath
besides	from among	in place of	on behalf of	within

POSTAL STATE AND POSSESSION ABBREVIATIONS

States

Alabama	AL
Alaska	AK
Arizona	AZ
Arkansas	AR
California	CA
Colorado	CO
Connecticut	CT
Delaware	DE
Florida	FL
Georgia	GA
Hawaii	HI
Idaho	ID
Illinois	IL
Indiana	IN
Iowa	IA
Kansas	KS
Kentucky	KY
Louisiana	LA
Maine	ME
Maryland	MD
Massachusetts	MA
Michigan	MI
Minnesota	MN
Mississippi	MS
Missouri	MO
Montana	MT
Nebraska	NE
Nevada	NV
New Hampshire	NH
New Jersey	NJ
New Mexico	NM
New York	NY
North Carolina	NC
North Dakota	ND
Ohio	OH
Oklahoma	OK
Oregon	OR
Pennsylvania	PA
Rhode Island	RI
South Carolina	SC
South Dakota	SD
Tennessee	TN
Texas	TX
Utah	UT
Vermont	VT
Virginia	VA
Washington	WA
West Virginia	WV
Wisconsin	WI
Wyoming	WY

District of Columbia	DC

U.S. Possessions

American Samoa	AS
Guam	GU
Puerto Rico	PR
Virgin Islands	VI

GUIDE TO MISUSED WORDS

a — an
The word *a* is used before a word that begins with a consonant sound.
> Danny painted *a* picture of his friends.

The word *an* is used before a word that begins with a vowel sound.
> Patty put *an* apple in her lunch sack.
> There is still *an* hour before lunch.

accept — except
The word *accept* is a verb that means to receive or to agree to.
> I *accept* your apology,

The word *except* is a preposition that means other than.
> You can take everything *except* the bike.

affect — effect
The word *affect* is a verb that means to influence.
> His inspirational words *affected* her deeply.

The word *effect* is a noun that refers to something brought on by a cause.
> What *effect* will the rain have on the baseball game?

already — all ready
Use the time word *already* to say that you have completed a task earlier.
> I *already* finished my homework.

Use the two words *all ready* to say that you are completely prepared.
> I am *all ready* to start my homework.

and — to
And is a conjunction that means also.
> Billy *and* I are going to the park.

To is used before a present-tense verb to form an infinitive. Don't use *and* instead of *to* in an infinitive.
> **Incorrect:** Come *and* get us at the park at 6:00.
> Try *and* get a video we'll all like.
> **Correct:** Come *to* get us at the park at 6:00.
> Try *to* get a video we'll all like.

between — among
Use the word *between* when speaking of two persons or things.
> Ryan must choose *between* a new soccer ball and a new baseball mitt.

Use the word *among* when speaking of more than two persons or things.
> The five groups split the history projects *among* themselves.

bring — take
The word *bring* means carry to.
> *Bring* the paper in from the porch.

The word *take* means carry away from.
> *Take* this report with you when you leave.

farther — further

The word *farther* is an adjective or adverb that means at a greater measurable distance or length. Think of the word *far*, which describes a long distance or length.

> Jim can jump *farther* than Kevin can.

The word *further* is an adjective or adverb that means more distant in time or degree; additional.

> How much *further* do we have to drive?

fewer — less

The word *fewer* refers to things that can be counted.

> We had *fewer* plants than we thought.

The word *less* refers to things that can be measured.

> The success of the show was *less* than expected.

good — well

Use the adjective *good* when describing a person or thing.

> That was a *good* movie.

Use the adverb *well* when telling how something is done.

> Dennis plays the trumpet *well*.

healthful — healthy

Healthful is used to describe things that promote good health.

> Taking vitamins and eating *healthful* food is important.

Healthy is used to describe the state of being in good health.

> I eat a balanced diet to remain *healthy*.

I — me

Use *I* in a compound subject when the speaker is part of the subject. A good test is to replace the compound with just *I*.

> **Correct:** *Mike* and *I* played video games with Tony.
> (Test: *I* played video games with Tony.)

> **Incorrect:** *Mike* and *me* played video games with Tony.
> (Test: *Me* played video games with Tony.)

Use *me* when the speaker receives the action of the verb. Again, a good test is to replace the compound with just *me*.

> **Correct:** Mike loaned *Tony* and *me* his video game.
> (Test: Mike loaned *me* his video game.)

in — into

Use *in* to refer to something inside a location.

> The towels are on the top shelf *in* the linen closet.

Use *into* to refer to a movement from outside to inside a location.

> Let's go *into* the restaurant—it's freezing out here!

> Dave went *into* his bedroom to get a change of socks.

its — it's

Its is a possessive pronoun.

> The dog sat next to *its* bone.

It's is a contraction of "it is."

> *It's* the perfect day for a picnic.

let — leave

Use the word *let* when speaking about allowing or permitting something.

> Will you *let* me ride your bike?

Use the word *leave* when speaking about going away from or to somewhere.

> We will *leave* for our meeting in one hour.

Also use *leave* to mean to allow to remain.

> **Correct:** *Leave* the tools by the peach tree.
> **Incorrect:** *Let* the boys alone!

lie — lay

The word *lie* is a verb that means "to rest or recline." The forms of *lie* are *lie, lies,* (is) *lying, lay,* and (have, has, or had) *lain*.

> Mark *will lie* on the sofa.
> Mark *is lying* on the sofa.
> He *lay* there for two hours.
> He *has lain* there for two hours.

The word *lay* is a verb that means "to put or place something." The forms of *lay* are *lay, lays, laying, laid,* and (have, has, or had) *laid*.

> Kathy, *lay* your coat on the bed.
> Kathy *is laying* her coat on the bed.
> She *laid* her coat on the bed.
> Kathy *has laid* her coat on the bed.

like — as if

Like is only a preposition. *Like* should never be followed by a verb.

> That sweater is just *like* one you already have.

Use *as if* as a subordinate conjunction to introduce a clause.

> It looks *as if* Gary and Nancy are getting along great.

loose — lose

Use the adjective *loose* to describe something that isn't tight.

> My tooth is *loose*.

Use the verb *lose* to mean not winning.

> We can't *lose* this game.

may — can

The word *may* is used when asking or giving permission.

> "*May* I borrow your math book?" asked Lisa.
> "Yes, you *may*," said Sandra.

The word *can* is used when talking about being able to do something.

> "*Can* you jump rope?" asked Ben.
> "I *can* jump rope," said Jeannie.

of — off

The word *of* is used to mean belonging to something, containing something, or about something.

> May I have a cup *of* milk?

Do not use the word *of* instead of *have*. Use *have* with the words *ought, must, might,* and *could*.

> **Incorrect:** He *could* of told me.
> **Correct:** He *could* have told me.

The word *off* is used to mean "away from" or "not on or touching" something.

> The dress fell *off* its hanger.

Do not use the word *off* instead of *from*.

> **Incorrect:** Helen borrowed some sugar *off* her neighbor.
> **Correct:** Helen borrowed some sugar *from* her neighbor.

Do not use the word *off* with the word *of*.

> **Incorrect:** Get *off of* the grass.
> **Correct:** Get *off* the grass.

principal — principle

A *principal* is the leader of a school. The *principal* is your *pal*.

> Our *principal*, Dr. Taylor, used to teach science.

When something is *principle*, it is important or first.

> The *principle* conductor never led the orchestra's rehearsals.

raise — rise

The word *raise* is a verb that means to "grow something" or "move upward." The forms of *raise* are *raise*(s), (is) *raising*, *raised*, and have *raised*.

> Ellen *is raising* the bottom shelf.
> We *will raise* tomatoes this year.

The word *rise* is a verb that means to "go up" or "get up." The forms of *rise* are *rise*(s), (is) *rising*, *rose*, and (have) *risen*.

> I *rise* at 6 each morning.
> The sun *has risen*.

say — go

Always use the word *say* instead of the informal *go* when writing dialogue or describing what someone said.

> **Bad:** "And then he *goes*, 'Whatever,' and just walks off."
> **Better:** "And then he *said*, 'Whatever' and just walked off."

since — because

The word *since* expresses a period of time.

> We've been swimming *since* 8 this morning.

The word *because* expresses a cause or reason.

> **Correct:** We're swimming *because* we love the exercise.
> **Incorrect:** We're swimming *since* we love it.

sit — set

The word *sit*(s) is used when speaking of resting or staying in one place.

> "Please, *sit* in the blue chair," said Mother.
> "Robby usually *sits* in the yellow chair," said Tony.

The word *set*(s) is used when speaking of putting or placing an object somewhere.

> Connie *set* the cups on the counter.
> She usually *sets* them in the sink.

that — which

Use *that* to introduce a clause without a comma.

> She took the bat *that* was signed by Cal Ripken.

Use *which* to introduce a clause following a comma.

> She stared at the bat, *which* lay broken on the floor, and burst into tears.

then — than

The word *then* means "at that time."

> We had dinner, and *then* we washed the dishes.

The word *than* introduces the second item in a comparison.

> I like the blue van better *than* the red sports car.

there — their — they're

The word *there* is used to mean in that place, to that place, or at that place.

> The ball rolled over *there*.

The word *there* is sometimes used with the words *is, are, was,* and *were.*

> *There* are five cookies on the plate.

The word *their* is used to show ownership or possession.

> The students picked up *their* books.

The word *they're* is a contraction. It means "they are."

> *They're* coming over tomorrow.

very — so

Both *very* and *so* can be used as adverbs, but do not use *so* in place of *very* to show amount or degree.

> **Incorrect:** Yuki is *so* cute.

> **Correct:** Yuki is *very* cute.

whose — who's

The word *whose* is a possessive pronoun.

> *Whose* is this cup?

The word *who's* is a contraction of "who is."

> *Who's* the owner of this cup?

your — you're

The word *your* is a possessive pronoun.
The word *you're* is a contraction of "you are."

> *You're* going to *your* lesson whether you like it or not!
> (you are)   (pronoun)

WEIGHTS AND MEASURES

U.S. Customary

Length
12 inches	= 1 foot
3 feet	= 1 yard
220 yards	= 1 furlong
8 furlongs	= 1 mile
5,280 feet	= 1 mile
1,760 yards	= 1 mile

Area
144 square inches	= 1 square foot
9 square feet	= 1 square yard
4,840 square yards	= 1 acre
640 acres	= 1 square mile
1 square mile	= 1 section
36 sections	= 1 township

Volume
1,728 cubic inches	= 1 cubic foot
27 cubic feet	= 1 cubic yard

Capacity (Dry)
2 pints	= 1 quart
8 quarts	= 1 peck
4 pecks	= 1 bushel

Capacity (Liquid)
16 fluid ounces	= 1 pint
4 gills	= 1 pint
2 pints	= 1 quart
4 quarts	= 1 gallon (8 pints)

Mass
437.5 grains	= 1 ounce
16 ounces	= 1 pound (7,000 grains)
14 pounds	= 1 stone
100 pounds	= 1 hundredweight [cwt]
20 cwt	= 1 ton (2,000 pounds)

Troy Weights
24 grains	= 1 pennyweight
20 pennyweights	= 1 ounce (480 grains)
12 ounces	= 1 pound (5,760 grains)

Measures
60 minims	= 1 fluid dram
8 fluid drams	= 1 fluid ounce
16 fluid ounces	= 1 pint

Apothecaries' Weights
20 grains	= 1 scruple
3 scruples	= 1 dram
8 drams	= 1 ounce (480 grains)
12 ounces	= 1 pound (5,760 grains)

Metric

Length
1 millimeter	= 1,000 micrometers
1 centimeter	= 10 millimeters
1 meter	= 1,000 millimeters
1 meter	= 100 centimeters
1 kilometer	= 1,000 meters

Area
1 square centimeter	= 100 square millimeters
1 square meter	= 10,000 square centimeters
1 square meter	= 1,000,000 square millimeters
1 square kilometer	= 1,000,000 square meters

Volume
1 milliliter	= 1 cubic centimeter
1 liter	= 1,000 milliliters
1 liter	= 0.001 cubic meter

Mass
1 gram	= 1,000 milligrams
1 kilogram	= 1,000 grams
1 metric ton	= 1,000 kilograms

APPROXIMATE CONVERSIONS FROM U.S. CUSTOMARY TO METRIC

Symbol	When You Know	Multiply by	To Find	Symbol
Length				
in	inches	2.5	centimeters	cm
ft	feet	30	centimeters	cm
yd	yards	0.9	meters	m
mi	miles	1.6	kilometers	km
Area				
in^2	square inches	6.5	square centimeters	cm^2
ft^2	square feet	0.09	square meters	m^2
yd^2	square yards	0.8	square meters	m^2
mi^2	square miles	2.6	square kilometers	km^2
	acres	0.4	hectares	ha
Mass				
oz	ounces	28	grams	g
lb	pounds	0.45	kilograms	kg
ST	short tons (2,000 lb)	0.9	metric ton	t
Volume				
tsp	teaspoons	5	milliliters	mL
tbsp	tablespoons	15	milliliters	mL
in^3	cubic inches	16	milliliters	mL
fl oz	fluid ounces	30	milliliters	mL
c	cups	0.24	liters	L
pt	pints	0.47	liters	L
qt	quarts	0.95	liters	L
gal	gallons	3.8	liters	L
ft^3	cubic feet	0.03	cubic meters	m^3
yd^3	cubic yards	0.76	cubic meters	m^3
Temperature				
°F	Fahrenheit	subtract 32 and divide by 1.8	Celsius	°C

APPROXIMATE CONVERSIONS FROM METRIC TO U.S. CUSTOMARY

Symbol	When You Know	Multiply by	To Find	Symbol
Length				
mm	millimeters	0.04	inches	in
cm	centimeters	0.4	inches	in
m	meters	3.3	feet	ft
m	meters	1.1	yards	yd
km	kilometers	0.6	miles	mi
Area				
cm^2	square centimeters	0.16	square inches	in^2
m^2	square meters	1.2	square yards	yd^2
km^2	square kilometers	0.4	square miles	mi^2
ha	hectares (10,000 m)	2.5	acres	a
Mass				
g	grams	0.035	ounces	oz
kg	kilograms	2.2	pounds	lb
t	metric ton (1,000 kg)	1.1	short tons	ST
Volume				
mL	milliliters	0.03	fluid ounces	fl oz
mL	milliliters	0.06	cubic inches	in^3
L	liters	2.1	pints	pt
L	liters	1.06	quarts	qt
L	liters	0.26	gallons	gal
m^3	cubic meters	35	cubic feet	ft^3
m^3	cubic meters	1.3	cubic yards	yd^3
Temperature				
°C	Celsius	multiply by 1.8 and add 32	Fahrenheit	°F

COOKING CONVERSIONS

A few grains/pinch/dash, etc. (dry)	=	Less than $\frac{1}{8}$ tsp
A dash (liquid)	=	A few drops
3 teaspoons	=	1 tablespoon
$\frac{1}{2}$ tablespoon	=	1-$\frac{1}{2}$ teaspoons
1 tablespoon	=	3 teaspoons
2 tablespoons	=	1 fluid ounce
4 tablespoons	=	$\frac{1}{4}$ cup
5-$\frac{1}{3}$ tablespoons	=	$\frac{1}{3}$ cup
8 tablespoons	=	$\frac{1}{2}$ cup
8 tablespoons	=	4 fluid ounces
10-$\frac{2}{3}$ tablespoons	=	$\frac{2}{3}$ cup
12 tablespoons	=	$\frac{3}{4}$ cup
16 tablespoons	=	1 cup
16 tablespoons	=	8 fluid ounces
$\frac{1}{8}$ cup	=	2 tablespoons
$\frac{1}{4}$ cup	=	4 tablespoons
$\frac{1}{4}$ cup	=	2 fluid ounces
$\frac{1}{3}$ cup	=	5 tablespoons plus 1 teaspoon
$\frac{1}{2}$ cup	=	8 tablespoons
1 cup	=	16 tablespoons
1 cup	=	8 fluid ounces
1 cup	=	$\frac{1}{2}$ pint
2 cups	=	1 pint
2 pints	=	1 quart
4 quarts (liquid)	=	1 gallon
8 quarts (dry)	=	1 peck
4 pecks (dry)	=	1 bushel
1 kilogram	=	approximately 2 pounds
1 liter	=	approximately 4 cups or 1 quart
1 cup	=	275 milliliters
1 pint	=	550 milliliters
1 quart	=	900 milliliters